D1429558

SHERIFF COURT PRACTICE

SHERIFF COURT PRACTICE

by

I. D. Macphail, Q.C., M.A., LL.B., LL.D.
Sheriff of Lothian and Borders at Edinburgh

SECOND EDITION
Volume 2

Edited by

C. G. B. Nicholson, C.B.E., Q.C., M.A., LL.B.
Sheriff Principal of Lothian and Borders

and

A. L. Stewart, Q.C., B.A., LL.B.
Sheriff of Tayside, Central and Fife at Dundee

Published under the auspices of
SCOTTISH UNIVERSITIES LAW INSTITUTE LTD

EDINBURGH
W. GREEN
2002

First published 1988
Second edition, Vol. 1, 1998
Second edition, Vol. 2, 2002

Published in 2002 by W. Green & Son Limited of
21 Alva Street,
Edinburgh, EH2 4PS

Typeset by LBJ Typesetting Ltd
of Kingsclere

Printed in Great Britain by MPG Books Ltd, Bodmin, Cornwall

No natural forests were destroyed to make this product; only farmed timber
was used and replanted.

A CIP catalogue record of this book is available from the British Library.

ISBN 0 414 01250 X

PREFACE TO VOLUME 2

At last the second edition of Macphail's Sheriff Court Practice is complete!

We stated in the preface to Volume 1 that Volume 2 would be published as soon as possible after the new summary cause and small claim rules came into existence. We envisaged that that would be "some months" after the publication of Volume 1. This volume is in fact appearing some four years after Volume 1, and this certainly calls for an explanation.

The reason for this apparently inordinate delay is that the new, revised rules for summary causes and small claims did not in fact materialise until the spring of 2002 instead of sometime in 1999, as had been confidently expected at the time when we wrote the preface of Volume 1. We understand that the problems faced by the Sheriff Court Rules Council which resulted in this lapse of time were caused by the large amount of rules relating to other matters—not least the implementation of the Scotland Act 1998 and the Human Rights Act 1998—which had to be given precedence over the new summary cause and small claim rules.

Although the new rules have now been approved by the Court of Session and came into force for all actions commenced on and after June 10, 2002, the financial limits of summary causes and small claims remain the same as they have been since 1988. This is so despite well-publicised proposals to increase the limits to £5,000 for summary causes and to £1,500 for small claims. It was generally understood that these increases would be brought into force at the same time as the new rules. Indeed the new summary cause rules, especially those dealing with actions of damages for personal injuries, are clearly intended to take account of the increased limits. The reason why these have still not been introduced is obscure. It is a matter of great regret that these increases have not yet been made and we express the hope that they will not be much longer delayed.

In the preface to Volume 1 we suggested that Volume 2 would deal not only with summary causes and small claims but would also have a chapter designed to update the material in Volume 1. Such a chapter seemed to us then to be a realistic prospect if Volume 2 was to appear only a few months after Volume 1. However, we have now reluctantly concluded that to produce an update covering developments in sheriff court practice over the last four years would be beyond our capabilities. There is therefore no updating chapter, and for this we apologise.

Sheriff Stewart wrote the chapter on summary causes in the first edition. He therefore undertook to write the chapters contained in this volume. His work was revised by Sheriff Principal Nicholson, but the main burden of preparing this volume fell upon Sheriff Stewart.

The chapter on summary causes in this edition does not precisely follow the arrangement of the equivalent chapter in the first edition. Sheriff Stewart considered that some improvements could be made in the order in which the topics covered by the chapter were taken. It is hoped that the new layout of the chapter will be of assistance to the reader. The small claims chapter is, of course, completely new. It follows the same pattern as the summary causes chapter.

Sheriff Stewart would like to express his gratitude to the members and secretariat of the Sheriff Court Rules Council for making available to him various drafts of the new rules. This enabled him to produce the manuscript of these chapters much more quickly than would have been the case if he had had to await the official publication of the Acts of Sederunt.

He also wishes to thank Mr Jeffrey Hope (solicitor, Dundee) and Mr Brian Woodcock (solicitor with Dundee City Council) for helping to guide him through the mysteries of housing law including the provisions of the Housing (Scotland) Act 2001, which is likely to come into force shortly after publication of this volume. Their assistance was invaluable.

Finally, we must once again express our gratitude to all at W. Green & Son Ltd who helped us with the production of this volume. Jill Barrington, commissioning editor, who remained remarkably calm and cheerful even when it seemed that the new rules were never going to appear and that publication would be indefinitely postponed, should be particularly mentioned.

We have endeavoured to state the law as at June 10, 2002, the date when the new rules came into effect.

GORDON NICHOLSON
ALASTAIR STEWART

Edinburgh
2002

CONTENTS

	PAGE
Preface to Volume 2	v
Table of Cases	ix
Table of Statutes	lxxxii
Table of Statutory Instruments	cxxv
Table of Scottish Statutory Instruments	cxxxvii
Table of Ordinary Cause Rules	cxxxix
Table of Summary Cause Rules	cxlix
Table of Summary Cause Rules (2002)	cli
Table of Summary Applications Rules	clvii
Table of Rules of the Court of Session	clix
Table of Abbreviations	clxi

PART VII—SUMMARY CAUSES AND SMALL CLAIMS

30. Summary Cause Procedure	3
31. Small Claim Procedure	93
Index	121

TABLE OF CASES

A, Appellant, Lanark Sh.Ct., Jan. 24, 1985, unreported. 26.310
A, Petr (1898) 6 S.L.T. 149. . . . . 26.408
A, Petrs, 1953 S.L.T. (Sh.Ct.) 45. . . . . 28.43
A (Adoption Placement), Re [1988] 1 W.L.R. 229; (1988) 132 S.J. 91. . . . . 28.82
A v. A (Child Abduction) (Habitual Residence) [1993] 2 F.L.R. 255; [1993] 1
 F.C.R. 819. . . . . 2.58
—— v. B (1834) 12 S. 347. . . . . 6.26
—— v. —— (1873) 10 S.L.R. 290. . . . . 9.119
—— v. ——, 1935 S.L.T. 12. . . . . 14.18
—— v. ——, 1955 S.C. 378, 1955 S.L.T. 436. . . . . 28.32
—— v. ——, Linlithgow Sh.Ct., Oct. 9, 1985, unreported. 13.61
—— v. B and C, 1971 S.C.(H.L.) 129. . . . . 28.84, 28.103, 28.107, 28.133, 28.152
—— v. C, 1922 S.L.T. 34. . . . . 10.60
—— v. Children's Hearing for Tayside Region, 1987 S.L.T. (Sh.Ct.) 126. . . . . 28.21
A and A v. G, 2nd Div., Apr. 12, 1994, unreported. 28.90
A and B v. C, 1977 S.C. 27. . . . . 28.133
—— v. ——, 1987 S.C.L.R. 514. . . . . 28.32, 28.76
AB (Adoption: Joint Residence), Re; *sub nom.* AB (A Minor) (Adopter: Unmar-
 ried Couple), Re; [1996] 1 F.L.R. 27; [1996] F.C.R. 633; [1995] Fam.Law
 663; (1995) 159 J.P.N. 827. . . . . 28.45, 28.121
AB v. CB, 1911 2 S.L.T. 99. . . . . 13.79
—— v. ——, 1937 S.C. 408; 1937 S.L.T. 288; 1937 S.N. 21. . . . . 4.08
—— v. ——, 1939 S.L.T. (Sh.Ct.) 11. . . . . 18.69
—— v. ——, 1985 S.L.T. 514. . . . . 28.114
AB v. CD (1836) 15 S. 158. . . . . 11.65
—— v. —— (1843) 6 D. 95. . . . . 19.22
—— v. —— (1905) 21 Sh.Ct.Rep. 303. . . . . 8.06, 12.20
—— v. ——, 1957 S.C. 415; 1958 S.L.T. 213. . . . . 2.11
AB and CB v. X's Curator, 1963 S.C. 124; 1963 S.L.T. 46. . . . . 28.05, 28.06, 28.28, 28.133
AB and CB (Petition of) to adopt X and Y, 1990 S.C.L.R. 809. . . . . 28.84, 28.112, 28.152
AB and CD, Petrs, 1992 S.C.L.R. 274; 1992 S.L.T. 1064 18.47, 28.01, 28.07, 28.08, 28.38,
 28.41, 28.90, 28.114, 28.132, 28.158
AB & Co. v. CD (1908) 25 Sh.Ct.Rep. 106. . . . . 11.47
AH and PH, Petrs, 1997 Fam.L.R. 84. . . . . 28.11, 28.120
AK v. Strathclyde R.C., Glasgow Sh.Ct., Sept. 6, 1982, unreported. 26.113
ASA International Ltd v. Nelson, Sh. Prin. Nicholson, Edinburgh Sh.Ct., Sept. 30,
 1998, unreported. 21.93
AW (Adoption Applications), Re [1993] 1 F.L.R. 62; [1992] Fam. Law 539. . . . . 28.82
Abbey National Building Society v. Strang, 1981 S.L.T. (Sh.Ct.) 4. . . . . 11.21, 21.48
Aberchirder Mags v. Banff District Committee (1906) 8 F. 571; (1906) 13 S.L.T.
 906. . . . . 19.33
Abercrombie v. Edgar & Crear Ltd, 1923 S.L.T. 271. . . . . 11.25, 29.15
Aberdeen v. Wilson (1872) 10 M. 971; (1872) 44 Sc.Jur. 540; (1872) 9 S.L.R. 621. . . 2.31
Aberdeen Cemetery Co. v. Clapperton (1918) 35 Sh.Ct.Rep. 102. . . . . 25.08
Aberdeen County Council v. Roger (1936) 53 Sh.Ct.Rep. 171. . . . . 26.56
Aberdeen Development Co. v. Mackie Ramsay & Taylor, 1977 S.L.T. 177. . . 2.113, 9.83,
 20.01, 20.05
Aberdeen Grit Co. Ltd v. Aberdeen Corporation, 1948 S.L.T. (Notes) 44. . . 12.15, 14.64
Aberdeen (Local Authority of) (1893) 1 S.L.T. 210. . . . . 26.326
Abidin Daver, The [1984] A.C. 398; [1984] 2 W.L.R. 196; [1984] 1 All E.R. 470. . . . 2.89,
 2.91
Abrahams Ltd v. Campbell, 1911 S.C. 353; 1911 1 S.L.T. 2; (1911) 48 S.L.R. 191. . . 2.29
Abse v. Smith [1986] Q.B. 536; [1986] 1 All E.R. 350. . . . . 1.32, 2.07
Acari v. Dumbartonshire C.C., 1948 S.C. 62. . . . . 25.29
Acutt v. Acutt, 1935 S.C. 525. . . . . 2.39
Adair v. Colville & Sons, 1926 S.C.(H.L.) 51; 1926 S.L.T. 590. . . . . 12.70, 18.05
—— v. J.C. Docherty & Sons, 1953 S.L.T. (Sh.Ct.) 58; (1953) 69 Sh.Ct.Rep. 161. . 18.117
Adams v. Great North of Scotland Ry (1890) 18 R.(H.L.) 1. 26.11
Adamson v. Roberts, 1951 S.C. 681; 1951 S.L.T. 355. . . . . 9.33
Adamson, Howie & Co. v. Guild (1867) 6 M. 347; (1867) 4 S.L.R. 156. . . . . 14.22

Addison v. Brown (1906) 8 F.443; (1906) 13 S.L.T. 855; (1906) 43 S.L.R. 335...... 6.19
—— v. ——, 1910 1 S.L.T. 185... 12.15
Addison v. Kellock (1906) 14 S.L.T. 410...................................... 14.38
Adelphi Hotel (Glasgow) Ltd v. Walker, 1960 S.C. 182; 1960 S.L.T. (Notes) 29.... 18.50
Administrator of Austrian Property v. Van Lorang, 1926 S.C. 598................ 2.109
Admiralty v. Aberdeen Steam Trawling and Fishing Co. Ltd, 1909 S.C. 335; 1909 1
    S.L.T. 2; (1909) 46 S.L.R. 254.. 15.53
Adoption Application (Payment for Adoption); *sub nom.* Adoption Application:
    Surrogacy AA212/86 [1987] Fam. 81; [1987] 3 W.L.R. 31; (1987) 15, J.P. 334;
    (1987) 131 S.J. 409; [1987] 2 All E.R. 826; [1987] 2 F.L.R. 291; (1987) 17
    Fam. Law 382; (1987) 137 New L.J. 267; (1987) 151 L.G. Rev. 432......... 28.82
Advance Building and Construction Services Ltd v. Cunningham, Kilmarnock
    Sh.Ct., Apr. 8, 1987, unreported...................................... 16.32
Advocate (H.M.) v. Airs, 1975 J.C. 64; 1975 S.L.T. 177............ 2.08, 2.18, 2.19, 2.21
—— v. Graham (1844) 7 D. 183.. 4.76
—— v. Murray (1866) 5 Irv. 232.. 15.27
—— v. Olsson, 1941 J.C. 63; 1941 S.L.T. 402............................... 16.68
—— v. Skene Black (1887) 1 White 365..................................... 15.27
Advocate (Lord) v. Argyllshire C.C., 1950 S.C. 304; 1950 S.L.T. 264............. 4.65
—— v. Arnold, 1951 S.C. 256; 1951 S.L.T. 116.............................. 4.122
—— v. Bank of India, 1993 S.C.L.R. 178; 1991 S.C.L.R. 320................. 11.14
—— v. Black, 1995 S.L.T. 540; 1994 S.C.L.R. 925........................... 2.14
—— v. Cooney, 1984 S.L.T. 434... 4.122
—— v. Duke of Hamilton (1891) 29 S.L.R. 213.............................. 4.76
—— v. Dumbarton D.C., O.H., Sept. 4, 1986, unreported.................... 4.77
—— v. Duncan Logan (Contractors) Ltd, 1964 S.L.T. (Notes) 35.............. 9.90
—— v. Gillespie, 1969 S.L.T. (Sh.Ct.) 10................................... 9.112
—— v. Gracie, 1951 S.C. 256; 1951 S.L.T. 116.............................. 4.122
—— v. Hunt (1867) 5 M.(H.L.) 1; (1867) 3 S.L.R. 223....................... 4.76
—— v. Johnston, 1983 S.L.T. 290.............. 10.17, 13.23, 17.07, 18.12, 18.18, 18.92
—— v. Johnston, 1985 S.L.T. 533; [1985] S.T.C. 527......................... 9.07
—— v. Meiklam (1860) 22 D. 1427.. 4.76
—— v. Miller's Trs (1884) 11 R. 1046; (1884) 21 S.L.R. 709................. 4.76
—— v. Mirrielees' Trs, 1943 S.C. 587, 1943 S.L.T. 103; 1944 S.L.T. 158; 1945
    S.C.(H.L.) 1... 4.76
—— v. Rizza, 1962 S.L.T. (Notes) 8................................ 4.118, 4.122
—— v. Royal Bank of Scotland, 1977 S.C. 155; 1976 S.L.T. 130........... 11.10, 29.33
—— v. Sinclair (1872) 10 M. 137; (1872) 10 S.L.R. 82...................... 23.45, 23.46
—— v. Stewart (1899) 36 S.L.R. 945; (1899) 6 S.L.T. 405.................... 4.78
—— v. Strathclyde Regional Council, O.H., Sept. 4, 1986, unreported........... 4.77
—— v. Tursi, 1998 S.L.T. 1035; 1997 S.C.L.R. 264..................... 3.05, 3.77
—— v. West End Construction, 1990 S.C.L.R. 777........................... 3.77
Affleck v. Affleck (1862) 24 D. 291; (1862) 34 Sc.Jur. 144..................... 11.06
Agnew v. Earl of Stair (1822) 1 Shaw's App. 333............................. 4.16
—— v. Laughlan, 1948 S.C. 656; 1948 S.L.T. 512............................ 4.33
—— v. Norwest Construction Co., 1935 S.C. 771; 1935 S.L.T. 517; 1935 S.N. 69... 11.14,
                                                                    19.26, 19.28
Agnew's Trs v. Macneel (1827) 5 S. 309 (N.E. 287)........................... 17.14
Ahmed's Tr. v. Ahmed (No. 1), 1993 S.L.T. 390.............................. 19.40
Aifanourios, The, 1980 S.C. 346; 1981 S.L.T. 233...................... 11.13, 24.06
Air 2000 Ltd v. Secretary of State for Transport (No. 2), 1990 S.L.T. 335......... 4.30
Air Canada v. Secretary of State for Trade (No. 2) [1983] 2 A.C. 394; [1983] 1 All
    E.R. 910.. 4.73, 4.74, 4.75, 15.45
Aird v. School Board of Tarbet, 1907 S.C. 22; (1906) 14 S.L.T. 387; (1906) 44 S.L.R.
    26... 18.13, 18.117
Aitchison v. McDonald, 1911 S.C. 174; 1910 2 S.L.T. 413; (1910) 48 S.L.R. 185.... 2.29,
                                                              2.32, 4.101, 24.12
—— v. Steven (1864) 3 M. 81... 14.51
Aitken v. Classen, 1928 S.C. 628; 1928 S.L.T. 422..................... 19.10, 19.55
—— v. Dick (1863) 1 M. 1038................................... 2.97, 6.06, 12.11
—— v. Motherwell and Wishaw Licensing Court, 1971 S.L.T. (Sh.Ct.) 25.. 26.49, 26.255
—— v. Norrie, 1966 S.C. 168; 1967 S.L.T. 4............. 12.42, 12.49, 12.50, 12.51, 12.65
—— v. Robertson (1877) 8 R. 434.. 18.100
Aitken's Trs v. Miles, 1921 S.C. 454; 1921 2 S.L.T. 32; (1921) 58 S.L.R. 433........ 4.14
Aitken (T. & R.) v. Cordner, 1958 S.L.T. (Sh.Ct.) 28; (1958) 74 Sh.Ct.Rep. 142.... 14.39
Aitkenhead v. Bunten & Co. (1892) 19 R. 803; (1892) 29 S.L.R. 659....... 11.70, 11.74,
                                                                          11.76

Al-Adsani v. Kuwait, *The Times*, Mar. 29, 1996; C.L.Y. 3663. . . . . 4.04
Albacora SRL v. Westcott & Laurence Line, 1966 S.C.(H.L.) 19; 1966 S.L.T. 253. . 16.84
Albyn Housing Society Ltd v. Taylor Woodrow Homes Ltd, 1985 S.L.T. 309. . . . . . . 2.12
Alcom Ltd v. Republic of Colombia [1984] A.C. 580; [1984] 2 All E.R. 6. . . . . 4.04
Alder v. Clark (1880) 7 R. 1093; (1880) 17 S.L.R. 740. . . . . 18.100
Alexander v. Campbell's Trs (1903) 5 F. 634; (1902) 10 S.L.T. 73. . . . . 11.47, 23.20
—— v. Graham (1842) 5 D. 218; (1842) 15 Sc.Jur. 61. . . . . 11.30
—— v. Perth C.C. (1939) 56 Sh.Ct.Rep. 20. . . . . 4.44, 12.53, 24.10
—— v. Picken, 1946 S.L.T. 91; 1945 S.N. 66. . . . . 12.15
Alexander (W.) & Sons v. Dundee Corporation, 1950 S.C. 123; 1950 S.L.T. 76. . . . . 9.30
Algeo v. Melville Dundas and Whitson Ltd, 1973 S.L.T. 90. 12.61
Alison v. Blenkhorn (1907) 23 Sh.Ct.Rep. 208. . . . . 26.32
Allan (1826) Shaw 172. . . . . 2.19
—— v. Alexander's Trs (1908) 16 S.L.T. 491. . . . . 2.27
—— v. Fleming (1845) 7 D. 908; (1846) 17 Sc.Jur. 472. . . . . 21.71
—— v. Scott, 1972 S.C. 59; 1972 S.L.T. 45. . . . . 16.100
Allan (Alexander) & Sons v. McGee, 1990 S.L.T. (Sh.Ct.) 2. . . . . 12.37, 13.15
Allan (James) & Sons (Contractors) Ltd v. Gourlay, 1956 S.L.T. (Sh.Ct.) 77. . 4.47, 12.29
Allan (Robert) & Partners v. Scottish Ideal Homes 1972 S.L.T. (Sh.Ct.) 32. . . . . . . 2.46
Allan's Exr v. Union Bank of Scotland, 1909 S.C. 206. . . . . 29.18
Allardice v. Wallace, 1957 S.L.T. 225. . . . . 16.33, 18.85, 18.109
Allen v. McCombie's Trs, 1909 S.C. 710; 1909 1 S.L.T. 296; (1909). 2.109, 4.40
Allen (David) & Sons Bill Posting Ltd v. Dundee and District Bill Posting Co. Ltd,
    1912 S.C. 970; 1912 1 S.L.T. 451; (1912) 49 S.L.R. 716. 2.34
Allen & Leslie (International) Ltd v. Wagley, 1976 S.L.T. (Sh.Ct.) 12. . . . . . 2.04, 18.92,
                                               25.08, 25.17, 25.32, 25.34, 25.35,
                                               25.39, 25.40, 25.41, 25.43, 25.44
Allgemeine Deutsche Credit Anstalt v. Scottish Amicable Life Assurance Society,
    1908 S.C. 33; (1908) 15 S.L.T. 427; (1908) 45 S.L.R. 29. . . . . 20.03
Allied Airways (Gandar Dower) Ltd v. Secretary of State for Air, 1950 S.C. 249;
    1950 S.L.T. 166. . . . . 2.100, 2.101
Allied Irish Banks v. GPT Sales and Services, 1995 S.L.T. 163; 1993 S.C.L.R. 778. . 11.19
Alloa Brewery Co. Ltd v. Parker, 1991 S.C.L.R. 70; affg. 1990 S.L.T. (Sh.Ct.) 57. . 18.05,
                                                                          18.19
Alpine v. Heritors of Dumbarton (1908) 16 S.L.T. 388. . . . . 12.26
Alston v. Alston's Trs, 1919 2 S.L.T. 22. . . . . 2.95, 2.96, 2.97
—— v. Macdougall (1887) 15 R. 78; (1887) 25 S.L.R. 74. . . . . 2.97, 4.32, 6.06, 6.20
Alston & Orr v. Allan, 1910 S.C. 304; 1910 S.L.T. 28. . . . . 19.16
Alston's Trs v. Lord Advocate (1896) 2 S.L.T. 150; (1896) 33 S.L.R. 278. . . . . 4.76
Alyth Light Symphony Band v. Ross, 1930 S.L.T. 150; (1929) 46 Sh.Ct.Rep. 62. . . . 4.101
Amarnath v. A.J. Drilling Ltd, 1993 S.C.L.R. 57. . . . . 16.41
American Mortgage Co. of Scotland v. Sidway, 1908 S.C. 500; (1908) 15 S.L.T.
    850. . . . . 3.99, 11.14, 29.24
Ammon v. Tod, 1912 S.C. 306; 1912 1 S.L.T. 118; (1912) 49 S.L.R. 244. . . . . . 18.16, 19.29
Ampliflaire Ltd v. The Chisholme Institute, 1995 S.C.L.R. 11. . . . . 18.12, 30.328
Anderson, 1912 S.C. 1144; 1912 2 S.L.T. 169; (1912) 49 S.L.R. 244. . . . . 15.19
Anderson v. Anderson (1855) 17 D. 804; (1855) 27 Sc.Jur. 415. . . . . 7.26
—— v. ——, 1981 S.L.T. 271. . . . . 12.42, 12.46
—— v. ——, 1989 S.C.L.R. 475. . . . . 22.42
—— v. Bank of Scotland (1836) 14 S. 316. . . . . 11.73
—— v. British Railways Board, 1973 S.L.T. (Notes) 20. . . . . 10.37, 10.52
—— v. Connacher (1850) 13 D. 405. . . . . 21.97
—— v. Dick (1901) 4 F. 68; (1901) 9 S.L.T. 225; (1901) 39 S.L.R. 42. . . . . 14.67
—— v. Dundee C.C., Dundee Sh.Ct., Oct. 26, 1998, unreported. 26.342
—— v. Garson (1875) 3 R. 254; (1875) 13 S.L.R. 166. . . . . 14.11
—— v. Glasgow D.C., 1987 S.L.T. 279. . . . . 2.121, 10.40
—— v. Harboe (1871) 10 M. 217; (1871) 44 Sc.Jur. 133. . . . . 3.100
—— v. Harrold, 1991 S.C.L.R. 135. . . . . 18.63
—— v. McFarlane (1899) 1 F.(J.) 36; (1899) 6 S.L.T. 291; (1899) 36 S.L.R. 315. . . . 16.62
—— v. McGown, 1911 S.C. 441; 1911 1 S.L.T. 173; (1911) 48 S.L.R. 417. . . . . 2.53
—— v. Moncrieff, 1966 S.L.T. (Sh.Ct.) 28. . . . . 21.98
—— v. Morrison (1905) 7 F. 561; (1905) 12 S.L.T. 784; (1905) 42 S.L.R. 428. . . . . 15.21,
                                                                          15.26
—— v. Neilans, 1940 S.L.T. (Sh.Ct.) 13. . . . . 26.183
—— v. Palombo, 1984 S.L.T. 332, 1986 S.L.T. 46. . . . . 4.74
—— v. St Andrew's Ambulance Association, 1942 S.C. 555; 1942 S.L.T. 278; 1942
    S.N. 42. . . . . 15.16, 15.54

Anderson v. Stoddart, 1923 S.C. 755; 1923 S.L.T. 449; (1923) 60 S.L.R. 483 . . . . 9.78
—— v. Thomson, 1985 S.L.T. (Sh.Ct.) 8 . . . . 14.38, 14.47
—— v. Urban, Glasgow Sh.Ct., Nov. 11, 1985, unreported 16.25
—— v. Wilson, 1972 S.C. 147; 1972 S.L.T. 170 . . . . 2.104, 2.105, 2.107, 9.126
Anderson Brown & Co. Ltd v. Morris, 1987 S.L.T. (Sh.Ct.) 96; 1987 S.C.L.R.
187 . . . . 18.19, 18.56
Anderson (J. & F.) v. Balnagown Estates Co., 1939 S.C. 168; 1939 S.L.T. 131; 1939
S.N. 1 . . . . 4.98, 10.09
Anderson (W.B.) & Sons Ltd v. Aytoun, 1960 S.L.T. (Notes) 60 . . . . 13.07
Anderson's Trs v. Donaldson & Co. Ltd, 1908 S.C. 38; (1907) 15 S.L.T. 409 . . . . 23.25
—— v. Skinner (1871) 8 S.L.R. 325 . . . . 4.07
Andoni (M.V.) v M.V. St Angus, 1945 S.C. 468; 1946 S.L.T. 26; 1945 S.N. 52 . . . . 19.14
Angus v. Glasgow Corporation, 1977 S.L.T. 206 . . . . 18.107
Anisminic Ltd v. Foreign Compensation Commission [1969] 2 A.C. 147; [1969] 2
W.L.R. 163; [1969] 1 All E.R. 208 . . . . 25.35
Annandale and Eskdale D.C. v. Northwest Water Authority, 1978 S.C. 187; 1979
S.L.T. 266 . . . . 2.13, 20.01
Antermony Coal Co. v. Wingate & Co. (1866) 4 M. 544; (1866) 38 Sc.Jur. 278 . . . . . 11.70
—— v. Wingate (1866) 4 M. 1017; (1866) 38 Sc.Jur. 517 . . . . 4.95
Appelby v. Glasgow Corporation, 1949 S.L.T. (Sh.Ct.) 72; (1949) 66 Sh.Ct.Rep. 25 14.30
Appleyard (Aberdeen) Ltd v. Morrison, 1979 S.L.T. (Sh.Ct.) 65 . . . 7.34, 7.35, 7.36, 18.12
Arbroath District Committee v. Provost of Carnoustie (1911) 28 Sh.Ct.Rep. 101. . 26.390
Arbuthnott v. Williamson (1909) 25 Sh.Ct.Rep. 255 . . . . 26.11
Arcari v. Dumbartonshire C.C., 1948 S.C. 62; 1948 S.L.T. 438 . . . . 18.01, 25.06, 25.32,
25.35, 25.37, 25.39, 25.40, 25.41, 25.42, 25.43,
25.45
Arch Joinery Contracts v. Arcade Building Services, 1992 S.L.T. 755; 1991 S.C.C.R.
638 . . . . 11.53, 11.58
Archer's Trs v. Alexander & Sons (1910) 27 Sh.Ct.Rep. 11 . . . . 18.06, 18.11, 18.12
Argyll (Duke of) v. Argyll (Duchess of), 1962 S.C.(H.L.) 88; 1962 S.L.T. 333 . . . . . . 8.57,
10.06, 10.18, 10.58
—— v. ——, 1962 S.C. 140 (revd, 1962 S.C.(H.L.) 88) 10.28, 15.105, 16.38
—— v. ——, 1963 S.L.T. (Notes) 42 (O.H.) 15.37, 15.105
—— v. Campbeltown Coal Co., 1924 S.C. 844; 1924 S.L.T. 514; (1924) 61 S.L.R.
555 . . . . 20.04
—— v. MacArthur (1941) 59 Sh.Ct.Rep. 91 . . . . 26.06
—— v. Muir, 1910 S.C. 96; 1909 2 S.L.T. 347; (1909) 47 S.L.R. 67 . . . . 2.29, 12.71, 12.72,
13.78, 18.50, 18.96
Argyllshire Weavers Ltd v. A. Macaulay (Tweeds) Ltd, 1962 S.C. 388; 1962 S.L.T.
310; 1962 S.L.T. (Notes) 96 (O.H.) 2.88, 2.89, 2.98, 8.19, 14.15, 15.78
Armia Ltd v. Daejan Developments Ltd, 1978 S.C. 152, 1979 S.C.(H.L.) 56, 1979
S.L.T. 147 . . . . 10.17
Armour v. Duff & Co., 1912 S.C. 120; 1911 2 S.L.T. 394; (1911) 49 S.L.R. 124 . . . . 19.11
—— v. Glasgow Royal Infirmary (1908) 16 S.L.T. 435 . . . . 11.70
—— v. Munro (1899) 7 S.L.T. 21; (1899) 36 S.L.R. 675 . . . . 2.34
Armour & Melvin v. Mitchell, 1934 S.C. 94; 1934 S.L.T. 90; 1933 S.N. 104 . . . 9.25, 12.36
Armstrong v. Thomson (1895) 2 S.L.T. 537 . . . . 4.115
Arnauld v. Boick (1704) Mor. 10159 . . . . 4.03
Arran and Easton Trs (Commissioner for) v. Carmichael (1949) 66 Sh.Ct.Rep. 64. . 12.37
Arrow Chemicals Ltd v. Guild, 1978 S.L.T. 206 . . . . 4.43, 4.50, 14.56
Arthur v. Lindsay (1895) 22 R. 417; (1895) 32 S.L.R. 334 . . . . 10.06
—— v. —— (1895) 22 R. 904; (1895) 3 S.L.T. 83; (1895) 32 S.L.R. 680 . . . . . 19.14, 19.55
Asbestos Insurance Coverage Cases [1985] 1 W.L.R. 331; [1985] 1 All E.R. 716;
(1985) 129 S.J. 189 . . . . 15.83
Ashcroft's Curator Bonis v. Stewart, 1988 S.L.T. 163 . . . . 10.18
Asher v. Macleod, 1948 S.L.T. 227; 1948 S.C. 55 . . . . 8.59
Assets Co. Ltd v. Falla's Tr. (1895) 22 R. 178; (1894) 2 S.L.T. 349 . . . . 9.119
—— v. Bain's Trs (1904) 6 F. 692; (1904) 11 S.L.T. 131; (1904) 41 S.L.R. 517;
(revsd on facts, (1905) 7 F.(H.L.) 104 (1905) 13 S.L.T. 147; (1905) 42 S.L.R.
835; [1905] A.C. 317) 2.123
Associated Leisure Ltd v. Associated Newspapers Ltd [1970] 2 Q.B. 450; [1970] 3
W.L.R. 101; [1970] 2 All E.R. 754 . . . . 9.12
Associated Portland Cement Manufacturers Ltd v. McInally, 1970 S.L.T. (Sh.Ct.)
9 . . . . 14.49, 14.53, 14.60, 14.61
Associated Provincial Picture Houses Ltd v. Wednesbury Corporation [1948] 1 K.B.
223; [1947] 2 All E.R. 680; (1947) 92 S.J. 26 . . . . 25.08
Atherlay v. Lanark C.C., 1968 S.L.T. (Sh.Ct.) 71 . . . . 26.255

Atholl (Duke of) v. Glover Incorporation of Perth (1899) 1 F. 658; (1899) 6 S.L.T. 351; (1899) 36 S.L.R. 481... 2.109
—— v. Robertson (1869) 8 M. 299; (1869) 42 Sc.Jur. 135; (1869) 7 S.L.R. 177..... 2.15, 2.125, 2.126, 2.129, 13.64
—— v. —— (1872) 10 M. 298; (1872) 44 Sc.Jur. 136.......................... 21.97
Atkinson & Wood v. Mackintosh (1905) 7 F. 598; (1905) 12 S.L.T. 856; (1905) 42 S.L.R. 461... 2.92, 2.98
Atlantic Engine Co. (1920) Ltd, 1955 S.L.T. 17................................. 4.62
Atlantic Star, The [1974] A.C. 436; [1973] 2 W.L.R. 795; [1973] 2 All E.R. 175..... 2.89, 2.98
Atlas Appointments Ltd v. Tinsley, 1995 S.L.T. 635; 1994 S.C.L.R. 729; 1997 S.C.L.R. 482 (I.H.)... 9.78
Att.-Gen. v. BBC [1981] A.C. 303; [1980] 3 W.L.R. 109; [1980] 3 All E.R. 161...... 2.13
—— v. English [1983] 1 A.C. 116; [1982] 3 W.L.R. 278; [1982] 2 All E.R. 903...... 2.20
Auld & Macdonald v. George Wimpey & Co. Ltd, 1077 S.L.T. (Notes) 23.. 13.71, 14.15, 14.34
Automobile Gas Producer Syndicate Ltd v. Caledonian Ry, 1909 1 S.L.T. 499..... 19.31
Avery v. Cantilever Shoe Co., 1942 S.C. 469; 1942 S.L.T. 275... 14.35, 14.49, 16.69, 16.71
—— v. New Park School for Boys, 1949 S.L.T. (Notes) 6........................ 9.29
Ayr (Burgh of) v. British Transport Commission, 1956 S.L.T. (Sh.Ct.) 3; (1956) 72 Sh.Ct.Rep. 73...................................... 2.128, 5.92, 15.77, 18.17
Ayr (Magistrates of) v. Lord Advocate, 1950 S.C. 102; 1950 S.L.T. 257............ 4.57
Ayr Road Trs v. Adams (1883) 11 R. 326; (1883) 21 S.L.R...................... 16.58
Ayr Toun Council, Petr (1891) 7 Sh.Ct.Rep. 196............................. 26.55
Ayr Toun Council v. Secretary of State for Scotland, 1965 S.C. 394; 1966 S.L.T.... 4.57
Ayton v. National Coal Board, 1965 S.L.T. (Notes) 24.............. 16.28, 19.11, 19.63
Azcarate v. Iturrizaga, 1938 S.C. 573; 1938 S.L.T. 390; 1938 S.N. 52........ 11.32, 11.35

B (Minors) (Abduction) (No. 2), Re [1993] 1 F.L.R. 993........................ 2.58
B (Child Abduction: Habitual Residence), Re [1994] 2 F.L.R. 915; (1994) 138 S.J. (LB) 176; *The Times*, July 5, 1994.................................... 2.58
B v. C, 1996 S.L.T. 1370......................... 28.01, 28.06, 28.07, 28.117, 28.120
—— v. L, *sub nom.* Brixey v. Lynas (No. 1) 1997 S.C.(H.L.) 1; 1996 S.L.T. 908; [1996] 2 F.L.R. 499; [1997] 1 F.C.R. 220; [1997] Fam.Law 10; 1996 S.C.L.R. 856 (HL), 1994 S.C.L.R. 835 (IH)................................... 18.114
Bacal Contracting Ltd v. Modern Engineering (Bristol) Ltd [1980] 2 All E.R. 655.. 11.59
Bacon v. Blair, 1972 S.L.T. (Sh.Ct.) 11..................................... 2.107
Bahai v. Rashidian [1985] 1 W.L.R. 1337; [1985] 3 All E.R. 385................. 2.128
Baikie v. Doull (1908) 24 Sh.Ct.Rep. 211.................................... 15.65
—— v. Glasgow Corporation, 1919 S.C.(H.L.) 13; (1919) 1 S.L.T. 126; (1919) 56 S.L.R. 141... 9.33
Bailey's Trs v. Bailey, 1954 S.L.T. 282..................................... 2.13
Baillie (1872) 10 M. 414; (1872) 9 S.L.R. 250................................ 19.27
Baillie (W. Jack) Associates v. Kennedy, 1985 S.L.T. (Sh.Ct.) 53...... 7.37, 12.25, 18.34, 30.128–30.130
Bain v. Assets Co. (1905) 7 F.(H.L.) 104.................................... 2.123
—— v. Lawson & Son (1899) 1 F. 576; (1899) 36 S.L.R. 417.................... 14.07
—— v. Whitehaven Ry (1850) 7 Bell's App. 79.............................. 9.18
Bain (William) & Co. (Joinery) Ltd v. Gilbert Ash (Scotland) Ltd, Glasgow Sh.Ct., Jan. 28, 1982, unreported....................................... 7.19
Bainbridge v. Bainbridge (1879) 6 R. 541................................... 14.04
—— v. Congdon [1925] 2 K.B. 261; [1925] 133 T.L.R. 286; [1925] 41 T.L.R. 480.. 26.268
Baird, Petrs, (1741) Mor. 16346; Ersk. I, vii, 13........................... 4.23, 4.24
Baird v. Baird, 1914 2 S.L.T. 260... 9.79
—— v. Barton (1882) 9 R. 970; (1882) 19 S.L.R. 731............... 18.35, 18.36, 18.37
—— v. Glendinning (1874) 2 R. 25; (1874) 12 S.L.R. 11............. 11.84, 17.22, 18.39
—— v. SMT Co. Ltd, 1948 S.C. 526; 1948 S.L.T. 411.............. 12.24, 12.26, 13.66
Baird (Wm) & Co. v. McBride, 1928 S.C. 487; 1928 S.L.T. 300; 1928 S.N. 31...... 19.27
Baird & Son (D.A.) v. Nisbet, 1995 S.C.L.R. 1127....................... 8.34, 14.06
Baird's Exrx v. Wylie, 1956 S.L.T. (Sh.Ct.) 10.............................. 14.64
Baird's Trs v. Leechman (1903) 10 S.L.T. 515............................... 4.43
Baker v. Glasgow Corporation, 1916 S.C. 199; 1915 2 S.L.T. 330; (1915) 53 S.L.R. 183.. 19.12
—— v. R [1975] A.C. 774; [1975] 3 W.L.R. 113; [1975] 3 All E.R. 55............. 18.13
Balfour v. Baird, 1959 S.C. 64; 1959 S.L.T. 273............................. 4.48

Balfour v. Foreign and Commonwealth Office [1994] 1 W.L.R. 681; [1994] 2 All
    E.R. 588; [1994] 1 C.R. 277. . . . . 4.74
Ballantine v. Reddie (1884) 22 S.L.R. 136. . . . . 13.34
Balthasar v. Mullane (1985) 84 L.G.R. 55; (1985) P. & C.R. 107. . . . . 26.174
Bank of Dubai Ltd v. Abbas [1997] I.L.Pr. 308. . . . . 3.08
Bank of East Asia Ltd v. Shepherd & Wedderburn W.S., 1994 S.C.L.R. 526. . . . . . . 15.58
Bank of Ireland v. Dewar, Paisley Sh.Ct., May 8, 1986, unreported. 12.68
Bank of Scotland v. Brunswick Developments (1987) Ltd, 1995 S.C. 272. . . . . 24.07
—— v. Davis, 1982 S.L.T. 20. . . . . 9.93
—— v. Graham's Tr., 1992 S.C. 79; 1993 S.L.T. 252; 1992 S.C.L.R. 306. . . . . 24.07
—— v. Rorie (1908) 16 S.L.T. 130. . . . . 11.70
—— v. SA Banque Nationale de Paris, 1996 S.L.T. 103. 3.60, 3.61
—— v. Seitz, 1990 S.L.T. 584; 1989 S.C.L.R. 270. 3.92, 11.14, 29.19
—— v. Shakeshaft, Dumbarton Sh.Ct., Dec. 29, 1977, unreported. 15.24, 15.29
—— v. W. & G. Fergusson (1898) 1 F. 96; (1898) 6 S.L.T. 205; (1898) 36 S.L.R.
    89. . . . . 9.28, 9.41, 10.04, 10.05
Bankhardt's Trs v. Scottish Amicable Society (1871) 9 M. 443. . . . . 11.14, 21.49, 29.21
Banks v. Cruden Building, 1992 S.C.L.R. 779. . . . . 7.29
—— v. Lang (1845) 17 Sc.Jur. 536. . . . . 11.82, 11.83
Bannatine's Trs v. Cunninghame (1872) 10 M. 317; (1872) 44 Sc.Jur. 244; (1872) 9
    S.L.R. 209. . . . . 18.36
Bannerman's Trs v. Bannerman, 1915 S.C. 398; 1915 1 S.L.T. 143; (1915) 52 S.L.R.
    315. . . . . 19.13, 21.71
—— v. Macqueen (1896) 3 S.L.T. 301; (1896) 33 S.L.R. 695. . . . . 19.10
Bannon v. Dumbarton C.C. (1934) 50 Sh.Ct.Rep. 301. . . . . 26.115
Banque Indo Suez v. Maritime Co. Overseas Inc. 1985 S.L.T. 117. . . . . 1.43, 19.18, 24.06,
    29.28
Barbour v. McGruer, 1968 S.L.T. (Notes) 52. . . . . 14.55
Barclay v. Chief Constable Northern Constabulary, 1986 S.L.T. 562. . . . . 2.115
—— v. Hannah, 1947 S.C. 245; 1947 S.L.T. (Notes) 3. . . . . 26.269
Barclay and Ewart's Reps v. Barclay (1850) 12 D. 1253. . . . . 11.73, 11.80
Barclay, Curle & Co. v. Sir James Laing & Sons Ltd, 1908 S.C. 82; (1908) 15 S.L.T.
    482; (1908) 45 S.L.R. 87. . . . . 11.30, 29.28
Baretdji v. Baretdji, 1985 S.L.T. 126. . . . . 16.39
Bargeport Ltd v. Adam, Glasgow Sh.Ct., Feb. 15, 1985 (unreported). 1.32
Bark v. Scott, 1954 S.C. 72; 1954 S.L.T. 210. . . . . 9.122
Barker v. Murdoch, 1979 S.L.T. 145. . . . . 18.116
—— v. Steel, 1951 S.L.T. (Sh.Ct.) 93; (1951) 67 Sh.Ct.Rep. 308. . . . . 18.41
Barnes (Flexible Packaging) Ltd v. Okhai (Flexible Packaging) Ltd, 1978 S.L.T.
    (Notes) 72. . . . . 5.93
Barnie (G. & A.) v. Stevenson, 1993 S.C.L.R. 318. . . . . 7.27
Baroness Gray v. Richardson (1874) 1 R. 1138. . . . . 15.59
Barr v. Bain (1896) 23 R. 1090; (1896) 4 S.L.T. 95; (1896) 33 S.L.R. 780. . . . . . . 8.63, 9.30
—— v. British Transport Commission, 1963 S.L.T. (Notes) 39. . . . . 11.73, 15.31
—— v. Commrs of Queensferry (1899) 1 F. 630; (1899) 6 S.L.T. 343; (1899) 36
    S.L.R. 448. . . . . 2.101
—— v. Neilson (1868) 6 M. 651; (1868) 40 Sc.Jur. 337; (1868) 5 S.L.R. 391. . . 4.42, 4.50
Barratt International Resorts Ltd v. Martin, 1994 S.L.T. 434. . . . . 3.24, 3.51
Barrell Enterprises, Re [1973] 1 W.L.R. 19. . . . . 5.78
Barrie v. Barrie's Tr., 1933 S.C. 132; 1933 S.L.T. 99; 1932 S.N. 106. . . . . 19.13
—— v. Caledonian Ry (1902) 5 F. 30; (1902) 10 S.L.T. 333; (1902) 40 S.L.R. 50. . 15.08,
    18.36, 18.117, 19.12
—— v. Hosie (1933) 49 Sh.Ct.Rep. 114; 1933 S.L.T. (Sh.Ct.) 39. . . . . 7.24
—— v. SMT Co. Ltd, 1936 S.L.T. 143; 1935 S.N. 122. . . . . 19.60
Barrow v. Bryce, 1986 S.L.T. 691. . . . . 9.33
Barry O'Trentham Ltd v. Lawfield Investments Ltd, May 3, 2002, O.H., unreported. . 30.78
Barstow v. Smith (1851) 13 D. 854; (1851) 23 Sc.Jur. 388. . . . . 11.72
Barton v. Caledon Shipbuilding and Engineering Co. Ltd, 1947 S.L.T. (Notes) 12. . 5.81,
    18.15
Barton v. Willaim Low & Co., 1968 S.L.T. (Notes) 27. . . . . 9.67, 10.17, 12.42, 12.61
Batchelor v. Pattison and Mackersy (1876) 3 R. 914; (1876) 13 S.L.R. 624. . . 9.12, 14.17,
    16.42, 19.25
—— v. Reilly, Glasgow Sh.Ct., Feb. 11, 1981, unreported. 14.22, 14.23, 14.24, 19.28,
    19.37
Batey (Wm) & Co. (Exports) Ltd v. Kent, 1987 S.L.T. 557. . . . . 24.06
Bathgate Storage and Distribution Co. Ltd v. Canada Permanent Trust Co. (U.K.)
    Ltd, Linlithgow Sh.Ct., June 13, 1984, unreported. 17.29

Battu v. Battu, 1979 S.L.T. (Notes) 7. . . . . 8.60, 8.64
Baxter v. Lothian Health Board, 1976 S.L.T. (Notes) 37. . . . . 15.90
Bayley v. Middleton, 1909 1 S.L.T. 493. . . . . 15.72, 16.11
BCP Group v. Customs & Excise Commissioners [1994] S.T.C. 41. . . . . 13.69
Beardmore & Co. v. Barry, 1928 S.C. 366; 1928 S.L.T. 208; 1928 S.N. 4. . . . . 18.50
—— v. ——, 1928 S.C.(H.L.) 47; 1928 S.L.T. 452; 1928 S.N. 96. . . . . 20.01, 20.04
Beardmore (Wm) & Co. Ltd v. Park's Exrx, 1932 S.L.T. 218. . . . . 10.30, 10.53
Beattie v. Glasgow Corporation, 1917 S.C.(H.L.) 22; 1916 2 S.L.T. 314; (1916) 54
    S.L.R. 24. . . . . 18.30, 18.48, 18.50
—— v. Halliday, Feb. 4, 1982, unreported. 18.115
Beattie & Son v. Pratt (1880) 7 R. 1171; (1880) 17 S.L.R. 796. . . 2.11, 11.26, 11.27, 11.40
Beck v. Newbold [1952] 2 All E.R. 412; [1952] 68 T.L.R. (Pt. 2) 332. . . . . 26.268
Becker v. Home Office [1972] 2 Q.B. 407; [1972] 2 W.L.R. 1193; 116 S.J. 256;
    [1972] 2 All E.R. 676. . . . . 16.16
Beedie v. Norrie, 1966 S.C. 207; 1966 S.L.T. 295. . . . . 12.42, 12.49, 12.63
Begg v. Begg (1887) 14 R. 497; (1887) 24 S.L.R. 367. . . . . 16.81
Belfrage v. Blyth (1910) 24 Sh.Ct.Rep. 295. . . . . 7.06
—— v. Davidson's Trs (1862) 24 D. 1132; (1862) 34 Sc.Jur. 561. . . . . 2.128
Belhaven Brewery Co. Ltd v. Swift, 1996 S.L.T. (Sh.Ct.) 127. . . . . 7.01
Bell v. Andrews (1885) 12 R. 961; (1885) 22 S.L.R. 640. . . . . 18.71
—— v. Blackwood, Morton & Sons Ltd, 1959 S.L.T. (Notes) 54. . . . . 16.30
—— v. Fiddes, 1996 S.L.T. 51. . . . . 7.19
—— v. John Davidson (Pipes) Ltd, (Sh.Ct.) 18; 1995 S.C.L.R. 192; 1995 S.L.T. 8.35,
    13.02, 13.12
—— v. McCurdie, 1981 S.C. 64; 1981 S.L.T. 159. . . . . 17.28
—— v. McGlennan, 1992 S.C. 41, 1992 S.L.T. 237. . . . . 2.130
—— v. Ogilvie (1863) 2 M. 336; (1863) 36 Sc.Jur. 162. . . . . 19.22, 19.25
—— v. Simpson, 1965 S.L.T. (Sh.Ct.) 9. . . . . 26.06
—— v. Strathern & Blair, 1953 S.L.T. (Notes) 23. . . . . 11.67, 11.71, 11.76
—— v. Thoro-Glaze, Alloa Sh.Ct., Sept. 17, 1982, unreported. . . . 30.127, 30.128, 30.328,
    30.329
—— v. Trotter's Trs (1841) 3 D. 380. . . . . 4.103
Bell Bros (H.P.) Ltd v. Aitken, 1939 S.C. 577; 1939 S.L.T. 453; 1939 S.N. 60. . . . . . 12.70,
    12.72
—— v. Hamilton (1945) 62 Sh.Ct.Rep. 31. . . . . 21.78
Bellenden (formerly Satterthwaite) v. Bellenden [1948] 1 All E.R. 343. . . . . 18.111
Bellenden v. Earl of Winchelsea (1825) 3 S. 367. . . . . 4.33
Bellshill Hosiery Co. v. Lanark C.C. (1948) 64 Sh.Ct.Rep. 206. . . . . 19.66
Bellway Ltd v. Strathclyde R.C., 1979 S.C. 92; 1980 S.L.T. 66. . . . . 12.70
Belmont Laundry Co. Ltd v. Aberdeen Steam Laundry Co. Ltd (1898) 1 F. 45;
    (1898) 6 S.L.T. 192; (1898) 36 S.L.R. 44. . . . . 4.41, 4.50, 8.57
Bendy Bros Ltd v. McAlister (1910) 26 Sh.Ct.Rep. 152. . . . . 29.83
Benicasa v. Dentalkit Srl (C-269/95) [1997] I.L.Pr. 343. . . . . 3.46, 3.51
Benjedward's Creditors (1753) Mor. 743. . . . . 11.14
Benmax v. Austin Motor Co. Ltd [1955] A.C. 370; [1955] 2 W.L.R. 418; [1955] 1 All
    E.R. 326. . . . . 18.108
Bennett v. Livingston Development Corporation, Linlithgow Sh.Ct., Oct. 29, 1979,
    unreported. 2.29, 30.72
—— v. MacLellan (1891) 18 R. 955; (1891) 28 S.L.R. 728. . . . . 4.104
Bentley v. Macfarlane, 1964 S.C. 76; 1964 S.L.T. 58. . 4.31, 4.32, 4.105, 4.108, 4.109, 9.99,
    9.117, 10.04, 10.09, 10.10, 10.24
Bernard's Exrx v. National Union of Mineworkers, 1971 S.C. 32; 1971 S.C. 32; 1971
    S.L.T. 177. . . . . 8.59, 8.60
Bernstein v. Skyviews & General Ltd [1978] Q.B. 479; [1977] 2 All E.R. 902; (1977)
    121 S.J. 157. . . . . 2.02
Berry, Petr, 1985 S.C.C.R. 106. . . . . 18.110, 18.111
Berry v. Taylor, 1993 S.L.T. 718; 1992 S.C.L.R. 910. . . . . 29.35
Bethune v. A. Stevenson & Co. Ltd, 1969 S.L.T. (Notes) 12. . . . . 2.123
Beton v. Beton, 1961 S.L.T. (Notes) 19. . . . . 11.41
Beveridge & Kellas v. Abercromby, 1996 S.C.L.R. 177. . . . . 12.39
Bhatia v. Tribax Ltd, 1994 S.L.T. 1201. . . . . 21.28, 21.36
Biggar Town Council, Petrs (1912) 28 Sh.Ct.Rep. 348. . . . . 25.09
Biggart v. Wilson, 1949 S.L.T. (Sh.Ct.) 26. . . . . 7.28
Bile Bean Manufacturing Co. v. Davidson (1906) 8 F. 1181; (1906) 14 S.L.T. 294;
    (1906) 43 S.L.R. 827. . . . . 2.12
Binnie v. Rederij Theodoro BV, 1993 S.C. 71. . . . . 9.60
Bird's Eye Foods Ltd v. Johnston, Cupar Sh.Ct., Feb. 3, 1977, unreported. . . 30.71, 30.72

Birkett v. James [1978] A.C. 297; [1977] 2 All E.R. 801. . . . . 5.99
Birnie v. Aberdeen Education Authority, 1937 S.L.T. (Sh.Ct.) 30; (1937) 53 Sh.Ct.
    Rep. 221. . . . . 26.115
—— v. McBain, 1914 1 S.L.T. 359; (1914) 30 Sh.Ct.Rep. 174. . . . . 11.54
Birrell v. Beveridge (1868) 6 M. 421; (1868) 40 Sc.Jur. 201. 16.95
—— v. Taylor (1884) 12 R. 151; (1884) 22 S.L.R. 103. . . . . 2.30
Birrell Ltd v. City of Edinburgh District Council, 1982 S.L.T. 111. . . . . 26.95
Bishop v. Bryce, 1910 S.C. 426; 1910 1 S.L.T. 317; (1910) 47 S.L.R. 317. . . . . 16.76
Bisset v. Ecclesfield (1864) 2 M. 1096. . . . . 9.30
Bissett v. Anderson (1847) 10 D. 233. . . . . 14.37
Black (1887) 1 White 365. . . . . 16.62
Black v. Bairds & Dalmellington Ltd, 1939 S.C. 472; 1939 S.L.T. 415; 1939 S.N.
    33. . . . . 15.53, 16.83
—— v. Black, 1990 S.C.L.R. 433 (Sh.Ct.). 6.04, 6.47
—— v. ——, 1990 S.C.L.R. 817; 1991 S.L.T. (Sh.Ct.) 5. . . . . 18.40
—— v. ——, 1990 S.L.T. (Sh.Ct.) 42. . . . . 16.39
—— v. British Railways Board, 1983 S.L.T. 146. . . . . 8.59, 8.60
—— v. Campbell & Cameron Ltd (1938) 54 Sh.Ct.Rep. 169. . . . . 12.69, 12.70, 12.72
—— v. Jehangeer Framjee & Co. (1887) 14 R. 678; (1887) 24 S.L.R. 476. . . 11.10, 11.25
—— v. John Williams & Co. (Wishaw), 1924 S.C.(H.L.) 22; 1924 S.L.T. 58; (1924)
    61 S.L.R. 26. . . . . 10.19, 10.29
—— v. Laidlaw (1844) 5 D. 1254. . . . . 13.36
—— v. McCallum (1924) 40 Sh.Ct.Rep. 108. . . . . 25.05, 25.29
—— v. Malcolm (1830) 8 S. 599. . . . . 11.76
—— v. Scott Lithgow Ltd, 1990 S.C. 322; 1990 S.L.T. 612. . . . . 2.128, 27.12, 27.14
—— v. Strathclyde R.C., Kilmarnock Sh.Ct., Aug. 27, 1982, unreported. 26.113
Black (J. & C.) (Haulage) Ltd v. Alltransport International Group Ltd, 1980 S.L.T.
    154; 1980 S.C. 57. . . . . 14.13, 18.05
Blackburn v. Head (1904) 11 S.L.T. 521. . . . . 23.44
Blade Securities Ltd, Petrs, 1989 S.L.T. 246. . . . . 29.24
Blaikie v. Aberdeen Ry (1852) 14 D. 590; (1852) 24 Sc.Jur. 288. . . . . 25.04
—— v. British Transport Commission, 1961 S.C. 44; 1961 S.L.T. 189. . . . . 9.33
Blair v. F. J. C. Lilley (Marine) Ltd, 1981 S.L.T. 90. . . . . 18.116
—— v. Sampson, Jan. 26, 1814, F.C. (1814–15, High Ct. of Justiciary, App. 501). . . . 2.15
—— v. Stirling, 1894 1 S.L.T. 599. . . . . 4.105
Blair Bryden Partnership, The v. Adair, 1995 S.L.T. (Sh.Ct.) 98; 1995 S.C.L.R. 358   8.42,
                                                                                                            13.01
Blake's Trs v. Jolly, 1920 1 S.L.T. 304; (1920) 57 S.L.R. 431. . . . . 13.78
Bland v. Chief Supplementary Benefit Officer [1983] 1 W.L.R. 262; [1983] 1 All
    E.R. 537; (1983) 127 S.J. 53. . . . . 18.49
Blandford v. Corsock Church of Scotland, 1950 S.L.T. (Sh.Ct.) 37; 66 Sh.Ct.Rep.
    166. . . . . 24.12
Blantyre (Lord) v. Glasgow Paisley and Greenock Ry (1851) 13 D. 570. . . . . 13.32
—— v. Lord Advocate (1876) 13 S.L.R. 213. . . . . 12.15
Blasquez v. Scott (1893) 1 S.L.T. 357. . . . . 19.27
Blau v. Sampson, Jan 26, 1814, F.C. (1814–15, High Ct. of Justiciary, App. 501). . . 2.129
Bliersbach v. MacEwen, 1959 S.C. 43; (1959) S.L.T. 81. . . . . 20.02
Bloe v. Bloe (1882) 9 R. 894; (1882) 19 S.L.R. 646. . . . . 19.27
Blow v. Ecuadorian Association Ltd (1903) 5 F. 444; (1903) 10 S.L.T. 603; (1903) 40
    S.L.R. 358. . . . . 11.72
Blue Sky Holdings Ltd v. Doran, Glasgow Sh.Ct., Dec. 13, 1982, unreported. 15.95
Blyth v. Edinburgh Mags (1905) 13 S.L.T. 459. . . . . 26.327
—— v. Watson, 1987 S.L.T. 616; 1987 G.W.D. 6–186. . . . . 19.23
Blyth Dry Docks & Shipbuilding Co. Ltd v. Commrs for Port of Calcutta, O.H.,
    Lord Emslie, Feb. 12, 1971, not reported on this point, 1972 S.L.T. (Notes)
    7. . . . . 2.14, 8.59
Blythe Building Co. Ltd v. Mason's Exrx (1936) 53 Sh.Ct.Rep. 180. . . . . 12.70
Blythswood Friendly Society v. O'Leary, 1966 S.L.T. (Sh.Ct.) 64. . . . . 23.13
Blythswood Motors Ltd v. Raeside, 1966 S.L.T. (Sh.Ct.) 13. . . . . 19.11
Boe v. Anderson (1857) 20 D. 11. . . . . 2.92
Boettcher v. Carron Co. (1861) 23 D. 322. . . . . 15.19
Bogan's Curator Bonis v. Graham, 1992 S.C.L.R. 920. . . . . 21.36
Bogie v. Bogie (1840) 3 D. 309. . . . . 4.14
Boland v. White Cross Insurance Association, 1926 S.C. 1066; 1926 S.L.T. 716; 1926
    S.N. 132. . . . . 11.14, 29.21
Bonar v. Trafalgar House Offshore Fabrication Ltd, 1996 S.C.L.R. 340. . . . . 21.30
Bond v. British Railways Board, 1972 S.L.T. (Notes) 47. . 14.31, 14.45, 14.53, 19.07, 19.12

Bone v. Morrison (1866) 5 M. 240; (1866) 39 Sc.Jur. 103. . . . . 4.105
—— v. School Board of Sorn (1886) 13 R. 768; (1886) 23 S.L.R. 537. . . . . . 25.32, 25.33, 25.34, 25.35
Boni v. McIver (1933) 49 Sh.Ct.Rep. 191. . . . . 23.24
Bonnar v. Simpson (1836) 1 Swin. 39. . . . . 16.62
Bonner v. Colvilles Ltd, 1968 S.L.T. (Sh.Ct.) 5. . . . . 8.60
Bonner's Tr. v. Bonner (1902) 4 F. 429; (1902) 9 S.L.T. 361; (1902) 39 S.L.R. 532. . . . . 18.71, 18.117
Bonnor v. Balfour Kilpatrick Ltd, 1974 S.C. 223; 1974 S.L.T. 187; 1975 S.L.T. (Notes) 3. . . . . 9.18, 9.70, 10.24, 10.56
Bonny v. Gillies (1829) 8 S. 13. . . . . 4.125
Bookless Bros v. Gudmundsson, 1921 S.C. 602; 1921, 1 S.L.T. 329; (1921) 58 S.L.R.. . . . . 14.18
Boots the Chemist Ltd v. G.A. Estates Ltd, 1993 S.L.T. 136; 1992 S.C.L.R. 859. . . . 21.36
Borders R.C. v. M. 1986 S.L.T. 222. . . . . 2.50
Borjesson v. Carlberg (1878) 5 R.(H.L.) 215; (1878) 3 A.C. 1322; (1878) 15 S.L.R. 779. . . . . 11.35, 24.06
Borland v. Lochwinnoch Golf Club, 1986 S.L.T. (Sh.Ct.) 13. . . . . 4.95, 4.99, 4.101
Borthwick v. Bank of Scotland, 1985 S.L.T. (Sh.Ct.) 49. . . 5.03, 13.50, 25.19, 30.04, 30.28
—— v. Borthwick (1896) 24 R. 211; (1896) 4 S.L.T. 185; (1896) 34 S.L.R. 164. . . . . 9.86, 12.09
—— v. ——, 1928 S.N. 155. . . . . 28.108
—— v. ——, 1929 S.L.T. 57. . . . . 15.102
—— v. Scottish Widows' Fund (1864) 2 M. 595; (1864) 36 Sc.Jur. 290. . . . . 2.127
Borthwick (Graham) Ltd v. Walco Developments (Edinburgh) Ltd, 1980 S.L.T. (Sh.Ct.) 93. . . . . 2.99
Bosco Design Services Ltd v. Plastic Sealant Services Ltd, 1979 S.C. 189; 1972 S.L.T. (Notes) 33. . . . . 7.08, 9.86, 21.75, 21.77
Boslem v. Paterson, 1982 S.L.T. 216. . . . . 6.46, 10.04, 10.41
Boss v. Lyle Shipping Co. Ltd, 1980 S.L.T. (Sh.Ct.) 65. . 11.68, 11.69, 11.70, 11.79, 16.90, 18.48
Boss Group Ltd v. Boss France SA [1997] 1 W.L.R. 351; [1996] 4 All E.R. 970; [1996] L.R.L.R. 403. . . . . 3.92
Bosville v. Lord Macdonald, 1910 S.C. 597; 1910 1 S.L.T. 141; (1910) 47 S.L.R. 328. . . . . 2.123
Boswell (David) Ltd v. William Cook Engineering Ltd, 1989 S.L.T. (Sh.Ct.) 61. . . . . 4.32
Boswell's Trs v. Pearson (1886) 24 S.L.R. 32. . . . . 21.99
Botterills of Blantyre v. Hamilton District Licensing Board, 1986 S.L.T. 14. . . . . . . 26.255
Boughen v. Scott, 1983 S.L.T. (Sh.Ct.) 94. . . . . 14.67
Boulting v. Elias, 1990 S.C. 135; 1990 S.L.T. 596. . . . . 4.38
Bourtreehill Baptist Church v. Cunningham District Licensing Board, Kilmarnock Sh.Ct., Dec. 15, 1977, unreported. 26.255
Boustead v. Gardner (1879) 7 R. 139; (1879) 17 S.L.R. 67. . . . . 9.12, 9.31
Bowers v. Strathclyde R.C., 1981 S.L.T. 122. . . . . 16.28, 18.116
Bowie v. Donaldson, 1922 S.C. 9; 1921 2 S.L.T. 236; (1921) 59 S.L.R. 26. . . . . . 2.28, 2.33
Bowman v. McKeown, *The Times*, Nov. 23, 1978; [1978] C.L.Y. 2399. . . . . 4.120
—— v. Wright (1877) 4 R. 322; (1877) 14 S.L.R. 250. . . . . 3.101
Bowman's Trs v. Scott (1901) 3 F. 450; (1901) 38 S.L.R. 557. . . . . 18.36, 18.117
Boyd v. Drummond, Robbie & Gibson, 1995 S.C.L.R. 178. . . . . 18.40, 21.78, 21.79
Boyes v. Eaton Yale & Towne Inc., 1978 S.L.T. (Notes) 6. . . . . 15.56
Boyle v. Glasgow Corporation, 1975 S.C. 238; 1979 S.L.T. (Notes) 77. . . . . . . 10.33, 12.51
—— v. Glasgow Royal Infirmary, 1969 S.C. 72; 1969 S.L.T. 137. . . . . 15.58
—— v. Gray, 1993 S.C.L.R. 272. . . . . 10.46
—— v. Olsen, 1912 S.C. 1235; 1912 2 S.L.T. 114; (1912) 49 S.L.R. 894. . . . . . 13.43, 14.54, 16.74
—— v. Rennies of Dunfermline, 1975 S.L.T. (Notes) 13. . . . . 21.25, 21.26
—— v. West of Scotland Ship-Breaking Co. Ltd, 1963 S.L.T. (Sh.Ct.) 54. . . . 10.20, 18.17
Boyne v. Grampian Regional Council, Aberdeen Sh.Ct., Apr. 14 1983, unreported. 26.113
Bracken v. Blasque (1891) 18 R. 819; (1891) 28 S.L.R. 632. . . . . 11.68, 11.75
Bradford v. McLeod, 1986 S.L.T. 244; 1985 S.C.C.R. 379. . . . . 2.128, 2.129
Bradford Equitable Building Society v. Thomson, 1965 S.L.T. (Sh.Ct.) 54. . , 12.68, 12.72
Bradie v. National Coal Board, 1951 S.C. 576; 1952 S.L.T. 32. . . . . 14.31, 19.15
Brady v. Barrow Steel Works Ltd [1965] 2 Q.B. 182; [1965] 2 W.L.R. 244; [1965] 2 All E.R. 639. . . . . 9.41
—— v. Miller's Properties Ltd (1935) 51 Sh.Ct.Rep. 315. . . . . 2.53
—— v. Napier & Son, 1944 S.C. 18; 1944 S.L.T. 187; 1943 S.N. 71. . . . . 2.29

Brakinrig v. Menzies (1841) 4 D. 274. . . . .   13.36, 13.37, 13.38
Brand v. Kent (1892) 20 R. 29; (1892) 30 S.L.R. 70. . . . .   11.31
—— v. Police Commrs of Arbroath (1890) 17 R. 790. . . . .   2.105
Brash v. Brash, 1966 S.C. 56; 1966 S.L.T. 157. . . . .   11.11, 11.12, 29.19
Brawnrigg Coal Co. Ltd v. Sneddon, 1911 S.C. 1064. . . . .   11.62
Breadalbane (Marquis of) v. McNab (1902) 20 Sh.Ct.Rep. 51. . . . .   8.65
—— v. Toberonochy State Quarry Co. (1916) 33 Sh.Ct.Rep. 154. . . . .   4.97, 23.17
Bremner v. TSB (Scotland) plc. 1993 S.L.T. (Sh.Ct.) 3; 1992 S.C.L.R. 662. . .   11.20, 11.26
Brennan v. Central SMT Co., 1947 S.N. 7; 1947 S.L.T. (Notes) 4; 1947 S.N. 7. . . . . .   1.40,
5.98, 18.05
—— v. Edinburgh Corporation, 1962 S.C. 36; 1962 S.L.T. 54. . . . .   16.71
Brenner and Noller v. Dean Witter Reynolds (C-318/93) [1994] E.C.R. I-4275. . . . . .   3.47
Bridge of Allan Water Co. v. Alexander (1868) 6 M. 321; (1868) 40 Sc.Jur. 177. . . .   26.95
Bridges v. Ewing (1830) 15 S. 8. . . . .   29.27
—— v. —— (1833) 11 S. 335. . . . .   13.78
Briggs v. Amalgamated Press Ltd, 1910 2 S.L.T. 298. . . . .   11.54
Bright v. Low, 1940 S.C. 280; 1940 S.N. 11. . . . .   14.45
Brims & Mackay v. Pattullo, 1907 S.C. 1106; (1907) 15 S.L.T. 198; (1907) 44 S.L.R.
319. . . . .   4.38
Bristow v. Menzies (1840) 2 D. 611. . . . .   11.36
Britain Steamship Co. Ltd v. Lithgows Ltd, 1975 S.L.T. (Notes) 20. . . . .   9.30, 9.102
British Anchor Pottery Co. Ltd v. Cowan & Co. (1950) 66 Sh.Ct.Rep. 279. . . . .   4.97, 7.24
British Artificial Silk Machines Ltd v. Liquidators of Scottish Amalgamated Silks
Ltd, 1935, unreported. 11.65
British Linen Co. v. Kansas Investment Co. (1895) 3 S.L.T. 138, 202. . . . .   29.29
British Medical Association v. Greater Glasgow Health Board, 1988 S.L.T. 538;
1989 S.L.T. 493; 1989 S.C.(H.L.) 65. . . . .   4.59, 4.65
British Motor Body Co. Ltd v. Thomas Shaw (Dundee) Ltd, 1914 S.C. 922; 1914 2
S.L.T. 131; (1914) 51 S.L.R. 812. . . . .   12.29
British Oxygen Co. v. South West Scotland Electricity Board, 1956 S.C.(H.L.) 112;
1956 S.L.T. 278; [1956] 3 All E.R. 199. . . . .   18.13
British Phonographic Industry Ltd v. Cohen, Cohen, Kelly, Cohen & Cohen Ltd,
1983 S.L.T. 137. . . . .   15.86
British Publishing Co. Ltd v. Hedderwick & Sons (1892) 19 R. 1008. . . . .   15.52
British Railways Board v. Glasgow Corporation, 1976 S.C. 224; 1975 S.L.T. 45. . . . .   2.131
—— v. Ross and Cromarty C.C., 1974 S.C. 27; 1974 S.L.T. 274. . . . .   19.45, 24.09
—— v. Strathclyde R.C., 1981 S.C. 90; 1982 S.L.T. 55. . . . .   9.28, 9.41, 10.38
British Relay Ltd v. Keay, 1976 S.L.T. (Sh.Ct.) 23. . . . .   1.27
British Westinghouse v. Provost of Aberdeen (1906) 14 S.L.T. 391. . . . .   26.32
Britton v. Central R.C., 1986 S.L.T. 207.   18.110, 18.111, 18.114
—— v. Maple & Co. Ltd, 1986 S.L.T. 70. . . . .   4.85
Broatch v. Pattison (1898) 1 F. 303; (1898) 6 S.L.T. 261. . . . .   2.31, 8.16, 18.27
Brock v. Buchanan (1851) 13 D. 1069; (1851) 23 Sc.Jur. 496. . . . .   2.54, 11.06, 25.04
Brodie v. Coplan (1906) 14 S.L.T. 35. . . . .   4.50
—— v. Ker, 1952 S.C. 216; 1952 S.L.T. 226. . . . .   2.38, 2.100, 2.101, 2.102
—— v. Wilson (1837) 15 S. 1195. . . . .   29.31
Brodie & Hall Ltd v. Di Placido (1938) 55 Sh.Ct.Rep. 82. . . . .   11.46, 12.68, 12.72
Brodt v. King, 1991 S.L.T. 272. . . . .   14.17, 14.32
Brook v. Hamilton (1852) 19 D. 701. . . . .   23.37
Brooks v. Brooks's Trs (1902) 4 F. 1014; (1902) 105 S.L.T. 217; (1902) 39 S.L.R.
816. . . . .   19.13
Brooks & Bohm Ltd v. Kitchencraft Co., 1944 S.C. 25; 1944 S.L.T. 217; 1943 S.N.
73. . . . .   18.117
Broomfield v. Greig (1868) 6 M. 992; (1868) 40 Sc.Jur. 568; (1868) 5 S.L.R. 635. . . .   9.30
Brotherson v. Livingston (1892) 20 R. 1; (1892) 30 S.L.R. 1. . . . .   2.30, 18.35
Brown v. Blaikie (1850) 13 D. 149; (1850) 23 Sc.Jur.47. . . . .   11.13
—— v. British Rail Property Board, 1983 S.L.T. (Sh.Ct.) 19. . . . .   18.12
—— v. Brown, 1929 S.L.T. (Sh.Ct.) 44. . . . .   19.28
—— v. ——, 1948 S.C. 5; 1948 S.L.T. 129, 1947 S.N. 169. . . . .   13.61, 13.66
—— v. ——, 1971 S.C. 22. . . . .   24.12
—— v. ——, 1985 S.L.T. 376. . . . .   18.110
—— v. Caterpillar Tractor Co. Ltd, O.H., Lord Cameron, Nov. 30., 1971, unre-
ported. 9.33
—— v. George Wilson (Stonehouse) Ltd, 1982 S.L.T. (Sh.Ct.) 96. . . . .   9.113, 9.114
—— v. Glenboig Union Fire Clay Co. Ltd, 1911 1 S.L.T. 27. . . . .   15.100
—— v. Hamilton D.C., 1983 S.C.(H.L.) 1. . . . .   2.38, 2.48, 12.69, 18.110,
18.111, 20.02, 21.75, 25.35

Brown v. Hastie & Co. Ltd (1904) 6 F. 1001. . . . . 10.05
—— v. Kirkcudbright Mags (1905) 8 F. 77; (1905) 43 S.L.R. 81. . . . . 26.327
—— v. Lee Constructions Ltd, 1977 S.L.T. (Notes) 61. . . . . 2.02
—— v. Lindley (1833) 12 S. 18; (1833) 6 Sc.Jur. 42. . . . . 11.76
—— v. Oliver & Co. (1895) 3 S.L.T. 43. . . . . 11.54
—— v. Redpath Brown & Co. Ltd, 1963 S.L.T. 219. . . . . 9.54
—— v. Rodger (1884) 12 R. 340; (1884) 22 S.L.R. 225. . . . . 9.78
Brown & Critchley v. Decorative Art Journals Co., 1922 S.C. 192; 1922 S.L.T. 117;
    (1922) 59 S.L.R. 241. . . . . 2.30, 18.04, 24.12
Brown & Sons v. Associated Fireclay Cos, 1937 S.C.(H.L.) 42; 1937 S.L.T. 435;
    1937 S.N. 72. . . . . 12.70,
Brown's Exrx v. N.B. Steel Foundry, 1968 S.L.T. 121. . . . . 9.28, 9.112, 16.84
Brown's Trs v. Horne, 1907 S.C. 1027; (1907) 15 S.L.T. 145; (1907) 44 S.L.R.
    795. . . . . 10.06, 13.36
Browne v. Orr (1872) 10 M. 397; (1872) 44 Sc.Jur. 225; (1872) 9 S.L.R. 232. . . . . . . 4.33
—— v. Thomson & Co., 1912 S.C. 359; 1912 1 S.L.T. 123; (1912) 49 S.L.R. 285. . . . 4.38
Brownlie v. Maitland, Aberdeen Sh.Ct., Nov. 5, 1985, unreported. 15.57, 15.60
—— v. Tennant (1855) 17 D. 422; (1855) 27 Sc.Jur. 179. . . . . 19.03
Brownrigg Coal Co. Ltd v. Sneddon, 1911 S.C. 1064; 1911 2 S.L.T. 96; (1911) 48
    S.L.R. 11.58, 11.59
Broxburn Oil Co. v. Morrison (1903) 5 F. 694, (1903) 10 S.L.T. 728. . . . . 13.28
Bruce v. British Motor Trading Corporation, 1924 S.C. 908; 1924 S.L.T. 723; (1924)
    61 S.L.R. 637. . . . . 6.22
—— v. Bruce, 1945 S.C. 353; 1945 S.L.T. 285; 1945 S.N. 38. . . . . 5.88
—— v. Calder (1903) 20 Sh.Ct.Rep. 288. . . . . 8.22, 12.15
—— v. Chief Constable of Edinburgh, 1962 S.L.T. (Sh.Ct.) 9; (1961) 77 Sh.Ct.Rep.
    80. . . . . 25.09, 25.11
—— v. Duncan (1793) Hume 596. . . . . 2.113
—— v. Evans (W. & A.S.), 1986 S.L.T. (Sh.Ct.) 20. . . . . 21.72, 21.74
—— v. Henderson (1889) 17 R. 276; (1889) 27 S.L.R. 223. . . . . 2.30
—— v. Irvine (1835) 13 S. 437; (1835) 7 Sc.Jur. 216. . . . . 18.04
—— v. Linton (1860) 23 D. 85; (1860) 33 Sc.Jur. 37. . . . . 16.55
—— v. McLellan, 1925 S.C. 103; 1924 S.L.T. 792. . . . . 14.53
—— v. Smith (1865) 1 S.L.R. 53. . . . . 11.68
Bruce Bros (Glasgow) Ltd v. McVittie (1943) 62 Sh.Ct.Rep. 20. . . . . 21.78
Brunt v. Brunt, 1954 S.L.T. (Sh.Ct.) 74; (1954) 70 Sh.Ct.Rep. 264. . . . . 26.125
Bryce v. Allied Ironfounders Ltd, 1969 S.L.T. (Notes) 29. . . . . 9.30, 9.70, 9.122
—— v. West Lothian D.C., 1979 S.L.T. (Sh.Ct.) 50. . . . . 14.49
Brydekirk (Minister of) v. Minister and Heritors of Hoddam (1877) 4 R. 798. . . . . . 16.102
Bryson v. Belhaven Engineering and Motors Ltd (1908) 15 S.L.T. 1043. . . . . 24.12
Bryson & Co. Ltd v. Glasgow Civil Service and Mercantile Guild (1915) 32
    Sh.Ct.Rep. 23. . . . . 4.101
Bryson & Manson v. Picken (1895) 12 Sh.Ct.Rep. 26. . . . . 26.32
Buccleuch (Duke of) v. Cowan (1866) 4 M. 475; affd (1876) 4 R.(H.L.) 14. . . . . 13.43
Buchan v. Lumsden (1837) 9 Sc.Jur. 449. . . . . 2.14
—— v. J. Marr (Aberdeen) Ltd, 1987 S.C.L.R. 96. . . . . 21.36
—— v. Thomson, 1976 S.L.T. 42. . . . . 4.38, 12.42, 12.45, 12.49, 12.62, 14.28
Buchan (E) v. His Creditors (1835) 13 S. 1112. . . . . 11.15, 29.29
Buchan Supply Stores v. Morgan, 1954 S.L.T. (Sh.Ct.) 7. . . . . 15.65
Buchanan v. Advocate (Lord) (1882) 9 R. 1218; (1882) 19 S.L.R. 842. . . . . 4.76
—— v. Alexander Cross & Sons Ltd, 1911 2 S.L.T. 33. . . . . 8.60
—— v. Corbett, Borthwick & Co. (1827) 5 S. 805 (N.E. 745). 12.18
—— v. Dickson, 1935 S.L.T. (Sh.Ct.) 20. . . . . 23.13
—— v. Lumsden (1837) 9 Sc.Jur. 449. . . . . 9.121
—— v. Peyton (1897) 4 S.L.T. 324. . . . . 11.54
—— v. Stevenson (1880) 8 R. 220. . . . . 11.55
Buchanan & French Ltd v. Watson (1910) 26 Sh.Ct.Rep. 246. . . . . 14.30
Buckie v. Kirk (1907) 15 S.L.T. 98. . . . . 15.27
Buick v. Jaglar, 1973 S.L.T. (Sh.Ct.) 6. . . . . 2.79
Buie v. Stiven (1863) 2 M. 208. . . . . 2.28, 2.34
Buik v. Pattullo (1855) 17 D. 568; (1855) 27 Sc.Jur. 242. . . . . 11.70
Bulmer (H.P.) Ltd v. J. Bollinger SA [1974] Ch. 401; [1974] 3 W.L.R. 202; [1974] 2
    All E.R. 1226. . . . . 13.69
Burgess v. Stag Garage Ltd, 1959 S.C. 387. . . . . 19.35
Burke v. C. Alexander & Partners (Transport) Ltd (1957) 73 Sh.Ct.Rep. 153. . 7.33, 7.35,
    14.10
—— v. Dunfermline Mags, 1932 S.N. 68. . . . . 14.39

Burmah Oil Co. v. Bank of England [1980] A.C. 1090; [1979] 3 W.L.R. 722; (1979)
123 S.J. 786. . . . . 4.74
Burmah Oil Co. (Burmah Trading) Ltd v. Lord Advocate, 1964 S.C.(H.L.) 117;
1964 S.L.T. 218. . . . . 4.54
Burn-Murdoch's Trs v. Thomson's Trs (1908) 15 S.L.T. 721. . . . . 15.39
Burnett v. Murray (1877) 14 S.L.R. 616. . . . . 11.54
Burns v. Burns (1879) 7 R. 355; (1879) 17 S.L.R. 223. . . . . 11.11, 11.36
—— v. Dixon's Iron Works, 1961 S.C. 102. . . . . 9.28, 10.19
—— v. Gillies (1906) 8 F. 460; (1906) 13 S.L.T. 734; (1906) 43 S.L.R. 322. . . . . 11.21
—— v. Glasgow Corporation, 1917 1 S.L.T. 301. . . . . 2.15
—— v. Waddell & Son (1897) 24 R. 325; (1897) 4 S.L.T. 231; (1897) 34 S.L.R.
264. . . . . 18.30, 18.36
Burroughs Machines Ltd v. Davie Crawford & Partners, 1976 S.L.T. (Notes) 35. . . . . 8.60
Burrows, Petr, (1905) 21 Sh.Ct.Rep. 215. . . . . 15.95
Burrows v. Burrows, 1996 S.C. 378; 1996 S.L.T. 1313. . . . . 23.37
—— v. Glasgow Corporation, 1916 1 S.L.T. 420. . . . . 15.61
Burton v. Chapel Coal Co., 1909 S.C. 430; 1909 1 S.L.T. 111; (1909) 46 S.L.R.
375. . . . . 2.108
Burtonport Fishermen's Co-operative v. Sans Unkles, 1994 S.C.L.R. 844. . . . . . 5.95, 8.34,
14.06
Busby v. Clark (1904) 7 F. 162; (1904) 12 S.L.T. 516; (1904) 42 S.L.R. 142. . . . 6.22, 6.25
Butler v. Adam Lynn Ltd, 1965 S.C. 137; 1965 S.L.T. 197. . . . . 18.116
—— v. Bowman, 1989 S.C.L.R. 770. . . . . 16.33
—— v. Glasgow Corporation (1930) 47 Sh.Ct.Rep. 72. . . . . 25.08, 25.47
Butler v. Thom, 1982 S.L.T. (Sh.Ct.) 57. . . . . 13.59
Butters Bros & Co. v. British Diatomite Co. (1906) 23 Sh.Ct.Rep. 6. . . . . 19.66
Buttes Gas and Oil Co. v. Hammer [1982] A.C. 888; [1981] 3 W.L.R. 787; [1981] 3
All E.R. 616. . . . . 2.36
Buxton v. Buxton (1845) 7 D. 1063. . . . . 5.76
Byrne v. Wm Baird & Co., 1929 S.C. 624; 1929 S.L.T. 493; 1929 S.N. 65. . . . . 19.27
—— v. Ross, 1993 S.L.T. 307; 1992 S.C.L.R. 898. . . . . 2.21, 9.30, 21.98

C, Petrs, 1993 S.L.T. (Sh.Ct.) 8; 1993 S.C.L.R. 14. . . . . 28.11, 28.67, 28.92
C (a minor) (adoption application), Re [1993] 1 F.L.R. 87; [1992] Fam. Law 538;
[1992] F.C.R. 337; (1992) 156 L.G. Rev. 566. . . . . 28.82
C (a minor) (adoption order: conditions), Re [1989] 1 A.C. 1 (H.L.). 28.90, 28.120
C (minors) (wardship: adoption), Re [1989] 1 F.L.R. 222. . . . . 28.30
C v. D, 1968 S.L.T. (Sh.Ct.) 39. . . . . 28.133
—— v. G [1985] 1 W.L.R. 647. . . . . 18.111
—— v. M, 1923 S.C. 1. . . . . 10.60
—— v. S, 1989 S.L.T. 168; 1989 S.C.; 1989 S.C.L.R. 124. . . . . 5.29
—— v. ——, 1996 S.L.T. 1387. . . . . 28.82
—— v. W, 1950 S.L.T. (Notes) 8. 2.15, 8.27, 9.14, 10.60
CB v. AB (1885) 12 R.(H.L.) 36; (1885) 22 S.L.R. 461; (1885) 10 A.C. 171. . . . . 2.123
Cadbury Bros Ltd v. T. Mabon Ltd 1962 S.L.T. (Sh.Ct.) 28, (1962) 78 Sh.Ct.Rep.
55. . . . . 2.15, 7.13, 9.122, 18.87
Caddell, 1936 S.L.T. (Sh.Ct.) 7; (1935) 52 Sh.Ct.Rep. 203. 26.118
Caddies v. Harold Houldsworth & Co. (Wakehead) Ltd, 1954 S.L.T. (Notes) 3. . . . . 18.50
Cadzow v. White, 1986 S.L.T. (Sh.Ct.) 21. . . . . 14.26
Cadzow Finance Co. Ltd v. Fleming, 1985 S.L.T. (Sh.Ct.) 37. . . . . 19.53
Cafferty v. Cheyne, 1939 J.C. 1; 1939 S.L.T. 78; 1938 S.N. 101. . . . . 16.83
Caird v. Sirne (1887) 14 R.(H.L.) 37; (1887) 12A A.C. 326; (1887) 24 S.L.R. 569. . . 17.08
Cairney v. Bulloch, 1994 S.L.T. (Sh.Ct.) 37, 1993 S.C.L.R. 901. . . . . 6.04, 6.46
—— v. Mags of Callander, 1958 S.L.T. (Notes) 40. . . . . 4.108, 4.112, 4.113
Cairns v. Anstruther (1838) 1 D. 24; affd (1841) 2 Rob. App. 29. . . . . 11.73
—— v. McGregor, 1931 S.C. 84; 1931 S.L.T. 38; 1930 S.N. 140. . . . . 4.112, 4.113
—— v. Murray (1884) 12 R. 167; (1884) 22 S.L.R. 116. . . . . 2.34
Cairns (R.W.) Ltd v. Busby East Church Kirk Session, 1985 S.L.T. 493. . . . . 26.255
Calbron v. United Glass Ltd, 1965 S.L.T. 366. . . . . 10.29
Calcranes v. Aberdeen Northern Transport, 1978 S.L.T. (Sh.Ct.) 52. . . . . 30.112
Calder v. Mackay (1860) 22 D. 741. . . . . 2.101
—— v. Rush, 1970 S.L.T. (Sh.Ct.) 51. . . . . 14.68
—— v. Simpson, 1994 S.L.T. (Sh.Ct.) 32; 1994 S.C.L.R. 27. 21.22
Calder Chemicals Ltd v. Brunton, 1984 S.L.T. (Sh.Ct.) 96. . . . . 2.04, 12.24, 12.25
Calderwood v. Dundee Mags., 1944 S.C. 24; 1944 S.L.T. 191; 1943 S.N. 70. . . . . . . 17.04

Caldwell v. Caldwell 1983 S.L.T. 610. . . . . 1.29
—— v. Dykes (1906) 8 F. 839; (1906) 14 S.L.T. 67; (1906) 43 S.L.R. 606. . . 12.25, 18.117
—— v. Hamilton, 1919 S.C.(H.L.) 100; 1919 2 S.L.T. 154; (1919) 56 S.L.R.
    529. . . . . 11.12, 11.15, 29.16
—— v. Surnpters [1972] Ch. 478; [1972] 2 W.L.R. 412; [1972] 1 All E.R. 567. . . . . 11.53,
    17.29
Caledonian and Dumbartonshire Ry v. Turner (1849) 12 D. 406. . . . . 11.69
Caledonian Fish Selling Marine Stores Co. Ltd v. Allard Hewson & Co. Ltd, 1970
    S.C. 168; 1970 S.L.T. 195. . . . . 3.101
Caledonian Ry v. Chisholm (1889) 16 R. 622; (1889) 26 S.L.R. 489. . . . . 19.16
—— v. Clyde Shipping Co., 1917 S.C. 107; 1916 2 S.L.T. 308; (1916) 54 S.L.R.
    105. . . . . 2.101
—— v. Cochran's Trs (1897) 24 R. 855; (1897) 5 S.L.T. 21; (1897) 34 S.L.R. 643. . 18.92
—— v. Colt (1860) 3 Macq. 833. . . . . 24.09
—— v. Glasgow Corporation (1900) 2 F. 871. . . . . 18.36
—— v. —— (1905) 7 F. 1020; (1905) 13 S.L.T. 350; (1905) 42 S.L.R. 773. . . . . 12.70
—— v. Greenock Corporation, 1922 S.C. 299; 1922 S.L.T. 211; (1922) 59 S.L.R.
    372. . . . . 19.66
—— v. Orr (1855) 17 D. 812. . . . . 14.05
—— v. Symington, 1912 S.C. 1033; 1912 2 S.L.T. 12; (1912) 49 S.L.R. 751. . 15.44, 15.63
Callaghan v. J. & A. Weir Ltd (1955) 71 Sh.Ct.Rep. 312. . . . . 9.22
Callaghan (Myles J.) Ltd (in receivership) v. Glasgow D.C., 1988 S.L.T. 227; (1987)
    3 B.C.C. 337. . . . . 4.88
Calver v. Howard, Baker & Co. (1894) 22 R. 1; (1894) 32 S.L.R. 3. . . . . 4.107
Cambuslang West Church Committee v. Bryce (1897) 25 R. 322; (1897) 5 S.L.T.
    240; (1897) 35 S.L.R. 245. . . . . 12.19, 12.20, 19.03
Cameron, Petr, 1996 S.C.L.R. 26. . . . . 3.31
—— v. Cameron, 1996 S.C. 17; 1996 S.L.T. 306. . . . . 2.58
—— v. Cuthbertson, 1924 S.L.T. (Sh.Ct.) 67. . . . . 29.72
Cameron v. Ferrier (1913) 29 Sh.Ct.Rep. 125. . . . . 15.47
—— v. Lord Advocate, 1952 S.C. 165; 1952 S.L.T. 409. . . . . 4.54, 4.65
—— v. McNeill (1822) 1 S. 389 (N.E. 364). 11.82
—— v. Woolfson, 1918 S.C. 190; 1918 1 S.L.T. 128; (1918) 55 S.L.R. 233. . . 15.38, 16.58,
    16.94
Cameron and Gunn v. Ainslie (1848) 10 D. 446; (1848) 20 Sc.Jur. 130. . . . . 4.67
Cameron & Waterson v. Muir & Son (1861) 23 D. 535; (1861) 33 Sc.Jur. 272. . . . . 11.88
Campbell (1893) 1 S.L.T. 157. . . . . 23.38, 23.40
—— v. Alexander & Sons Ltd, 1934 S.L.T. 52; 1933 S.N. 90. . . . . 14.48
—— v. Ayr C.C. (1905) 13 S.L.T. 193. . . . . 8.22
—— v. Brown (1829) 3 W. & S. 441. . . . . 18.04
—— v. Caledonian Ry (1852) 14 D. 441. . . . . 17.07, 18.85, 1898
—— v. Campbell (1863) 1 M. 217; (1863) 35 Sc.Jur. 163. . . . . 9.110
—— v. —— (1865) 3 M. 501; (1865) 37 Sc.Jur. 238. . . . . 2.110
—— v. —— (1866) 4 M. 867; (1866) 38 Sc.Jur. 450. . . . . 2.125
—— v. ——, 1934 S.L.T. 45; 1933 S.N. 79. . . . . 19.05
—— v. ——, 1956 S.C. 285; 1957 S.L.T. 84. . . . . 13.66
—— v. ——, 1960 S.L.T. (Notes) 20. . . . . 13.61
—— v. Campbell's Trs, 1957 S.L.T. (Sh.Ct.) 53; (1957) 73 Sh.Ct.Rep. 210. . . . . . . 4.104
—— v. Cordale Investment Ltd, 1985 S.L.T. 305. . . . . 10.19, 10.21
—— v. Earl of Crawfurd (1783) Mor. 3973. . . . . 15.74
—— v. Fotheringham (1826) 4 S. 766 (N.E. 774). 10.04
—— v. Henderson, 1948 S.L.T. (Notes) 71. . . . . 15.29
—— v. ——, 1949 S.C. 172. . . . . 10.29, 16.02
—— v. Herron, 1948 J.C. 127; 1948 S.L.T. 515. . . . . 25.06
—— v. Lindsay, 1967 S.L.T. (Sh.Ct.) 30. . . . . 14.30
—— v. McAllister (1893) 1 S.L.T. 14. . . . . 4.116
—— v. McCance, 1929 S.L.T. 26; 1928 S.N. 145. . . . . 11.89, 18.05
—— v. Macpherson (1905) 22 Sh.Ct.Rep. 88. . . . . 6.05
—— v. Rossi, 1975 S.L.T. (Sh.Ct.) 25. . . . . 14.39
—— v. Train, 1910 S.C. 147; 1909 2 S.L.T. 458; (1909) 47 S.L.R. 200. . . . . 2.30
—— v. Watson's Tr. (1898) 25 R. 690. . . . . 11.21
Campbell and Cowan & Co. v. Train, 1910 S.C. 147; 1909 2 S.L.T. 458; (1909) 47
    S.L.R. 200. . . . . 13.46
Campbell & Henry v. Hunter (1910) 27 Sh.Ct. Rep 26. . . . . 5.88
Campbell's Trs v. Kinloch, 1925 S.L.T. 189; 192 S.N. 23. . . . . 2.30
—— v. O'Neill, 1911 S.C. 188; 1910 2 S.L.T. 392; (1910) 48 S.L.R. 115. . . . . . 18.04, 23.09
Campbells v. Murray, 1972 S.L.T. 249. . . . . 23.37

Campbeltown Building Co. v. Campbeltown Commrs (1894) 10 Sh.Ct.Rep. 16. . . . . 25.08
Canada Trust Co. v. Stolzenberg (No. 2) [1998] 1 W.L.R. 547. . . . . 3.76
Cannon (P.) (Garages) Ltd v. Lord Advocate, 1983 S.L.T. (Sh.Ct.) 50. . . . . . . 4.74, 15.55,
                                                                                                     15.86
Cant v. Eagle Star Insurance Co., 1937 S.L.T. 444; 1937 S.N. 61. . . . . 2.101
Cantors Properties (Scotland) Ltd v. Swears & Wells Ltd, 1977 S.L.T. (Notes) 30;
      affd 1978 S.C. 310; 1980 S.L.T. 165. . . . . 2.112, 9.124
Caprice v. Boswell (1986) 16 Fam. Law 52; (1985) 149 J.P. 703. . . . . 2.21
Carlos Leasing v. Taylor, 1986 S.L.T. (Sh.Ct.) 53. . . . . 19.36, 19.57
Carmichael v. Anstruther (1866) 4 M. 841. . . . . 2.112
—— v. Ashrif, 1985 S.C.C.R. 461. . . . . 5.26
—— v. Caledonian Ry (1868) 6 M. 671; (1868) 40 Sc.Jur. 347, (1868) 5 S.L.R.
      4131. . . . . 14.41
—— v. Sexton, 1986 S.L.T. 16. . . . . 15.94
—— v. Wingate 1990 S.L.T. (Sh.Ct.) 64. . . . . 1.31
Carnbroe Chemical Co. Ltd v. Lanark Middle Ward (1927) 43 Sh.Ct.Rep. 163. . . . . . 9.41
Carrigan v. Cleland (1907) 15 S.L.T. 543. . . . . 4.14
Carroll v. Scots Shipbuilding & Engineering Co. Ltd, 1969 S.L.T. (Notes) 46. . . . . . . 9.28
Carron v. Cowan & Co., Nov 28, 1809, F.C. 4.03
Carron Co. v. Stainton's Trs (1857) 19 D. 932. . . . . 21.11
Carruthers v. Caledonian Ry (1854) 16 D. 425. . . . . 9.68
Carruthers' Tr. v. Finlay & Wilson (1897) 24 R. 363; (1897) 4 S.L.T. 223; (1897) 34
      S.L.R. 254. . . . . 19.31
Carson v. Howard Doris Ltd, 1981 S.C. 278; 1981 S.L.T. 273. . . . . 10.41, 12.49
—— v. McDowall (1908) 24 Sh.Ct.Rep. 324. . . . . 18.37, 19.28
Carswell & Son v. Finlay (1887) 24 S.L.R. 643. . . . . 8.62, 10.06, 16.28
Carter v. Allison, 1966 S.C. 257; 1967 S.L.T. 17. . . . . 8.59, 9.25, 9.119
Carthwaite v. Carthwaite [1964] P. 356. . . . . 2.01
Carvana v. Glasgow Corporation, 1976 S.L.T. (Sh.Ct.) 3. . . . . 25.09, 25.11
Cassells v. Cassells, 1955 S.L.T. (Sh.Ct.) 41; (1955) 71 Sh.Ct.Rep. 113. . . . . 26.125
Cassells v. Stewart (1879) 6 R. 936. . . . . 29.25
Cassidy v. Cassidy, 1986 S.L.T. (Sh.Ct.) 17. . . . . 18.08
—— v. Celtic Football and Athletic Co. Ltd, 1995 S.L.T. (Sh.Ct.) 95; 1995 S.C.L.R.
      395. . . . . 19.40
Cassils & Co. v. Absalon (1907) 15 S.L.T. 48. . . . . 15.77, 15.78
Castanho v. Brown & Root (U.K.) Ltd [1981] A.C. 557; [1980] 3 W.L.R. 991; [1981]
      1 All E.R. 143. . . . . 2.19
Castlegreen Storage & Distributors Ltd v. Schreiber, 1982 S.L.T. 269. . . . . . . 14.16, 14.29
Castlehill Ltd v. Scott, Glasgow Sh.Ct., Oct. 2, 1979, unreported. 10.25, 10.31
Cathcart v. Board of Agriculture, 1915 S.C. 166; 1914 2 S.L.T. 379. . . . . 26.13
—— v. Cathcart (1899) 1 F. 781; (1899) 7 S.L.T. 3; (1899) 36 S.L.R. 596. . . . . 18.86
—— v. Cathcart's Trs (1906) 13 S.L.T. 909. . . . . 4.27
Cavendish Pharmacies Ltd v. Stephensons Ltd, 1998 S.L.T. (Sh.Ct.) 66. . . . . 12.68
Cecil v. Marchioness of Huntly (1905) 13 S.L.T. 189. . . . . 15.29
Cellular Clothing Co. v. Schulberg, 1952 S.L.T. (Notes) 73. . . . . 19.11, 19.12
Central Motor Engineering Co. v. Galbraith, 1918 S.C. 755; 1918 2 S.L.T. 177;
      (1918) 55 S.L.R. 702. . . . . 9.22, 9.131
Central R.C. v. B, 1985 S.L.T. 413. . . . . 18.11, 25.38
—— v. Barbour European Ltd, 1982 S.L.T. (Sh.Ct.) 49. . . . . 25.09, 26.335, 26.411
—— v. M, 1991 S.C.L.R. 300. . . . . 28.133, 28.152
Central SMT Co. Ltd v. Lanarkshire C.C., 1949 S.C. 450. . . . . 13.79
—— v. Cloudsley, 1974 S.L.T. (Sh.Ct.) 70. . . . . 12.53, 24.10
Central Trading Corporation v. James Mills (Montrose) Ltd, 1982 S.L.T. (Sh.Ct.)
      30. . . . . 11.63
Cessford v. Millport Commissioners (1899) 15 Sh.Ct.Rep. 362. . . . . 26.327
Chalmers v. Atlas Steel Foundry and Engineering Co. Ltd, 1964 S.L.T. (Notes) 98   14.31
—— v. Chalmers, 1982 S.L.T. 79. . . . . 9.121
—— v. —— 1983 S.L.T. 535. . . . . 13.23
Chalmers' Trs v. Watson (1860) 22 D. 1060; (1860) 32 Sc.Jur. 480. . . . . 4.105
Chamber's Trs v. Smith (1878) 5 R.(H.L.) 151. . . . . 29.26, 29.31
Channel Tunnel Group and France Manche S.A. v. Balfour Beatty Group [1993]
      A.C. 334; [1993] 2 W.L.R. 262; [1993] 1 All E.R. 664. . . . . 2.99
Chapman v. James Dickie & Co. (Drop Forgings) Ltd, 1985 S.L.T. 380. . . . . 10.20
—— v. Balfour (1875) 2 R. 291; (1875) 12 S.L.R. 195. . . . . 11.73
Charteris v. Charteris, 1967 S.C. 33; 1967; S.L.T. 172. . . . . 15.31
Cheek v. Santa Fe (U.K.) Ltd, 1978 S.L.T. (Sh.Ct.) 60. . . . . 9.119
Chiesa v. Greenshields, 1958 S.L.T. (Sh.Ct.) 58; (1958) 74 Sh.Ct.Rep. 171. . . . . 13.54

Chiron Corp. v. Evans Medical Ltd [1996] F.S.R. 863; (1996) 19(11) I.P.D. 2, Pat.
    Ct.. .... 3.26
Christie (1873) 1 R. 237. .... 4.23
—— v. Birrells, 1910 S.C. 986; 1910 2 S.L.T. 182; (1910) 47 S.L.R. 853. .... 12.37
—— v. Fife Coal Co. (1899) 2 F. 192; (1899) 7 S.L.T. 250; (1899) 37 S.L.R. 134. .. . 14.67
Chung v. Wigtown District Licensing Board, 1993 S.L.T. 1118. .... 26.255
Civil Service Building Society v. MacDougall, 1988 S.L.T. 687; 1988 S.C.L.R. 157. . 15.58,
    15.89
Clark, Petr, Apr. 26, 1984, unreported. 2.07
Clark v. Campbell (1873) 1 R. 281; (1873) 11 S.L.R. 138. .... 2.14, 11.70
—— v. Clark, 1967 S.C. 296; 1967 S.L.T. 108. .... 9.22
—— v. Comrie, 1910 1 S.L.T. 404. .... 18.20
—— v. Duncan (1833) 12 S. 158. .... 23.20
—— v. Hinde, Milne & Co. (1884) 12 R. 347. .... 29.83
—— v. Laddaws, 1994 S.L.T. 792; 1994 S.C.L.R. 521. .... 19.64
—— v. Loos (1855) 17 D. 306; (1855) 27 Sc.Jur. 133. .... 11.33
—— v. McLean, 1995 S.L.T. 235; 1994 S.C.L.R. 564. .... 18.114
—— v. National Bank of Scotland (1890) 27 S.L.R. 628. .... 29.18
—— v. Prydes 1959 S.L.T. (Notes) 16. .... 2.123
—— v. Scottish Amicable Assurance Society, 1922 S.L.T. (Sh.Ct.) 88; (1922) 38
    Sh.Ct.Rep. 170. .... 29.21, 21.49
—— v. Stirling (1839) 1 D. 955. .... 21.89
—— v. R.B. Tennant Ltd, 1962 S.C. 578. .... 8.59
—— v. Watson, 1982 S.L.T. 450. .... 13.04, 13.13, 17.28
Clark & Macdonald v. Bain (1895) 23 R. 102; (1895) 3 S.L.T. 159; (1895) 33 S.L.R.
    86. .... 5.83, 5.87
Clark's Exr v. Clark, 1953 S.L.T. (Notes) 58. .... 13.72, 13.78
Clarke v. Clarke's Trs, 1925 S.C. 693; 1925 S.L.T. 498, 1925 S.N. 93. .... 21.10
—— v. Chadburn [1985] 1 W.L.R. 78; (1984) 128 S.J. 767; [1985] 1 All E.R. 211;
    [1984] I.R.L.R. 350; (1984) 81 L.S. Gaz. 3094. .... 4.57
—— v. Edinburgh and District Tramways Co. Ltd, 1914 S.C. 775; 1914 2 S.L.T. 39;
    (1914) 51 S.L.R. 681. .... 9.35, 15.02
—— v. ——, 1919 S.C.(H.L.) 35; 1919 1 S.L.T. 247; (1919) 56 S.L.R. 303. .... 18.103
—— v. McNab (1888) 15 R. 670; (1888) 25 S.L.R. 389. .... 11.87, 19.09
—— v. Muller (1884) 11 R. 418; (1884) 21 S.L.R. 290. .... 11.54
—— v. Newmarch (1836) 14 S. 488. .... 11.76
—— v. Scott (1896) 23 R. 442; (1896) 3 S.L.T. 257; 1896 33 S.L.R. 318. .... 24.10
Clarkson v. Hastie, 1962 S.L.T. (Notes) 8. .... 12.25
Classic Cinema Ltd v. Motherwell D.C., 1977 S.L.T. (Sh.Ct.) 69. ...... 25.09, 25.11, 25.47
Clavering v. McCunn (1881) 19 S.L.R. 139. .... 15.56, 16.24
Cleave and Son Ltd v. Letters & Co. Ltd (1929) 45 Sh.Ct.Rep. 223. .... 30.133
Clegg v. McKirdy & MacMillan, 1932 S.C. 442; 1932 S.L.T. 250. .... 14.57
Cleghorn v. Fairgrieve, 1982 S.L.T. (Sh.Ct.) 17. .... 19.11
Cleland v. Campbell, 1998 S.L.T. 642. .... 21.26
—— v. Clason and Clark (1849) 11 D. 601; (1850) 7 Bell's App. 153. .... 5.75
Clements v. Edinburgh Corporation (1905) 7 F. 651; (1905) 13 S.L.T. 59. .... 19.41
—— v. Macaulay (1866) 4 M. 583; (1866) 38 Sc.Jur. 309. .... 2.88, 2.89
Clinton (Lord) v. Brown (1874) 1 R. 1137; (1874) 11 S.L.R. 665. .... 19.11
Clippens Oil Co. Ltd v. Edinburgh and District Water Trs (1905) 7 F. 914; (1905)
    42 S.L.R. 698; (1905) 13 S.L.T. 220. .... 10.29, 10.30
—— v. —— (1906) 8 F. 731; (1906) 13 S.L.T. 985; (1906) 43 S.L.R. 540. .... 21.92
Clugston v. Scottish Women's Friendly Society (1914) 30 Sh.Ct.Rep. 150. .... 10.04
Cluny Investment Services v. Macandrew & Jenkins, 1992 S.C.L.R. 478. .... 11.23
Clyde Caravans (Langbank) Ltd v. Renfrew C.C., 1962 S.L.T. (Sh.Ct.) 20. .... 26.161
Clyde Nail Co. Ltd v. A. C. Moore & Co. Ltd, 1949 S.L.T. (Notes) 43; (1961) 77
    Sh.Ct.Rep. 128. .... 14.67, 19.52
Clydesdale Bank v. D. & H. Cohen, 1943 S.C. 244; 1943 S.L.T. 245; 1943 S.N.
    10. .... 2.100, 8.19, 13.79
—— v. McColl (1941) 59 Sh.Ct.Rep. 159. .... 21.71
—— v. Paton (1896) 23 R.(H.L.) 22; (1896) 4 S.L.T. 7; (1896) 33 S.L.R. 533. . 2.15, 9.14,
    10.60
—— v. Walker & Bain, 1926 S.C. 72. .... 2.76
Clydesdale Bank plc v. Scottish Midland Co-operative Society Ltd, 1995 S.C.L.R.
    1151. .... 29.45
Clyne v. Murray (1831) 9 S. 338. .... 24.15
Coatbridge Health Studios Ltd v. Alexander George & Co. Ltd, 1992 S.L.T. 717. . 14.08,
    14.12

Coates v. Lothian R.C., Linlithgow Sh.Ct., Jan. 3, 1986, unreported............. 26.113
Cobb v. Baker Oil Tools (U.K.) Ltd, 1984 S.L.T. 232..................... 14.25, 14.27
Cobban v. British Transport Commission [1955] C.L.Y. 3535................... 9.104
Cobham v. Minter, 1986 S.L.T. 336.............................. 4.109, 12.46
Cochran v. Paton & Co. (1919) 36 Sh.Ct.Rep. 3.............................. 12.25
Cochrane v. Paul (1857) 20 D. 178................................ 2.94, 2.98, 2.113
Cockburn v. Clark (1885) 12 R. 707; (1885) 22 S.L.R. 475................. 21.73, 21.74
Cohen (George), Sons & Co. v. Jamison & Paterson, 1963 S.C. 289; 1963 S.L.T.
  35.. 11.43, 11.45
Coin Controls Ltd v. Suzo International (U.K.) Ltd and others, Laddie J., Mar. 26,
  1997.. 3.26
Colbeck Bros Ltd v. Wallace Todd & Co. (1923) 39 Sh.Ct.Rep. 315.............. 19.06
Colbron v. United Glass Ltd, 1965 S.L.T. 366; 1965 S.L.T. (Notes) 59..... 10.17, 11.89
Colchester Estates (Cardiff) v. Carlton Industries plc [1986] Ch. 80; [1984] 2 W.L.R.
  693; [1984] 2 All E.R. 601... 18.08
Cole-Hamilton v. Boyd, 1962 S.C. 247, (1963) S.C.(H.L.) 1; 1962 S.L.T. 180; 1963
  S.L.T. 157... 4.108
Collie & Co. v. Mitchell, 1935 S.L.T. 16... 5.89
Collier v. Ritchie & Co. (1884) 12 R. 47; (1884) 22 S.L.R. 38................... 11.54
Collins v. Barrowfield United Oddfellows, 1915 S.C. 190; (1914) 42 S.L.R. 388.... 26.201
—— v. N.B. Banking Co. (1851) 13 D. 541.................................. 15.34
Collum v. Glasgow Corporation, 1964 S.L.T. 199............................. 14.30
Colonial Mutual Group (U.K. Holdings) Ltd v. Johnston, 1995 S.C.L.R. 1165...... 8.36,
                                                                        14.07
Colville v. Colville, 1988 S.L.T. (Sh.Ct.) 23........................... 18.25, 22.90
Colvin v. Montgomery Preservations Ltd, 1995 S.L.T. (Sh.Ct.) 15; 1995 S.C.L.R.
  40... 8.35, 13.01, 13.02
Comer v. James Scott & Co. (Electrical Engineers) Ltd, 1976 S.L.T. (Notes) 72... 15.56
Comet Products U.K. Ltd v. Hawkex Plastics Ltd [1971] 2 Q.B. 67; [1971] 2 W.L.R.
  361; [1971] 1 All E.R. 1141... 2.21
Comex Houlder Diving Ltd v. Colne Fishing Co. Ltd, 1987 S.L.T. 443............. 4.49
Commercial Aluminium Windows Ltd v. Cumbernauld Development Copn, 1987
  S.L.T. (Sh.Ct.) 91.. 29.35
Commercial Bank of Scotland Ltd v. Eagle Star Insurance Co. Ltd, 1950 S.L.T.
  (Notes) 30.. 11.14
Commerzbank Aktiengesellschaft v. Large, 1977 S.C. 375........................ 9.91
Commission for Racial Equality v. Amari Plastics Ltd [1982] Q.B. 1194; [1982] 2
  W.L.R. 972; [1982] 2 All E.R. 499.................................. 26.373
Customs and Excise (Commissioners of), Applicants, 1992 S.L.T. 11........ 29.91, 29.92
Commrs. of Highland Roads v. Machray, Croall & Co. (1858) 20 D. 1165......... 2.125
Comrie v. Gow & Sons (1931) 47 Sh.Ct.Rep. 159............................. 25.19
Conacher v. Conacher (1857) 20 D. 252.................................. 11.82
Connell v. Ferguson (1857) 19 D. 482; (1857) 29 Sc.Jur. 228.......... 2.11, 2.13, 2.14,
                                                                    9.14, 9.67, 9.118
—— v. Ferguson (1861) 23 D. 683....................................... 21.61
—— v. Grierson (1865) 3 M. 1166...................................... 13.71, 13.73
Connelly v. DPP [1964] A.C. 1254; [1964] 2 W.L.R. 1145; [1964] 2 All E.R. 401.... 2.05,
                                                                          2.07
Connelly (A.P.) v. RTZ Corporation plc [1997] 4 All E.R. 335................... 2.89
Conney v. Kilpatrick, 1990 G.W.D. 5–285............................... 24.04
Connolly v. Edinburgh Northern Hospitals, 1974 S.L.T. (Notes) 53.............. 15.88
Connor v. Andrew Main & Sons, 1967 S.L.T. (Notes) 71...................... 12.50
Constant v. Christensen, 1912 S.C. 1371; 1912 2 S.L.T. 62; (1912) 50 S.L.R. 27..... 2.76
Construction Industry Training Board v. James Duncan (Plumbers) Ltd, Glasgow
  Sh.Ct., Mar. 13, 1985, unreported.................................. 12.70
Consultants and Technologists North Sea Ltd v. Scott, 1986 S.L.T. 685........... 7.30
Continental Bank v. Aeakos Compania [1994] 1 W.L.R. 588; [1994] 2 All E.R. 540;
  [1994] 1 Lloyd's Rep. 505... 3.60
Continental Illinois National Bank and Trust Co. of Chicago v. Papanicolaou [1986]
  2 Lloyd's Rep. 441... 12.36
Convery v. Kirkwood, 1985 S.L.T. 483................................. 16.30
Conway v. Dalziel (1901) 3 F. 918..................................... 10.17
—— v. Rimmer [1968] A.C. 910; [1968] 2 W.L.R. 998; [1968] 1 All E.R. 874..... 4.73, 15.55
Conzemius Ltd v. Findlay (1924) 41 Sh.Ct.Rep. 337......................... 11.32
Cook v. Crane, 1922 S.C. 631; 1922 S.L.T. 397; (1922) 59 S.L.R. 466.. 16.97, 18.81, 18.82
—— v. Kinghorn (1904) 12 S.L.T. 186................................... 11.54
—— v. McGinnes, 1982 S.L.T. (Sh.Ct.) 101.............................. 13.61

Cook v. Robertson's Exr 1960 S.L.T. (Sh.Ct.) 4, (1959) 75 Sh.Ct.Rep. 161. . . 10.25, 17.08
Cookney v. Laverty, 1967 S.L.T. (Notes) 89. . . . . 12.64, 13.80
Cooney v. Kilpatrick, 1989 S.C. 61; 1989 S.L.T. 457; 1989 S.C.L.R. 266. . . . . 11.52, 11.54
Cooper v. Cooper, 1987 S.L.T. (Sh.Ct.) 37. . . . . 22.47
Cooper v. Frame & Co. (1893) 20 R. 920; (1893) 1 S.L.T. 125; (1893) 30 S.L.R.
    807. . . . . 11.52, 11.53, 11.54
Cooper & Co. v. Deutsche Bank, Berlin (1914) 31 Sh.Ct.Rep. 67. . . . . 4.03
Cooper (Owen) Estates v. Lexden and Winstree RDC (1964) 63 L.G.R. 66; P. &
    C.R. 233, D.C.. . . . . 26.161
Coppola v. Midlothian District Licensing Board, 1983, S.L.T. (Sh.Ct.) 95. . . . . . . 26.255
Coral (Joe) (Racing) Ltd v. Hamilton D.C., 1981 S.C. 285; 1981 S.L.T. (Notes)
    106. . . . . 26.38
Cordiner, Petr, 1973 J.C. 16; 1973 S.L.T. 125. . . . . 2.25, 21.92
Cormack v. Crown Estate Commrs, 1983 S.L.T. 179. . . . . 25.19
—— v. Waters (1846) 8 D. 889. . . . . 14.22, 14.24
Cornhill Insurance Co. Ltd v. Fraser, Owen & Co. Ltd (1936) 53 Sh.Ct.Rep. 168. . . 2.42,
    20.02
Cornwall v. Walker (1871) 8 S.L.R. 442. . . . . 19.29
Corson v. Macmillan, 1927 S.L.T. (Sh.Ct.) 13. . . . . 11.22
Corvi v. Ellis, 1969 S.C. 312; 1969 S.L.T. 350. . . . . 4.48, 14.37
Costine's Trs v. Costine (1878) 5 R. 782, (1878) 15 S.L.R. 446. . . . . 21.71
Costorphine v. Kasten (1898) 1 F. 287; (1898) 6 S.L.T. 238; (1898) 36 S.L.R. 174. . . 6.26
Coul v. Ayr C.C., 1909 S.C. 422; 1909 1 S.L.T. 144; (1909) 46 S.L.R. 338. . . . 10.25, 18.82
Couper v. McGuiness (1948) 64 Sh.Ct.Rep. 249. . . . . 20.05
Coutts v. J.M. Piggins Ltd, 1983 S.L.T. 320. . . . . 5.86, 17.12
—— v. Wear, (1914) 2 S.L.T. 86. . . . . 2.109
Cowan v. Farnie (1836) 14 S. 634. . . . . 4.125, 12.19, 19.23
—— v. Liqrs of Western Bank (1860) 22 D. 1260; (1860) 32 Sc.Jur. 564. . . . . 11.44
—— v. Stewart (1872) 10 M. 735; (1872) 44 Sc.Jur. 424; (1872) 9 S.L.R. 471. . . . . . 2.16
Cowan & Sons v. Duke of Buccleuch (1876) 4 R.(H.L.) 14; (1876) 14 S.L.R. 189;
    (1876) 2 A.C. 344. . . . . 4.38
Cowie v. Atlantic Drilling Co. Ltd, 1995 S.L.T. 1151; 1995 S.C.L.R. 335. . . . 21.21, 21.22,
    21.23
—— v. Carron Co., 1945 S.C. 280; 1945 S.L.T. 237; 1945 S.N. 26. . . . . 10.13, 14.15, 14.34
—— v. Kiddie (1897) 5 S.L.T. (Sh.Ct.) 331; (1897) 14 Sh.Ct.Rep. 26. . . . . 26.32
Coxall v. Stewart, 1976 S.L.T. 275. . . . . 9.121, 21.02, 21.04
Coyle v. National Coal Board, 1959 S.L.T. 114. . . . . 2.100
Cozy Legs of Scotland v. Razno & Co. Ltd, 1991 S.L.T. (Sh.Ct.) 52. . . . . 7.29
Craig v. Brunsgaard, Kjosterud & Co. (1896) 23 R. 500; 3 S.L.T. 265. . . . . 3.100
—— v. Craig (1906) 14 S.L.T. 469; (1906) 44 S.L.R. 100. . . . . 18.37, 19.15, 19.55
—— v. Lorn District Committee of Argyll C.C. (1911) 28 Sh.Ct.Rep. 14. . . . . 26.327
—— v. Walker, 1930 S.N. 144. . . . . 15.19
Craig Line Steamship Co. Ltd v. N.B. Storage and Transit Co., 1915 S.C. 113; 1914
    2 S.L.T. 326; (1914) 52 S.L.R. 65. . . . . 4.03
Craig-Na-Brro Sales v. Munro Furniture Ltd, 1974 S.L.T. (Sh.Ct.) 107. . . . . 8.05
Craven (Earl of) v. Lord Elibank's Trs (1854) 16 D. 811. . . . . 4.10, 4.16
Craw v. Malcolm (1908) 24 Sh.Ct.Rep. 268. . . . . 14.26
Crawford v. Kennedy (1694) Mor. 7866. . . . . 4.76
—— v. Ritchie (1837) 16 S. 107. . . . . 11.33
Crawford Bros v. Commrs of Northern Lighthouses, 1925 S.C.(H.L.) 22; 1925
    S.L.T. 341; 1925 S.N. 61. . . . . 2.101
Crawfurd v. Ballantine's Trs (1833) 12 S. 113; (1833) 6 Sc.Jur. 71. . . . . 11.82
Cray v. McHardy (1862) 24 D. 1043. . . . . 2.104
Crédit Chimique v. James Scott Engineering Ltd, 1979 S.C. 406; 1982 S.L.T. 131. . . 2.89,
    2.91, 2.92, 9.120
Crédit Suisse Financial Products v. Société Générale d'Entreprises [1997] I.L.Pr.
    165 (C.A.). 3.51
Creed v. Christie and Ferguson, 1991 S.L.T. (Sh.Ct.) 44. . . . . 10.17, 13.15
Crendon Timber Engineering Ltd v. Miller Construction Ltd, 1996 S.L.T. (Sh.Ct.)
    102. . . . . 5.97, 18.56
Cresswell v. Hodgson [1951] 2 K.B. 92; [1951] 1 All E.R. 710. . . . . 26.269
Crichton v. Wood, 1981 S.L.T. (Notes) 66. . . . . 2.43, 16.24
Crichton Bros v. Crichton (1902) 5 F. 178; (1902) 40 S.L.R. 60. . . . . 11.54
Crighton v. Lord Rossie (1573) Mor. 2178. . . . . 4.16
Cringean v. McNeil, 1996 S.L.T. (Sh.Ct.) 136; 1996 S.C.L.R. 184 (Sh.Ct.). 7.06
Critchley v. Campbell (1884) 11 R. 475; (1884) 21 S.L.R. 326. . . . . 14.68
Crolla v. Edinburgh District Licensing Board, 1983 S.L.T. (Sh.Ct.) 11. . . . . 26.255

Crombie v. British Transport Commission, 1961 S.C. 108. . . . .   14.38, 19.12
Crompton (Alfred) Amusement Machines Ltd v. Commissioners of Customs and
    Excise [1974] A.C. 405; [1973] 2 All E.R. 1169. . . . .   4.74
Cropper v. Smith (1884) 26 Ch.D. 700. . . . .   5.102
Croskery v. Gilmour's Trs (1890) 17 R. 697; (1890) 27 S.L.R. 490. . . . .   4.48
Cross v. Noble, 1975 S.L.T. (Notes) 33. . . . .   12.51
Cross & Sons v. Bordes (1879) 6 R. 934; (1879) 16 S.L.R. 539. . . . .   11.84, 18.70
Crossan v. Caledonian Ry (1902) 5 F. 187; (1902) 10 S.L.T. 562; (1902) 40 S.L.R.
    167. . . . .   19.38
Crow v. Crow, 1986 S.L.T. 270. . . . .   23.42
Crudens Ltd v. Tayside Health Board, 1979 S.C. 142. . . . .   2.105, 2.108
Cruickshank v. Gow & Sons (1888) 15 R. 326; (1888) 25 S.L.R. 292. . . . .   9.78
Cruickshank Fraser & Co. v. Caledonian Ry (1876) 3 R. 484. . . . .   9.24
Culbert v. Ramsay, 1951 S.L.T. (Notes) 16. . . . .   9.68
Cullen v. Brown (1860) 22 D. 1090. . . . .   11.67, 11.77, 11.80, 12.18
——— v. Buchanan (1862) 24 D. 1280; (1862) 34 Sc.Jur. 616. . . . .   11.30, 11.33
Cullen's Exrs v. Kilmarnock Theatre Co., 1913 1 S.L.T. 290; 1914 2 S.L.T. 334. . . . .   19.05
Cumming v. Scottish Daily Record, *The Times*, June 8, 1995. . . . .   2.93, 3.76
——— v. Stewart, 1928 S.C. 709; 1928 S.L.T. 421; 1928 S.N. 76. . . . .   12.10
——— v. Williamson (1842) 4 D. 1304; (1842) 14 Sc.Jur. 419. . . . .   11.44
Cuningham v. Home (1760) Mor. 747. . . . .   11.13
Cunningham v. Black (1883) 10 R. 441. . . . .   2.29
——— v. Cunningham, 1965 S.C. 78; 1965 S.L.T. (Notes) 12. . . . .   18.69, 18.98
——— v. Skinner (1902) 4 F. 1124; (1902) 10 S.L.T. 148; (1902) 39 S.L.R. 722. . . . . .   2.106,
                                                                                                                        11.53, 11.65
——— v. Smith (1880) 7 R. 424; (1880) 17 S.L.R. 269. . . . .   4.23
——— v. Western SMT Co. Ltd (1945) 61 Sh.Ct.Rep. 99. . . . .   14.39
Cunninghame-Jardine v. Cunninghame-Jardine's Trs, 1979 S.L.T. 298. . . . . . .   21.02, 21.05
Curran v. HAT Painters (Scotland) Ltd, 1987 S.L.T. 98. . . . .   21.22, 21.26
Currie v. Cowan & Co., 1911 2 S.L.T. 467. . . . .   4.115
——— v. McKnight (1896) 24 R.(H.L) 1; (1896) 4 S.L.T. 161; (1896) 34 S.L.R. 93;
    [1897] A.C. 97. . . . .   2.76
Currie's Trs v. Bothwell, 1954 S.L.T. (Sh.Ct.) 87; (1954) 70 Sh.Ct.Rep. 233. . . . .   21.66
Custom Made Commercial (C-288/92) [1994] E.C.R. I-2913. . . . .   3.92
Cuthbert v. Cuthbert's Trs, 1908 S.C. 967; (1908) 16 S.L.T. 164; (1908). 11.15, 29.29
——— v. Stuart-Gray (1904) 21 Sh.Ct.Rep. 31. . . . .   8.06
Cuthill v. Burns (1862) 24 D. 849. . . . .   5.87
Cutlar v. McLeod's Tr. (1876) 13 S.L.R. 308. . . . .   14.40

D (A MINOR) (ADOPTION: PARENTAL AGREEMENT), RE [1990] F.C.R. 615. . . . .   28.06
D (an infant), Re [1977] A.C. 602. . . . .   28.133
D and another (minors) (adoption reports: confidentiality), Re [1995] 4 All ER 385. . . . . . .
                                                                                                                        28.87
D v. C.D. (1908) 15 S.L.T. 911. . . . .   15.102
——— v. F, 1994 S.C.L.R. 417. . . . .   28.18
——— v. Grampian Regional Council, 1995 S.L.T. 519; 1995 S.C.L.R. 516. . . . .   28.122
——— v. National Society for the Prevention of Cruelty to Children [1978] A.C. 171;
    [1977] 2 W.L.R. 201; [1977] 1 All E.R. 589. . . . .   15.55
——— v. Strathclyde Regional Council, 1991 S.C.L.R. 185 (Notes). 28.21
——— v. Strathclyde Region, 1988 S.C.L.R. 592. . . . .   28.21
D and D v. F (1993) 17 *Adoption & Fostering* 3.57. . . . .   28.18
DSQ Property Co. Ltd v. Lotus Cars Ltd [1987] 1 W.L.R. 127. . . . .   11.57
DTL Gas Supplies Ltd v. Protan Srl, 1998 G.W.D. 31–1578. . . . .   18.34
DTZ Debenham Thorpe v. I. Henderson Transport Services, 1995 S.L.T. 553; 1995
    S.C.L.R. 345. . . . .   5.95, 5.96 8.34, 18.56, 14.06
Dairon v. Dairon (1900) 3 F. 320; (1900) 3 S.L.T. 303; (1900) 38 S.L.R. 179. . . . . . .   19.59
Dalgleish v. Glasgow Corporation, 1976 S.C. 32; 1976 S.L.T. 157. . . . .   18.08, 18.113
——— v. Leitch (1889) 2 White 302. . . . .   18.92
——— v. Mitchell (1886) 23 S.L.R. 552. . . . .   14.23
——— v. Scott (1822) 1 S. 506 (N.E. 469). 1.27
Dalhanna Knitwear Co. Ltd v. Mohammed Ali, 1967 S.L.T. (Sh.Ct.) 74. . . . .   2.79
Dalkeith Police Commrs v. Duke of Buccleuch (1889) 16 R. 575; (1889) 26 S.L.R.
    435. . . . .   19.14
Dallas v. J. & F. Anderson, 1977 S.L.T. (Sh.Ct.) 88. . . . .   11.46, 11.60, 11.65
Dallas & Co. v. McArdle, 1949 S.C. 481; 1949 S.L.T. 375. . . . .   8.59, 8.60
Dalmahoy and Wood v. Mags of Brechin (1859) 21 D. 210; (1859) 31 Sc.Jur. 119. .   11.89

Dalton & Co. v. Boyle & Co. (1909) 26 Sh.Ct.Rep. 53. . . . . 18.37
Dalzell v. Dalzell, 1985 S.L.T. 286. . . . . 14.64
Dalziel v. Scott (1831) 3 Sc.Jur. 591. . . . . 11.83
Dampskibsselskabet Neprune v. Blasquez (1908) 15 S.L.T. 1046. . . . . 11.70
Daniel v. Foster, 1989 S.L.T. (Sh.Ct.) 43; 1989 S.C.L.R. 378. . . . . 3.09
Danvaern Production v. Schufabriken Otterbeck [1995] E.C.R. I-2053. . . . . 3.40
Darling v. Gray (1892) 19 R.(H.L.) 31. . . . . 4.40
D'Arpino v. Glasgow Town Council (1935) 51 Sh.Ct.Rep. 228. . . . . 26.108
Darroch v. Kerr, 1909 S.C. 112. . . . . 16.60
Data Controls (Middlesborough) Ltd v. British Railways Board, 1991 S.L.T. 426;
    1991 S.C.L.R. 359. . . . . 5.03, 13.59, 30.29
Davenport v. Corinthian Motor Policies at Lloyds 1991 S.L.T. 774; 1992 S.C.L.R.
    221. . . . . 3.93
Davidson v. Anderson, 1921 S.C. 369. . . . . 7.25
—— v. Charteris (1738) Mor. 16899. . . . . 6.23
—— v. Davidson (1860) 22 D. 749; (1860) 32 Sc.Jur. 305. . . . . 28.108
—— v. —— (1891) 18 R. 884; (1891) 29 S.L.R. 688. . . . . 3.90, 6.02, 6.08, 18.35, 28.36
—— v. Davidson's Trs, 1952 S.L.T. (Notes) 3. . . . . 13.79
—— v. Duncan, 1981 S.C. 83. . . . . 18.81, 18.82
—— v. McFadyean, 1942 J.C. 95; 1943 S.L.T. 47; 1942 S.N. 24. . . . . 16.82
—— v. Murray (1784) Mor. 761. . . . . 11.13
—— v. North of Scotland Hydro-Electric Board, 1954 S.C. 230; 1954 S.L.T. 175. . . 18.21
—— v. Panti, 1915 1 S.L.T. 273. . . . . 14.37
—— v. Robertson (1827) 5 S. 751 (N.E. 702). 12.09
—— v. Shipmasters' Society of Aberdeen (1897) 5 S.L.T. 34. . . . . 2.85
—— v. Watson, 1925 S.C. 883; 1925 S.L.T. 588; 1925 S.N. 110. . . . . 13.34
—— v. Whatmough, 1930 S.L.T. 536; 1930 S.N. 102. . . . . 4.113, 14.65
Davidson & Syme, W.S. v. Booth, 1971 S.L.T. (Notes) 11. 5.90
Davidson, Pirie & Co. v. Dihle's Reps (1900) 2 F. 640; (1900) 7 S.L.T. 384; (1960)
    37 S.L.R. 446. . . . . 4.106, 12.11
Davie v. Edinburgh Corp., 1977 S.L.T. (Notes) 5; 1978 S.L.T. (Notes) 37. . . . . . 9.30, 9.33
—— v. Edinburgh Mags, 1951 S.C. 720; 1952 S.L.T. 74. . . . . 9.121
—— v. ——, 1953 S.C. 34; 1953 S.L.T. 54. . . . . 16.83
—— v. Stark (1876) 3 R. 1114; (1876) 13 S.L.R. 666. . . . . 8.58
Davies v. BICC Ltd, 1980 S.L.T. (Sh.Ct.) 17. . . . . 10.37
—— v. Davies, Edinburgh Sh.Ct., July 1, 1982, unreported. 2.104
—— v. Direct Loans Ltd [1986] 1 W.L.R. 823; [1986] 2 All E.R. 783. . . . . 26.213
—— v. Hunter, 1933 S.L.T. 158. . . . . 8.60
Davis (Jack) Publicity Ltd v. Kennedy, Paisley Sh.Ct., Dec. 18, 1984, unreported. . 9.111,
    10.24, 10.58, 11.82, 11.83,
    12.25, 13.14
Davis's Tutor v. Glasgow Victoria Hospitals, 1950 S.C. 382; 1950 S.L.T. 392. . . . . . . 4.14
Dawson v. Dawson, 1956 S.L.T. (Notes) 58. . . . . 16.76
—— v. McLean (1896), unreported. 17.03
De Duca v. Sillitoe (1936) 52 Sh.Ct.Rep. 18. . . . . 12.03
De Melo v. Bazazi, 1995 S.L.T. (Sh.Ct.) 57, 1995 S.C.L.R. 564. . . . . 14.06, 14.10
Dean v. Walker (1873) 11 M. 759; (1873) 45 Sc.Jur. 468; (1873) 10 S.L.R. 535. . . . . 19.14
Dean Warwick Ltd v. Borthwick, 1981 S.L.T. (Notes) 18. . . . . 11.58
Deane v. Lothian R.C., 1986 S.L.T. 22. . . . . 21.89
Deans of Chapel Royal v. Johnstone (1869) 7 M (H.L.) 19. 4.76
Deer District Committee v. Shanks and McEwan, 1911 1 S.L.T. 314. . . . . 26.390
Delta Sales & Marketing Ltd v. Nugent, 1991 S.C.L.R. 461. . . . . 14.74
Dempster v. Potts (1836) 14 S. 521. . . . . 11.72
—— v. Wallace Hunter & Co. (1834) 12 S. 844. . . . . 19.41
Dennison v. Paisley Ry (1899) 16 Sh.Ct.Rep. 17. . . . . 26.95
Derber v. J. Smith Stewart and Co. Ltd, 1957 S.L.T. (Sh.Ct.) 53; (1957) 73 Sh.Ct.
    Rep. 181. . . . . 11.65, 18.41
D'Ernesti v. D'Ernesti (1882) 9 R. 655; (1882) 19 S.L.R. 436. . . . . 11.69, 11.70, 11.71
Derrick v. Derrick (1900) 8 S.L.T. 321. . . . . 11.54
Dessau v. Daish (1897) 24 R. 976; (1897) 5 S.L.T. 74; (1897) 34 S.L.R. 739. . . . . 11.67,
    11.68, 11.69, 11.71
Devos (N.V.) Gebroeder v. Sunderland Sportswear Ltd, 1987 S.L.T. 331. . . . . 9.30
Devotion II, The, 1979 S.C. 80. . . . . 14.41
Dewar v. Dewar's Trs (1906) 14 S.L.T. 238. . . . . 4.25
—— v. John Dewar & Sons Ltd (1899) 2 F. 249. . . . . 2.38
Dexter & Carpenter v. Waugh & Robertson, 1925 S.C. 28; 1924 S.L.T. 765. . . . . 15.31

Dick v. Blairgowrie Town Council (1910) 27 Sh.Ct.Rep. 243. . . . .   15.65
—— v. Mcllwham (1828) 6 S. 798. . . . .   4.17
Dick & Parker v. Langloan Iron and Chemical Co. Ltd (1904) 21 Sh.Ct.Rep. 139. .   11.26
Dick & Stevenson v. Mackay (1880) 7 R. 778; (1880) 17 S.L.R. 565. . . . .   16.91
—— v. Woodside Steel and Iron Co. (1888) 16 R. 242; (1888) 26 S.L.R. 165. . . . . .   10.05
Dickey v. British Mexican Ry (1893) 1 S.L.T. 273. . . . .   11.68, 11.75
Dickson v. Bryan (1889) 16 R. 673; (1889) 26 S.L.R. 511.   2.31
—— v. Graham (1887) 4 R. 717; (1887) 14 S.L.R. 471. . . . .   2.54
—— v. Murray (1866) 4 M. 797. . . . .   2.42, 12.67, 12.71
—— v. United Dominions Trust Ltd (No. 2), 1983 S.L.T. 189. . . . .   2.97, 29.67
—— v. United Dominions Trust Ltd, 1988 S.L.T. 19.   2.112, 4.111
Dickson & Walker v. John Mitchell & Co., 1910 S.C. 139; 1909 2 S.L.T. 390; (1909)
    47 S.L.R. 110. . . . .   2.27, 2.29
Dickson's Trs (1894) 2 S.L.T. 61. . . . .   26.408
Differ v. GKN Kwikform Ltd, 1990 S.L.T. (Sh.Ct.) 49. . . . .   14.12
Dinardo Partnership Ltd v. Thomas Tait & Sons Ltd, 1995 S.C.L.R. 941. . . . .   8.35, 13.01
Dingley v. Chief Constable, Strathclyde Police, 1997 S.C.L.R. 376. . . . .   19.06
—— v. Black (1934) 51 Sh.Ct.Rep. 171. . . . .   11.54
Dingwall v. Cunninghame D.C., Kilmarnock Sh.Ct., Jan. 26, 1978, unreported. . . .   26.255
—— v. Burns (1871) 9 M. 582. . . . .   4.17
—— v. Dingwall, 1958 S.L.T. (Notes) 41. . . . .   16.24
—— v. J Wharton (Shipping) Ltd [1961] 2 Lloyd's Rep. 213. . . . .   16.76
Director-General of Fair Trading v. Boswell, 1979 S.L.T. (Sh.Ct.) 9. .   25.01, 25.14, 25.25,
                                                                                                    25.41, 26.404
Disblair Estates Ltd v. Jackson, Aberdeen Sh.Ct., Nov. 23, 1982, unreported. 23.08,
                                                                                                        30.261
Dixon Street Motors v. Associated Rentals Ltd, 1980 S.L.T. (Sh.Ct.) 46. . . . . . .   1.11, 7.28
Dobbie v. Duncanson (1872) 10 M. 810; (1872) 9 S.L.R. 521. . . . .   18.87, 19.05
—— v. Forth Ports Authority, 1974 S.C. 40. . . . .   15.56
—— v. Thomson (1880) 7 R. 983. . . . .   2.30
Dobell, Beckett & Co. v. Neilson (1905) 12 S.L.T. 747. . . . .   19.40
Docherty v. Docherty, 1981 S.L.T. (Notes) 24. . . . .   6.27
—— v. Glasgow Tramways and Omnibus Co. (1895) 2 S.L.T. 406; (1895) 32 S.L.R.
    353. . . . .   4.115
—— v. McAlpine & Sons (1899) 2 F. 128; (1899) 37 S.L.R. 87. . . . .   8.60
—— v. McClynn, 1983 S.L.T. 645. . . . .   2.07, 4.24, 15.102
—— v. McGlynn, 1985 S.L.T. 237. . . . .   15.103, 15.105
—— v. Royal Bank of Scotland, 1962 S.L.T. (Notes) 102.   8.64
Docherty & Co. (R.J.) v. Horne, 1967 S.L.T. (Sh.Ct.) 27.   21.73
Docherty and Graham v. McLellan, 1912 S.C.(J.) 102; 1912 S.L.T. 196; (1912) 6
    Adam 700; (1912) 49 S.L.R. 997. . . . .   16.52
Dodd v. Hilson (1874) 1 R. 527. . . . .   21.95
Dodds v. Ayr C.C., 1954 S.C. 86. . . . .   25.31
Doherty v. Norwich Union Fire Insurance Society Ltd, 1974 S.C. 213; 1975 S.L.T.
    41. . . . .   4.33, 5.72, 12.67, 12.68, 12.69
Doig v. Randsgrove Ltd, 1980 S.L.T. (Notes) 16. . . . .   10.18
Dominion Technology Ltd v. Gardner Cryogenics Ltd (No. 1) 1993 S.L.T. 828. . . . .   18.89
Don v. Don (1848) 10 D. 1046; (1848) 20 Sc.Jur. 387. . . . .   15.73
Donaghy v. Rollo, 1964 S.C. 278.   4.32, 10.04, 10.09, 10.10
Donald v. Baird (1907) 15 S.L.T. 427. . . . .   8.59, 8.60, 8.64
—— v. Donald, 1913 S.C. 274; 1912 2 S.L.T. 436; (1912) 50 S.L.R. 155. . . . . . .   2.42, 12.67,
                                                                                            12.68, 12.69, 12.70, 12.72
—— v. Hodgart's Trs (1893) 21 R. 246; (1893) 1 S.L.T. 366. . . . .   21.05
—— v. Rutherford, 1984 S.L.T. 70. . . . .   2.121, 8.59, 8.60, 10.40, 10.41
—— v. Strathclyde PTE, 1986 S.L.T. 625. . . . .   18.116
Donaldson v. Findlay, Bannatyne & Co. (1846) 5 Bell's App. 105. . . . .   11.43
Donnan v. Glasgow Corporation, 1970 S.L.T. (Sh.Ct.) 30.   26.116
Donnelly v. Donnelly, 1986 S.L.T. 305. . . . .   2.79
Donoghue v. Stevenson, 1932 S.C. (H.L.) 31; [1932] A.C. 562; 1932 S.L.T. 317. . . .   18.03
Doohan v. National Coal Board, 1959 S.C. 310; 1959 S.L.T. 308. . . . .   11.68
Dorman, Long & Co. v. Harrower (1899) 1 F. 1109; (1899) 7 S.L.T. 121; (1899) 36
    S.L.R. 879. . . . .   4.44, 12.53, 24.10
Dormer v. Melville Dundas & Whitson Ltd, 1987 S.C.L.R. 655. . . . .   10.41
Dornoch Parish Council (1929) 46 Sh.Ct.Rep. 33. . . . .   26.56
Dougan v. Cruickshank & Co. Ltd, 1954 S.L.T. (Notes) 73. . . . .   14.48
Doughton v. Doughton, 1958 S.L.T. (Notes) 34. . . . .   9.79
Doughty Shipping Co. Ltd v. North British Ry Co., 1909 1 S.L.T. 267. . . . .   4.32

Douglas v. Douglas, 1966 S.L.T. (Notes) 43. . . . . 15.56, 15.58
—— v. Frew (1910) 26 Sh.Ct.Rep. 355. . . . . 23.30
—— v. Hogarth (1901) 4 F. 148; (1901) 9 S.L.T. 254; (1901) 39 S.L.R. 118. . . 4.43, 4.48,
4.50
—— v. McKinlay (1902) 5 F. 260; (1902) 10 S.L.T. 480; (1902) 40 S.L.R. 238. . . . . 11.54,
11.64, 11.65
Douglas and Heron v. Armstrong (1779) Mor. 3700. . . . . 6.26
Douglas, Heron & Co. v. Palmer (1777) 5 Br. Supp. 449. 11.12
Douglas's C. B. v. Douglas, 1974 S.L.T. (Notes) 67. . . . . 21.21
Dove v. Henderson (1865) 3 M. 339; (1865) 37 Sc.Jur. 161. . . . . 11.40, 11.41
Dowgray v. Gilmour, 1907 S.C. 715; (1907) 14 S.L.T. 906; (1907) 44 S.L.R. 559. . . . 15.62
Dresser U.K. Ltd v. Falcongate Ltd [1992] 1 Q.B. 523. . . . . 2.93
Drew v Robertson (1903) 11 S.L.T. 67. . . . . 11.54
—— v. Western SMT Co., 1947 S.C. 222; 1947 S.L.T. 92; 1946 S.N. 150. . . . . 17.18
Drummond v. Hunter (1869) 7 M. 347; (1869) 41 Sc.Jur. 203; (1869) 6 S.L.R. 231. . 2.29
—— v. Leslie (1835) 13 S. 684; (1835) 10 Fac. 158. . . . . 13.39
Drummond & Dobie v. Boyd (1834) 12 S. 454. . . . . 11.28
Drummond's Trs v. Peel's Trs 1929 S.C. 484; 1929 S.L.T. 450. . . . . 1.42, 4.07, 4.12,
4.14, 4.18, 4.23, 4.24, 4.25, 4.26, 4.28, 7.01
Dryburgh v. Caledonian Insurance Co., 1933 S.N. 85. . . . . 2.101
—— v. Currys Group plc, 1988 S.C.L.R. 316. . . . . 7.37
—— v. Gordon (1896) 24 R. 1; (1896) 4 S.L.T. 113; (1896) 34 S.L.R. 19. . . . . 11.39
—— v. National Coal Board, 1962 S.C. 485. . . . . 10.18, 10.37, 10.56, 16.37
Drysdale v. Lawson (1842) 4 D. 1061. . . . . 11.06
—— v. Reid (1920) 36 Sh.Ct.Rep. 124. . . . . 4.112
Drysdale (A.F.) Ltd v. Menzies, 1998 G.W.D. 32–1667. . . . . 19.06, 19.16
Dudgeon v. Forbes (1832) 10 S. 810. . . . . 15.21, 15.24
Duff v. West Craig Ltd (1935) 51 Sh.Ct.Rep. 315. . . . . 2.53
—— v. Wood (1858) 20 D. 1231. . . . . 11.27
Duggan v. Strathclyde R.C., Glasgow Sh.Ct., Aug. 17, 1983, unreported. 26.113
Duggie v. A. Tulloch & Sons Ltd, 1983 S.L.T. (Sh.Ct.) 66. . . . . 18.82
Duguid v. Wilh Wilhelmsen Enterprises Ltd A/S, 1988 S.L.T. 118. . . . . 21.23
Dumbartonshire C.C. v. Clydebank Commissioners (1901) 4 F. 111; (1901) 9 S.L.T.
236; (1901) 39 S.L.R. 57. . . . . 25.47
Dumez France (C-220/88) [1990] E.C.R. I-49. . . . . 3.93
Dumfries and Galloway R.C. v. M, 1990 S.C. 31. . . . . 28.16
—— v. O, 1994 S.C.L.R. 661. . . . . 2.128
Dunbar v. Dunbar, 1912 S.C. 19; 1911 2 S.L.T. 349 (*sub nom.* A.B. v. C.B.); (1911)
49 S.L.R. 16. . . . . 13.59, 13.66
—— v. Edinburgh Corporation, 1961 S.L.T. (Sh.Ct.) 45; (1961) 77 Sh.Ct.Rep. 60. . 26.89
—— v. Macadam (1884) 11 R. 652; (1884) 21 S.L.R. 458. 18.100
Dunbar & Co. v. Scottish County Investment Co., 1920 S.C. 210; 1920 1 S.L.T. 136;
(1920) 57 S.L.R. 179. . . . . 2.38, 2.43, 20.02
Dunblane and Lecroft Parish Council, Petrs (1923) 40 Sh.Ct.Rep. 3. . . . . 26.55
Duncan v. Cammell Laird & Co. [1942] A.C. 624; [1942] 1 All E.R. 587. . . . . 4.73
—— v. Duncan (1830) 8 S. 641; (1830) 2 Sc.Jur. 298. . . . . 11.71
—— v. Dundee Licensing Authority, 1962 S.L.T. (Sh.Ct.) 15. . . . . 25.46
Duncan v. Fife Coal Co. (1905) 7 F. 958; (1905) 13 S.L.T. 370; (1905) 42 S.L.R. 822. . 8.60
—— v. Lodijensky (1904) 6 F. 408; (1904) 11 S.L.T. 684; (1904) 41 S.L.R. 322. . . . . 2.35,
2.53, 23.14
—— v. Ramsay (1906) 23 Sh.Ct.Rep. 181. . . . . 23.44
—— v. Salmond (1874) 1 R. 839; (1874) 11 S.L.R. 358. . . . . 14.17, 19.06, 19.11
—— v. Wilson, 1940 S.C. 221; 1940 S.L.T. 186; 1940 S.N. 10. . . . . 17.27, 18.106
Duncan's Trs v. Steven (1897) 24 R. 880; (1897) 34 S.L.R. 657. . . . . 4.44, 24.10
Dundas v. Hogg, 1937 S.L.T. (Sh.Ct.) 1; (1936) 52 Sh.Ct.Rep. 329. . . . . 26.11
Dundas' Trs v. Dundas' Trs, 1912 S.C. 375; 1912 1 S.L.T. 141; (1912) 49 S.L.R. 417. . . . .
19.13
Dundee General Hospitals v. Bell's Trs. 1952 S.C. (H.L.) 78; 1952 S.L.T. 270; [1952]
1 All E.R. 896. . . . . 17.12
Dundee Magistrates v. Taylor and Grant (1863) 1 M. 701. . . . . 11.30, 11.33
Dunlop v. Brown (1903) 11 S.L.T. 522. . . . . 4.27
—— v. Crawford (1886) 13 R. 973; (1886) 23 S.L.R. 702. . . . . 9.30
—— v. Dunlop, 1959 S.L.T. (Notes) 5. . . . . 21.11
—— v. ——, 1992 S.C.L.R. 989. . . . . 16.46
—— v. McGowans, 1980 S.C.(H.L.) 73; 1980 S.L.T. 129. . . . . 2.113
—— v. Weir (1823) 2 S. 167. . . . . 29.27
Dunlop Pneumatic Tyre Co. Ltd v. Rose (1901) 3 F. 635. . . . . 21.96

Dunlop's Trs v. Farquharson, 1956 S.L.T. 16. . . . .   19.23, 21.57
—— v. Lord Belhaven (1852) 14 D. 825. . . . .   15.73
Dunn v. Dunn's Trs, 1930 S.C. 131; 1930 S.L.T. 86; 1929 S.N. 119. . . . .   18.106
Dunning v. United Liverpool Hospitals' Board of Governors [1973] 1 W.L.R. 586;
    [1973] 2 All E.R. 454; (1973) 117 S.J. 167. . . . .   15.88
Dunsmore v. Dunsmore, 1986 S.L.T. (Sh.Ct.) 9. . . . .   23.43
Dunsmore's Tr. v. Stewart (1891) 19 R. 4; (1891) 29 S.L.R. 22. . . . .   11.54
Durnin v. William Coutts & Son, 1955 S.L.T. (Notes) 9.   9.104
Duthie v. Caledonian Ry (1898) 25 R. 934; (1898) 6 S.L.T. 44; (1898) 35 S.L.R. 726. .   4.48
—— v. Milne, 1946 S.L.T. (Sh.Ct.) 14; (1946) 63 Sh.Ct.Rep. 9. . . . .   2.73, 26.319
Duthie Bros & Co. v. Duthie (1892) 19 R. 905; (1892) 29 S.L.R. 808. . . . .   10.31
Duthie's Trs, Petrs, 1966 S.L.T. (Sh.Ct.) 24. . . . .   2.66
Dye v. Reid (1931) 9 S. 342. . . . .   15.73
Dyer v. Balfour Beatty Construction (Northern) Ltd, 1997 S.C.L.R. 783. . . . .   8.61
—— v. Hyslop, 1995 S.C.L.R. 161. . . . .   2.72
Dyet v. National Coal Board, 1957 S.L.T. (Notes) 18. . . . .   16.81
Dykes v. Merry and Cuninghame (1869) 7 M. 603; (1869) 41 Sc.Jur. 355; (1869) 6
    S.L.R. 405. . . . .   2.30, 13.40

ERDC Construction Ltd v. H.M. Love & Co. 1995 S.L.T. 254. . . . .   2.100
Eadie v. Glasgow Corporation, 1908 S.C. 207; (1908) 15 S.L.T. 612; (1908) 45
    S.L.R. 171. . . . .   12.19, 12.20
Eadie Cairns v. Programmed Maintenance Painting, 1987 S.L.T. 777. . . . .   9.67
Eagle Lodge Ltd v. Keir and Cawder Estates Ltd, 1964 S.C. 31; 1964 S.L.T. 13. . . . .   4.32,
                                                                                                    8.59
Eagle Star Insurance Co. Ltd v. Edward, 1982 S.C.L.R. 145. . . . .   12.24
East Hook Purchasing Corporation Ltd v. Ben Nevis Distillery (Fort William) Ltd,
    1985 S.L.T. 442. . . . .   10.06
East Kilbride D.C. v. King, 1996 S.L.T. 30. . . . .   25.30
East Lothian D.C. v. National Coal Board, 1982 S.L.T. 460. . . . .   26.285
Ebrahem v. Ebrahem, 1989 S.L.T. 808; 1989 S.C.L.R. 540. . . . .   15.43
Edgar v. Lord Advocate, 1965 S.C. 67. . . . .   9.122
Edinburgh and District Water Trs v. Clippens Oil Co. (1899) 1 F. 899; (1899) 7
    S.L.T. 36; (1899) 36 S.L.R. 710. . . . .   2.108, 2.113, 8.41, 9.07
Edinburgh Corporation v. Kirkcudbright Education Authority, 1954 S.L.T. (Sh.Ct.)
    39; (1953) 70 Sh.Ct.Rep. 73. . . . .   25.17
Edinburgh D.C. v. Robbin, 1994 S.L.T. (Sh.Ct.) 51; 1994 S.C.L.R. 43. . . . .   18.12, 18.30
—— v. Round and Robertson, 1987 S.L.T. (Sh.Ct.) 117. . . . .   2.48, 2.131
Edinburgh Entertainments Ltd v. Stevenson, 1925 S.C. 848; 1925 S.L.T. 557; 1925
    S.N. 107. . . . .   11.58
Edinburgh Magistrates v. Lord Advocate, 1912 S.C. 1085; 1912 S.L.T. 133; (1912)
    49 S.L.R. 873. . . . .   4.77
—— v. Macfarlane (1857) 20 D. 156. . . . .   4.33
—— v. Warrender (1862) 1 M. 13. . . . .   8.55
Edinburgh Modern Quarry Co. Ltd v. Eagle Star Insurance Co. Ltd, 1965 S.L.T.
    (Notes) 91. . . . .   5.100, 11.58, 11.86, 11.89
Edinburgh North Constituency Association S.N.P. Club v. Thomas H. Peck Ltd,
    1978 S.L.T. (Sh.Ct.) 76. . . . .   25.33
Edinburgh Northern Tramways Co. v. Mann (1891) 18 R. 1140; (1891) 29 S.L.R.
    51. . . . .   18.50
Edinburgh Oil Gas-Light Co. v. Clyne's Trs (1835) 13 S. 413. . . . .   13.39
Edinburgh Street Tramways Co. v. Torbain (1876) 3 R. 655, (1876) 4 R.(H.L.) 87;
    (1876) 3 A.C. 58; (1876) 14 S.L.R. 729. . . . .   2.32
Edington v. Astley (1829) 8 S. 192; (1829) 2 Sc.Jur. 69. . . . .   5.90
—— v. Dunbar Steam Laundry Co. (1903) 11 S.L.T. 117. . . . .   12.19, 19.03
Edwards v. Edwards [1958] P. 235; [1958] 2 W.L.R. 956; [1958] 2 All E.R. 179. . . . .   2.19
Elas v. SMT Co., 1950 S.C. 570; 1950 S.L.T. 397. . . . .   19.40
Elder v. Manson, 1964 S.L.T. (Land Ct.) 15. . . . .   26.277
Elder's Trs v. Elder (1895) 22 R. 505; (1895) 2 S.L.T. 579; (1895) 32 S.L.R. 365. . .   2.109,
                                                                                                    21.70
Elefanten Schuh v. Jaqqmain (150/80) [1981] E.C.R. 1671. . . . .   3.54
Ellerman Lines Ltd v. Clyde Navigation Trs, 1909 S.C. 690; 1909 1 S.L.T. 249;
    (1909) 46 S.L.R. 472. . . . .   4.42, 4.48
Elliot v. Erikson, 1960 S.L.T. (Sh.Ct.) 28; (1960) 76 Sh.Ct.Rep. 104. . .   11.68, 13.80, 18.89
Elliott v. Aitken (1869) 7 M. 894. . . . .   11.83
—— v. Galpern, 1927 S.C. 29; 1926 S.L.T. 759; 1926 S.N. 141. . . . .   2.43

Elliot v. North British Ry (1921) 38 Sh.Ct.Rep. 17. . . . . 12.25
Ellis v. Ellis (1870) 8 M. 805; (1870) 42 Sc.Jur. 447; (1870) 7 S.L.R. 497. . . . 12.12, 12.18
—— v. Fraser (1840) 3 D. 264. . . . . 9.22
—— v. Macdonald, 1980 S.L.T. 11. . . . . 18.69, 18.98
—— v. Menzies & Co. (1901) 9 S.L.T. 243. . . . . 11.29
Ellison (S.D.) & Co. (Scotland) v. Asgher, Paisley Sh.Ct., Feb. 14, 1985, unreported. . 7.33
Ellon Castle Estates Co. Ltd v. Macdonald, 1975 S.L.T. (Notes) 55. . . . . 9.26, 9.114
Elmslie v. Pauline (1905) 7 F. 541; (1905) 12 S.L.T. 784; (1905) 42 S.L.R. 401. . . . . 11.70
Elrick v. Elrick, 1973 S.L.T. (Notes) 68. . . . . 15.36
Emerald Airways Ltd v. Nordic Oil Services Ltd, 1996 S.L.T. 403. . . . . 29.28
Emerald Stainless Steel Ltd v. South Side Distribution Ltd, 1982 S.C. 61; 1983
    S.L.T. 162. . . . . 4.88, 9.18
Emmerson v. Emmerson (1939) 55 Sh.Ct.Rep. 146. . . . . 18.69
Empson v. Smith [1966] 1 Q.B. 426; [1965] 3 W.L.R. 380; (1965) 109 S.J. 493;
    [1965] 2 All E.R. 881. . . . . 4.05
Emslie v. Tognarelli's Exrs, 1969 S.L.T. 20. . . . . 10.37
Engineers and Managers' Association v. Advisory, Conciliation and Arbitration
    Service [1980] 1 W.L.R. 302; [1980] 1 All E.R. 896; (1980) 124 S.J. 202. . . . 18.113
English's Coasting and Shipping Co. Ltd v. British Finance Co. Ltd (1886) 13 R.
    430; (1886) 23 S.L.R. 289. . . . . 11.57
Epps v. Newton, 1951 S.C. 582; 1952 S.L.T. 97. . . . . 19.52
Equity and Law Life Assurance Society v. Tritonia Ltd, 1943 S.C.(H.L.) 88; 1944
    S.L.T. 24; 1943 S.N. 22; [1943] A.C. 584. . . . . 1.32
Eriks Allied Polymer Ltd v. Hydracrat Ltd, Hamilton Sh.Ct., Dec. 8, 1982,
    unreported. 10.54, 14.12
Erskine v. Walker's Trs (1883) 10 R. 717; (1883) 20 S.L.R. 457. . . . . 11.73, 11.80
Esso Petroleum Co. Ltd v. Hall Russell & Co. Ltd, 1995 S.C.L.R. 36. . . . . 2.123
—— v. ——, 1988 S.L.T. 874. . . . . 20.01
—— v. Law, 1956 S.C. 33. . . . . 2.104, 2.106, 8.18, 8.19, 14.03
—— v. Southport Corporation [1956] A.C. 218. . . . . 9.07
Eurocopy (Scotland) plc v. British Geological Survey, 1997 S.C.L.R. 392; 1997
    G.W.D. 4–133. . . . . 5.78, 5.87, 5.94, 5.95, 18.42, 18.56
Evans v. McIntyre Aberdeen Sh.Ct., Mar. 17, 1980, unreported. 1.31
Ewart v. Brown (1882) 10 R. 163; (1882) 20 S.L.R. 105. . . . . 19.11
Ewing v. Hare and Glasgow (1823) 2 S. 534 (N.E. 467). 11.67
—— v. McLelland (1860) 33 Sc. J. 1. . . . . 29.19
Exchange Loan Co. v. Levenson (1904) 21 Sh.Ct.Rep. 33. . . . . 4.41
Exchange Telegraph Co. v. White, 1961 S.L.T. 104. . . . . 21.84
Exven Ltd v. Lurnsden, 1982 S.L.T. (Sh.Ct.) 105. . . . . 26.09
Eyres v. Hunter (1711) Mor. 7596. . . . . 4.76

F (A Minor) (Child Abduction), Re [1992] 1 Family Law Reports 548. . . . . 2.58
F (A Minor) (Wardship: Appeal), Re [1976] Fam. 238; [1976] 2 W.L.R. 189; [1976]
    1 All E.R. 417. . . . . 18.112
F v. Management Committee and Managers of Ravenscraig Hospital, 1988 S.C.
    158. . . . . 25.38, 25.41, 25.43, 25.45
Fagan v. Fagan, 1991 S.L.T. (Sh.Ct.) 2. . . . . 18.42, 18.47
Fairholme's Trs v. Graham, 1943 S.L.T. 158; 1942 S.N. 57. . . . . 2.102
Fairley v. Elliot (1839) 1 D. 399; (1839) 11 Sc.Jur. 257. . . . . 11.69
—— v. McGown (1836) 14 S. 470; (1836) 11 Fac. 385. . . . . 13.39
—— v. National Coal Board, 1965 S.L.T. (Notes) 17. 10.18, 16.37
Fairlie v. Fairlie's Trs (1903) 11 S.L.T. 51. . . . . 12.19, 12.20
Fairlights Assets Co. Ltd v. Wright, Johnston & Mackenzie, 1948 S.L.T. (Notes)
    79. . . . . 15.80
Falconer v. Brown (1893) 1 Adam 96; (1893) 21 R. (J.) 1; (1893) 1 S.L.T. 277
    (1893) 31 S.L.R. 52. . . . . 16.39, 16.75
—— v. Stephen (1849) 11 D. 1338. . . . . 15.81
Falkingham v. Lothian R.C., 1983 S.L.T. (Sh.Ct.) 2. . . . . 15.88
Farquhar v. Farquhar, 1948 S.L.T. (Notes) 25. . . . . 14.18
Farrans v. Roxburgh C.C., 1969 S.L.T. 35. . . . . 2.105, 2.106
Farrell v. Long (C-295/95) [1997] 3 W.L.R. 613. . . . . 3.32
Faulkner v. Love [1977] Q.B. 937; [1977] 2 W.L.R. 477; [1977] 1 All E.R. 791. . . . 26.174
Faulks v. Park (1854) 17 D. 247. . . . . 14.37
—— v. Whitehead (1854) 16 D. 718; (1854) 26 Sc.Jur. 308. . . . . 11.68, 11.75
Fearn v. Cowpar (1899) 7 S.L.T. 68. . . . . 12.14

Feeney v. United Biscuits, 1993 S.C.L.R. 965. . . . . 29.40
Feld British Agencies Ltd v. James Pringle Ltd, 1961 S.L.T. 123. . . 4.38, 4.39, 4.41, 12.36
Fennel v. Cameron, 1968 S.L.T. (Sh.Ct.) 30. . . . . 19.11
Fenton v. Thorley [1903] A.C. 443. . . . . 27.15
Ferguson v. Ferguson, 1936 S.C. 808; 1936 S.L.T. 549; 1936 S.N. 77. . . . . 15.36, 16.41
—— v. Johnston (1886) 13 R. 635; (1886) 23 S.L.R. 508. 19.63
—— v. Leslie (1873) 11 S.L.R. 16. . . . . 11.55
—— v. Livingstone, Oban Sh.Ct., Jan. 10, 1985, unreported. 14.08
—— v. McGrandles, 1993 S.L.T. 822 (O.H.). 21.19
—— v. Maclennan Salmon Co. Ltd, 1990 S.C. 45; 1990 S.L.T. 658 (2nd Div) 1990
    S.L.T. 428; 1990 S.C.L.R. 79 (O.H.). 14.37
—— v. Tennant, 1978 S.C.(H.L.) 19; 1978 S.L.T. 165. . . . . 21.93
Ferguson, Davidson & Co. v. Paterson and Dobbie (1898) 1 F. 227; (1898) 6 S.L.T.
    219; (1898) 36 S.L.R. 153. . . . . 4.125, 4.127, 10.04, 10.10, 12.20
Ferguson, Lamont & Co's Tr. v. Lamont (1889) 17 R. 282; (1889) 27 S.L.R. 227. . . 11.55
Ferguson and Menzies Ltd v. J.W. Soils Supplies Ltd, 1998 G.W.D. 30–1529. . . . . . . 8.38
Ferguson's Tr. v. Reid, 1931 S.C. 714; 1931 S.L.T. 502; 1931 S.N. 85. . . 5.92, 18.15, 18.17
Fergusson v. Skirving (1852) 1 Macq. 232; (1852) 24 Sc.Jur. 473. . . . . 5.84
Fernie v. Bell (1894) 2 S.L.T. 311. . . . . 9.107
Ferns v. Management Committee and Manager of Ravenscraig Hospital, 1987
    S.L.T. (Sh.Ct.) 76. . . . . 26.304
Ferrier v. Berry (1828) 6 S. 982. . . . . 12.09
—— v. Coull (1906) 22 Sh.Ct.Rep. 263. . . . . 26.187
—— v. Crockart, 1937 S.L.T. 206. . . . . 9.94
Feuars in Orkney v. Stewart (1741) Mor. 11986. . . . . 4.38
Field, dec'd (In the estate of) (No. 2) [1965] 1 W.L.R. 1336; [1965] 2 All E.R. 653;
    (1965) 109 S.J. 335. . . . . 16.68
Fife C.C. v. Thoms (1898) 25 R. 1097; (1898) 35 S.L.R. 868. . . . . 15.53, 15.75
Fife's Trs (Duke of) v. George Wimpey & Co., 1943 S.C. 377; 1944 S.L.T. 41; 1943
    S.N. 23. . . . . 2.38
Fife's Trs (Earl of) v. Commissioners of Woods and Forests (1849) 11 D. 889. . . . . . . 4.76
Fillets (Aberdeen) Ltd v. Aberdeen Harbour Board, Aberdeen Sh.Ct., June 14,
    1984, unreported. 30.04
Findlay, Petr, 1975 S.L.T. (Sh.Ct.) 46. . . . . 2.66
—— v. Findlay (No. 2), 1995 S.L.T. 492. . . . . 2.58
—— v. National Coal Board, 1965 S.L.T. 328. . . . . 12.42, 12.45, 12.49, 12.53, 12.63
Fine v. Edinburgh Life Assurance Co., 1909 S.C. 636; 1909 1 S.L.T. 233; (1909) 46
    S.L.R. 480. . . . . 19.27
Fingland & Mitchell v. Howie, 1926 S.C. 319; 1926 S.L.T. 283; 1926 S.N. 14. . . . . . . 2.54
Finklestone v. Smellie (1916) 32 Sh.Ct.Rep. 244. . . . . 11.55, 12.10
Finlay v. Bush, 1925 S.L.T. (Sh.Ct.) 140; (1925) 41 Sh.Ct.Rep. 171. . . . . 16.47
—— v. Finlay, 1962 S.L.T. (Sh.Ct.) 43; (1961) 78 Sh.Ct.Rep. 62. . . . . 4.07, 4.23, 4.25
Finlay (James) Corporation Ltd v. McCormack, 1986 S.L.T. 106. . . . . 13.79
Finnie v. Logie (1859) 21 D. 825. . . . . 9.35, 9.36
First Edinburgh Starr-Bowkett Building Society v. Munro (1883) 11 R. 5. . . . . 26.201
Firth v. Anderson, 1954 S.L.T. (Sh.Ct.) 27; (1953) 70 Sh.Ct.Rep. 52. . . . . 9.118
Fischer & Co. v. Andersen (1896) 23 R. 395; (1896) 3 S.L.T. 230; (1896) 33 S.L.R.
    306. . . . . 4.125, 4.126, 7.21, 7.22, 8.23
Fisher v. Bontine (1827) 6 S. 330. . . . . 15.57
—— v. Weir, 1964 S.L.T. (Notes) 99. . . . . 11.11, 11.29
Fishof v. Cheapside Bonding Co. Ltd, 1972 S.L.T. (Notes) 7. . . . . 4.38, 4.39
Flanagan v. Dempster Moore & Co. Ltd, 1928 S.C. 308; 192 8 S.L.T. 258. . . . . 14.54
Flannigan v. British Dyewood Co., 1971 S.C. 110; 1971 S.L.T. 208. . . . . 2.94, 2.97
Fleming v. Dickson (1862) 1 M. 188; (1862) 35 Sc.Jur. 96. . . . . 1.11, 25.13, 25.30,
    25.34, 26.55
—— v. Eadie & Son (1897) 25 R. 3; (1897) 5 S.L.T. 136; (1897) 35 S.L.R. 1. . 5.77, 5.81,
    8.59, 18.15
—— v. Gemmill, 1908 S.C. 340; (1908) 15 S.L.T. 691; (1908) 45 S.L.R. 281. . 4.42, 4.43,
    4.47, 4.48, 4.50
—— v. McGillivray, 1946 S.C. 1; 1945 S.L.T. 301. . . . . 4.50, 11.89
—— v. McLagan (1879) 6 R. 588; (1879) 16 S.L.R. 316. . . . . 20.03
—— v. North of Scotland Banking Co. (1881) 9 R. 11; (1881) 19 S.L.R. 4. . 18.36, 18.117
—— v. —— (1882) 9 R. 659; (1882) 19 S.L.R. 412. . . . . 19.14
—— v. Paterson, 1948 S.C. 564; 1948 S.L.T. 412. . . . . 11.89
—— v. Twaddle (1828) 7 S. 92. . . . . 29.29, 29.73
Fleming & Ferguson v. Paisley Magistrates, 1948 S.C. 547; 1948 S.L.T. 457. . . . . . . 21.76

Fleming Bros (Stuctural Engineers) Ltd v. Ford Motor Co. Ltd, 1969 S.L.T. (Notes) 54... 14.39
Fletcher v. Davidson (1874) 2 R. 71; (1874) 12 S.L.R. 27....................... 18.04
Fletcher's Trs v. Fletcher (1888) 15 R. 862; (1888) 25 S.L.R. 606.............. 19.33
Florence v. Smith, 1913 S.C. 393; 1912 2 S.L.T. 451; (1912) 50 S.L.R. 267........ 11.70
Flynn v. Faulds (1948) 64 Sh.Ct.Rep. 265; 1949 S.L.T. (Sh.Ct.) 17............... 10.05
Fookes v. Slaytor [1978] 1 W.L.R. 1293; [1979] 1 All E.R. 137; (1978) 122 S.J. 489..... 9.112
Foote v. Foote, 1963 S.L.T. (Sh.Ct.) 51; (1963) Sh.Ct.Rep. 164.................. 6.22
Forbes v. H.M. Advocate, 1963 J.C. 68.. 16.62
—— v. Forbes, 1965 S.L.T. 109............................... 18.104, 18.105, 18.106
—— v. ——, 1993 S.C. 271; 1994 S.L.T. 16; 1993 S.C.L.R. 348........ 2.25, 21.96, 21.99
—— v. ——, 1994 S.L.T. 307.. 21.99
—— v. Forbes's Trs, 1957 S.C. 325; 1957 S.L.T. 102........................ 5.86, 8.58
—— v. Johnstone, 1995 S.C. 220; 1995 S.L.T. 158; 1995 S.C.L.R. 154.... 7.29, 7.30, 7.33
—— v. Underwood (1886) 13 R. 465; (1886) 23 S.L.R. 324.................. 2.88, 2.89
Forbes (J.C.) Ltd v. Duignan, 1974 S.L.T. (Sh.Ct.) 74...................... 9.26, 9.114
Forbes Smith (D.) & Johnston v. Kate, 1975 S.L.T. (Sh.Ct.) 33................. 4.98
Ford (1844) 6 D. 1163; (1844) 16 Sc.Jur. 506................................. 11.70
—— v. Bell Chandler, 1977 S.L.T. (Sh.Ct.) 90......................... 21.82, 26.126
—— v. Ford (1912) 28 Sh.Ct.Rep. 226.. 10.05
Forrest v. Dunlop (1875) 3 R. 15; (1875) 13 S.L.R. 2.................... 2.104, 14.03
—— v. Low's Trs, 1907 S.C. 1240; (1907) 15 S.L.T. 330; (1907) 44 S.L.R. 925..... 15.38
—— v. MacGregor, 1913 1 S.L.T. 372... 15.97
Forsyth v. Hare & Co. (1834) 13 S. 42; (1834) 10 Fac. 35...................... 4.94
—— v. John Dickinson Group Ltd, 1984 S.L.T. (Sh.Ct.) 51................ 13.47, 30.29
—— v. Pringle Taylor & Lamond Lawson (1906) 14 S.L.T. 658............. 15.72, 15.77
—— v. Scott's Trs, 1947 S.L.T. (Sh.Ct.) 46; (1947) 63 Sh.Ct.Rep. 136............. 9.78
—— v. Stoddart (A. F.) & Co., 1985 S.L.T. 51 2.121, 10.40, 10.41, 18.110, 18.111, 18.114
Forth & Clyde Construction Co. Ltd v. Trinity Timber & Plywood Co. Ltd, 1984 S.L.T. 94... 4.88
Forth Tugs Ltd v. Wilmington Trust Co., 1987 S.L.T. 153.................. 3.101, 4.04
Foster v. Craigmillar Laundry Ltd, 1980 S.L.T. (Sh.Ct.) 100................... 18.08
—— v. Foster's Trs, 1923 S.C. 212; 1923 S.L.T. 59; (1923) 60 S.L.R. 155.......... 2.92
Fowler v. Brown, 1916 S.C. 597; 1916 1 S.L.T. 280; (1916) 53 S.L.R. 416......... 9.124
—— v. Fowler (No. 2), 1981 S.L.T. (Notes) 78............................... 18.68
Fox v. Taher [1997] I.L.Pr. 441... 3.61
Foxley v. Dunn, 1978 S.L.T. (Notes) 35................................. 9.26, 9.114
Francesco v. De Meo, 1908 S.C. 7; (1908) 15 S.L.T. 387; (1908) 45 S.L.R. 13....... 2.16
Frank v. H.M. Advocate, 1938 J.C. 17; 1938 S.L.T. 109; 1937 S.N. 107........... 16.71
Fraser v. Cameron (1892) 19 R. 564; (1892) 29 S.L.R. 446.................... 4.115
—— v. Church of Scotland General Trs, 1986 S.L.T. 692...................... 9.99
—— v. Dunbar (1839) 1 D. 882....................................... 4.112, 12.14
—— v. Fraser (1903) 11 S.L.T. 70..................................... 18.87, 19.05
—— v. Linlithgow Education Authority (1923) 39 Sh.Ct.Rep. 262.............. 26.115
—— v. Lord Lovat (1850) 7 Bell's App. 171................................. 2.105
—— v. Mackenzie (1874) 12 S.L.R. 74...................................... 11.62
—— v. McMurrich, 1924 S.C. 93; 1923 S.L.T. 757; (1923) 61 S.L.R. 57.......... 11.54
—— v. McNeill, 1948 S.C. 517; 1948 S.L.T. 417.............................. 18.50
—— v. Pattie (1847) 9 D. 903... 4.27
—— v. Savings Investment Trust Ltd (1912) 28 Sh.Ct.Rep. 224............. 7.30, 21.51
—— v. Smith, 1937 S.N. 67.. 16.46, 16.60
—— v. Stronach (1885) 23 S.L.R. 76....................................... 16.11
Fraser (J. & J.) v. Smith, 1937 S.C. 667; 1937 S.L.T. 510; (1937) S.N. 55.... 18.20, 18.65, 18.71
Fraser & Son Ltd v. Bute Gift Co. Ltd (1958) 74 Sh.Ct.Rep. 154.............. 18.117
Fraser-Johnston Engineering Co. v. Jeffs, 1920 S.C. 222; 1920 1 S.L.T. 131; (1920) 57 S.L.R. 214.. 9.119, 11.10
Free Church of Scotland v. McRae (1905) 7 F. 686; (1905) 13 S.L.T. 77; (1905) 42 S.L.R. 632... 2.128
Friedmann v. Austay (London) Ltd [1954] 1 W.L.R. 466; [1954] 1 All E.R. 594; (1954) 98 S.J. 162... 11.53
Friel v. Chief Constable of Strathclyde, 1981 S.C. 1; 1981 S.L.T. 113.... 4.73, 4.74, 15.55, 15.86, 15.88
Frimokar (U.K.) Ltd v. Mobile Technical Plant (International) Ltd, 1990 S.L.T. 180; 1989 S.C.L.R. 767.. 11.45, 14.74
Fritz's Agency Ltd v. Moss Empires Ltd (1922) 38 Sh.Ct.Rep. 124............... 29.21
Frizell v. Thomson (1860) 22 D. 1176.................................. 23.37, 23.28

Fry v. N.E. Ry (1882) 10 R. 290; 20 S.L.R. 209............................... 14.53
Fryers v. Joseph Simmers & Sons, 1986 G.W.D. 5–105........................ 9.33
Fulton v. Earl of Eglinton and Winton (1895) 22 R. 823; (1895) 3 S.L.T. 61;
  (1895).. 2.106
Fulton Clyde Ltd v. J. F. McCallum & Co., 1960 S.C. 78; 1960 S.L.T. 253......... 12.36
Fulwood (S.S.) Limited v. Commissioners of the Harbour of Dumfries and
  Navigation of the River Nith, 1907 S.C. 735; (1907) 14 S.L.T. 364; (1907) 44
  S.L.R. 566.. 17.23, 19.26
Furnheim v. Watson, 1946 S.L.T. 297, 1946 J.C. 99; 1946 S.L.T. 297; 1946 S.N. 42. . 1.24,
                                                                          16.65, 16.68
Fyfe v. Croudace Ltd, 1986 S.L.T. 528..................................... 2.116

G, Petr, 1955 S.L.T. (Sh.Ct.) 27; 71 Sh.Ct.Rep. 44........................... 28.43
G v. G (Minors: Custody Appeal) [1985] 1 W.L.R. 647; [1985] 2 All E.R. 225.... 18.110,
                                                                  18.112, 18.113
G v. O, unreported.. 28.114
G. & A. (Hotels) Ltd v. THB Marketing Services, 1983 S.L.T. 497............... 4.91
GAS Construction Co. Ltd v. Schrader, 1992 S.L.T. 528....................... 14.11
GEA Airexchangers Ltd v. James Howden & Co. Ltd, 1984 S.L.T. 264........... 9.30
GUD Pension Trustee Ltd v. Quinn, 1994 S.C.L.R. 1105...................... 29.40
GUR Corporation v. Trust Bank of Africa Ltd [1986] 3 All E.R. 449; [1986]...... 4.04
GUS Catalogue Order Ltd v. Oxborrow, 1987 S.C.L.R. 617............... 30.71, 30.72
GUS Property Management Ltd v. Littlewoods Mail Order Stores Ltd, 1982
  S.C.(H.L.) 157.. 10.17
Gairdner v. Macarthur, 1915 S.C. 589; 1915 1 S.L.T. 277; (1915) 52 S.L.R. 427.... 10.25,
                                                                              18.98
—— v. Macarthur, 1916 S.C.(H.L.) 130.................................... 18.99
—— v. Young (1874) 2 R. 173; (1874) 12 S.L.R. 140....................... 16.91
Gaitens v. Blythswood Shipping Co., 1948 S.L.T. (Notes) 49.................. 9.68
Galashiels Provident Building Society v. Newlands (1893) 20 R. 821; (1893) 30
  S.L.R. 730.. 25.30, 26.201
Gale v. Bennett (1857) 19 D. 665... 11.70
Gall v. Gall (1870) 9 M. 177; (1870) 43 Sc.Jur. 92; (1870) 8 S.L.R.............. 16.71
—— v. Loyal Glenbogie Friendly Society (1900) 2 F. 1187; (1900) 8 S.L.T. 140;
  (1900) 37 S.L.R. 911.. 9.82
Gallacher (Fatal Accident Inquiry), 1993 S.C.L.R. 781........................ 27.14
—— v. Gallacher, 1996 S.C.L.R. 174...................................... 5.71
Gallagher v. Edinburgh Corporation, 1929 S.L.T. 356; 1929 S.N. 58........ 11.54, 11.64
Gallier v. Lothian Regional Council, O.H., June 28, 1985, unreported........... 15.58
Galloway v. Galloway, 1947 S.C. 330..................................... 15.65
—— v. McClelland (1917) 33 Sh.Ct.Rep. 242.............................. 26.10
—— v. McGhie (1869) 41 Sc.Jur. 400..................................... 2.31
—— Water Power Co. v. Carmichael, 1937 S.C. 135................... 15.19, 15.20
Gamble v. Unison Scotland, 1997 S.C.L.R. 803; 1997 G.W.D. 15–639............ 18.34
Ganley v. Scottish Boatowners Mutual Insurance Association, 1967 S.L.T. (Notes)
  45... 9.26, 9.114
Garden, Haig-Scott & Wallace v. Prudential Approved Society for Women, 1927
  S.L.T. 393; 1927 S.N. 8... 12.26
Gardiner v. Main (1894) 22 R. 100.. 24.10
Gardiners v. Victoria Estates Co. Ltd (1885) 13 R. 80; (1885) 23 S.L.R. 55....... 19.16
Gardner v. Beresford's Trs (1877) 4 R. 1091............................... 18.50
—— v. Hastie, 1928 S.L.T. 497; 1928 S.N. 101............................. 8.60
—— v. J. Robertson (Canisters) Ltd (1960) 76 Sh.Ct.Rep. 167................ 17.08
Garrioch v. Glass, 1911 S.C. 453; 1911 1 S.L.T. 89.......................... 18.117
Garvie's Trs v. Still, 1972 S.L.T. 29....................................... 2.36
Gas Power and By-Products Co. Ltd v. Power Gas Corpn Ltd, 1911 S.C. 27; 1910 2
  S.L.T. 241; (1910) 48 S.L.R. 38................................... 4.35, 12.15
Gatoil International Inc. v. Arkwright-Boston Manufacturers Mutual Insurance Co.,
  1985 S.C.(H.L.) 1; 1985 S.L.T. 68; [1985] A.C. 255; [1985] 1 All E.R. 129... 11.13,
                                                                    11.32, 24.06
Gatt v. Angus Shipping Co. Ltd (1907) 14 S.L.T. 749........................ 13.43
Gauldie v. Arbroath Mags, 1936 S.C. 861; 1936 S.N. 89...................... 21.93
Gaunt v. Marco's Leisure Ltd, 1995 S.C.L.R. 966..................... 18.19, 18.56
Gavin v. Henderson & Co., 1910 S.C. 357; 1910 1 S.L.T. 191; (1910) 47 S.L.R. 460. . 4.43
Gedge v. Royal Exchange Assurance Corporation [1900] 2 Q.B. 214; 1900 W.L.
  30310.. 2.12

Geils v. Geils (1851) 1 Macq 36; (1851) 13 D. 31; (1851) 23 Sc.Jur. 435..... 2.104, 9.115
General Billposting Co. Ltd v. Glasgow Corporation (1939) 55 Sh.Ct.Rep. 104.... 25.08
General Guarantee Corporation v. Alexander, 1918 S.C. 662; 1918 2 S.L.T. 30;
    (1918) 55 S.L.R. 645.. 2.29, 2.31
George v. George C. Peebles & Son, 1998 S.L.T. 685........................... 21.36
George Hotel (Glasgow) Ltd v. Prestwick Hotels Ltd, 1961 S.L.T. (Sh.Ct.) 61;
    (1961) 77 Sh.Ct.Rep. 97.. 11.82, 21.79
Gerber v. Greggs Bakeries Ltd, Hamilton Sh.Ct., Oct. 18, 1981, unreported....... 23.08
Gerrard, Petr, 1984 S.L.T. 108; 1984 S.C.C.R. 1............................... 16.14
Gibb v. Lee (1908) 16 S.L.T. 260; (1908) 45 S.L.R. 833........................ 11.19
Gibbon (Edward) (Aberdeen) Ltd v. Edwards, 1992 S.L.T. (Sh.Ct.) 86........... 9.114
Gibson, Petr., 1984 S.L.T. 61.. 15.106
—— v. Adams (1875) 3 R. 144; (1875) 13 S.L.R. 47............................ 8.64
—— v. Barbour's Reps (1846) 8 D. 427; (1846) 18 Sc.Jur. 193.................. 12.09
—— v. British Insulated Callenders' Construction Co. Ltd, 1973 S.C.(H.L.) 15;
    1973 S.L.T. 2... 16.84
—— v. Clark (1895) 23 R. 294; (1895) 3 S.L.T. 197....... 2.54, 2.97, 6.46, 11.06, 25.04
—— v. Droopy and Brown Ltd, 1989 S.L.T. 173............................... 10.39
—— v. Ewan (1852) 15 D. 211; (1852) 2 Stuart 49, 117....................... 13.33
—— v. Gibson, 1970 S.L.T. (Notes) 60..................................... 4.08
—— v. Irvine (1900) 7 S.L.T. 391... 4.43
—— v. Lord Advocate, 1975 S.C. 136; 1975 S.L.T. 134..................... 4.57
—— v. Strathclyde R.C., 1992 S.C.L.R. 902..................... 9.33, 10.17, 13.23
Gibson & Simpson v. Pearson, 1992 S.L.T. 894, 1992 S.C.L.R. 771..... 2.106, 2.108, 7.19
Gibson's Trs v. Fraser (1877) 4 R. 1001; (1877) 14 S.L.R. 631............. 10.05, 10.14
—— v. Gibson (1869) 7 M. 1061; (1899) 7 S.L.T. 65; (1899) 36 S.L.R. 777........ 12.10
—— v. Wilson (1899) 1 F. 1016; (1899) 7 S.L.T. 65; (1899) 36 S.L.R. 777........ 19.13
Gifford v. Buchanan, 1983 S.L.T. 613...................................... 26.398
—— v. Traill (1829) 7 S. 854... 20.01
Gilchrist v. National Cash Register Co. Ltd, 1929 S.C. 272; 1929 S.L.T. 222; 1929
    S.N. 10... 15.39
Gilfillan v. National Coal Board, 1972 S.L.T. (Sh.Ct.) 393.................. 9.30
Gilillan v. Lanark C.C. (1902) 9 S.L.T. 432; (1902) 10 S.L.T. 274.............. 8.60
Gill v. Anderson (1859) 21 D. 723; (1959) 31 Sc.Jur. 386.................... 12.18
—— v. National Coal Board [1955] C.L.Y. 3497............................ 15.56
Gillanders v. Gillanders, 1966 S.C. 54; 1966 S.L.T. 120................... 11.11
Gillespie v. Cochran Dickie & Mackenzie, Paisley Sh.Ct., Feb. 13, 1985, unreported.... 24.14
—— v. Duncan (1933) 50 Sh.Ct.Rep. 60................................. 10.30
—— v. Paisley Road Trust (1900) 7 S.L.T. 350.......................... 4.43
—— v. Riddell, 1908 S.C. 629; (1908) 15 S.L.T. 1069; (1908) 45 S.L.R. 514; affd.
    1909 S.C.(H.L.) 3... 20.03
Gillon v. Simpson (1859) 21 D. 243; (1859) 31 Sc.Jur. 130.................... 13.37
Gillon's Trs v. Gillon (1903) 40 S.L.R. 461; (1903) 10 S.L.T. 742............. 5.89
Gillon's Trs and Rottenburg v. Duncan (1896) 24 R. 35..................... 5.89
Gilmour v. Donnelly (1899) 7 S.L.T. 267................................. 11.54
—— v. Scottish Clan Motorways Ltd, 1928 S.N. 19..................... 9.22, 9.131
Girvan, Petr, 1985 S.L.T. 92.. 13.79
Giulianotti v. Arbroath Licensing Authority, 1962 S.L.T. (Sh.Ct.) 18; (1961) 77
    Sh.Ct.Rep. 148... 25.09
Glacken v. National Coal Board, 1951 S.C. 82; 1951 S.L.T. 75............... 15.60
Glaser v. Glaser, 1997 S.L.T. 456..................................... 28.112
Glasgow (City of) Union Ry v. Hunter (1870) 8 M.(H.L.) 156; (1870) 42 Sc.Jur.
    430.. 26.93
Glasgow and S.W. Ry v. Ayr Mags, 1911 S.C. 298; 1911 1 S.L.T. 176; (1910) 48
    S.L.R. 211.. 19.17, 19.55
—— v. Boyd & Forrest, 1918 S.C.(H.L.) 14; 1918 1 S.L.T. 10; (1918) 55 S.L.R.
    117....................................... 2.106, 2.108, 2.110, 2.111, 8.41
Glasgow City and District Ry v. Macbrayne (1883) 10 R. 894; (1883) 20 S.L.R. 602.. 2.02
Glasgow Corporation v. Central Land Board, 1956 S.C.(H.L.) 1; 1956 S.L.T. 41.... 4.65,
                                                                     4.73, 15.55
—— v. General Accident Fire and Life Assurance Corporation Ltd, 1914 S.C. 835;
    1914 2 S.L.T. 64; (1914) 51 S.L.R. 712..................... 18.34, 18.94, 21.69
—— v. Glasgow Churches Council, 1944 S.C. 97; 1944 S.L.T. 317; 1944 S.N. 7..... 1.11,
                                                                25.06, 25.08
—— v. Mickel, 1922 S.C. 228; 1922 S.L.T. 160; (1922) 59 S.L.R. 153........... 26.201
—— v. Railwaymen's Club (1915) 31 Sh.Ct.Rep. 220........................ 9.85
—— v. Regent Oil Co. Ltd, 1971 S.L.T. (Sh.Ct.) 61....................... 12.15

Glasgow District of Order of Foresters v. Stevenson (1899) 2 F. 14; (1899) 7 S.L.T.
   163; (1899) 37 S.L.R. 54. . . . . 26.201
Glasgow District Subway Co. v. Albin & Son (1895) 23 R. 81; (1895) 3 S.L.T. 138;
   (1895) 33 S.L.R. 54. . . . . 26.95
—— v. McCallum (1896) 12 Sh.Ct.Rep. 148. . . . . 19.42, 26.349
Glasgow Gas-Light Co. v. Glasgow Working Men's Total Abstinence Society (1866)
   4 M. 1041; (1866) 38 Sc.Jur. 530. . . . . 17.03, 17.07
Glasgow Lock Hospital, Petrs, 1929 S.L.T. (Notes) 26. . . . . 26.407
Glasgow Magistrates v. Glasgow District Subway Co. (1893) 21 R. 52   18.29, 25.01, 26.32
Glasgow Navigation Co. Ltd v. Iron Ore Co. Ltd. 1910 S.C.(H.L.) 63; [1910] A.C.
   293; 1910 1 S.L.T. 345; (1910) 47 S.L.R. 507. . . . . 2.13
Glasgow Parish Council v. United Collieries Trs (1907) 15 S.L.T. 232. . . . . 26.32
Glasgow Procurators v. Colquhoun (1900) 2 F. 1192; (1900) 37 S.L.R. 909. . . . . 2.105
Glasgow Shipowners Association v. Clyde Navigation Trs (1885) 12 R. 695; (1885)
   22 S.L.R. 374. . . . . 2.112, 4.35, 8.22, 12.15
Glasgow University Court v. Lord Advocate, 1961 S.C. 246; 1961 S.L.T. 345. . . . . . . 26.85
Glasgow Working Men's Building Society v. Kirkwood (1888) 4 Sh.Ct.Rep. 165. . . 26.197
Glasser v. Glasser, 1997 S.L.T. 456. . . . . 15.43
Glassford, The v. The City of Edinburgh (1904) 12 S.L.R. 159; (1904) 7 F. 213;
   (1904) 12 S.L.T. 481. . . . . 18.85
Glebe Sugar Refining Co. v. Greenock Harbour Trs, 1921 S.C.(H.L.) 72; 1921 2
   S.L.T. 26; (1921) 58 S.L.R. 435; [1921] A.C. 66. . . . . 16.42
Glen v. Dumbarton Commissioners (1897) 13 Sh.Ct.Rep. 244. . . . . 25.08
Glen Music Co. Ltd v. Glasgow D.C., 1983 S.L.T. (Sh.Ct.) 26. . . . . 11.25
Goldie v. Chrysler Motors Ltd (1939) 55 Sh.Ct.Rep. 99. . . . . 14.16, 14.18, 14.26, 19.12
Goodall v. Bilsland, 1909 S.C. 1152; 1909 1 S.L.T. 376; (1909) 46 S.L.R. 555. . . . . . 4.125
Goodhall v. Mackill (1891) 8 S.L.R. 40. . . . . 11.72
Goodwin v. Farming Agricultural Finance Ltd, 1996 S.C.L.R. 545. . . . . 19.18
Goold v. Evans [1951] 2 T.L.R. 1189. . . . . 16.92
Gordon v. Bruce & Co. (1897) 24 R. 844; (1897) 5 S.L.T. 13; (1897) 34 S.L.R.
   633. . . . . 11.32, 13.40
—— v. Davidson (1864) 2 M. 758; (1864) 36 Sc.Jur. 376. . . . . 9.67, 9.70, 13.05
—— v. —— (1865) 3 M. 938; (1865) 37 Sc.Jur. 494. 19.26, 19.27
—— v. Duncan (1827) 5 S. 544 (N.E. 511). 11.11
—— v. Gordon (1822) 2 S. 93 (N.E. 86). 11.80
—— v. —— (1823) 2 S. 572 (N.E. 493). 11.67, 11.80
—— v. Gordon's Trs (1866) 4 M. 501; (1866) 38 Sc.Jur. 232. . . . . 2.15, 2.125, 2.129
—— v. Graham (1874) 1 R. 1081; (1874) 11 S.L.R. 623. . . . . 18.34, 18.35
—— v. Henderson (1922) 38 Sh.Ct.Rep. 293. . . . . 4.115
—— v. Hill (1841) 3 D. 517. . . . . 11.25
—— v. Mayfair Homes Ltd, 1994 S.C.L.R. 862. . . . . 8.34
—— v. Nakeski-Cumming 1924 S.C. 939; 1924 S.L.T. 640; 1924 S.L.R. 588. . . . . 1.32
—— v. Orrok (1849) 11 D. 1358. . . . . 15.26
—— v. Purves (1902) 10 S.L.T. 446, (1903) 11 S.L.T. 38. . . . . 10.04, 10.10, 12.20
Gordon D.C. v. Acutt, 1991 S.L.T. (Sh.Ct.) 78. . . . . 30.279
Gordon's Trs v. Forbes (1904) 6 F. 455; (1904) 11 S.L.T. 697; (1904) 41 S.L.R.
   346. . . . . 11.68, 11.70
Gorman v. National Coal Board, 1975 S.L.T. (Notes) 8. . . . . 10.37
Gorman v. Wright, 1916 S.C.(J.) 44; (1916) 7 Adam 765; 1916 2 S.L.T. 54; (1916) 53
   S.L.R. 617. . . . . 2.126, 2.128
Gorrie & Sons v. Northern Laundry Co. Edinburgh Ltd (1910) 27 Sh.Ct.Rep. 66. . 11.45,
   11.46
Gottlieb v. Fons Patent Inkwell Ltd, 1917 1 S.L.T. (Sh.Ct.) 331; (1916) 33
   Sh.Ct.Rep. 70. . . . . 2.33, 30.133
Goudie v. Goudie (1903) 11 S.L.T. 27. . . . . 23.41
Gould v. Gould, 1966 S.C. 88; 1966 S.L.T. 131. . . . . 15.56
—— v. McCorquodale (1869) 8 M. 165; (1869) 42 Sc.Jur. 72; (1869) 7 S.L.R. 108. . . 4.33
Govan v. McKillop, 1909 S.C. 562; 1909 1 S.L.T. 168; (1909) 46 S.L.R. 416. . 19.51, 19.52
—— v. National Coal Board, 1987 S.L.T. 511. . . . . 15.56
—— v. Thomson, Dec. 20, 1814, F.C. 4.07
Govan Old Victualling Society Ltd v. Wagstaff (1907) 14 S.L.T. 716; (1907) 44
   S.L.R. 295. . . . . 2.106, 9.115
Govan Rope and Sail Co. Ltd v. Weir & Co. (1897) 24 R. 368; (1897) 34 S.L.R.
   310; (1897) 4 S.L.T. 245. . . . . 10.22
Govers & Co. v. Findlay & Wallace, 1923 S.L.T. (Sh.Ct.) 127; (1922) 39 Sh.Ct. Rep.
   201. . . . . 11.55, 11.60, 11.65

Gow v. Henry (1899) 2 F.48; (1899) 7 S.L.T. 203; (1899) 37 S.L.R. 40. . 8.19, 8.60, 14.31,
    14.65
—— v. Portobello Co-operative Society (1926) 43 Sh.Ct.Rep. 127.............. 26.201
Gow's Trs v. Mealls (1875) 2 R. 729; (1875) 12 S.L.R. 458..................... 2.13
Gowan's Trs v. Gowans (1889) 27 S.L.R. 210............................... 21.69
Gracey v. Sykes, 1994 S.C.L.R. 909....................................... 8.42, 13.01
Gracie v. Gracie, 1910 S.C. 899; 1910 2 S.L.T. 144; (1910) 47 S.L.R. 458.... 11.14, 11.21
Graham v. Farquhar (1893) 1 S.L.T. 63................................. 2.20, 8.32
—— v. Galli, 1980 S.L.T. (Sh.Ct.) 2...................................... 10.04
—— v. Graham, 1968 S.L.T. (Notes) 42............................... 4.32, 4.105
—— v. Graham's Trs (1901) 4 F. 1; (1901) 9 S.L.T. 205; (1901) 39 S.L.R. 3....... 11.68
—— v. Macfarlane (1869) 7 M. 640...................................... 29.27
—— v. National Coal Board, 1964 S.L.T. (Sh.Ct.) 53................... 13.73, 13.75
—— v. Sprot (1847) 9 D. 545; (1847) 19 Sc.Jur. 221...................... 15.73
—— v. Wylie & Lochhead Ltd, 2nd Div., Feb. 17, 1949, unreported........ 7.33 14.10
—— v. Young, 1927 S.L.T. (Sh.Ct.) 25; (1926) 43 Sh.Ct. Rep 3.................. 13.52
—— v. Robert Younger Ltd, 1955 J.C. 28; 1955 S.L.T. 250................. 2.19, 21.92
Graham Builders Merchants Ltd v. The Royal Bank of Scotland plc, 1992 S.C.L.R.
    402... 15.58
Grahame v. Secretary of State for Scotland, 1951 S.C. 368; 1951 S.L.T. 312; 1951
    S.L.C.R. 35.. 2.104, 2.108, 8.41,
Grampian Hydraulics (Buckie) Ltd v. Dauntless Marine Engineering & Supply Co.
    Ltd, 1992 S.L.T. (Sh.Ct.) 45; 1992 S.C.L.R. 301.................. 9.67, 9.114
Grangemouth and Forth Towing Co. Ltd v. Netherlands East Indies Govt., 1942
    S.L.T. 228; 1942 S.N. 19... 14.37
Grant v. Allen [1980] 1 All E.R. 720....................................... 26.174
—— v. Countess of Seafield, 1926 S.C. 274; 1926 S.L.T. 144; 1925 S.N. 160....... 15.19,
    15.24, 15.28, 15.31
—— v. ——, 1926 S.L.T. 213... 15.24, 15.28
—— v. ——, 1926 S.L.T. 726; 1926 S.N. 22.............................. 14.18
—— v. Gauld (Peter G.) & Co., 1985 S.L.T. 545....................... 10.26
—— v. Giffnock Collieries Ltd (1928) 44 Sh.Ct.Rep. 211..................... 19.06
—— v. Grant (1908) 24 Sh.Ct.Rep. 114................................. 16.03
—— v. Hill (1792) Mor. 786....................................... 11.34, 29.30
—— v. McAlister (1948) 64 Sh.Ct.Rep. 261................................ 12.36
—— v. Macdonald (1867) 4 S.L.R. 189.................................. 11.71
Grant (Wm) and Sons Ltd v. Wm Cadenhead Ltd, 1985 S.L.T. 291.............. 21.92
Grant (William) & Sons International Ltd v. Marie Brizard & Roger International
    SA, 1996 S.C.L.R. 987.................................. 3.60, 3.61, 3.93
Grant's Trs v. McDonald, 1939 S.C. 448; 1939 S.L.T. 391; 1939 S.N. 32........... 21.71
Gray v. Boyd, 1996 S.L.T. 60; 1995 S.C.L.R. 1075; 1994 S.C.L.R. 923............. 9.114
—— v. Caledonian Ry, 1912 S.C. 339; 1912 1 S.L.T. 76; (1912) 49 S.L.R. 219...... 4.38,
    21.13
—— v. Coupar Angus Town Council (1905) 21 Sh.Ct.Rep. 214................... 25.09
—— v. Gray, 1968 S.C. 185; 1968 S.L.T. 254............ 18.30, 18.110, 18.111, 18.114,
—— v. ——, 1993 S.C.L.R. 580... 26.125
—— v. ——, 1996 S.C.L.R. 531... 18.12
—— v. Ireland (1884) 11 R. 1104; (1884) 21 S.L.R. 766........................ 11.65
—— v. Low (1856) 18 D. 628; (1856) 28 Sc.Jur. 382.......................... 8.06
—— v. McHardy (1862) 24 D. 1043...................................... 2.109
—— v. Rivet Bolt and Nut Co. Ltd, 1912 2 S.L.T. 341....................... 8.60
—— v. SSPCA (1890) 17 R. 789; 27 S.L.R. 906......................... 10.22, 10.29
—— v. Weir (1891) 19 R. 25... 23.18
Great Australian Gold Mining Co. v. Martin (1877) 5 Ch.D. 1.................. 9.12
Green v. Maxwell Property Development Co., 1976 S.L.T. (Sh.Ct.) 65....... 9.67, 13.05
—— v. Miller's Debt Recovery Services, 1954 S.L.T. (Sh.Ct.) 26; (1953) 70 Sh.Ct.
    Rep. 59.. 21.49
Greengairs Rovers F.C. v. Blades (1910) S.L.T. (Sh.Ct.) 23; 26 Sh.Ct.Rep. 280..... 4.101
Greenhorn v. J. Smart & Co. (Contractors) Ltd, 1979 S.C. 427; 1980 S.L.T. 70.... 10.18,
    10.34, 10.37, 10.38, 10.52, 13.09
Greenline Carriers (Tayside) Ltd v. City of Dundee District Council, 1991 S.L.T.
    673... 17.27
Greenock Parochial Board v. Miller and Brown (1877) 4 R. 737; (1877) 14 S.L.R.
    489... 18.36
Greenock Port and Harbour Trs v. British Oil and Cake Mills Ltd, 1944 S.C. 70;
    1944 S.L.T. 293; 1944 S.N. 1.................................. 13.72, 13.79
Gregson v. Grant, 1910 2 S.L.T. 16; (1916) 48 S.L.R. 6.................... 2.19, 8.16

Gribb v. Gribb, 1993 S.L.T. 178. . . . . 13.67
Gribben v. Gribben, 1976 S.L.T. 266. . . . . 2.21, 21.96, 21.97, 21.98
Grieg v. City of Glasgow Friendly Society, 1939 S.L.T. (Sh.Ct.) 31. . . . . 26.201
Grier v. Wimpey Plant and Transport Ltd 1994 S.L.T. 714; 1994 S.C.L.R. 454. . . . . . 5.94,
                                                                                    18.48, 18.98
Grierson v. Greenock Licensing Court, 1969 S.L.T. (Sh.Ct.) 33. . . . . 26.255
—— v. McGarva (1934) 50 Sh.Ct.Rep. 88. . . . . 16.97
Grieve v. Batchelor & Buckling, 1961 S.C. 12; 1961 S.L.T. 151. . . . . 5.94, 18.98
Grieve's Trs v. Grieve, 1907 S.C. 963; (1907) 15 S.L.T. 91; (1907) 44 S.L.R. 737. . . 19.26,
                                                                                           19.27
Griffin v. Lord Advocate, 1950 S.C. 448; 1951 S.L.T. 245. . . . . 4.57
Grimason v. National Coal Board, 1986 S.L.T. 286. . . . . 10.38, 10.52
Grimes v. Grimes, 1995 S.C.L.R. 268. . . . . 8.37, 14.14, 22.53, 22.54
Grindall v. John Mitchell (Grangemouth) Ltd, 1987 S.L.T. 137. . . . . 4.110
Group 4 Total Security Ltd v. Ferrier, 1985 S.L.T. 287. . . . . 21.91
—— v. Jaymarke Developments Ltd, 1995 S.C.L.R. 303. . . . . 5.93, 8.34, 8.35, 14.06
Groupo Torras v. Al-Sabah [1996] 1 Lloyd's Rep. 7. . . . . 3.60
Grunwald v. Hughes, 1965 S.L.T. 209. . . . . 4.41
Guardian Royal Exchange Group v. Moffat, 1986 S.L.T. 262. . . . . . . 7.28, 7.30, 7.31, 7.37
Gubay v. Kington [1984] 1 W.L.R. 163; [1984] 1 All E.R. 513; (1984) 128 S.J. 100. . 18.13
Guinness, Mahon & Co. v. Coats Iron and Steel Co. (1891) 18 R. 441; (1891) 28
       S.L.R. 285. . . . . 10.25
Gunn v. Breadalbane (Marquis of) (1849) 11 D. 1040. . . . . 14.37
—— v. Hunter (1886) 13 R. 573; 23 S.L.R. 395. . . . . 14.35, 14.38, 14.68
—— v. McAdam & Son, 1949 S.C. 31; 1949 S.L.T. 20. . . . . . 9.28, 9.29, 9.132, 10.19, 17.12
Gunn, Collie & Topping v. Purdie, 1946 S.L.T. (Sh.Ct.) 11. . . . . 11.45, 12.25
Gunn & Co. v. Couper (1871) 10 M. 116; (1871) 44 Sc.Jur. 74; (1871) 9 S.L.R.
       98. . . . . 11.72, 11.77
Gunstone v. Scottish Women's Amateur Athletic Association, 1987 S.L.T. 611. . . . . . 4.33
Gupta v. Laurie, 1994 S.C.L.R. 176; (*sub nom.* Gupta v. Gupta's Tr, 1994 S.L.T.
       1052). 18.12, 30.328
Gupta's Trustee v. Gupta, 1996 S.C. 82 1996 S.L.T. 1098. . . . . 18.12
Guthrie v. McEachern (1826) 5 S. 135 (N.E. 124). 21.74
—— v. McKimmie's Tr., 1952 S.L.T. (Sh.Ct.) 49; (1952) 68 Sh.Ct.Rep. 175. . . . . . . 21.10
—— v. Morren (1939) 55 Sh.Ct.Rep. 172. . . . . 29.27
Gysin v. Pochin (Joinery) Ltd, 1970 S.L.T. (Notes) 9. . . . . 14.53

H (A Minor) (Adoption: Non-patrial), Re [1982] 3 All E.R. 84. . . . . 28.91
H (infants) (adoption: parental consent), Re [1977] 2 All E.R. 339. . . . . 28.75
H v. McGregor, 1973 S.C. 95. . . . . 26.61
—— v. Sweeney, 1982 J.C. 70. . . . . 5.25
Haberstich v. McCormick & Nicholson, 1974 S.C. 241; 1975 S.L.T. 181. . . . . 5.88
Hackett v. Allan, Dunoon Sh.Ct., May 15, 1984, unreported. 8.58, 9.30, 9.122, 13.21
Hackston v. Hackston, 1956 S.L.T. (Notes) 38. . . . . 2.73
Haddow v. Glasgow District Licensing Board, 1983 S.L.T. (Sh.Ct.) 5. . . . . 26.255
Hadinton (Countess of) v Richardson (1822) 1 S. 387. . . . . 11.25
Hadkinson v. Hadkinson [1952] P. 285 [1952] 2 T.L.R. 416; [1952] 2 All E.R. 567,
       C.A. 5.91
Hadmor Productions Ltd v. Hamilton [1983] 1 A.C. 191; [1982] 1 All E.R. 1042. . 18.110
Haggerty v. Nisbet, 1933 S.L.T. 188; 1933 S.N. 16. . . . . 14.18, 14.30
Haigh & Ringrose Ltd v. Barrhead Builders Ltd, 1981 S.L.T. 157. . . . . 9.36
Haldane v. Allan, 1956 S.L.T. 325; 1956 J.C. 41. . . . . 26.14
—— v. Speirs (1872) 10 M. 537; (1872) 44 Sc.Jur. 305; (1872) 9 S.L.R. 317. . . . . . . 8.57
Halkerston v. Wedderburn (1781) Mor. 10493. . . . . 2.02
Hall v. Associated Newspapers Ltd, 1979 J.C. 1; 1978 S.L.T. 241. . . . . . . 2.05, 2.19, 5.91
—— v. Hall (1891) 18 R. 690; (1891) 28 S.L.R. 476. . . . . 2.128
—— v. ——. 1987 S.L.T. (Sh.Ct.) 15. . . . . 23.42, 23.43
—— v. Newland's Trs (1859) 22 D. 333; (1859) 32 Sc.Jur. 140. . . . . 11.75, 11.79
Halley v. Watt, 1956 S.C. 370; 1956 S.L.T. 111. . . . . 2.123
Halliburton Manufacturing and Service Ltd v. Bingham Blades & Partners, 1984
       S.L.T. 388. . . . . 2.100
—— v. Picts (Construction) Co. Ltd, 1986 S.L.T. (Sh.Ct.) 24. . . . . 14.21, 14.26, 14.29
Halliday v. Rolland Decorators Ltd, 1994 S.C.L.R. 305. . . . . 9.67
—— v. Semple 1960 S.L.T. (Sh.Ct.) 11 (1959) 75 Sh.Ct.Rep. 188. . . . . 26.11
Halloran v. Greater Glasgow Passenger Transport Executive, 1976 S.L.T. 77. . . . . . . 15.02
Hallowell v. Niven (1843) 5 D. 655; (1843) 15 Sc.Jur. 312. . . . . 4.110, 12.12

Hamill v. Newalls Insulation Co., 1987 S.L.T. 478. . . . . 2.121
Hamilton (1861) 24 D. 31. . . . . 4.23
—— v. Anderson (1856) 18 D. 1003; (1856) 28 Sc.Jur. 459. 1.02
—— v. —— (1858) 3 Macq. 363; (1858) 20 D.(H.L.) 16. . . . . 5.98, 10.60
—— v. British Coal Corporation, 1990 S.L.T. 287. . . . . 13.67
—— v. Bruce's Trs (1857) 19 D. 745; (1857) 29 Sc.Jur. 346. . . . . 11.33, 11.41
—— v. Christie (1857) 19 D. 712. . . . . 14.12
—— v. Dutch East India Co. (1732) 1 Pat. App. 69. . . . . 2.105
—— v. Emslie (1860) 7 M. 173, 176. . . . . 29.78
—— v. Hamilton (1877) 4 R. 688; (1877) 14 S.L.R. 448. . . . . 2.29
—— v. ——, 1948 S.L.T. (Notes) 8. . . . . 18.48, 18.96
—— v. ——, 1988 S.C.L.R. 773. . . . . 19.40, 1966
—— v. John Brown & Co. (Clydebank) Ltd, 1969 S.L.T. (Notes) 18. . . 9.28, 10.19, 16.84
—— v. McLauchian (1908) 16 S.L.T. 341. . . . . 2.12, 19.12
—— v. Monkland Iron and Steel Co. (1863) 1 M. 672; (1863) 35 Sc.Jur. 387. . . . . . 11.19
—— v. Murray & Co. (1830) 9 S. 143. . . . . 6.04, 9.121
—— v. Robertson (1878) 5 R. 839. . . . . 9.30
—— v. Santi (1916) 32 Sh.Ct.Rep. 73. . . . . 9.33, 9.131
Hamilton (John) & Co. v. John Fleming & Co. Ltd, 1918 1 S.L.T. 229. . . . . 14.37
Hamilton (Lord) v. Glasgow Dairy Co., 1933 S.C. 18; 1933 S.L.T. 7; 1932 S.N. 89. . 14.30
Hamilton D.C. v. Sneddon, 1980 S.L.T. (Sh.Ct.) 36. . . . . 30.29
Hamilton Leasing Ltd v. Clark, 1974 S.L.T. (Sh.Ct.) 95. . . . . 4.43, 7.09
Hamilton's (Duke of) Trs v. Woodside Coal Co. (1897) 24 R. 294; (1897) 4 S.L.T.
    241; (1897) 34 S.L.R. 257. . . . . 8.63, 15.53
Hamlyn & Co. v. Talisker Distillery (1894) 21 R.(H.L.) 21; (1894) 2 S.L.T. 12;
    (1894) 31 S.L.R. 642; [1894] A.C. 202. . . . . 2.99, 2.100, 2.101
Hammersmith LBC v. Magnum Automated Forecourts Ltd [1978] 1 W.L.R. 50;
    [1977] 1 All E.R. 401; [1977] 76 L.G.R. 159; [1977] 121 S.J. 259; (1978)
    J.P.L. 106, C.A.. . . . . 26.167
Hancock's Curator Bonis v. Ellis, 1980 S.L.T. (Notes) 27. . . . . 21.25, 21.26
Handren v. Scottish Construction Ltd, 1967 S.L.T. (Notes) 21. . . . . 21.36
Hannah v. Hannah's Trs 1958 S.L.T. (Notes) 9. . . . . 4.33
—— v. Lord Advocate, 1970 S.L.T. (Sh.Ct.) 46. . . . . 4.66, 6.22
Hannan v. Kendal, O.H., Lord Kincaimey, Mar. 30., 1897, unreported. 11.19
Hansen v. Donaldson (1873) 1 R. 237; (1873) 11 S.L.R. 590. . . . . 15.19, 15.21
Hanslam v. Kirkcudbright C.C., 1962 S.L.T. (Sh.Ct.) 47. 26.161
Hardie v. Brown, Barker & Bell (1907) 15 S.L.T. 539. . . . . 11.62
Hardnec Flooring Co. v. Forbes, 1975 S.L.T. (Sh.Ct.) 9. . . . . 19.11
Hardy v. British Airways Board, 1983 S.L.T. 45. . . . . 4.48, 14.29
—— v. Robinson 1985 S.L.T. (Sh.Ct.) 40. . . . . 1.06, 5.97, 14.03, 14.11,
                                                              18.12, 18.34, 18.56, 18.69, 30.13
Hare v. Stein (1882) 9 R. 910; (1882) 19 S.L.R. 652. . . . . 14.19
Harker v. Dickson (1856) 18 D. 793. . . . . 11.80
Harkes v. Mowat (1862) 24 D. 701. . . . . 4.38
Harkness v. Harkness, 1962 S.L.T. (Sh.Ct.) 32; (1961) 77 Sh.Ct.Rep. 165. . . . . 18.88
Harland Engineering Co. v. Stark's Trs, 1913 2 S.L.T. 448. 2.95
Harley v. Kinnear Moodie & Co. Ltd, 1964 S.L.T. 99; 1964 S.L.T. 64. . . . . . 11.68, 11.73
Harper v. Connor's Trs (1927) 43 Sh.Ct.Rep. 138. . . . . 9.94
—— v. James Dunlop & Co. Ltd (1902) 5 F. 208; (1902) 10 S.L.T. 407; (1902) 40
    S.L.R. 174. . . . . 9.30
—— v. Inspector of Rutherglen (1881) 8 R. 784. . . . . 25.37
—— v.—(1903) 6 F. 23; (1903) 11 S.L.T. 369; (1903) 41 S.L.R. 16. . . . . . . 18.01, 25.45
Harris School Board v. Davidson (1881) 9 R. 371; (1881) 19 S.L.R. 265. . . . . 21.64
—— v. Harris, C.A., Apr. 8, 1952, unreported. 16.39
—— v. Lamont, 1925 S.L.T. (Sh.Ct.) 141; (1925) 41 Sh.Ct.Rep. 243. . . . . . . 12.24, 12.26
—— v. Roberts, 1983 S.L.T. 452. . . . . 10.41, 12.49, 12.51
Harrison v. Butters, 1968 S.L.T. (Notes) 90. . . . . 11.70
Harrods (Buenos Aires) Ltd, Re [1992] Ch. 72. . . . . 3.03
Hart v. Grant & Wylie (1907) 23 Sh.Ct.Rep. 186. . . . . 11.22
—— v. Thorntons W.S., 1995 S.C.L.R. 642. . . . . 8.48, 13.01
Hartley v. H.M. Advocate, 1979 S.L.T. 26; 1979 S.L.T. (News) 189. . . . . 16.73
Hartnett v. Hartnett, 1997 S.C.L.R. 525. . . . . 8.08, 22.38, 25.25
Harvey v. Dyce (1876) 4 R. 265. . . . . 1.13
—— v. Farquhar (1870) 8 M. 971; (1870) 42 Sc.Jur. 564. . . . . 11.65
—— v. Gibson (1826) 4 S. 809 (N.E. 816); (1826) Fac. 158. . . . . 25.04
—— v. Glasgow Corporation, 1915 S.C. 600; 1915 1 S.L.T. 286; (1915) 52 S.L.R.
    395. . . . . 19.05

Harvey v. Harvey's Trs (1860) 22 D. 1310; (1860) 32 Sc.Jur. 613. . . . . 2.13
—— v. Lindsay (1875) 2 R. 980. . . . . 5.88
—— v. Smith (1904) 6 F. 511; (1904) 11 S.L.T. 667; (1904) 41 S.L.R. 292. . . . . 9.88
Hastie (J. & A.) v. Edinburgh D.C., 1981 S.L.T. (Sh.Ct.) 92. . . . . 30.223
Hastings Black Corporation Ltd v. A.I.R. (Air Conditioning and Refrigeration) Ltd,
    Glasgow Sh.Ct., Oct. 4, 1984, unreported. 4.89
Hattie v. Leitch (1889) 16 R. 1128. . . . . 16.93
Haughton v. North British Ry (1892) 20 R. 113; (1892) 30 S.L.R. 111. . . . . 10.29
Hawthorne v. Milne, 1956 S.L.T. (Sh.Ct.) 85; (1956) 72 Sh.Ct.Rep. 323. . . . . 18.82
Hay v. Dufourcet & Co. (1880) 7 R. 972. . . . . 29.29
Hay's Trs v. Young (1877) 4 R. 398; (1877) 14 S.L.R. 282. . . . . 21.83
Hayes v. Robinson, 1984 S.L.T. 300. . . . . 4.33, 9.67
Hayhoe v. Hydro Plant, 1976 S.L.T. (Sh.Ct.) 78. . . . . 9.24
Hayward v. Edinburgh Royal Infirmary, 1955 S.L.T. (Notes) 69. . . . . 14.30
Hazle v. Turner (1840) 2 D. 886. . . . . 2.02
Healey v. A. Massey & Son, 1961 S.C. 198; 1961 S.L.T. 198. . . . . 9.25, 9.67
Heddle v. Gow (1880) 18 S.L.R. 96. . . . . 2.29
—— v. Leith Magistrates (1898) 25 R. 801; (1898) 4 S.L.T. 335. . . . . 25.33
Hegard v. Hegard, 1981 S.L.T. (Notes) 45. . . . . 11.53, 11.57, 11.64
Hegarty & Kelly v. Cosmopolitan Insurance Corporation Ltd, 1913 S.C. 377; 1913 1
    S.L.T. 18; (1913) 50 S.L.R. 256. . . . . 2.101
Heggie & Co. v. Stark and Selkrig (1826) 4 S. 510 (N.E. 518). 9.94, 19.03, 19.05
Henderson (1933) 50 Sh.Ct.Rep. 17. . . . . 26.09
—— v. Adamson, 1998 S.C.L.R. 365. . . . . 8.08
—— v. Campbell Bros, 1937 S.C. 91; 1937 S.L.T. 135; 1936 S.N. 117. . . . . 10.03
—— v. Grant (1896) 23 R. 659; (1986) 3 S.L.T. 311; (1896) 33 S.L.R. 483. . . . . 2.30
—— v. Henderson, 1953 S.L.T. 270. . . . . 15.28, 15.31
—— v. Huzzard (1934) 50 Sh.Ct.Rep. 300. . . . . 23.18
—— v. McCown, 1916 S.C. 821; 1916 2 S.L.T. 65; (1916) 53 S.L.R. 627. . . . . 15.57, 15.60
—— v. Nelson (1913) 29 Sh.Ct.Rep. 233. . . . . 23.30
—— v. Outram and Co. Ltd, 1993 S.C.L.R. 162;. 11.29, 11.30
—— v. Paul (1867) 5 M. 628; (1867) 39 Sc.Jur. 307. . . . . 13.39
—— v. Peeblesshire C.C., 1972 S.C. 195; 1972 S.L.T. (Notes) 35 No 1972 Volume . 14.47
—— v. Richardson (1848) 10 D. 1035; (1848) 20 Sc.Jur. 382. . . . . 11.19
—— v. Robb (1889) 16 R. 341; (1889) 26 S.L.R. 222. . . . . 4.110
—— v. Singer (U.K.) Ltd, 1983 S.L.T. 198. . . . . 10.41
—— v. Smith (1750) Mor. 6563. . . . . 24.15
—— v. Thomson (Patrick) Ltd, 1911 S.C. 246; 1910 2 S.L.T. 443; (1910) 48 S.L.R.
    200. . . . . 9.82, 15.02, 15.08
—— v. Warden (1845) 17 Sc.Jur. 271. . . . . 1.17
Henderson (Glen) Stuggart Ltd v. Henderson, Ayr Sh.Ct., May 18, 1992, unre-
    ported. 18.13
Henderson's Trs (1831) 9 S. 618. . . . . 11.19
—— v. Dunfermline District Committee of Fife C.C. (1896) 12 Sh.Ct.Rep. 58. . . . 2.128,
                                                                                                        2.129
Hendry v. Fordyce (1952) 69 Sh.Ct.Rep. 191. . . . . 26.10
—— v. Hendry, 1916 1 S.L.T. 208, 1916 2 S.L.T. 135; 53 S.L.R. 757. . . . . 14.32
Henley's Tyre and Rubber Co. Ltd v. Swan, 1929 S.L.T. (Sh.Ct.) 48; (1929) 45
    Sh.Ct. Rep. 50. . . . . 11.23, 11.30
Henry v. Morrison (1881) 8 R. 692; (1881) 18 S.L.R. 438. . . . . 2.31
Hepburn v. Scottish Power plc, 1997 S.C. 80; 1997 S.L.T. 859; 1997 S.C.L.R. 295. . . 15.54
—— v. Tait (1874) 1 R. 875; (1874) 11 S.L.R. 502. . . . . 4.112, 4.113, 4.125, 11.55
Hepburn & Ross v. Tritonia Ltd, 1951 S.L.T. (Sh.Ct.) 6; (1950) 66 Sh.Ct.Rep.
    290. . . . . 14.22, 14.24
Hepburn's Trs v. R (1894) 21 R. 1024; (1894) 2 S.L.T. 103. 21.71
Herbertson v. Ascomit Co. Ltd, 1992 S.L.T. 1115. . . . . 21.24
Herdman v. Young (1744) Mor. 13987. . . . . 9.14
Heriot v. Thomson (1833) 12 S. 145. . . . . 14.52
Heriot-Hill v. Heriot-Hill (1906) 14 S.L.T. 182. . . . . 9.121, 13.23
Heritage House Ltd v. Brown, 1995 S.L.T. (Sh.Ct.) 101; 1995 S.C.L.R. 783. . . . . . . 12.35
Heron v. Winfields Ltd (1894) 22 R. 182; 2 S.L.T. 349; (1894) 32 S.L.R. 137. . . . . . 3.99,
                                                                                                        11.13, 29.27
Herron v. Kennon, 1986 S.L.T. 260. . . . . 21.22, 21.23
Hertz v. Itzig (1865) 3 M. 813. . . . . 29.32
Herzberg v. Herzberg, 1952 S.L.T. (Sh.Ct.) 65; (1952) 68 Sh.Ct. Rep. 174. . . . . 11.73
Hester v. MacDonald, 1961 S.C. 370; 1961 S.L.T. 414. . . . . 1.31
Hewat v. Edinburgh Corporation, 1944 S.C. 30; 1944 S.L.T. 193; 1943 S.N. 76. . . . . 16.86

Heyman v. Darwins Ltd [1942] A.C. 356; [1942] 1 All E.R. 337. . . . . 2.101
Higgins v. Burton, 1969 S.L.T. (Notes) 52. . . . . 15.55
—— v. Glasgow Corporation, 1954 S.L.T. (Sh.Ct.) 73; (1954) 70 Sh.Ct.Rep. 187. . . 13.79,
    13.82
High-Flex (Scotland) Ltd v. Kentallen Mechanical Services Co., 1977 S.L.R.
    (Sh.Ct.) 91. . . . . 2.07, 11.34, 29.30
Highgate & Co. v. British Oil and Guano Co. Ltd, 1914 2 S.L.T. 241. . . . . 26.32
Hill v. Black, 1914 S.C. 913; 1914 2 S.L.T. 123; (1914) 51 S.L.R. 811. . . . . 2.09
—— v. College of Glasgow (1849) 12 D. 46. . . . . 29.24
—— v. Sneddon, Campbell & Munro, 1931 S.C. 164. . . . . 11.54
Hillhead Garage Ltd v. Bunten & Miller (1924) 40 Sh.Ct.Rep. 208. . . . . 7.06
Hilton v. Walkers (1867) 5 M. 969; (1867) 39 Sc.Jur. 538; (1867) 3 S.L.R. 283. . . . . 13.38,
    13.39
Hislop v. MacRitchie's Trs (1879) 7 R. 384. . . . . 4.114
—— v. —— (1881) 8 R.(H.L.) 95; (1881) 8 R.(H.L.) 95; (1881) 19 S.L.R. 57; (1881)
    6 App. Cas. 560. . . . . 4.32
Hoare v. Mackay (1905) 13 S.L.T. 588. . . . . 23.24
Hobbs v. Fawcett, 1983 S.L.T. (Sh.Ct.) 15. . . . . 10.41
Hobday v. Kirkpatrick's Trs, 1985 S.L.T. 197. . . . . 21.10
Hodge v. British Coal Corporation, 1992 S.L.T. 484; 1992 S.C.L.R. 529. . . . . 10.20
Hodgson v. Hodgson's Trs, 1984 S.L.T. 97. . . . . 6.10
Hoey v. Hoey (1884) 11 R. 578; (1884) 21 S.L.R. 407. . . . . 16.81
Hogan v. Cunningham (1915) 32 Sh.Ct.Rep. 67; 1916 1 S.L.T. 320. . . . . 16.97
Hogg v. Frew, 1951 S.L.T. 397. . . . . 15.38
Hoggan v. McKeachie, 1960 S.C. 461; 1960 S.L.T. (Notes) 64. . . . . 7.28
Holmes v. McMurrich, 1920 S.C. 632; 1920 2 S.L.T. 76; (1920) 57 S.L.R. 523. . . . . . 11.70
—— v. Tassie (1828) 6 S. 394. . . . . 18.05
Holt v. National Bank of Scotland, 1927 S.L.T. 664; 1927 S.N. 142. . . . . 19.27, 19.28
Home v. Hardy (1842) 4 D. 1184. . . . . 15.81
Home-Drummond v. Douglas (1904) 20 Sh.Ct.Rep.. . . . . 21.98
—— v. McLachlan, 1908 S.C. 12; (1908) 15 S.L.T. 403; (1908) 45 S.L.R. 15. . . . . . . 21.92
—— v. Norman (1902) 19 Sh.Ct.Rep. 16. . . . . 21.90
Honeyman's Exrs v. Sharp, 1978 S.C. 223; 1979 S.L.T. 177. 8.58
Hood v. Gordon (1896) 23 R. 675; (1896) 33 S.L.R. 491. . . . . 19.46
Hook v. McCallum (1905) 7 F. 528; (1905) 42 S.L.R. 399; (1905) 12 S.L.T. 770. . . . . 4.50
Hope v. Gemmell (1898) 1 F. 74; (1898) 6 S.L.T. 204; (1898) 36 S.L.R. 81. . . . . 16.92
—— v. Hope (1956) 72 Sh.Ct.Rep. 244. . . . . 18.50
—— v. Hope's Trs (1898) 1 F.(H.L.) 1; (1898) 6 S.L.T. 132; (1898) 35 S.L.R. 971;
    [1899] A.C. 1. . . . . 9.36
—— v. Landward Committee of Parish Council of Inveresk (1906) 8 F. 896; (1906)
    43 S.L.R. 679; (1906) 14 S.L.T. 161. . . . . 12.18
Hope Bros v. Morrison, 1960 S.C. 1; 1960 S.L.T. 80. 8.59, 8.65
Hope's Tr. v. Hope (1904) 11 S.L.T. 625. . . . . 29.29
Hopes and Lavery v. H.M. Advocate, 1960 J.C. 104; 1960 S.L.T. 264. . . . . 19.62
Hopetoun (Earl of) v. Horner (1842) 4 D. 877; (1842) 14 Sc.Jur. 313. . . . . 11.76
—— v. Scots Mining Co. (1859) 21 D. 218. . . . . 2.97
Hopkin v. Ayr Local Taxation Officer, 1964 S.L.T. (Sh.Ct.) 60. . . . . 25.40, 26.382
Hopkinson Ltd v. McGrory, Glasgow Sh.Ct., Apr. 1952, unreported. 2.15, 7.13, 7.19
—— v. Sanders, 1941 S.L.T. (Sh.Ct.) 36; (1941) 57 Sh.Ct.Rep. 11. . . . 12.67, 12.68, 12.69,
    12.70
—— v. Scottish Radio and Sounding Co. Ltd (1954) 70 Sh.Ct.Rep. 297. . . . . 14.37
Hopkinson (George) Ltd v. Carr, 1955 S.L.T. (Sh.Ct.) 80. . . . . 2.15, 7.13, 7.19
Hopkirk v. Wilson (1855) 18 D. 299; (1855) 28 Sc.Jur. 129. 2.28
Hopper & Co. v. Walker (1903) 20 Sh.Ct.Rep. 137. . . . . 29.19
Horak v. Lord Advocate, 1984 S.L.T. 201. . . . . 4.67, 20.07, 20.10
Horn v. McLean (1830) 8 S. 329; (1830) 5 Fac. 279. . . . . 2.54
Horn & Co. Ltd v. Tangyes Ltd (1906) 8 F. 475. . . . . 11.64, 18.41
Horne & Ross v. Ram (1848) 11 D. 141. . . . . 4.31
Horsburgh v. Morton (1825) 3 S. 596 (N.E. 409). 23.17
Horton v. Horton, 1992 S.L.T. (Sh.Ct.) 37; 1992 S.C.L.R. 197. . . . . 22.42
Hoth v. Cowan, 1926 S.C. 58; 1925 S.L.T. 636, 1925 S.N. 120. . . . . 2.101
Houison-Craufurd's Trs v. Davies, 1951 S.C. 1; 1951 S.L.T. 25. . . . . 2.102
Housing of the Working Classes Act 1890, Re, ex p. Stevenson [1892] 1 Q.B. 609. . . . 18.49
Houston v. British Road Services Ltd, 1967 S.L.T. 329. . . . . 14.62
—— v. Gault, 1925 S.C. 429; 1925 S.L.T. 255; 1925 S.L.T. 255; 1925 S.N. 31. . . . . . 18.36
Houstoun Local Authority v. McPhedran (1890) 6 Sh.Ct.Rep. 267. . . . . 26.93
Howard v. Hamilton D.C., 1985 S.L.T. (Sh.Ct.) 42. . . . . 26.50

Howden v. Rocheid (1868) 6 M. 300... 4.110
—— v. Viscountess Hawarden (1864) 2 M. 637; (1864) 36 Sc.Jur. 314............. 2.95
Howden (James) & Co. Ltd v. Powell Duffryn Steam Coal Co. Ltd, 1912 S.C.
    920.. 2.101
Howitt v. Alexander & Sons, 1948 S.C. 154; 1948 S.L.T. 334... 14.31, 14.32, 19.07, 19.14,
                                                                            19.15
Huber v. Banks, 1986 S.L.T. 58... 11.19
Huckstep v. Dunfermline District Education Sub-Committee, 1954 S.L.T. (Sh.Ct.)
    109; (1954) 70 Sh.Ct.Rep. 345.. 26.115
Huewind Ltd v. Clydesdale Bank plc, 1996 S.L.T. 369; [1995] 5 Bank L.R. 35...... 24.07
—— v. ——, 1995 S.L.T. 392.. 24.07
Hughes v. Lord Advocate, 1963 S.C.(H.L.) 31; 1963 S.L.T. 150; [1963] 2 W.L.R.
    779; 107 S.J. 232; [1963] 1 All E.R. 705.................................. 4.14
—— v. ——, 1993 S.C.L.R. 155... 29.29
—— v. Scott (1940) 56 Sh.Ct.Rep. 176...................................... 7.06
Hughes's Tr. v. Hughes, 1925 S.C. 25; 1924 S.L.T. 764................... 11.84, 18.39
Hughes's Tutrix v. Glasgow D.C., 1982 S.L.T. (Sh.Ct.) 70..................... 9.68
Hughson v. Lerwick Police, 1956 S.L.T. (Sh.Ct.) 18; (1956) 72 Sh.Ct.Rep 57...... 26.183
Hulme v. Hulme, 1990 S.L.T. (Sh.Ct.) 25; 1990 S.C.L.R. 181.................. 18.39
Hume v. Baillie (1852) 14 D. 821; (1852) 24 Sc.Jur. 462................ 11.13, 29.27
Hume's Trs v. Ralston's Trs (1834) 12 S. 727; (1834) 6 Sc.Jur. 410............... 21.71
Humphries v. S, 1986 S.L.T. 683... 2.13
Hunt v. Rutherford (1855) 17 D. 305; (1855) 27 Sc.Jur. 133............... 12.24, 12.26
Hunter (1908) 15 S.L.T. 716.. 6.45
—— v. Chief Constable of West Midlands Police [1982] A.C. 529; (1981) 2 W.L.R.
    906; (1981) 3 All E.R. 727; (1981) 125 S.J. 829........................... 2.19
—— v. Darngavil Coal Co. (1900) 3 F. 10; (1900) 38 S.L.R. 6.................. 8.60
—— v. Hunter, 1993 S.C.L.R. 785..................................... 18.25, 22.90
—— v. John Brown & Co., 1961 S.C. 231................................... 2.123
—— v. LMS Ry, 1938 S.L.T. 598; 1939 S.L.T. 297....................... 9.80, 9.100
—— v. McLean, 1948 S.L.T. (Notes) 83..................................... 8.64
—— v. Russell (1901) 3 F. 596; (1901) 8 S.L.T. 476; (1901) 38 S.L.R. 420........ 14.37
Hunter & Son v. Weir, 1955 S.L.T. (Sh.Ct.) 101; (1955) 71 Sh.Ct.Rep. 343........ 19.18
Huntly (Marquis of) v. Nicol (1858) 20 D. 374; (1858) 20 Sc.Jur. 211....... 2.104, 17.14
—— v. —— (1896) 23 R. 610; (1896) 3 S.L.T. 297; (1896) 33 S.L.R. 432.......... 5.86
Hutcheon v. Hamilton District Licensing Board, 1978 S.L.T. (Sh.Ct.) 44.... 25.01, 25.18,
                                                                    25.23, 26.255
Hutcheon and Partners v. Hutcheon, 1979 S.L.T. (Sh.Ct.) 61.................... 4.97
Hutcheon's Exr v. Hutcheon (1941) 58 Sh.Ct.Rep. 158......................... 2.43
Hutchison, 1965 S.C. 240.. 5.89
—— v. Davidson, 1945 S.C. 395; 1945 S.N. 46; 1946 S.L.T. 11............. 10.27, 18.81
—— v. Dougall's Trs 1912 2 S.L.T. 516..................................... 4.07
—— v. Ferrier (1846) 8 D. 1228; (1846) 18 Sc.Jur. 587.................. 4.31, 9.99
—— v. Hutchison, 1912 1 S.L.T. 219........................... 3.99, 11.13, 29.27
—— v. ——, 1962 S.C. 596; 1962 S.L.T. (Notes) 11........................ 14.18
—— v. Hutchison's Trs (1902) 10 S.L.T. 562; (1902) 40 S.L.R. 200.............. 19.31
—— v. Magistrates of Innerleithen, 1933 S.L.T. 52; 1932 S.N. 115.............. 2.104
—— v. Robson (1930) 47 Sh.Ct.Rep. 109.................................... 18.19
Hynd v. West Fife Co-operative Ltd, 1980 S.L.T. 41..... 10.34, 10.35, 10.37, 10.56, 10.59
Hynds v. Hynds, 1966 S.C. 201; 1966 S.L.T. 282.................. 2.105, 2.106, 2.107
Hyslop v. Flaherty, 1933 S.C. 588; 1933 S.L.T. 499...................... 14.08, 14.12

IANNELLI v. Stevenson, 1977 S.L.T. (Sh.Ct.) 5............................... 18.82
Immanuel (Owners of) v. Denholm & Co. (1887) 15 R. 152.................... 9.18
Imperial Hotel (Aberdeen) Ltd v. Vaux Breweries Ltd, 1978 S.C. 86; 1973 S.L.T. 13.. 4.89
Imperial Tobacco Ltd v. Att.-Gen. [1979] Q.B. 555; [1979] 2 All E.R. 592........ 23.09
—— v. —— [1981] A.C. 718; [1980] 1 All E.R. 866........................ 23.09
Inch v. Inch (1856) 18 D. 997; (1856) 28 Sc.Jur. 452........................ 16.75
Ingles's Tr. v. Ingle, 1996 S.L.T. 26; 1995 S.C.C.R. 934.................... 25.30
Inglis v. LMS Ry, 1941 S.C. 551; 1941 S.L.T. 408; S.N. 48.................. 18.116
—— v. McIntyre (1862) 24 D. 541... 29.05
—— v. National Bank of Scotland Ltd, 1909 S.C. 1038; 1909 1 S.L.T. 518; (1909) 46
    S.L.R. 730... 8.58, 9.122
—— v. ——, 1911 S.C. 6; 1910 2 S.L.T. 207; 48 S.L.R. 9.................. 18.37
—— v. Robertson & Baxter (1898) 25 R.(H.L.) 70.......................... 29.27
—— v. Smith (1859) 21 D. 822... 2.30

Inglis and Bow v. Smith and Aikman (1867) 5 M. 320; (1867) 39 Sc.Jur. 139...... 11.34
Inglis' Trs v. Macpherson, 1910 S.C. 46; 1909 2 S.L.T. 363; (1909) 47 S.L.R. 43... 16.97, 21.03, 23.30
Inland Revenue v. Gibb, 1963 S.L.T. (Notes) 66........................ 12.68, 12.70
Innes v. Dunbar (1534) Mor. 7320... 12.68
—— v. McDonald (1899) 1 F. 380; (1899) 6 S.L.T. 273......................... 18.37
Innes' Reps v. Duke of Gordon (1827) 6 S. 279; (1827) 3 Fac. 260.............. 2.128
Insurance Co. (X) v. A and B, 1936 S.C. 225; 1936 S.L.T. 188.................. 25.46
Interatlantic (Namibia) (Pty) Ltd v. Okeanski Ribolov Ltd, 1996 S.L.T. 819....... 11.13
International General Electrical Co. of New York Ltd v. Comms of Customs and
    Excise [1962] Ch. 784; [1962] 3 W.L.R. 20; (1962) 106 S.J. 327; [1962] 2 All
    E.R. 398... 4.57
Interplan (Joiners and Shopfitters) Ltd v. Brown, Paisley Sh.Ct., June 26, 1984,
    unreported... 4.38, 10.05, 10.09
Inverurie Magistrates v. Sorrie, 1956 S.C. 175; 1956 S.L.T. (Notes) 17........... 21.83
Iona Hotels Ltd (In receivership), Petrs, 1991 S.L.T. 11; (*sub nom.* Iona Hotels v.
    Craig) 1990 S.C. 330; 1990 S.C.L.R. 614........................ 11.10, 29.33
Ireland v. Taylor [1949] 1 K.B. 300; [1948] 2 All E.R. 450; (1948) 92 S.J. 408...... 16.78
Irvine v. Gow (1910) 26 Sh.Ct.Rep. 174................................ 11.33, 25.38
—— v. Irvine (1857) 19 D. 284.. 16.24
—— v. Powrie's Trs, 1915 S.C. 1006; 1915 2 S.L.T. 108; (1915) 52 S.L.R. 775...... 15.98
—— v. Reid (1921) 37 Sh.Ct.Rep. 108....................................... 11.70
—— v. Strathclyde R.C., 1995 S.L.T. (Sh.Ct.) 28; 1994 S.C.L.R. 388............ 29.76
Irving v. Aberdeen and District Milk Marketing Board (1941) 59 Sh.Ct.Rep. 1..... 2.102
—— v. Irving, 1998 S.C.L.R. 373.. 18.39
Isaacs v. Robertson [1985] 1 A.C. 97; [1984] 3 W.L.R. 705; [1984] 3 All E.R. 140... 5.91
Islip Pedigree Breeding Centre v. Abercromby, 1959 S.L.T. 161.......... 18.104, 18.108

J AND J v. C's Tutor, 1948 S.C. 636...................... 28.01, 28.07, 28.96, 28.100
Jack v. Black, 1911 S.C. 691; 1911 1 S.L.T. 124; (1911) 48 S.L.R. 81............. 14.48, 18.117, 23.18
—— v. Carmichael (1894) 10 Sh.Ct.Rep. 242.......... 11.60, 11.65, 18.32, 18.40, 23.13
—— v. Glasgow Corporation, 1965 S.L.T. 227................................ 12.49
—— v. Jack, 1953 S.L.T. (Sh.Ct.) 26; (1952) 69 Sh.Ct.Rep. 34................. 14.49
—— v. ——, 1962 S.C. 24; 1962 S.L.T. 21.................................. 9.121
—— v. King (1932) 47 Sh.Ct.Rep. 242................................ 19.05, 26.10
—— v. MacKay, 1990 S.C.L.R. 816... 4.32
—— v. Umpherston (1837) 15 S. 833; (1837) 9 Sc.Jur. 388................... 18.05
—— v. Waddell's Trs, 1918 S.C. 73; 1917 2 S.L.T. 235.................. 23.24, 29.72
—— v. Wardrop, 1928 S.L.T. (Sh.Ct.) 9; (1927) 44 Sh.Ct.Rep. 61.............. 16.47
Jack, Son & Co. v. Laing, 1929 S.C. 426; 1929 S.N. 31........................ 19.27
Jackson v. Clyde Navigation Trust, 1961 S.L.T. (Sh.Ct.) 35; (1960) 77 Sh.Ct.Rep.
    41.. 14.58
—— v. McKay, 1923 S.C. 286; 1923 S.L.T. 151; (1923) 60 S.L.R. 190............ 16.90
Jacobs v. Brett (1875) 20 L.R.Eq. 1.. 2.38
—— v. Provincial Motor Cab Co. Ltd, 1910 S.C. 567; 1910 1 S.L.T. 392; (1910) 47
    S.L.R. 756... 14.48
Jaffray v. Murray (1830) 8 S. 667... 15.35
James v. James (1886) 13 R. 1153; (1886) 23 S.L.R. 819...................... 11.29
Jameson v. Sharp (1887) 14 R. 643; (1887) 25 S.L.R. 473....... 9.87, 11.25, 21.49, 29.38
Jamieson v. Allan McNeil & Son, 1974 S.L.T. (Notes) 9................. 9.30, 9.34
—— v. Jamieson, 1952 S.C.(H.L.) 44; 1952 S.L.T. 257; [1952] A.C. 525; [1952] 1
    T.L.R. 833; [1952] 116 J.P. 226; [1952] 1 All E.R. 875; reversing 1st Div. 1951
    S.L.T. 174; 1951 S.C. 286 [1953] S.L.T. (News) 125....................... 9.33
Japan Leasing (Europe) plc v. Weir's Tr., 1998 S.L.T. 224; 1997 S.C.L.R. 519..... 18.34
Japp v. Adams, 1939 S.C. 439; 1939 S.L.T. 283; 1939 S.N. 31................. 19.49
Jardine v. Mags of Moffat, 1907 S.C. 1065; (1907) 15 S.L.T. 133.............. 18.35
Jarlath (Sister), Petr, 1980 S.L.T. (Sh.Ct.) 72.......................... 25.05, 25.13
Jarrett v. Barclays Bank [1997] I.L.Pr. 531................................ 3.24
Jarvie v. Laird, 1974 S.L.T. (Sh.Ct.) 75.................................... 9.114
—— v. Sharp, 1992 S.L.T. 350...................................... 21.28, 21.36
Jarvie's Trs v. Bannatyne, 1927 S.C. 34; 1926 S.L.T. 777; 1926 S.N. 140.......... 12.68
Jarvis v. Chief Constable of Strathclyde, 1976 S.L.T. (Sh.Ct.) 66............... 26.183
Jeffray v. Angus, 1909 S.C. 400; 1909 1 S.L.T. 84; 46 S.L.R. 388.............. 18.01
Jenic Properties Ltd v. Andy Thornton Architectural Antiques, 1992 S.L.T. (Sh.Ct.)
    5; 1992 S.C.L.R. 16... 3.52

Jenkins v. Gascoigne, 1907 S.C. 1189; (1907) 15 S.L.T. 269; (1907) 44 S.L.R. 861. . .   2.54
—— v. Glasgow Coporation, 1934 S.L.T. 53; 1933 S.N. 111.   15.57
—— v. Robertson (1867) 5 M.(H.L.) 27; (1867) 39 Sc.Jur. 384. . . . .   2.106
—— v. —— (1869) 7 M. 739; (1869) 41 Sc.Jur. 386; (1869) 6 S.L.R. 465. . .   4.112, 4.113,
                                                              8.60, 11.52, 11.56, 11.64
Joel v. Gill (1859) 22 D. 6. . . . .   9.79
Johannesburg Municipal Council v. Stewart & Co. Ltd, 1911 1 S.L.T. 359. . . . .   15.78
Johnson v. Gill, 1978 S.C. 74. . . . .   26.10
—— v. Grant, 1923 S.C. 789; 1923 S.L.T. 501; (1923) 60 S.L.R. 508. . . . .   2.08, 21.99
—— v. Johnson (1910) 26 Sh.Ct.Rep. 134. . . . .   11.23, 11.32
—— v. Taylor Bros & Co. Ltd [1920] A.C. 144. . . . .   6.06
Johnston v. Dewart, 1992 S.L.T. 186; 1991 S.C.L.R. 447. . . . .   7.28
—— v. Brodie (1862) 24 D. 973. . . . .   18.35
—— v. Johnston (1903) S.L.R. 499. . . . .   2.19, 16.96
—— v. ——, 1965 S.L.T. (Sh.Ct.) 29. . . . .   6.04, 6.20, 6.47
—— v. ——, 1985 S.L.T. 510. . . . .   14.30
—— v. Laird & Son, 1915 2 S.L.T. 24. . . . .   11.54
—— v. Lithgows Ltd, 1964 S.L.T. (Notes) 96. . . . .   14.57
—— v. MacFarlane, 1987 S.C.L.R. 104. . . . .   23.38
—— v. Robson, 1995 S.L.T. (Sh.Ct.) 26. . . . .   23.37
—— v. South of Scotland Electricity Board, 1968 S.L.T. (Notes) 7. . . . .   15.53
—— v. Wallace (1954) 71 Sh.Ct.Rep. 80. . . . .   11.53
—— v. Young (1890) 18 R. (J.) 6; (1890) 28 S.L.R. 30. . . . .   23.18
Johnstone (1885) 12 R. 468. . . . .   4.27
—— v. Arnotts (1830) 8 S. 383; (1830) 2 Sc.Jur. 173. . . . .   4.46
—— v. Clyde Navigation Trs, Dec. 16, 1948, HL; (1949) 93 S.J. 132; (1949) 82
     Ll.L.R. 187. . . . .   9.28
—— v. Henderson (1906) 8 F. 689; (1906) 13 S.L.T. 944; (1906) 43 S.L.R. 486. . . .   11.55
Johnstone's Exrs v. Harris, 1977 S.L.T. (Notes) 10, 1977 S.C. 365; 1977 S.L.T.
     (Notes) 10. . . . .   8.64, 16.30
Johnstone & Clark (Engineers) Ltd v. Lockhart, 1995 S.L.T. 440. . . . .   7.19
Jones v. Admiralty (The), 1956 S.L.T. (Sh.Ct.) 20; (1955) 72 Sh.Ct.Rep. 67. .   18.50, 18.54
—— v. Jones, 1993 S.C.L.R. 151. . . . .   13.73, 18.15, 18.46
—— v. Lanarkshire Health Board, 1990 S.L.T. 19. . . . .   10.39
—— v. ——, 1991 S.L.T. 714. . . . .   10.39
—— v. McDermott (Scotland), 1986 S.L.T. 551. . . . .   10.18, 10.37
—— v. National Coal Board [1957] 2 Q.B. 55; [1957] 2 W.L.R. 760; [1957] 2 All
     E.R. 155; [1957] 101 S.J. 319. . . . .   16.39, 16.40
Jones Sewing Machine Co. Ltd v. Smart, 1987 G.W.D. 5–162. . . . .   4.98
Jopp v. McHardy (1890) 2 Guthrie's Sh.Ct. Cas. 145. . . . .   29.27
Jordan v. Court Line Ltd, 1947 S.C. 29; 1947 S.L.T. 134; 1946 S.N. 111. . . . .   16.76, 17.27,
                                                                                          18.106
—— v. Jordan, 1983 S.L.T. 539. . . . .   18.107
Jubert v. Church Commissioners for England, 1952 S.C. 160; 1952 S.L.T. 99. . .   2.91, 2.92
Junner v. North British Ry (1877) 4 R. 686; (1877) 14 S.L.R. 438. . . . .   15.102

K, Petr, 1986 S.C.C.R. 709. . . . .   28.108
KHR Financings Ltd v. Jackson, 1977 S.L.T. (Sh.Ct.) 6. . . . .   30.333
Kalfelis v. Bankhaus Schröder (189/87) [1988] E.C.R. 5565.   3.93
Karl Construction Ltd v. Palisade Properties plc, 2002 S.L.T. 312. . . . .   30.78
Karlshamns Oljefabriker, A/B v. Monarch Steamship Co., 1949 S.C.(H.L.) 1; 1949
     S.L.T. 51. . . . .   19.12
Kaur v. Lord Advocate, 1980 S.C. 319; 1981 S.L.T. 322. . . . .   13.69
Kay v. Ayrshire and Arran Health Board, *The Scotsman*, Jan. 15, 1982. . . . .   4.14
—— v. ——, 1986 S.L.T. 435, 1987 S.L.T. 577; (1986) 31 J.L.S. 94. . . . .   17.28
—— v. G.P. Inveresk Corporation, 1988 S.C.L.R. 422. . . . .   21.21
—— v. Morrison's Reps, 1984 S.L.T. 175. . . . .   4.106, 9.80
Kay's Tutor v. Ayrshire and Arran Health Board, 1985 S.L.T. 435, 1987 S.L.T.
     577. . . . .   4.120
Kaye v. Hunter, 1958 S.C. 208. . . . .   25.08, 25.35, 25.39
Kearie (James E.) Ltd v. Maycretes Sales Ltd, 1949 S.L.T. (Notes) 25. . . . . . .   5.89, 17.03,
                                                                                    17.06, 18.85, 18.98
Kearney's Exrs v. John Finlay MacLeod and Parker, 1965 S.C. 450; 1965 S.L.T.
     404. . . . .   18.47
Keel v. Keel, 1985 S.L.T. (Sh.Ct.) 52. . . . .   13.71, 13.73, 13.74

Keenan v. Glasgow Corporation, 1923 S.C. 611; 1923 S.L.T. 392; (1923) 60 S.L.R.
    403.. 9.38, 9.68, 9.85
—— v. Rolls-Royce Ltd, 1969 S.C. 322; 1970 S.L.T. 90......................... 9.31
—— v. Scottish Wholesale Co-operative Society Ltd, 1914 S.C. 959; 1914 2 S.L.T.
    213; (1914) 51 S.L.R. 839.. 16.76
Keith v. Archer (1836) 15 S. 116................................. 4.10, 4.14, 4.26
—— v. Dunfermline Town Council, 1968 S.L.T. (Sh.Ct.) 51.................... 26.255
—— v. Outram & Co. (1877) 4 R. 958; (1877) 14 S.L.R. 591................... 10.29
Kelly v. Cornhill Insurance Co., 1964 S.C. (H.L.) 46; 1964 S.L.T. 81............. 20.04
—— v. Docherty, 1991 S.C.C.R. 312.................................... 16.62
—— v. Edmund Nuttall Sons & Co. (London) Ltd, 1965 S.C. 427; 1965 S.L.T.
    418... 9.47, 10.24, 16.101
—— v. Fyfe Douglas Co. Ltd, 1965 S.L.T. (Notes) 87.............. 5.100, 11.86, 19.23
—— v. Holloway Bros (London) Ltd, 1960 S.L.T. (Notes) 69................... 10.37
—— v. Kelly, 1986 S.L.T. 101... 12.68
Kelso School Board v. Hunter (1874) 2 R. 228; (1874) 12 S.L.R. 354.... 2.24, 9.82, 21.84
Keltie v. Wilson (1828) 7 S. 208....................................... 24.15
Kelvin v. Whyte, Thomson & Co., 1909 1 S.L.T. 477.......................... 16.04
Kennedy v. Clyde Shipping Co., 1908 S.C. 895; (1908) 45 S.L.R. 736; (1908) 16
    S.L.T. 121.. 5.88
—— v. Crawford (1899) 7 S.L.T. 26...................................... 11.54
—— v. Fort William Police Commissioners (1877) 5 R. 302; (1877) 15 S.L.R. 91... 11.35
—— v. Glasgow Corporation (1959) 70 Sh.Ct.Rep. 239, 1954 S.L.T. (Sh.Ct.) 56;
    (1954) 70 Sh.Ct.Rep. 239.. 17.18
—— v. Hamilton Bros Oil and Gas Ltd, 1986 S.L.T. 110.................. 11.62, 11.64
—— v. Kennedy (1910) 27 Sh.Ct.Rep. 71................................. 11.33
—— v. ——, 1991 S.C.L.R. 443; 1992 S.L.T. (Sh.Ct.) 39.................... 18.117
—— v. M, 1993 S.L.T. 717.. 28.134
—— v. Macdonald (1876) 3 R. 813; (1876) 13 S.L.R. 525...................... 2.97
—— v. Macrae, 1946 S.C. 118; 1946 S.L.T. 198............................. 18.18
—— v. Norwich Union Fire Insurance Society, 1994 S.L.T. 617; 1993 S.C.L.R.
    735.. 10.17, 13.23
—— v. S, 1986 S.L.T. 679.. 2.104
—— v. Strathclyde R.C., Glasgow Sh.Ct., Aug. 9, 1982, unreported............. 26.113
—— v. Wise (1890) 17 R. 1036; (1890) 27 S.L.R. 813........................ 2.105
Kent v. Glasgow Corporation, 1974 S.L.T. (Sh.Ct.) 44....................... 26.113
Kerr (1822) Shaw 68... 2.19
—— v. Advocate (H.M.), 1958 J.C. 14; 1958 S.L.T. 82................... 15.11, 15.16
—— v. Alexander, Edinburgh Sh.Ct., July 14, 1978, unreported........... 10.29, 24.03
—— v. Annandale Steamship Co., 1927 S.L.T. (Sh.Ct.) 31; (1926) 43 Sh.Ct.Rep.
    44... 25.35
—— v. Brown (John) & Co. Ltd, 1965 S.C. 144; 1965 S.L.T. 237............... 10.06
—— v. Employers' Liability Assurance Corp. Ltd (1899) 2 F. 17; (1899) 7 S.L.T.
    179; (1899) 37 S.L.R. 21.. 19.05
—— v. Ferguson (R. & W.), 1931 S.C. 736; 1931 S.L.T. 475, 540..... 3.99, 11.15, 11.25,
    29.21
—— v. Hood, 1907 S.C. 895; (1907) 15 S.L.T. 14; (1907) 44 S.L.R. 652........... 2.42
—— v. Strathclyde R.C., 1968 S.L.T. (Sh.Ct.) 42........................... 18.79
—— v. Toole (1948) 66 Sh.Ct.Rep. 116................................... 18.76
Kessack v. Kessack (1899) 1 F. 398; (1899) 8 S.L.T. 286; (1899) 36 S.L.R. 296..... 16.91
Ketley (A.) v. Scott [1981] I.C.R. 241.................................. 26.213
Ketteman v. Hansel Properties Ltd [1987] 2 W.L.R. 312; [1987] A.C. 189; (1987)
    131 S.J. 134; [1988] 1 All E.R. 38; [1987] 1 FTLR 284; (1987) 85 L.G.R. 409;
    (1987) 36 Build. L.R. 1; [1987] 1. E.G.L.R. 237; affm, [1984] 1 W.L.R. 1274;
    [1985] 1 All E.R. 352... 2.114, 10.14
Key v. Primrose (1709) Mor. 46.. 2.40
—— v. Scottish Chemist Supply Co., 1956 S.L.T. (Notes) 43............... 10.60, 14.35
Killin v. Weir (1905) 7 F. 526; (1905) 12 S.L.T. 737; (1705) 42 S.L.R. 393..... 4.38, 4.39
Kilmarnock and Loudoun D.C. v. Young, 1993 S.L.T. 505.......... 26.56, 26.84, 26.325
Kilmarnock Magistrates v. Mather (1869) 7 M. 548; (1869) 41 Sc.Jur. 290; (1869) 6
    S.L.R. 355... 4.31, 9.99
—— v. Reid (1897) 24 R. 388... 2.54, 13.31
Kilmarnock Theatre Co. v. Buchanan, 1911 S.C. 607......................... 11.58
Kilmaurs Dairy Association Ltd v. Brisbane and Beattie's Dairies (1927) 43
    Sh.Ct.Rep. 210; 1927 S.L.T. (Sh.Ct.) 65......................... 12.68, 12.70
Kilpatrick Parish Council v. Row Parish Council, 1911 2 S.L.T. 32............... 15.27
Kilrenny (Magistrates of) v. Johnston (1828) 6 S. 624....................... 2.95

Kincaid (John G.) & Co v. Taggart, 1974 S.C. 15............................. 6.46
King v. King (1841) 4 D. 124... 2.128
Kinloch v. Barclays Bank plc, 1995 S.C.L.R. 975........................... 29.73
—— v. Lourie (1853) 16 D. 197... 9.78
Kinnaird v. Donaldson, 1922 S.C.L.R. 694.......................... 5.85, 12.51
—— v. McLean, 1942 S.C. 448; 1942 S.L.T. 217........................... 4.40
Kinnaird & Sons v. Millar (1931) 47 Sh.Ct.Rep........................... 2.33
Kinnersly v. Husband, Edinburgh Sh.Ct., Mar. 24, 1987, unreported............. 10.06
Kinnes v. Fleming (1881) 8 R. 386; (1881) 18 S.L.R. 245.................. 18.41, 18.42
Kintore (Earl of) v. Earl of Kintore's Trs (1886) 13 R. 997; (1886) 23 S.L.R. 715... 2.55,
                                                                              23.45
—— v. Pirie (1904) 12 S.L.T. 385; (1904) 42 S.L.R. 5.................. 18.37, 19.09
—— v. Pirie & Sons (1906) 8 F. 1058; (1906) 12 S.L.T. 131; affd, (1906) 8 F.(H.L.)
        16; (1906) 14 S.L.T. 215... 21.95
Kippen v. Oppenheim (1846) 8 D. 957; (1848) 18 Sc.Jur. 489.................... 23.23
Kirk v. Scottish Gas Board, 1968 S.C. 328; 1969 S.L.T. 18................... 4.14, 4.23
Kirkham v. Cementation Co. Ltd 1964 S.L.T. (Notes) 33................. 8.32, 10.45
Kirkonnel v. Barnbarroch (1628) Mor. 3682............................... 6.46
Kirkpatrick v. Maxwelltown Town Council, 1912 S.C. 288; 1912 1 S.L.T. 65; (1912)
        49 S.L.R. 261... 25.23
Kirkwood v. Campbell (1926) 43 Sh.Ct.Rep. 7............................. 10.05
—— v. City of Glasgow D.C., 1988 S.L.T. 430............................. 14.13
Kirkwood & Co. (Fashions) Ltd v. Glasgow D.C., Glasgow Sh.Ct., Jan. 12, 1981,
        unreported.. 15.90
Kleinwort Benson (C-346/93) [1995] E.C.R. I-615............................ 3.70
Kleinwort Benson Ltd v. Glasgow City Council [1996] Q.B. 678................. 3.93
Knight v. Freeto (1863) 2 M. 386....................................... 11.72
Kontos v. Kontos, 1990 S.C.L.R. 293.................................... 19.18
Korner v. Shennan, 1949 S.L.T. (Notes) 42............................... 18.48
Kruger Stores (Pty) Ltd v. Kopman (1957) 1. S.A.L.R. 645.................. 11.59
Krupp v. Menzies, 1907 S.C. 903; (1907) 15 S.L.T. 36; (1907) 44 S.L.R. 657........ 8.64

L/F FøROYA FISKASOLA v. Charles Mauritzen Ltd, 1978 S.L.T. (Sh.Ct.) 27.......... 9.91
L.M. & S. Ry v. Turnbull, 1926 S.L.T. 264.............................. 2.38
LNE Ry v. Reid Bros (1944) 61 Sh.Ct.Rep. 22............................ 7.24
Lacey v. Russell, 1966 S.L.T. (Sh.Ct.) 76.............................. 19.63
Lacy v. Lacy (1869) 7 M. 369... 16.97
Ladbroke Racing (Stratclyde) Ltd v. Cunninghame District Licensing Court, 1978
        S.L.T. (Sh.Ct.) 50.. 26.38
Ladbrokes the Bookmakers v. Hamilton D.C., 1977 S.L.T. (Sh.Ct.) 86...... 25.20, 25.32,
                                                                         25.33, 25.34
Ladgroup Ltd v. Euroeast Lines SA, 1997 S.L.T. 916 (O.H.).................... 24.06
Lai Wee Lian v. Singapore Bus Service (1978) Ltd [1984] A.C. 729; [1984] 3 W.L.R.
        63; (1984) 128 S.J. 432... 17.25, 18.83, 25.27
Laidlaw v. Dunlop (1831) 9 S. 579; (1831) 3 Sc.Jur. 365.................... 2.100
—— v. Smith (1834) 12 S. 538.. 2.97, 14.19
—— v. —— (1838) 16 S. 367; affd, (1841) 2 Rob. 490.............. 11.34, 29.20, 29.30
Laing v. Lord Advocate, 1973 S.L.T. (Notes) 81.......................... 4.60, 4.62
—— v. Harper (1829) 7 S. 335.. 23.23
—— v. Nixon (1866) 4 M. 327... 15.22
Laing's Sewing Machine Co. v. Norrie & Sons (1877) 5 R. 29; (1877) 15 S.L.R. 22   12.15
Laird v. Scott, 1914 S.L.T. 368.. 15.33
Lamb v. Thompson (1901) 4 F. 88; (1901) 9 S.L.T. 220; (1901) 39 S.L.R. 80   18.01, 18.04
Lambert (A.) Flat Management v. Lomas [1981] 1 W.L.R. 898; (1981) 125 S.J.
        218... 26.167
Lamonby v. Foulds Ltd, 1928 S.C. 89; 1928 S.L.T. 42, 1927 S.N. 149.......... 2.31, 2.34
Lamont v. Dublin and Glasgow Steam Packet Co., 1908 S.C. 1017............... 18.42
—— v. Hall, 1964 S.L.T. (Sh.Ct.) 25.................................... 10.26, 24.12
—— v. Lamont, 1939 S.C. 484... 13.66
—— v. Strathclyde R.C., Campbeltown Sh.Ct., Aug. 1, 1986, unreported......... 25.33
Lamont & Co. v. Reid (1925) 42 Sh.Ct.Rep. 262.......................... 14.21, 14.29
Lanark C.C. v. Airdrie Mags (1906) 8 F. 802; (1906) 14 S.L.T. 92............. 25.31
—— v. Docherty, 1959 S.L.T. (Sh.Ct.) 12; (1959) 75 Sh.Ct.Rep. 28............ 8.05
—— v. Frank Doonin Ltd, 1974 S.L.T. (Sh.Ct.) 13................. 17.08, 25.28, 26.315
Lanarkshire C.C. v. East Kilbride C.C., 1967 S.C. 235.................... 2.102, 9.120
Lanarkshire Health Board v. Banafaa, 1987 S.L.T. 229.................... 4.32, 10.17

Lanarkshire Speedway and Sports Stadium Ltd v. Gray, 1970 S.L.T. (Notes) 54. . . .   12.46
Landcatch Ltd v. Sea Catch plc, 1993 S.L.T. 451. . . . .   29.14
Lang v. Glasgow Court House Commissioners (1871) 9 M. 768; (1871) 43 Sc.Jur.
    422; (1871) 8 S.L.R. 514. . . . .   26.93
Lang (G. D.) Lanarkshire Mining Co. v. Clarkson, Airdrie Sh.Ct., Oct. 9, 1989,
    unreported. 18.63
Lapsley v. Lapsley (1915) 31 Sh.Ct.Rep. 330. . . . .   11.30
La Reunion Européenne and Others v. Shielhoff's Bevrachtingskantoor and Others
    (C-51/97). 3.93
Latif v. Motherwell District Licensing Board, 1994 S.L.T. (Notes) 411. . . . .   26.255
Latta, 1977 S.L.T. 127. . . . .   4.07
Lattimore v. Singleton, Dunn & Co., 1911 2 S.L.T. 360. . . . .   11.19
Lauder v. National Bank of Scotland Ltd, 1918 1 S.L.T. 43. . . . .   5.81, 18.15
Lauderdale (Earl of) v. Scrymgeour Wedderburn (1904) 7 F. 1045. . . . .   15.57, 15.62
—— v. —— (1903) 11 S.L.T. 194. . . . .   13.78
—— v. ——, 1911 S.C. 4; 1910 2 S.L.T. 209; (1910) 48 S.L.R. 3. . . . .   13.24, 19.55
Laughland v. Galloway, 1968 J.C. 26; 1968 S.L.T. 272. . . . .   2.128
Laurence v. Gray (1908) 25 Sh.Ct.Rep.19; (1908) 16 S.L.T. 466. . . . .   18.34
Laurenson v. Gordon (1901) 18 Sh.Ct.Rep. 319. . . . .   18.37
Lauriston v. Lauriston (1953) 69 Sh.Ct.Rep. 337. . . . .   14.18, 14.22
Law v. Chartered Institute of Patent Agents [1919] 2 Ch. 276; 1919 W.N. 120. . . . .   2.128
—— v. Law, Hamilton Sh.Ct., May 21, 1992, unreported.   18.70
Lawrence v. J.D. McIntosh & Hamilton, 1981 S.L.T. (Sh.Ct.) 73. . . . .   10.38
—— v. Knight, 1972 S.C. 26. . . . .   14.66, 14.68
—— v. Sir William Arrol & Co., 1958 S.C. 348. . . . .   9.28, 10.19
Lawrence Jack Collections v. Hamilton 1976 S.L.T. (Sh.Ct.) 18. . . . .   1.27
Lawrence's Will Trust, Re, [1972] Ch. 418; [1971] 3 W.L.R. 188; [1971] 3 All E.R.
    433; (1971) 115 S.J. 550. . . . .   17.29
Lawrie v. Pearson (1888) 16 R. 62; (1888) 26 S.L.R. 37. . . . .   11.54
Lawson v. Donaldson (1893) 10 Sh.Ct.Rep. 110. . . . .   15.42
—— v. Lawson 1996 S.L.T. (Sh.Ct.) 83. . . . .   18.82
—— v. Low (1845) 7 D. 960. . . . .   14.24
—— v. Swan National Car Rental Ltd, Glasgow Sh.Ct., Sept. 27, 1985,
    unreported. 15.40, 16.17
—— v. Young (1891) 7 Sh.Ct.Rep. 319. . . . .   11.69, 11.78, 18.32, 18.48, 18.50
Lawson's Trs v. British Linen Co. (1874) 1 R. 1065.   11.67, 11.69
Learmonts v. Shearer (1866) 4 M. 540. . . . .   11.14, 21.49, 29.26
Leddy v. Rudport, Sh. Prin. O'Brien, Duns Sh.Ct., Mar., 1981, unreported. 18.63
Lee v. Alexander (1882) 10 R. 230; (1882) 20 S.L.R. 155. . . . .   19.12, 19.14
—— v. National Coal Board, 1955 S.C. 151; 1955 S.L.T. 202. . . . .   9.131
—— v. Pollock's Trs (1906) 8 F. 857; (1906) 14 S.L.T. 115; (1906) 43 S.L.R. 657. .   14.22,
                                                                                14.23, 14.24, 14.26
Lee & Brown v. Menzies (1896) 12 Sh.Ct.Rep. 273. . . . .   11.45
Lees v. Gordon, 1929 S.L.T. 400; 1929 S.N. 88. . . . .   14.38
Lees v. Marr Typefounding Co. (1887) 4 R. 1088. . . . .   2.54
Lees' Trs v. Dun, 1912 S.C. 50, 1913 S.C.(H.L.) 12. . . . .   2.123
Legerwood v. McKenna (1868) 7 M. 261. . . . .   9.94, 19.03
Leggat v. Burgh of Barrhead (1902) 19 Sh.Ct.Rep. 7. . . . .   25.33
Leggat Bros v. Gray, 1912 S.C. 230; 1912 1 S.L.T. 49; (1911) 49 S.L.R. 189. . . . . . .   12.68
Leigh & Co. (R.S.) v. Berger & Co., 1958 S.L.T. (Sh.Ct.) 21; (1957) 74 Sh.Ct.Rep.
    55. . . . .   21.75
Leighton v. Harland & Wolff Ltd, 1953 S.L.T. (Notes) 34.   16.42
Leitch v. Scottish Legal Burial Society (1879) 9 M. 40. . . . .   25.32, 25.33
Leith Dock Commrs v. Miles (1866) 4 M.(H.L.) 14; (1866) 38 Sc.Jur.279. . . . .   2.107
Leith Harbour and Docks Commissioners v. N.B. Ry (1904) 12 S.L.T. 192. . . . . . .   24.10
Leith (Magistrates of) v. Gibb (1882) 9 R. 627 (1882) 19 S.L.R. 399. . . . .   19.42
—— v. Lennon (1875) 3 R. 152; (1875) 13 S.L.R. 84. . . . .   18.48, 18.49
—— v. —— (1881) 18 S.L.R. 313. . . . .   19.12
Leith-Buchanan v. Hogg, 1931 S.C. 204; 1931 S.L.T. 164; 1930 S.N. 130. . . . .   4.31
Lennie v. Lennie, 1948 S.C. 466; affd, 1950 S.C.(H.L.) 1. . . . .   16.38
—— v. Mackie & Co. (1907) 23 Sh.Ct.Rep. 85. . . . .   29.31
Lennox v. National Coal Board, 1955 S.C. 438; 1956 S.L.T. 203. . . . .   8.32, 9.25, 10.45
Leny v. Milne (1899) 15 Sh.Ct.Rep. 76. . . . .   12.23, 12.25
Leonard v. Lindsay & Benzine (1886) 13 R. 958; (1886) 23 S.L.R. 657. . . . .   21.95
Lep Industrial Holdings Ltd v. Adsil Products Ltd, Ayr Sh.Ct., Oct. 31, 1991,
    unreported. 18.117
Leslie v. Leslie, 1983 S.L.T. 186. . . . .   9.54

Lethem v. Evans, 1918 1 S.L.T. 27. . . . . 19.13
Leur-Bloem v. Inspecteur der Belastingdienst/Onderemingen Amsterdam 2
  (C-28/95) [1998] C.M.L.R. 157. . . . . 3.70
Leven (Earl of) v. Balfour (1711) Mor. 10930. . . . . 4.76
Leven and Melville (Earl of) v. Cartwright (1861) 23 D. 1038;(1861) 33 Sc.Jur.521 2.109
Lever v. Greenock Motor Services Co., 1949 S.C. 88; 1949 S.L.T. 94. . . . . 19.15
Levern (Distributors) Ltd v. St. Vincent Credit Co. 1966 S.L.T. (Sh.Ct.) 57. . . . . . . 18.19
Levison v. Jewish Chronicle Ltd, 1924 S.L.T. 755. . . . . 2.19, 8.16
Levy v. Gardiner, 1964 S.L.T. (Notes) 68; 1965 S.L.T. (Notes) 86. . . . . 2.98, 11.30
Lewis, Petr, 1963 S.L.T. (Sh.Ct.) 6. . . . . 1.27
——, Paisley Sh.Ct., Feb. 3, 1978, unreported. 1.27
Lewis (B.) (Upholstery) Ltd v. Hewitt, 1987 S.C.L.R. 580. . . . . 19.60
Lewis (Presbytery of) v. Fraser (1874) 1 R. 888; (1874) 11 S.L.R. 512. . . . . 25.04
Leys v. Leys (1886) 13 R. 1223; (1866) 23 S.L.R. 834. 2.19, 5.91
Liddall v. Ballingry Parish Council, 1908 S.C. 1082; (1908) 16 S.L.T. 58; (1908) 45
  S.L.R. 816. . . . . 25.47, 26.56
Lieber v. Gobel (C-292/93) [1994] E.C.R. I-2335. . . . . 3.24
Lindie v. H.M. Advocate, 1974 J.C. 1; 1974 S.L.T. 208. . . . . 16.82
Lindsay v. Anchor Lline Lyd [1948] C.L.Y. 4715. . . . . 9.68
—— v. Barr (1826) 4 S. 748 (N.E. 756). 18.04
—— v. Earl of Wemyss (1872) 10 M. 708; (1872) 44 Sc.Jur. 389; (1872) 9 S.L.R.
  458. . . . . 23.24
—— v. Giles (1844) 6 D. 771; (1844) 16 Sc.Jur. 357. . . . . 17.29
—— v. La Martona Rubber Estates Ltd, 1911 2 S.L.T. 468. 29.24
—— v. Lindsay (1827) 5 S. 288. . . . . 11.73
—— v. —— (1939) 56 Sh.Ct.Rep. 88. . . . . 13.59
—— v. London and North West Ry (1860) 22 D. 571. . . . . 29.18
—— v. Stivens, 1967 S.L.T. (Sh.Ct.) 84. . . . . 11.82
—— v. Walker's Trs (1877) 4 R. 870; (1877) 14 S.L.R. 560. . . . . 13.40
Linfai v. Stivens, 1967 S.L.T. (Sh.Ct.) 84. . . . . 21.79
Links & Co. Ltd v. Jesner (1953) 69 Sh.Ct.Rep. 261. . . . . 9.78
Lipton v. Powell [1921] 2 K.B. 51; 1921 W.N. 26. . . . . 2.12
Liquidator of the Universal Stock Exchange Co. Ltd v. Howat (1891) 19 R. 128. . . 16.58,
  16.94
Liquidators of Benhar Coal Co. v. Turnbull (1883) 10 R. 558. . . . . 11.25
Liquidators of Western Bank v. Douglas (1860) 22 D. 447. . . . . 4.41, 4.48, 9.121
Liszewski v. Thomson, 1942 J.C. 55; 1942 S.L.T. 147; 1941 S.N. 87. . . . . 16.65, 16.68
Little v. Burns (1881) 9 R. 118; (1881) 19 S.L.R. 105. . . . . 14.38
—— v. Stevenson & Co. (1896) 23 R.(H.L.) 12; (1896) 3 S.L.T. 328; (1896) 33
  S.L.R. 514; [1996] A.C. 108. . . . . 17.05
Littlejohn v. Clancy, 1974 S.L.T. (Notes) 68. . . . . 21.25
—— v. Reynolds (1890) 6 Sh.Ct.Rep. 321. . . . . 11.48
Littlewood's Warehouses v. Adam, Edinburgh Sh.Ct., 1977 (reported in the
  commentary to GUS Catalogue Order Ltd v. Oxborrow, 1987 S.C.L.R.
  617). 30.71
Livingston v. Johnson (1830) 8 S. 594. . . . . 13.36
—— v. Kinloch (1795) Mor. 769. . . . . 29.21
—— v. Murrays (1830) 9 S. 161. . . . . 15.73
Livingstone v. Gillies, 1930 S.L.T. (Sh.Ct.) 25. . . . . 2.14
—— v. H.M. Advocate, May 23, 1974, Crown Office Circular No. 1278. . . . . 16.39
—— v. Livingstone (1886) 14 R. 43. . . . . 11.15, 29.29
—— v. McFarlane (1842) 5 D. 1; (1842) 15 Sc.Jur. 101. . . . . 11.39
Llanfyllin Rural District Council v. Holland (1964) 62 L.G.R. 459; (1964) 16 P. &
  C.R. 140, D.C.. . . . . 26.161
Llewellyn v. Hebbert, 1983 S.L.T. 370. . . . . 3.101
Lloyd's Bank Ltd v. Bauld, 1976 S.L.T. (Notes) 53. . . . . 9.114
Lloyd's Register of Shipping (C-439/93) [1995] E.C.R. 1-961. . . . . 3.35
Lobban v. Philip 1995 S.C.L.R. 1104. . . . . 15.43
Lochead v. Graham (1883) 11 R. 201. . . . . 29.71
Lochgelly Iron and Coal Co. Ltd v. Sinclair, 1907 S.C. 442; (1907) 14 S.L.T. 783;
  (1907) 44 S.L.R. 364. . . . . 19.26
Lochgilphead T.C. v. McIntyre (1940) 59 Sh.Ct.Rep. 179. . . . . 23.17
Lochrie v. McGregor, 1911 S.C. 21; 190 2 S.L.T. 251; (1910) 48 S.L.R. 41. . . . . 6.15
Lockhart v. Ferrier (1832) 11 S. 236. . . . . 11.67
Lockyer v. Ferryman (1876) 3 R. 882; (1876) 13 S.L.R. 572. . . . . 2.106
—— v. —— (1877) 4 R.(H.L.) 32; (1877) 2 App. Cas. 519. . . . . 2.104
—— v. Sinclair (1846) 8 D. 582. . . . . 15.35

Logan (Daniel) & Son v. Rodger, 1952 S.L.T. (Sh.Ct.) 99. . . . . 12.26
Lombard North Central Ltd v. Wilson, Glasgow Sh.Ct., Oct. 7, 1980, unreported. . . 29.78
London and Edinburgh Shipping Co. v. The Admiralty, 1920 S.C. 309; 1920 1 S.L.T.
 222; (1920) 57 S.L.R. 252. . . . . 16.28, 16.29
Longmuir v. Longmuir (1850) 12 D. 926. . . . . 2.94
Longworth v. Hope (1865) 3 M. 1049. . . . . 2.89
Loosefoot Entertainment Ltd v. Glasgow District Licensing Board, 1991 S.L.T. 843;
 1990 S.C.L.R. 584. . . . . 26.255
Lornie v. Perthshire Highland District Committee (1909) 25 Sh.Ct.Rep. 124. . . . . . . 25.47
Lossie Hydraulic Co. v. Ecosse Transport Ltd 1980 S.L.T. (Sh.Ct.) 94. . . . . 9.26, 9.114
Lothian v. Lothian, 1965 S.L.T. 368. . . . . 14.64
Lothian Hotels v. Ferer, 1981 S.L.T. (Sh.Ct.) 52. . . . . 14.67, 19.50
Lothian R.C. v. A, 1992 S.L.T. 858; 1992 S.C.L.R. 376. . . . . 28.06, 28.07, 28.35,
 28.40, 28.101, 28.110, 28.115, 28.160, 28.165
—— v. A, Edinburgh Sh.Ct., July 13, 1979, unreported. 25.27
—— v. Lord Advocate, 1993 S.L.T. 1132; 1993 S.C.L.R. 565. . . . . 27.22
—— v. S, 1986 S.L.T. (Sh.Ct.) 37. . . . . 25.25
—— v. ——, Sh. Prin. Nicholson, Edinburgh Sh.Ct., Feb. 14, 1991, unreported. . . . 18.81,
 28.133
Louden (Wm) & Sons Ltd v. Frank Doonin Ltd, Glasgow Sh.Ct., May 9,
 unreported. 2.100
Loudon v. Young (1856) 18 D. 856; (1856) 28 Sc.Jur. 389. . . . . 13.78
Love v. Love, 1907 S.C. 728; (1907) 15 S.L.T. 12; (1907) 44 S.L.R. 649. . . . . 9.119
—— v. Low (1905) 12 S.L.T. 817. . . . . 11.71
—— v. Montgomerie and Logan, 1982 S.L.T. (Sh.Ct.) 60. . . . . 18.69
—— v. Scottish Amicable Building Society, 1940 S.L.T. 295. 4.34
—— v. Spences Ltd (1895) 3 S.L.T. 170. . . . . 14.37
Low (Alexander) and Sons v. Mckenzie, 1972 S.L.T. (Sh.Ct.) 10. . . . . 10.06
Lowe v. Bristol Motor Omnibus Co., 1934 S.C. 1; 1933 S.L.T. 625; (1933) S.N. 75. . 16.71
Lowson v. Lowson (1902) 4 F. 692; (1902) 39 S.L.R. 444. . . . . 11.70
Loyal Orange Lodge No. 493 v. Roxburgh D.C., 1980 S.C. 141; 1981 S.L.T. 33. . . 26.292
Lucarelli v. Buchanan, 1954 S.L.T. (Sh.Ct.) 46. . . . . 12.68
Lucas's Tr. v. Campbell & Scott (1894) 21 R. 1096; (1894) 2 S.L.T. 101; (1894) 31
 S.L.R. 788. . . . . 11.10, 21.49, 29.29
Lucovich (1885) 12 R. 1090; (1885) 22 S.L.R. 729. . . . . 3.100
Ludlow v. Strang, 1938 S.C. 551; 1939 S.L.T. 466; 1938 S.N. 52. . . . . 18.35, 18.36
Lumsden v. Lang's Trs, 1940 S.L.T. (Sh.Ct.) 6; (1939) 55 Sh.Ct.Rep. 223. . . . . 16.41
Lund v. Briggs & Sons Ltd, Airdrie Sh.Ct., Mar. 20, 1981, unreported. 15.65
Lunn v. Watt, 1911 2 S.L.T. 479. . . . . 15.19
Lusk v. Tait (1899) 15 Sh.Ct.Rep. 249. . . . . 23.32
Luss Estates Co. v. B.P. Oil Grangemouth Refinery Ltd, 1981 S.L.T. 97. . . . . 9.117
Luxmoore v. Red Deer Commission, 1979 S.L.T. (Notes) 53. . . . . 2.106, 14.65
Lyall & Wood v. Thomson, 1993 S.L.T. (Sh.Ct.) 21. . . . . 21.72, 21.73
Lyell v. Harthill Thistle Pipe Band (1905) 21 Sh.Ct.Rep. 294. . . . . 15.29
Lyle v. Smith, 1954 S.L.T. (Sh.Ct.) 11; (1954) 71 Sh.Ct.Rep. 28. . . . . 21.77
Lynch v. Stewart (1871) 9 M. 860; (1871) 43 Sc.Jur. 522; (1871) 8 S.L.R. 572. . . . . . 10.58
Lyons v. Anderson (1880) 8 R. 24; (1880) 18 S.L.R. 5. . . . . 23.27
Lyon's Trs v. Smith, 1922 S.L.T. (Sh.Ct.) 42; (1921) 37 Sh.Ct.Rep. 251. . . . . 23.34
Lythgoe v. Banks, 1993 S.N. 76. . . . . 19.27

M., PETR, 1953 S.C. 277. . . . . 28.43
M. v. Children's Hearing for Strathclyde Region, 1988 S.C.L.R. 592. . . . . 28.21
—— v. Kennedy, 1993 S.C. 115; 1993 S.C.L.R. 69. . . . . 16.62
—— v. M, 1967 S.L.T. 157. . . . . 9.35, 9.37
—— v. S, 1909 1 S.L.T. 192. . . . . 10.60
M. Publications (Scotland) Ltd v. Meiland, 1981 S.L.T. (Notes) 72. . . . . 4.90, 9.70
MAC Electrical and Heating Engineers Ltd v. Calscot Electrical (Distributors) Ltd,
 1989 S.C.L.R. 498. . . . . 9.30
MDW Developments v. Kilmarnock and Loudon D.C., Kilmarnock Sh.Ct., July 5,
 1986, unreported. 26.50
M.H. Credit Corp. Ltd v. Gill, Linlithgow Sh.Ct., Dec. 1983, unreported. 7.26, 7.27
M.Y. v. Strathclyde R.C., Glasgow Sh.Ct., Aug. 16, 1982, unreported. 26.113
McAdam v. Martin's Trs (1872) 11 M. 32. . . . . 29.18
Macalister v. Macalister, 1978 S.L.T. (Notes) 78. . . . . 22.47
McAlister v. Swinburne (1873) 1 R. 166; (1873) 11 S.L.R. 62. 11.54
McAllister v. H.M. Advocate, 1985 S.L.T. 399; 1985 S.C.C.R. 36. . . . . 6.46

McAllister v. Duthie (1867) 5 M. 912; (1867) 39 Sc.Jur. 509. . . . .   11.82, 11.83
Macandrew v. Crerar, 1929 S.C. 699; 1929 S.L.T. 540; 1929 S.N. 79. . . . .   23.37
McArthur v. Boucher (1887) 15 R. 117; (1887) 25 S.L.R. 138. . . . .   18.20
Macarthur v. Bruce (1760) Mor. 803. . . . .   11.34
McArthur v. Raynesway Plant Ltd, 1980 S.L.T. 74. . . . .   9.33, 10.42, 10.52
Macaskill v. Nicol, 1943 S.C. 17; 1943 S.L.T. 147; 1942 S.N. 53. . 5.92, 18.16, 18.17, 18.70
McAthey v. Patriotic Investment Co. Ltd, 1910 S.C. 584; 1910 1 S.L.T. 121; (1910)
      47 S.L.R. 315. . . . .   14.64, 14.65
McAulay v. Cowe (1873) 1 R. 307; (1873) 11 S.L.R. 156. . . . .   2.97, 14.19
McBain v. Wallace & Co. (1881) 8 R. (H.L.) 106; (1881) 6 App. Cas. 588; (1881) 18
      S.L.R. 734. . . . .   8.41
MacBean v. West End Clothiers Co. Ltd, 1918 S.C. 221; (1918) 55 S.L.R. 497. . . . .   11.65
Macbeth v. Innes (1873) 11 M. 404; (1873) 45 Sc.Jur. 270; (1873) 10 S.L.R. 255. . . .   1.21
Macbeth Currie & Co. v. Matthew, 1985 S.L.T. (Sh.Ct.) 44. . . .   4.118, 19.24, 19.40, 19.41
Macbeth & Maclagan v. Macmillan, 1914 S.C.(J.) 165; (1914) 7 Adan 493; 1914 2
      S.L.T. 30; (1914) 51 S.L.R. 676. . . . .   1.32
McBride v. Lewis, 1922 S.L.T. 380. . . . .   15.02
McCaffer v. Allan (1896) 4 S.L.T. 27 (1896) 33 S.L.R. 601. . . . .   5.86, 17.04, 17.07
McCafferty v. McCabe (1898) 25 R. 872; (1898) 6 S.L.T. 7; (1898) S.L.R. 679. . . . . .   8.60
——— v. McCafferty, 1986 S.L.T. 651. . . . .   18.114
McCaig v. Maitland (1887) 14 R. 295; (1887) 24 S.L.R. 219. . . . .   2.109, 21.70
McCall v. Gattens (1905) 13 S.L.T. 149. . . . .   11.54
——— v. Sharpe and Bayne (1862) 24 D. 393; (1862) 34 Sc.Jur.195. . . . .   4.125
McCallum, Applicant, 1990 S.L.T. (Sh.Ct.) 90; 1990 S.C.L.R. 399. . . . .   29.74
McCallum, 1925 S.L.T. (Sh.Ct.) 56; (1924) 41 Sh.Ct.Rep. 51. . . . .   25.29
——— v. Cohen (1915) 32 Sh.Ct.Rep. 39. . . . .   2.14, 9.121
——— v. Forth Iron Co. (1861) 23 D. 729; (1861) 33 Sc.Jur. 371. . . . .   2.85
——— v. Paterson, 1969 S.C. 85; 1969 S.L.T. 177. . . . .   16.84
McCann v. Miller Insulation and Engineering Ltd, 1986 S.L.T. 147. . . . .   21.22, 21.24
——— v. St Andrews Links Trust (Trs of), Cupar Sh.Ct., June 3, 1983, unreported. . .   15.87
McCardle v. McCardle's J.F. (1906) 8 F. 419; (1906) 13 S.L.T. 664; (1906) 43 S.L.R.
      268. . . . .   2.128
McCarroll v. McKinstery, 1923 S.C. 94; 1923 S.L.T. 96; (1923) 60 S.L.R. 99. . . . . . .   2.110,
                                                                                                                                     18.04
McCarthy v. Abowall (Trading) Ltd 1992 S.L.T. (Sh.Ct.) 65; 1992 S.C.L.R. 264. . . . .   3.52
McChesney v. Harper, 1993 S.C.L.R. 170. . . . .   5.88
McChristie v. EMS Promotions Ltd, 1991 S.L.T. 934. . . . .   14.11, 18.56
McCluskey v. Sir Robert McAlpine & Sons Ltd, 1994 S.C.L.R. 650. . . . .   18.114
McCluskie v. National Coal Board, 1961 S.C. 87; 1961 S.L.T. (Notes) 6. . . . .   10.37, 10.52
McClymont v. McCubbin, 1994 S.C. 573; 1995 S.L.T. 1248. . . . .   24.07
MacColl v. MacColl, 1946 S.L.T. 312; 1946 S.N. 80. . . . .   15.105, 16.57
McColl v. McColl, 1949 S.L.T. (Notes) 11. . . . .   9.79
——— v. ———, 1992 S.C.L.R. 187. . . . .   18.46
——— v. McDonald, 1933 S.L.T. (Sh.Ct.) 4. . . . .   7.33
——— v. Strathclyde R.C., 1981 S.L.T. (Notes) 70. . . . .   16.56, 16.57
McConnachie, 1914 S.C. 853; (1914) 2 S.L.T. 71; 1914 51 S.L.R. 716. . . . .   3.100
McConnel v. Pringle (1960) 76 Sh.Ct.Rep. 67. . . . .   9.67
McConnell & Reid v. Smith, 1911 S.C. 635; 1911 1 S.L.T. 333; (1911) 48 S.L.R.
      564. . . . .   2.101
McConochie v. Binnie (1847) 9 D. 791. . . . .   4.14
McCormick v. Campbell (1924) 42 Sh.Ct.Rep. 124.   3.90, 6.02
MacCormick v. Lord Advocate, 1953 S.C. 396; 1953 S.L.T. 255. . . . .   4.57
McCraddie v. Markham, Glasgow Sh.Ct., Dec. 20, 1961, unreported. 14.04
McCrae v. Bryson, 1922 S.L.T. 664, 1923 S.C. 896. . . . .   11.64, 13.72, 14.55
McCrattan v. Renfrew D.C., 1983 S.L.T. 678. . . . .   10.37, 10.52
McCrindle v. Sandilands, 1980 S.L.T. (Notes) 12. . . . .   9.54
McCrone v. Boots Farm Sales Ltd, 1981 S.C. 68; 1981 S.L.T. 103. . . . .   9.30
McCrone, Macbeth, Currie & Co., 1968 S.L.T. (Notes) 24. . . . .   9.54
McCuaig v. McCuaig, 1909 S.C. 355; 1909 1 S.L.T. 60; (1909) 46 S.L.R. 287. . . . . .   4.108,
                                                                                                                             4.112, 11.56
McCubbin v. Turnbull (1850) 12 D. 1123. . . . .   16.64
McCue v. Scottish Daily Record and Sunday Mail Ltd, 1988 S.C.L.R. 742; 1998
      G.W.D. 23–1153. . . . .   5.92, 11.61, 11.65, 14.11, 11.79, 11.84, 18.20, 18.70
McCulloch v. G. & C. Moore, 1928 S.N. 114; 1928 S.L.T. 646. . . . .   14.38
——— v. Glasgow Corporation, 1918 S.C. 155; 1918 1 S.L.T. 41; (1918) 55 S.L.R.
      178. . . . .   15.02
——— v. McCulloch, 1990 S.L.T. (Sh.Ct.) 63; 1990 S.C.L.R. 155. . . . .   7.06

McCulloch v. McCulloch's Trs (1903) 6 F.(H.L.) 3; (1903) 11 S.L.T. 429; (1903) 41
  S.L.R. 88; [1904] A.C. 55. . . . . 19.13
—— v. McLaughlin 1930 J.C. 8; 1930 S.L.T. 49; 1929 S.N. 105. . . . . 1.39
—— v. Neilson, Hamilton Sh.Ct., Nov. 11, 1983, unreported. 13.74
McCusker v. Saveheat Cavity Wall Insulation Ltd, 1987 S.L.T. 24. . . . 9.28, 18.106, 18.115
McDade v. Glasgow Corporation, 1966 S.L.T. (Notes) 4. . . . . 15.02
McDermid (R.) Ltd v. Muir Crawford (Builders) Ltd, 1978 S.L.T. (Sh.Ct.) 17. . . . . 2.128,
  14.50
McDermott v. Western SMT Co., 1937 S.C. 239; 1937 S.L.T. 286; 1937 S.N. 9. . . . . 4.50,
  18.21
Macdonald v. Baird & Co. Ltd (1927) 43 Sh.Ct.Rep. 73. . . . . 9.85
MacDonald v. Brown (1835) 13 S. 594, 2 Sh. & McL. 103, (1837) 15 S. 770, (1841) 3
  D. 871. . . . . 4.17
Mcdonald v. Burns (1938) 54 Sh.Ct.Rep. 229. . . . . 4.103
Macdonald v. Cameron (1882) 10 R. 172. . . . . 13.28
—— v. Denoon, 1928 S.L.T. 439; 1928 S.N. 89. . . . . 18.04
—— v. Forsyth (1898) 25 R. 870; (1898) 5 S.L.T. 380; (1898) 35 S.L.R. 634. . . . . . . 10.30
—— v. G 101 Off Sales Ltd, 1988 S.C.L.R. 448. . . . . 19.15
—— v. Glasgow Western Hospitals, 1954 S.C. 453; 1954 S.L.T. 226. . . . . 9.29
McDonald v. Glass (1883) 21 S.L.R. 45; (1883) 11 R. 57. . . . . 9.26
Macdonald v. Greenock Dockyard Co. Ltd, 1959 S.L.T. (Sh.Ct.) 6; (1958) 74
  Sh.Ct.Rep. 201. . . . . 10.17
McDonald v. Kelly, 1995 S.C.L.R. 187. . . . . 2.128
Macdonald v. Macdonald (1842) 1 Bell's App. 819. 2.112, 2.113
McDonald v. McDonald (1912) 29 Sh.Ct.Rep. 157. . . . . 13.44
Macdonald v. Macdonald (1956) 72 Sh.Ct.Rep. 171. . . . . 18.48
—— v. ——, 1970 S.L.T. (Notes) 71. . . . . 16.24
MacDonald v. MacDonald, 1985 S.L.T. 244. . . . . 16.38
McDonald v. McDonalds (1881) 8 R. 357. . . . . 15.76
Macdonald v. McEachen (1880) 7 R. 574; (1880) 17 S.L.R. 392. . . . . 18.87, 19.06
—— v. Mackenzie, 1947 J.C. 169; 1748 S.L.T. 27; 1947 S.N. 146. . . . . 2.16, 16.52
—— v. Mackessack (1888) 16 R. 168; (1888) 26 S.L.R. 124. . . . . 2.54, 18.05, 21.80
McDonald v. Ross, 1929 S.C. 240; 1929 S.L.T. 178; 1928 S.N. 161. . . . . 2.29
McDonald v. Secretary of State for Scotland, 1994 S.C. 234. 4.57
Macdonald v. Simpsons (1882) 9 R. 696; (1882) 19 S.L.R. 471. . . . . 11.52
—— v. Sinclair (1843) 5 D. 1253; (1843) 15 Sc.Jur. 511. . . . . 6.26
—— v. SMT Co., 1948 S.C. 529. . . . . 14.39, 14.57
McDonald v. Western SMT Co., 1945 S.C. 47; 1945 S.L.T. 112; 1944 S.N. 58. . . . . 15.102
—— v. Wingate (1825) 3 S. 494 (N.E. 344); (1825) 21 F.C. 700. . . . . 11.25
Macdonald (D.) & Bros Ltd v. Cosmos Decorators Ltd, 1969 S.L.T. (Sh.Ct.) 9. . . 18.117
McDonald's Trs v. Stewart (1891) 18 R. 491; (1891) 28 S.L.R. 363. . . . . 11.68
McDonnell v. McShane, 1967 S.L.T. (Sh.Ct.) 61. . . . . 16.02, 16.90
McDonough v. Focus DIY Ltd, 1994 S.L.T. 596; 1993 S.C. 539; 1993 S.C.L.R.. . . . . 7.29
McDougall (1878) 5 R. 1014. . . . . 17.14
—— v. Buchanan (1867) 6 M. 120; (1867) 40 Sc.Jur. 67; (1867) 5 S.L.R. 99. . . . . . . 2.54
—— v. Chitnavis, 1937 S.C. 390; 1937 S.L.T. 421; 1937 S.N. 20. . . . . 2.11
Macdougall v. Cunningham (1901) 9 S.L.T. 100. . . . . 11.65
McDougall v. Duke of Argyll (1864) 3 M. 248. . . . . 26.324
—— v. James Jones & Sons Ltd, O.H., Nov. 27, 1970, unreported. 16.50
McDougall (D. & J.) Ltd v. Argyll and Bute D.C., 1986 S.L.T. 564. . . . . 8.60, 8.64
—— v. ——, 1987 S.L.T. 7. . . . . 2.100
McDowall v. Campbell (1838) 16 S. 629. . . . . 13.43
—— v. McGhee, 1913 2 S.L.T. 238. . . . . 4.32
—— v. Stewart (1871) 10 M. 193; (1871) 44 Sc.Jur. 116; (1871) 9 S.L.R. 140. . . . . . 19.52
McElroy v. McAllister, 1949 S.C. 110; 1749 S.L.T. 139. . . . . 9.18
McElroy & Sons v. Tharsis Sulphur and Copper Co. (1879) 6 R. 1119; (1879) 16
  S.L.R. 683. . . . . 19.10, 19.55
McEwan v. Pattison (1865) 3 M. 779; (1865) 37 Sc.Jur. 399. . . . . 19.11
—— v. Sharp (1899) 1 F. 393; (1899) 36 S.L.R. 292. . . . . 18.34
—— v. Steedman & McAlister, 1913 S.C. 761; 1913 1 S.L.T. 298. . . . . 21.95
McEwen v. Blair and Morrison (1822) 1 S. 313 (N.E. 289). 11.34
McFadyen v. St Cuthbert's Co-operative Association [1951] C.L.Y. 3992. . . . . 14.55
—— v. Wilson, Kilmarnock Sh.Ct., Jan 20, 1984, unreported. 2.09, 10.24
McFarlane v. Crawford (1919) 35 Sh.Ct.Rep. 78. . . . . 2.54
Macfarlane v. Friendly Society of Stornoway (1870) 8 M. 438; (1870) 42 Sc.Jur. 209;
  (1870) 7 S.L.R. 259. . . . . 2.29

MacFarlane v. MacDougall, 1932 S.L.T. (Sh.Ct.) 36; (1931) 47 Sh.Ct.Rep. 325..... 2.33, 12.38
Macfarlane v. Macfarlane, 1947 S.L.T. (Notes) 34....................... 8.64, 12.70
—— v. ——, 1956 S.C. 472; 1956 S.L.T. 33..................................... 9.25
McFarlane v. McFarlane, Sh. Prin. Mowat Airdrie Sh.Ct., Sept. 19, 1991, unreported... 18.81
—— v. ——, 1995 S.C.L.R. 794................................ 18.02, 18.25, 22.55
Macfarlane v. Raeburn, 1946 S.C. 67.. 18.81
—— v. Thompson (1884) 12 R. 232; (1884) 22 S.L.R. 179..................... 18.19
McFarquhar v. British Railways Board, 1967 S.L.T. (Notes) 102................. 10.06
McFeetridge v. Stewarts & Lloyds Ltd, 1913 S.C. 773; 1913 1 S.L.T. 325; (1913) 50 S.L.R. 505... 2.104, 9.126
Macfie v. Blair (1884) 22 S.L.R. 224.. 19.16
—— v. Scottish Rights of Way Society (1884) 11 R. 1094; (1884) 21 S.L.R. 742.... 8.22, 12.15
McGarry v. O'Connor, 1991 S.L.T. (Sh.Ct.) 43................................. 7.37
McGarva v. McBrierly, 1917 1 S.L.T. 324; (1917) 33 Sh.Ct.Rep. 283.............. 11.33
McGaughey v. Livingstone, 1992 S.L.T. 386; 1991 S.C.L.R. 412.................. 4.07
McGeachy v. Standard Life Assurance Co., 1972 S.C. 145....................... 5.22
McGeouch v. Strathclyde R.C., 1985 S.L.T. 321............................... 9.33
McGhee v. Ellingham (1932) 49 Sh.Ct.Rep. 282............................... 16.97
McGhie v. British Transport Commission, 1964 S.L.T. (Notes) 56.......... 10.18, 16.37
McGibbon v. Sanchez, 1998 G.W.D. 15–736..................... 16.33, 18.85, 18.109
McGildowney v. Hart (1910) 27 Sh.Ct.Rep. 37................................. 11.69
Macgillivray v. Mackintosh (1891) 19 R. 103; (1891) 29 S.L.R. 103......... 18.37, 19.04
McGinn v. Meiklejohn Ltd, 1969 S.L.T. (Notes) 49............................. 15.02
McGlone v. British Railway Board, 1966 S.C.(H.L.) 1; 1966 S.L.T. 2.... 4.14, 9.28, 16.84
McGlynn v. National Coal Board, O.H., Lord Stott, July 9, 1971, unreported...... 9.37
McGourlich v. Renfrew D.C. (1982) 73 SCOLAG 58......................... 26.328
McGovern v. Central R.C., 1982 S.L.T. (Sh.Ct.) 110.......................... 26.178
McGowan v. Belling & Co. Ltd, 1983 S.L.T. 77........................... 15.17, 16.24
—— v. Cartner, 1996 S.L.T. (Sh.Ct.) 10; 1995 S.C.L.R. 312.......... 13.07, 14.12, 16.48
—— v. City of Glasgow Friendly Society, 1913 S.C. 991; 1913 2 S.L.T. 40; (1913) 50 S.L.R. 783... 12.70, 26.201
McGown v. Cramb (1897) 24 R. 481; (1897) 4 S.L.T. 289; (1897) 34 S.L.R. 347.... 10.06
—— v. Erskine, 1978 S.L.T. (Notes) 4....................................... 15.90
McGraddie v. Clark, 1966 S.L.T. (Sh.Ct.) 36.................... 6.04, 6.06, 6.21, 6.22
McGrath v. Glasgow Coal Co. Ltd, 1909 S.C. 1250; 1909 2 S.L.T. 92; (1909) 46 S.L.R. 890... 9.68, 9.104
—— v. National Coal Board, H.L., May 4, 1954, unreported.................... 16.84
McGrattan v. Renfrew D.C., 1983 S.L.T. 678................................. 10.52
MacGregor v. Berwickshire C.C., 1967 S.L.T. (Sh.Ct.) 13..................... 26.255
McGregor v. D, 1981 S.L.T. (Notes) 97....................................... 2.104
Macgregor v. Macfarlane (1914) 31 Sh.Ct.Rep. 104...................... 2.14, 9.121
MacGregor v. MacGregor, 1946 S.L.T. (Notes) 13......................... 9.14, 10.60
McGregor v. Mackechnie (1918) 34 Sh.Ct.Rep. 174............................ 9.85
Macgregor v. McKinnon (1915) 32 Sh.Ct.Rep. 3.......................... 6.09, 25.19
McGregor v. Rooney, O.H., Lord Hunter, Feb. 5, 1971, unreported....... 11.89, 18.05
—— v. Lord Strathallan (1862) 24 D. 1006; (1862) 34 Sc.Jur. 493............. 18.04
—— v. Wimpey Construction Ltd, 1991 S.C.L.R. 868.................... 14.25, 18.56
McGregor's Trs v. Kimbell, 1912 S.C. 261; 1912 1 S.L.T. 14; (1912) 49 S.L.R. 214.. 19.33
McGruer (1898) 15 Sh.Ct.Rep. 38... 25.05
McGuffie v. Forth Valley Health Board, 1991 S.L.T. 231....................... 10.24
McGuire v. Union Cold Storage Co. Ltd, 1909 S.C. 384; 1909 1 S.L.T. 38; (1909) 46 S.L.R. 323... 18.65, 18.91
McHarg, Rennie & Lindsay v. Tauber, 1953 S.L.T. (Sh.Ct.) 10; (1953) 69 Sh.Ct.Rep. 27... 19.63
McHugh v. Leslie, 1961 S.L.T. (Notes) 65.................................... 16.30
McIlwraith v. Lochmaddy Hotel Ltd, 1995 S.C.L.R. 595........................ 9.67
McInally v. Kildonan Homes Ltd, 1979 S.L.T. (Notes) 89....................... 11.41
McInnes v. McInnes, 1990 S.C.L.R. 327...................................... 22.47
Macinsure Brokers Ltd v. Mackenzie & Co., 1984 S.L.T. (Sh.Ct.) 66.. 14.16, 14.22, 14.26
McIntosh v. British Railways Board (No. 1), 1990 S.C. 338; 1990 S.L.T. 637....... 13.67
—— v. Potts (1905) 7 F. 765; (1905) 13 S.L.T. 108............................ 23.24
—— v. Walker Steam Trawl Fishing Co. Ltd, 1971 S.L.T. (Notes) 75........ 9.28, 10.19
McIntyre v. Armitage Shanks Ltd, 1979 S.C. 248; 1979 S.L.T. 110............ 8.59, 8.60
Macintyre v. Caledonian Ry (1909) 25 Sh.Ct.Rep. 329......................... 11.20

MacIntyre v. Cleveland Petroleum Co. Ltd, 1967 S.L.T. 95. . . . . 2.13
—— v. Elie and Earlsferry Town Council, 1967 S.L.T. (Sh.Ct.) 78. . . . . 26.255
—— v. Ellams & Curry, 1938 S.L.T. 413; 1939 S.N. 98. . . . . 14.57
—— v. McIntyre, 1920 1 S.L.T. 207. . . . . 4.08, 15.27, 15.102
—— v. National Coal Board, 1978 S.L.T. (Sh.Ct.) 32. . . . . 15.56
Macintyre Bros v. Smith, 1913 S.C. 129; 1913 1 S.L.T. 148; (1913) 50 S.L.R. 261. . . 13.39
McIsaac v. Leonard (1915) 31 Sh.Ct.Rep. 303. . . . . 10.60
MacIver, Applicant, 1991 S.C.L.R. 870. . . . . 29.71, 29.78
McIver v. McIver, 1996 S.C.L.R. 225. . . . . 2.19, 2.25, 21.92, 21.96, 21.99, 25.36
Maciver v. Mackenzie, 1942 J.C. 51; 1942 S.L.T. 144; 1941 S.N. 88. . . . . 16.24
Mackay v. Boswall-Preston, 1916 S.C. 96; 1915 2 S.L.T. 291; (1915) 53 S.L.R. 79. . . 11.55
—— v. Campbell, 1966 S.C. 237; 1966 S.L.T. 329; affd, 1967 S.C.(H.L.) 53; 1967
      S.L.T. 337 (H.L.). 8.65, 21.77, 21.80
—— v. Dick & Stevenson (1881) 8 R.(H.L.) 37; (1881) 18 S.L.R. 387; (1881) 6
      App. C.S. 252. . . . . 17.05, 17.07, 17.08
—— v. Macdonald, 1928 S.C. 776. . . . . 18.01
McKay v. McIntosh, 1952 S.L.T. (Sh.Ct.) 88. . . . . 12.36
Mackay v. Mackay, 1914 S.C. 200; 1914 1 S.L.T. 29; (1914) 51 S.L.R. 200. . . . . 4.105
—— v. Mackenzie (1894) 21 R. 894; (1894) 2 S.L.T. 69; (1894) 31 S.L.R. 746. . . . . . 5.89,
                                                                               17.03, 18.85, 18.98
Mackay & Son v. Leven Police Commissioners (1893) 20 R. 1093; (1893) 30 S.L.R.
      919. . . . . 2.100, 2.101
Mackays v. James Deas and Son Ltd, 1977 S.L.T. (Sh.Ct.) 10. . . . . 18.12
McKechnie v. Halliday (1856) 18 D. 659; (1856) 28 Sc.Jur. 283. . . . . 19.23
McKechnie's Trs v. Meiklam's Trs, 1909 2 S.L.T. 266, 340. . . . . 26.32
McKellar v. Dallas's Ltd, 1928 S.C. 503; 1928 S.L.T. 306; 1928 S.N. 36. . . . . 21.77
Mackellar v. Mackellar (1898) 25 R. 883; (1898) 6 S.L.T. 18; (1898) 35 S.L.R.
      695. . . . . 19.33
McKelvie v. Scottish Steel Scaffolding Co., 1938 S.C. 278; 1938 S.L.T. 159; 1938
      S.N. 13. . . . . 7.30, 7.33, 14.12
McKenna v. British Transport Commission, 1960 S.L.T. (Notes) 30. . . . . 10.06
—— v. McKenna, 1984 S.L.T. (Sh.Ct.) 92. . . . . 2.04
—— v. Wain, Ayr Sh.Ct., July 27, 1983, unreported. 23.44, 23.46
Mackenzie v. Balerno Paper Mill Co. (1883) 10 R. 1147; (1883) 20 S.L.R. 757. . . . 11.43,
                                                                        11.46, 11.47, 11.84, 21.79
—— v. Blakeney (1879) 7 R. 51; (1879) 17 S.L.R. 5. . . . . 12.24
—— v. British Linen Co. (1879) 17 S.L.R. 241. . . . . 15.28
—— v. Calder (1868) 6 M. 833; (1868) 40 Sc.Jur. 443; (1868) 5 S.L.R. 499. . . . . 12.67
—— v. Cameron (1894) 21 R. 427; (1894) 1 S.L.T. 480; (1894) 31 S.L.R. 347. . . . . . 25.30
—— v. Coulthart (1889) 16 R. 1127; (1889) 26 S.L.R. 764. . . . . 21.99
—— v. Digby Brown & Co., 1992 S.L.T. 891; 1992 S.C.L.R. 339. . . . . 21.19
—— v. Drummond's Exrs (1868) 6 M. 932; (1868) 40 Sc.Jur. 537; (1868) 5 S.L.R.
      605. . . . . 3.101, 12.09
—— v. Fairfields Shipbuilding and Engineering Co. Ltd, 1964 S.C. 90. . . . . . . 10.37, 10.56
McKenzie v. H. D. Fraser & Sons, 1990 S.C. 311; 1990 S.L.T. 629; 1990 S.C.L.R.
      785. . . . . 14.38, 19.09
Mackenzie v. Girvan (1840) 3 D. 318. 13.35, 13.37, 13.38, 13.40
McKenzie v. Jones (1926) 42 Sh.Ct.Rep. 289. . . . . 10.05, 16.96
Mackenzie v. Macallister, 1909 S.C. 367; 1909 1 S.L.T. 62; (1909) 46 S.L.R. 288. . . . 4.42,
                                                                           4.43, 4.47, 4.50
McKenzie v. McKenzie, 1943 S.C. 108; 1943 S.L.T. 169; 1942 S.N. 64. . . . . 16.76
Mackenzie v. Mackenzie, 1951 S.C. 163; 1951 S.L.T. 114. . . . . 5.98, 5.100, 10.29
—— v. Maclennan, 1916 S.C. 617. . . . . 24.04
—— v. Munro (1869) 7 M. 676; (1869) 41 Sc.Jur. 374; (1869) 6 S.L.R. 438. . . . . 10.28
—— v. —— (1894) 22 R. 45; 1894 2 S.L.T. 290; (1894) 32 S.L.R. 43. . . . . 8.05, 18.05
—— v. North British Ry (1879) 17 S.L.R. 129. . . . . 18.04
MacKenzie v. R. McKenzie & Co. [1956] C.L.Y. 12121 (O.H.). 3.101
MacKenzie v. West Lothian D.C., 1979 S.C. 433. . . . . 9.14
MacKenzie v. John R. Wyatt (Musical Enterprises) Ltd, 1974 S.L.T. (Sh.Ct.) 8. . . . . 14.07,
                                                                18.12, 18.19, 18.30, 18.34, 18.70
Mackenzie & Co. v. Finlay (1868) 7 M. 27. . . . . 29.29, 29.71
MacKenzie's Exrx v. Morrison's Trs, 1930 S.C. 830; 1930 S.L.T. 616; 1930 S.N. 84. . 2.123
MacKenzie's Trs v. Sutherland (1895) 22 R. 233; (1895) 32 S.L.R. 172. . . . . 21.71
McKeown v. Palmers Scaffolding (Scotland) Ltd, 1962 S.L.T. (Notes) 10. . . . 14.53, 14.55
McKerchar v. McQuarrie (1887) 14 R. 1038. . . . . 12.24
McKerron v. Highland R.C., Inverness Sh.Ct., Sept. 2, 1983, unreported. 26.113

Mackersy v. Davis & Sons (1895) 22 R. 368; (1895) 32 S.L.R. 277; (1895) 2 S.L.T.
515... 4.43
McKidd v. Manson (1882) 9 R. 790; (1882) 19 S.L.R. 603.............. 1.43, 6.06, 7.06
Mackie v. Glasgow Corporation, 1924 S.L.T. 510............................. 10.39
—— v. Mackie (1897) 5 S.L.T. 42... 13.79
—— v. —— (1953) 69 Sh.Ct.Rep. 167....................................... 14.18
—— v. Riddell (1874) 2 R. 115; (1874) 12 S.L.R. 115...................... 9.30
—— v. Strachan, Kinmond & Co. (1896) 23 R. 1030; (1896) 35 S.L.R. 764........ 12.70
McKie v. Western SMT Co., 1952 S.C. 206; 1952 S.L.T. 191.................... 15.55
Mackie & Stark v. Cruikshank (1896) 4 S.L.T. 84............................ 15.82
MacKillop v. Mactaggart, 1939 S.L.T. 65; 1939 S.N. 9............... 11.18, 11.35
McKinlay v. McKinlay (1849) 11 D. 1022; (1849) 21 Sc.Jur. 368............ 11.71, 11.82
McKinnan v. Keith, 1912 S.L.T. 501.. 8.60
McKinnell v. White, 1971 S.L.T. (Notes) 61................................ 4.14
Mackinnon v. Donaldson, Lufkin and Jenrette Securities Corpn [1986] Ch. 482;
[1986] 2 W.L.R. 453; [1986] 1 All E.R. 653................................ 15.94
—— v. Guildford (1894) 2 S.L.T. 309................................. 15.72, 15.76
McKinnon v. Hamilton (1866) 4 M. 852...................................... 29.78
Mackinnon (L.) & Son v. Coles, Aberdeen Sh.Ct., Jan. 13, 1984, unreported..... 18.12,
                                                                          30.328
MacKinnon's Trs v. MacNeil (1897) 24 R. 981......................... 2.13, 17.28
McKinstery v. Plean Colliery Co. Ltd (1910) 27 Sh.Ct.Rep. 62................ 18.37
Mackintosh v. Galbraith and Arthur (1900) 3 F. 66; (1900) 8 S.L.T. 241........ 14.57
—— v. Mackintosh (1835) 13 S. 884..................................... 4.31, 9.99
—— v. Macqueen (1828) 6 S. 784... 15.51
—— v. Miller (1864) 2 M. 452; (1864) 36 Sc.Jur. 218................... 11.33, 11.41
—— v. Smith and Lowe (1864) 2 M. 1261.................................... 7.19
—— v. —— (1865) 3 M.(H.L.) 6; (1865) 4 Macq. 913; (1865) 37 Sc.Jur. 318.. 2.106, 7.19
Mackintosh's Tr. v. Stewart's Tr. (1906) 8 F. 467; (1906) 13 S.L.T. 846 (1906) 43
S.L.R. 363... 2.110
McLachian v. Black (1822) 1 S. 217 (N.E. 206)............................. 1.27
—— v. Flowerdew (1851) 13 D. 1345....................................... 15.39
Maclachlan v. Glasgow, 1925 S.L.T. (Sh.Ct.) 77..................... 24.12, 24.15
McLachlan v. Rutherford (1854) 16 D. 937................................. 18.05
Maclagan v. Marchbank 1911 S.L.T. 184; (1911) 27 Sh.Ct.Rep. 282........... 2.54
Maclaine Watson & Co. v. International Tin Council [1989] Ch. 253........... 4.06
McLaren v. Ferrier (1865) 3 M. 833.................................. 5.81, 8.15
—— v. Manson (1857) 20 D. 218; (1857) 30 Sc.Jur. 113................ 21.73, 21.74
MacLaren v. Preston (1893) 1 S.L.T. 75................................... 29.21
McLaren v. Procurator Fiscal for the Lothian and Borders, 1992 S.L.T. 844; 1991
S.C.L.R. 872... 4.82
McLauchlan v. McLauchlan's Trs, 1941 S.L.T. 43............................ 4.34
—— v. Reilly (1892) 20 R. 41; (1892) 30 S.L.R. 81........................ 23.18
McLaughlan, Brown & Co. v. Morrison (1902) 18 Sh.Ct..Rep. 206............. 12.70
McLaughlin v. A. A. Stuart & Sons (Glasgow) Ltd, 1955 S.L.T. (Notes) 2...... 14.48
—— v. Douglas & Kidston (1863) 4 Irv. 273; (1863) 35 Sc.Jur. 322... 16.62, 16.63, 16.64
—— v. Scott's Shipbuilding and Engineering Co. Ltd, 1960 S.L.T. (Notes) 58..... 13.12
McLean v. Auchinvole (1824) 3 S. 190 (N.E. 129).......................... 19.29
—— v. British Railways Board, 1966 S.L.T. 39............................ 10.42
—— v. Galbraith Stores, 1935 S.C. 165; 1935 S.L.T. 135; 1934 S.N. 109..... 14.48, 14.53
Maclean v. Galloway, 1979 S.L.T. (Sh.Ct.) 32............................. 2.102
McLean v. Glasgow Corporation, 1933 S.L.T. 396; 1933 S.N. 46........... 4.32, 13.78
—— v. Hassard (1903) 10 S.L.T. 593...................................... 8.60
Maclean v. Inverness Road Trs (1891) 7 Sh.Ct.Rep. 246.................... 26.385
McLean v. MacBrayne Ltd (1916) 33 Sh.Ct.Rep. 74......................... 17.15
—— v. McGarvey (1908) 16 S.L.T. 130..................................... 11.70
—— v. Marwhirn Developments Ltd, 1976 S.L.T. (Notes) 47................. 20.04
—— v. Renfrew Mags (1930) 47 Sh.Ct.Rep. 42............................. 25.47
—— v. Thomas O'Connor Autos, 1967 S.L.T. (Sh.Ct.) 41...... 5.100, 11.89, 16.47, 19.23
—— v. Victoria Spinning Co. Ltd, 1971 S.L.T. (Notes) 10................. 10.20
Maclean of Ardgour v. Maclean, 1941 S.C. 613; 1941 S.L.T. 339; 1942 S.L.T. 46;
1941 S.N. 56.. 5.83, 5.86
Macleay v. Macdonald, 1928 S.C. 776; 1928 S.L.T. 463; 1929 S.C. 371; 1929 S.L.T.
319................................... 18.68, 18.86, 18.98, 21.99, 28.134
McLeish v. Glasgow Bonding Co. Ltd, 1965 S.L.T. 39...................... 15.106
McLellan v. Kirkcudbright C.C., 1962 S.L.T. (Sh.Ct.) 43; (1962) 78 Sh.Ct.Rep.30.. 26.161
MacLellan & Co. Ltd v. Jesner, 1952 S.L.T. (Sh.Ct.) 39; (1952) 68 Sh.Ct.Rep. 141.. 9.78

Maclennan v. Luth, 1951 S.L.T. (Sh.Ct.) 103; (1951) 67 Sh.Ct.Rep. 21............ 19.11
McLennan v. Moray and Nairn Joint C.C., 1955 S.L.T. (Sh.Ct.) 14; (1955) 71 Sh.Ct.
    Rep. 21.. 26.115
McLeod v. Advocate (H.M.), 1939 J.C. 68; 1939 S.L.T. 556; 1939 S.N. 81......... 16.39
Macleod v. Alexander Sutherland Ltd, 1977 S.L.T. (Notes) 44.................. 21.80
—— v. Davidson (1887) 14 R. 298; (1887) 24 S.L.R. 224...................... 6.18
—— v. Dobson (1900) 16 Sh.Ct.Rep. 33, 104........................... 2.02, 26.187
—— v. Glen Talla Ltd, Kilmarnock Sh.Ct., June 12, 1986, unreported............ 14.37
McLeod v. Leslie (1868) 5 S.L.R. 687.. 15.82
Macleod v. Lewis (Justices of the Peace) (1892) 20 R. 218; (1892) 30 S.L.R. 186... 2.20,
    8.32
MacLeod v. MacLeod, 1928 S.L.T. (Sh.Ct.) 27............................... 24.04
McLeod v. Munro (1930) 47 Sh.Ct.Rep. 21.................................. 19.50
MacLeod v. Sinclair, 1981 S.L.T. (Notes) 38................................ 10.38
—— v. Speirs (1884) 5 Coup. 387; (1884) 11 R.(J.) 26; (1884) 21 S.L.R. 530... 1.02, 2.19
McLeod v. Tancred Arrol & Co. (1890) 17 R. 514; (1890) 27 S.L.R. 348...... 8.59, 8.60
MacLeod v. Woodmuir Miners Welfare Society Social Club, 1961 J.C. 5; 1960
    S.L.T. 349.. 16.24
Macleod's Judicial Factor v. Busfield, 1914 2 S.L.T. 268; (1914) 52 S.L.R. 13...... 4.78
McLinden v. British Steel Corporation, 1972 S.L.T. (Sh.Ct.) 25............ 10.20, 17.12
MacLinden v. Colvilles Ltd, 1967 S.L.T. (Notes) 80.......................... 14.57
McLintock v. Prinzen & Van Glabbeek (1902) 4 F. 948; (1902) 10 S.L.T. 157;
    (1902) 39 S.L.R. 760... 11.46, 21.80
McMahon v. Matheson (1899) 1 F. 896; (1899) 7 S.L.T. 47; (1899) 36 S.L.R. 704.. 18.86,
    18.88
McManus v. Speirs Dick and Smith Ltd, 1989 S.L.T. (Sh.Ct.) 45................. 9.114
McMenemy v. Argyll Stores Ltd, 1992 S.L.T. 971; 1992 S.C.L.R. 971............. 21.30
—— v. James Dougal & Sons Ltd, 1960 S.L.T. (Notes) 84...................... 9.29
McMichael v. UK (1995) 20 E.H.R.R. 205.................................... 28.87
McMillan v. Advocate (H.M.), 1983 S.L.T. 24; 1982 S.C.C.R. 309............... 6.12
—— v. Central SMT Co., 1947 S.L.T. (Notes) 3; 1947 S.N. 20.................. 14.52
—— v. Hassan (1945) 61 Sh.Ct.Rep. 91..................................... 16.90
—— v. Mackinlay, 1926 S.C. 673; 1926 S.L.T. 436; 1926; S.N. 75.......... 4.113, 4.115
—— v. MacPhee (1914) 30 Sh.Ct.Rep. 342................................... 26.03
McMillan & Son v. Rowan & Co. (1903) 5 F. 317............................ 26.32
McMorran v. Glover (1937) 53 Sh.Ct.Rep. 87............................... 11.31
McMurray v. Wallis (1950) 66 Sh.Ct.Rep. 234............................... 8.05
Macnab v. Nelson, 1909 S.C. 1102; 1909 2 S.L.T. 68; (1909) 46 S.L.R. 817........ 14.08
McNair v. Dunfermline Corporation, 1953 S.C. 183; 1953 S.L.T. 65.......... 4.43, 14.56
McNairn v. McNairn, 1959 S.L.T. (Notes) 35.......................... 11.14, 29.19
McNamara (1866) Ark. 521... 15.27
McNaught v. British Railways Board, 1979 S.L.T. (Notes) 99.............. 9.24, 9.112
—— v. Milligan (1885) 13 R. 366; (1885) 23 S.L.R. 236....................... 4.98
Macnaughtan v. Thurman (1907) 24 Sh.Ct.Rep. 80........................... 11.55
Macnaughton v. Macnaughton, 1949 S.C. 42; 1949 S.L.T. 10.................... 19.40
—— v. Macnaughton's Trs, 1953 S.C. 387; 1953 S.L.T. 240.......... 2.13, 20.01, 20.04
McNeil v. National Coal Board, 1966 S.C. 72; 1966 S.L.T. 237....... 4.40, 14.54, 18.117
McNeilie v. H.M. Advocate, 1929 J.C. 50; 1929 S.L.T. 145; 1928 S.N. 157......... 16.82
McNeill v. McArthur, 1997 S.L.T. 926; 1997 S.C.L.R. 252................. 18.20, 18.45
MacNeill v. MacNeill, 1929 S.L.T. 251; 1929 S.N. 18........................ 15.105
McNicol v. Buko Ltd, 1986 S.L.T. 12........................... 21.22, 21.24, 21.26
McNiven v. Glasgow Corporation, 1920 S.C. 584; 1920 2 S.L.T. 57; (1920) 57 S.L.R.
    514.. 6.24
—— v. Orr (1905) 22 Sh.Ct.Rep. 9... 7.26
McPhail v. Lanarkshire County Council, 1951 S.C. 301; 1951 S.L.T. 32, 167....... 10.37
—— v. Lothian R.C., 1981 S.C. 119; 1981 S.L.T. 173........................ 4.88
McPhee v. Glasgow Corporation, 1910 1 S.L.T. 380.......................... 15.08
Macphee v. Glasgow Corporation, 1915 S.C. 990; 1915 2 S.L.T. 88; (1915) 52 S.L.R.
    772.. 15.02
McPhee v. Heatherwick, 1977 S.L.T. (Sh.Ct.) 46.............. 2.104, 2.105, 2.106
McPhendron and Currie v. McCallum (1888) 16 R. 45....................... 11.29
Macpherson Petr., 1989 S.L.T. (Sh.Ct.) 53.................................. 1.27
McPherson v. British Railways Board, 1985 S.L.T. 467.................... 14.38, 19.49
—— v. Cameron's Exr, 1942 S.L.T. (Sh.Ct.) 26............................. 20.22
Macpherson v. Ellen (1914) 30 Sh.Ct.Rep. 206.............................. 2.02
—— v. Macdonald Fraser & Co.. Ltd (1905) 12 S.L.T. 824................. 8.22, 12.15
—— v. Wright (1885) 12 R. 942.. 29.31

McQuater v. Fergusson, 1911 S.C. 640; 1911 1 S.L.T. 295. . . . . 9.94, 19.03, 25.46
McQuator v. Wellwood (1908) 16 S.L.T. 110. . . . . 11.54
McQueen v. Armstrong (1908) 24 Sh.Ct.Rep. 377. . . . . 23.18
Macqueen v. Mackie & Co. Distillers, 1920 S.C. 544; 1920 2 S.L.T. 31; (1920) 57
 S.L.R. 486. . . . . 15.53
McRae (Alexander) (1841) Bell's Notes to Hume, ii, 270. . . . . 16.65
MacRae v. British Transport Commission, 1957 S.C. 195; 1957 S.L.T. (Notes) 30. . 15.58
Macrae v. Edinburgh Street Tramways Co. (1885) 13 R. 265; (1885) 23 S.L.R. 185 14.45
—— v. Reed & Mallik Ltd, 1961 S.C. 68; 1961 S.L.T. 96. 21.36
—— v. Sutherland (1889) 16 R. 476. . . . . 11.64
Macrae's Tr. v. Macrae (1945) 62 Sh.Ct.Rep. 48. . . . . 11.55
McRostie v. Halley (1850) 12 D. 816; (1850) 22 Sc.Jur. 353. . . . . 8.57
MacShannon v. Rockware Glass Ltd [1978] A.C. 795; [1978] 2 W.L.R. 362; [1978] 1
 All E.R. 625; (1978) 122 S.J. 81. . . . . 9.114
McSheehy v. MacMillan, 1993 S.L.T. (Sh.Ct.) 10; 1992 S.C.L.R. 603. . . . . 2.105, 2.109
McSkimming v. Royal Bank of Scotland plc, 1997 S.L.T. 515; 1996 S.C.L.R. 547. . . 11.34,
 29.30
McSourley v. Paisley Mags (1902) 10 S.L.T. 86. . . . . 9.37
McTaggart v. McDouall (1867) 5 M. 534; (1867) 39 Sc.Jur. 274. . . . . 9.83, 21.13
Mactaggart v. MacKillop, 1938 S.L.T. 100; 1938 S.N. 26. . . . . 11.19, 11.25
—— v. ——, 1938 S.L.T. 559. . . . . 15.46, 15.50
McTague v. LNER [1948] C.L.Y. 4684. . . . . 16.76
McTernan v. Bennell (1898) 1 F. 333; (1898) 6 S.L.T. 122; (1898) 36 S.L.R. 239. . . . 6.06
Macvean v. Maclean (1873) 11 M. 506; (1873) 45 Sc.Jur. 470; (1873) 10 S.L.R. 312 . 8.59
McVinnie v. McVinnie, 1995 S.L.T. (Sh.Ct.) 81; 1995 S.C.L.R. 480. . . . . 15.43, 28.112
McWilliam v. McWilliam, 1990 S.C.L.R. 373. . . . . 19.03
—— v. Robertson (1911) 27 Sh.Ct.Rep. 219. . . . . 16.97
McWilliams v. McWilliams, 1963 S.C. 259. . . . . 26.125
Magee & Co. (Belfast) Ltd v. Bracewell Harrison & Coton, 1980 S.L.T. (Notes) 102 . 9.54
—— v. ——, 1981 S.L.T. 107. . . . . 4.48, 14.64
Maguire v. Burges, 1909 S.C. 1283; 1909 2 S.L.T. 219; (1909) 46 S.L.R. 925. . . . . . . 4.33
Mahon v. Air New Zealand Ltd [1984] A.C. 808; [1984] 3 W.L.R. 884; [1984] 3 All
 E.R. 201; (1984) 128 S.J. 752. . . . . 16.38, 17.27
Mahoney v. Officer, 1995 S.L.T. (Sh.Ct.) 49; 1994 S.C.L.R. 1059. . 5.95, 8.34, 14.06, 18.56
Main v. Lanarkshire & Dumbartonshire Ry (1893) 21 R. 323; (1893) 1 S.L.T. 383;
 (1893) 31 S.L.R. 239. . . . . 25.31, 26.347
—— v. Rankin & Sons, 1929 S.C. 40; 1929 S.L.T. 20; 1928 S.N. 118. . . . . 4.113
Mainschiffahrts-Genossenschaft v. Les Gravieres Rhenanes (C-106/95) [1997]
 I.L.Pr. 411. . . . . 3.51, 3.92
Mair v. National Coal Board, 1962 S.L.T. (Sh.Ct.) 53; (1962) 78 Sh.Ct.Rep. 40. . . . 13.75
—— v. Simpson's Motors Ltd, 1966 S.C. 198; 1966 S.L.T. 294. . . . . 12.62
Maitland v. Bingorama Ltd, 1977 S.L.T. (Sh.Ct.) 58. . . . . 17.12
—— v. Maitland (1885) 12 R. 899; (1885) 22 S.L.R. 418. . . . . 13.79
Malcolm v. Campbell (1889) 17 R. 255; (1889) 27 S.L.R. 207. . . . . 8.55
—— v. Macintyre (1877) 5 R. 22; (1877) 15 S.L.R. 8. . . . . 18.34, 18.36, 18.94
—— v. Moore (1901) 4 F. 23; (1901) 9 S.L.T. 212; (1901) 395 S.L.R. 26. . . . . 14.37
—— v. Stewart (1829) 7 S. 715. . . . . 15.28
Malcolmson v. Sampson (1927) 44 Sh.Ct.Rep. 88. . . . . 14.18, 14.29
Malone v. Glasgow D.C., Glasgow Sh.Ct., Nov. 20, 1979, unreported. . 18.55, 18.70, 23.34
Maltby v. D.J. Freeman & Co. [1978] 1 W.L.R. 431; [1978] 2 All E.R. 913; (1978)
 122 S.J. 212. . . . . 19.20
Maltman v. Tarmac Civil Engineering Ltd, 1967 S.C. 177; 1967 S.L.T. 141; 1967
 S.L.T. (Notes) 102. . . . . 2.110, 2.111, 11.64
Maltman's Factor v. Cook (1867) 5 M. 1076. . . . . 15.28
Manchester and County Bank Ltd v. Moore, 1909 S.C. 246; (1909) 16 S.L.T. 595;
 (1909) 46 S.L.R. 222. . . . . 18.20, 18.65
Manders v. Lacon Floors Ltd, 1993 S.C.L.R. 311. . . . . 5.78, 5.88, 5.90, 7.36, 19.06
Manor Lifts Ltd v. J. H. Gray (Builders) Ltd, 1989 S.L.T. (Sh.Ct.) 63. . . . . . . 14.46, 14.66
Mansfield v. Walker's Trs (1883) 11 S. 813; (1833) 5 Sc.Jur. 569. . . . . 11.24
Manson, Petr, J.C., May 27, 1977, unreported. 2.24
Manson v. British Gas Corporation 1982 S.L.T. 77. . . . . 1.36, 15.60
—— v. Chief Constable of Strathclyde, *The Scotsman*, Dec. 16, 1983. . . . . 2.19
—— v. Smith (1871) 9 M. 492; (1871) 8 S.L.R. 346. . . . . 1.21
Marco v. Merrens, 1964 S.L.T. (Sh.Ct.) 74. . . . . 2.79
Margrie Holdings Ltd v. City of Edinburgh District Council, 1994 S.L.T. 971. . . . . . 2.108
Marinari (C-364/93) [1995] E.C.R. 1–2719. . . . . 3.93

Marks & Spencer Ltd v. British Gas Corporation, 1983 S.L.T. 196. . . . . 15.54
—— v. ——, 1985 S.L.T. 17. . . . . 14.39, 14.67, 19.18
Marr & Sons v. Lindsay (1881) 8 R. 784; (1881) 18 S.L.R. 535. . . . . 18.01
Marsh v. Baxendale, (I.H.) 1995 S.L.T. 198; 1994 S.C.L.R. 239; (O.H.) 1995 S.L.T.
    195; 1995 S.C.L.R. 239. . . . . 18.16, 18.17, 18.70
—— v. Taylor, 1992 S.L.T. (Sh.Ct.) 28. . . . . 16.33, 18.63
Marshall v. Black, 1981 S.L.T. 228. . . . . 10.42, 10.52, 12.10
—— v. Callander and Trossachs Hydropathic Co. Ltd (1896) 24 R. 33; (1896) 4
    S.L.T. 117; (1896) 34 S.L.R. 5. . . . . 17.14, 18.40, 18.86, 21.76
—— v. Cannon (1848) 21 Sc.Jur. 63. . . . . 11.73
—— v. Hynd (1828) 6 S. 384. . . . . 12.09
—— v. Wm Sharp and Sons, 1991 S.L.T. 114; 1991 S.C.L.R. 104. . . . . 16.102
Marshall & Nimmo & Co. (1847) 10 D. 328. . . . . 29.21
Marshall & Sons v. Robertson (1904) 21 Sh.Ct.Rep. 243. . . . . 11.20
Martin v. Bell-Ingram, 1986 S.L.T. 575. . . . . 10.24
—— v. Ellis, 1978 S.L.T. (Sh.Ct.) 38. . . . . 26.255
—— v. Lindsay (1894) 21 R. 759. . . . . 4.114, 4.115
—— v. McKinsley, 1980 S.L.T. (Notes) 15. . . . . 21.19
—— v. McLean (1844) 6 D. 981; (1844) 16 Sc.Jur. 437. . . . . 9.30
—— v. Stopford-Blair's Exrs (1879) 7 R. 329; (1879) 17 S.L.R. 208. . . . . 2.98
—— v. Underwood (1827) 5 S. 783 (N.E. 730). 11.79
Martin's Exrx v. McGhee, 1914 S.C. 628; 1914 1 S.L.T. 365; (1914) 51 S.L.T. 499. . 12.09
Marshall v. Callander and Trossachs Hydropathic Co. Ltd (1896) 24 R. 33; (1896) 4
    S.L.T. 17; (1896) 34 S.L.R. 5. . . . . 18.68
Masinimport v. Scottish Mechanical Light Industries Ltd, 1972 S.L.T. (Notes) 76;
    1976 S.C. 102. . . . . 11.78, 11.89
—— v. ——, 1st Div., May 15, June 7 and Sept. 25, 1973, unreported. 11.79
Mason (1830) 5 Murray 129 (note). 16.12
—— v. Foster Wheeler Power Products Ltd, 1984 S.L.T. (Sh.Ct.) 5. . 12.25, 12.26, 18.117
Mather v. Smith (1858) 21 D. 24; (1858) 31 Sc.Jur. 11. . . . . 14.12
Mather (Alexander) & Son v. John Wilson & Co. Ltd (1908) 15 S.L.T. 946. . 29.22, 29.23
Matheson v. Fraser, 1911 2 S.L.T. 493. . . . . 6.22, 21.89
Mathewson v. Yeaman (1900) 2 F. 873; (1900) 8 S.L.T. 23; (1900) 37 S.L.R. 681. . . 18.05
Mathieson v. Hawthorns & Co. Ltd (1899) 1 F. 468; (1899) 6 S.L.T. 311; (1899) 36
    S.L.R. 356. . . . . 12.70, 12.72
Mathieson Gee (Ayrshire) Ltd v. Quigley, 1952 S.C.(H.L.) 38; [1952] W.N. 193;
    (1952) 96 S.J. 295. . . . . 2.12
Matthew v. Ballingall (1844) 6 D. 1135. . . . . 19.41
Matthews v. Munster (1888) 20 Q.B.D. 141; [1886.90] All E.R. Rep. 251. . . . . 5.98
—— v. Scottish Legal Aid Board, 1995 S.C.L.R. 184. . . . . 14.74
Matuszcsyk v. National Coal Board, 1955 S.C. 418; 1955 S.L.T. 101. . . . . 2.104, 2.108
Mauritzen (Charles) Ltd v. Baltic Shipping Co., 1948 S.C. 646; 1948 S.L.T. 300. . . . 2.101
Mavor v. Governors of Aberdeen Educational Trust (1902) 10 S.L.T. 156. . . 4.108, 12.14
Mavor & Coulson v. Grierson (1892) 19 R. 868; (1892) 29 S.L.R. 766. . . . . 14.68
Maxton v. Bone (1866) 13 R. 912; 23 S.L.R. 645. . . . . 11.84, 18.39
Maxwell v. Controller of Clearing House, 1923 S.L.T. (Sh.Ct.) 137. . . . . 29.72
Maxwells (Dundee) Ltd v. Adam, 1911 2 S.L.T. 149. . . . . 18.12
May v. Malcolm (1825) 4 S. 76 (N.E. 79); (1825) 21 Fac. 838. . . . . 11.25
Mazs v. Dairy Supply Co. Ltd, 1978 S.L.T. 208. . . . . 10.52
Meadows Removals v. Berry, 1992 S.C.L.R. 960. . . . . 18.36
Meagher v. Meagher [1961] I.R. 96. . . . . 26.319
Mearns v. British Transport Commission, 1960 S.L.T. (Notes) 56. . . . . 16.30
Mecca Ltd v. Edinburgh Corporation, 1967 S.L.T. (Sh.Ct.) 43. . . . . 26.255
Mecklermedia Corporation v. D.C. Congress GmbH, *The Times*, Mar. 27, 1997. . . . . 3.60
Meechan v. British Railways Board, 1989 S.C.L.R. 772. . . . . 9.33
Meek v. Milne, 1985 S.L.T. 318. . . . . 10.37
Meekison v. Uniroyal Englebert Tyres Ltd, 1995 S.L.T. (Sh.Ct.) 63; 1995 S.C.C.R.
    273. . . . . 19.21, 28.129
Meiklejohn v. Stevenson (1870) 8 M. 890; (1870) 42 Sc.Jur. 531 (1870) 7 S.L.R.
    565. . . . . 16.56, 16.70
Mellis (1872) S.L.R. 630. . . . . 11.32
Melrose v. Spalding (1868) 6 M. 952; (1868) 40 Sc.Jur. 545; (1868) S.L.R. 565. . . . . 17.03
Melrose-Drover Ltd v. Heddle (1905) 7 F. 852; (1905) 13 S.L.T. 197. . . . . 11.54
Melrose Parish Council v. Hawick Parish Council, 1912 S.C. 1029; 1912 2 S.L.T. 47;
    (1912) 49 S.L.R. 749. . . . . 2.29, 2.34
Menzies v. Baird, 1912 1 S.L.T. 84. . . . . 15.39
—— v. Caldwell (1834) 12 S. 772; (1834) 6 Sc.Jur. 437. . . . . 12.19

Menzies v. Menzies (1890) 17 R. 881; (1890) 27 S.L.R. 721. . . . . 10.26
—— v. —— (1893) 20 R.(H.L.) 108; (1893) 30 S.L.R. 530; [1893] W.N. 48. . 2.106, 9.115
—— v. Templeton (1896) 12 Sh.Ct.Rep. 323. . . . . 11.46, 11.84, 18.19, 21.79
Mercer v. Maxwell (1850) 12 D. 756; (1850) 22 Sc.Jur. 265. 12.09
Merchandise Funds Co. Ltd v. Maxwell, 1978 S.L.T. (Sh.Ct.) 19. . . . . 17.12
Merchants Facilities (Glasgow) Ltd v. Keenan, 1967 S.L.T. (Sh.Ct.) 65. . . . . 21.78
Meri Mate Ltd v. City of Dundee D.C., 1994 S.C.L.R. 960. 26.167
Meron v. Umland (1896) 3 S.L.T. 286. . . . . 24.06
Merrick Homes Ltd v. Duff, 1996 S.L.T. 932. . . . . 11.60, 11.65
—— v. Duff (No. 2), 1997 S.L.T. 53. . . . . 11.61, 19.64, 19.66
Merry & Cuninghame v. District Committee of Middle Ward of Lanarkshire, 1926
    S.L.T. (Sh.Ct.) 107; (1926) 43 Sh.Ct.Rep. 163. . . . . 19.06
Merson v. Coia, 1959 S.L.T. (Sh.Ct.) 33; (1958) 75 Sh.Ct.Rep. 32. . . . . 13.03, 13.07
Mess v. Mutch (1929) S.L.T. (Sh.Ct.) 22; (1928) 45 Sh.Ct.Rep. 54. . . . . 7.36
Methven Simpson Ltd v. Gray & Goskirk (1905) 22 Sh.Ct.Rep. 342. . . . . 8.59, 8.60
Metric Modules International Ltd v. Laughton Construction Co. Ltd, 1995 S.C.L.R.
    676. . . . . 11.62, 11.65
Mica Insulator Co. Ltd v. Bruce Peebles & Co. Ltd, 1907 S.C. 1293; (1907) 15
    S.L.T. 50; (1907) 44 S.L.R. 674. . . . . 19.33, 19.51, 19.52
Mickel v. McCoard, 1913 S.C. 1036; 1913 2 S.L.T. 106; (1913) 50 S.L.R. 853. . . . . . 19.33
Micosta SA v. Shetland Islands Council, 1983 S.L.T. 483. . . . . 15.54, 15.88
Microwave Systems (Scotland) Ltd v. Electro-Physiological Instruments Ltd, 1971
    S.C. 140; 1971 S.L.T. (Notes) 38. . . . . 4.31, 9.99, 9.117
Middleton v. Booth, 1986 S.L.T. 450. . . . . 23.13
—— v. Leslie (1829) 19 R. 801; (1892) 29 S.L.R. 657. . . . . . 9.82, 17.14, 21.76, 21.80, 25.28
—— v. Middleton, 1972 S.C. 188; 1972 S.L.T. (Notes) 29. . . . . 9.112
Milburn, 1946 S.C. 301. . . . . 2.21
Mill v. Fildes, 1982 S.L.T. 147. . . . . 24.06
Millar v. Millar (1907) 15 S.L.T. 205. . . . . 11.11
—— v. ——, Sh. Prin. Nicholson Edinburgh Sh.Ct., Mar. 29, 1990, unreported. . . . 18.78
—— v. ——, 1992 S.L.T. (Sh.Ct.) 69. . . . . 18.19
—— v. Mitchell (1860) 22 D. 833; (1860) 32 Sc.Jur. 346. . . . . 8.64
Millar & Lang v. Polak (1907) 14 S.L.T. 788. . . . . 11.15
—— v. Poole (1907) 15 S.L.T. 76. . . . . 11.15, 29.27
Millars of Falkirk v. Turpie, 1976 S.L.T. (Notes) 66. . . . . 18.104
Miller v. Campbell's Trs 1965 S.L.T. (Notes) 57. . . . . 14.65
—— v. Chapelside Chemical Co. (1887) 3 Sh.Ct.Rep. 83. . . . 1.24, 4.119, 7.01, 8.06, 14.03
—— v. Chief Constable of Strathclyde Police, Kilmarnock Sh.Ct., Jan. 27, 1978,
    unreported. 26.183
—— v. McCallum (1840) 3 D. 65; (1840) 16 Fac. 17. . . . . 18.04
—— v. Mac Fisheries, 1922 S.C. 157; 1922 S.L.T. 94; (1922) 59 S.L.R. 182. . 2.110, 2.111,
                                                                                                                            10.25
—— v. McLean (1831) 9 S. 923. . . . . 11.29
—— v. McPhun (1895) 22 R. 600; (1895) 3 S.L.T. 6; (1895) 32 S.L.R. 471. . . . . 14.68
—— v. National Coal Board, 1960 S.C. 376; 1961 S.L.T. 77. . . . . 6.06, 10.35, 12.57
—— v. Smith (J.M.) Ltd (1908) 16 S.L.T. 268. . . . . 11.54
—— v. South of Scotland Electricity Board, 1958 S.C.(H.L.) 20; 1958 S.L.T.. . . . . . . 9.33
—— v. Wilson (1749) Mor. 15148. . . . . 24.15
Miller (Christie) v. Bain (1879) 6 R. 1215. . . . . 21.98
Miller & Son v. Oliver & Boyd (1906) 8 F. 390. . . . . 2.101, 2.105
Miller Group (The) Ltd v. Tasker, 1993 S.L.T. 207. . . . . 23.40
Miller (James N.) & Sons v. Anderson, 1991 S.C.L.R. 407. . . . . 19.18
Miller, Peel, Hughes, Rutherford & Co. v. Forrester (1897) 5 S.L.T. 71. . . . . 4.41
Milligan v. Tinne's Trs, 1971 S.L.T. (Notes) 64. . . . . 19.44, 19.45, 19.47, 19.52
Millom and Askam Hematite Co. v. Simpson (1897) 14 Sh.Ct.Rep. 206; (1897) 5
    S.L.T. 196. . . . . 18.30, 18.55
Mills v. Allen [1953] 2 Q.B. 341; [1953] 3 W.L.R. 356; [1953] 2 All E.R. 634. . . . . . 26.269
Milmor Properties Ltd v. W. and T. Investment Co. Ltd, 1999 S.C.L.R. 910 (Notes);
    2000 S.L.T. (Sh.Ct.) 2. . . . . 30.05
Miln v. Mudie (1828) 6 S. 967. . . . . 2.02
Miln's Judicial Factor v. Spence's Trs, 1929 S.L.T. 279; 1929 S.N. 49. . . . . 19.45, 19.46
Milne v. Birrell (1902) 4 F. 879. . . . . 11.40
—— v. Darroch (1937) 53 Sh.Ct.Rep. 3. . . . . 23.13
—— v. Milne, 1994 S.C.L.R. 437. . . . . 23.42, 23.43
—— v. Wakelin, 1933 S.L.T. 274. . . . . 15.57
Milne & Co. v. Aberdeen District Committee (1899) 2 F. 220. . . . . 9.12, 9.30
Milne Home v. Dunse Police Commissioners (1882) 9 R. 924. . . . . 19.14

Minister of Pensions v. Higham [1948] 2 K.B. 153; [1948] All E.R. 863; [1948]
    L.J.R. 1438. . . . . 18.08
Minister of Social Security v. Connolly, 1967 S.L.T. 121. . . . . 4.68
Mintons v. Mawley & Co. (1882) 20 S.L.R. 126. . . . . 19.53
Miro Windows v. Mrugala, 1992 S.L.T. (Sh.Ct.) 66. . . . . 18.19
Mitchell (1893) 20 R. 902; (1893) 1 S.L.T. 105; (1893) 30 S.L.R. 801. . . . . . . 25.04, 25.05
—— v. Aberdeen Insurance Committee, 1918 S.C. 415; 1918 1 S.L.T. 316; (1918)
    55 S.L.R. 376. . . . . 9.47, 9.119
—— v. Baird (1902) 4 F. 809; (1902) 10 S.L.T. 119; (1902) 39 S.L.R. 682. . . . 9.94, 19.03
—— v. Grierson (1894) 21 R. 367; (1874) 1 S.L.T. 448; (1874) 31 S.L.R. 301. . . . . . . 4.38
—— v. HAT Contracting Services Ltd (No. 3), 1993 S.L.T. 1196. . . . . 21.28
—— v. Laing, 1998 S.L.T. 203. . . . . 21.33
—— v. Mitchell, 1954 S.L.T. (Sh.Ct.) 45; (1954) 70 Sh.Ct.Rep. 127. . . . . . . 15.102, 28.108
—— v. Redpath Engineering Ltd, 1990 S.L.T. 259; 1988 S.C.L.R. 581. . . . . 14.57
—— v. Sellar, 1915 S.C. 360; 1915 1 S.L.T. 128; 1915 52 S.L.R. 300. . . . . 10.25
Mitchell & Mitchell, 1992 S.C.L.R. 252. . . . . 22.29
Mitchell Construction Co. (Scotland) Ltd v. Brands Transport and Demolitions Ltd
    1975 S.L.T. (Notes) 58. . . . . 1.40, 5.98, 9.67, 18.05
Mitchell's Trs v. Aspin, 1971 S.L.T. 29; affd, 1971 S.L.T. 166. . . . . 2.107
Mitchell-Gill v. Buchanan, 1921 S.C. 390; 1921 1 S.L.T. 197; (1921) 58 S.L.R. 371. . 26.11
Mitchells v. Nicoll (1890) 17 R. 795. . . . . 14.37
Moffat v. Marconi Space and Defence Systems Ltd, 1975 S.L.T. (Notes) 60. . . . . . . 9.112
Mohammed v. Mohammed, 1954 S.L.T. (Sh.Ct.) 93. . . . . 9.22, 9.26
Moncrieff v. Waugh (1859) 21 D. 216. . . . . 2.123
Monklands D.C. v. Baird, 1987 S.C.L.R. 88. . . . . 13.47, 30.31
Monkman v. Monkman, 1988 S.L.T. (Sh.Ct.) 37. . . . . 18.35
Montecchi Shimco (U.K.) Ltd [1979] W.L.R. 1180; (1978) 123 S.J. 55. . . . . 12.36
Montefiore v. Mendav Motor Components Ltd [1918] 2 K.B. 241; [1918.1919] All
    E.R. Rep. 1188; (1918) 62 S.J. 585. . . . . 2.12
Montgomerie v. AB (1845) 7 D. 553; (1845) 17 Sc.Jur. 272. . . . . 15.72, 15.76
Montgomery v. Zarifi, 1917 S.C. 62; affd, 1918 S.C.(H.L.) 128; 1916 2 S.L.T. 232;
    1918 2 S.L.T. 110; (1918) 55 S.L.R. 597. . . . . 2.92
Montgomery (Thomas) & Sons v. W.B. Anderson & Sons Ltd, 1979 S.L.T. 101. . . . . . 4.85
Montrose Mags v. Birnie (1829) 8 S. 108. . . . . 21.95
Moodie v. Dempster, 1931 S.C. 553; 1931 S.L.T. 324; 1931 S.W. 35. . . . . 4.07, 4.28, 12.13
—— v. Maclean, 1981 S.L.T. (Notes) 53. . . . . 21.22, 21.26
Moore v. Electoral Registration Officer, 1980 S.L.T. (Sh.Ct.) 39. . . . . 26.117
—— v. Greater Glasgow Health Board, 1978 S.C. 123; 1979 S.L.T. 42. . . . . . . 15.58, 15.89
—— v. Harland & Wolff, 1937 S.C. 707; 1937 S.L.T. 603; 1937 S.N. 65. . . . . 16.76
—— v. Secretary of State for Scotland, 1985 S.L.T. 38. 2.19, 4.120
—— v. Stephen & Sons, 1954 S.C. 331; 1954 S.L.T. 289. . . . . 8.58
Moran v. King, 1975 S.L.T. (Notes) 77. . . . . 10.20
More v. Brown & Root Wimpey Highland Fabricators Ltd, 1983 S.L.T. 669. . . . . . . 15.54
Moreton v. McDonald (1849) 11 D. 1417; (1849) 21 Sc.Jur. 540. . . . . 15.22
Morgan v. Morgan, 1998 S.C.L.R. 681. . . . . 22.38
Morgan, Gellibrand & Co. v. Dundee Gem Line S.S. Co. Ltd (1890) 18 R. 205;
    (1890) 28 S.L.T. 171. . . . . 10.29
Moriarty v. Evans Medical Supplies Ltd [1958] 1 W.L.R. 66; [1957] 3 All E.R. 718;
    [1957] (102) S.J. 67. . . . . 18.13
Morley v. Jackson (1888) 16 R. 78; (1888) 26 S.L.R. 52. . . . . 10.04
Morran v. Glagow Council of Tenants' Associations, 1994 S.C.L.R. 1065. . . . . . 5.95, 8.34,
    14.06, 18.56
Morris v. Goldrich, 1953 S.L.T. (Sh.Ct.) 43; (1953) 69 Sh.Ct.Rep. 169. . . . . 15.28
—— v. Morris, 1993 S.C.L.R. 144. . . . . 2.58
Morison (Alex) & Co. v. McCulloch, 1984 S.L.T. (Sh.Ct.) 88. . . . . 21.73
Morrison v. Barton (No. 2), 1994 S.L.T. 685. . . . . 14.31, 14.53
—— v. J. Kelly and Sons Ltd, 1970 S.C. 65; 1970 S.L.T. 198. . . . . 18.106
—— v. Kirk, 1912 S.C. 44; 1911 2 S.L.T. 355; (1911) 49 S.L.R. 36. . . . . 23.38
—— v. Lipp's Exrs, 1947 S.L.T. (Notes) 59. . . . . 8.64
—— v. McArdle, 1967 S.L.T. (Sh.Ct.) 58. . . . . 9.111
—— v. Morrison's Exrx, 1912 S.C. 892; 1912 1 S.L.T. 384; (1912) 49 S.L.R. 578. . . 4.105,
    11.65
—— v. Panic Link Ltd, 1994 S.L.T. 232; 1993 S.C. 631; 1993 S.L.T. 602; 1993
    S.C.L.R. 386. . . . . 2.89, 2.103, 3.52
—— v. Ramsay (1948) 64 Sh.Ct.Rep. 160. . . . . 13.34
—— v. Scotstoun Marine Ltd, 1979 S.L.T. (Notes) 76. . . . . 10.33
—— v. Smith (1876) 4 R. 9; (1876) 14 S.C.R. 17. . . . . 14.12

Morrison v. Somerville (1860) 22 D. 1082. . . . . 7.09
—— v. Vallance's Exrs, 1907 S.C. 999; (1907) 15 S.L.T. 206; (1907) 44 S.L.R. 790. . 6.04,
 6.20
—— v. Waters & Co. (1906) 8 F. 867; (1906) 14 S.L.T. 127. . . . . 14.57
Morrison's Associated Cos Ltd v. James Rome & Sons Ltd, 1946 S.C. 160; 1964
 S.L.T. 249. . . . . 9.07, 9.28, 9.28, 10.19
Morrow v. Enterprise Sheet Metal Works (Aberdeen) Ltd, 1986 S.L.T. 697. . . . . . . 17.05
—— v. Neil, 1975 S.L.T. (Sh.Ct.) 65. . . . . 24.03, 24.04, 24.05
Mortensen v. Peters (1906) 5 Adam 121; (1906) 8 F.(J.) 93; (1906) 14 S.L.T. 227;
 (1906) 43 S.L.R. 872. . . . . 2.02
Morton v. Liddle, 1996 J.C. 194; 1996 S.L.T. 1143. 24.03, 24.04
—— v. O'Donnell, 1979 S.L.T. (Notes) 26. . . . . 14.48, 14.60, 14.61
—— v. Smith (1902) 9 S.L.T. 396. . . . . 11.37, 11.69, 11.70, 11.78
Morton (Earl of) v. Fleming, 1921 1 S.L.T. 205. . . . . 15.53, 15.62
Morton's (Earl of) Trs v. Fife C.C. (1952) 68 Sh.Ct.Rep. 97. . . . . 26.89
Moss v. Penman, 1994 S.C. 41; 1994 S.L.T. 19; 1993 S.C. 300; 1993 S.C.L.R. 374. . . 24.09
Moss' Empires v. Assessor for Glasgow, 1917 S.C.(H.L.) 1; 1916 2 S.L.T. 215 (1916)
 54 S.L.R. 12. . . . . 18.92, 25.35
Motordrift A/S v. Trachem Co. Ltd, 1982 S.L.T. 127. . . . . 2.99, 2.101, 13.72
Motor Plants Ltd v. D. Stewart & Co. Ltd, 1909 1 S.L.T. 478. . . . . 11.45, 11.58
Moubray's Trs v. Moubray (1883) 10 R. 460. . . . . 2.129, 5.86
Mouland v. Ferguson, 1979 S.L.T. (Notes) 85. . . . . 21.36
Mountstar Metal Corporation Ltd v. Cameron, 1987 S.L.T. (Sh.Ct.) 106. . . . . 23.30
Mowat v. Kerr, 1977 S.L.T. (Sh.Ct.) 62. . . . . 11.30, 11.32, 11.33, 18.11, 25.38
Mowatt v. Shore Porters Society, 1965 S.L.T. (Notes) 10. . . . . 10.37
Mowbray v. D.C. Thomson Co. Ltd. 1996 S.L.T. 846. . . . . 18.70
Mowbray v. Secretary of State, 1992 S.L.T. (Sh.Ct.) 84; 1992 S.C.L.R. 328; 1991
 S.C.L.R. 328. . . . . 15.65, 18.42
—— v. Secretary of State for Scotland, 1998 Civ. Pract. B., 20.11. . . . . 18.70
—— v. Valentine, 1998 S.C.L.R. 305. . . . . 2.130
Moyes v. Burntisland Shipping Co., 1952 S.C. 429; 1952 S.L.T. 417. . . 10.28, 10.29, 11.89
Muir v. Barr (1849) 11 D. 487. . . . . 14.22, 14.24
—— v. Chief Constable of Edinburgh, 1961 S.L.T. (Sh.Ct.) 41; (1961) 77
 Sh.Ct.Rep. 30. . . . . 25.46
—— v. Glasgow Corporation, 1917 2 S.L.T. 106. . . . . 4.35, 12.15
—— v. ——, 1955 S.L.T. (Sh.Ct.) 23; (1954) 71 Sh.Ct.Rep. 48. . . . . . . 25.01, 25.14, 25.20
—— v. Milligan (1868) 6 M. 1125; (1868) 40 Sc.Jur. 631. . . . . 2.19, 5.91
—— v. Milne, Paisley Sh.Ct., June 7, 1984, unreported. 14.12
—— v. More Nisbett (1881) 19 S.L.R. 59. . . . . 11.07
—— v. Muir (1906) 8 F. 365; (1906) 13 S.L.T. 658; (1906) 43 S.L.R. 240. . . . . 2.101
—— v. ——, 1994 S.C.L.R. 182. . . . . 1.23
—— v. National Bank Ltd (1943) 59 Sh.Ct.Rep. 51. . . . . 6.15, 9.49, 9.105
—— v. Stevenson (1850) 12 D. 512. . . . . 4.125
Muir & Rutherford (1933) 49 Sh.Ct.Rep. 214. . . . . 12.19
Muir & Son v. Robert Muir & Co. Ltd, 1910 1 S.L.T. 414. . . . . 9.96
Muir & Weir v. Petrie (1910) 22 Sh.Ct.Rep. 151. . . . . 6.09, 25.19
Muir (Malcolm) Ltd v. Jamieson, 1947 S.C. 314. . . . . 2.106
Muir's Sequestration (1911) 27 Sh.Ct.Rep. 327. . . . . 6.15, 9.105
Muirhead v. Advocate (H.M.), 1983 S.L.T. 545; 1983 S.C.C.R. 133. . . . . 15.31
—— v. Douglas, 1979 S.L.T. (Notes) 17. . . . . 2.19, 5.91
—— v. Gilmour, 1909 1 S.L.T. 235; (1909) 46 S.L.R. 425. . . . . 2.34
—— v. Miller (1877) 4 R. 1139; (1877) 14 S.L.R. 425. . . . . 11.15
Muldoon v. Carntyne Steel Castings Co. Ltd, 1965 S.L.T. (Notes) 63. . 10.05, 10.06, 10.18
Mullan v. Anderson, 1993 S.L.T. 835; 1993 S.C.L.R. 506. . . . . 5.03, 13.59, 30.29
Mullen v. Harmac Ltd, 1993 S.C. 643; 1994 S.L.T. 926. . . . . 7.29
Mulvenna v. The Admiralty, 1926 S.C. 854. . . . . 29.29
Mulvey v. Mulvey (1922) 39 Sh.Ct.Rep. 256. . . . . 18.10, 18.37
Munn v. Macgregor (1854) 16 D. 385; (1854) 26 Sc.Jur. 182. . . . . 15.21
Munro v. Anderson-Grice Engineering Co. Ltd, 1983 S.L.T. 295. . . . . 10.41
—— v. Liquidator of Balnagown Estates Co., 1949 S.C. 49; 1949 S.L.T. 85. . 21.76, 21.80
—— v. Macdonald's Exrs (1866) 4 M. 687. . . . . 13.79
—— v. Mudie (1901) 9 S.L.T. 53. . . . . 11.54
Munro and Miller (Pakistan) v. Wyvern Structures Ltd, 1996 S.L.T. 135. . . . . 16.48
Munro's Trs v. Munro, 1971 S.C. 280; 1971 S.L.T. 313. . . . . 4.14, 4.25, 4.26
Murdison v. Scottish Football Union (1896) 23 R. 449; (1896) 3 S.L.T. 273; (1896)
 33 S.L.R. 337. . . . . 9.30, 10.29, 10.30

Murdoch v. Murdoch, 1973 S.L.T. (Notes) 73. . . . . 21.84, 21.94
—— v. Young, 1909 2 S.L.T. 450. . . . . 9.79, 11.62
Murphy v. McKeand (1866) 4 M. 444; (1866) 38 Sc.Jur. 207. . . . . 18.42
—— v. Muir, 1927 S.L.T. (Sh.Ct.) 55; (1927) 43 Sh.Ct.Rep. 235. . . . . 2.33, 19.06
—— v. Richards & Co., 1922 S.L.T. (Sh.Ct.) 135. . . . . 9.85
Murphy (S.W.) Ltd v. Alloa Town Council, 1971 S.L.T. (Sh.Ct.) 20. . . . . 26.255
Murray v. Edinburgh D.C., 1981 S.L.T. 253. . . . . 9.33
—— v. Kilmaurs Snooker Club, Kilmamock Sh.Ct., Sept. 18, 1986, unreported. . . . 11.83
—— v. Murray (1845) 7 D. 1000. . . . . 11.77
—— v. ——, 1957 S.L.T. 41; 1956 S.C. 376 (O.H.). 2.107
—— v. Nicholls, 1983 S.L.T. 194. . . . . 9.30
—— v. Rennie & Angus (1897) 24 R. 1026; (1897) 5 S.L.T. 80; (1897) 34 S.L.R.
    709. . . . . 19.33
—— v. Seath, 1939 S.L.T. 348; 1939 S.N. 49. 2.105, 2.112, 9.124
—— v. Wyllie, 1916 S.C. 356; 1916 1 S.L.T. 87; (1916) 53 S.L.R. 263. . . . . 9.36
Murray's Trs v. Trs for St Margaret's Convent (1906) 8 F. 1109; (1906) 14 S.L.T.
    307; (1906) 43 S.L.R. 774. . . . . 4.34
—— v. Wilson's Exrs, 1945 S.C. 51; 1945 S.L.T. 118; 1944 S.N. 70. . . . . 9.67, 16.23, 16.24
Murray & Cruden Ltd v. Walker, 1955 S.L.T. (Sh.Ct.) 9. . . . . 14.39
Murray (J. & C.) v. Wallace Marrs & Co., 1914 S.C. 114. . . . . 29.29
Murray Williamson Builders Ltd v. Sweets Services Ltd, 1992 S.C.L.R. 555. . . . . 19.60
Music Hire Service (Manchester) Ltd v. Roccio, 1961 S.L.T. (Notes) 13. . . . . 9.110, 10.17
Mutch v. Robertson, 1981 S.L.T. 217. . . . . 18.14
Mutual Shipping Corporation v. Bayshore Shipping Co. Ltd [1985] 1 W.L.R. 625;
    (1985) 128 S.J. 219; [1985] 1 All E.R. 520; [1985] 1 Lloyd's Rep. 189; (1985)
    82 L.S. Gaz. 1329, CA. 5.87
Myers v. Elamn [1940] A.C. 282; [1939] 4 All E.R. 484. . . . . 19.23

N (CHILD ABDUCTION: HABITUAL RESIDENCE), RE [1993] 2 F.L.R. 124. . . . . 2.58
N v. Hutcheson (1979) 39 SCOLAG 188. . . . . 2.13
NWL Ltd v. Woods [1979] 1 W.L.R. 1294. . . . . 21.91
Naim v. S.E. Lancashire Insurance Co., 1930 S.C. 606; 930 S.L.T. 458; 1930 S.N.
    36. . . . . 4.113
Naim Bros v. Robertson, 1954 S.L.T. (Sh.Ct.) 44; (1954) 70 Sh.Ct.Rep. 166. . . . . . . 19.55
Nakeski-Cumming v. Gordon's Judicial Factor, 1923 S.C. 770; 1923 S.L.T. 482;
    (1923) 60 S.L.R. 486. . . . . 11.64
Napier v. Leith (1860) 22 D. 1262. . . . . 15.39
Napier Co. (Arbroath) Ltd v. S.M. Frangos, 1995 S.C.L.R. 804. . . . . 10.06
Napier (N.G.) Ltd v. Corbett (1959) 79 Sh.Ct.Rep. 23. . . . . 13.79
National Bank v. McQueen (1881) 18 S.L.R. 683. . . . . 29.18
National Bank of Scotland v. MacQueen (1881) 18 S.L.R. 683. . . . . 29.29
National Bank of Scotland Nominees Ltd v. Adamson, 1932 S.L.T. 492; 1932 S.N.
    85. . . . . 12.68, 12.69
National Cash Register Co. Ltd v. Hunter (1915) 32 Sh.Ct.Rep. 121. . . . 6.04, 6.15, 9.105
National Coal Board v. Knight Bros, 1972 S.L.T. (Notes) 24. . . . . 12.48
——v. Thomson, 1959 S.C. 353; 1960 S.L.T. 89. . . . . 4.48, 24.10
National Commercial Bank of Scotland v. Assessor for Fife, 1963 S.C. 197; 1963
    S.L.T. 329. . . . . 25.17
National Exchange Co. v. Drew and Dick (1858) 20 D. 837; (1858) 30 Sc.Jur.
    484. . . . . 15.34, 15.76
Neale (F.J.) (Glasgow) Ltd v. Vickery, 1973 S.L.T. (Sh.Ct.) 88. . . . . 11.14
Nederlandse Scheepshypotheekbank v. Cam Standby Ltd, 1994 S.C.L.R. 956. . . . . . 29.28
Neil v. Edinburgh & Leith Tramways Co. (1903) 10 S.L.T. 524. . . . . 13.43
—— v. McNair (1901) 3 F.(J.) 85; (1901) 3 Adam 384; (1901) 9 S.L.T. 59; (1901) 38
    S.L.R. 804. . . . . 12.68, 12.70
—— v. South-East Lancashire Insurance Co., 1930 S.C. 629; 1930 S.L.T. 343; 1929
    S.N. 8. . . . . 11.54
Neill v. Neill [1948] C.L.Y. 4887. . . . . 21.09
—— v. Smith (1953) 70 Sh.Ct.Rep. 105. . . . . 11.78
Neill's Trs v. Macfarlane's Trs, 1952 S.C. 356; 1952 S.L.T. 369. . . . . . . 25.30, 25.41, 25.45
Neilson v. Househill Coal and Iron Co. (1842) 4 D. 1187. . . . . 9.15, 9.112
—— v. Smith (1821) Hume 31. . . . . 11.13
—— v. Wilson (1822) 1 S. 314 (N.E. 290). 11.79
—— v. —— (1890) 17 R. 608; (1890) 27 S.L.R. 505. . . . . 4.46, 4.47, 4.98
Nelson v. Cordon (1874) 1 R. 1093. . . . . 2.97
—— v. Dowden, Glasgow Sh.Ct., Oct. 20, 1981, unreported. 7.15, 21.94

Nelson v. Duraplex Industries Ltd, 1975 S.L.T. (Notes) 31. . . . . 21.21, 21.22, 21.23
—— v. Gordon (1874) 1 R. 1093; (1874) 11 S.L.R. 631. . . . . 2.97, 14.19
—— v. J. Wilson & Sons (1912) S.L.R. 90. . . . . 18.39, 18.46
Nelson, Donkin & Co. v. Browne (1876) 3 R. 810; (1876) 13 S.L.R. 523. . . . . 2.30
Nelson (Hugh) & Co. v. Glasgow Corporation, 1908 S.C. 879. . . . . 19.27
Nero v. Gunn & Cameron (1886) 2 Sh.Ct.Rep. 342. . . . . 11.68, 11.76
Neste Chemicals SA v. DK Line SA; The Sargasso [1994] 3 All E.R. 180; [1994] 2
    Lloyd's Rep. 6; *The Times*, April 4, 1994, C.A.; affirming [1993] 1 Lloyd's
    Rep. 424. . . . . 2.93
Neville v. Neville, 1924 S.L.T. (Sh.Ct.) 43; (1921) 40 Sh.Ct.Rep. 151. . . . . 21.89
New Mining and Exploring Syndicate Ltd v. Chalmers & Hunter, 1909 S.C. 1390;
    1909 2 S.L.T. 236; (1909) 46 S.L.R. 1002. . . . . 11.58, 11.61, 18.110, 18.111
Newcastle Building Society v. White, Kilmarnock Sh.Ct., May 16, 1985,
    unreported. 8.63, 18.17
Newhart Developments Ltd v. Co-operative Commercial Bank Ltd [1978] 1 Q.B.
    814; [1978] 1 W.L.R. 636; (1977) 121 S.J. 847; [1978] 2 All E.R. 896, C.A.. . . 4.89
Nicholson v. Murray (1927) 43 Sh.Ct.Rep. 108. . . . . 23.34
Nicol v. Blott, 1986 S.L.T. 677. . . . . 21.91
—— v. McIntosh, 1987 S.L.T. 104. . . . . 10.06
Nicol (D. & J.) v. Dundee Harbour Trs 1915 S.C.(H.L.) 7. . . . . 4.29, 4.30, 4.33
Nicol Homeworld Contracts Ltd v. Charles Gray Builders Ltd, 1986 S.L.T. 317. . . . . 12.42,
                                                                            12.46, 12.62
Nicoll v. Reid (1877) 5 R. 137; (1877) 15 S.L.R. 89. . . . . 4.98
Nicolson v. Johnstone (1872) 11 M. 179; (1872) 45 Sc.Jur. 110; (1872) 10 S.L.R.
    104. . . . . 16.102
—— v. Maclachlan and Brown, 1985 S.L.T. 132. . . . . 15.31
Nimmo v. Alexander Cowan & Sons, 1967 S.C.(H.L.) 79; 1967 S.L.T. 277; [1967]
    W.L.R. 1169; [1967] 3 All E.R. 187. . . . . 9.31
Nimmo's Exrs v. White's Exrs, 1976 S.L.T. 70. . . . . 12.42, 12.46
Nisbet v. Cairns (1864) 2 M. 863; (1864) 36 Sc.Jur. 423. . . . . 16.28
—— v. Macleod (1923) 39 Sh.Ct.Rep. 248. . . . . 7.30, 7.31
—— v. Marley Roof Tile Co. Ltd, 1988 S.C.L.R. 56. . . . . 21.26
—— v. Mitchell-Innes (1880) 7 R. 575; (1880) 17 S.L.R. 438. . . . . 21.95
Niven v. Clyde Fasteners Ltd, 1986 S.L.T. 344. . . . . 11.82
—— v. Holmes, 1979 S.L.T. (Sh.Ct.) 15. . . . . 14.12
—— v. Tudhope, 1982 S.C.C.R. 365. . . . . 16.78
Nivison v. Howat (1883) 11 R. 182; (1883) 21 S.L.R. 104. . . . . 12.70
Noble v. Magistrates of Inverness (1825) 3 S. 516 (N.E. 358). 12.19, 12.20
—— v. Noble, 1921 1 S.L.T. 57. . . . . 11.11, 11.29, 11.32
—— v. ——, 1979 S.L.T. (Notes) 75. . . . . 21.23, 21.25
—— v. ——, 1990 S.L.T. (Sh.Ct.) 15. . . . . 18.19
Nobel's Explosives Co. v. British Dominions General Insurance Co., 1919 S.C. 455;
    1919 1 S.L.T. 225; (1919) 56 S.L.R. 298. . . . . 14.30
Nordsoen, The v. Mackie, Koth & Co., 1911 S.C. 172; 1910 2 S.L.T. 292; (1910) 48
    S.L.R. 91. . . . . 11.31
Norfolk (Duke of) v. Wilson, 1950 S.L.T. (Notes) 11. . . . . 17.03, 18.98
Norris v. Norris, 1992 S.L.T. (Sh.Ct.) 51; 1992 S.C.L.R. 395. . . . . 18.02, 18.25, 22.90
Nortech v. Aeroskip Sports, 1996 S.L.T. (Sh.Ct.) 94. 14.07, 18.19
North v. Stewart (1870) 17 R.(H.L.) 60; (1890) 15 App. Cas. 452; (1890) 28 S.L.R.
    397. . . . . 3.101, 6.06, 11.25
North British Ry v. Bernards Ltd (1900) 7 S.L.T. 329. . . . . 14.66
—— v. Birrel's Trs, 1918 S.C.(H.L.) 33; 1917 2 S.L.T. 271; (1917) 55 S.L.R. 102. . . 20.01
—— v. Brown, Gordon & Co. (1857) 19 D. 840. . . . . 9.117
—— v. Carter (1870) 8 M. 998; (1870) 42 Sc.Jur. 611; (1870) 7 S.L.R. 643. . . . . 9.121
—— v. Garroway (R. & J.) (1893) 20 R. 397; (1893) 30 S.L.R. 446. . . . . 15.54, 15.74
—— v. Lanarkshire and Dumbartonshire Ry (1897) 24 R. 564; (1897) 4 S.L.T. 316;
    (1897) 34 S.L.R. 415. . . . . 2.108, 2.112
—— v. McArthur (1889) 17 R. 30; (1889) 27 S.L.R. 34. . . . . 2.29, 2.30
—— v. N.B. Grain Storage and Transit Co. (1897) 11 R. 687; (1897) S.L.T. 352;
    (1897) 34 S.L.R. 563. . . . . 13.80
—— v. Newburgh and North Fife Ry, 1911 S.C. 710; 1911 1 S.L.T. 266 (1911) 48
    S.L.R. 450. . . . . 2.100
—— v. White (1881) 9 R. 97; (1881) 19 S.L.R. 59. . . . . 11.13, 11.70
North Central Wagon & Finance Co. Ltd v. McGiffen, 1958 S.L.T. (Sh.Ct.) 62;
    (1958) 74 Sh.Ct.Rep. 204. . . . . 21.78
North of Scotland Bank Ltd v. Mackenzie, 1925 S.L.T. 352. . . . . 15.39

North-Western Salt Co. v. Electrolytic Alkali Co. [1914] A.C. 461; [1914.15] All
  E.R. Rep. 752; (1914) 58 S.J. 338. . . . . 2.12
Northamber plc v. Ian Benson (t/a Kyle Micros), 1990 S.C.L.R. 140. . . . . 3.07
Norwich Pharmacal Co. v. Commissioners of Customs and Excise [1974] A.C. 133;
  [1973] 3 W.L.R. 164; (1973) 117 S.J. 567. . . . . 4.74

OATES v. Redpath Brown & Co., 1926 S.L.T. 211; 1926 S.N. 23. . . . . 8.60
Oatman v. Provost of Magistrates Councillors of Buckhaven (1914) 30 Sh.Ct.Rep.
  258. . . . . 26.327
O'Brien v. A. Davies & Son Ltd, 1961 S.L.T. 85 (O.H.). 29.19
—— v. O'Brien (1910) 26 Sh.Ct.Rep. 268. . . . . 2.16
O'Connor v. Auld (W. G.) & Co. (Engineering) Ltd, 1970 S.L.T. (Notes) 16. . 9.22, 9.112
—— v. McRobb, 1975 S.L.T. (Sh.Ct.) 42. . . . . 17.12
O'Donnell v. Murdoch McKenzie & Co., 1966 S.C.(H.L.) 58 (revsd 1967 S.C.(H.L.)
  63). 16.84
—— v. Robertson (A. M. & G.), 1965 S.L.T. 155. . . . . 14.35, 14.68, 19.12
—— v. Wilson, 1910 S.C. 799; 1910 2 S.L.T. 3; (1910) 47 S.L.R. 707. . . . . 25.01
Officers' Superannuation and Provident Fund v. Cooper, 1976 S.L.T. (Sh.Ct.) 2. . . . 29.29
Officers of Ordnance v. Edinburgh Magistrates (1860) 22 D. 446. . . . . 4.78
—— v. McDonald (1825) 3 S. 629 (N.E. 442). 13.78
Ogilvie v. Perth Kitchen Centres Ltd, 1993 S.L.T. (Sh.Ct.) 60. . . . . 10.57
Ogston v. Stewart (1896) 23 R.(H.L.) 16; [1896] A.C. 120; (1896) 3 S.L.T. 332;
  (1896) 33 S.L.R. 516. . . . . 4.67
O'Hanlon v. John G. Stein & Co. Ltd, 1965 S.C.(H.L.) 23; 1965 S.L.T. 125; [1965] 2
  W.L.R. 496. . . . . 9.28, 10.19
O'Hare v. Reaich, 1956 S.L.T. (Sh.Ct.) 78; 1956 Sh.Ct.Rep. 21. . . . . 11.14
—— v. Western Heritable Investment Co., 1965 S.C. 97; 1965 S.L.T. 182. . . . . 10.37
O'Keefe v. Grieve's Trs, 1917 1 S.L.T. 305. . . . . 19.30, 19.31
Oliphant v. Douglas (1633) Mor. 15002. . . . . 6.24
Oliver v. Oliver, 1989 S.L.T. (Sh.Ct.) 2. . . . . 18.46
—— v. Robertson (1869) 8 M. 82; (1869) 42 Sc.Jur. 41; (1869) 7 S.L.R. 44. . . . . . . 11.66
Olsen v. Keddie, 1976 S.L.T. (Sh.Ct.) 64. . . . . 7.33, 7.35, 11.89
Ommanney v. Smith (1851) 13 D. 678; (1851) 23 Sc.Jur. 303. . . . . 2.125, 2.129
Ondix International Ltd (NV) v. James Landay Ltd, 1963 S.C. 270; 1963 S.L.T.
  (Notes) 68. . . . . 11.68, 11.69, 11.70, 11.75, 11.76, 12.39
Orchard v. South Eastern Electricity Board [1987] Q.B. 565; [1987] 2 W.L.R. 102;
  [1987] 1 All E.R. 95. . . . . 19.23
Ord v. Wright (1738) Mor. 10479. . . . . 23.44
Oriel Ltd, Re [1986] 1 W.L.R. 180; [1985] 3 All E.R. 216. . . . . 2.70
Orphanus v. Queen Mary College [1985] A.C. 761; [1985] 2 W.L.R. 703; [1985] 2
  All E.R. 241. . . . . 26.374
Orr v. Glasgow, Airdrie and Monklands Junction Ry (1857) 20 D. 327. . . . . 13.82
—— v. Metcalfe, 1973 S.C. 57; 1973 S.L.T 133. . . . . 9.93, 21.13
—— v. Smith (1891) 28 S.L.R. 589. . . . . 19.42
Orr Ewing's Trs (1884) 12 R. 343; (1885) 13 R.(H.L.) 1; (1885) 22 S.L.R. 911. . . . . . 2.92,
  12.16
Orr Pollock & Co. (Printers) Ltd v. Mulholland, 1983 S.L.T. 558. . . . . . 7.28, 8.04, 18.111
Orttewell v. Gilchrist, 1998 S.L.T. (Sh.Ct.) 63; 1998 G.W.D. 9–466. . . . . . . 18.117, 19.09
O'Sullivan v. Kerr, O.H., Lord Emslie, June 10, 1970, unreported. 9.39
Oswald v. Fairs, 1911 S.C. 257; 1911 1 S.L.T. 114; (1911) 48 S.L.R. 279. . . . 10.22, 12.67,
  12.72
Ovens & Sons v. Bo'ness Coal Gas-Light Co. (1891) 28 S.L.R. 255. . . . . 19.40
Overbury v. Peek (1863) 1 M. 1058; (1863) 35 Sc.Jur. 604. . . . . 11.67, 11.68, 11.71
Overseas League v. Taylor, 1951 S.C. 105; 1951 S.L.T. 212. . . . . 9.78
Ower v. Crichton (1902) 10 S.L.T. 279. . . . . 8.23, 14.15
Oyston v. Turnbull (1875) 13 S.L.R. 69. . . . . 4.127

P v. H.M. Advocate, 1991 S.C.C.R. 933. . . . . 16.62
—— v. Lothian R.C., 1989 S.L.T. 739; 1989 S.C. 200. . . . . 28.133, 28.166
—— v. P, 1940 S.C. 389; 1940 S.L.T. 334; 1940 S.N. 30. . . . . 14.30
P. & W. MacLellan Ltd v. Peattie's Trs (1903) 6 F. 1031. . . . . 13.21
PTKF Kordinent v. VMPTO Progress, 1994 S.L.T. 235 (O.H.). 2.89, 3.99, 3.100
Pagan & Osborne v. Haig, 1910 S.C. 341; 1910 1 S.L.T. 122; (1910) 47 S.L.R. 440. . 2.27,
  2.37, 2.38
Paisley and Barrhead District Ry v. Coats (1902) 19 Sh.Ct.Rep. 12. . . . . . . 26.347, 26.349

Paisley Parish Council v. Glasgow and Row Parish Councils, 1907 S.C. 674; (1907)
    S.C. 674; (1907) 14 S.L.T. 853; (1907) 44 S.L.R. 520. . . . .   2.29
Palmer v. S.E. Lancashire Insurance Co. Ltd, 1932 S.L.T. 68; 1931 S.N. 121. . . . . . .   2.101
Palumbo v. James Jack (Hyndford) Ltd, 1977 S.L.T. (Sh.Ct.) 95. . . . .   12.38, 18.30, 18.36,
                                                                            18.39, 18.48
Paolo v. Parias (1897) 24 R. 1030; (1897) 5 S.L.T. 93; (1897) 34 S.L.R. 780. . . . . . .   19.27
Park v. Colvilles Ltd, 1960 S.C. 143; 1960 S.L.T. 200. . . . .   19.46
—— v. Park (1876) 3 R. 850; (1876) 13 S.L.R. 550. . . . .   4.14
—— v. Wilson and Clyde Coal Co. 1929 S.C.(H.L.) 38. . . . .   1.42, 5.98
Park, Dobson & Co. v. William Taylor & son, 1929 S.C. 571; 1929 S.L.T. 415; 1929
    S.N. 59. . . . .   11.14, 29.21
Park Motors v. Blackmore, 1964 S.L.T. (Sh.Ct.) 30. . . . .   9.131
Parker v. Welsh (1894) 2 S.L.T. 122. . . . .   12.14
Parkinson (Sir Lindsary) & Co. Ltd v. Triplan [1973] 2 All E.R. 273; (1973) 117 S.J.
    146. . . . .   11.58, 11.60
Parks v. Earl of Stair (1854) 16 D. 1165. . . . .   12.11
—— v. Tayside R.C., 1989 S.L.T. 345; (*sub nom.* P v. Tayside R.C.), 1989 S.C.L.R.
    165. . . . .   15.55, 15.88
Parnell v. Walter (1889) 16 R. 917; (1889) 27 S.L.R. 1. . . . .   3.99, 11.14, 29.25
Parratt v. Ceiling Decor Ltd, 1998 S.C.L.R. 556. . . . .   19.66
Partick Town Council v. Muir & Sons (1905) 21 Sh.Ct. Rep. 196. . . . .   26.390
Paterson v. Cowan (1826) 4 S. 477 (N.E. 482); (1826) 1 Fac. 383. . . . .   11.25
—— v. Kidd's Trs (1896) 23 R. 737; (1896) 4 S.L.T. 11; (1896) 33 S.L.R. 568   5.81, 18.15
—— v. MacDonald (1880) 7 R. 958; (1880) 17 S.L.R. 659. . . . .   23.44
—— v. McDonald (1880) 7 R. 958. . . . .   2.55
—— v. Magistrates of St Andrews (1880) 7 R. 712; (1880) 17 S.L.R. 225. . . . .   14.64
—— v. Paterson (1899) 2 F. 81; (1899) 7 S.L.T. 201; (1899) 37 S.L.R. 60. . . . .   13.80
—— v. ——, 1919 1 S.L.T. 12. . . . .   15.50, 15.61
—— v. ——, 1958 S.C. 141; 1958 S.L.T. 205. . . . .   2.106, 22.48
—— v. Scottish Solicitors' Discipline Tribunal, 1984 S.L.T. 3. . . . .   9.24
—— v. United Scottish Herring Drifter Insurance Co., 1927 S.N. 75 141. . . . .   2.101
—— v. Wallace, 1909 S.C. 20; 1909 16 S.L.T. 540; (1909) 46 S.L.T. 97. . . . . . .   10.03, 10.05
—— v. Whitelaw (1899) 15 Sh.Ct. Rep. 256; (1899) 7 S.L.T. 55. . . . .   18.37
—— v. Wright (1937) 53 Sh.Ct. Rep. 108. . . . .   11.54
Paterson & Son v. McInnes (1950) 66 Sh.Ct.Rep. 226. . . . .   21.48, 21.51
Paterson & Sons v. Kit Coffee Co. Ltd. (1908) 16 S.L.T. 180. . . . .   16.24
Pathirana v. Pathirana [1967] 1 A.C. 233; [1966] 3 W.L.R. 666. . . . .   26.319
Paton v. McKnight (1897) 24 R. 554; (1897) 4 S.L.T. 331; (1897) 34 S.L.R. 445. . . .   10.31
—— v. Paton's Trs (1901) 8 S.L.T. 455. . . . .   11.54, 19.31
Pattullo v. Dundee Corporation, 1969 S.L.T. (Sh.Ct.) 31.   26.255
Paul v. Henderson (1867) 5 M. 1120; (1867) 39 Sc.Jur. 605. . . . .   13.39, 18.04
—— v. Macrae (1887) 3 Sh.Ct. Rep. 338. . . . .   7.26
Paxton v. Advocate (H.M.), 1984 S.L.T. 367. . . . .   2.19
—— v. Brown, 1908 S.C. 406; (1908) 15 S.L.T. 662; (1908) 45 S.L.R. 323. . . . .   2.19, 4.38,
                                                                            4.39, 10.10, 13.50
—— v. McKain, 1983 S.L.T. (Sh.Ct.) 88. . . . .   10.24
Paynter v. Rutherford, 1940 S.L.T. (Sh.Ct.) 18; (1939) 55 Sh.Ct.Rep. 305. . . .   26.06, 26.11
Peacock v. Sutton, 1998 G.W.D. 15–766.   14.40, 14.51, 18.117
Pearce v. Pearce, 1945 S.L.T. 17; 1944 S.N. 22. . . . .   16.41
Pearce & Co. v. Owners of S.S. "Hans Maersk", 1935 S.C. 703; 1935 S.L.T. 430;
    1935 S.N. 60. . . . .   14.68
Pearce Bros v. Irons (1869) 7 M. 571; (1869) 41 Sc.Jur. 302; (1869) 6 S.L.R. 372 . .   13.32,
                                                                            13.33
Pearson v. Educational Institute of Scotland, 1998 S.L.T. 189. . . . .   18.89
—— v. McGavin (1866) 4 M. 754. . . . .   14.12
—— v. Naydler [1977] 1 W.L.R. 899. . . . .   11.57, 11.59
Pearson and Jackson v. Alison (1871) 9 M. 473; (1871) 43 Sc.Jur. 279; (1871) 8
    S.L.R. 330. . . . .   7.24
Pease, Wrays and Trigg v. Smith & Jameson (1822) 1 S. 452 (N.E. 420). . . .   11.73, 11.77,
                                                                            11.80
Peden v. Peden, 1957 S.C. 409; 1958 S.L.T. 31. . . . .   4.67
Peel v. Drummond's Trs, 1929 S.C. 484. . . . .   4.10
Peggie v. Keddie, 1932 S.C. 721; 1932 S.L.T. 372. . . . .   14.55
Pegler v. Northern Agricultural Implement Co. (1877) 4 R. 435; (1877) 14 S.L.R.
    302. . . . .   9.22, 13.79
Peline v. Sterne (L.) & Co. Ltd (1963) 79 Sh.Ct.Rep. 136. . . . .   18.82, 18.85

Penman v. Douglas (1739) Mor. 10481. . . . . 23.44
—— v. White, 1957 S.C. 338. . . . . 8.55, 8.64
Penman & Sons v. Crawford (1903) 20 Sh.Ct.Rep. 123. . . . . 14.46
Penny v. Scott (1894) 22 R. 5; (1894) 2 S.L.T. 241; (1894) 32 S.L.R. 9. . . . . . 18.92, 25.33
Peppard & Co. Ltd v. Bogoff [1962] I.R. 180. . . . . 11.59
Percival v. Bairds & Scottish Steel Ltd, 1952 S.L.T. (Sh.Ct.) 80; (1952) 68
    Sh.Ct.Rep. 242. . . . . 9.36
Percy v. Percy, 1923 S.L.T. 295. . . . . 4.27
Performing Rights Society v. Rangers F.C. Supporters' Club, Greenock, 1974 S.C.
    49; 1974 S.L.T. 151. . . . . 18.103
Permament Houses (Holdings) Ltd v. Caledonian Properties Ltd, 1987 S.L.T. 552. . 3.101
Perman v. Binny's Trs, 1925 S.L.T. 123. . . . . 16.46
Perry v. Garner [1953] 1 Q.B. 335; [1953] 2 W.L.R. 271; [1953] 1 All E.R. 285. . . . 26.331
Perry (C.R.) Ltd v. Connell, 1981 S.L.T. (Sh.Ct.) 190. . . . . 14.39
Perry (Howard E.) & Co. Ltd v. British Railways Board [1980] 1 W.L.R. 1375. . . . . 17.29
Perth (Earl of) v. Lady Willoughby de Eresby's Trs (1875) 2 R. 538; (1877) 5
    R.(H.L.) 26; (1877) 3 App. Cas. 297. . . . . 2, 104, 2.108, 2.113
Peterhead Harbours Trs v. Chalmers, 1984 S.L.T. 130. . . . . 26.208
Petrie v. Angus (1889) 2 White 358. . . . . 2.19
—— v. Forsyth (1874) 2 R. 214; (1874) 12 S.L.R. 157. . . . . 5.83
Petroleum Industry Training Board v. Jenkins, 1982 S.L.T. (Sh.Ct.) 43. . . . . 9.93
Petty v. Harris, 1977 S.L.T. (Notes) 27. . . . . 14.18
Philip v. Gordon (1848) 11 D. 175; (1849) 21 Sc.Jur. 39. . . . . 4.125, 12.19, 19.23
—— v. Reid, 1927 S.C. 224; 1927 S.L.T. 168; 1926 S.N. 172. . . . . 14.13, 18.05
—— v. Willson, 1911 S.C. 1203; 1911 2 S.L.T. 158; (1911) 48 S.L.R. 947. . . . . 19.31
Phoenix Fireplace Builders v. McCubbin, 1953 S.L.T. (Sh.Ct.) 75; (1953) 69 Sh.Ct
    Rep. 315. . . . . 12.39
Phonographic Performance Ltd v. McKenzie, 1982 S.L.T. 272. . . . . 21.92
Phosphate Sewage Co. v. Lawson & Son's Tr. (1878) 5 R. 1125. . . . . 2.108
—— v. Molleson (1876) 3 R.(H.L.) 77; (1876) 1 App. Cas. 780. . . . . 13.71
—— v. —— (1879) 6 R.(H.L.) 113; (1879) 16 S.L.R. 822; (1879) 4 App. Cas. 801   2.110,
                                                                                        2.113
Pickard v. Pickard, 1963 S.C. 604; 1963 S.L.T. 56. . . . . 20.02
—— v. Reid, 1953 S.L.T. (Sh.Ct.) 5; (1953) 69 Sh.Ct.Rep. 63. . . . . 19.11
Picken v. Arundale & Co. (1872) 10 M. 987; (1872) 44 Sc.Jur. 568; (1872) 9 S.L.R.
    640. . . . . 8.62, 9.25
Pinkerton v. Chief Constable of Strathclyde Police, Kilmarnock Sh.Ct., Oct. 11,
    1976, unreported. 26.183
Pirie v. Collie (1851) 13 D. 841. . . . . 4.27
—— v. Leask, 1964 S.C. 103; 1964 S.L.T. 107. . . . . 10.25, 18.98
Pirie & Sons v. Kintore (1906) 8 F.(H.L.) 16; [1906] A.C. 478; (1906) 14 S.L.T. 215;
    (1906) 43 S.L.R. 838. . . . . 7.15
Pirrie v. McNeil, 1922 S.L.T. 160. . . . . 18.15
Pitoy v. Steel (1960) 76 Sh.Ct. Rep. 79. . . . . 18.85
Pittalis v. Sherefettin [1986] Q.B. 868; [1986] 2 All E.R. 227. . . . . 5.78
Plasticisers Ltd v. Stewart & Sons (Hacklemakers) Ltd, 1972 S.C. 268; 1973 S.L.T.
    58. . . . . 19.45
Plotzker v. Lucas, 1907 S.C. 315; (1907) 14 S.L.T. 67; (1907) 44 S.L.R. 245. . . . . 4.95
Po, The [1991] 2 Lloyd's Rep. 206; (1991) 135 S.J. (LB) 37; *The Times*, May 15 1991. . 3.03
Polland v. Sturrock's Exrs, 1952 S.C. 535; 1953 S.L.T. 18; 1955 S.L.T. (Notes) 77. . . 21.10
Pollard v. Galloway and Nivison (1881) 9 R. 21; (1881) 19 S.L.R. 12. . . . . 21.71
Pollich v. Heatley, 1910 S.C. 469; 1910 1 S.L.T. 203; (1910) 47 S.L.R. 402. . . . . 19.03
Pollock v. Campbell, 1962 S.L.T. (Sh.Ct.) 89; (1962) 78 Sh.Ct.Rep. 174. . . . 11.06, 26.319
—— v. Ewing (1869) 7 M. 815; (1869) 6 S.L.R. 522. 2.55, 23.44
—— v. North British Ry (1901) 3 F. 727; (1901) 8 S.L.T. 94; (1901) 37 S.L.R.
    881. . . . . 21.80, 25.28
—— v. Scott (1844) 6 D. 1297; (1844) 16 Sc.Jur. 551. . . . . 11.48
—— v. Thomson (1858) 21 D. 173; (1858) 31 Sc.Jur. 101. . . . . 2.105
Pollock & Son v. Crawford (1900) 16 Sh.Ct. Rep. 124. . . . . 19.31
Pollock, Whyte & Waddell v. Old Park Forge Ltd (1907) 15 S.L.T. 3. . . . . 11.19
Pollok v. Workman (1900) 2 F. 354. . . . . 4.40
Pollok School v. Glasgow Town Clerk, 1946 S.C. 373; 1946 S.L.T. 125, 365; 1947
    S.C. 605; 1948 S.L.T. 45. . . . . 5.86, 18.14
Pompa's Trs v. Edinburgh Magistrates, 1942 S.C. 119; 1942 S.L.T. 118. . . . . . 10.34, 10.35
Ponton's Exrs v. Ponton, 1913 S.C. 598; 1913 1 S.L.T. 182; (1913) 50 S.L.R. 412. . . 9.119
Poor Clares Colletines (Edinburgh Trs for the Religious Community of) v. Burns,
    1939 S.L.T. (Sh.Ct.) 2. . . . . 4.103

Poorcock v. Sutton, 1998 G.W.D. 15–766. . . . . 18.17
Port Glasgow Property Investment Co. v. Port Glasgow Mags (1909) 25 Sh.Ct.Rep.
    86. . . . . 25.08
Porteous v. Cordiners of Glasgow (1830) 8 S. 908; (1830) 5 Fac. 742. . . . . 2.42
—— v. Pearl Life Assurance Co. (1901) 8 S.L.T. 430. . . . . 11.56
—— v. Rutherford, 1980 S.L.T. (Sh.Ct.) 129. . . . . 24.03
Porter v. Feudenherg [1915] 1 K.B. 857; [1914.15] All E.R. 918. . . . . 4.03
Porter Speirs (Leicester) Ltd v. Cameron [1950] C.L.Y. 5329. . . . . 11.45
Porterfield v. Stewart (1821) 1 S. 9 (N.E. 6). 2.129
Portland (Duke of) v. Wood's Trs, 1926 S.C. 640; 1927 S.C.(H.L.) 1; 1926 S.L.T.
    417; 734; 1926 S.N. 62, 140. . . . . 10.24, 18.50
Portobello (Magistrates of) v. Magistrates of Edinburgh (1882) 10 R. 130. . . 18.11, 25.37,
                                                                     25.38, 25.41
Postel Properties Ltd v. Miller & Santhouse plc, 1993 S.L.T. 353; 1992 S.C.L.R.
    799. . . . . 21.75
Potter v. Hamilton (1870) 8 M. 1064; (1870) 42 Sc.Jur. 625. 11.56
—— v. McCulloch, 1987 S.L.T. 308. . . . . 21.30, 21.31
Potter & Co. v. Braco de Prata Printing Co. Ltd (1891) 18 R. 511. . . . . 9.33
Pow v. Pow, 1987 S.L.T. 127. . . . . 11.11, 11.36
Powell v. Long (1896) 23 R. 955; (1896) 4 S.L.T. 70; (1896) 33 S.L.R. 693. . . . . 11.54
Pragnell-O'Neill v. Lady Skiffington, 1984 S.L.T. 282. . . . . 16.76
Prawdzic-Lazarska v. Prawdzic-Lazarski, 1954 S.C. 98; 1954 S.L.T. 41. . . . . 9.18
Prentice v. Chalmers, 1985 S.L.T. 168. . . . . 9.33, 21.36
Prestwick Investment Trust v. Jones, 1981 S.L.T. (Sh.Ct.) 55. . . . . 23.03, 23.30, 26.98
Price v. Fernando, 1995 S.C.L.R. 23. . . . . 5.95, 8.34, 14.06, 14.09, 30.261
Primrose, Thomson & Co. v. Crawford (1911) 29 Sh.Ct.Rep. 243. . . . . 7.24
Prince v. Secretary of State for Scotland, 1985 S.C. 8; 1985 S.L.T. 74. . . . . 13.69
Pringle v. Bremner and Stirling (1867) 5 M.(H.L.) 55. . . . . 9.33, 9.67
Prise v. Aberdeen Licensing Court, 1974 S.L.T. (Sh.Ct.) 48. . . . . 25.09, 25.11
Pritchard, decd., *Re* [1963] Ch. 502; [1963] Ch. 502; [1963] 2 W.L.R. 685; [1963] 1
    All E.R. 873; (1963) 107 S.J. 154. . . . . 9.41
Professional and Civil Service Supply Association Ltd v. Lawson, 1913 2 S.L.T. 55   11.55
Project Contract Services Ltd v. Fraoli, 1980 S.C. 261; 1980 S.L.T. (Notes) 101. . . . . 5.87,
                                                                    7.15, 17.19
Property Managers & Factors (Edinburgh) Ltd v. Federal Republic of Nigeria,
    Edinburgh Sh.Ct., Aug. 22, 1983, unreported. 2.17, 4.04
Property and Reversionary Investment Corporation Ltd v. Secretary of State for the
    Environment [1975] 1 W.L.R. 1504; [1975] 2 All E.R. 436; (1975) 119 S.J.
    274. . . . . 19.20
Pryde v. Proctor and Gamble Ltd, 1971 S.L.T. (Notes) 18. . . . . 9.18
Public Utilities Commission of D.C. v. Pollak (1952) 343 U.S. 451. . . . . 2.128
Pugh v. Duke of Leeds (1777) 2 Cowp. 714. . . . . 6.13
Purdie v. Kincaid & Co. Ltd, 1959 S.L.T. (Sh.Ct.) 64; (1959) 75 Sh.Ct.Rep. 100. . . . 14.04
—— v. William Allan & Sons, 1949 S.C. 477; 1950 S.L.T. 29. . . . . 18.116
Purryag v. Greater Glasgow Health Board, 1996 S.L.T. 794 (O.H.). 21.36
Purves v. Block (1867) 5 M. 1003. . . . . 2.29, 2.31
—— v. Graham, 1924 S.C. 477; 1924 S.L.t. 446; (1924) 61 S.L.R. 360. . . . . 25.19
—— v. North British Ry (1840) 10 D. 853. . . . . 13.71
—— v. Strathclyde Industrial Services, Dumbarton Sh.Ct., Oct. 21, 1983, unre-
    ported. 7.33, 7.37
Purvis v. Douwie (1869) 7 M. 764; (1869) 41 Sc.Jur. 396. . . . . 12.24

Quinn v. Bowie (No. 2), 1987 S.L.T. 576; 1987 S.C.L.R. 592. . . . . 14.40
—— v. Cameron & Robertson, 1956 S.C. 244; 1957 S.C.(H.L.) 22; 1957 S.L.T. 2,
    143. . . . . 9.112
—— v. Gardner & Sons Ltd (1888) 15 R. 776. . . . . 13.28
—— v. Lees, 1994 S.C.C.R. 159. . . . . 16.62
—— v. Peacock & Co. (1916) 33 Sh.Ct.Rep. 205. . . . . 2.76

R (Wardship: Child Abduction), Re [1993] 1 Fam. 249. . . . . 2.58
R v. O, unreported. 28.114
—— v. Acton Crown Court, ex p. Varney [1984] Crim.L.R. 638. . . . . 26.183
—— v. Bellamy [1986] Crim. L.R. 54. . . . . 16.62
—— v. Bono (1913) 29 T.L.R. 635. . . . . 15.95
—— v. Denbigh Justices, ex p. Williams [1974] Q.B. 759; [1974] 3 W.L.R. 45; 118
    S.J. 478 [1974] 2 All E.R. 1052; [1974] Crim L.R. 442, D.C.. . . . . 5.19

R v. Dunmow Justices, ex p. Anderson [1964] 1 W.L.R. 1039; [1964] 2 All E.R. 943. . . . . .
26.14
—— v. Goldstein [1983] 1 W.L.R. 151; [1983] 1 All E.R. 434; (1983) 126 S.J. 84;
(1983) Crim. L.R. 249. . . . . 13.11
—— v. Governor of Brixton Prison, ex. p. Walsh [1985] A.C. 154; [1984] 3 W.L.R.
205; [1984] 2 All E.R. 609; (1984) 128 S.J. 482. . . . . 16.16
—— v. Grossman (1981) 73 Cr.App. 302; [1981] Crim. L.R. 396. . . . . 15.94
—— v. Guildhall Magistrates' Ct., ex p. Jarret-Thorpe [1977] C.L.Y. 1993; *The
Times*, Oct. 6, 1977. . . . . 4.05
—— v. Hayes (1976) 64 Cr.App.R. 194; [1977] 1 W.L.R. 234; [1977] 2 All E.R.
288. . . . . 16.62
—— v. Immigration Appeal Tribunal, ex p. Weerasuriya [1983] 1 All E.R. 195;
[1982] Imm. A.R. 23. . . . . 25.11
—— v. Liverpool JJ., *ex p.* Topping [1983] 1 W.L.R. 119; [1983] 1 All E.R. 490. . . . 2.128
—— v. Lothian R.C., 1987 S.C.L.R. 362. . . . . 18.113, 28.133
—— v. Marlborough St. Stipendiary Magistrate, ex p. Simpson (1980) 70 Cr.App.R.
291; [1980] Crim. L.R. 305. . . . . 15.95
—— v. Secretary of State for Foreign and Commonwealth Affairs, ex p. Trawnik
[1986] *The Times*, Feb. 21; [1986] C.L.Y. 950. 4.53
—— v. Secretary of State for the Home Department, ex p. Greenwood, [1986] *The
Times*, Aug. 2. . . . . 16.16
—— v. Secretary of State for the Home Department, ex p. Kirkwood [1984] 1
W.L.R. 913. . . . . 4.59
—— v. Waterfield [1975] 1 W.L.R. 711; (1975) 119 S.J. 300; [1975] 2 All E.R. 40. . . 5.26
—— v. Westminster City Council, ex p. Residents' Association of Mayfair [1991]
C.O.D. 182. . . . . 11.57
RHM Bakeries (Scotland) Ltd v. Strathclyde R.C., 1985 S.L.T. 3. . . . . 9.113
Rackstraw v. Douglas, 1919 S.C. 354; 1919 1 S.L.T. 158; (1919) 56 S.L.R. 253. . . . 10.09
Radford & Bright Ltd v. D.M. Stevenson & Co. (1904) 6 F. 429; (1904) 11 S.L.T.
695; (1904) 41 S.L.R. 330. . . . . 11.33
Rae v. Calor Gas Ltd, 1995 S.L.T. 244; 1995 S.C.L.R. 261 (I.H.). 6.25
—— v. Rae, Glasgow Sh.Ct., Jan. 26, 1984, unreported. 10.06
—— v. ——, 1991 S.L.T. 454; 1991 S.C.L.R. 188 (Ex Div.); reversing 1990 S.C.L.R.
543 (Sh.Ct.). 13.67, 23.37, 23.42
—— v. Swanson (1905) 21 Sh.Ct.Rep. 291; (1905) 13 S.L.T. 424. . . . . 4.43
Rae Associates v. Sneddon, Edinburgh Sh.Ct., Apr. 12, 1983, unreported. 19.50
Raes v. Meek (1889) 16 R.(H.L.) 31; (1889) 27 S.L.R. 8; (1889) 14 App. Cas. 558. . . 4.33
Rafferty v. Weir Housing Corporation Ltd, 1966 S.L.T. (Notes) 23. . . . . 10.19
Railton v. Jacques (1834) 13 S. 26. . . . . 10.44
—— v. Mathews and Leonard (1844) 6 D. 1348; (1844) 16 Sc.Jur. 576. . . . . 11.68, 11.71,
11.76
Raimes, Clark & Co. v. Swan's Tr. (1902) 10 S.L.T. 316. . . . . 2.29
Rainsford-Hannay v. Smith, 1934 S.L.T. 491; 1934 S.N. 93. . . . . 16.97
Raiston v. Jackson, 1994 S.L.T. 771. . . . . 23.37
Ram v. Yadh, Glasgow Sh.Ct., Mar. 5, 1982, unreported. 7.33, 7.38, 18.08
Ramsay v. McLaren, 1936 S.L.T. 35; 1935 S.N. 108. . . . . 4.77
—— v. Shaw [1949] C.L.Y. 4626. . . . . 18.30
Ramsay's Trs v. Souter (1864) 2 M. 891. . . . . 14.33, 14.35, 14.43, 14.46, 14.60
Rank Leisure Services Ltd v. Motherwell and Wishaw Burgh Licensing Court, 1976
S.L.T. (Sh.Ct.) 70. . . . . 25.08, 25.09, 25.11, 25.24, 25.33, 26.43
Ranken v. Nolan (1842) 4 D. 832. . . . . 11.70
—— v. Ranken, 1971 S.L.T. (Notes) 55. . . . . 18.35
Rankin v. Waddell, 1949 S.C. 555; 1949 S.L.T. 433. . . . . 14.55
Rankine (1821) 1 S. 118 (N.E. 117). 4.14
—— v. Roberts (1873) 1 R. 225; (1873) 11 S.L.R. 89. . . . . 16.91
Ransohoff & Wissler v. Burrell (1897) 25 R. 284; (1897) 35 S.L.R. 229. . . . . 2.101
Raphael v. Wilcon Homes Northern, 1994 S.C.L.R. 940 (O.H.). 2.100
Rattray v. Rattray (1897) 25 R. 315; (1897) 5 S.L.T. 245; (1897) 35 S.L.R. 294. . . . 15.105
Ratty v. Hughes, 1996 S.C.L.R. 160. . . . . 7.28, 7.37
Ravelston S.S. Co. v. Sieberg Bros, 1946 S.C. 349; 1946 S.L.T. 375; 1946 S.N. 51. . . 16.41
—— v. ——, 1947 S.L.T. (Notes) 12. . . . . 14.04
Rawlings v. General Trading Co. [1921] 1 K.B. 635; [1921] W.N. 23. . . . . 2.12
Rayment v. Jack, 1988 S.L.T. 647; 1988 S.C.L.R. 535. . . . . 7.29
Rayner (J.H.) Ltd v. Dept of Trade [1989] Ch. 72. 4.06
Reavis v. Clan Line Steamers, 1926 S.C. 215; 1926 S.L.T. 68; 1925 S.N. 151. . . . . . 15.47
Rediffusion Ltd v. McIlroy, 1986 S.L.T. (Sh.Ct.) 33. . . . . 30.329
Redman v. McRae, 1991 S.L.T. 785. . . . . 21.28, 21.36

Redpath v. McCall, 1963 S.L.T. (Sh.Ct.) 47; (1963) 79 Sh.Ct.Rep. 182............ 9.114
Redpath Dorman Long Ltd v. Cummins Engine Co. Ltd, 1981 S.C. 370; 1982 S.L.T.
    489.. 10.23
—— v. Tarmac Construction Ltd, 1982 S.C. 14; 1982 S.L.T. 442....... 2.100, 2.101, 9.67
Reed Stenhouse (U.K.) Ltd v. Brodie, 1986 S.L.T. 354......................... 21.89
Rees v. Lowe, 1990 S.L.T. 507; 1990 J.C. 96; 1989 S.C.C.R. 664................ 16.62
Reeve v. Dykes (1829) 7 S. 632; (1829) 1 Sc.Jur. 183......................... 19.32
Rehman v. Ahmad, 1993 S.L.T. 741... 24.07
Reiach v. Sinclair, 1954 S.L.T. (Sh.Ct.) 71.................................. 7.32
Reid v. Advocate (H.M.), 1984 S.L.T. 391; 1984 S.C.C.R. 153............. 18.50, 18.51
—— v. Clark, 1914 2 S.L.T. 68.. 6.46
—— v. Edinburgh Acoustics (No. 2), 1995 S.L.T. 982; 1995 S.C.L.R. 791......... 19.23
—— v. Henderson (1841) 3 D, 1102... 13.36
—— v. Mitchell (1899) 16 Sh.Ct.Rep. 61...................................... 21.92
—— v. Moore (1893) 20 R. 712... 9.30
—— v. North Isles District Committee of Orkney C.C., 1912 S.C. 627; 1912 1 S.L.T.
    310; (1912) 49 S.L.R. 511........................... 12.24, 12.26, 19.06, 19.61
—— v. Plant Welding Equipment Ltd, 1980 S.L.T. (Notes) 7... 21.21, 21.22, 21.23, 21.26
—— v. Reid (1839) 1 D. 400.. 4.07
—— v. Russell, 1971 S.L.T. (Sh.Ct.) 15..................................... 16.47
—— v. Smart (J.) & Co. Ltd, 1981 S.L.T. (Notes) 20......................... 21.22
—— v. Tudhope, 1986 S.L.T. 136; 1985 S.C.C.R. 268.......................... 2.09
Reidford v. Liston, 1931 S.L.T. 418; 1931 S.N. 76.......................... 23.41
Reilly v. Doocey, 1951 S.L.T. (Notes) 54................................... 19.23
—— v. Smith (1904) 6 F. 662; (1904) 12 S.L.T. 46; (1904) 41 S.L.R. 516........... 4.43
Reilly Glen & Co. v. Beaton, 1964 S.L.T. (Sh.Ct.) 73............... 8.05, 8.06, 14.03
Rellis v. Hart, 1993 S.L.T. 738.. 2.58
Renfrew and Brown v. Magistrates of Glasgow (1861) 13 D. 1003.... 11.67, 11.69, 11.73
Renfrew D.C. v. Gray, Paisley Sh.Ct., Oct. 2, 1985, unreported................. 30.332
Rennie (1849) 11 D. 1021... 4.27
—— v. Campbell Bros, 1929 S.L.T. 27; 1928 S.N. 146......................... 11.54
—— v. James, 1908 S.C. 681; (1908) 15 S.L.T. 945; (1908) 45 S.L.R. 528......... 2.112
Rennie & Playfair v. Aitken, June 8, 1811, F.C............................. 19.27
Reynolds v. Mackenzie, Kilmarnock Sh.Ct., May 30, 1986, unreported...... 14.19, 14.65
Riach v. Wallace (1899) 1 F. 718; (1899) 6 S.L.T. 365; (1899) 36 S.L.R. 520....... 10.08
Ribble Paper Mills Ltd v. Clyde Paper Mills Ltd, 1972 S.L.T. (Notes) 25.... 9.67, 13.05,
                                                                            16.24
Richards & Wallington (Earthmoving) Ltd v. Whallings Ltd, 1982 S.L.T. 66... 4.85, 9.78,
                                                                            11.19
Richardson v. Fleming (1867) 5 M. 586...................................... 15.57
—— v. Richardson, 1957 S.L.T. 30... 19.27
—— v. ——, 1957 S.L.T. (Notes) 45.. 2.107
—— v. ——, 1991 S.L.T. (Sh.Ct.) 7; 1991 S.C.L.R. 209.................. 18.08, 18.39
—— v. Wilson (1879) 7 R. 237; (1879) 17 S.L.R. 122......................... 8.32
Richmond v. Grahame (1847) 9 D. 633.. 4.47
Riddell v. Lanarkshire and Ayrshire Ry (1904) 6 F. 432; (1904) 11 S.L.T. 689;
    (1904) 41 S.L.R. 319.. 14.41
—— v. Riddell (1890) 18 R. 1; (1890) 28 S.L.R. 1........................... 15.27
Rieley v. Kingslaw Riding School, 1975 S.C. 28; 1975 S.L.T. 61........... 10.25, 18.113
Rigby v. Fletcher (1833) 11 S. 256... 29.18
Riggs v. Drummond (1861) 23 D. 1251; (1861) 33 Sc.Jur. 628................. 15.57
Rigg's Exr v. Urquhart (1902) 10 S.L.T. 503................................ 19.10
Riley v. Ellis, 1910 S.C. 934; 1910 2 S.L.T. 84; (1910) 47 S.L.R. 788.............. 11.15
—— v. McLaren (1853) 16 D. 323... 15.27
Rintoul & Co. v. Bannatyne (1862) 1 M. 137; (1862) 35 Sc.Jur. 80............. 11.30
Risi v. Lennox Properties Ltd, 1993 S.C.L.R. 227........................... 7.28
Ritchie v. Cleary, 1995 S.C.L.R. 561................................. 8.42, 13.01
—— v. EFT Industrial Ltd, 1997 S.C.L.R. 955; 1997 G.W.D. 28–1400, Sh.Ct....... 21.02
—— v. Leith Docks Commissioners (1902) 10 S.L.T. 395...................... 15.16
—— v. McIntosh (1881) 8 R. 747....................................... 11.52, 11.54
—— v. McLachlan (1870) 8 M. 815; (1870) 42 Sc.Jur. 477; (1870) 7 S.L.R. 500.... 11.20,
                                                                            11.26
—— v. Maersk Co. Ltd, 1994 S.C.L.R. 1038................................... 8.34
Rixson v. Rixson, 1990 S.L.T. (Sh.Ct.) 5; 1989 S.C.L.R. 472................ 18.39
Road Transport Industry Training Board v. John Duncan Removals Ltd 1975 S.L.T.
    (Sh.Ct.) 2... 1.32
Rob's Trs v. Hutton (1866) 4 M. 546; (1866) 38 Sc.Jur. 278................. 11.70

Robb v. Dickson (1901) 9 S.L.T. 224. . . . . 11.55
—— v. Dundee D.C., 1980 S.L.T. (Notes) 91. . . . . 9.30, 9.33
—— v. Elgin (1877) 14 S.L.R. 473. . . . . 18.34
—— v. Independent West Middlesex Assurance Co. (1853) 5 D. 1025. . . . . . 11.78, 11.80
—— v. Logiealmond School Board (1875) 2 R. 417; (1875) 12 S.L.R. 286. . . . 9.47, 9.112,
13.12, 16.101
—— v. —— (1875) 2 R. 698; (1875) 12 S.L.R. 469. . . . . 19.11
Roberts v. Crawford (1884) 22 S.L.R. 135. . . . . 6.22
—— v. Fettes (1901) 10 S.L.T. 319. . . . . 12.68
—— v. Logan, 1966 S.L.T. 77. . . . . 9.114
Robertson (1842) 1 Broun 152. . . . . 16.76
—— (1896) 4 S.L.T. 114. . . . . 11.39
Robertson, Petr, 1978 S.L.T. (Sh.Ct.) 30. . . . . 2.66
Robertson v. Black & Watson (1901) 18 Sh.Ct.Rep. 98. . . . . 18.35
—— v. Brandes, Schönwald & Co. (1906) 8 F. 815; (1906) 14 S.L.T. 90; (1906) 43
S.L.R. 635. . . . . 2.101
—— v. British Bakeries Ltd, 1991 S.C.L.R. 450. . . . . 21.30
—— v. Cockburn (1875) 3 R. 21; (1875) 13 S.L.R. 15. . . . . 2.54, 9.82, 21.76
—— v. Crane Hire (Paisley) Ltd, 1982 S.L.T. 505. . . . . 10.33, 12.49
—— v. Duke of Atholl (1905) 8 F. 150; (1905) 13 S.L.T. 577; (1905) 42 S.L.R.
601. . . . . 4.112, 4.113, 8.60, 11.56, 11.64
—— v. Lord Advocate (Mar. 25, 1950), 1965 S.C. 400. . . . . 4.57
—— v. McCaw, 1911 S.C. 650; 1911 1 S.L.T. 346; (1911) 48 S.L.R. 577. . . . . 11.53
—— v. McDonald (1829) 7 S. 272. . . . . 21.89
—— v. Murphy (1867) 6 M. 114; (1867) 40 Sc.Jur. 61; (1867) 5 S.L.R.. . . . . 8.57, 8.59
—— v. Park, Dobson & Co. (1896) 24 R. 30; (1896) 4 S.L.T. 114; (1896) 34 S.L.R.
3. . . . . 11.40
—— v. Robertson (1897) 4 S.L.T. 358. . . . . 15.21
—— v. Ross (1873) 11 M. 910; (1873) 45 Sc.Jur. 556; (1873) 10 S.L.R. 636. . 4.125, 24.05
—— v. Steuart (1874) 1 R. 532; (1874) 11 S.L.R. 427. . . . . 16.81
Robertson & Co. v. Bird & Co. (1897) 24 R. 1076; (1897) 5 S.L.T. 81; (1897) 34
S.L.R. 867. . . . . 9.25
—— v. Exley, Dimsdale & Co. (1833) 11 S. 320. . . . . 11.73, 11.77
—— v. Robertson, Paisley Sh.Ct., Dec. 4, 1986, unreported. 2.100
Robertson (W. & A.) v. Gerrard (1908) 16 S.L.T. 100. . . . . 2.101
Robertson's Trs v. Roberts, 1982 S.L.T. 22. . . . . 23.38
Robeson v. Waugh (1874) 2 R. 63. . . . . 9.30
Robinson, Re [1912] 1 Ch. 717; 1912 W.N. 80. . . . . 2.12
Robinson v. National Bank of Scotland, 1916 S.C.(H.L.) 154; 1916 1 S.L.T. 336;
(1916) 53 S.L.R. 390. . . . . 19.11
—— v. Reid's Trs (1900) 2 F. 928; (1900) 8 S.L.T. 47; (1900) 37 S.L.R. 718. . . . . . . 4.43
Robson v. Bywater (1870) 8 M. 757; (1870) Sc.Jur. 366. . . . . 2.123
—— v. Robson, 1973 S.L.T. (Notes) 4. . . . . 14.64
Roburn Construction v. William Irvine (South) & Co. [1991] B.C.C. 726; *The
Times*, September 3, 1991. . . . . 11.57, 11.58, 11.59, 11.60
Rodden v. Whatlings Ltd, 1961 S.C. 132; 1960 S.L.T. (Notes) 96. . . . . 9.18
Rodenhurst v. Chief Constable of Grampian Police, 1992 S.C. 1; 1992 S.L.T. 104. . 25.08,
25.35, 25.39
Rodger v. Weir, 1917 S.C. 300; 1917 1 S.L.T. 114; (1917) 54 S.L.R. 254. . . . . 4.115
Rodgers v. Clydesdale, 1995 S.C.L.R. 1163 (Notes) (Sh.Ct.). 10.60
Roe v. Roe (1915) 32 Sh.Ct.Rep. 30. . . . . 9.18
Roger v. J. & P. Cochrane & Co., 1910 S.C. 1; 1909 2 S.L.T. 277; (1909) 47 S.L.R. 5. . 9.93
—— v. Roger (1896) 6 S.L.T. 233. . . . . 15.36
Rogers v. Home Secretary [1973] A.C. 388; [1972] 3 W.L.R. 278; (1972) 116 S.J.
696; [1972] 2 All E.R. 1057, H.L.. . . . . 2.16, 4.74, 4.75
—— v. Orr, 1939 S.C. 492; 1939 S.L.T. 403; 1939 S.N. 54. 15.55
Rogers (Charles) & Son v. G. & H. Mullen, 1957 S.L.T. 23. . . . . 18.117, 19.08
Rogerson v. Rogerson, 1964 S.L.T. (Notes) 89. . . . . 15.61
—— v. Rogerson's Tr (1885) 22 S.L.R. 673. . . . . 11.54
Rolfe v. Drummond (1862) 1 M. 39; (1862) 35 Sc.Jur. 36. 11.44
Rolled Steel Products (Holdings) Ltd v. British Steel Corporation [1986] Ch. 246;
[1985] 2 W.L.R. 908; [1985] 3 All E.R. 1; (1984) 128 S.J. 629. . . . . 17.01
Rollo v. British Railways Board, 1980 S.L.T. (Notes) 103. 10.37
Rondel v. Worsley [1969] 1 A.C. 191. . . . . 16.42
Roney v. Tarakan Petroleum Oil Syndicate, 1910 1 S.L.T. 272. . . . . 21.49
Ronson Nominees Ltd v. Mitchell, 1982 S.L.T. (Sh.Ct.) 18. . . . . 4.65
Roofcare Ltd v. Gillies, 1984 S.L.T. (Sh.Ct.) 8. . . . . 16.102, 18.14

Rooney v. Cormack (1895) 23 R. 11; (1895) 3 S.L.T. 133; (1895) 33 S.L.R. 7...... 4.27,
    19.03
—— v. F.W. Woolworth plc, 1990 S.L.T. 257; 1989 S.C.L.R. 557............... 14.38
Rorie v. Rorie, 1967 S.L.T. 75.. 2.112, 9.124
Rose v. Johnston (1878) 5 R. 600; (1878) 15 S.L.R. 325................... 9.30, 10.24
Rose Street Foundry and Engineering Co. v. Lewis & Sons, 1917 S.C. 341; 1917 1
    S.L.T. 153... 4.41, 4.50
Ross v. British Railways Board, 1972 S.C. 154; 1972 S.L.T. 174............ 16.30, 21.36
—— v. Brunton (1914) 30 Sh.Ct.Rep. 141................................ 21.51
—— v. Edinburgh D.C., 1977 S.L.T. (Sh.Ct.) 39.......................... 26.289
—— v. Glasgow Corporation, 1919 2 S.L.T. 209.......................... 15.02
—— v. Invergordon Distillers Ltd, 1961 S.C. 286; 1961 S.L.T. 358.......... 3.17
—— v. Ross (1887) 5 R. 1013; (1887) 15 S.L.R. 664....................... 3.99
—— v. —— (1895) 22 R. 461; (1895) 2 S.L.T. 577; (1895) 32 S.L.T. 337......... 13.79
—— v. —— (1901) 2 S.L.T. 117... 7.24
—— v. ——, 1909 2 S.L.T. 117.. 12.15
—— v. ——, 1920 S.C. 530; 1920 2 S.L.T. 4; (1920) 57 S.L.R. 461.... 18.29, 25.29, 26.32
—— v. ——, 1927 S.C.(H.L.) 4; 1927 S.L.T. 2; 1926 S.N. 29.............. 18.48, 18.50
—— v. ——, 1928 S.C. 600; 1928 S.L.T. 357; 1928 S.N. 29............... 2.110, 2.111
—— v. Shaw (1849) 11 D. 984; (1849) 21 Sc.Jur. 349...................... 11.67
—— v. Tennant's Trs (1877) 5 R. 182; (1877) 15 S.L.R. 109................ 4.14
Ross & Coulter v. Inland Revenue, 1948 S.C.(H.L.) 1; 1948 S.L.T. 303......... 18.110
Rosslyn (Earl of) v. Lawson (1872) 9 S.L.R. 291........................ 9.94
Ross-shire C.C. v. Macrae-Gilstrap, 1930 S.C. 808; 1930 S.L.T. 587; 1930 S.N. 81.. 25.39,
    25.41
Rothesay Town Council, Petrs (1898) 14 Sh.Ct.Rep. 189...................... 25.09
Rothfield v. Cohen, 1919 1 S.L.T. 138.................................. 2.94, 2.98
—— v. North British Ry, 1920 S.C. 805; 1920 2 S.L.T. 269; (1920) 57 S.L.R. 661... 20.05
Rothman's of Pall Mall (Overseas) Ltd v. Saudi Arabian Airlines Corporation
    [1981] Q.B. 368; [1980] 3 W.L.R. 642; [1980] 3 All E.R. 359; (1980) 124 S.J.
    542... 2.77
Rothwell v. Stuart's Trs (1898) 1 F. 81; (1898) 6 S.L.T. 215; (1898) 36 S.L.R. 97.... 9.25
Rowan v. Mercer (1863) 4 Irv. 377..................................... 7.26
Rowe v. Elliot, 1973 S.L.T. (Notes) 41................................. 18.05
—— v. Rowe (1872) 9 S.L.R. 492...................................... 11.07, 18.15
Rowlett v. Rowlett [1955] C.L.Y. 3510................................. 9.79
Roxburgh v. Commercial Bank of Scotland (1903) 19 Sh.Ct.Rep. 248; (1903) 11
    S.L.T. 30.. 14.19
—— v. Dinardo, 1981 S.L.T. 291...................... 2.73, 2.99, 2.101, 26.319
Roxburgh C.C. v. Dalrymple's Trs (1894) 21 R. 1063; (1894) 2 S.L.T. 76; (1894) 31
    S.L.R. 906... 25.33, 25.34, 26.385
Roxburgh Lunacy Board v. Selkirk Parish Council (1902) 4 F. 468; (1902) 9 S.L.T.
    419... 25.30
Roxburghe (Duke of) (1875) 2 R. 715; (1875) 12 S.L.R. 472......... 18.30, 18.34, 18.36
Roy v. Carron Co., 1967 S.L.T. (Notes) 84............................ 10.21
—— v. Turner (1891) 18 R. 717; (1891) 28 S.L.R. 509.................. 11.10, 11.25
—— v. Wright (1826) 5 S. 107 (N.E. 98).............................. 9.15, 9.16
Roy (D.) (Roofs and Floors) Ltd v. McCorquodale, 1979 S.L.T. (Sh.Ct.) 33........ 9.114
Roy, Nicholson, Becker & Day v. Clarke, 1984 S.L.T. (Sh.Ct.) 16............ 14.67
Royal Bank of Scotland v. Fairholm (1770) Mor.App. "Adjudication", No. 3...... 11.14
—— v. Gillies, 1987 S.L.T. 54.. 18.01
—— v. McKerracher, 1968 S.L.T. (Sh.Ct.) 77...................... 4.42, 4.43, 7.09
—— v. Mason, 1995 S.L.T. (Sh.Ct.) 32; 1994 S.C.L.R. 558................. 7.06
—— v. Skinner, 1931 S.L.T. 382...................................... 29.18
Royal Bank of Scotland plc v. Briggs, 1982 S.L.T. (Sh.Ct.) 46.............. 9.93
—— v. Geddes, 1983 S.L.T. (Sh.Ct.) 32................................ 9.93
—— v. Law, 1995 S.C. 508; 1996 S.L.T. 83............................. 29.21
Royal Blind Asylum and School, The v. Lothian R.C., 1981 S.L.T. (Sh.Ct.) 109... 26.358
Royal Life Insurance Ltd v. Douglas, 1998 S.C.L.R. 405................... 5.96, 8.34
Royle v. Gray, 1973 S.L.T. 31.. 2.23
Ruby v. W. Alexander & Sons, 1949 S.C. 642; 1949 S.L.T. 372.............. 19.36
Rukat v. Rukat [1975] Fam. 63; [1975] 2 W.L.R. 201; [1975] 1 All E.R. 343; (1974)
    119 S.J. 30... 16.67
Rush v. Fife R.C., 1984 S.L.T. 391.......................... 1.32, 11.53, 11.65
Russel v. Gillespie (1859) 3 Macq. 757, (1859) 21 D.(H.L.) 13............ 2.106
Russell v. Allan (1877) 5 R. 22....................................... 18.36, 18.94
—— v. Dickson, 1997 S.C. 269; 1997 G.W.D. 22–1058 *The Times*, June 23, 1997.... 1.13

Russell v. Johnston (1827) 6 S. 255. . . . . 11.40
Russo's Tr, Petr, 1981 S.L.T. (Sh.Ct.) 26. . . . . 19.09, 19.18
Rutherford v. Harvey & McMillan, 1954 S.L.T. (Notes) 28. . . . . 2.123
—— v. Licences and General Insurance Co. Ltd, 1934 S.L.T. 47; 1933 S.N. 110. . . 4.112,
4.113, 8.60, 8.64
—— v. Virtue, 1993 S.C.L.R. 886. . . . . 2.31, 10.04, 13.50, 18.114
Rutherfurd v. Nisbett's Trs (1832) 11 S. 123. . . . . 2.104
Rutherglen Parish Council v. Glenbucket Parish Council (1896) 3 S.L.T. 251; (1896)
33 S.L.R. 368. . . . . 19.42
Ruthven (Lord) v. Drummond, 1908 S.C. 1154; (1908) 16 S.L.T. 335; (1908) 45
S.L.R. 901. . . . . 11.30
—— v. Pulford & Son, 1909 S.C. 951; 1909 1 S.L.T. 405; (1909) 46 S.L.R. 612. . . . 11.15,
29.29
Ruthven v. Ruthven (1905) 13 S.L.T. 69 (1905) 42 S.L.R. 562. . . . . 5.79
Rutten v. Cross Medical Ltd [1997] I.L.Pr. 199. . . . . 3.92
Ryan v. Little, 1910 S.C. 219; 1909 2 S.L.T. 47. . . . . 23.24
—— v. McBurnie, 1940 S.C. 173; (1940) S.L.T. 139; (1940) S.N. 2. . . . . 2.104, 2.109
—— v. Paterson (1972) J.C.L. 111. . . . . 16.52

S, Petr, 1953 S.L.T. 220. . . . . 28.43
S (a minor) (blood transfusion: adoption order condition), Re [1994] 2 F.L.R.
416. . . . . 28.120
S (A Minor) (Custody: Habitual Residence), Re [1997] 3 W.L.R. 597 (H.L.). 3.31
S v. O, unreported. 28.114
Sadler v. Webster (1893) 21 R. 107; (1893) 1 S.L.T. 302; (1893) 31 S.L.R. 89. . . . . . 12.70
Sagnata Investments Ltd v. Norwich Corporation [1971] 2 Q.B. 614; [1971] 3
W.L.R. 133; [1971] 2 All E.R. 1441. . . . . 25.09, 25.11
Salaried Staff London Loan Co. Ltd v. Swears and Wells Ltd, 1985 S.L.T. 326. . . . . 21.80
Saleem v. Hamilton District Licensing Board, 1993 S.L.T. 1092; 1993 S.C.L.R.
266. . . . . 13.07, 16.48, 25.20
Salsbury v. Woodland [1970] 1 Q.B. 324; [1969] 3 W.L.R. 29; [1969] 3 All E.R. 863;
(1969) 113 S.J. 327. . . . . 16.92
Samson & Co. v. Hough (1886) 13 R. 1154; (1886) 23 S.L.R. 828. . . . . 15.21, 15.28
Sandeman's Trs, 1947 S.C. 304; 1947 S.L.T. 299; 1947 S.N. 27. . . . . 4.68
Sanderson v. McManus, 1995 S.C.L.R. 902. 18.13, 18.82, 28.133
—— v. ——, 1997 S.C.L.R. 281. . . . . 18.03, 18.13
Sanderson & Son v. Armour & Co., 1922 S.C.(H.L.) 117; 1922 S.L.T. 285; (1922) 59
S.L.R. 268. . . . . 2.99, 2.101
Sandilands v. Sandilands (1848) 10 D. 1091. . . . . 11.69, 15.21
Sandlan v. H.M. Advocate, 1983 S.L.T. 519; 1983 S.C.C.R. 71. . . . . 16.80
Santa Fe International Corp. v. Napier Shipping SA, 1985 S.L.T. 430. . . . . 15.78
Sargasso, The [1994] 3 All E.R. 180; [1994] 2 Lloyd's Rep. 6; *The Times*, April 4,
1994. . . . . 2.93
Sama (Harry) Ltd v. Barnett & Co. Sales (Central) Ltd, 1954 S.L.T. (Sh.Ct.) 105. . 15.60
Sarrio SA v. Kuwait Investment Authority [1997] 3 W.L.R. 1143; [1997] 4 All E.R.
929 [1997] I.L.Pr. 441. . . . . 3.60
Saudi Distribution Services Ltd v. Kane, 1985 S.L.T. (Sh.Ct.) 9. . . . . 2.97
Sawers v. Kinnair (1897) 25 R. 45. . . . . 23.18
Schaw v. Black (1889) 16 R. 336; (1889) 26 S.L.R. 220. . . . . 4.34
Schroder Leasing Ltd v. Fraser, Paisley Sh.Ct., Apr. 25, 1986, unreported. 7.28, 7.32,
7.37
Science Research Council v. Nassé [1980] A.C. 1028; [1979] 3 W.L.R. 762; [1979] 3
All E.R. 673; (1979) 123 S.J. 768. . . . . 4.73, 15.54, 15.74
Scobie v. Dumfries & Galloway R.C., 1991 S.L.T. (Sh.Ct.) 33. . . . . 29.40
Scotsman Publications Ltd v. SOGAT, 1986 S.L.T. 646. . . . . 21.88, 21.92
Scott v. Brown [1982] 2 Q.B. 724; [1891, 94] All E.R. Rep. 654. . . . . 2.12
—— v. Christie (1856) 19 D. 178. . . . . 12.27
—— v. Cook (1886) 24 S.L.R. 34. . . . . 12.70
—— v. Cormack Heating Engineers Ltd, 1942 S.C. 159. . . . . 8.63
—— v. Edina Garages Ltd, Edinburgh Sh.Ct., Apr. 2, 1982, unreported. 19.49
—— v. Hawkins, Sh. Prin. Caplan, Kilmarnock Sh.Ct., Dec. 19, 1984, unreported. . 14.08,
18.70, 23.04
—— v. Johnston (1885) 12 R. 1022. . . . . 11.54
—— v. MacDonald (1885) 12 R. 1123; (1885) 22 S.L.R. 666. . . . . 2.108
—— v. Mills's Trs, 1923 S.C. 726; 1923 S.L.T. 436; (1923) 60 S.L.R. 459. . . . . 5.89, 12.10
—— v. National Coal Board, 1979 S.L.T. (Sh.Ct.) 38. . . . . 16.33

Scott v. Portsoy Harbour Co. (1900) 8 S.L.T. 38. . . . . 15.61
—— v. Roy (1886) 13 R. 1173; (1886) 23 S.L.R. 855. . . . . 11.54
—— v. Scott (1839) 1 D. 1176. . . . . 21.95
—— v. —— [1913] A.C. 417; [1911, 1913] All E.R. 1. . . . . 5.19, 5.22
—— v. ——, 1913 2 S.L.T. 278. . . . . 15.36
—— v. ——, 1924 S.C. 843; 1924 S.L.T. (624; (1924) 61 S.L.R. 560. . . . . 11.71, 11.76
—— v. ——, 1958 S.L.T. (Sh.Ct.) 40; (1958) 74 Sh.Ct.Rep. 73. . . . . 20.04
—— v. Scott's Tr., 1914 S.C. 704; 1914 1 S.L.T. 468; (1914) 51 S.L.R. 613. . . . . 11.54
—— v. Wilson (1829) 7 S. 566. . . . . 9.94, 19.03
Scott & Sons v. Del Sel, 1923 S.C.(H.L.) 37; 1923 S.L.T. 204; (1923) 60 S.L.R. 437 2.101
Scott, Simpson & Wallis v. Forrest & Turnbull (1897) 24 R. 877; (1897) 5 S.L.T. 33;
    (1897) 34 S.L.R. 655. . . . . 15.61
Scott's Trs, 1957 S.L.T. (Notes) 45. . . . . 26.409
Scottish Amalgamated Silks Ltd v. Macalister, 1930 S.L.T. 593; 1930 S.N. 121. . . . . 12.68,
                                                                                              12.69
Scottish Enterprise v. Southbank Glass Co. Ltd, 1992 S.C.L.R. 785. . . . . 7.29
Scottish Flavour Ltd v. Watson, 1982 S.L.T. 78. . . . . 11.82, 21.79
Scottish Gas Board v. Alexander 1963 S.L.T. (Sh.Ct.) 27; (1963) 79 Sh.Ct.Rep. 86. . 1.32
—— v. Kerr's Trs, 1956 S.L.T. (Sh.Ct.) 69; (1956) 72 Sh.Ct.Rep. 139. . . . . 26.266
Scottish Heritages Co. Ltd v. N.B. Property Investment Co. Ltd (1885) 12 R. 550;
    (1885) 22 S.L.R. 361. . . . . 4.116
Scottish Marine Insurance Co. v. Turner (1853) 1 Macq. 334; (1853) 15 D.(H.L.) 33;
    (1853) 25 Sc.Jur. 274. . . . . 9.25, 16.28
Scottish Milk Agency Ltd v. Leiper (1931) 47 Sh.Ct.Rep. 106. . . . . 12.25
Scottish National Orchestra Society Ltd v. Thomson's Exr, 1969 S.L.T. 325. . . . . 9.18
Scottish N.E. Ry v. Napier (1859) 21 D. 700; (1859) 31 Sc.Jur. 350. . . . . . 9.21, 9.23, 9.60
Scottish Omnibuses Ltd v. Gillies, Dumbarton Sh.Ct., Feb. 1978, unreported. 15.59
Scottish Special Housing Association v. Maxwell, 1960 S.C. 391; 1960 S.L.T. (Notes)
    64. . . . . 2.29, 13.23
Scottish and Universal Newspapers Ltd v. Smith, 1982 S.L.T. 160. . . . . 18.110, 18.111,
                                                                               18.114, 21.91, 21.93
Scoular v. McLaughlan (1864) 2 M. 955; (1864) 36 Sc.Jur. 465. . . . . 18.05
Scullion v. Scullion, 1990 S.C.L.R. 577. . . . . 2.58
Seafield Trs v. General Trs of Church of Scotland, 1928 S.L.T. (Sh.Ct.) 18; (1928)
    44 Sh.Ct.Rep. 1891. . . . . 26.86
Seaforth's Trs v. Macauley (1844) 7 D. 80. . . . . 11.36
Seaman v. Butters, 1911 2 S.L.T. 198. . . . . 11.70
Seath v. Glasgow D.C., 1985 S.L.T. 407. . . . . 26.289
Secker v. Cameron, 1914 S.C. 354; 1914 1 S.L.T. 214. . . . . 2.55, 23.44
Secretary of State for Social Services v. Caro Accessories Ltd, Airdrie Sh.Ct., Sept.
    19. 1983, unreported. 13.41, 14.08
Secretary for State for Trade and Industry v. Houston, 1994 S.L.T. 775; 1994
    S.C.L.R. 209. . . . . 15.54
Selangor United Rubber Estates Ltd v. Cradock [1968] 1 W.L.R. 1555; (1968) 112
    S.J. 744; [1969] 1 W.L.R. 1773; (1968) 113 S.J. 896. . . . . 4.93
Selby v. Baldry (1867) 5 S.L.R. 64. . . . . 17.03
Sellar v. Highland Ry, 1918 S.C. 838; 1919 S.C.(H.L.) 19; 1919 1 S.L.T. 149; (1919)
    56 S.L.R. 216. . . . . 2.126, 2.127
Sellars v. IMI Yorkshire Imperial Ltd, 1986 S.L.T. 629. . . 8.27, 10.34, 10.37, 10.48, 10.60
Semple v. Macnair and Crawford (1907) 15 S.L.T. 448. . . . . 2.73
Shankland & Co. v. McGildowny, 1912 S.C. 857; 1912 1 S.L.T. 410; (1912) 49 S.L.R.
    564. . . . . 11.10, 11.12, 11.15, 29.16
Shanks v. Gray, 1977 S.L.T. (Notes) 26. . . . . 19.52
—— v. Nisbet (1900) 16 Sh.Ct.Rep. 316. . . . . 26.07
Shaw v. Browne (1886) 2 Sh.Ct.Rep. 203. . . . . 18.37
—— v. Caledonian Ry (1888) 15 R. 504; (1888) 25 S.L.R. 561. . . . . 12.16
—— v. Dow & Dobie (1869) 7 M. 449; (1869) 41 Sc.Jur. 246; (1869) 6 S.L.R. 297. . 3.99
—— v. Renton & Fisher Ltd, 1977 S.L.T. (Notes) 60. . . . . 8.59, 8.60, 9.54
—— v. Shaw [1979] Fam. 62; [1979] 3 W.L.R. 24; (1979) 123 S.J. 142; [1979] 3 All
    E.R. 1; (1979) 9 Fam. Law 187. . . . . 4.05
—— v. Shaw's Trs (1876) 3 R. 813; (1876) 13 S.L.R. 526. . . . . 4.31, 4.32, 13.78
—— v. Strathclyde R.C., 1988 S.L.T. 313. . . . . 20.01, 20.04
—— v. William Grant (Minerals) Ltd, 1989 S.L.T. 121; 1988 S.C.L.R. 416. . . . . 24.07
Shaw & Shaw v. J. & T. Boyd Ltd, 1907 S.C. 646. . . . . 19.40
Shaw Stewart v. Corbet, May 30, 1830, F.C. (notes p. 146). 2.125
Sheaf Steamship Co. v. Compania Transmediterranea, 1930 S.C. 660; 1930 S.L.T.
    445. . . . . 2.74, 2.76, 3.99

Sheard v. Haldane (1867) 5 M. 636. . . . . 15.22
Shearer v. Nicoll, 1935 S.L.T. 313; 1935 S.N. 57. . . . . 23.18
Shedden v. Patrick (1852) 14 D. 721; affd (1854) 17 D.(H.L.) 18. . . . . 9.30
Sheltered Housing Management Ltd v. Aitken, 1998 S.C.L.R. 59. . . . . 18.20, 18.45
Shepherd v. Elliot (1896) 23 R. 695; (1896) 3 S.L.T. 330; (1896) 33 S.L.R. 495. . . . 19.07,
                                                               19.10
—— v. Henderson (1881) 9 R.(H.L.) 1; (1881) 19 S.L.R. 577; (1881) 7 App. Cas.
    49. . . . . 17.08
Sheridan v. Peel, 1907 S.C. 577; (1907) 14 S.L.T. 820; (1907) 44 S.L.R. 406. . . . . . . 15.60
Sherrin v. Brand [1956] 1 Q.B. 403; [1956] 2 W.L.R. 131; [1956] 1 All E.R. 194;
    (1956) 100 S.J. 34. . . . . 26.269
Shevchuk v. National Coal Board, 1982 S.L.T. 557. 17.27, 18.106
Shevill v. Press Alliance (C-68/93) 1995 E.C.R. 1–415. . . . . 3.93
Shiell v. Guthrie's Trs (1874) 1 R. 1083. . . . . 29.89
Shiels v. Shiels' Trs (1874) 1 R. 502. . . . . 13.37, 13.40
Shinas v. Fordyce (1777) 5 Brown's Supp. 572. . . . . 4.126
Shirra v. Robertson (1873) 11 M. 660; (1873) 45 Sc.Jur. 412; (1873) 10 S.L.R.
    445. . . . . 18.30, 18.35
Shirreff v. Brodie (1836) 14 S. 825. . . . . 14.24
Shivas' Tr. v. Shivas' Trs (1883) 27 J. of J. 556. . . . . 11.30
Shoker v. Buchanan, Edinburgh Sh.Ct., Nov. 18, 1983, unreported. 30.137
Short's Tr. v. Chung (No. 2), *The Times*, May 18, 1998. . . . . 2.108
Shotts Iron Co. v. Kerr (1871) 10 M. 195; (1871) 44 Sc.Jur. 117; (1871) 9 S.L.R. 142. . 2.31
Sidlaw Industries Ltd v. Cable Bet Ltd, 1979 S.L.T. (Notes) 40. . . . . 14.31, 14.35, 19.14
Sim v. McConnell (1936) 52 Sh.Ct.Rep. 324. . . . . 26.11
—— v. Robinow (1892) 19 R. 665; (1892) 29 S.L.R. 585. . . . . 2.89
Sim (James) Ltd v. Haynes, 1968 S.L.T. (Sh.Ct.) 76. . . . . 8.12
Sime v. Linton (1897) 24 R.(J.) 70; (1897) 2 Adam 288; (1897) 5 S.L.T. 30; (1897)
    34 S.L.R. 664. . . . . 16.92
Sime, Sullivan & Dickson's Tr. v. Adam, 1908 S.C. 32. . . . . 12.27
Simla Bank v. Home (1870) 8 M. 781; (1870) 42 Sc.Jur. 443; (1870) 7 S.L.R. 487. . 11.67,
                                                11.68, 11.69
Simpson v. Allan (1894) 1 S.L.T. 590; (1894) 31 S.L.R. 572. 11.64
—— v. Bruce, 1984 S.L.T. (Sh.Ct.) 38. . . . . 2.03, 6.02
—— v. Imperial Chemical Industries Ltd, 1983 S.L.T. 601. . . . . 13.43
—— v. Royal Burgh of Inverurie, Aberdeen Sh.Ct., Feb. 7, 1974, unreported. 9.41
Simpson, Boath & Co., Petrs, 1981 S.C. 153. . . . . 2.19, 5.91
Simpson's Trs v. Fox, 1954 S.L.T. (Notes) 12. . . . . 21.68
Sinclair v. Baikie (1884) 11 R. 413; (1884) 21 S.L.R. 275. . . . . 11.84, 18.39
—— v. Bayley-Lunnon, 1969 S.L.T. (Sh.Ct.) 18. . . . . 12.23
—— v. Brown (1841) 3 D. 871. . . . . 2.125
—— v. Brown Bros (1882) 10 R. 45; (1882) 20 S.L.R. 12. . . . . 19.12
—— v. Caithness Flagstone Co. (1898) 25 R. 703; (1898) 35 S.L.R. 541; (1898) 5
    S.L.T. 364. . . . . 4.50
—— v. Fleming (1909) 25 Sh.Ct.Rep. 268. . . . . 4.45
—— v. Gardner (1915) 32 Sh.Ct.Rep. 211. . . . . 21.78
—— v. Glasgow and London Contract Corporation Ltd (1904) 6 F. 818; (1904) 12
    S.L.T. 175; (1904) 41 S.L.R. 608. . . . . 11.58
—— v. Lochgelly Iron and Coal Co. Ltd (1905) 13 S.L.T. 103. . . . . 8.60
—— v. Lothian R.C., 1981 S.L.T. (Sh.Ct.) 13. . . . . 25.17, 26.115
—— v. McColl (1894) 10 Sh.Ct.Rep. 144. . . . . 18.42
—— v. Mossend Iron Co. (1854) 17 D. 258; (1855) 27 Sc.Jur. 105. . . . . 16.102
—— v. National Coal Board, 1963 S.C. 586; 1963 S.L.T. 296. . . . . 9.31
—— v. Royal Bank of Scotland, 1983 S.L.T. 256. . . . . 19.13, 19.14, 19.45
—— v. Samuels, 1948 S.L.T. (Notes) 44. . . . . 13.03, 13.07
—— v. Sinclair (1833) 12 S. 61. . . . . 11.82
—— v. ——, 1986 S.L.T. (Sh.Ct.) 54. . . . . 22.47
—— v. Spence (1883) 10 R. 1077; (1883) 20 S.L.R. 726. . . . . 25.25, 26.327
—— v. Staples (1860) 22 D. 600; (1860) 32 Sc.Jur. 209. . . . . 11.14, 29.24
—— v. Stark (1828) 6 S. 336; (1828) 3 F.C. 371. 4.14, 4.17, 4.18
Singer v. Gray Tool Co. (Europe) Ltd, 1984 S.L.T. 149. . . 4.49, 12.48, 14.26, 14.29, 14.64
Singer Manufacturing Co. v. Jessiman (1881) 8 R. 695; (1881) 18 S.L.R. 496. . 2.31, 18.30
Singh v. Singh, 1997 G.W.D. 20–930. . . . . 2.58
Skerret v. Oliver (1896) 23 R. 468; (1896) 3 S.L.T. 257; (1896) 33 S.L.R. 323. . . . . . . 9.88
Skinner's Tr. v. Keith (1887) 14 R. 563; (1887) 24 S.L.R. 414. . . . . 12.18
Skiponian Ltd v. Barratt Developments (Scotland) Ltd, 1983 S.L.T. 313. . . . 16.35, 16.36,
                                               16.37, 18.110, 18.111

Slater v. Grampian Regional Council, 1991 S.L.T. (Sh.Ct.) 72; 1991 S.C.L.R. 344. . 29.40
Sloan v. B, 1991 S.L.T. 530. . . . . 5.23, 26.61
—— v. North East Fife District Licensing Board, 1978 S.L.T. (Sh.Ct.) 62. . . . . 26.254
Slorach v. Kerr, 1921 S.C. 285. . . . . 4.40
Small & Co. v. Dundee Police Commissioners (1884) 12 R. 123. . . . . 25.08
Smart v. Bargh, 1949 S.C. 57; 1949 S.L.T. 91. . . . . 9.35, 9.112
—— v. Miller, 1966 S.L.T. (Sh.Ct.) 80. . . . . 7.25, 7.28
—— v. Wilkinson, 1928 S.C. 383; 1928 S.L.T. 243; 1928 S.N. 8. . . . . 12.37
Smart (J.) & Co. v. Stewart, 1911 2 S.L.T. 340 S.L.R. 92; (1911) 49 S.L.R. 66. . . . . 19.31
Smeaton v. Dundee Corporation, 1941 S.C. 600; 1942 S.L.T. 47. . . . . . 14.35, 14.42, 14.43,
                                                                      14.48, 14.49
Smellie v. Smellie, 1953 S.L.T. (Notes) 53. . . . . 11.89
—— v. Thomson (1868) 6 M. 1024; (1868) 40 Sc.Jur. 538. . . . . 13.78
Smith, Petr, 1985 S.L.T. 461. . . . . 15.88
Smith v. Alexander Baird Ltd, 1993 S.C.L.R. 563. . . . . 15.43
—— v. Barclay, 1962 S.C. 1; 1962 S.L.T. 117. . . . . 21.09
—— v. Berry's Tr., 1995 S.C.L.R. 1132. . . . . 18.34
—— v. British Rail Engineering Ltd, 1985 S.L.T. 463. . . . . 14.38, 19.09, 19.49
—— v. Conner & Co. Ltd, 1979 S.L.T. (Sh.Ct.) 25. . . . . 6.22
—— v. Foster, 1949 S.C. 269; 1949 S.L.T. 163. . . . . 4.67
—— v. Gow (1895) 2 S.L.T. 473. . . . . 15.102
—— v. Hutchison, 1926 S.L.T. (Sh.Ct.) 50; (1925) 42 Sh.Ct.Rep. 183. . . . . 12.68
—— v. Kippen (1860) 22 D. 1495; (1860) 32 Sc.Jur. 681. . . . . 9.94
—— v. Kirkwood (1897) 24 R. 872; (1897) 5 S.L.T. 22; (1897) 34 S.L.R. 652. . . . . . 18.04,
                                                                      18.05, 18.08
—— v. Liverpool and London and Globe Insurance Co. (1887) 14 R. 931; (1887)
      24 S.L.R. 672. . . . . 2.127, 2.128
—— v. L.M.S. Ry, 1948 S.C. 125; 1948 S.L.T. 235. . . . . 19.15
—— v. Lord Advocate, 1932 S.L.T. 374; 1932 S.N. 70. . . . . 4.63, 4.65, 4.116
—— v. ——, 1980 S.C. 227; 1981 S.L.T. 19. . . . . 4.53, 4.62, 4.63
—— v. ——, 1995 S.L.T. 379. . . . . 27.22
—— v. McAulay (1846) 9 D. 190. . . . . 5.84
—— v. McColl's Trs, 1910 S.C. 1121; 1910 1 S.L.T. 117; (1910) 47 S.L.R. 291. . . . . 20.03
—— v. Middleton, 1972 S.C. 30; 1972 S.L.T. (Notes) 3. . . . . 21.35, 21.36
—— v. Norval (1828) 6 S. 852. . . . . 11.69, 11.70
—— v. Scottish Legal Life Assurance Society, 1912 S.C. 611; 1912 1 S.L.T. 270;
      (1912) 49 S.L.R. 457. . . . . 26.201
—— v. Smith's Tr (1900) 8 S.L.T. 226. . . . . 4.27
—— v. Stewart & Co., 1960 S.C. 329; 1961 S.L.T. 2. . . . . 2.97, 6.06
—— v. Tasker, 1955 S.L.T. 347. . . . . 4.106
—— v. Taylor, 1972 S.L.T. (Lands Tr.) 34. . . . . 2.36
—— v. Watson, 1912 S.C. 553; 1912 1 S.L.T. 257; (1912) 49 S.L.R. 411. . . . . . 16.57, 16.95
Smith & Kinnear v. Burns (1847) 9 D. 1344. . . . . 29.21
Smith's Trs v. McCheyne (1879) 16 S.L.R. 592. . . . . 11.55
Smith-Shand's Trs v. Forbes, 1921 S.C. 820; 1921 2 S.L.T. 151; (1921) 58 S.L.R.
      554. . . . . 4.38, 4.39, 10.10
Sneddon v. Addie & Sons' Collieries, 1927 S.N. 164. . . . . 2.30
Société du Gaz de Paris v. Armateurs Francais, 1925 S.C. 332; 1925 S.L.T. 196. . . . . 2.89
Society of Accountants in Edinburgh v. Lord Advocate, 1924 S.L.T. 194. . . . . 25.46
—— v. Scottish Health Board, 1924 S.L.T. 199. . . . . 25.46
Sokha v. Secretary of State for the Home Department, 1992 S.L.T. 1049. . . . . 2.89
Somerville v. National Coal Board, 1963 S.C. 666; 1963 S.L.T. 334. . . . . 14.45
Somerwell v. Somerwell (1900) 8 S.L.T. 84. . . . . 15.45, 15.73, 15.74
Sonntag v. Waidmann (C-172/91) [1993] E.C.R. I-1963; [1993] 1 L. Pr. 466. . . . . 3.05
Source Ltd v. Tuv Rheinland Holding AG [1997] 1.L.Pr. 514 (CA). 3.92, 3.93
Soutar v. Kilroe, 1994 S.C.L.R. 757 (Sh.Ct.). 20.03
—— v. Mulhern, 1907 S.C. 723; (1907) 14 S.L.T. 862; (1907) 44 S.L.R. 563. . . . . . . 2.29
South India Shipping Corporation v. Export-Import Bank of Korea [1985] 1 W.L.R.
      585; [1985] 2 All E.R. 219. . . . . 6.41
South Side Sawmills Ltd v. Buchanan, 1963 S.L.T. (Sh.Ct.) 19; (1963) 79 Sh.Ct.Rep.
      56. . . . . 3.90, 6.02
Sovfracht (v./O) v. Van Udens Scheepvart en Agentuur Maatschappij [1943] A.C.
      203; [1943] 1 All E.R. 76. . . . . 4.03
Spalding v. Inveresk Paper Co. Ltd, 1971 S.L.T. (Notes) 47. . . . . 10.06, 10.16,
                                                                      10.17, 10.51, 10.52
—— v. Valentine (1883) 10 R. 1092; (1883) 20 S.L.R. 724. 9.78
Spaulding & Co. v. Marjoribanks (1903) 11 S.L.T. 71. . . . . 6.22

Speirs v. Caledonian Ry, 1921 S.C. 889; 1921 2 S.L.T. 123; (1921) 58 S.L.R. 573... 15.39
—— v. Peat, 1987 S.C.L.R. 369; 1987 G.W.D. 9–307. . . . . 5.93
—— v. Speirs (1938) 54 Sh.Ct.Rep. 208. . . . . 11.11
Spence v. Davie, 1993 S.L.T. (Sh.Ct.) 38. . . . . 2.03
—— v. Paterson's Trs (1873) 1 R. 46. . . . . 2.123
—— v. Spence, 1914 S.C. 887; 1914 2 S.L.T. 113; (1914) 51 S.L.R. 766. . . . . 9.86
—— v. Wilson, 1998 S.L.T. 688. . . . . 21.36
Spiliada Maritime Corporation v. Cansulex Ltd [1987] A.C. 460; [1986] 3 W.L.R.
    972; [1986] 3 All E.R. 843. . . . . 2.89, 2.90, 2.91
Spottiswoode v. Hopkirk (1853) 16 D. 59. . . . . 9.83, 17.13, 21.04
Sproat v. Mure (1826) 5 S. 66 (N.E. 61). 9.14
Sproll v. Walker (1899) 2 F. 73; (1899) 7 S.L.T. 195. . . . . 14.37
Squire Light & Sound Ltd v. Vidicom Systems Ltd, 1987 S.C.L.R. 538; 1987
    G.W.D. 12–437. . . . . 7.09, 17.02
Staff v. Allan, 1971 S.L.T. (Notes) 61. . . . . 14.67
Stafford v. McLaurin (1875) 3 R. 148; (1875) 13 S.L.R. 83. . . . . 11.11
Stallworth v. H.M. Advocate, 1978 S.L.T. 93. . . . . 16.13, 16.14
Standard Shipowners' Mutual Association v. Taylor 23 R. 870; (1896) 4 S.L.T. 57;
    (1896) 33 S.L.R. 647. . . . . 2.29
Stanley Howard (Construction) v. Davis, 1988 S.L.T. (Sh.Ct.) 30. . . . . 2.100
Stanley Ltd v. Hamway, 1911 2 S.L.T. 2; (1911) 48 S.L.R. 757. . . . . 9.37
Star Fire and Burglary Insurance Co. Ltd v. Davidson & Sons Ltd (1902) 4 F. 997;
    (1902) 39 S.L.R. 768. . . . . 11.58
Stark's Trs v. Duncan (1906) 8 F. 429; (1906) 13 S.L.T. 737; (1906) 43 S.L.R. 288. . 2.08,
    2.23, 21.97
Station Garage v. Masson, 1978 S.L.T. (Sh.Ct.) 65. . . . . 16.47
Steedman v. Steedman (1886) 23 S.L.R. 856. . . . . 16.14
Steel v. Steel (1898) 25 R. 715; (1898) 5 S.L.T. 376. . . . . 13.40, 23.44
—— v. Steel and Buchanan (1826) 4 S. 527 (N.E. 535). 11.68
Steel-Maitland v. British Airways Board, 1981 S.L.T. 110. . . . . 2.02
Steele v. Lanarkshire Middle Ward District Committee, 1928 S.L.T. (Sh.Ct.) 20;
    (1928) 44 Sh.Ct.Rep. 249. . . . . 25.46
Steen v. Macnicol, Feb. 28, 1967, unreported. 4.14
Stein v. Stein, 1936 S.C. 268; 1936 S.L.T. 103; 1936 S.N. 13. 9.79
Stenhouse v. Stenhouse's Trs (1903) 10 S.L.T. 684. . . . . 19.31
Stenhouse London Ltd v. Allwright, 1972 S.C. 209; 1972 S.L.T. 255. . . . . 11.14, 21.49
Stephen v. Skinner (1860) 22 D. 1122; (1860) 32 Sc.Jur. 509. 11.54
—— v. Woodend Bowling Club, 1994 S.L.T. (Sh.Ct.) 9. . . . . 26.256
Stephenson v. Dunlop (1841) 4 D. 248. . . . . 11.71
Stephenson & Co. v. Dobbins and Bibby (1852) 14 D. 510; (1852) 24 Sc.Jur. 255. . . . 7.26
Stepney B.C. v. Joffe [1949] 1 K.B. 599; [1949] 1 All E.R. 256; (1949) 93 S.J. 119. . 25.09,
    25.11
Stern v. Bruce Peebles & Co. Ltd, 1909 2 S.L.T. 297; (1909) 47 S.L.R. 77. . . . . 11.70
Steuart v. Ree (1885) 12 R. 563; (1885) 22 S.L.R. 366. . . . . 6.20, 6.22
Steuart v. Young's Paraffin Light and Mineral Oil Co. (1898) 6 S.L.T. 69. . . 2.100, 2.101
Steven v. Broady Norman & Co., 1928 S.C. 351; 1928 S.N. 3; 1928 S.L.T. 290. . . . . . 4.43,
    4.48, 9.83
Stevens v. Campbell (1873) 11 M. 772; (1873) 45 Sc.Jur. 542; (1873) 10 S.L.R.
    608. . . . . 11.41
—— v. Motherwell Entertainments Ltd, 1914 S.C. 957; 1914 2 S.L.T. 170; (1914) 51
    S.L.R. 818. . . . . 10.29, 11.89
—— v. Thomson, 1971 S.L.T. 136. . . . . 4.106, 10.35, 10.36, 10.52
Stevens, Son & Co. v. Grant (1887) 5 R. 19; (1887) 15 S.L.R. 7. . . . . 2.30
Stevenson v. Fraser & Carmichael (1914) 30 Sh.Ct.Rep. 277; 1914 2 S.L.T. 224. . . . 12.37
—— v. Glasgow Corporation, 1908 S.C. 1034; (1908) 16 S.L.T. 302; (1908) 45
    S.L.R. 860. . . . . 9.34
—— v. Kyle (1849) 11 D. 1086; (1849) 21 Sc.Jur. 416. . . . . 15.56, 16.24
—— v. Lee (1886) 13 R. 913; (1886) 23 S.L.R. 649. . . . . 11.55
—— v. Midlothian D.C., 1983 S.C.(H.L.) 50; 1983 S.L.T. 433. . 11.52, 11.53, 11.54, 11.65
—— v. Pontifex & Wood (1887) 15 R. 125; (1887) 25 S.L.R. 120. . . . . 2.113, 9.83
—— v. Sharp, 1910 S.C. 580; 1910 1 S.L.T. 275; (1910) 47 S.L.R. 511. . . . . 2.29
—— v. Wilson (1941) 58 Sh.Ct.Rep. 74. . . . . 6.09
Stewart v. Advocate (Lord) (1857) 2 Irv. 614; (1857) 29 Sc.Jur. 344. . . . . 1.17
—— v. Callaghan, 1996 S.L.T. (Sh.Ct.) 12. . . . . 15.72, 15.83
—— v. Colvilles Ltd 1963 S.L.T. (Sh.Ct.) 15; (1963) 79 Sh.Ct.Rep. 64. . . . . . 17.08, 17.18
—— v. Gelot (1871) 9 M. 1057; (1871) 43 Sc.Jur. 583; (1871) 8 S.L.R. 688. . . . . 2.111
—— v. Earl of Galloway (1770) Mor. 7004. . . . . 13.37

Stewart v. Glasgow Corporation, 1958 S.C. 28; 1958 S.L.T. 137............ 16.31, 16.76
—— v. Greenock Harbour Trs (1868) 6 M. 954; (1868) 40 Sc.Jur. 550; (1868) 5
    S.L.R. 615... 2.106
—— v. Highlands & Islands Development Board, 1991 S.L.T. 787.............. 12.51
—— v. Jarvie, 1938 S.C. 309....................................... 29.34
—— v. Kennedy (1889) 16 R. 521; (1889) 26 S.L.R. 390................. 15.65, 18.50
—— v. Lothians Construction (Edinburgh) Ltd, 1972 S.L.T. (Notes) 75...... 5.98, 7.23,
    14.13, 18.05
—— v. Macbeth & Gray (1882) 10 R. 382; (1882) 20 S.L.R. 266.......... 11.29, 11.31
—— v. McDaid, 1987 S.C.L.R. 342.................................... 14.10, 14.12
—— v. Macdonald (1860) 22 D. 1514; (1860) 32 Sc.Jur. 701.................... 6.46
—— v. Reid, 1934 S.C. 69; 1934 S.L.T. 81; 1933 S.N. 98..................... 1.27
—— v. Royal Bank of Scotland plc, 1994 S.L.T. (Sh.Ct.) 27.............. 11.14, 29.19
—— v. Secretary of State for Scotland, 1995 S.L.T. 895; 1996 S.L.T. 1203......... 1.09
—— v. Steen, 1987 S.L.T. (Sh.Ct.) 60; 1987 S.C.C.R. 34...................... 11.58
—— v. Stewart (1906) 8 F. 769; (1906) 13 S.L.T. 997; (1906) 43 S.L.R. 522... 2.95, 5.98,
    14.22
—— v. ——, 1984 S.L.T. (Sh.Ct.) 58.................. 2.19, 5.100, 9.114, 11.86, 19.23
Stewart (A.C.) and Partners v. Coleman, 1989 S.L.T. 430...................... 10.09
Stewart's Exrs v. Stewart, 1994 S.L.T. 466.................................. 9.36
Stirling v. Dunn (1831) 9 S. 562... 15.82
Stirling Maxwell's Trs v. Kirkintilloch Police Commissioners (1883) 11 R. 1; (1883)
    21 S.L.R. 1.. 18.37
Stirling Parish Council v. Dunblane Parish Council, 1912 S.C. 316; 1912 1 S.L.T.
    32.. 25.30
—— v. Perth Parish Council (1898) 25 R. 964; (1898) 6 S.L.T. 56; (1898) 35 S.L.R.
    735.. 2.29
Stirling Park & Co. v. Digby Brown & Co., 1996 S.L.T. (Sh.Ct.) 17.............. 19.22
Stoddart v. British Transport Commission, 1956 S.L.T. 71...................... 10.14
—— v. R. J. Macleod Ltd, 1963 S.L.T. (Notes) 23..................... 14.42, 14.45
Stone v. Aberdeen Marine Insurance Co. (1849) 11 D. 1041.................... 15.29
—— v. Macdonald, 1979 S.C. 363; 1979 S.L.T. 288...................... 9.67, 13.05
—— v. Mountford, 1995 S.L.T. 1279....................................... 21.26
Stonehaven Town Council v. E. Williams Promotions, 1954 S.L.T. (Sh.Ct.) 105;
    (1955) 72 Sh.Ct.Rep. 30... 9.105
Storrie v. Mitchell, 1937 S.L.T. 624; 1937 S.N. 115.......................... 19.41
—— v. Murray, 1974 S.L.T. (Sh.Ct.) 45.................................... 15.100
Stothart v. Johnston's Trs (1822) 2 Mur. 549.............................. 19.27
Stott v. Gray (1834) 12 S. 828... 2.32
Stout v. U.K. Atomic Energy Authority, 1979 S.L.T. 54..................... 4.50, 9.36
Stow's Trs v. Silvester (1900) 8 S.L.T. 253................................. 11.70
Strachan v. Caledonian Fish-Selling and Marine Stores Co. Ltd, 1965 S.L.T. (Notes)
    63; 1963 S.C. 157.. 10.18, 16.37
—— v. McDougle (1835) 13 S. 954....................................... 29.21
—— v. Pharmaceutical Society of Great Britain (1901) 8 S.L.T. 373.............. 2.37
—— v. Steuart (1870) 9 M. 116; (1870) 43 Sc.Jur. 47; (1870) 8 S.L.R. 105........ 11.46
Strain v. Strain (1886) 13 R. 1029; (1886) 23 S.L.R. 739..................... 25.37
—— v. Strain (1890) 17 R. 566; (1890) 27 S.L.R. 586....................... 19.27
Strang v. Brown & Son (1882) 19 S.L.R. 890.............................. 19.14
—— v. Steuart (1864) 2 M. 1015; (1864) 4 M.(H.L.) 5...................... 2.55, 4.33
Strangford (Viscountess) v. Hurlet & Campsie Alum. Co. (1861) 23 D. 534; (1861)
    33 Sc.Jur. 221.. 11.88
Strathallan v. Glenlyon's Trs (1837) 15 S. 971; (1837) 9 Sc.Jur. 441.............. 4.33
Strathan v. Steuart (1870) 9 M. 116..................................... 14.05
Strathclyde (Chief Constable of) v. Hamilton and District Bookmaker's Club, 1977
    S.L.T. (Sh.Ct.) 78.. 25.33
Strathclyde Region (Assessor for) v. Dass Nicholas, 1981 S.L.T. (Notes) 116....... 5.87
Strathclyde Regional Council, Petrs, 1996 S.C.L.R. 109.............. 28.28, 18.41, 28.95
—— v. A, First Division, Jan. 29, 1993, unreported.......................... 28.133
—— v. B, Glasgow Sh.Ct., Feb. 17, 1984, unreported; 1997 Fam.L.B. 142... 15.55, 25.24,
    25.26, 28.106
—— v. Dales of Dalry Ltd, Kilmarnock Sh.Ct., Oct. 13, 1981, unreported........ 26.335
—— v. 85 Sound Club, Kilmarnock Sh.Ct., May 25, 1983, unreported.......... 26.256
—— v. F, 1995 G.W.D. 33–1677 (Sh.Ct.)................................... 28.40
—— v. T, 1984 S.L.T. (Sh.Ct.) 18... 25.27
—— v. Tudhope, 1983 S.L.T. 22; 1982 S.C.C.R. 286......................... 26.167
Strathmore Group Ltd v. Credit Lyonnais, 1994 S.L.T. 1023................... 9.54

Strichen Endowments (Governors of) v. Diverall (1891) 19 R. 79; (1891) 29 S.L.R.
102. . . . . 18.30, 18.34, 18.35
Strichen Parish Council v. Goodwillie, 1908 S.C. 835; (1908) 16 S.L.T. 70; (1908)
S.L.R. 684. . . . . 25.32, 26.55, 26.56
Stroud v. Stroud, 1994 S.L.T. (Sh.Ct.) 7; 1993 S.C.L.R. 763. . . . . 18.02, 18.25, 22.55
Struthers v. Kirkintilloch Magistrates, 1951 S.L.T. (Notes) 77. . . . . 6.04
Stuart v. Carron Co., 1948 S.L.T. (Notes) 43. . . . . 19.10
—— v. Cowan & Co. (1883) 10 R. 581. . . . . 29.27
—— v. Potter, Choate & Prentice, 1911 1 S.L.T. 377; (1911) 48 S.L.R. 657. . . . . 9.18
Studd v. Cook (1883) 10 R.(H.L.) 53; (1883) 20 S.L.R. 566; (1883) 8 App. Cas. 577. . 4.27
Sturrock v. Deas & Co., 1913 1 S.L.T. 60. . . . . 14.37
Summerlee Iron Co. Ltd v. Caledonian Ry, 1911 S.C. 458; 1911 1 S.L.T. 103. . . . . 10.13,
21.77
—— v. Duff, 1920 S.C. 291. . . . . 24.15
—— v. Lindsay, 1907 S.C. 1161. . . . . 4.29
Sundt & Co. v. Watson (1914) 31 Sh.Ct.Rep. 156. . . . . 12.70
Sutherland v. Duncan, 1996 S.L.T. 428. . . . . 10.49, 13.02
—— v. Edinburgh District Licensing Board, 1984 S.L.T. 241. . . . . 26.255
—— v. Glasgow Corporation, 1951 S.C.(H.L.) 1; 1951 S.L.T. 185. . . . . 17.08, 18.99
—— v. Goalen (1855) 17 D. 509; (1855) 27 Sc.Jur. 212. . . . . 13.34
—— v. Leith Provident Co-operative Society, 1964 S.C. 151; 1964 S.L.T. (Notes)
63. . . . . 16.35
—— v. Prestongrange Coal and Fire-Brick Co. Ltd (1888) 15 R. 494; (1888) 25
S.L.R. 359. . . . . 16.92
—— v. Squair (1898) 25 R. 656; (1898) 5 S.L.T. 336; (1898) 35 S.L.R. 312. . . . . 2.54
—— v. Thomson (1876) 3 R. 485; (1876) 13 S.L.R. 311. . . . . 2.53
Sutherland (Duke of) v. Reed (1890) 18 R. 252; (1890) 29 S.L.R. 217. . . . . . . 2.85, 2.106
Sutherland (James) & Sons v. Pottinger, 1989 S.L.T. 679. 13.64
Sutherlands of Peterhead (Road Hauliers) Ltd v. Allard Hewson & Co. Ltd, 1972
S.L.T. (Notes) 83. . . . . 3.100, 11.19
Sutie v. Ross (1705) Mor. 816. . . . . 29.32
Svenska Petroleum AB v. HOR Ltd, 1986 S.L.T. 513. . . . . 11.30, 24.06
Swallowfield v. Custom and Excise Commissioners [1994] S.T.C. 41. . . . . 13.69
Swan v. Blaikie, 1992 S.C.L.R. 405. . . . . 18.31
—— v. Kirk, 1932 S.L.T. (Sh.Ct.) 9; (1931) 47 Sh.Ct.Rep. 217. . . . . . . 11.33, 18.11, 25.38
Swan & Sons Ltd v. Speirs (1925) 41 Sh.Ct.Rep. 218. . . . . 11.55, 11.65
Swanson v. Gardner & Co. Ltd (1916) 33 Sh.Ct.Rep. 117. 12.24
—— v. Manson, 1907 S.C. 426; (1907) 14 S.L.T. 737. . . . . 4.33
Swirles v. Isles, 1930 S.C. 696; 1930 S.L.T. 428; 1930 S.N. 59. . . . . 4.113
Sydie v. A. A. Stuart & Sons (Contractors) Ltd, 1968 S.L.T. (Sh.Ct.) 93. . . . . 5.86, 18.12,
18.18
Symington v. Campbell (1894) 21 R. 434; (1894) S.L.T. 478; (1894) 31 S.L.R. 372. . 4.32,
4.105, 4.109
—— v. Symington (1874) 1 R. 1006. . . . . 11.10, 11.25, 11.38
—— v. —— (1875) 3 R. 205; (1875) 3 S.L.R. 124. . . . . 11.11, 11.36, 30.78
Symington, Son & Co. Ltd v. Larne Shipbuilding Co. Ltd, 1911 2 S.L.T. 32. . . . . . . 7.09
Szczepanski v. Szczepanski (1985) 15 Fam. Law 120. . . . . 2.21

T, PETR, 1997 S.L.T. 724; 1996 S.C.L.R. 897; [1997] Fam. Law 8; [1997] Fam. Law
225; *The Times*, August 20, 1996. . . . 28.01, 28.07, 28.38, 28.41, 28.46, 28.75, 28.79,
28.84, 28.87, 28.94, 28.96, 28.100, 28.112, 28.131, 28.133, 28.152
T (Minor) (adoption: validity of order), Re [1986] 2 F.T.R. 31. . . . . 28.16
T v. T, 1987 S.L.T. (Sh.Ct.) 74. . . . . 9.82
—— v. Secretary of State for Scotland, 1987 S.C.L.R. 65. . . . . . . 25.17, 25.38, 25.40, 25.45,
26.304
TSB Scotland PLC v. Haynes, Edinburgh Sh.Ct., June 28, 1990. . . . . 18.73
Tahir v. Tahir (No. 2) 1995 S.L.T. 451. . . . . 2.42
Tait v. Johnston (1891) 18 R. 606; (1891) 28 S.L.R. 431. . . . . 3.90, 6.02, 6.45,
6.46, 28.36, 30.17
—— v. Lees (1903) 5 F. 304; (1903) 10 S.L.T. 528; (1903) 40 S.L.R. 253. . . . . 2.34
—— v. Main, 1989 S.L.T. (Sh.Ct.) 81; 1989 S.C.L.R. 106. . . . . 11.31, 11.33, 24.06
Tait & Co. v. Wallace (1894) 2 S.L.T. 261. . . . . 19.31
Tallis v. H.M. Advocate, 1982 S.C.C.R. 91. . . . . 16.39
Tatry, The (C-406/92) [1994] E.C.R. I-5439. . . . . 3.11, 3.60, 3.61
Tavendale v. Burgh of Motherwell and Wishaw, 1962 S.C. 216; 1962 S.L.T. 228. . . . 14.57

Taylor v. Brick, 1982 S.L.T. 25.................................... 2.11, 2.100, 2.102
—— v. Calvert [1978] 1 W.L.R. 899; [1978] 2 All E.R. 630.................... 26.174
—— v. Drummond (1848) 11 D. 223; (1848) 21 Sc.Jur. 53..................... 12.24
—— v. Fairlie's Trs (1833) 6 W. & S. 301................................. 11.54
—— v. Haughey, 1982 S.C.C.R. 360.. 16.65
—— v. Scottish and Universal Newspapers Ltd, 1981 S.C. 408; 1982 S.L.T. 172.... 4.88,
4.89
—— v. Simon Carves Ltd, 1958 S.L.T. (Sh.Ct.) 23; 1958 74 Sh.Ct.Rep. 41........ 9.112
—— v. Steel-Maitland, 1913 S.C. 978; 1913 2 S.L.T. 29; (1913) 50 S.L.R. 776...... 12.26
—— v. Taylor, 1919 1 S.L.T. 169....................................... 11.70, 11.72
Taylor (Robert) & Partners (Edinburgh) v. William Gerrard, 1995 S.C.L.R. 1131;
1996 S.L.T. (Sh.Ct.) 105.. 13.71
Taylor's Trs v. McGavigan (1896) 23 R. 945; (1896) 33 S.L.R. 707.............. 18.05
Tayside R.C., Petrs, 1987 G.W.D. 9–262................................... 28.38
Telford's Exr v. Blackwood (1866) 4 M. 369..................... 11.11, 11.30, 29.27
Temple (John) Ltd v. Logan, 1973 S.L.T. (Sh.Ct.) 41........................ 1–27
Tenlon v. Seaton (1885) 12 R. 1179...................................... 11.65
Tennant v. Houston, 1987 S.L.T. 317..................................... 2.128
Tennent Caledonian Breweries Ltd v. Gearty, 1980 S.L.T. (Sh.Ct.) 71...... 10.04, 13.50,
25.19, 30.02, 30.04
Tennents v. Romanes (1881) 8 R. 824; (1881) 18 S.L.R. 583.............. 18.19, 18.37
Terrell v. Ker (1900) 2 F. 1055; (1900) 8 S.L.T. 74; (1900) 37 S.L.R. 807......... 10.06
Terry v. Murray, 1947 S.C. 10; 1946 S.N. 95; 1947 S.L.T. 8............. 2.15, 7.06, 7.13
Thames Cleaning Co. Ltd v. British Rail Transport Ship Management (Scotland)
Ltd, Stranraer Sh.Ct., May 12, 1981, unreported.................... 18.09, 18.20
Thiem's Trs v. Collie (1899) 7 S.L.T. 4.................................... 29.67
Thirtle v. Copin (1912) 29 Sh.Ct.Rep. 13................................. 25.19
Thom v. Andrew (1888) 15 R. 780; (1888) 25 S.L.R. 595........... 11.52, 11.54, 11.64
—— v. Bridges and Macqueen (1857) 19 D. 721; (1857) 29 Sc.Jur. 311..... 4.110, 12.12
—— v. Caledonian Ry (1902) 9 S.L.T. 440................................. 11.54
—— v. McBeth (1875) 3 R. 161.................................... 23.39, 23.40
Thom & Sons v. Burrell (1929) 45 Sh.Ct.Rep. 187.......................... 26.32
Thomas v. Thomas, 1947 S.C.(H.L.) 45............................ 18.104, 18.105
Thompson v. Crawfurd, 1979 S.L.T. (Notes) 91....................... 12.09, 12.10
—— v. Fairfeld Shipbuilding & Engineering Co., 1954 S.C. 354................. 14.30
—— v. Lynn, 1995 S.C.L.R. 1090.................................... 18.47, 18.48
—— v. Strathclyde R.C., Glasgow Sh.Ct., Aug. 5, 1983, unreported............. 26.113
Thompson & Co. v. King (1883) 10 R. 469; (1883) 20 S.L.R. 313............... 18.37
Thoms v. Bain (1888) 15 R. 613... 11.74
—— v. Thom's Tr, 1907 S.C. 343; (1907) 14 S.L.T. 635; (1907) 44 S.L.R. 265...... 19.40
Thomson v. Barclay (1883) 10 R. 694; (1883) 20 S.L.R. 440............... 2.30, 23.18
—— v. Broughty Ferry Commissioners (1898) 6 S.L.T. 202; (1898) 14 Sh.Ct.Rep.
365.. 26.327
—— v. Edinburgh and District Tramways Co. Ltd (1901) 3 F. 355; (1901) 8 S.L.T.
352; (1901) 38 S.L.R. 263... 19.03
—— v. Fullerton (1842) 5 D. 379.. 29.24
—— v. Glasgow Corporation, 1962 S.C.(H.L.) 36; 1962 S.L.T. 105.... 8.40, 10.02, 10.14,
10.15, 10.16, 10.17, 10.20, 10.25, 16.38,
16.39, 16.87, 16.96, 18.110, 18.111, 18.114
—— v. Gordon (1869) 7 M. 687; 41 Sc.Jur. 347; (1869) 6 S.L.R. 444............. 15.51
—— v. Greig, 1967 S.L.T. (Notes) 113.................................... 12.49
—— v. Hughson & Co. (1861) 23 D. 679; (1861) 33 Sc.Jur. 318...... 10.06, 10.24, 10.44
—— v. Jamieson, 1986 S.L.T. 72.. 15.16
—— v. Paxton (1849) 11 D. 1113.. 13.79
—— v. Simons & Co. Ltd (1943) 60 Sh.Ct.Rep. 106......................... 19.06
—— v. Stirling D.C., 1985 S.L.T. (Lands Tr.) 4............................ 2.09
—— v. Thomson [1887] 14 R. 634.. 4.07
—— v. ——, 1979 S.L.T. (Sh.Ct.) 11..................................... 18.40
—— v. Watson Ltd (1943) 61 Sh.Ct.Rep. 67............................... 15.47
—— v. Wiggins Teape Ltd, 1981 S.L.T. (Sh.Ct.) 85.................... 6.04, 6.15, 6.20
—— v. Woodthorpe (1863) 1 M. 635................................ 11.77, 11.79
—— v. Yorkshire Building Society, 1994 S.C.L.R. 1014...................... 4.111
Thomson & Co. v. Bowater & Sons, 1918 S.C. 316; 1918 1 S.L.T. 200; (1918) 55
S.L.R. 293.. 15.64, 15.65
—— v. Dailly (1897) 24 R. 1173; (1897) 4 S.L.T. 291; (1897) 34 S.L.R. 850....... 14.37
—— v. Pattison Elder & Co. (1895) 22 R. 432; (1895) 2 S.L.T. 546.............. 9.30
Thomson (D.C.) & Co. v. D'Agostino (1985) 30 J.L.S. 381.................... 19.40

Thomson Ship Cranes Ltd, *The Scotsman*, December 9, 1971. . . . . 1.32
Thomson's Trs v. Livingston (1863) 2 M. 114. . . . . 4.15, 4.16
Thorburn v. Dempster (1900) 2 F. 583; (1900) 7 S.L.T. 364; (1900) 37 S.L.R. 415. . . 3.54,
                                                                        9.108, 9.109, 9.112
—— v. Hoby & Co. (1853) 15 D. 767; (1853) 25 Sc.Jur. 640; (1853) 2 Stuart 468. . 15.73
Thorburn (John) and Sons v. Border Hervexters Ltd, 1992 S.L.T. 549; 1992
    S.C.L.R. 144. . . . . 16.102
Thorne v. Smith [1947] K.B. 307; [1947] 1 All E.R. 39; (1947) 91 S.J. 54. . . . . 26.269
—— v. Strathclyde R.C., 1984 S.L.T. 161. . . . . 15.88, 15.89
Thorniewood United F.C. Social Club v. Hamilton, 1982 S.L.T. (Sh.Ct.) 97. . 14.08, 14.12
Thornton, 1967 S.L.T. (Sh.Ct.) 71. . . . . 1.28
—— v. North Star Fishing Co. Ltd, 1983 S.L.T. 530. . . . . 13.71
Tingman v. Tingman (1854) 17 D. 122; (1854) 27 Sc.Jur. 35. . . . . 11.70
Titchener v. British Railways Board, 1981 S.L.T. 208. . . . . 10.21
Tito v. Waddell [1975] 1 W.L.R. 1303; [1975] 3 All E.R. 997; (1975) 119 S.J. 680. . 16.92,
                                                                                16.93
Tobermory Magistrates v. Capaldi, 1938 S.L.T. (Sh.Ct.) 38; (1938) 54 Sh.Ct.Rep.
    175. . . . . 25.47
Todd v. H.M. Advocate, 1984 S.L.T. 123. . . . . 16.58
—— v. Kelso Co-operative Society, 1953 S.L.T. (Sh.Ct.) 2. . . . . 26.201
—— v. Macdonald, 1960 J.C. 93; 1960 S.L.T. (Notes) 53. . . . . 16.81, 16.82
—— v. Neilars, 1940 S.L.T. (Sh.Ct.) 12. . . . . 26.183
—— v. Todd, 1966 S.L.T. 50. . . . . 18.117
Todd and Higginbotham v. Glasgow Corporation (1879) 16 S.L.R. 718. . . . . . 14.23, 14.28
Tolan v. Stewart (1913) 30 Sh.Ct.Rep. 280. . . . . 9.30
Tolland v. William Reid (Sports) Ltd, 1970 S.L.T. (Notes) 19. . . . . 5.78
Torbet v. Borthwick (1849) 11 D. 694. . . . . 12.18
Torrance v. Craufuird (1822) 1 S. 301 (N.E. 280). 9.94, 19.03
Tosh v. Ogilvy (1873) 1 R. 254; (1873) 11 S.L.R. 119. . . . . 15.27, 16.62
Tough v. Tough, Aberdeen Sh.Ct., Nov. 22, 1978, unreported. 21.96
Town and County Bank v. Lilienlield (1900) 8 S.L.T. 227. . . . . 11.70
Towning & Sons v. Watson & Son, 1968 S.L.T. (Sh.Ct.) 27. . . . . 19.60
Tradden v. Sweetman (1862) 24 D. 1360. . . . . 11.80
Trade Development Bank v. David W. Haig (Bellshill) Ltd, 1983 S.L.T. 107. . 9.67, 13.05
Train v. Little, 1911 S.C. 736; 1911 1 S.L.T. 345; (1911) 48 S.L.R. 619. . . . . 11.78
Train & McIntyre Ltd v. Forbes, 1925 S.L.T. 286; 1925 S.N. 33. . . . . . 15.72, 15.75, 15.76
Trainer v. Renfrewshire Upper District Committee, 1907 S.C. 1117; (1907) 15
    S.L.T. 201; (1907) 44 S.L.R. 835. . . . . 18.69, 21.93
Trappes v. Meredith (1871) 10 M. 38. . . . . 29.26
Travers v. Neilson, 1967 S.C. 155; 1967 S.L.T. 64. . . . . 12.45
Trawnik v. Lennox [1985] 1 W.L.R. 532; (1985) 129 S.J. 225; [1985] 2 All E.R. 368. . 4.53
Traynor v. Henderson, 1972 S.L.T. (Sh.Ct.) 73. . . . . 18.108
Traynor's Exrs v. Baird's & Scottish Steel Ltd, 1957 S.C. 311; 1957 S.L.T. 71. . . . . . 9.83
Treacher v. Galloway (1845) 7 D. 1099; (1845) 17 Sc.Jur. 567. . . . . 19.41
Treasury Solicitor v. Regester [1978] 1 W.L.R. 446; [1978] 2 All E.R. 920; (1977)
    122 S.J. 163. . . . . 19.20
Trepca Mines Ltd, Re [1960] 1 W.L.R. 24; [1959] 3 All E.R. 798 (1959) 104 S.J.
    32. . . . . 16.67
Troc Sales Ltd v. Kirkcaldy District Licensing Board, 1982 S.L.T. (Sh.Ct.) 77. . . . . 25.31,
                                                                        25.32, 25.46, 26.38, 26.255
Trojan Plant Hue Co. Ltd v. Durafencing (Northern) Ltd, 1974 S.L.T. (Sh.Ct.) 3. . 18.82
Trowsdale's Tr. v. Forcett Ry (1870) 9 M. 88; (1870) 43 Sc.Jur. 51; (1870) 8 S.L.R.
    82. . . . . 11.15, 29.27
Tulloch v. Baind (1859) 21 D. 807. . . . . 12.20
—— v. Davidson (1858) 20 D. 1045. . . . . 9.15
Tulloh v. Tulloh (1861) 23 D. 639. . . . . 9.30
Turnbull v. Campbell (1859) 21 D. 1021; (1859) 31 Sc.Jur. 595. . . . . 2.110
—— v. Frame, 1966 S.L.T. 24. . . . . 4.50
Turnbull & Son v. Scott (1899) 15 Sh.Ct.Rep. 268. . . . . 29.29
Turner v. Galway (1882) 19 S.L.R. 892. . . . . 24.06
—— v. Garstrang RDC (1965) 64 L.G.R. 28. . . . . 26.161
—— v. Gray (1821) 3 S. 235 (N.E. 165). 18.04
—— v. Tunnock's Trs (1864) 2 M. 509. . . . . 13.44
—— v. Turner, 1930 S.L.T. 393; 1930 S.N. 40. . . . . 15.105
—— v. Wilson, 1954 S.C. 296; 1954 S.L.T. 131. . . . . 12.24, 12.25, 26.10
Turner's Ltd v. Hay, 1963 S.L.T. (Sh.Ct.) 45; (1963) 79 Sh.Ct.Rep. 180. . . . . 9.114

Turner's Trs v. Steel (1900) 2 F. 363; (1900) 7 S.L.T. 287; (1900) 37 S.L.R. 250. . .   18.30,
                                                                                          18.34
Tweedie (1829) Shaw 222. . . . .   16.62
—— v. Tweedie, 1966 S.L.T. (Notes) 89. . . . .   11.11, 11.29
Twibill v. Niven & Co. (1897) 12 Sh.Ct.Rep. 313. . . . .   26.32

UCB Bank plc v. Dundas & Wilson C.S., 1990 S.C. 377; 1991 S.L.T. 90; 1990
    S.C.L.R. 827. . . . .   14.67, 14.39
Uden v. Burrell (1914) 30 Sh.Ct.Rep. 224. . . . .   11.32
Ulferts Fabriker A.B. v. Form and Colour Ltd, 1977 S.L.T. (Sh.Ct.) 19. . . . .   9.114
Underhill v. Ministry for Food [1950] 1 All E.R. 591; (1950) 94 S.J. 194. . . . .   4.57
Unigate Foods Ltd v. Scottish Milk Marketing Board, 1975 S.C.(H.L.) 75; 1975
    S.L.T. (Notes) 76. . . . .   2.13, 9.67, 16.23, 16.24, 20.04, 21.02
Union Bank of Australia v. Harrison Jones & Devlin Ltd (1910) 11 C.L.R. 492. . . .   23.09
Union Bank of Scotland v. Macmillan (1930) 47 Sh.Ct.Rep. 15. . . . .   19.28
—— v. Mills (1926) 42 Sh.Ct.Rep. 141. . . . .   29.18
Union Bank of Scotland Ltd v. Fulton, 1929 S.L.T. (Sh.Ct.) 37; (1928) 45
    Sh.Ct.Rep. 62. . . . .   16.96
Union Carbide Corporation v. B.P. Chemicals Ltd, 1995 S.C.L.R. 524. . . . .   3.66
United Creameries Co. v. Boyd & Co., 1912 S.C. 617; 1912 1 S.L.T. 297; (1912) 49
    S.L.R. 460. . . . .   25.19, 25.24, 25.25, 26.32
United Dominions Trust v. McDowell 1984 S.L.T. (Sh.Ct.) 10. . . . .   2.12, 2.15, 7.13
—— v. Stark 1981 S.L.T. (Sh.Ct.) 58. . . . .   1.38
Upham (JWA) Ltd v. Torode, 1982 S.C. 5. . . . .   24.06
Upper Crathes Fishings Ltd v. Barclay, 1991 S.C.L.R. 151. . . . .   23.37
Ure v. Ure, 1947 S.C. 305; 1947 S.L.T. 179; 1947 S.N. 55. . . . .   16.90, 18.49
Urquhart v. British Railways Board, 1982 S.L.T. 308. . . . .   10.17, 10.18
—— v. Grigor (1857) 19 D. 853; (1857) 29 Sc.Jur. 399. . . . .   12.27, 14.17

V v. B (A Minor) (Abduction) [1991] 1 F.L.R. 266; [1991] Fam. Law 138; [1991]
    F.C.R. 451. . . . .   2.58
VAG Finance Ltd v. Smith, 1988 S.L.T. (Sh.Ct.) 59; 1988 S.C.L.R. 598. . . . .   18.12
Valentine v. Grangemouth Coal Co. (1897) 5 S.L.T. 47; (1897) 35 S.L.R. 12. . . . . . .   21.49
Valery v. Scott (1876) 3 R. 965; (1876) 13 S.L.R. 622. . . . .   9.18
Vallance v. Easson Bros, 1949 S.L.T. (Notes) 7. . . . .   13.08
Valley v. Wiggins Teape Ltd, 1979 S.L.T. (Notes) 50. . . . .   9.35
Van den Boogard v. Laumen (C-220/95) [1997] Q.B. 759; [1997] 3 W.L.R. 284;
    [1997] All E.R. (EC) 517. . . . .   3.05, 3.32
Van Engers, Roeclofs & Co. v. Ellis Hughes (1898) 6 S.L.T. 90. . . . .   15.62
Van Uden v. Burrell, 1916 S.C. 391; 1926 1 S.L.T. 117; (1916) 53 S.L.R. 400. . . . . . .   4.03
Van Uden Maritime BV v. Kommanditgesellschaft in Firma DECO-LINE, Peter
    Determann KG (C-391/95), Opinion of Att. Gen. Leger, June 10, 1977. . . . . . .   3.65
Varney (Scotland) Ltd v. Lanark T.C., 1974 S.C. 245; 1976 S.L.T. 46. . . . . . .   2.132, 18.13
Vaughan v. Davidson (1854) 16 D. 922. . . . .   11.85, 11.86
Verrico (J.) & Co. Ltd v. Australian Mutual Provident Society, 1972 S.L.T. (Sh.Ct.)
    57. . . . .   11.14, 29.19
Vervaeke v. Smith [1983] 1 A.C. 145; [1982] 2 W.L.R. 855 [1982] 2 All E.R. 144;
    (1982) 126 S.J. 295. . . . .   2.104
Vidlocker v. McWilliam, 1964 S.L.T. (Notes) 6. . . . .   11.68, 11.69
Vincent v. Anderson (1919) 36 Sh.Ct.Rep. 182. . . . .   23.40
—— v. Chalmers & Co's Tr. (1887) 5 R. 43; (1877) 15 S.L.R. 27. . . . .   11.30, 11.31, 11.32
Visionhire v. Dick, Kilmarnock Sh.Ct., Sept. 18, 1984, unreported. 30.43, 30.72
"Vitruvia" S.S. Co. v. Ropner Shipping Co., 1924 S.C. (H.L.) 31; 1924 S.L.T. 83;
    (1924) 61 S.L.R. 52. . . . .   10.19

W (A Minor), Re [1985] 3 All E.R. 449. . . . .   28.91
W v. C (1939) Sh.Ct.Rep. 261. . . . .   28.103
—— v. Sunderland MBC [1980] 1 W.L.R. 1101; [1980] 2 All E.R. 514; (1980) 124
    S.J. 272. . . . .   16.38
Waddell v. Dumfries & Galloway R.C., 1979 S.L.T. (Sh.Ct.) 45. . . . . . .   25.31, 25.33, 26.50
—— v. Hope (1843) 6 D. 160. . . . .   4.112, 11.03, 11.85, 11.86, 12.14
—— v. Stirling C.C. (1942) 59 Sh.Ct.Rep. 78. . . . .   26.324
—— v. Waddell (1836) 15 S. 151. . . . .   29.29
—— v. Waddell's Tr., 1932 S.L.T. 201. . . . .   29.26
Waddington v. Buchan Poultry Products Ltd, 1961 S.L.T. 428. . . . .   15.56
Wagon Finance Ltd v. O'Lone, 1995 S.C.L.R. 149. . . . .   18.19

Wailes Dove Bitumatic Ltd v. Plastic Sealant Services Ltd, 1979 S.L.T. (Sh.Ct.) 41. . 7.31, 7.33, 18.08
Walden v. Campbell, 1940 S.L.T. (Sh.Ct.) 39. . . . . 13.54, 13.55
Walker v. Crawford (1902) 10 S.L.T. 362. . . . . 2.100
—— v. Cumming (1868) 6 M. 318; (1868) 40 Sc.Jur. 175; (1868) 5 S.L.R. 220. . . . . . 9.30
—— v. Dunn, 1995 S.C.L.R. 588. . . . . 21.19
—— v. Infabco Diving Services Ltd, 1983 S.L.T. 633. . . . . 21.24, 21.26, 21.28
—— v. Junor (1903) 5 F. 1035; (1903) 11 S.L.T. 189; (1903) 40 S.L.R. 745. . . . . 21.97
—— v. Kelty's Tr. (1839) 1 D. 1066; affd (1843) 2 Bell's App. 57); (1839) 14 Fac. 1018. . . . . 11.52, 11.56
—— v. McGruther & Marshall Ltd, 1982 S.L.T. 345. . . . . 16.76
—— v. McNeil, 1981 S.L.T. (Notes) 21. . . . . 19.06, 19.33, 19.45
—— v. United Creameries Ltd, 1928 S.L.T. (Sh.Ct.) 21; (1928) 44 Sh.Ct.Rep. 148   21.51
—— v. Walker (1903) 5 F. 320; (1903) 10 S.L.T. 551; (1903) 40 S.L.R. 271. . . 4.27, 4.113
—— v. ——, 1947 S.L.T. (Notes) 8; 1947 S.N. 21. . . . . 14.18
—— v. ——, 1995 S.C.L.R. 187. . . . . 14.18, 14.20
—— v. Waterlow (1869) 7 M. 751; (1869) 6 S.L.R. 466. . . . . 19.46
—— v. Wotherspoon (1916) 35 Sh.Ct.Rep. 74. . . . . 18.19, 18.30
Walker's Tr. v. Walker (1878) 5 R. 678; (1878) 1 S.L.R. 383. . . . . 21.64
Walker & Co. v. Shaw-Stewart (1855) 2 Macq. 424. . . . . 13.36
Wallace (1830) 9 S. 40. . . . . 4.23
—— v. Braid (1900) 2 F. 754; (1900) 37 S.L.R. 569. . . . . 2.106
—— v. Earl of Eglinton (1836) 14 S. 599; (1836) 8 Sc.Jur. 274. . . . . 12.18
—— v. Henderson (1875) 2 R. 999. . . . . 21.04
—— v. —— (1876) 4 R. 264; (1876) 14 S.L.R. 181. . . . . 11.89
—— v. Morrison & Co. Ltd, 1927 S.N. 170. . . . . 8.60
—— v. Scottish Special Housing Association, 1981 S.L.T. (Notes) 60. . . . . . . 10.23, 18.81
Wallace (George) Builders Ltd v. Clydebank Parish Church Congregational Board, Paisley Sh.Ct., May 24, 1984, unreported. . . . .
Walls v. Walls, 1953 S.L.T. 269. . . . . 4.27, 4.28
Walls' Trs v. Drynan (1888) 15 R. 359; (1888) 25 S.L.R. 275. . . . . 2.11, 2.17, 3.101, 6.06, 9.119
Warburton v. Hamilton (1826) 4 S. 631 (N.E. 639). 19.27
Ward v. Coltness Iron Co., 1944 S.C. 318; 1944 S.L.T. 405; 1944 S.N. 26. . . . . 9.07
—— v. Walker, 1920 S.C. 80; 1920 1 S.L.T. 2; (1920) 57 S.L.R. 121. . . . . . 4.14, 4.23, 4.25
Ward (Alexander) & Co. Ltd v. Samyang Navigation Co. Ltd, 1975 S.C.(H.L.) 26; 1975 S.L.T. 126; [1975] 1 W.L.R. 673; [1975] 2 All E.R. 424; affg 1975 S.L.T. 50; rvsg 1973 S.L.T. (Notes) 80. . . . . 3.100, 4.92, 9.117, 9.119, 11.10, 13.12
Wardell, Petr, 1993 S.C.L.R. 398. . . . . 1.27
Wardrope v. Duke of Hamilton (1876) 3 R. 876. . . . . 2.15, 9.14, 10.60
Wards v. Kelvin Tank Services Ltd, 1984 S.L.T. (Sh.Ct.) 39. . . . . 11.16, 11.27
Warrand v. Watson, 1907 S.C. 432; (1907) 14 S.L.T. 694; (1907) 44 S.L.R. 311. . . . 19.03, 19.06
Waterhouse v. Barker [1924] 2 K.B. 759; [1924] All E.R. 777. . . . . 15.93, 15.95
Watmore v. Burns (1839) 1 D. 743; (1839) 14 Fac. 822. . . . . 13.37
Watson v. Babcock Power, 1987 S.C.L.R. 624. . . . . 13.67
—— v. Cowan, 1913 1 S.L.T. 435. . . . . 15.39
—— v. Foley, 1955 S.L.T. (Sh.Ct.) 28; (1955) 71 Sh.Ct.Rep. 47. . . . . 8.05
—— v. Frame (1983) 28 J.L.S. 421. . . . . 10.35
—— v. Livingstone (1902) 5 F. 171; (1902) 10 S.L.T. 421; (1902) 40 S.L.R. 267. . . . 16.02
—— v. McEwan (1905) 7 F.(H.L.) 109; (1905) 13 S.L.T. 340; (1905) 42 S.L.R. 837; [1905] A.C. 480. . . . . 15.16
—— v. McHugh, 1992 S.L.T. (Sh.Ct.) 35; 1992 S.C.L.R. 164. . . . . 17.21
—— v. Russell (1894) 21 R. 433; (1894) 1 S.L.T. 478; (1894) 31 S.L.R. 352. . . 5.79, 5.81, 18.15
—— v. Speedie Bros Ltd (1932) 49 Sh.Ct.Rep. 83. . . . . 14.39
—— v. Stewart (1872) 10 M. 494; (1872) 44 Sc.Jur. 269; (1872) 9 S.L.R. 295. . . . . . 18.41
—— v. Thomson, 1990 S.L.T. 374, 1991 S.L.T. 683. . . . . 4.110
—— v. Watson (1898) 6 S.L.T. 201. . . . . 12.11
—— v. ——, 1934 S.C. 374; 1934 S.L.T. 275; 1934 S.N. 34. . . . . 15.105
—— v. Williamson (1895) 3 S.L.T. 21. . . . . 11.54
Watson (Charles B.) (Scotland) Ltd v. Glasgow District Licensing Board, 1980 S.L.T. (Sh.Ct.) 37. . . . . 25.20, 25.34, 26.38, 26.255
Watson (R. & W.) Ltd v. David Traill & Sons Ltd, 1972 S.L.T. (Notes) 38. . 12.42, 12.48
Watson Gow & Co. v. Glasgow Assessor, 1910 S.C. 807. . . . . 6.12
Watt v. Advocate (Lord), 1979 S.C. 120; 1979 S.L.T. 137. . . . . 12.70, 25.35
—— v. Coughlan (1902) 10 S.L.T. 89. . . . . 2.97

Watt v. Smith's Trs (1901) 9 S.L.T. 215. . . . . 10.08
—— v. Thomson (1868) 6 M. 1112; (1870) 8 M.(H.L.) 77; (1873) 11 M. 960; (1874)
    1 R. (H.L.) 21. . . . . 2.19, 8.16
—— v. Watt, 1978 S.L.T. (Notes) 55. . . . . 14.08
Watt & Co. Ltd v. McEwan (1954) 70 Sh.Ct.Rep. 326. . . . . 18.117
Watt Bros & Co. v. Foyn (1879) 7 R. 126. . . . . 18.04
Wauchope v. North British Ry (1860) 23 D. 191. . . . . 21.04
Weatherall v. Jack, 1995 S.C.L.R. 189. . . . . 8.36
Webb v. Webb (C-294/92) [1994] E.C.R. 1–1717, 1996 S.L.T. (News) A1–A2. . . . . . 3.24
Webb's Exrs v. Reid (1906) 14 S.L.T. 323. . . . . 23.32, 23.34, 26.100
Webster v. Lord Advocate, 1984 S.L.T. 13. . . . . 17.24
—— v. ——, 1985 S.L.T. 361. . . . . 21.84, 21.93, 21.94
—— v. Simpson's Motors, 1967 S.L.T. 287. . . . . 15.38, 15.39, 19.40
—— v. Webster (1896) 33 S.L.R. 369; (1896) 3 S.L.T. 255. . . . . 11.74
Webster Engineering Services v. Gibson, 1987 S.L.T. (Sh.Ct.) 101. . . . . 30.15, 30.329
Weems v. Mathieson (1861) 1 Macq. 215; (1861) 33 Sc.Jur. 621. . . . . 18.85
Weir v. Buchanan (1876) 4 R. 8. . . . . 11.52, 11.53
—— v. Otto (1870) 8 M. 1070; (1870) 42 Sc.Jur. 628; (1870) 7 S.L.R. 708. . . 11.11, 11.36
—— v. Stevenson (1885) 1 Sh.Ct.Rep. 161. . . . . 14.32, 14.46
—— v. Tudhope (1892) 19 R. 858; (1892) 29 S.L.R. 803. . . . . 18.19, 18.70
Weissenbruch v. Weissenbruch, 1965 S.L.T. 139. . . . . 2.108
Welsbach Incandescent Gas Co. v. McMann (1901) 4 F. 395; (1901) 9 S.L.T. 387;
    (1901) 39 S.L.R. 270. . . . . 21.97
Welsh v. Advocate (H.M.), 1986 S.L.T. 664; 1986 S.C.C.R. 233. . . . . 6.46
—— v. Cousin (1899) 2 F. 277; (1899) 37 S.L.R. 199. . . . . 14.65
—— v. Duncan (1893) 20 R. 1014; (1893) 30 S.L.R. 933. 2.29
—— v. Thornhome Services, 1994 S.C.L.R. 1021. . . . . 14.06
Welsh (Andrew) Ltd v. Thornhome Services, 1994 S.C.L.R. 1021. . 8.34, 8.38, 8.44, 18.56
Wescott v. James Dickie & Co., 1991 S.L.T. 200. . . . . 13.67
West v. Cow, 1929 S.C. 783; 1929 S.L.T. 598. . . . . 19.28
—— v. Hair (1926) 43 Sh.Ct.Rep. 118. . . . . 7.25
—— v. Secretary of State for Scotland, 1992 S.C. 385; 1992 S.L.T. 636; 1992
    S.C.L.R. 504. . . . . 21.75, 25.35
West Cumberland Farmers Ltd v. Director of Agriculture of Sri Lanka, 1985 S.L.T.
    296. . . . . 24.06
—— v. Ellon Hinengo Ltd, 1988 S.L.T. 294. . . . . 3.99, 3.100
West Lothian D.C., Linlithgow Sh.Ct., Sept. 20, 1985, unreported. 25.05
Western Bank v. Baird (1863) 2 M. 127. . . . . 15.47
—— v. Baird's Trs (1866) 4 M. 1071. . . . . 21.11
—— v. Buchanan (1865) 4 M. 97. . . . . 9.94, 19.03
Western Ranches Ltd v. Nelson's Trs (1898) 25 R. 527; (1898) 5 S.L.T. 201; (1898)
    35 S.L.R. 448. . . . . 15.28
Western SMT Co. Ltd v. Greenock Magistrates, 1957 S.L.T. (Notes) 22. . . . . 9.90
Westwood v. Keay (1949) 66 Sh.Ct.Rep. 147. . . . . 9.67, 12.26
Wheatley v. Anderson, 1927 S.C. 133; 1927 S.L.T. 127; 1926 S.N. 175. . . . . . . 15.53, 15.61
White v. Lord Morton's Trs (1866) 4 M.(H.L.) 53; (1866) 1 L.R. Sc. App. 70. . . . . . 2.106
—— v. McEwen's Trs (1873) 11 M. 602; (1873) 10 S.L.R. 395. . . . . 5.88, 5.89
—— v. Steel (1894) 21 R. 649; (1894) 1 S.L.T. 575; (1894) 31 S.L.R. 542. . . . . 4.14
—— v. White, 1984 S.L.T. (Sh.Ct.) 30. . . . . 26.125
White & Carter (Councils) Ltd v. McGregor, 1962 S.C.(H.L.) 1. . . . . 21.75
Whitehall v. Whitehall, 1957 S.C. 30; 1957 S.L.T. 96. . . . . 4.72, 15.60
—— v. ——, 1958 S.C. 252; 1958 S.L.T. 268. . . . . 4.14, 15.102
Whitehead v. Blaik (1893) 20 R. 1045; (1893) 30 S.L.R. 916. . . . . 4.115
Whitehouse v. Jordan [1981] 1 W.L.R. 246; [1981] 1 All E.R. 267. . . . . 18.108
—— v. Strathclyde R.C., Dunoon Sh.Ct., Feb. 18, unreported. 18.81
Whitelaw v. Fultan (1871) 10 M. 27; (1871) 44 Sc.Jur. 37; (1871) 9 S.L.R. 25. . . . . . 2.54
Whiteley (Wm.) Ltd v. Dobson, Molle & Co. Ltd (1902) 10 S.L.T. 71. . . . . 15.78
Whitson v. Blairgowrie District Committee (1897) 24 R. 519; (1897) 4 S.L.T. 307;
    (1897) 34 S.L.R. 395. . . . . 26.385
Whyte v. City of Perth Co-operative Society, 1932 S.C. 482; 1932 S.L.T. 349; 1932
    S.N. 42. . . . . 11.65
—— v. Gerrard (1861) 24 D. 102; (1861) 34 Sc.Jur. 58. . . . . 18.34
—— v. Kilmarnock District Committee of Ayr C.C., 1912 2 S.L.T. 15. . . . . 24.01
—— v. Smith Anderson & Co. Ltd, 1974 S.L.T. (Notes) 75. . . . . 16.79
—— v. Walker, 1983 S.L.T. 441. . . . . 2.121, 10.41, 10.46
—— v. Whyte (1895) 23 R. 320; (1895) 3 S.L.T. 225; (1895) 33 S.L.R. 227. . 18.15, 18.98
Wick v. Wick (1898) 1 F. 199; (1898) 36 S.L.R. 180. . . . . 14.38

Widdop (H.) & Co. Ltd v. J. & J. Hay Ltd, 1961 S.L.T. (Notes) 35. . . . . 9.67
Wildridge v. Anderson (1897) 2 Adam 399; (1897) 25 R.(J.) 27; (1897) 5 S.L.T. 206;
    (1897) 35 S.L.R. 125. . . . . 2.126, 2.128
Wilkinson v. Kinneil Cannel and Coking Coal Co. (1897) 24 R. 1001; (1897) 34
    S.L.R. 533. . . . . 4.14, 4.115
—— v. Richards, 1967 S.L.T. 270. . . . . 14.47, 14.54
—— v. Wilkinson (1963) Sh.Ct.Rep. 47. . . . . 7.08
Will v. Sneddon, Campbell & Munro, 1931 S.C. 164; 1931 S.L.T. 125; 1930 S.N.
    151. . . . . 11.52, 11.63, 11.65
Will (W.H.) & Sons Ltd v. Manning's Tr, 1951 S.L.T. (Sh.Ct.) 29. . . . . 11.24
Williams v. Cleveland and Highland Holdings Ltd, 1993 S.L.T. 398. . . . . 23.39
—— v. Forth Valley Health Board, 1983 S.L.T. 376. . . . . 10.41
—— v. Summerfield [1972] 2 Q.B. 513; [1972] 3 W.L.R. 131; [1972] 2 All E.R.
    1334; (1972) 116 S.J. 413. . . . . 15.95
Williamson v. H.M. Advocate, 1979 J.C. 36; 1978 S.L.T. (Notes) 58. . . . . 16.51
—— v. Harris, 1981 S.L.T. (Sh.Ct.) 56. . . . . 18.17, 18.36, 18.70
—— v. John Williams (Wishaw) Ltd, 1971 S.L.T. (Sh.Ct.) 2. . . . . 10.30, 19.16, 19.36, 19.55
—— v. McPherson, 1951 S.C. 438; 1951 S.L.T. 283. . . . . 14.60
—— v. Stewart (1910) 27 Sh.Ct.Rep. 240. . . . . 26.10
Will's Trs v. Cairngorm Canoeing and Sailing School Ltd, 1973 S.L.T. (Notes) 63. . 8.64,
    8.65
Wilson (1885) 13 R. 342. . . . . 6.45, 16.08, 16.09
—— v. Agnew (1828) 6 S. 927. . . . . 12.11
—— v. Bennet (1904) 6 F. 269; (1904) 11 S.L.T. 580. . . . . 2.105
—— v. Brakenridge (1888) 15 R. 587; (1888) 25 S.L.R. 394. . . . . 18.35
—— v. Clyde Rigging and Boiler Scaling Co., 1959 S.C. 328; 1959 S.L.T. (Notes)
    59. . . . . 9.112
—— v. Cook, 1954 S.L.T. (Sh.Ct.) 17; (1953) 69 Sh.Ct.Rep. 353. . . . . 4.98
—— v. Cumming, 1970 S.L.T. (Sh.Ct.) 44. . . . . 2.36, 26.277
—— v. Dunlop, Bremner & Co. Ltd, 1921 1 S.L.T. 35. . . . . 2.95
—— v. Ferguson, 1957 S.L.T. (Sh.Ct.) 52; (1957) 73 Sh.Ct.Rep. 194. . . . . 13.53
—— v. Glasgow Tramways Co. (1877) 5 R. 981; (1878) 15 S.L.R. 656. . . . . . . 2.99, 12.70
—— v. Hay, 1977 S.L.T. (Sh.Ct.) 52. . . . . 13.51, 13.54, 13.55
—— v. IBA, 1979 S.C. 351; 1979 S.L.T. 279. . . . . 9.118
—— v. Imrie Engineering Services, 1993 S.L.T. 235. . . . . 16.94
—— v. Junor (1907) 15 S.L.T. 182. . . . . 2.95, 13.64
—— v. Lothian R.C., 1995 S.L.T. 991; 1995 S.C.L.R. 634. . . . . 9.41, 10.04
—— v. Mackie (1875) 3 R. 18; (1875) 13 S.L.R. 8. . . . . 11.19, 11.35
—— v. MacQueen, 1925 S.L.T. (Sh.Ct.) 130; (1925) 41 Sh.Ct.Rep. 278. . . . . 16.55
—— v. Mersey Insulation Co. Ltd, 1987 S.L.T. 238. . . . . 10.17
—— v. Murphy, 1936 S.L.T. 564; 1936 S.N. 106. 2.104, 2.105
—— v. Rapp, 1911 S.C. 1360; 1909 2 S.L.T. 295; (1909) 47 S.L.R. 257. . . . . . 13.43, 14.47,
    14.54
—— v. Stronach (1862) 24 D. 271. . . . . 29.67
—— v. Thomas Usher & Son, 1934 S.C. 322; 1934 S.L.T. 307; 1934 S.N. 18. . . . . . . 16.76,
    16.81, 16.91
—— v. Wallace (1858) 20 D. 764; (1858) 30 Sc.Jur. 415. . . . . 2.34
—— v. Wilson, 1981 S.L.T. 101. . . . . 11.11, 11.16, 11.36
—— v. Young (1896) 4 S.L.T. 73. . . . . 15.19
Wilson's Exrs v. Bank of England, 1925 S.L.T. 81. 15.57, 15.62
Wilson's Trs v. Wilson's Factor (1869) 7 M. 457; (1869) 41 Sc.Jur. 244; (1869) 6
    S.L.R. 285. . . . . 18.87, 19.05
Wilson & Clyde Coal Co. v. Cairnduff, 1911 S.C. 647. . . . . 24.15
Wilson & McFarlane v. Stewart & Co. (1898) 25 R. 655; (1898) 5 S.L.T. 363; (1898)
    35 S.L.R. 538. . . . . 2.100, 9.120
Wimpey Construction (UK) Ltd v. Martin Black & Co. (Wire Ropes) Ltd, 1988
    S.C. 264. . . . . 19.57
Winchester v. Ramsay, 1966 S.C. 41; 1966 S.L.T. 97. . . . . 12.42, 12.61, 12.64
Wines (H.D.) (Inverness) Ltd v. Inverness District Licensing Board, 1981 S.C. 318;
    1982 S.L.T. 73. . . . . 25.17, 26.255
Winnik v. Dick, 1984 S.L.T. 185. . . . . 10.24
Winning v. Napier, Son & Co. Ltd, 1963 S.C. 293; 1963 S.L.T. 43. . . . . 14.11, 14.12
Winter v. Kerr (1895) 12 Sh.Ct.Rep. 77. . . . . 11.44, 12.70, 12.72
Winter (David) & Sons Ltd v. George Craig & Sons Ltd, 1995 S.L.T. 1331; 1995
    S.C.L.R. 109. . . . . 8.34, 14.06
Wisely v. John Fulton Plumbers Ltd, 1998 S.L.T. 1026. . . . . 21.36
Wishart v. Howatson (1897) 5 S.L.T. 84. . . . . 2.95

Wither v. Cowie, 1990 S.C.C.R. 741. . . . . 13.69
Withers v. Lattimore (1920) 37 Sh.Ct.Rep. 147. . . . . 11.68
Wolf and Wolf v. Forfar Potato Co., 1984 S.L.T. 100. . . . . 13.09
Wolfson v. Edelman, 1952 S.L.T. (Sh.Ct.) 87; (1952) 68 Sh.Ct.Rep. 307. . . . . 2.42
——— v. Glasgow District Licensing Board, 1980 S.C. 136; 1981 S.L.T. 17. . . 18.13, 26.252
Wolthekker v. Northern Agricultural Co. (1862) 1 M. 211; (1862) 35 Sc.Jur. 156. . . 11.35
Wood v. Miller, 1960 S.C. 86; 1960 S.L.T. (Notes) 7. . . . . 14.42, 14.48, 19.40
——— v. North British Ry (1899) 1 F. 562; (1899) 6 S.L.T. 323. 2.105
——— v. Philips, 1994 S.L.T. 142. . . . . 10.18
——— v. Wood's Trs (1904) 6 F. 640; (1904) 12 S.L.T. 20; (1904) 41 S.L.R. 489. . . . . 19.05
Wood's Trs v. Wood (1900) 2 F. 870; (1900) 8 S.L.T. 34; (1900) 37 S.L.R. 671. . . . 12.24,
   12.26
Woodbury v. Sutherland's Trs, 1938 S.C. 689; 1938 S.L.T. 510; 1938 S.N. 69. . . . . . . 8.19
——— v. ———, 1939 S.L.T. 93; 1939 S.N. 69. . . . . 10.29, 10.30
Woods v. ACS Motors Ltd, 1930 S.C. 1035; 1930 S.L.T. 717; 1930 S.N. 114. . . . . . . 2.123
——— v. British Steel Corporation, 1974 S.L.T. (Notes) 24. . . . . 19.15
——— v. Co-operative Insurance Society, 1924 S.C. 692; 1924 S.L.T. 529; (1924) 61
   S.L.R. 489. . . . . 2.12, 2.101
——— v. Minister of Pensions, 1952 S.C. 529; 1953 S.L.T. 49. . . . . . . 18.110, 18.111, 18.114
Woodward v. Woodward, 1910 2 S.L.T. 248. . . . . 19.41
Wordie Property Co. Ltd v. Secretary of State for Scotland, 1984 S.L.T. 345. . . . . . . 25.08
Wordie's Trs v. Wordie, 1916 S.C.(H.L.) 126; 1916 1 S.L.T. 246. . . . . 19.13
Wright v. Buchanan, 1917 S.C. 73. . . . . 29.89
——— v. Guild & Wyllie (1893) 30 S.L.R. 785. . . . . 9.30
——— v. Valentine (1910) 26 Sh.Ct.Rep. 26. . . . . 15.47
——— v. Wightman (1875) 3 R. 68; (1875) 13 S.L.R. 29. . . . . 2.54
Wright, Walter & Co. Ltd v. Cowdray, 1973 S.L.T. (Sh.Ct.) 56. . . . . 18.85, 18.86
Writers to the Signet v. Mackersy, 1924 S.C. 776; 1924 S.L.T. 549; (1924) 6 S.L.R.
   532. . . . . 6.01
Wycombe D.C. v. Jeffways & Pilot Coaches (1983) 81 L.G.R. 662. . . . . 26.167
Wyld v. Silver [1962] 1 W.L.R. 863; [1962] 2 All E.R. 809; (1962) 106 S.J. 409. . . . . 11.53
Wylie v. H.M. Advocate, 1966 S.L.T. 149. . . . . 2.19, 16.62, 16.69
——— v. Corrigan, 1998 G.W.D. 34–1731. . . . . 21.09
Wyllie v. Fisher, 1907 S.C. 686; (1907) 14 S.L.T. 894. . . . . 18.117

X v. Y, 1922 S.L.T. 158. . . . . 15.102
——— v. ———, 1945 S.L.T. (Sh.Ct.) 2. . . . . 12.10
——— v. ———, 1994 S.C.L.R. 775. . . . . 28.59, 28.99, 28.101, 28.115

Y (Minors) (Adoption Jurisdiction), Re [1985] Fam. 136; [1985] 3 W.L.R. 601;
   [1985] 3 All E.R. 33; [1986] 1 F.L.R. 152; (1985) 16 Fam. Law 26. . . . . 28.43
Yates v. Robertson (1891) 18 R. 1206; (1891) 29 S.L.R. 911. 16.55
Yau v. Ogilvie & Co., 1985 S.L.T. 91. . . . . 15.88
Yellowlees v. Alexander (1882) 9 R. 765; (1882) 19 S.L.R. 539. . . . . 13.44
Young, Petrs, (1828) 7 S. 220. . . . . 4.23, 4.26
——— v. Aktiebolaget Ofverums Bruk (1890) 18 R. 163. . . . . 11.12, 29.27
——— v. Armour, 1921 1 S.L.T. 211. . . . . 2.20, 8.32
——— v. Carter (1907) 14 S.L.T. 411, 829. . . . . 11.70
——— v. Evans, 1968 S.L.T. (Notes) 57. . . . . 9.119
——— v. Mitchells (1874) 1 R. 1011; (1874) 11 S.L.R. 582. . . . . 2.105
——— v. National Coal Board, 1957 S.C. 99; 1957 S.L.T. 266. . . . . 15.53, 15.54, 15.65
——— v. Nith Commissioners (1880) 7 R. 891. . . . . 17.14, 19.03, 19.05
——— v. North British Ry (1887) 14 R.(H.L.) 53; (1887) 12 App. Cas. 544; (1887) 24
   S.L.R. 763. . . . . 4.67
——— v. O'Rourk (1826) 4 S. 617 (N.E. 625). 2.42
——— v. Roberton (1830) 9 S. 59. . . . . 2.42
——— v. Young's Trs 1957 S.C. 318; 1957 S.L.T. 205. . . . . 2.104, 2.106
Young (John) (Bellshill) Ltd v. Jay, Hamilton Sh.Ct., May 21, 1992, unreported. . . 18.70
Young & Co. v. Graham (1860) 23 D. 36. . . . . 9.47
Young's Exrx v. Armour, 1957 S.L.T. (Sh.Ct.) 42; (1956) 73 Sh.Ct.Rep. 21.78
Yuille v. Daks Simpson Ltd, 1984 S.L.T. 115. . . . . 12.47
——— v. Lawrie (1823) 2 S. 155 (N.E. 140). 23.25

Z v. Z, 1954 S.L.T. (Sh.Ct.) 47; (1954) 70 Sh.Ct.Rep. 169. 28.100
Zagrodnik v. Zagrodnik, 1952 S.C. 258. . . . . 18.113
Zannetos v. Glenford Investment Holdings Ltd, 1982 S.L.T. 453. . . . . 5.81

TABLE OF STATUTES

1429 Lawburrows Act.......... 24.02
1581 Lawburrows Act.......... 24.02
     Breach of Arrestment Act
        (c. 23)......... 11.34, 29.30
1584 Decrees in Absence Act
        (c. 10)............... 21.70
1592 Citation Act (c. 59)....... 11.19
1594 Declinature Act (c. 22)..... 2.125
     Ejection   Caution   Act
        (c. 27)............... 23.13
1597 Lawburrows Act (c. 273).... 24.02
1600 Crown Proceedings Act
        (c. 23)................ 4.76
1661 March Dykes Act (c. 41).... 2.55,
                     23.44, 23.45, 23.46
     Diligence Act (c. 344)....... 2.40
1669 March Dykes Act (c. 17).... 2.55,
                     23.45, 23.46
1681 Declinature Act (c. 13)..... 2.125
1686 Interlocutors Act (c. 4)...... 5.83
     Evidence Act (c. 30).. 16.53, 16.60
1693 Citation Act (c. 21)........ 11.19
     Court of Session Act
        (c. 42)................ 5.19
1695 Division of Commonties
        Act (c. 38)...... 2.55, 23.37
     Runrig Lands Act (c. 51).... 2.55
1672 Ajudications Act (c. 45)..... 2.40
1770 Entail Improvement Act
        (10 Geo. 3, c. 51)..... 26.259
     s. 11 .... 26.259
     s. 26 .... 26.259
     s. 33 .... 26.260
1808 Herring Fishery (Scotland)
        Act (48 Geo. 3,
        c. 110)
     s. 60 .... 2.02
1809 Public Records (Scotland)
        Act (49 Geo. 3, c. 42)... 5.38
1815 Jury Trials (Scotland) Act
        (55 Geo. 3, c. 42)
     s. 6 .... 2.110
1822 Riotous   Assemblies
        (Scotland) Act (3
        Geo. 4, c. 33)........ 26.108
     s. 10 .... 26.108
1825 Jurors (Scotland) Act (6
        Geo. 4, c. 22)
     s. 3 .... 1.12
     Court of Session Act (6
        Geo. 4, c. 120)
     s. 4 .... 11.82
     s. 40 .... 18.99
     s. 57 .... 2.75
1830 Court of Session Act (11
        Geo. 4 & Will, 4,
        c. 56)
     s. 21 .... 2.74
     s. 22 .... 2.74
     s. 33 .... 2.39, 2.56

1838 Debtors (Scotland) Act (1
        & 2 Vict. c. 114)
     s. 21 ...... 11.28, 11.32, 11.33
     s. 22 .... 11.25, 29.38
        (2) 29.38
     s. 32 .... 11.19
     Sheriff Courts (Scotland)
        Act (1 & 2 Vict.
        c. 119).......... 16.97, 21.03
     s. 15 .... 2.53
     s. 21 .... 2.74
1840 Entail Sites Act (3 & 4
        Vict. c. 48).......... 26.261
     s. 1 .... 26.261
     s. 3 .... 26.261
     Evidence (Scotland) Act
        (3 & 4 Vict. c. 59)
     s. 3 .... 16.46, 16.52, 16.53
1845 Lands Clauses Consolida-
        tion (Scotland) Act (8
        & 9 Vict. c. 19) 26.92, 26.348
     s. 9 .... 26.95
     s. 15 .... 26.92
     s. 16 .... 26.92
     s. 21 .... 26.93
     s. 22 .... 26.93, 26.356
     ss 23–52 .... 26.93
     s. 56 .... 26.93, 26.94
     s. 57 .... 26.93, 26.94
     s. 60 .... 26.94
     s. 80 .... 22.107
     s. 84 .... 26.95
     s. 87 .... 26.95
     s. 89 .... 26.95
     s. 97 .... 26.95
     s. 114 .... 26.95
     s. 139 .... 26.95
     Railways Clauses Consol-
        idation (Scotland) Act
        (8 & 9 Vict. c. 20).... 26.201,
                               26.412
     s. 3 .... 26.347
     s. 6 .... 26.348
     s. 7 .... 26.349
     s. 8 .... 26.349
     s. 11 .... 26.349
     s. 25 .... 26.348
     s. 30 .... 26.350
     s. 31 .... 26.350
     s. 32 .... 26.348
     s. 33 .... 26.348
     s. 34 .... 36.348
     s. 35 .... 26.348
     s. 36 .... 26.348
     s. 37 .... 26.348
     s. 39 .... 26.350
     s. 51 .... 26.352
     s. 53 .... 26.351
     s. 54 .... 26.351
     s. 57 .... 26.352

1845 Railways Clauses Consol-
        idation (Scotland) Act
        —*cont.*
        s. 60 . . . . 26.353
        s. 61 . . . . 26.353
        s. 63 . . . . 26.353
        s. 134 . . . . 26.347
        s. 147 . . . . 26.347
        s. 150 . . . . 25.31, 26.347
1846 Citations (Scotland) Act (9
        & 10 Vict. c. 67)
        s. 1 . . . . 11.19
1847 Harbours, Docks and Piers
        Clauses Act (10 & 11
        Vict. c. 27) 26.207
        s. 7 . . . . 26.207
        s. 26 . . . . 26.207
        s. 46 . . . . 26.208
        s. 57 . . . . 26.208
        s. 79 . . . . 26.209
        s. 80 . . . . 26.209
        s. 85 . . . . 26.209
        s. 92 . . . . 26.209
        s. 94 . . . . 26.209
1850 Court of Session Act (13
        & 14 Vict. c. 36)
        s. 16 . . . . 2.39, 2.56
        s. 19 . . . . 2.39
1852 Evidence (Scotland) Act
        (16 & 17 Vict. c. 20)
        s. 1 . . . . 16.02
        s. 4 . . . . 16.81
1853 Sheriff Courts (Scotland)
        Act (16 & 17 Vict.
        c. 80)
        s. 2 . . . . 7.31
        s. 4 . . . . 10.60
1855 Burial Grounds (Scotland)
        Act (18 & 19 Vict.
        c. 68) 26.55
        s. 5 . . . . 26.55
        s. 10 . . . . 26.56
        s. 18 . . . . 26.57
        s. 32 . . . . 26.55, 26.57
1856 Court of Exchequer
        (Scotland) Act (19 &
        20 Vict. c. 56)
        s. 24 . . . . 4.78
1857 Registration of Leases
        (Scotland) Act (20 &
        21 Vict. c. 26) 26.265
        s. 6 . . . . 26.265
        Crown Suits (Scotland)
        Act (21 & 22 Vict.
        c. 42) 4.71, 11.21
        s. 1 . . . . 4.63
        s. 2 . . . . 4.64
        s. 3 . . . . 4.64
        s. 4 . . . . 4.65
        s. 5 . . . . 4.63
1858 Confirmation of Executors
        (Scotland) Act (21 &
        22 Vict. c. 56)
        s. 3 . . . . 2.66, 3.86
1858 Legitimacy Declaration
        Act (21 & 22 Vict.
        c. 93)
        s. 9 . . . . 2.39
1861 Conjugal Rights
        (Scotland) Amend-
        ment Act (24 & 25
        Vict. c. 86)
        s. 8 . . . . 22.52
1863 Church of Scotland Courts
        Act (26 & 27 Vict.
        c. 47) 26.80
        s. 2 . . . . 26.80
1864 Fish Teinds (Scotland) Act
        (27 & 28 Vict. c. 33) . . . 26.81
        s. 2 . . . . 26.81
        s. 4 . . . . 26.81
        s. 5 . . . . 26.81
        s. 5 . . . . 26.81
        s. 7 . . . . 26.81
1867 Hypothec Amendment
        (Scotland) Act (30 &
        31 Vict. c. 42)
        s. 7 . . . . 23.22
1868 Judgments Extension Act
        (31 & 32 Vict. c. 54) . . . 11.68,
                                                11.69
        Promissory Oaths Act (31
        & 32 Vict. c. 72)
        s. 6 . . . . 1.07, 1.14
        Sched. 2, Pt II 1.07, 1.14
        Entail Amendment
        (Scotland) Act (31 &
        32 Vict. c. 84) 26.262,
                                                26.263
        s. 3 . . . . 26.262
        s. 4 . . . . 26.262
        s. 14 . . . . 26.260
        Ecclesiastical Buildings
        and Glebes (Scotland)
        Act (31 & 32 Vict.
        c. 96) 26.82
        s. 3 . . . . 26.82
        ss 4–20 . . . . 26.82
        Court of Session Act (31
        & 32 Vict. c. 100)
        s. 24 . . . . 2.106
        s. 29 . . . . 10.25
        s. 39 . . . . 14.27
        s. 62 . . . . 10.25
        s. 69 . . . . 18.101
        s. 72 . . . . 10.25, 18.98
        s. 103 . . . . 2.127
        Titles to Land Consolida-
        tion (Scotland) Act
        (31 & 32 Vict. c. 101)
        s. 155 . . . . 11.38
        s. 157 . . . . 11.39
        Salmon Fisheries
        (Scotland) Act (31 &
        32 Vict. c. 123) 26.186
        s. 26 . . . . 26.186
1871 Dogs Act (34 & 35 Vict.
        c. 56) 26.14
        s. 2 . . . . 26.14

1871 Promissory Oaths Act (34
     & 35 Vict. c. 72)
     s. 2 .... 1.07
     Regulation of Railways
     Act (34 & 35 Vict.
     c. 78)............... 26.354
     s. 7(1) 26.354
        (2) 26.354
        (3) 26.354
        (4) 26.354
     s. 16(3) 26.354
     Pedlars Act 1871 (34 & 35
     Vict. c. 96)........... 26.401
     s. 3 .... 26.401
     s. 15 .... 26.401
1872 Railway Rolling Stock
     Protection Act 1872
     (25 & 36 Vict. c. 50).. 26.355
     s. 2 .... 26.355
     s. 3 .... 26.355
     s. 4 .... 26.355
     s. 5 .... 26.355
     s. 6(1) 26.355
     s. 52 .... 26.355
1874 Building Societies Act (37
     & 38 Vict. c. 42)
     s. 1 .... 26.53
     s. 4 .... 26.53
     s. 32 .... 26.53
     Conveyancing (Scotland)
     Act (37 & 38 Vict.
     c. 94)
     s. 10 .... 2.66
     s. 35 .... 23.39
1876 Sheriff Courts (Scotland)
     Act (39 & 40 Vict.
     c. 70)
     s. 14(1) 7.31
     s. 29 .... 18.101
     s. 34 .... 5.87
     s. 35 .... 3.86
     s. 50 .... 5.36
     s. 52 .... 25.15
     s. 54 .... 1.36
1877 Writs   Execution
     (Scotland) Act 1877
     (40 & 41 Vict. c. 40)
     s. 2 .... 5.38
     Sheriff Courts (Scotland)
     Act (40 & 41 Vict.
     c. 50)
     s. 8(4) 2.74
     s. 11 .... 12.67
1879 Bankers' Books Evidence
     Act (42 & 43 Vict.
     c. 11)
     s. 6 .... 15.93, 15.94
     s. 7 .... 15.93, 15.94, 15.95
     s. 8 .... 15.96
     s. 9 .... 15.97
     s. 10 .... 15.93, 15.94
1880 Judicial Factors (Scotland)
     Act (43 & 44 Vict.
     c. 4)................ 11.07
     s. 4 .... 2.68
     s. 4(1) 2.68, 12.05

1880 Judicial Factors (Scotland)
     Act—cont.
     s. 4(1A) 2.68
        (b)(ii) 12.05
1882 Inferior Courts Judgments
     Extension Act (45 &
     46 Vict. c 31).... 11.68, 11.69
     Civil   Imprisonment
     (Scotland) Act (45 &
     46 Vict. c. 42).. 24.01, 26.125
     s. 4 .... 26.125
     s. 6 .... 24.02
     s. 6(2) 24.02, 24.03
        (3) 24.03, 24.04
        (4) 24.04
        (6) 24.04
        (7) 24.04
     Entail (Scotland) Act (45
     & 46 Vict. c. 53)...... 26.263
     s. 3 .... 26.263
     s. 4 .... 26.263
     s. 5 .... 26.263
     s. 6 .... 26.263
     s. 11 .... 26.263
     Bills of Exchange Act (45
     & 46 Vict. c. 61)
     s. 100 .... 11.45
     Citation   Amendment
     (Scotland) Act (45 &
     46 Vict. c. 77)......... 6.29
     s. 3 .... 6.19, 6.20, 6.22,
                       30.91, 30.92
     s. 4 .... 6.21, 6.22, 16.08
     s. 6 .... 6.18, 16.08
     s. 7 .... 6.19
1885 Sea Fisheries (Scotland)
     (Amendment) Act (48
     & 49 Vict. c. 70)...... 26.187
     s. 1 .... 26.187
     s. 7 .... 3.34, 26.187
     s. 8 .... 3.34, 26.187
1886 Burial Grounds (Scotland)
     Amendment Act (49
     & 50 Vict. c. 21)...... 26.57
1889 Judicial Factors (Scotland)
     Act (52 & 53 Vict.
     c. 39)
     s. 11A 2.68
1890 Partnership Act (53 & 54
     Vict. c. 39)........... 26.319
     s. 35 .... 2.73, 26.318
        (f) 2.73
     s. 39 .... 2.73, 26.318
     s. 40 .... 26.319
     s. 42(1) 26.319
     s. 45 .... 26.318
1891 Stamp Act (54 & 55 Vict.
     c. 39)
     s. 14 .... 13.80
        (1) 2.16
     Crofters Common Grazing
     Regulations Act (54
     & 55 Vict. c. 41)...... 26.02
     s. 5 .... 26.02

1891 Sheriff Courts (Scotland)
Act 1891 (54 & 55
Vict. c. 58)
s. 4(2) 26.401
1892 Sheriff Courts (Scotland)
Extracts Act (55 & 56
Vict. c. 17)
s. 4 .... 17.15, 21.80
s. 7(1) 29.13
s. 8 .... 1.28, 11.18
s. 9 .... 9.93
s. 77(2) 1.28
Sched. 1 .... 21.80
para. 1 .... 7.16
Statute Law Revision Act
(55 & 56 Vict. c. 19)... 10.60,
26.347
1893 Sheriff Courts Consignations (Scotland) Act
(56 & 57 Vict. c. 44).. 30.231
s. 4 .... 11.49
s. 5 .... 11.48
1894 Arbitration (Scotland) Act
(57 & 58 Vict. c. 13)... 26.32
s. 2 .... 26.32
s. 3 .... 26.32
s. 4 .... 26.32
s. 6 .... 26.32
Heritable   Securities
(Scotland) Act (57 &
58 Vict. c. 44).... 2.55, 26.97
s. 3 .... 23.28
s. 4 .... 23.29
s. 5 .... 23.03, 23.29, 26.98
s. 6 .... 23.31, 26.99
s. 7 .... 23.31, 26.99
s. 8 .... 23.32, 26.100
s. 9 .... 23.32
s. 11 .... 23.33, 26.101
s. 12(1) 23.34
(2) 23.35
s. 15 .... 23.29, 26.97
s. 16 .... 23.36
Sched. B 23.28
Sched. C 23.28
Sched. D 23.32, 26.100
Merchant   Shipping   Act
(57 & 58 Vict. c. 60).. 26.392
s. 494 .... 26.392
s. 495 .... 26.392
s. 496 .... 26.392
s. 497 .... 26.392
s. 503 .... 21.32
1895 Courts   of   Law   Fees
(Scotland) Act (58 &
59 Vict. c. 14)
s. 2 .... 1.23, 1.45
Local   Government
(Scotland) Act (58 &
59 Vict. c. 52)
s. 21 .... 26.55
s. 22 .... 26.55
Fatal   Accidents   Inquiry
(Scotland) Act (58 &
59 Vict. c. 34)........ 27.01

1897 Public Health (Scotland)
Act (60 & 61 Vict.
c. 38)............... 26.324
s. 32(4) 26.325
s. 41 .... 26.327
s. 47(4) 26.327
(5) 26.327
s. 52(3) 26.326
s. 54(1) 26.326
(3) 26.326
s. 55(1) 26.326
(3) 26.326
s. 69(1) 26.236
(2) 26.236
s. 76 .... 26.327
s. 90 .... 26.327
s. 94 .... 26.327
s. 146 .... 26.328
(2) 26.55
s. 148 .... 26.328
s. 154 .... 26.324
s. 156 .... 26.325
s. 157 .... 26.324
s. 158 .... 26.324
s. 162 .... 26.327
s. 164 .... 26.327
1898 Vexatious   Actions
(Scotland) Act (61 &
62 Vict. c. 35)... 2.113, 2.130,
4.118
s. 1 .... 4.122, 4.123
s. 1A 4.123
1900 Moneylenders Act (63 &
64 Vict. c. 51)........ 26.213
1905 Railway Fires Act 1905 (5
Edw. 7, c. 11)........ 26.356
s. 2(2) 26.356
(2) 26.356
(3) 26.356
1906 Dogs Act (6 Edw. 7, c. 32).. 26.14
s. 1(4) 26.14
Fatal Accidents and Sud-
den Deaths Inquiry
(Scotland) Act (7
Edw. 6, c. 35)........ 27.01
1907 Sheriff Courts (Scotland)
Act (7 Edw. 7, c. 51).... 1.01,
1.35, 22.107, 26.103, 28.132
s. 3 .... 30.2
s. 3(a) 2.03
(d) 5.01, 12.68, 25.12
(e) ... 4.95, 4.101, 6.43, 9.77
(f) 1.17
(h) 5.71, 10.28, 13.25,
14.03, 14.11, 17.02, 17.23,
18.33, 18.37, 19.05, 30.328
(n) 4.101, 9.77
(o) 4.101, 9.77
(p) 5.09, 25.01, 25.14
(3) 5.02
s. 4 ...... 2.02, 2.03, 2.74, 2.76,
25.12, 30.16
s. 5 .... 30.18
s. 5(1) 20.02

1907 Sheriff Courts (Scotland)
    Act—*cont.*
    s. 5(2) 2.57
       (B) 2.39, 2.57
      (3) 2.55, 23.37
      (4) ... 2.40, 2.42, 2.53, 12.69,
                  23.01
      (5) 2.78, 24.11, 24.12
    s. 5A 2.53, 21.80, 26.103,
                  23.41
      (2) 17.22
        (a) 21.80
        (b) 21.80
    s. 6 .... 25.12, 30.16
      (a) 3.38
      (j) 25.12
    s. 7 .... 2.27, 2.28, 18.93
    s. 11 .... 1.07
    s. 14 .... 1.08
    s. 17 .... 1.17
    s. 27 .. 5.71, 10.25, 10.27, 11.61,
      11.65, 11.82, 11.83, 13.25,
      14.11, 15.65, 16.97, 18.10,
      18.11, 18.25, 18.32, 18.44,
      18.79, 18.81, 18.82, 18.92,
      18.95, 18.96, 19.06, 25.29,
             25.36, 28.132
      (a) 18.38, 21.93
      (b) 11.46, 18.39, 21.79
      (c) 13.81, 18.41
      (d) 13.25, 18.42
      (e) 7.37, 18.43
      (f) 13.81, 13.83, 18.11,
      18.43, 18.47, 19.28, 21.93
      (h) 18.39
    s. 28 .. 5.27, 11.61, 11.65, 14.11,
      15.65, 18.10, 18.11, 18.92,
      18.93, 18.96, 19.06, 25.29,
                  25.36
      (1) 18.94, 18.95, 28.132
        (a) 11.84
        (b) 13.81
        (c) 7.37
        (d) .. 11.84, 13.81, 13.83,
        16.90, 18.96, 19.28,
           21.79, 21.93
      (2) 18.92
    s. 29 .... 11.05, 16.90, 18.38,
      18.58, 18.68, 18.70, 18.71,
            18.101, 21.93
    ss 34–37 .... 23.12, 30.282
    s. 34 .... 30.263
      (a) 30.264
      (b) 30.264
    s. 35 .... 23.12, 30.263
    s. 36 .... 30.262, 30.263, 30.265
    s. 37 ..... 23.12, 30.262, 30.263,
                  30.266
    s. 38 ..... 23.12, 30.262, 30.267,
                  30.275
    s. 38A 23.12
    s. 39 .... 1.35
    s. 50 .... 15.04, 15.87, 25.14,
      25.15, 25.16, 25.24, 25.25,
             25.26, 25.27

1907 Sheriff Courts (Scotland)
    Act—*cont.*
    Sched. 1 .. 1.22, 1.35, 5.02, 5.36,
      10.01, 10.54, 11.25, 12.67
      r. 15 .... 4.17
      r. 29 .... 7.30
      r. 30 .... 7.30
      r. 71 .... 16.13
1912 Protection of Animals
    (Scotland) Act (2 & 3
    Geo. 5, c. 14).... 26.15, 26.21
    s. 2 .... 26.15
    s. 3 .... 26.16
    s. 12(1) 26.17
    s. 13 .... 26.15
1913 Sheriff Courts (Scotland)
    Act (2 & 3 Geo. 5,
    c. 28)............... 22.107
1914 Entail (Scotland) Act (4 &
    5 Geo. 5, c. 43)....... 26.264
    s. 4(a) 26.264
1916 Registration of Business
    Names Act (6 & 7
    Geo. 5, c. 58)
    s. 8(1)(c) 4.87
1920 Administration of Justice
    Act (10 & 11 Geo. 5,
    c. 81)............... 11.69
1921 Trusts (Scotland) Act (11
    & 12 Geo. 5, c. 58)
    s. 2 .... 4.105
    s. 22 .... 2.44, 2.69, 26.407
    s. 23 .... 2.44, 2.69, 26.408
    s. 24 .... 2.44, 2.69, 26.409
    s. 24A .. 2.44, 2.69, 3.97, 26.407,
              26.408, 26.409
    s. 29A 2.44
    s. 34 .... 26.407, 26.408, 26.409
1922 Celluloid and Cinemato-
    graph Film Act 1922
    (12 & 13 Geo. 5,
    c. 35)............... 26.329
    s. 1(3) 26.329
    s. 8(1) 26.330
      (2) 26.330
    s. 10 .... 26.329, 26.330
1923 Industrial Assurance Act
    (13 & 14 Geo. 5, c. 8) 26.196
    s. 32(1) 26.196
1924 Conveyancing (Scotland)
    Act (14 & 15 Geo. 5,
    c. 27)............... 26.104
    s. 23(5) 26.104
      (6) 26.105
    s. 33 .... 23.36
    s. 34 .... 23.36
    s. 44 .... 11.38
      (3)(a) 11.42
    Sched. K, Form No. 8 .. 26.104
1925 Church of Scotland (Prop-
    erty and Endow-
    ments) Act (15 & 16
    Geo. 5, c. 32).... 26.57, 26.83
    s. 2(1)(b) 26.83
      (2) 26.83, 26.84

1925	Church of Scotland (Property and Endowments) Act—*cont.*	
	s. 7	26.82
	s. 16	26.85
	s. 22(2)(h)	26.85
	s. 28	26.86
	s. 28(2)	26.86
	(4)	26.86
	(5)	26.86
	s. 35(1)	26.87
	Sched. IIB	26.83
	Sched. VI, para. 1	26.85
	Sched. XI	26.86
	Performing Animals (Regulation) Act (15 & 16 Geo. 5, c. 38)	
	s. 2(1)	26.18
	s. 6(a)	26.18
	(b)	26.18
1926	Execution of Diligence (Scotland) Act (16 & 17 Geo. 5, c. 16)	
	s. 3	11.18
	s. 4	6.19, 30.92
	Judicial Proceedings (Regulation of Reports) Act (16 & 17 Geo. 5, c. 61)	5.28, 20.12
1927	Moneylenders Act (17 & 18 Geo. 5, c. 21)	26.213
	Sheriff Courts and Legal Officers (Scotland) Act (17 & 18 Geo. 5, c. 35)	
	s. 1	1.21
	s. 1(2)	1.29
	(4)	1.21
	s. 2	1.21
	s. 3	1.21
	s. 5	1.21
	s. 6	1.21
	s. 8(1)	1.29
1929	Local Government (Scotland) Act (19 & 20 Geo. 5, c. 25)	
	s. 1(1)	26.55
	s. 2(1)(e)	26.55
	Government Annuities Act 1929 (19 & 20 Geo. 5, c. 29)	26.322
	s. 48(1)	26.322
	(3)	26.322
	s. 61(1)	26.323
1930	Adoption of Children (Scotland) Act (20 & 21 Geo. 5, c. 37)	28.01
	Land Drainage (Scotland) Act (20 & 21 Geo. 5, c. 20)	26.257
	s. 1(1)	26.257
	(2)	26.257
	(3)	26.257
	(4)	26.257

1930	Land Drainage (Scotland) Act—*cont.*	
	s. 1(5)	26.257
	(6)	26.257
	(7)	26.257
	s. 2(1)	26.258
	(2)	26.258
	(3)(i)	26.258
	(ii)	26.258
	(4)	26.257, 26.258
1933	Foreign Judgments (Reciprocal Enforcement) Act (23 & 24 Geo. 5, c. 13)	2.105, 11.69
	Administration of Justice (Scotland) Act (23 & 24 Geo. 5, c. 41)	
	s. 3(1)	4.122
	Church of Scotland (Property and Endowments) (Amendment) Act (23 & 24 Geo. 5, c. 44)	26.88
	s. 9(2)	26.88
	(3)	26.88
1936	Public Order Act (26 Geo. 5 & 1 Edw. 8, c. 6)	26.292
	Courts of Justice Act (N.I.)	11.68
1937	Harbours, Piers and Ferries (Scotland) Act (1 Edw. 8 & 1 Geo. 6, c. 28)	26.211
	s. 15(2)	26.211
	Children and Young Persons (Scotland) Act (1 Edw. 8 & 1 Geo. 6, c. 37)	
	s. 46	5.29
	Public Records (Scotland) Act (1 Edw. 8 & 1 Geo. 6, c. 43)	
	s. 2(2)	15.99
	Methylated Spirits (Sale by Retail) (Scotland) Act (1. Edw. 8 & 1 Geo. 6, c. 48)	26.402
	s. 2(3)	26.402
1938	Conveyancing Amendment (Scotland) Act (1 & 2 Geo. 6, c. 24)	
	s. 1	26.407
	Nursing Homes Registration (Scotland) Act 1938 (1 & 2 Geo. 6, c. 73)	26.397
	s. 3(3)	26.397
1939	Reorganisation of Offices (Scotland) Act (2 & 3 Geo. 6, c. 20)	
	s. 1(8)	4.68
1940	Law Reform (Miscellaneous Provisions) (Scotland) Act (3 & 4 Geo. 6, c. 42)	26.126, 26.257
	s. 1	21.81

1940 Law Reform (Mis-
cellaneous Provisions)
(Scotland) Act—*cont.*
s. 1(1)(i) 21.81, 26.126
    (ii) 21.81
    (iii) 21.81
    (iv) 21.81
    (2) 21.82, 26.126
    (3) 21.82
s. 3 .... 12.63, 18.21, 24.09
    (1) 4.49
    (2) 4.49, 12.48, 14.64
1944 Law Officers Act (7 & 8
Geo. 6, c. 25)
s. 2 .... 4.63
1945 Law Reform (Contributory
Negligence) Act (8 &
9 Geo. 6, c. 28)... 9.57, 9.128,
                           17.08
s. 1 .... 21.32
    (2) 17.18
s. 3(1) 17.18
1947 Naval Forces (Enforcement of Maintenance
Liabilities) Act (10 &
11 Geo. 6, c. 24)
s. 1 .... 4.70
National Health Service
(Scotland) Act 1947
(10 & 11 Geo. 6,
c. 27)
Sched. 11, Pt 1 .... 26.326
Fire Services Act (10 & 11
Geo. 6, c. 41)........ 26.176
s. 1(2) 26.177
s. 26(2)(h) 26.176
s. 36(14) 26.177
Acquisition of Land
(Authorisation Pro-
cedures) (Scotland)
Act (10 & 11 Geo. 6,
c. 42)
Sched. 2 .... 26.92
Crown Proceedings Act
(10 & 11 Geo. 6,
c. 44)........... 4.52, 12.30
s. 13 .... 4.77
s. 17(1) 4.65
s. 21(1) 4.56, 4.57, 4.58
    (2) 4.59
s. 26(1) 4.79
s. 31 .... 4.77
s. 35(2)(a) 4.81, 7.17
    (b) 4.60
    (c) 4.61
    (d) 4.62
s. 38(2) 4.53, 4.56
    (3) 4.53
    (4) 4.53
s. 40(1) 4.53
    (2)(c) 4.53
    (f) 4.77
    (3) 4.53
s. 42 ...... 4.57, 4.58, 4.59, 4.77
s. 43 ...... 4.57, 4.58, 4.59, 4.77
    (a) 4.77

1947 Crown Proceedings Act—
cont.
s. 44 .... 4.54, 4.55, 13.63, 13.66
s. 45(1) 4.80
    (2) 4.80
    (3) 4.80
    (4) 4.80
s. 46 .... 4.70
s. 47 ... 4.72, 12.03, 15.03, 15.86
s. 50 .... 4.60, 4.81
s. 51(2) 4.53
1948 National Assistance Act
(11 & 12 Geo. 6,
c. 29)............... 26.280
s. 47(1) 26.280
    (2) 26.280
    (3) 26.280
    (4) 26.280
    (5) 26.280
    (12) 26.280
s. 65(c) 26.280
Sched. 7, Pt III 26.236
British Nationality Act (11
& 12 Geo. 6, c. 56)
s. 31 .... 2.39
Sched. 4 .... 2.39
1949 Tenancy of Shops
(Scotland) Act (12, 13
& 14 Geo. 6, c. 25)... 26.266
s. 1 .... 26.266, 30.02, 30.04
    (1) 26.266
    (2) 26.266
    (3) 26.266
    (5) 26.266
Lands Tribunal Act (12, 13
& 14 Geo. 6, c. 42)
s. 1 .... 2.36
s. 1(6) 26.94, 26.95
    (8)(a) 26.94, 26.95
s. 2 .... 2.36
s. 3 .... 2.36
s. 4 .... 2.36
Prevention of Damage by
Pests Act (12, 13 & 14
Geo. 6, c. 55)........ 26.331
s. 4(1) 26.331
    (5) 26.331
    (6) 26.331
s. 15(1) 26.332
    (2) 26.332
    (5) 26.332
Coast Protection Act (12,
13 & 14 Geo. 6, c. 74).. 26.89
s. 13(3) 26.89
    (9)(a) 26.89
s. 25(4) 26.90
Registered Designs Act
(12, 13 & 14 Geo. 6,
c. 87)
s. 27 .... 2.46
National Health Service
(Amendment) Act
(12, 13 & 14 Geo. 6,
c. 93)
s. 7(4) 2.73

1950 International Organisations (Immunities and
Privileges) Act (14
Geo. 6, c. 14).......... 4.06
Maintenance Orders Act
(14 Geo. 6, c. 37)....... 3.78
1951 Pet Animals Act (14 & 15
Geo. 6, c. 35).... 26.19, 26.21
s. 1(4) 26.19
(8) 26.19
s. 7(3) 26.19
Nurses (Scotland) Act (14
& 15 Geo. 6, c. 55)... 26.299
s. 28(1) 26.299
(4) 26.299
s. 31(1) 26.299
s. 32 .... 26.299
National Assistance
(Amendment) Act (14
& 15 Geo. 6, c. 57)
s. 1(2) 26.280
Rag, Flock and Other Fill-
ing Materials Act (14
& 15 Geo. 6, c. 63)... 26.333
s. 14(1) 26.333
Sched., para. 3 .... 26.333
para. 4 .... 26.333
Reserve and Auxiliary
Forces (Protection of
Civil Interests) Act
(14 & 15 Geo. 6,
c. 65)................ 26.34
s. 25 .... 26.34
s. 38 .... 26.35
s. 39 .... 26.35
1952 Judicial Offices (Salaries,
etc.) Act (15 & 16
Geo. 6 & 1 Eliz. 2,
c. 12)
s. 3 .... 1.14
1954 Protection of Animals
(Amendment) Act (2
& 3 Eliz. 2, c. 40)
s. 1(1) 26.16A
s. 1(3) 26.16A
1955 Army Act (3 & 4 Eliz. 2,
c. 18)
s. 150 .... 4.70
s. 151 .... 4.70
s. 152 .... 4.70
Air Force Act (3 & 4 Eliz.
2, c. 19)
s. 150 .... 4.70
s. 151 .... 4.70
s. 152 .... 4.70
1956 Administration of Justice
Act (4 & 5 Eliz. 2,
c. 46)
s. 45 .... 2.76
s. 47 .... 2.76, 24.06
(1) 11.13
(2) 11.13

1956 Agriculture (Safety,
Health and Welfare
Provisions) Act (4 & 5
Eliz. 2, c. 49)......... 26.03
s. 3(5) 26.03
s. 25(1), (3) 26.03
1957 Naval Discipline Act (5 &
6 Eliz. 2, c. 53)
s. 128E 4.70
1958 Maneouvres Act (7 & 8
Eliz. 2, c. 7).......... 26.96
s. 7(4) 26.96
Matrimonial Proceedings
(Children) Act (6 & 7
Eliz. 2, c. 40)
s. 11(1) 22.35
Agricultural Marketing
Act (6 & 7 Eliz. 2,
c. 47)................ 26.04
s. 18(1) 26.04
(2) 26.04
(5) 26.04
(5)(a) 26.04
(b) 26.04
(7) 26.04
Local Government
(Omnibus Shelters
and Queue Barriers)
(Scotland) Act (6 & 7
Eliz. 2, c. 50)......... 26.281
s. 6 .... 26.281
Interest on Damages
(Scotland) Act (6 & 7
Eliz. 2, c. 61).... 14.41, 14.51
s. 1(1) 21.35
(1A) 21.35
(1B) 14.40
Merchant Shipping (Lia-
bility of Shipowners
and Others) Act (6 &
7 Eliz. 2, c. 62)
s. 2 .... 21.32
1959 Building (Scotland) Act (7
& 8 Eliz. 2, c. 24)...... 26.50
s. 6(5) 26.50
s. 6B(2)(a) 26.50
(b) 26.50
s. 10 .... 26.51
(1B) 26.50
s. 11 .... 26.50, 26.51
s. 13 .... 26.51
(2) 26.50
s. 16 .... 26.51
(1) 26.50
(a) 26.50
(b) 26.50
(c) 26.50
(d)–(g) 26.50
(3) 25.31, 26.50, 26.51
s. 17 .... 26.51
(6) 26.51, 26.52
(7) 26.51
s. 18(4) 26.52
(9) 26.52
Sched. 6 .... 26.50

1959 Deer (Scotland) Act (7 & 8 Eliz. 2, c. 40)
 s. 25A(2) 26.31
1960 Radioactive Substances Act (8 & 9 Eliz. 2, c. 34)
 s. 9 .... 26.327
 Sched. 1, Pt II, para. 13 26.327
 Companies Act (Northern Ireland) (c. 22 (N.I.)).... 3.71
 Mental Health (Scotland) Act (8 & 9 Eliz. 2, c. 61)
 s. 108 .... 1.12
 Caravan Sites and Control of Development Act (8 & 9 Eliz. 2, c. 62).. 26.161
 s. 5(3) 26.161
 s. 7(1) 26.161
 s. 8(2), (4) 26.161
 s. 26(2) 26.162
 s. 32(1)(c) 26.161
  (1)(i) 26.162
  (2) 26.161
  (2)(b) 26.161
 Pt 1 .... 26.174
1961 Carriage by Air Act (9 & 10 Eliz. 2, c. 27)........ 2.02
 Sched. 1 .... 2.77
 Factories Act (9 & 10 Eliz. 2, c. 34)............. 26.120
 s. 169 .... 26.120
 s. 170 .... 26.120
 Criminal Justice Act (9 & 10 Eliz. 2, c. 39)
 s. 29(1) 16.16
 Flood Prevention (Scotland) Act (9 & 10 Eliz. 2, c. 41)....... 26.91
 s. 8(3) 26.91
 Sheriffs' Pensions (Scotland) Act (9 & 10 Eliz. 2, c. 42)
 s. 6(1) 1.08
 Mock Auctions Act (9 & 10 Eliz. 2, c. 47)....: 29.89
 Trustee Investments Act (9 & 10 Eliz. 2, c. 62).. 21.40, 30.53
1962 Civil Aviation (Euro-control) Act (10 & 11 Eliz. 2, c. 8)
 s. 7(3) 3.87
 Recorded Delivery Service Act (10 & 11 Eliz. 2, c. 27)................ 6.29
 s. 1 .... 6.19, 16.08, 30.91, 30.92
 s. 2 .... 6.19, 30.92
 s. 27(3) 26.357
 s. 29(2) 26.357
  (4) 26.357
 s. 30 .... 26.357
 s. 31(1) 26.357
  (2) 26.357
  (4) 26.357
 s. 66 .... 26.357

1962 Recorded Delivery Service Act—*cont.*
 Sched........... 6.19, 30.92
 Building Societies Act (10 & 11 Eliz. 2, c. 37)..... 26.53
 Pipelines Act (10 & 11 Eliz. 2, c. 58)......... 26.357
 s. 15(7) 26.357
 s. 27(3) 26.357
 s. 29(2) 26.357
  (4) 26.357
 s. 30 .... 26.357
 s. 31(1) 26.357
  (2) 26.357
  (4) 26.357
 s. 66 .... 26.357
1963 Betting, Gaming and Lot-teries Act (c. 2)........ 26.38
 s. 2 .... 26.38
 s. 4 .... 26.38
 s. 9 .... 26.38
 s. 51 .... 26.42
 Sched. 1, para. 1(b) 26.38
  para. 24 .... 26.38
  para. 28(1) 26.40
   (2) 26.40
  para. 28A 26.40
  para. 28D 26.40
   (2) 26.40
 Sched. 2, para. 7 .... 26.41
 Sched. 3, para. 13(3) 26.41
 Sheriff Courts (Civil Juris-diction and Pro-cedure) (Scotland) Act (c. 22)
 s. 3 .... 30.02, 30.04, 30.240, 30.292, 30.297
 Children and Young Per-sons Act (c. 3)
 s. 57(1) 5.29
  (4) 5.29
 Sched. 3, para. 50 .... 16.16
 Offices, Shops and Rail-way Premises Act (c. 41)............... 26.121
 s. 46(11) 26.121
 s. 71(1) 26.122
  (2) 26.122
  (3) 26.122
 Animal Boarding Estab-lishments Act (c. 43)... 26.20
 s. 1(1) 26.20
  (4) 26.20
  (9) 26.20
 s. 3(3) 26.21
  (4) 26.21
 s. 5(2) 26.20
 Land Compensation (Scotland) Act (c. 51)
 s. 1 .... 2.36
 s. 8 .... 2.36
 Sched. 2, para. 2(1) 26.240
1964 Succession (Scotland) Act (c. 41)............... 26.398
 s. 16(1) 26.398
  (3)(b) 26.398

1964	Succession (Scotland) Act	
	—cont.	
	s. 20	4.105
	s. 35	1.12
	Sched. 2, para. 1	20.19
	Riding Establishments Act	
	(c. 70).	26.403
	s. 1(5)	26.403
	(10)	26.403
	Fishery Limits Act (c. 72)	
	s. 1	2.02
	s. 3	2.02
	Sched.	2.02
	Diplomatic Privileges Act	
	(c. 81)	
	s. 4	4.05
	Sched. 1, art. 31	4.05
	art. 37(2)	4.05
	(3)	4.05
1965	Industrial and Provident	
	Societies Act (c. 12). .	26.197,
		26.205
	s. 22	26.197
	s. 32	26.197
	s. 42(3)(b)	26.198
	(4)	26.198
	s. 55(a)(ii)	26.199
	s. 56	26.199
	s. 58(6)(a)	26.199
	s. 60(2)	26.200
	(3)(b)	26.201
	(7)(a)	26.201
	(b)(i)	26.201
	(ii)	26.201
	(9)	26.201
	Law Commissions Act	
	(c. 22)	
	s. 2	1.14
	Gas Act (c. 36)	
	s. 17(4)	27.03
	Carriage of Goods by	
	Road Act (c. 37)	
	s. 10	11.63
	Sched., art. 31(5)	11.63
	Registration of Births,	
	Deaths and Marriages	
	(Scotland) Act (c. 49). .	26.359
	s. 10(3)	26.361
	s. 16(3)	26.359
	s. 18(2)(c)	26.360
	s. 20	2.57
	(1)(i)	26.360
	(ii)	26.360
	(iii)	26.360
	s. 25(3)	26.359
	s. 42(5)	2.57, 26.360
1966	Law Reform (Mis-cellaneous Provisions) (Scotland) Act (c. 19)	
	s. 1	11.15
	s. 2(1)	4.70
	s. 8	2.57, 22.92
	(1)	22.02
	(3)	22.95
1966	Docks and Harbours Act	
	(c. 28).	26.212
	s. 34(1)	26.212
	(2)	26.212
	(4)	26.212
	Housing (Scotland) Act	
	(c. 49).	9.41
1967	Agriculture Act (c. 22).	26.05
	s. 21(1)	26.05
	(2)	26.05
	(4)	26.05
	(a)	26.05
	(b)	26.05
	(12)	26.05
	Legal Aid (Scotland) Act	
	(c. 43)	
	s. 16(1)(b)(ii)	11.53
1968	Consular Relations Act	
	(c. 18)	
	s. 12	4.05
	Sched. 1, art. 43	4.05
	45	4.05
	Firearms Act (c. 27)	25.10, 26.183
	s. 21(6)	26.184
	s. 28A(6)	26.183
	s. 29(2)	26.183
	s. 30A(6)	26.183
	s. 30B(3)	26.183
	s. 30C(2)	26.183
	s. 34(5)	26.183
	s. 36(3)	26.183
	s. 37(3)	26.183
	s. 38(7)	26.183
	s. 44(1)	26.183
	(2)	25.10, 26.183
	(3)	25.10, 26.183
	s. 52(4)	26.185
	Sched. 5, Pt III	26.183
	para. 2	26.183
	para. 3	26.183
	para. 4	26.183
	para. 8	26.184
	para. 9	26.184
	Agriculture (Mis-cellaneous Provisions) Act (c. 34)	
	s. 14(3)	26.95
	Sched. 4, paras 4.5	26.95
	Health Services and Public Health Act 1968	
	(c. 46).	26.334
	s. 71(2)	26.334
	s. 72(1)	26.334
	(2)	26.334
	Sewerage (Scotland) Act 1968 (c. 47).	26.335
	s. 3	26.411
	(2)	26.335
	s. 10(3)	26.336
	s. 14(5)	26.337
	s. 15(2)	26.337
	s. 21(2)	26.337
	s. 33(2)	26.338
	s. 41	26.339
	s. 43	26.340

1968 International Organisations Act (c. 48)
s. 12(5) 4.06
Sched. 1 .... 4.06
Social Work (Scotland)
Act (c. 49)...... 2.56, 26.282
s. 16 .... 4.10, 25.38, 28.25
s. 17 .... 4.10
s. 18 .... 4.10
s. 61(1) 26.282
(1A) 26.282
(2) 26.282
s. 64(4) 26.282
s. 78(1) 26.283
s. 83(1) 26.283
Sched. 2, Pt. II, para. 7 ... 5.29
Sched. 5, para. 1 .... 26.282
para. 4 .... 26.282
para. 7 .... 26.282
Caravan Sites Act (c. 52). . 26.163,
26.174
s. 1(2) 26.163
(3) 26.163
s. 4(1)–(4) 26.163
(5) 26.163
s. 5 .... 26.163
Theatres Act (c. 54)....... 26.155
s. 14(1) 26.155
s. 15 .... 26.156
Hovercraft Act (c. 59)
s. 2(1) 2.02
Gaming Act (c. 65)........ 26.43
s. 9 .... 26.45
s. 11 .... 26.43
(2) 26.43
s. 34(1) 26.47
s. 52(1) 26.43
Sched. 2, para 33(1) 26.43
para. 34(1) 26.43
para. 45 .... 26.44
para. 47(1) 26.44
para. 61 .... 26.44
Sched. 4 .... 26.45
para. 1(1) 26.45
para. 9–18 .... 26.45
para. 21 .... 26.45
Sched. 7 .... 26.46
Sched. 8, paras 1–4 ...... 26.46
Sched. 9, para. 15 .... 26.47
Sched. 10, para. 2 .... 5.38
Pt II 26.45
Pt III 26.46
Law Reform (Mis-
cellaneous Provisions)
(Scotland) Act (c. 70)
s. 10 .... 2.79
(2)(a) 2.105
s. 12 .... 2.79, 2.105
Sched. 3 .... 20.19
Sea Fisheries Act (c. 77)
s. 5.10 .... 26.187
Sched. 1, para. 24 ...... 26.187
para. 28 .... 26.187
para. 29 .... 26.187

1969 Mines and Quarries (Tips)
Act (c. 10)........... 26.315
s. 13(2) 26.317
(7) 26.317
s. 15(1) 26.315
s. 16(4) 26.315
(5) 26.315
s. 18(2) 26.317
(7) 26.317
s. 19 .... 26.315
s. 20(5) 26.316
s. 21 .... 26.316
s. 22(1) 26.316
Mines and Quarries (Tips)
Act—
s. 24 .... 26.316
(2) 26.316
(4) 26.316
s. 35(a) 26.315
Sched. 2, para. 6(4) 26.316
Employers' Liability
(Defective Equip-
ment) Act (c. 37)
s. 1 .... 12.47
Age of Majority (Scotland)
Act (c. 39)
s. 1(1) 4.10
Children and Young Per-
sons Act (c. 54)
Sched. 5, para. 6 .... 16.16
Sched. 6 .... 16.16
1970 Taxes Management Act
(c. 9)............... 26.250
s. 2(4) 1.12, 1.16
s. 8(1) 15.57
s. 20(1) 26.250
s. 20C(3) 26.250
s. 20D(1)(b) 26.250
s. 63 .... 26.251
s. 64 .... 29.04
Administration of Justice
Act (c. 31)
s. 2 .... 2.75
Riding Establishment Act
(c. 32)
s. 2(2) 26.403
Conveyancing and Feudal
Reform (Scotland)
Act (c. 35)...... 23.04, 23.10,
26.105
s. 1 .... 2.36
s. 2 .... 2.36
s. 3 .... 2.36
s. 4 .... 2.36
s. 5 .... 2.36
s. 6 .... 2.36
s. 7 .... 2.36
s. 18(2) 23.04
(b) 26.105
s. 20(3) 23.04, 26.105
(4) 26.105
s. 22(1) 23.04, 26.105
(2) 26.105
(3) 23.04, 26.105

1970　Conveyancing and Feudal
　　　　Reform　(Scotland)
　　　　Act—*cont.*
　　　　s. 24 . . . . 26.105
　　　　　　(1) 23.04
　　　　s. 28 . . . . 26.105
　　　　　　(1) 23.04
　　　　s. 29(1) 26.105
　　　　　　(2) 23.04, 26.105
　　　　　　(3) 25.32, 26.105
　　　　s. 39(1) 26.100
　　　　s. 50 . . . . 2.36
　　　　Pt II 26.105
　　　　Building　(Scotland)　Act
　　　　　　(c. 38)
　　　　s. 4 . . . . 26.50
　　　　Sched. 1, Pt 1,
　　　　　para. 3(b) 26.50
　　　　　para. 5(a) 26.50
1971　Rent　(Scotland)　Act
　　　　　(c. 28)
　　　　s. 38 . . . . 2.36
　　　　Sched. 5 . . . . 2.36
　　　　Interest　on　Damages
　　　　　(Scotland) Act (c. 31). . 16.30
　　　　s. 1 . . . . 21.35
　　　　　　(1) 14.40
　　　　Armed Forces Act (c. 33)
　　　　s. 59 . . . . 4.70
　　　　s. 61(1) 4.70
　　　　Fire　Precautions　Act
　　　　　(c. 40). 26.178
　　　　s. 1(2) 26.179
　　　　s. 2 . . . . 26.179
　　　　s. 3 . . . . 26.178
　　　　s. 4(1) 26.178
　　　　s. 5 . . . . 26.178
　　　　s. 8(4)–(7) 26.178
　　　　s. 9(1) 26.178
　　　　　　(2) 26.178
　　　　s. 10(1) 26.179
　　　　　　(2) 26.179
　　　　s. 10A(1) 26.179
　　　　　　(2) 26.179
　　　　s. 28(2) 26.180
　　　　　　(3) 26.180
　　　　　　(5) 26.180
　　　　s. 43(1) 26.178
　　　　Redemption　of　Standard
　　　　　Securities　(Scotland)
　　　　　Act (c. 45)
　　　　s. 1(d) 26.105
　　　　Sheriff　Courts　(Scotland)
　　　　　Act (c. 58). . . . 1.01, 1.35, 1.44
　　　　s. 1 . . . . 1.44, 1.45
　　　　s. 2(1) 1.03
　　　　s. 3 . . . . 5.09
　　　　　　(2) 1.04
　　　　s. 4 . . . . . . 26.13, 26.186, 26.207,
　　　　　　　　　　　　　26.327, 26.354
　　　　　　(2) 1.06, 26.401
　　　　s. 5(1) 1.07
　　　　s. 5A 1.08
　　　　s. 6(1) 1.08
　　　　　　(3) 1.08
　　　　s. 7 . . . . 1.16, 2.03, 30.17

1971　Sheriff　Courts　(Scotland)
　　　　　Act—*cont.*
　　　　s. 8 . . . . 1.14, 1.46
　　　　s. 9 . . . . 1.44, 1.45
　　　　s. 10(1) 1.09, 1.44
　　　　　　(1A) 1.09, 1.11, 2.129
　　　　　　(2) 1.15, 1.17
　　　　　　(3) 1.17
　　　　s. 11(1) 1.10, 1.44
　　　　　　(1A) 1.10, 1.11, 2.129
　　　　　　(1B) 1.10
　　　　　　(2) 1.15, 1.17
　　　　　　(3)(a) 1.10
　　　　　　　(b) 1.17
　　　　　　(6) 1.17
　　　　　　(7) 1.10
　　　　s. 12 . . . . 1.08, 1.14
　　　　s. 13(1) 1.08
　　　　　　(2) 1.08
　　　　s. 14(2) 1.15
　　　　　　(3) 2.03
　　　　　　(a) 1.15
　　　　　　(b) 1.15
　　　　　　(4) 1.15
　　　　s. 15 . . . . 1.47, 1.48
　　　　　　(1) 1.38, 1.44, 5.99
　　　　　　(2) . . . 1.15, 1.38, 1.39, 1.40
　　　　s. 16 . . . . 1.38, 1.48
　　　　　　(1) 1.44, 5.99
　　　　　　(a) 1.47
　　　　　　(b) 1.15, 1.47, 2.03
　　　　　　(2) 1.15, 1.47
　　　　s. 17 . . . . 1.38, 1.47, 1.48
　　　　　　(1) 5.11
　　　　　　(a) 5.15
　　　　　　(2) 5.13
　　　　　　(3) 5.14
　　　　s. 18 . . . . 1.44, 1.48
　　　　s. 19 . . . . 1.08
　　　　s. 20 . . . . 1.29, 1.44
　　　　s. 23 . . . . 1.49
　　　　　　(7) 1.49
　　　　s. 24 . . . . 1.49
　　　　s. 25 . . . . 1.49
　　　　　　(2) 5.11
　　　　s. 32 . . . . 1.36, 1.37
　　　　s. 33 . . . . 1.37
　　　　　　(4) 1.37
　　　　s. 34 . . . . 1.37
　　　　s. 35 . . . . 5.07, 26.270, 31.02
　　　　　　(1) 5.06, 30.02, 30.18
　　　　ss 35(1)(a)–(d) 30.04
　　　　s. 35(1)(a) 23.09
　　　　　　(b) 23.14, 30.285
　　　　　　(c) . . . 2.31, 21.75, 23.02,
　　　　　　　　　　　　　23.09, 30.261
　　　　　　(2) 5.08, 30.03, 31.02
　　　　　　(3) 31.02, 31.116
　　　　　　(4) 31.02
　　　　s. 36A 31.44
　　　　s. 36B . . . 31.103, 31.123, 31.125
　　　　　　(1) 31.123
　　　　　　(2) 31.123
　　　　　　(3) 31.124

1971 Sheriff Courts (Scotland) Act—*cont.*
s. 36B(3)(a) 31.124
    (b) 31.124
s. 37 .... 30.27, 31.18
    (1)(a) 5.08, 8.66, 13.46, 16.33, 19.49, 30.28, 30.34
    (b) 5.03, 8.66, 13.58, 13.60, 20.11, 30.29
    (2) 5.03, 13.47, 30.30, 30.133, 31.18
    (a) .. 13.47, 30.29, 30.34
    (b) 13.47, 30.29
    (2A) 2.61, 13.61, 18.24, 28.38, 28.97
    (2B) 5.03, 13.48, 31.22
    (a) 13.48, 30.32, 31.18
    (b) 13.48, 30.32, 31.18
    (2C) 5.03, 13.49, 30.33, 31.21, 31.22
    (3) 13.06, 13.61
    (a) .. 13.48, 18.24, 28.38, 30.33
    (b) 13.47, 30.29
    (4) 13.45, 13.58, 13.61, 31.18
s. 38 .... 2.27, 30.34, 31.137, 30.328, 30.345
    (a) 30.328
    (b) .. 30.328, 31.347, 31.348
s. 41 .... 30.02
    (1) 21.75
s. 45(2)–(4) 31.02
    (3) 5.02, 31.328
Sched. 1,
    para. 1 ... 3.86, 23.29, 26.207
Sched. 2 .... 2.27
Mineral Workings (Offshore Installations) Act (c. 61)
s. 6(5) 27.03
Diplomatic and Other Privileges Act (c. 64)
Sched. 4.05
Banking and Financial Dealings Act (c. 80)
s. 1 .... 5.12
    (3) 5.12
Sched. 1 .... 5.12
1972 Island of Rockall Act (c. 2)
s. 1 .... 2.02
Superannuation Act (c. 11)
Sched. 6 .... 1.21
Maintenance Orders (Reciprocal Enforcement) Act (c. 18)... 3.78, 5.34
Matrimonial Proceedings (Polygamous Marriages) Act (c. 38)
s. 2(2) 22.15

1972 Administration of Justice (Scotland) Act (c. 39)
s. 1 ... 3.65, 12.02, 12.04, 12.05, 15.01, 15.46, 15.60, 24.01, 30.152, 30.169, 30.173, 30.174, 30.316, 31.94
    (1) 15.84, 15.85, 15.86, 15.87, 15.88, 15.89, 15.90, 15.101, 30.169, 30.170
    (1A) 15.03, 15.08, 15.84, 30.169, 30.170
    (b) 12.03, 12.04
    (2) 12.03, 15.03, 15.85, 15.90
    (b) 15.87
    (3) 12.04
    (4) 12.03, 15.03, 15.86
s. 4 .... 1.36, 9.93
Finance Act (c. 41)........ 19.58
National Health Service (Scotland) Act (c. 58)
Sched. 6, para. 45 ...... 26.327
    para. 50 .... 26.326
    para. 55 .... 26.326
    para. 83 .... 26.280
    para. 138 .... 26.334
    para. 139 .... 26.334
Gas Act (c. 60)
s. 39(2) 26.357
    (3) 26.357
Poisons Act (c. 66)........ 26.300
s. 5(1) 26.300
    (3) 26.300
    (4) 26.300
    (6)(a) 26.300
European Communities Act (c. 68)
Sched. 1 .... 30.63
1973 Fair Trading Act (c. 41)... 26.404
s. 32(2) 26.405
s. 34 .... 26.404
    (1) 26.404
ss 35–40 .... 26.404
s. 41(2)(a) 26.404
    (b) 26.404
    (3) 26.404
s. 42(2)(b) 26.404
Pt III 26.404
Domicile and Matrimonial Proceedings Act (c. 45)............... 13.77
s. 7 .... 2.39
s. 8 .... 2.39, 22.03
    (2) 2.58
    (3) 2.58
    (4) 2.58
s. 10 .... 2.59
    (1) 2.59
    (1A) 2.59
    (2) 2.59
s. 11 .... 22.27
s. 12(4) 2.58
Sched. 3 ..... 2.60, 22.06, 22.27
    para. 3(1) 22.29

1973 Domicile and Matrimonial
    Proceedings   Act—
    cont.
  Sched. 3—*cont.*
    para. 3(2) 22.28
    para. 4(a) 22.07
    para. 7 .... 22.07
    para. 8 .... 22.28
    para. 9(1) 22.29
       (2) 22.29
       (4) 22.07
    para. 10(1) 22.30
       (2) 22.30
    para. 11(1) 22.31
      (2)(a) 22.31
       (b) 22.31
       (3) 22.31
       (4) 22.31
  Prescription and Limita-
    tion (Scotland) Act
    (c. 52)
  s. 6(1) 2.119, 10.38
  s. 8A 4.49, 12.53, 24.10
  s. 17 ...... 10.40, 10.41, 10.42,
              12.51, 21.17
    (1) 2.115, 10.38
    (2) 2.115
     (a) 2.115
     (b) 2.115
    (3) 2.116, 10.40
  s. 18 .. 10.40, 10.41, 10.42, 12.51
    (1) 2.116
    (2) 2.117, 2.118
    (3) 2.118
    (4) 2.118
    (5) 2.118
  s. 18A 10.40, 10.41
    (1) 2.119
    (2) 2.119
    (3) 2.119
    (4)(a) 2.119
     (b) 2.119
  s. 18B 2.120
    (1) 2.120
    (2) 2.120
    (3) 2.120
  s. 19A 2.121, 10.40, 10.41,
            10.42, 12.51
    (1) 2.121
    (2) 2.121
    (3) 2.121
  s. 22(1) 2.115
    (2) 2.115
    (3) 2.115
  Sched. 1,
    para. 1(d) 2.114, 2.119
       2(g) 2.114
       (gg) 2.114
  Breeding of Dogs Act
    (c. 60)................ 26.22
  s. 1(1) 26.22
    (5) 26.22
    (10) 26.22
  s. 3(3) 26.21
  s. 5(2) 26.22

1973 Local   Government
    (Scotland) Act (c. 65)... 1.04,
                  26.284
  s. 32(1) 26.284
    (2) 26.284
    (3) 26.284
    (4) 26.284
    (5) 26.284
    (6) 26.284
  s. 75(2) 26.285
    (3) 26.285
  s. 76 .... 26.285
  s. 169(1) 26.55
  s. 190 .... 6.39
  s. 202(9) 26.286
  s. 205(3) 1.18
    (7) 1.18
  s. 210 .... 1.12
  s. 214 .... 2.02
  s. 231 .... 26.287
  s. 232 .... 26.287
  s. 235(1) 6.39
    (3) 6.39
  Sched. 1, para. 1 .... 1.05
    para. 18 .... 2.58
  Sched. 27 ...... 26.324, 26.326,
             26.327, 26.328
  Pt 1, para. 1(1) 1.20
       (3) ... 1.20, 26.347,
                 26.349
    para. 2 .... 26.327
    para. 63(a) 26.86
    para. 65 .... 26.86
  Pt II, para. 202 .... 2.02
1974 Health and Safety at Work
    etc. Act (c. 37)
  s. 14(7) 27.03
  Land   Tenure   Reform
    (Scotland) Act (c. 38)
  s. 9 .... 23.05, 30.02, 30.261
    (6) 23.05, 30.02
    (7) 7.18, 23.05
  Consumer   Credit   Act
    (c. 39)......... 12.42, 26.213
  s. 16 .... 30.117
  s. 127 .... 26.214
  s. 128 .... 26.214
  s. 129 .... 17.21, 26.214, 30.117
  s. 129(1)(c) 30.117
    (2)(a) 30.117
     (b) 30.117
  s. 130 .... 26.214
  s. 131 .... 26.214
  ss 132, 136 .... 26.214
  s. 137(1) 26.213
  s. 138 .... 26.213
  s. 139(1)(a) 26.213
    (b) 26.213
    (c) 26.213
    (2) 26.213
    (6) 26.213
  s. 189 .... 30.117
  s. 189(1) 26.213, 26.214
  Control of Pollution Act
    (c. 40)................ 26.164
  s. 3(1) 26.166

1974 Control of Pollution Act
—*cont.*
  s. 13(1) 26.164
      (2) 26.164
      (3) 26.164
          (a) 26.164
          (b) 26.164
      (5) 26.165
      (6) 26.165
  s. 16(1) 26.166
      (2) 26.166
  s. 30(1) 26.166
      (2) 26.164
  s. 58(1) 26.167
      (3) 26.167
      (8) 26.167
  s. 59(1) 26.168
      (2)(a) 26.168
          (h) 26.168
      (4) 26.168
      (7)(a) 26.168
  s. 60 . . . . 26.345
      (2) 26.169
      (7) 26.169
  s. 61 . . . . 26.345
      (1) 26.170
      (4) 26.170
      (6) 26.170
  s. 63(1) 26.171
      (2) 26.171
  s. 65 . . . . 26.345
      (6) 26.171
      (7) 26.171
  s. 66(1) 26.171
      (7) 26.171
  s. 67 . . . . 26.345
      (5) 26.171
  s. 70(4) 26.172
  s. 85(2) 26.172
  s. 87(6) 26.172
  s. 91(1) 26.173
      (5)(b) 26.173
  s. 98 . . . . 26.173
  s. 106(6) 26.164, 26.165,
          26.166, 26.167, 26.168,
          26.169, 26.171, 26.172
  Pt III 26.172
  Friendly Societies Act
      (c. 46). 26.202
  s. 22 . . . . 26.202
  s. 80(2)(b) 26.204
  s. 83(b) 26.204
  s. 99(3) 26.203
      (4) 26.203
      (5) 26.203
  s. 103 . . . . 4.102, 6.44
1975 District Courts (Scotland)
      Act (c. 20)
  s. 3(1) 24.02
  Criminal   Procedure
      (Scotland) Act (c. 21)
  s. 140 . . . . 16.52
  s. 321(5) 16.13
  s. 343 . . . . 16.52
  s. 344(1) 16.62
  s. 461 . . . . 5.29

1975 Criminal   Procedure
      (Scotland) Act—*cont.*
  Sched. 10, Pt I 2.74, 5.29,
                                  16.52
  Reservoirs Act (c. 23). 26.410
  s. 17(5) 26.410
      (9) 26.410
  House of Commons Dis-
      qualification   Act
      (c. 24)
  s. (1)(1)(a) 1.08
  Sched. 1, Pt I 1.06
  Evidence (Proceedings in
      Other   Jurisdictions)
      Act (c. 34)
  ss 1–4 . . . . 30.187
  s. 1 . . . . 15.41, 30.191
  s. 2 . . . . 15.41
      (2)(b) 15.83
      (4) 15.83
  s. 3 . . . . 15.41
  s. 4 . . . . 15.41
  Litigants in Person (Costs
      and   Expenses) Act
      (c. 47). . 4.121, 30.224, 31.127
  Mobile Homes Act (c. 49)
      Sched., Pt II, para. 2 . . 26.163
  Guard Dogs Act (c. 50). 26.23
  s. 3(1) 26.23
      (4) 26.21
  s. 4(1) 26.23
      (2) 26.23
  s. 7 . . . . 26.23
  Safety of Sports Grounds
      Act (c. 52). 26.157
  s. 1 . . . . 26.157
  s. 2 . . . . 26.157
  s. 3(1) 26.157
  s. 5 . . . . 26.157
  s. 10(1) 26.158
      (3) 26.158
  s. 10A(1) 26.158
      (8) 26.158
      (9) 26.158
  s. 17 . . . . 26.157
  Sex   Discrimination Act
      (c. 65). 26.362, 26.369
  s. 59(1) 26.363
      (4) 26.363
      (5a) 26.363
      (5b) 26.363
  s. 66(1) 26.368
      (2) 26.368
      (5A) 26.368
      (7) 26.368
      (8) 26.368
  s. 68(1)(b) 26.364
      (2) 26.364
      (3) 26.364
  s. 71(1) 26.365
  s. 72(2)(a) 26.366
      (3)(a) 26.366
          (b) 26.366
  s. 76(2)(b) 26.368
      (3) 26.366

1975 Sex Discrimination Act—
     cont.
     s. 77(2) 26.367
        (5) 26.367
     Pt III 26.368
     Children Act (c. 72)
     s. 51(1) 22.40
     s. 53 .... 28.121
     Petroleum and Submarine
        Pipelines Act (c. 74)
     s. 27(5) 27.03
1976 Damages (Scotland) Act
     (c. 13)..... 9.98, 12.17, 27.02
     s. 1(4) 18.116
     s. 5 .... 21.14
     Sched. 1 ... 2.118, 21.14, 30.321
     Fatal Accidents and Sud-
        den Deaths Inquiries
        (Scotland) Act (c. 14)... 1.30,
           1.32, 27.03, 27.05, 27.22
     s. 1 .... 27.05
        (1)(a) 27.02, 27.03
           (ii) 27.04
        (b) 27.02, 27.05
        (2) 27.02
        (3) 27.07
        (4) 27.04
     s. 2(1) 27.06
        (2) 27.06
        (3) 27.06
     s. 3(1) 27.08
        (2) 27.08
     s. 4(1) 27.09
        (2) 27.09
        (3) 27.11
        (4) 27.12
        (5) 27.12
        (6) 27.12
        (7) 27.10, 27.11
     s. 5(1) 27.13
        (2) 27.13
     s. 6(1) 27.14, 27.17, 27.20,
            27.22
        (a) ... 27.14, 27.19, 27.20
        (b) ... 27.14, 27.19, 27.20
        (c) ... 27.14, 27.18, 27.19
        (d) 27.14, 27.19
        (2) 27.14
        (3) 27.21
        (4) 27.21
        (5) 27.21
     s. 7 .... 27.02
        (1)(h) 27.23
     s. 8(2) 27.01
     s. 9 .... 27.03
        Sched. 2 .... 27.01
     Lotteries and Amusements
        Act (c. 32)............ 26.48
     s. 5 .... 26.48
     Sched. 1, para. 6 .... 26.48
     Sched. 3, para. 1(1)(d) ... 26.49
        para. 1(2)(c) 26.49
        para. 6 .... 26.49
        para. 12 .... 26.49
        para. 13 .... 26.49

1976 Restrictive Practices Court
        Act (c. 33)............. 2.36
     Dangerous Wild Animals
        Act (c. 38)............ 26.24
     s. 2(1) 26.24
        (8) 26.24
     Divorce (Scotland) Act
        (c. 39)
     s. 11 .... 4.07, 12.13
     Finance Act (c. 40)
        Sched. 6 .... 26.250
     Licensing (Scotland) Act
        (c. 66)... 26.43, 26.47, 26.252,
            26.290
     s. 17(4) 26.252
        (5) 26.252
        (6) 26.252
     s. 18A 26.252
        (3) 26.252
        (6) 26.252
     s. 25(4C) 26.252
     s. 26(2), (4), (10) 26.252
     s. 31(8) 26.252
     s. 32(1), (7) 26.252
     s. 35(4) 26.252
     s. 38 .... 26.252
     s. 39 .... 26.31, 26.255
        (1) 26.43, 26.255
        (2) 26.255
        (2A) 26.255
     s. 39(3) 25.17, 26.255
        (4) 25.07, 26.39, 26.43,
            26.47, 26.49
          (a) 26.255
          (b) 26.255
          (c) 26.255
          (d) 26.255
        (5) 26.47, 26.255
        (6) 26.43, 26.47, 26.49
          (a) 26.39, 26.255
          (b) 26.39
        (7) 26.39, 26.43, 26.49,
            26.255
        (8) 26.31, 25.34, 26.39,
          26.43, 26.47, 26.49, 26.555
        (9) 1.36
     s. 44(a)–(e) 26.253
     s. 53 .... 26.254
     s. 56(1) 26.256A
        (2) 26.256A
     s. 65(8) 26.254
     s. 101 .... 26.252
     s. 102(1) 5.38
     s. 104 .... 26.256
     s. 105 .... 26.256
     ss 108–10 .... 26.256
     s. 117(2) 26.256
     s. 133(1) 26.38
        (4) ... 26.38, 26.39, 26.43,
            26.47, 26.49
     Sched. 4,
        paras 2, 7, 9, 10 ...... 26.254
     Pt II 26.252, 26.255
     Pt III 26.253, 26.255
     Pt V 26.254, 26.255
     Pt VII 26.255, 26.256

1976	Race Relations Act (c. 74)	26.369
	s. 50(4)	26.370
	(5)	26.370
	s. 57(1)	26.376
	(2)(b)	26.376
	s. 59(1)(b)	26.373
	(2)	26.373
	(3)	26.373
	s. 62(1)	26.371
	s. 63(2)(a)	26.372
	(b)	26.372
	(3)(b)	26.372
	(4)	26.372
	s. 67(4)	26.375
	s. 68(4)	26.372
	s. 72(2)	26.374
	(5)	26.374
	Sched. 4, para. 5(2)	26.368
	para. 8(a)	26.368
	(b)	26.366
	Pt III	26.376
	Fishery Limits Act (c. 86)	
	s. 2	26.187
1977	Presumption of Death (Scotland) Act (c. 27)...	4.67, 7.25, 14.02, 14.03, 14.72
	s. 1	13.62
	(1) 2.65, 20.06, 20.07	
	(4)	2.65
	(5)	20.10
	(6) 13.62, 20.11	
	s. 2(1)	20.12
	(a)	20.13
	(b)	20.13
	(2)(a)	20.13
	(b)	20.13
	(c)	20.13
	s. 3	20.14
	(1)	2.65
	s. 4(1)	20.18
	(2)	20.18
	(3)	20.18
	(4) 13.62, 20.18	
	s. 5	20.18
	(2)	20.18
	(4)	20.18
	s. 6(1)	20.16
	s. 7	20.17
	s. 8	20.18
	s. 9(1)	20.12
	(2)	20.12
	(3)	20.12
	s. 10	20.12
	s. 12 .... 20.15, 20.18	
	s. 14	20.12
	s. 17 .... 20.07, 20.16	
	Patents Act (c. 37)	
	s. 98(1)	2.46
	Rent Act (c. 42)	
	Sched. 23, para. 49(a) ...	26.180
	Criminal Law Act (c. 45)	
	Sched. 12	16.16
1978	Oaths Act (c. 19)	
	s. 4(1)	16.63
	(2)	16.63
1978	Oaths Act—*cont.*	
	s. 5	16.63
	(1)	16.64
	(4)	16.64
	s. 6(1)	16.64
	Adoption (Scotland) Act (c. 28)....	28.04, 28.09, 28.36, 28.116, 28.150, 28.193
	s. 1	28.12
	s. 3	28.12
	s. 6 .. 28.01, 28.06, 28.08, 28.64, 28.65, 28.79, 28.87, 28.108, 28.149, 28.156, 28.158, 28.160, 28.190	
	(1)(a) .. 28.09, 28.48, 28.160	
	(b)	28.11
	(i) 28.10, 28.85	
	(2)	28.10
	s. 6A	28.150
	s. 7	28.11
	s. 11 .... 28.12, 28.18, 28.65	
	(3)	28.21
	s. 12(1) 28.42, 28.44	
	(2)	28.42
	(3) 28.25, 28.42	
	s. 12(3A)	28.42
	(5)	28.44
	(6)	28.120
	(7)	28.44
	(8)	28.44
	(9)	28.119
	s. 13	28.12
	(1) 28.43, 28.51	
	(2) 28.43, 28.51	
	(3)	28.43
	s. 14(1)	28.45
	(1A) 28.45, 28.48	
	(1B) 28.45, 28.48, 28.53	
	(2)(a)	28.50
	(c)	28.50
	s. 15(1)	28.48
	(aa) 28.46, 28.52, 28.57	
	(b)	28.46
	(2)(a)	28.50
	(c)	28.50
	(3)	28.47
	(a)	28.47
	(b)	28.47
	s. 16	28.02
	(1)	28.31
	(a)	28.135
	(i)	28.93
	(ii)	28.93
	(iii)	28.93
	(b)(i) 28.31, 28.73	
	(2) 28.06, 28.28, 28.34, 28.59	
	(4) 28.31, 28.54	
	s. 17	28.37
	s. 18 .... 28.02, 28.12, 28.93, 28.135	
	(1) ... 28.17, 28.31, 28.139, 28.144, 28.159, 28.160	
	(a)	28.140

1978 Adoption (Scotland) Act
—*cont.*

s. 18(2) 28.137, 28.140,
28.141, 28.167
(a) 28.140
(b) 28.141
(3) 28.138, 28.159
(5) .. 28.25, 28.135, 28.139,
28.154
(6) 28.146, 28.155,
28.159, 28.160, 28.172,
28.185
(7) 28.146, 28.160
(a) 28.159
(8) 28.136, 28.160
(9) 28.167
s. 19 ..... 28.12, 28.155, 28.195
(1) 28.185
(b) 28.174
(2), (3) 28.150, 28.172,
28.185
(4) 28.173
(a) 28.173
s. 20 .... 28.12, 28.155
(1) 28.186
(1A) 28.186
(2) 28.194
(3) 28.190
(4)(a) 28.191
(b) 28.191
(5) 28.191, 28.192
s. 21 .... 28.12, 28.186
(1) 28.195
(2) 28.195
s. 22 .... 28.12
(1) 28.20, 28.22, 28.65,
28.67, 28.175
(2) 28.63, 28.65
(3) 28.65
s. 22A 28.17
(1) 28.22, 28.23
s. 23 .. 28.12, 28.63, 28.64, 28.96
s. 24(1) 28.49, 28.127
(2) 28.82
(3) .. 28.08, 28.116, 28.156,
28.159, 28.160
s. 25(1) 28.123
(2) 28.123
s. 25A 28.40, 28.99
s. 27 .... 28.12, 28.175
s. 28 .... 28.12
(1) 28.175
(2)(a) 28.175
(b) 28.175
(4) 28.175
(6) 28.175
s. 29(1), (2) 28.178, 28.180
s. 30 .... 28.12
(1) 28.175
(b) 28.175
(2) 28.175
(3) 28.126, 28.175
(6) 28.126
s. 31 .... 28.12
(1) 28.175
s. 35(1) 28.12

1978 Adoption (Scotland) Act
—*cont.*

s. 39(1)(b) 28.42, 28.52
(2) 28.47
s. 45 .... 28.12
(1) 28.130
(4) 28.130
(5) 28.130
s. 46(1) 28.47, 28.183
s. 49 .... 28.51
(1) 28.51, 28.57
(2) 28.51
s. 50 .... 28.51
s. 51 .... 28.82
s. 51A(3) 28.82
s. 56 .... 28.36, 28.195
s. 56(1), (2) 28.36
(3) 28.37
(4) 28.37
s. 57 .... 5.20, 28.40, 28.109
s. 58(1)(a) 28.68
(b) 28.68, 28.144
(2) 28.70
(a) 28.69
(b) 28.152
(3) 28.54
s. 65(1) 28.12, 28.18, 28.24,
28.29, 28.30, 28.44, 28.136
(3) 28.21
(6) 28.137, 28.141
Sched. 1, para. 1... 28.118, 28.130
para. 1(5) 28.130
(7) 28.130
Interpretation Act (c. 30)
s. 3 .... 9.17
s. 5 .... 1.06, 2.03, 10.03, 18.85,
18.90, 25.32, 25.41
s. 7 .... 6.20
s. 22 .... 1.06, 2.03
s. 23 ... 1.06, 10.03, 18.85, 18.90
Sched. 1 ..... 1.06, 2.03, 10.03,
18.85, 18.90, 25.32,
25.41, 26.13
para. 4(1) 28.181
para. 4(1)(a), (b) 28.181
para. 4(2) 28.181, 28.182
Sched. 2,
Pt 1, para 4(1)(a) .. 1.06, 2.03
Pt 11, para 6 .... 1.06
State Immunity Act (c. 33).. 10.04
s. 1(1) 4.04
(2) 2.17
s. 2 .... 4.04
s. 12 .... 4.04
s. 13 .... 4.04
s. 14(1) 4.04
s. 20 .... 4.05
Rating (Disabled Persons)
Act (c. 40)........... 26.358
s. 6(5) 26.358
(5A) 26.358
(6) 26.358

1978 National Health (Scotland) Act (c. 58)
    Sched. 6, para. 90 . . . . . . 26.299
1979 Carriage by Air and Road Act (c. 28)
    Sched. 1, art. 28 . . . . 2.77
    Land Registration (Scotland) Act (c. 33). 26.106, 26.267
    s. 6(1)(c) 11.38
    s. 9(1), (4) 26.106
    s. 20(6) 26.106
    (8) 26.106
    s. 21(3) 26.106
    (5) 26.106
    s. 22A 26.267
    (1) 26.106
    (2) 26.106
    (8) 26.106
    (9) 26.106
    Credit Unions Act (c. 34). . 26.205
    s. 1(1) 26.205
    Banking Act (c. 37)
    Sched. 6, para. 1 . . . . . . 15.97
    Sale of Goods Act (c. 54)
    s. 11(5) 11.45
    s. 39 . . . . 11.13
    s. 40 . . . . 11.13
    s. 58 . . . . 11.45
1980 Protection of Trading Interests Act (c. 11)
    s. 6 . . . . 3.71, 3.87
    Slaughter of Animals (Scotland) Act (c. 13). . 26.25
    s. 4 . . . . 26.25
    s. 5(5) 26.25
    s. 12 . . . . 26.25
    s. 13 . . . . 26.27
    s. 15(4) 25.32, 26.25
    Education (Scotland) Act (c. 44). 5.20, 26.113
    s. 28A 26.113
    (1) 26.113
    (3) 26.113
    (4) 26.113
    s. 28B–E 26.113
    s. 28E(3) 26.113
    s. 28F 26.113
    (1) 26.113
    (2) 26.113, 26.114, 26.116
    (3) 26.114, 26.116
    (a) 26.113
    (b) 26.113
    (c) 26.113
    (4) 26.113, 26.114, 26.116
    (5) 26.113, 26.116
    (a) 26.113
    (b) 26.113
    (6) 26.113, 26.116
    (7) 26.116
    (8) 26.113, 26.114, 26.116
    s. 28F(9) . . 25.32, 26.113, 26.114

1980 Education (Scotland) Act —*cont.*
    s. 28G–H 26.113
    s. 28H(1)–(3) 26.114
    (5) 26.115
    (6) 26.114
    (7) 26.114
    s. 39(3) 26.115
    (4) 26.115
    s. 44(2) 26.115
    s. 60(2) 26.115
    s. 65(1), (2), (3), (5), (8) 26.116
    s. 100(1) 1.12
    s. 135(1) 26.114
    Sched. 2, para. 4 . . . . 1.12
    Water (Scotland) Act 1980 (c. 45). 26.411
    s. 25 . . . . 26.412
    s. 26 . . . . 26.412
    s. 27 . . . . 26.412
    (1) 26.411
    (3) 26.411
    s. 28 . . . . 26.412
    (2) 26.412
    ss 29–36 . . . . 26.412
    s. 37 . . . . 26.412, 26.413
    s. 38(3) 26.412
    s. 71(2) 26.414
    s. 104(1) 26.411
    Solicitors (Scotland) Act (c. 46). 26.278
    s. 4 . . . . 1.33
    s. 20(1)(b) 1.33
    s. 24 . . . . 1.33
    s. 25 . . . . 1.33
    s. 28F(3)(c) 25.26
    (5) 25.07
    s. 32(1) 30.19
    (2)(a) 30.19
    s. 61A(1) 21.72
    s. 62(1) 19.30
    (2) 19.30
    s. 65(2) 6.19, 30.92
    Sched. 4, Pt II, para. 12 . . . . 26.278
    Law Reform (Miscellaneous Provisions) (Scotland) Act (c. 55). . 24.11, 24.12
    s. 1 . . . . 13.61
    (1)(d) 1.08
    s. 10(a) 1.09, 2.129
    (b) 1.10, 2.129
    s. 12(2) 10.40
    s. 13 . . . . 2.44
    (a)(ii) 26.407
    (iii) 26.407
    (b) 26.408
    (c) 26.409
    (d) . . 26.407, 26.408, 26.409
    s. 14(1) 2.68
    (b) 2.69
    s. 15(a) 2.78

1980 Law Reform (Mis-
   cellaneous Provisions)
   (Scotland) Act—*cont.*
   s. 16 . . . . 13.47, 13.48,
        13.58, 13.60, 13.61
     (a) 30.27
     (b) 2.61
   s. 17 . . . . 26.32
   s. 18(3) 30.27
   s. 19 . . . . 2.130, 4.123
   s. 23 . . . . 10.40, 12.51
     (a) 2.121
   Sched. 1, Pt I 1.08
   Sched. 3 . . . . 2.27, 2.78
  Criminal   Justice
   (Scotland) Act (c. 62)
   s. 42 . . . . 2.22
   s. 58 . . . . 3.34
   s. 59 . . . . 3.34
   s. 60 . . . . 3.34
   s. 61 . . . . 3.34
   s. 62 . . . . 3.34
   s. 63 . . . . 3.34
   s. 64 . . . . 3.34
   s. 65 . . . . 3.34
   s. 66 . . . . 3.34
   s. 67 . . . . 3.34
  Local Government, Plan-
   ning and Land Act
   (c. 65)
   Sched. 2, para. 10(1) 26.164
   para. 10(2)(a) 26.164
       (3) 26.165
       (4) 26.165
   para. 14(a) 26.171
1981 International Organisations Act (c. 9). 4.06
  Merchant Shipping Act
   (c. 10)
   s. 1 . . . . 21.32
  Energy Conservation Act
   (c. 17). 26.124
   s. 24(2) 26.124
  Judicial Pensions Act
   (c. 20)
   s. 6 . . . . 1.08
   s. 16 . . . . 1.08
   s. 17 . . . . 1.08
   s. 18 . . . . 1.08
   s. 19 . . . . 1.08
   s. 20 . . . . 1.08
   s. 21 . . . . 1.08
   s. 22 . . . . 1.08
   s. 23 . . . . 1.08
   s. 24 . . . . 1.08
   s. 25 . . . . 1.08
   s. 26 . . . . 1.08
   s. 27 . . . . 1.08
   s. 28 . . . . 1.08
   s. 29 . . . . 1.08
  Animal Health Act (c. 22). . 26.28
   s. 92(3) 26.28
   Sched. 5 . . . . 26.26
  Zoo Licensing Act (c. 37). . . 26.29
   s. 18(1)(b) 26.29

1981 Zoo Licensing Act—*cont.*
   s. 18(4) 26.29
     (6) 26.29
  Contempt of Court Act
   (c. 49). 5.28
   s. 1 . . . . 2.20
   s. 2 . . . . 2.20
   s. 3 . . . . 2.20
   s. 4 . . . . 2.20
     (2) 2.20, 5.22, 5.30
   s. 5 . . . . 2.20
   s. 9 . . . . 2.20, 5.27, 16.55
   s. 11 . . . . 5.30
   s. 15 . . . . 21.99
     (1) 2.24
     (2) 21.99
      (a) 2.24
     (3) 2.22, 2.24, 21.99
      (a) 2.24
  Supreme Court Act (c. 54)
   s. 6 . . . . 2.75
   s. 33 . . . . 15.85
   s. 35 . . . . 15.85
  Education (Scotland) Act
   (c. 58)
   s. 1 . . . . 25.07, 25.26, 25.32
     (1) 5.20, 26.113
   s. 4(1) 26.116
   s. 28F(3)(c) 5.20
   Sched. 8 . . . . 26.116
  Matrimonial   Homes
   (Family Protection)
   (Scotland) Act (c. 59). . . 5.21,
    8.02, 15.43; 18.114, 22.02,
    22.15, 22.46, 22.52, 22.105,
     22.106, 23.42, 29.81
   s. 2(1)(e) 22.15
   s. 3(1) 22.15
     (2) 22.15
     (3) 22.107
     (a) 23.42
     (b) 23.42
     (c) 23.42
     (d) 23.42
     (4) 22.79, 22.107
   s. 4 . . . . 22.15
     (a) 22.15
     (6) 22.79
   s. 5 . . . . 22.80
   s. 6(2) 22.107
     (4) 26.106
   s. 7 . . . . 22.15
     (1) 22.77, 22.78, 22.79,
            23.43
     (4) 22.81
   s. 8(1) 22.78
   s. 11 . . . . . . 22.77, 22.107, 29.81
   s. 13 . . . . 22.15, 22.61
   s. 14 . . . . 26.76
   s. 15 . . . . 26.76
     (1) 22.79
     (2) 22.80
     (4) 22.82
     (5) 22.80, 22.82
   s. 16 . . . . 1.30, 26.76

1981 Matrimonial Homes (Family Protection) (Scotland) Act—*cont.*
s. 17 .... 1.30, 22.15, 26.76
s. 18 .... 22.15, 22.78
  (1) 22.79
s. 19 .... 23.42, 23.43
British Nationality Act (c. 61)
  Sched. 7 .... 2.39
1982 Civil Aviation Act (c. 16)... 26.36
s. 71 .... 26.36
s. 76 .... 2.02
s. 86 .... 3.87
s. 91 .... 2.77
Deer (Amendment) (Scotland) Act (c. 19)
s. 11 .... 26.31
Oil and Gas (Enterprise) Act (c. 23)
s. 23 .... 2.02, 3.71, 3.87
  (1) 27.03
  (2) 27.03
  (6)(a) 27.03
    (b) 27.03
    (c) 27.03
    (d) 27.03
Civil Jurisdiction and Judgments Act (c. 27).. 28.50, 30.16, 31.63
s. 1 .... 7.12, 11.05
  (1) 13.68, 30.63
s. 2(1) 3.04
s. 3(1) 3.04
  (2) 3.04
  (3) 3.04
s. 3B 3.68
s. 10(2) 3.21
  (3) 3.49, 3.50
s. 16(1) 3.69
    (a) 3.25
  (2) 3.69
  (3) 3.70, 3.78
  (4) 3.70
s. 17(1) 3.71
s. 20(1) 3.03, 3.77
  (2) 3.78
  (3) 3.78
  (4) 3.78
  (5) 3.78
s. 21(1) 3.78
  (2) 3.79
  (3) 3.79
s. 22(1) 2.93, 3.53, 3.78
  (2) 3.78
  (4) 3.78
s. 23 .... 3.78
s. 24(2) 3.66, 11.02
    (a) 11.70
s. 27 .... 3.65
s. 28 .... 3.65, 3.66
s. 41 .... 7.12
  (2) 3.07, 30.20, 30.21, 31.14

1982 Civil Jurisdiction and Judgments Act—*cont.*
s. 41(3) 3.08, 30.21, 31.14
  (4) 3.09, 30.20, 30.21, 31.14
  (5) 3.08, 3.91
  (6) 3.07, 3.08
  (7) 3.12
s. 42 .... 7.12
  (1) 3.13
  (3) 3.15
  (4) 3.16
  (5) 3.17
  (6) 3.18
  (7) 3.18
  (8) 3.16
s. 43(2) 3.19
  (3) 3.19
  (4) 3.19
  (5) 3.19
s. 45(3) 3.21
s. 46(1) 3.22, 4.54
  (3) 3.22
    (a) 4.54
s. 49 .... 2.93, 3.78
s. 50 .... 3.08, 3.13
Sched. 1 .. 2.63, 3.02, 6.30, 7.12
  art. 1 .... 3.05, 3.44, 3.107
  art. 2 .... 3.06
  art. 3 .... 3.11, 3.98, 3.103
  art. 4 .... 3.12, 3.45
  art. 5(5) 3.42, 3.46, 3.47
    (6) 2.44, 3.21
  art. 7 .... 3.42, 3.45
  art. 8 .... 3.42, 3.44
    r. 1 .... 3.93, 3.96, 3.103
    r. 9 .... 3.42, 3.44
    r. 10 .... 3.42, 3.44
    r. 11 .... 3.43, 3.44
    r. 12 .... 3.44
    r. 12A 3.44
    r. 13 .... 3.46, 3.47
    r. 14 .... 3.46, 3.47
    r. 15 .... 3.46, 3.48
    r. 17 .... 2.44, 3.23
    r. 21 .... 2.93, 3.60
    r. 22 .... 2.93
    r. 23 .... 2.93
    r. 52 .... 3.10
    r. 57 .... 2.76
Sched. 2 .... 3.02
  art. 3 .... 13.68, 30.63
Sched. 3 .... 3.02
Sched. 3A 3.02
Sched. 3B 3.02
Sched. 3C 2.63, 3.68, 6.30, 7.12
  art. 5(6) 2.44
  art. 17(2) 2.44
Sched. 4 .. 2.63, 3.02, 3.03, 3.41, 3.47, 3.51, 3.63, 3.69, 3.70, 3.71, 3.74, 3.77
  art. 2 .... 3.72
  art. 3 .... 3.72
  art. 5(1) 3.92

1982 Civil Jurisdiction and
      Judgments Act—*cont.*
  Sched. 4—*cont.*
    art. 5(3) 3.73, 3.93, 3.104
    art. 5(4) 3.93
    art. 5(5) 3.96
    art. 5(6) 2.44, 3.23
        (8) 3.73
        (8)(b) 3.103, 3.105
        5A 3.19, 3.25, 3.73,
                              3.106
    art. 6(1) 3.38
        (2) 3.39
    art. 13 .... 3.49, 3.50
    art. 14 .... 3.49, 3.50
    art. 15 .... 3.49, 3.50
    art. 16 .. 3.03, 3.23, 3.24, 3.25,
                        3.28, 3.75
        (2) 3.19, 3.20
    art. 17 .... 2.44, 3.52, 3.75
    art. 18 .... 3.54
    art. 19 .... 3.55
    art. 20 .... 3.55, 3.59
    art. 24 .... 3.65
  Sched. 5 .... 3.25, 3.71
  Sched. 5, para. 1 .... 3.25
  Sched. 8 .... 25.12, 26.32, 30.16
    r. 1 .... 2.04, 3.90, 3.92, 3.93,
          3.94, 3.96, 3.104, 21.46,
                      21.53, 21.83
    r. 2 .... 3.90, 3.90A
        (1) 3.91
        (2) 3.92
        (3) 3.93
        (4) 3.94
        (5) 2.63, 3.95
        (6) 3.50, 3.96
        (7) 2.44, 3.97
        (8) 3.98, 3.99, 3.103
        (9) 3.50, 3.103, 21.46,
                              21.53
        (10) 2.04, 2.53, 3.93,
                        3.104, 21.83
        (11) 3.105
        (12) 3.19, 3.25, 3.106
        (13) 2.47, 3.107
        (14) 2.46, 3.27, 3.108
        (15) 3.109
        (a) .. 3.38, 4.47, 21.46,
                              21.53
        (b) 3.39
    r. 3 .... 3.50, 3.90A, 3.110
    r. 3(6) 3.50, 3.112
    r. 4 ... 2.36, 3.23, 3.54, 3.90A,
                              3.113
        (1) 3.111
        (a) ... 2.36, 3.24, 23.01
        (b) ... 3.19, 3.25, 3.106
        (d) 3.28
        (2) 3.26
        (3) 3.54, 3.111, 3.113
    r. 5 .. 2.36, 3.53, 3.90A, 3.112
        (1) 3.53
        (2) 3.53
        (3) 2.44, 3.53

1982 Civil Jurisdiction and
      Judgments Act—*cont.*
  Sched. 8—*cont.*
    r. 5(4) 2.44, 3.53
        (5) 3.53
        (6) 3.53
    r. 6 .... 3.54, 3.112
    r. 7 .... 2.11, 2.36, 3.55, 3.113
    r. 8 .... 2.11, 2.36, 3.55, 3.113
  Sched. 9 .. 2.76, 3.02, 3.77, 3.78,
                  3.79, 3.80, 3.106
    para. 1 .... 3.80
    para. 2 .... 3.81
    para. 3 .... 3.82
    para. 4 .... 3.25, 3.83
    para. 5 .... 3.84
    para. 6 .... 2.76, 3.85
    para. 7 .... 3.86
    para. 8 .... 3.87
    para. 9 .... 3.87
    para. 10 .... 3.87
    para. 11 .... 3.87
    para. 12 .... 3.87
    para. 13 .... 3.87
    para. 14 .... 3.85, 3.87
  Sched. 14 .... 26.104
Merchant Shipping (Liner
      Conferences)   Act
      (c. 37)
  s. 7(1) 2.36
Civic Government (Scot-
      land) Act (c. 45)..... 26.286,
                              26.288
  s. 2 .... 26.288
      (2) 26.288
  s. 3(1) 26.288
      (2) 26.288
      (3) 26.288
      (4) 26.288
  s. 6(1) 26.298
  s. 10 .... 26.289
  s. 13 .... 26.289
  s. 24 .... 26.289
  s. 28 .... 26.289
  s. 32 .... 26.289
  s. 38 .... 26.289
  s. 39 .... 26.289
  s. 40 .... 26.289
  s. 41 .... 26.289
  s. 41A 26.289
  s. 42 .... 26.289
  s. 43 .... 26.289
  s. 45 .... 26.291
  s. 62 .... 26.292
  s. 63 .... 26.292
      (1) 26.292
  s. 64 .... 26.292
      (1) 26.292
      (2) 26.292
      (3) 26.292
      (4) 26.292
      (5) 26.292
      (6) 26.292
      (7) 26.292
      (8) 26.292
      (9) 26.292

1982 Civic Government (Scotland) Act—*cont.*
s. 65 .... 26.292
s. 66 .... 26.292
s. 76(1) 26.293
    (2) 26.293
    (3) 26.293
    (4) 26.293
    (5) 26.293
s. 84 .... 26.294
s. 87 .... 26.295
s. 88(1), (3) 26.298
    (4) 26.298
s. 91 .... 26.295
s. 92 .... 26.295
s. 95 .... 26.295
s. 96 .... 26.295
s. 102(1) 26.298
s. 104 .... 26.296
s. 106(1) 26.295
    (2) 26.295
    (3) 26.295
    (4) 26.295
    (5) 26.295
    (6) 26.295
s. 110(1) 26.286
    (2)(b) 26.286
s. 119(9) 26.297
    (10) 26.297
    (16) 26.297
Sched. 1 .... 26.289
    para. 18 .... 26.290
        (1) 26.290
        (2) 26.290
        (3) 26.290
        (4) 26.290
        (5) 26.290
        (6) 26.290
        (7) 26.290
        (8) 26.290
        (9) 26.290
        (11) 26.290
        (12) 26.290
Sched. 2, para. 24 ...... 26.291
    para. 9(5)(c) 26.291
        (d) 26.291
    para. 21(1) 26.298
    para. 24(2)(b) 26.291
Pt VIII .. 26.295, 26.296, 26.298
Criminal Justice Act (c. 48). 21.99
Insurance Companies Act (c. 50)
s. 3 .... 11.65
s. 4 .... 11.65
Administration of Justice Act (c. 53)
s. 12 .... 21.29
    (1) 30.318
        (a) 21.29, 21.30
        (b) 21.29
    (2) 21.30
        (a) 30.318, 30.319
    (3) 21.31

1982 Administration of Justice Act—*cont.*
s. 12(4) 21.30
    (a) 30.318
    (5) 21.32
s. 13(1) 21.29
s. 14 .... 21.14
1983 Representation of the People Act (c. 2). 26.117
s. 56(1)(a) 26.117
    (b) 26.117
    (d) 26.117
s. 57 .... 26.117
    (1)(b) 26.117
    (2) 26.117
s. 73(1) 26.118
s. 78(1) 26.118
    (2) 26.118
    (4) 26.118
    (7) 26.118
s. 79(2) 26.118
s. 86(1) 26.118
    (1A) 26.118
    (11) 26.118
s. 128(1) 26.119
    (3)(b) 26.119
s. 134(1)(b) 26.119
s. 146(1), (5) 26.119
s. 167 .... 26.119
    (1A) 26.119
s. 204(3) 26.118
Merchant Shipping Act (c. 5)
s. 12 .... 21.32
British Fishing Boats Act (c. 8). 26.188
s. 3 .... 26.188
Divorce Jurisdiction, Courts Fees and Legal Aid (Scotland) Act (c. 12)
s. 1 .... 2.39, 2.57
s. 4 .... 1.23, 1.45
Sched. 1, para. 11 .... 13.61
    para. 12 .... 2.61, 13.61
Mobile Homes Act (c. 34) 26.174
s. 1(1), (2) 26.174
    (5) 26.174
s. 2(2) 26.174
    (3) 26.174
    (4) 26.174
s. 4 .... 26.175
s. 5(1) 26.174, 26.175
Sched. 1, Pt II 26.174
Mental Health (Scotland) Act (c. 36). 5.38, 22.24
s. 21(5) 25.43
s. 29(4) 25.38
s. 33(4) 25.07
s. 40(6) 25.43
s. 50(5) 25.07
s. 123 .... 1.12

1983 Matrimonial and Family
    Proceedings Act
    (c. 42).......... 22.02, 22.46
    s. 28 .... 22.66
        (2)(c) 2.59
    s. 30(1) 22.66
    Prescription and Limita-
    tion (Scotland) Act
    (c. 45)
    s. 1 .... 4.49, 12.53, 24.10
    s. 2 .. 2.115, 2.116, 10.38, 10.40,
                            12.51
    s. 3 .... 2.115
    Sched. 1, para. 8(a) 2.121
    Cable and Broadcasting
    Act (c. 46)
    Sched. 5, para. 5(3) 5.29
        para. 39(1) 2.20
    Rent (Scotland) Act
    (c. 58)
    s. 44 .... 2.36
    Sched. 4 .... 2.36
1984 Telecommunications Act
    (c. 12).............. 26.320
    Sched. 2, para. 1(1) 26.320,
                            26.321
        para. 5 .... 26.320
        para. 6(2) 26.320
        para. 7 .... 26.320
            (5) 26.320
        para. 8(1) 26.320
            (2) 26.320
            (3) 26.320
            (4) 26.320
        para. 14(1) 26.321
            (3) 26.321
            (4) 26.321
            (5) 26.321
        para. 17(1) 26.321
            (2) 26.321
            (5) 26.321
            (8) 26.321
            (9) 26.321
        para. 19(2) 26.321
            (5) 26.321
        para. 20(1) 26.321
            (3) 26.321
        para. 21 .... 26.321
    Rating and Valuation
    (Amendment)
    (Scotland) Act (c. 31)
    s. 5(2)(a) 26.358
        (b) 26.358
    Data Protection Act
    (c. 35).............. 26.377
    s. 21(8) 26.377
    s. 24(1) 26.377
        (3) 26.377
    s. 25(1) 26.377
    Mental Health (Scotland)
    Act (c. 36).......... 26.301
    s. 17(1)(a) 26.301
    s. 18(1)(b) 26.301
        (2) 26.301
        (3) 26.301

1984 Mental Health (Scotland)
    Act—*cont.*
    s. 19(1) 26.301
    s. 21 .... 26.306, 26.313
        (1) 26.301
            (a) 26.301
            (b) 26.301
        (2)(a) 26.301
        (3A) 26.301
        (4) 26.301
        (5) 26.301
    s. 22(1) 26.301
    s. 23 .... 26.301
    s. 24 .... 26.302
    s. 26 .... 26.302
        (6) 26.302
    s. 26A(1), (2) 26.302
        (7) 26.302
    s. 29(4) 26.304
    s. 30(1) 26.303
        (2) 26.303
        (6) 26.303
    s. 33(2) 26.302, 26.303
        (3)(b) 26.307
        (4) 26.302, 26.303
    s. 34(2) 26.303
    s. 35(2) 26.303
    s. 35A 26.305, 26.306
    s. 35D 26.305
    s. 35F 26.305
    s. 36.39 .... 26.307
    s. 40 .... 26.306, 26.307
    ss 41, 42 .... 26.307
    s. 45(1) 26.308
    s. 47(6) 26.307
    s. 50(5) 26.307
    s. 51(2) 26.307
    s. 52(2) 26.307
    s. 56(1) 26.309
        (2) 26.309
        (3) 26.309
    s. 57(1) 26.309
        (2) 26.309
    s. 63(1), (2) 26.310
    s. 64(1)–(7) 26.310
    s. 65(1) 26.310
    s. 66(1) 26.312
        (2) 26.312
        (3) 26.312
    s. 68 .... 26.310
    s. 70(1) 26.313
        (2) 26.313
    s. 71(1) 26.314
        (2) 26.314
        (4) 26.314
        (5) 26.314
    s. 113 ... 26.301, 26.303, 26.304
    s. 125(1) 26.314
    Pt V 26.313, 26.314
    Roads (Scotland) Act
    (c. 54).............. 26.385
    s. 1(5) 26.385
        (7) 26.385
    s. 13(7) 26.385
    s. 16(3) 26.386

1984 Roads (Scotland) Act—
cont.
s. 35(7) 26.385
s. 49 .... 26.285
s. 57(6) 26.385
s. 59(1) 26.385
s. 63(3) 26.385
s. 66(3) 26.385
s. 74(4) 26.385
s. 84(1) 26.386
s. 90(4) 26.385
s. 91(1) 26.385
    (2) 26.385
    (3) 26.385
    (6) 26.385
    (9) 26.385
s. 93(2) 26.385
    (3) 26.385
    (4) 26.385
    (6) 26.385
s. 96(4) 26.390
    (5) 26.390
s. 99(4) 26.385
s. 112(7) 26.386
s. 114(5) 26.386
s. 115(2) 26.387
s. 140(1) 26.388
    (8) 26.388
s. 142 .... 26.389
s. 151(1) 26.385
Sched. 9,
    para. 3(3)(a) 26.349
             (b) 26.349
             (c) 26.349
          (6)(a) 26.351
             (b(i) 26.351
               (ii) 26.351
          (15)(a) 26.351,
                          26.352
             (b) 26.351,
                          26.352
             (c) 26.351
          (21) 26.352
    para. 48 .... 26.281
    para. 55(2)(c) 26.357
    para. 64(2) 26.335
             (4) 26.339
    Sched. 11 .... 26.349
Foster Children (Scotland)
    Act (c. 56)............ 26.58
s. 1 .... 28.18
s. 3 .... 28.17
s. 9 .... 26.58
s. 10 .... 26.58
s. 11(1) 26.58
s. 12 .... 26.59
    (1)(a) 26.59
       (b) 26.59
    (2) 26.59
       (a) 26.58
       (b) 26.58
    (3) 26.59

1984 Rent (Scotland) Act
    (c. 58)........ 26.222, 26.268
s. 1 .... 26.269
s. 2 .... 26.269
s. 3 .... 26.269
s. 5 .... 26.268
s. 7 .... 26.272
    (1) 26.268
    (2) 26.268
s. 8 .... 26.271
s. 11(1) 26.269
    (a) 26.269
    (b) 26.269
    (2) 26.269
s. 12(1) 26.269
    (2) 26.269
    (5) 26.269
s. 21 .... 26.269
s. 23 .... 26.270
    (1) 26.270
s. 23A 26.270
s. 24(3) 26.270
    (6) 26.270
s. 25(2) 26.277
s. 29 .... 26.270
    (4) 26.271
s. 31(2) 26.271
s. 32(4) 26.271
    (5) 26.271
s. 39 .... 26.271
s. 45(2) 26.271
s. 60(3) 26.271
s. 77 .... 26.272
s. 87(1) 26.273
    (5) 26.273
s. 91 .... 26.274
s. 92 .... 26.274
s. 93(1) 26.274
    (2) 26.274
    (3) 26.275
    (5) 26.274
    (6) 26.274, 26.276
    (8) 26.275
    (9) 26.275
s. 97(1)(a), (2) 26.268
    (3) 26.275
    (8) 26.275
    (9) 26.275
s. 102(1) 26.277
    (2) 26.277
    (3) 26.276
s. 103(1) 26.220, 26.268,
            26.271, 26.274, 26.276
    (2) 26.268, 26.271
s. 104 .... 26.276
s. 106(1) 26.276
s. 110 .... 26.276
Sched. 1, para. 7 .... 26.276
Sched. 2, Pt 1 .... 26.269
    Pt I, case 7 .... 26.269
       case 8 .... 26.269
    Pt II 26.269
    Pt V 26.271
    Pt IX 26.274

1985 Companies Act (c. 6)
s. 4 . . . . 2.72
s. 5 . . . . 2.72
s. 6 . . . . 2.72
s. 25(1) 4.84
(2) 4.84
s. 27 . . . . 4.84
s. 28(7) 4.85
s. 30 . . . . 4.84
s. 127 . . . . 2.72
s. 135 . . . . 2.72
s. 136 . . . . 2.72
s. 137 . . . . 2.72
s. 138 . . . . 2.72
s. 139 . . . . 2.72
s. 140 . . . . 2.72
(2) 2.72
s. 287(2) 3.17
s. 359 . . . . 2.72
s. 382(2) 15.56
s. 409(1) 2.70
s. 425 . . . . 2.72
s. 426 . . . . 2.72
s. 427 . . . . 2.72
s. 427A 2.72
s. 428 . . . . 2.72
s. 429 . . . . 2.72
s. 430 . . . . 2.72
s. 430A 2.72
s. 430B 2.72
s. 430C 2.72
s. 430D 2.72
s. 430E 2.72
s. 430F 2.72
s. 438 . . . . 4.93
s. 459 . . . . 2.72
s. 460 . . . . 2.72
s. 461 . . . . 2.72
s. 463(1) 29.33
s. 653(2) 2.72
(2A) 2.72
(2B) 2.72
s. 680 . . . . 4.91
s. 691(1)(b)(ii) 6.41
s. 695(1) 6.41
(2) 6.41
s. 725(1) 6.40, 11.21, 11.22
s. 726 . . . . 11.57
(2) 11.57, 11.62
s. 735(1)(a) 6.40
s. 744 . . . . 2.71, 6.41
s. 745(1) 11.57
Sched. 2 . . . . 3.25, 3.71
Business Names Act (c. 7)
s. 5 . . . . 4.96, 4.99
(1) 4.87
(2) 4.87
Cinemas Act (c. 13). 26.159
s. 16(1) 26.159
Family Law (Scotland) Act
(c. 37). 30.302
s. 1 . . . . 22.59, 22.71
s. 2 . . . . 2.61
(1) 22.68
s. 3(1)(d) 7.13

1985 Family Law (Scotland) Act
—cont.
s. 7(2) 22.72
s. 8(1)(aa) 22.15
(ba) 22.15
(2) 3.32
(3) 8.02, 22.52, 22.60
s. 9 . . . . 3.32
(1)(c) 3.32
(d) 3.32
(e) 3.32
s. 13(1)(d) 2.12, 2.15
s. 14(2) 22.61
(4) 22.61
s. 16(1)(b) . . . 8.02, 22.52, 22.60
(3) 8.02, 22.52, 22.60
s. 18 . . . 2.42, 8.02, 22.15, 22.52,
22.60, 22.65
s. 19 . . . 6.08, 11.11, 11.36, 11.37
s. 20 . . . . 15.49
s. 23 . . . . 30.02, 30.240
s. 25 . . . . 29.73
Sched. 1, para. 1 . . . . 2.57
Sched. 2 . . . . 3.80
Food and Environment
Protection Act (c. 48). . 26.190
Sched. 2,
para. 7(1)–(3) 26.190
Representation of the
People Act (c. 50)
s. 204(3) 26.118
(5) 26.119
Sched. 2, para. 1 . . . . 26.117
Sched. 4, para. 26 . . . . . . 26.118
para. 30(a) 26.118
para. 56 . . . . 26.119
Child Abduction and
Custody Act (c. 60)
s. 4 . . . . 2.39
s. 8 . . . . 2.39
s. 16 . . . . 2.134
s. 20 . . . . 2.134
s. 23(2) 22.40
s. 27 . . . . 2.39
Bankruptcy (Scotland) Act
(c. 66)
s. 6(5) 2.70
s. 9 . . . . 2.70
(1) 2.70
(2) 2.70
(3) 2.70
(4) 2.70
(5) 2.70
s. 16 . . . . 2.70
s. 34(4) 2.42
s. 36(2)(d) 11.10
(5) 2.42
s. 37(4) 11.10, 29.34, 29.83
s. 39(2)(b) 4.110, 12.12
s. 56 . . . . 3.83
s. 73(1) 2.42, 2.70
s. 75(1) 29.34
Sched. 7, para. 4 . . . . 2.68
para. 24 . . . . 29.34, 29.58

1985 Housing (Consequential Provisions) Act (c. 71)
Sched. 2, para. 59 ...... 26.268
Weights and Measures Act (c. 72)............... 26.416
s. 79(3) 26.416
(4) 26.416
Law Reform (Miscellaneous Provisions) (Scotland) Act (c. 73)
s. 2 .... 26.106, 26.267
s. 8 .... 7.01
(1) 24.07
(2) 24.07
(3) 24.07
(4) 24.07
(5) 24.07
(6) 24.07
(7) 24.07
(8) 24.07
(9) 20.02
s. 9(1) 24.08
(2) 24.08
(3) 24.08
(4) 24.08
(5) 24.08
(6) 24.08
(7) 24.07, 24.08
(8) 24.08
s. 12(2) 2.119
(3) 2.121
(4) 2.115
(5) 2.114
s. 14 ...... 13.67, 28.38, 30.26
(1)(b) 12.05
s. 15(3)(b) 15.86
s. 17 .. 2.53, 21.80, 23.41, 26.103
s. 18 .... 13.60, 13.61
(1) 5.08, 30.03, 31.02
(3) 13.48, 13.49
(a) 5.03
(b) 13.48
(4) 2.27
s. 19 .... 12.03, 15.03
s. 20 .... 1.08
s. 23(1) 1.12
s. 47 .... 1.21
s. 49 .... 4.70, 29.17
s. 51 .... 26.301, 26.307
s. 52 .... 26.49
Sched. 2, para. 13 .... 1.37
Sched. 4 .... 1.08, 1.14, 3.83
1986 Law Reform (Parent and Child) (Scotland) Act (c. 9)
s. 2(1) 4.10
(4) 4.10
(8) 4.10
s. 3 .... 28.26
s. 4 .... 28.29
s. 6 .... 2.07, 15.104
(1) 15.104
(2) 15.104
(3) 15.104

1986 Law Reform (Parent and Child) (Scotland) Act —*cont.*
s. 6(4) 15.104
s. 7 .... 2.39
(1) 2.64
(2) 2.64
(3) 2.64
(h) 2.64
(5) 2.39
(6) 2.64
Sched. 1,
para. 8(3)(c) 26.360
para. 8(5) 26.360
para. 9 .... 26.283
para. 11 .... 2.61, 2.118
Sched. 2 ..... 2.02, 2.39, 2.57, 26.283
Patents, Designs and Marks Act (c. 39)
Sched. 2, Pt I,
para. 1(2)(j) 2.46, 3.71, 3.108
Finance Act (c. 41)
s. 100 .... 20.19
Insolvency Act (c. 45)....... 3.71, 26.199
s. 6(1) 2.72
(4) 2.72
(5) 2.72
(6) 2.72
s. 8(1) 2.71
s. 9(1) 2.71
s. 51(2) 2.71
s. 55 .... 4.88
(3) 29.33
s. 100(3) 2.72
s. 108 .... 2.72
s. 110 .... 2.72
s. 112 .... 2.72
s. 113 .... 4.91
s. 116 .... 4.90
s. 120(3) 2.71, 27.54
(a), (b), (c) 27.54
(4) 2.71
(5) 2.71
s. 126(1) 4.91
(2) 4.91
s. 130(2) 4.91
(3) 4.91
s. 165(1)(b) 2.72
(3) 4.90
s. 167(1) 4.90
(3) 4.90
s. 169(1) 4.90
(2) 12.12
s. 185 .... 29.83
(1) 29.34
(b) 2.72
s. 198 .... 5.23
s. 201(3) 2.72
s. 204(5) 2.72
s. 212 .... 2.72
s. 213 .... 2.72
s. 214 .... 2.72
s. 215 .... 2.72

1986 Insolvency Act—*cont.*
    s. 251 . . . . 2.71
    Sched. 2, para. 1 . . . . 4.88
        para. 5 . . . . 4.88
    Sched. 4, Pt. II, para. 4 . . . 4.90
    Sched. 13, Pt. I 2.72
    Sched. 14 . . . . 26.199
    Company Directors Dis-
      qualification Act
      (c. 46)
    s. 2(2) 2.71
    s. 3(4) 2.71
    s. 4(2) 2.71
    s. 6(3) 2.71
    s. 10(1) 2.71
    Legal Aid (Scotland) Act
      (c. 47). 26.279
    s. 14 . . . . 27.10
    s. 15 . . . . 27.10
    s. 18(2) 5.100, 19.09
        (a) 26.279
        (b)(i) 26.279
          (ii) 26.279
        (c) 26.279
        (3) 26.279
        (4) 26.279
    s. 29(12) 26.279
    s. 30 . . . . 2.22
    s. 38(1)(a) 11.53
    Sched. 2, Pt II,
      para. 3(c) 31.04
    Building Societies Act
      (c. 53). 15.97, 26.53
    s. 90 . . . . 26.53
    s. 108 . . . . 26.53
        (3) 26.53
    s. 119(1) 26.53
    Sched. 15,
      paras 1, 2 & 15 . . . . 26.53
    Sched. 19, Pt 1 . . . . 26.53
    Family Law Act (c. 55). 2.58,
               3.81, 3.82, 22.03
    Pt I 2.04
    s. 9 . . . . 2.62
    s. 10 . . . . 2.62
    s. 11 . . . . 2.62
    s. 16(1) 2.62
        (2) 2.62
    s. 33(1) 22.39
    s. 35(3) 2.04, 22.40
        (a) 6.06
    s. 42(4) 22.08
    Financial Services Act
      (c. 60). 3.71
    s. 172 . . . . 2.72
    Sched. 12 . . . . 2.72
    Salmon Act (c. 62). 26.189
    s. 11(9) 26.189
        (10) 26.189
    Public Order Act (c. 64). . . 26.109
    s. 24(2) 26.109
    Sched. 2, para. 1(3) 26.292
1987 Coal Industry Act (c. 3)
    Sched. 1, para. 46 . . . . 26.388

1987 Debtors (Scotland) Act
    (c. 18). . 1.32, 6.14, 6.16, 6.23,
      7.02, 7.03, 7.04, 10.11, 26.127,
        26.154, 29.13, 29.14, 29.40,
        29.66, 29.70, 29.73, 29.81
    s. 1 . . . . . . 17.21, 26.127, 30.116
        (1) 6.07, 30.116
        (5) 30.116
    s. 3 . . . . 26.127, 29.13
    s. 5 . . . . 26.128
    s. 6 . . . . 24.11
    s. 8(3) 29.85
    s. 9(2) 29.48
        (b) 29.65
        (9) 29.85
        (12) 29.84
    s. 10 . . . . 26.128
    s. 15 . . . . 26.127, 26.128
    s. 16 . . . . . . 29.27, 29.74, 29.76,
                29.81, 29.86
        (1) 29.27
        (a)–(f) 29.76
        (2) 29.76
        (4) 29.74, 29.81
    s. 17(1), (2) 29.77
    s. 18(1) 29.77
        (2) 2.78, 29.77
    s. 19(1) 29.78
        (2) 29.72
    s. 20(2) 29.78
        (c) 29.72
        (3) 29.77
        (4) 29.78
        (6) 29.79
        (d) 29.81
        (7) 29.79
    s. 21(1) 2.78, 26.129
        (a) 29.79
        (b) 29.78, 26.129
        (4) 29.81
        (7) 29.80
        (8), (9) 29.78
    s. 22 . . . . 11.25
        (2) 29.72
        (3) 2.78, 29.80
        (4) 29.80
        (5) 2.78, 29.80
    s. 23 . . . . 2.78
        (1) 29.81, 26.130
        (2) 29.84, 26.130
    s. 24 . . . . 2.78, 24.11
        (1) 26.131, 29.81
        (2) 29.81
        (3) 26.131, 29.81
    s. 25 . . . . 29.84
    s. 26 . . . . . . 26.132, 29.75, 29.85
    s. 27 . . . . 2.78, 29.85
        (1) 26.133
        (2) 26.133, 29.85
        (3) 29.85
        (4) 26.133
        (5) 29.86
    s. 28(1) 26.134, 29.82, 29.84
        (2) 29.84
        (4) 2.78, 26.135, 29.82

1987 Debtors (Scotland) Act—
cont.
s. 28(5) 2.78
    (6) 2.78, 26.135, 29.82,
                                29.84
s. 29(1) 29.82
    (2) 2.78, 29.82, 29.84
        (a) 26.136
        (b) 26.136
    (3) 2.78, 26.137
    (4) 26.137, 29.82
    (5) 29.82
s. 30 . . . . 24.11
    (1) 26.138
    (2) 26.138, 29.86
    (5) 29.86
s. 31(2)(c) 29.87
    (3) 29.88
s. 32 . . . . 29.68
    (1)–(5) 29.87
s. 35(1) 26.138, 29.88
    (2) 26.138, 29.88
    (3) 26.138
    (9), (10) 29.88
s. 36 . . . . 29.88
s. 37(5)–(7) 29.89
s. 38 . . . . 29.89
s. 39 . . . . 29.90
    (3) 26.139
s. 39(5) 29.90
s. 40(1) 29.72
    (2) 26.140, 29.72
    (5) 29.84
s. 41 . . . . 29.73
    (2) 29.74
    (3) 26.140, 29.74
    (5) 29.74
    (6) 29.84
    (7), (8) 29.74
s. 42(1) 26.141
    (3) 26.141
    (4) 26.141
s. 43(1) 26.142
    (5) 26.142
s. 46 . . . . 26.144
    (1) 29.40
        (a) 29.41
    (2) 29.40
s. 47(1) 29.43
s. 49 . . . . 29.44
s. 50 . . . . 29.46
    (1) 26.145, 29.46
    (2) 26.145
    (3) 26.146, 29.46
s. 51(1) 29.53
    (2)(a) 29.52
        (b) 29.55
s. 52 . . . . 29.50
    (1)(c) 29.51
s. 53(1) 29.53
s. 54(1) 29.51
    (2) 29.51
    (3) 29.51
s. 55 . . . . 26.147, 29.54
    (1) 29.54

1987 Debtors (Scotland) Act—
cont.
s. 55(2) 29.51, 29.54
    (5)–(8) 29.54
s. 56(1), (2) 29.55
s. 57(1) 29.45, 29.53
    (4), (6) 29.49, 29.57
s. 58(1) 29.58
s. 59(4), (5) 29.59
s. 60 . . . . 26.148
    (1)(b) 29.59
    (8) 26.148
    (9) 26.148, 29.60
s. 62(4) 26.149
    (5) 26.149, 29.62
    (9) 26.149
s. 63 . . . . 29.60
s. 64 . . . . 29.60
s. 65 . . . . 26.150
    (1), (2) 29.61
    (5), (8) 29.63
s. 66 . . . . 26.151
    (1)(a), (b) 29.64
    (4) 29.63
    (6) 29.63
s. 69(2) 29.43, 29.52
    (3) 29.43, 29.52
    (4) 29.45
    (5) 29.49
s. 70(1) 29.42, 29.52
    (2) 29.42, 29.52
    (3) 29.42
s. 72(2), (4) 29.48
s. 73 . . . . 29.40, 29.44
    (1) 29.46, 29.54, 29.59,
                                29.62
    (2) 29.29
s. 74 . . . . 26.251
s. 75 . . . . 1.27
s. 76 . . . . 1.27
s. 78 . . . . 1.27
s. 79 . . . . 1.27
    (1)(b) 26.139
s. 80 . . . . 1.27
    (6) 1.27
s. 81 . . . . 1.27
s. 82 . . . . 1.27
s. 83 . . . . 1.27, 1.28
s. 84 . . . . 1.27
s. 85 . . . . 1.27
s. 86 . . . . 1.27
s. 87(2)(a) 29.77
s. 90(1) 29.42, 29.67
    (2) 29.67
    (3) 29.69
    (5)–(7) 29.69
s. 97 . . . . 26.154
s. 101 . . . . 29.92
s. 103(1) 26.152, 30.345
    (2) 26.152
s. 106 . . . . 22.10, 29.50
Sched. 2 . . . . 29.44
Sched. 3 . . . . 29.60
Sched. 4 . . . . 26.153, 26.251
Sched. 5 . . . . 26.153, 26.251

1987 Debtors (Scotland) Act—
  cont.
    Sched. 6,
      para. 3 .... 11.25
      para. 4 .... 26.208
    Sched. 6,
      para. 26 .... 26.276
      para. 28(b) 29.58
    Pt III 29.13, 29.29
  Banking Act (c. 22)........ 29.12
  Housing (Scotland) Act
    (c. 26)........ 26.215, 26.268,
                              26.357
    s. 44 .... 30.268
    ss 44–46 .... 26.215
    s. 47 .... 23.06
        (1) 23.06, 26.215
        (2) 30.268
        (3) 30.268
    s. 48 .... 26.215
        (1) 30.273, 30.280
        (2)(a) 30.272, 30.279
    s. 49 .... 26.216
    s. 50 .... 26.216
    s. 51(1) 26.216
        (2) 26.216
        (3), (4) 26.217
    s. 57 .... 26.218
    s. 88 .... 26.240
        (1), (6) 26.219
    s. 97 .... 26.220
        (5) 26.220
        (6) 26.220
    s. 99(1)–(3) 26.221
    s. 102 .... 26.220, 26.221
    s. 103 .... 26.222
    s. 108(1) 26.225
    s. 109 .... 26.225
    s. 110 .... 26.226
    s. 111(1) 26.225
    s. 113 .... 26.223
    s. 114(1) 26.227
    s. 115 .... 26.227
    s. 116 .... 26.227
    s. 120 .... 26.240
    s. 121 .... 26.240
        (1), (3) 26.227
    s. 125 .... 26.227, 26.241
    s. 127 .... 26.357
    s. 129 .... 26.219, 26.227
    s. 157 .... 26.228
        (5) 26.228
    s. 158 .... 26.228
        (4) 26.228
    s. 160 .... 26.229
    s. 161 .... 26.229
    s. 162 .... 26.229
    s. 163(1), (2) 26.229
    s. 166 .... 26.230
    s. 167 .... 26.230
    s. 169(1) 26.230
    s. 170(1) 26.230
        (2) 26.230
    s. 173 .... 26.231
    s. 174 .... 26.231
    s. 178(1) 26.232

1987 Housing (Scotland) Act—
  cont.
    s. 181(1) 26.234
        (4) 26.234
    s. 184 .... 26.236
    s. 185 .... 26.235
    s. 186(1) 26.232
        (3) 26.232
    s. 188(4) 26.233
    s. 190(4) 26.237
    s. 275 .... 26.239
    s. 276 .... 26.239
    s. 299(1) 26.238
    s. 309 .... 26.240
        (1) 26.240
        (2) 26.240
    s. 322(1) 26.241
        (2) 26.241
    s. 323(1) 26.242
        (a) 26.242
        (b) 26.242
        (c) 26.242
    s. 324 .... 26.226
        (1) 26.224
        (3) 26.243
        (4) 26.243
        (5) 26.226, 26.243
        (7) 26.243
    Sched. 5, paras 5, 6 ..... 26.218
    Sched. 8, para. 5 .... 26.240
    Sched. 10, para. 3 ...... 26.223,
                              26.224
      para. 5(1) 26.224
    Sched. 11, para. 3(1) 26.236
      para. 3(2) 26.236
        (4) 26.236
      para. 4 .... 26.236
      para. 5(1) 26.233
    Sched. 20, para. 4 ...... 26.239
      para. 5 .... 26.239
    Sched. 23, para. 9 ...... 26.357
    Pt IV 26.222
    Pt V 26.225
    Pt VI 26.242
    Pt VIII 26.231, 26.237
    Pt XIV 26.238
    Pt XV 26.240
  Fire Safety and Safety of
    Places of Sports Act
    (c. 27).............. 26.160
    s. 9(1) 26.179
    s. 19(1) 26.157
    s. 22 .... 26.157
    s. 23 .... 26.158
    ss 26–29 .... 26.160
    s. 30(1)–(4), (7) 26.160
    s. 44(1) 26.289
    s. 49 .... 26.157
        (2) 26.179
    Sched. 2 .... 26.157
    Sched. 5, para. 4 .... 26.179
      para. 6 .... 26.157
  Registered Establishments
    (Scotland) Act (c. 40)
    s. 1(1) 26.282

1987 Consumer Protection Act
(c. 43). 26.406
s. 15 . . . . 26.406
s. 14(8) 26.406
1988 Civil Evidence (Scotland)
Act (c. 32)
s. 1 . . . . 16.76
(1) 20.19, 21.98, 27.14
s. 2 . . . . 15.12, 28.94, 28.112
(1) 15.43, 30.156, 31.85
s. 3 . . . . 15.38
s. 6(1) 16.24, 27.14
Court of Session Act
(c. 36)
s. 26(4) 2.27
s. 32(3) 16.97
(4) 17.03
s. 33 . . . . 13.64
s. 52 . . . . 18.99
Sched. 2 . . . . 18.99
Housing (Scotland) Act
(c. 43). 26.244, 30.268
s. 12 . . . . 26.244, 30.268
s. 14 . . . . 26.246
s. 18 . . . . 26.245
(4) 30.272, 30.279
s. 19 . . . . 26.245, 30.268
(2) 30.268
s. 20(1) 30.273, 30.280
s. 21 . . . . 26.246
s. 22(1) 26.247
(2) 26.247
s. 23 . . . . 26.270
s. 24 . . . . 26.270
s. 27 . . . . 26.270
s. 29 . . . . 26.248
s. 30(1) 26.249
(2) 26.249
s. 32 . . . . 26.244
s. 39(1), (2) 26.270
s. 46(1) 26.269
s. 47(11) 26.268
s. 90 . . . . 26.270
Sched. 5 . . . . 26.245, 30.268
Ground 6 . . . . 26.247
Ground 9 . . . . 26.247
Sched. 9, para. 4 . . . . 26.268,
26.271
Pt III 26.270
Copyright, Designs and
Patents Act (c. 48)
s. 99 . . . . 2.46
s. 102(5) 2.46
s. 114 . . . . 2.46
s. 115 . . . . 2.46
s. 152 . . . . 2.46
s. 195 . . . . 2.46
s. 204 . . . . 2.46
s. 205 . . . . 2.46
s. 230 . . . . 2.46
s. 231 . . . . 2.46
s. 232 . . . . 2.46
s. 235(5) 2.46
s. 251 . . . . 2.46
Sched. 4 . . . . 2.46

1988 Road Traffic Act (c. 52). . . 26.381
s. 90(1) 26.381
(2) 26.381
(3) 26.381
s. 92 . . . . 26.382
(5) 26.382
s. 93 . . . . 26.382
s. 99(1)(b) 26.382
(3) 26.382
s. 99C 26.382
s. 100(1) 26.382
(a) 26.382
(b) 26.382
(c) 26.382
(2) 26.382
s. 115A(1) 26.383
s. 116(4) 26.383
s. 119(1) 26.383
(3) 26.383
s. 151(5) 12.06
s. 152(1)(a) 12.06
(2) 12.06
(3) 12.06
Road Traffic Offenders
Act (c. 53). 26.384
s. 42(1) 26.384
(2) 26.384
(3) 26.384
(4) 26.384
1989 Road Traffic (Driver
Licensing and Infor-
mation Systems) Act
1989 (c. 22)
s. 2(1) 26.383
s. 16 . . . . 26.383
Sched. 2, para. 6 . . . . 26.383
Finance Act (c. 26)
s. 146 . . . . 26.250
Companies Act (c. 40)
s. 110(2) 2.72
Sched. 19, para. 11 . . . . 2.72
Children Act (c. 41). 26.59
s. 71 . . . . 26.59
s. 77(6), (10) 26.59
Sched. 10, para. 33 . . . . . . 28.53
Prisons (Scotland) Act
(c. 45)
s. 34 . . . . 27.04
1990 Criminal Justice (Inter-
national Co-opera-
tion) Act (c. 5). 26.111
s. 25(1) 26.111
(2) 26.111
(4) 26.111
(5) 26.111
s. 26 . . . . 26.111
Food Safety Act (c. 16). . . . 26.191
s. 11 . . . . 26.191
s. 12 . . . . 26.191
s. 37 . . . . 26.193
(1) 26.191
(3) 26.192, 26.194
(4) . . 26.191, 26.193, 26.194

1990 Food Safety Act—*cont.*
    s. 37(5), (6) 26.192, 26.193,
                      26.194
    s. 39(1) 26.191
    Pt II 26.191
    National Health Service
      and Community Care
      Act (c. 19)
    Sched, 9, para. 10 ...... 26.282
    Access to Health Records
      Act 1990 (c. 23)...... 26.378
    s. 8(1) 26.378
      (2) 26.378
      (5) 26.378
    Human Fertilisation and
      Embryology Act
      (c. 37).......... 4.11, 28.47
    s. 30(9) 28.25
    Law Reform (Mis-
      cellaneous Provisions)
      (Scotland) Act (c. 40).. 26.33
    s. 9 .... 2.44
      (4) 2.44
    s. 36(3) 21.72
    s. 66 .... 2.99, 26.33
    s. 70(3) 15.104
    Sched. 7 .... 2.99
    Sched. 8, para. 11(2) 26.255
      para. 11(3) 26.255
      para. 26 .... 1.37
      para. 36(12) 2.22
    Broadcasting Act (c. 42)
    Sched. 1, para. 12 .... 2.20
      para. 14 .... 2.20
      para. 15 .... 2.20
    Sched. 7 .... 26.33
    Sched. 20, para. 31(1) 2.20
    Environmental Protection
      Act (c. 43)........... 26.341
    s. 8(2) 26.342
    s. 79 .... 26.341
      (1)(a) 26.341
        (b) 26.345
        (d) 26.345
        (e) 26.345
        (f) 26.345
        (g) 26.345
        (ga) 26.345
    s. 80 .... 26.345
      (1) 26.345
      (3) ... 25.10, 26.341, 26.345
      (4) 26.341
    s. 80A(3) 26.345
    s. 81(3) 26.341
    s. 82(1) 26.342
      (2) 26.342
      (3) 26.342
      (4) 26.341
      (5) 26.342
      (8) 26.342
      (11) 26.342
      (13) 26.342
    Sched. 3, para. 1A(2) ... 26.341
      para. 2(3) 26.342
      para. 2(8) 26.342

1991 Civil Jurisdiction and
      Judgments Act (c. 12)... 3.68
    Sched. 2, para. 24 .... 2.93
    New Roads and Street
      Works Act (c. 22)..... 26.391
    s. 158(1) 26.391
    Natural Heritage
      (Scotland) Act (c. 28) 26.415
    s. 24 .... 26.415
    Coal Mining Subsidence
      Act (c. 45)........... 26.318
    s. 40 .... 26.318
    s. 41 .... 26.318
    s. 42(1) 26.318
    Mental Health (Deten-
      tion) (Scotland) Act
      (c. 47)
    s. 1 .... 26.302
    s. 2 .... 26.301
    Child Support Act (c. 48)... 22.96,
      22.99, 30.293, 30.298, 30.301
    s. 3 .... 22.12
      (1) 30.298, 30.300
    s. 4 .... 22.12
    s. 6 .... 22.12
    s. 7 .... 22.12
    s. 8 .... 2.57
      (6) 22.11, 22.12, 30.298,
                  30.299, 30.300
      (7) 22.11, 22.12, 30.298,
                  30.299, 30.300
      (8) 22.11, 22.12, 30.298,
                  30.299, 30.300
      (9) 30.298
      (10) ... 22.11, 22.12, 30.298,
                  30.299, 30.300
    s. 10 .... 22.98, 30.302
      (5) 22.98
    s. 11 .... 22.11, 30.299
    s. 32(5) 26.60
    s. 33(1) 30.299
      (2) 26.60
    s. 44 .... 30.298
    s. 54 .... 22.96, 30.299
    s. 55 ...... 22.12, 22.96, 30.298,
                  30.300
    Age of Legal Capacity
      (Scotland) Act (c. 50)... 2.62,
          4.10, 4.14, 4.20,
          4.21, 28.28, 28.58
    s. 1 .... 6.23
      (1) 4.12, 28.28
      (b) 4.22, 21.43, 30.56
      (3)(f) 2.15
        (i) 4.12
        (ii) 4.12
      (g) 28.28
      (5) 4.19
    s. 2(4) 4.12, 28.108
      (4A) 4.11
      (5) 4.19
    s. 3(2)(d) 4.22
    s. 4(a) 4.12
    s. 5 .... 4.10
      (1) 4.11

1991	Age of Legal Capacity (Scotland) Act—*cont.*	
	s. 5(3)	4.22
	(4)	4.11
	s. 8	2.116
	s. 9	6.23
	(c)	4.12
	Sched. 1	15.104
	para. 35	2.61
	Agricultural Holdings (Scotland) Act (c. 55)	26.06, 26.09
	s. 8(1)	26.07
	(8)	26.07
	s. 20	23.07
	(1)	23.07
	s. 21	30.282
	s. 60	26.09
	s. 61	26.09
	(1)	26.32
	s. 63(3)(b)	26.12
	s. 67	26.13
	s. 68(1)	26.06
	(4)	26.06
	s. 69(1)	26.06
	(2)	26.06
	s. 77	26.08
	s. 88(1)	26.34
	Sched. 7	26.09
	para. 17	26.09
	para. 19	26.09
	para. 20	26.10
	para. 21	26.10
	para. 22	26.10
	para. 23	26.11
	para. 24	26.11
	Sched. 11, paras 2–4	26.34
	Armed Forces Act (c. 62)	
	s. 14	4.70
	s. 15	4.70
1992	Social Security Administration Act (c. 5)	
	s. 109	29.50
	s. 117	13.41
	s. 187	11.15
	Local Government (Finance) Act (c. 14)	
	Sched. 13, para. 2	26.328
	Friendly Societies Act (c. 40)	26.206
	s. 80	26.206
	(1)	26.206
	(3)	26.206
	(4)	26.206
	(5)	26.206
	(6)	26.206
	s. 82(1)	26.206
	(4)	26.206
	s. 83	26.200
	Trade Union and Labour Relations (Consolidation) Act (c. 52)	26.123
	s. 1	4.100
1992	Trade Union and Labour Relations (Consolidation) Act—*cont.*	
	s. 10	4.100
	s. 82(2), (3)	26.123
	(9)	26.123
	s. 127	4.100
	s. 221(1)	21.88
1993	Judicial Pensions and Retirement Act (c. 8)	1.08, 1.14
	s. 1	1.08
	s. 2	1.08
	s. 3	1.08
	s. 4	1.08
	s. 5	1.08
	s. 6	1.08
	s. 7	1.08
	s. 8	1.08
	s. 9	1.08
	s. 10	1.08
	s. 11	1.08
	s. 12	1.08
	s. 13	1.08
	s. 16	1.08
	s. 17	1.08
	s. 18	1.08
	s. 19	1.08
	s. 20	1.08
	s. 22	1.08
	s. 23	1.08
	s. 24	1.08
	s. 26(1)	1.08
	(5)	1.08
	(11)	1.08
	s. 27	1.08
	(1)	16.41
	s. 28	1.08
	s. 29	1.08
	s. 30	1.08
	s. 31	1.08
	Sched. 5	1.08
	Sched. 6, para 10	1.08
	Sched. 7	1.08
	Prisoners and Criminal Proceedings (Scotland) Act (c. 9)	
	s. 20	1.14
	Sched. 2	1.14
	Clean Air Act (c. 11)	
	s. 24(1)	26.343
	(4)(b)	26.343
	s. 35(1)	26.343
	(2)	26.343
	s. 54(1)(a)	26.344
	(b)	26.344
	(2)	26.344
	s. 56(3)	26.343
	(4)(b)	26.343
	Noise and Statutory Nuisance Act (c. 40)	26.345
1994	Value Added Tax Act (c. 23)	26.112
	s. 91(1)	26.112

1994 Value Added Tax Act—
          cont.
        Sched. 11,
          para. 10(3)(h) 26.112
      Trade Marks Act (c.26)
        s. 16 . . . .   2.46
        s. 19 . . . .   2.46
        s. 20 . . . .   2.46
        s. 64 . . . .   2.46
        s. 75 . . . .   2.46
        s. 76 . . . .   2.46
      Local Government etc.
          (Scotland) Act (c. 39). . . 1.03,
                                       1.04
        s. 2 . . 26.31, 26.41, 26.48, 26.55,
                   26.108, 26.157, 28.12
        s. 4 . . . .   26.55
        s. 23(1) 26.48
        s. 29(2) 1.12, 25.01
          (7) 1.12
        s. 86 . . . .   26.74
        s. 102 . . . .   26.336
        s. 180(1) . . . 26.18, 26.20, 26.22,
                   26.23, 26.288, 29.19
        Sched. 13, ...   26.164
          para. 3(2) 26.55
          para. 13 . . . .   26.18
          para. 31(3) 26.280
          para. 36 . . . .   26.19
          para. 52 . . . .   26.50
          para. 59(3) 26.41
            (4) 26.41
          para. 61 . . . .   26.20
          para. 75(4)(a) 26.335
            (18) 26.337
          para. 91 . . . .   26.22
          para. 95(8) 26.173
          para. 101 . . . .   26.23
          para. 104(2) 26.48
            (4) 26.49
          para. 119(17) 26.411
          para. 129(2) 26.288
            (5) 26.292
            (6) 26.292
          para. 135(4) 26.385
          para. 137(2) 26.268
      Deregulation and Con-
          tracting Out Act
          (c. 40)
        Sched. 5, para. 3 . . . .   2.72
1995 Civil Evidence (Family
          Mediation) (Scotland)
          Act (c. 6)
        s. 1 . . . .   22.36
      Jobseekers Act (c. 18)
        Sched. 2 . . . .   11.15
      Merchant Shipping Act
          (c. 21). 26.393
        s. 34(1)(b) 29.40
        s. 61 . . . .   26.393
        s. 62 . . . .   26.393
        s. 63 . . . .   26.393
        s. 64 . . . .   26.393
        s. 65 . . . .   26.393

1995 Merchant Shipping Act—
          cont.
        s. 69 . . . .   26.393
        s. 193(1) 1.12
        s. 229 . . . .   2.75
        s. 268(1) 26.394
          (2) 26.394
          (4) 26.394
          (5) 26.394
          (8) 26.394
          (9)(b) 26.394
        s. 269(1) 26.395
          (2) 26.395
          (4)(b) 26.394
        s. 271(6) 27.03
        Sched. 8, para. 1(2) 1.12
        Sched. 13 . . . .   11.13
      Environment Act (c. 25)
        s. 107 . . . .   26.341
        Sched. 17, para. 3 . . . . . .   26.341
          para. 4(b) 26.341
            (c) 26.341
            (d) 26.341, 26.342
          para. 6(a) 26.342
            (b) 26.342
            (c) 26.342
            (d) 26.342
            (f) 26.342
          para. 7 . . . .   26.341
            (b) 26.341
      Children (Scotland) Act
          (c. 36). 2.15, 5.28, 22.01,
              26.61, 26.279, 28.01, 28.04,
              28.05, 28.06, 28.09, 28.21,
              28.22, 28.26, 28.29, 28.69,
                     28.121, 31.33
        s. 1(1) 4.11, 28.26
          (b)(ii) 4.22
          (2)(a) 4.11
          (3) 2.61, 18.24, 28.24
        s. 2(b) 4.22
          (1) 28.26
          (2) 4.11
          (4) 2.61, 18.24, 28.24
          (7) 4.11
        s. 3(1) 4.11
          (a) 28.25
          (b) 28.25
          (5) 4.11
          (6) 28.121
        s. 4 . . . . 4.11, 28.26, 28.146
        s. 5(3) 28.124
        s. 7 . . . .   4.11, 28.29
        s. 11 . . . . . 2.56, 2.61, 4.11, 7.12,
              8.02, 8.08, 14.14, 18.68,
              22.02, 22.08, 22.23, 22.49,
              22.52, 22.58, 22.73, 22.74,
              22.75, 22.76, 28.26, 28.89,
              28.122, 28.146, 28.190
          (1) 2.62, 4.22, 28.45,
              28.121, 28.154, 28.166
          (d) 21.43, 22.102,
                     30.57, 31.33
          (2)(a) 28.25

1995 Children (Scotland) Act—
cont.
s. 11(2)(g) 14.14, 22.02
      (h) .. 14.14, 22.02, 26.79,
                            28.29
      (3) 28.45
          (a) 28.154
          (b) 28.166
      (4)(b) 28.154
      (7)(a) 22.103
          (b) 22.103
      (10) 22.23
s. 12(1) 22.23
s. 13 ...... 21.37, 21.43, 22.102,
          30.55, 30.56, 30.57, 31.33
      (1) 21.37, 21.43, 30.48,
                            30.56
      (2) 21.37, 21.43, 30.48,
                            30.56
      (3) 21.43, 30.56
s. 14(1) 2.61
      (2) 2.61, 2.62
s. 15(1) 4.11
      (2) 5.71
      (6) 4.12
s. 16(1) 28.21
s. 17 .... 28.175
      (6) 28.137
s. 25 .... 28.137
s. 33(1) 28.137
s. 34(2) 26.282
s. 44 .... 5.20, 5.29
      (5) 5.29
s. 51 .... 26.279
      (1)(a) 26.62
          (b) 26.62
      (3) 26.62
      (11) 5.29
          (a)(i) 26.63
          (b) 26.63
      (14) 26.63
      (15)(a) 26.70
          (b)   26.62, 26.72, 26.73
s. 52(2) 22.100
s. 53(2)(b) 28.125, 28.167
s. 54 .... 22.100, 28.89
      (1) 28.124, 28.167
      (2) 28.124
          (c) 28.167
      (3) 22.101, 28.167
s. 55 .... 26.69
s. 57 .... 5.18, 26.61
      (1) 26.70
      (2) 26.70
s. 58 .... 26.71, 26.73
s. 59(2) 26.72
      (4) 26.72
      (9) 26.73
s. 60(6)(a) 26.72
      (7) 26.73
      (12) 26.73
      (13) 26.73
s. 65(7) 26.64
      (8)(b) 26.65
      (9) 26.65, 26.66

1995 Children (Scotland) Act—
cont.
s. 66(1) 26.67
      (2) 26.67
      (3)(a) 26.67
      (5) 26.67
      (8) 26.67
s. 67(1) 26.67
      (2) 26.67
s. 68 .... 22.101
      (2) 26.64
      (4) 26.64
      (8) 26.64
      (10) 26.66, 26.68
s. 69 .... 22.101
s. 70 .... 28.21
s. 72(5) 28.15
s. 73(4) 28.15
      (c)(ii) 28.22, 28.23
      (5) 28.22
      (8)(a)(i) 28.22
      (13) 28.22
      (14) 28.23, 28.92
s. 75(14) 28.159
s. 76 .... 26.75
      (2)(b) 26.75
      (c) 26.75
      (4) 26.75
s. 77(2), (3) 26.76
      (7) 26.76
s. 78(1) 26.76
      (3) 26.283
      (6), (14) 26.75
s. 79(3) 26.75
s. 80(1) 26.283
      (2) 25.12, 26.75
      (6) 26.283
s. 81(2) 26.283
s. 85(1), (2) 26.68
      (3)(a)–(c) 26.68
      (5) 26.68
      (6) 26.68
s. 86 .. 2.134, 5.23, 25.38, 28.25,
                      28.89, 28.13
      (2) 26.74
      (3)(a) 28.25
      (4) 26.74
      (5) 26.74
      (6)(a) 26.68
          (b) 26.68
s. 87(4)(a) 26.74
      (b) 26.74
s. 88(3) 26.74
      (5) 26.74
s. 91(4) 26.77
s. 92 .... 26.279
s. 93(2) 28.23
      (b) 26.62, 26.279
      (5) 5.20, 5.23, 25.26,
                      26.62, 26.66
s. 97 .... 28.53
s. 98 .... 28.139
s. 101 .... 28.69
s. 103(1) 28.24
s. 105(4) 2.15, 26.283

1995 Children (Scotland) Act—
  cont.
  Sched. 2,
    paras 8, 9 .... 28.50
    para. 11(a) 28.139
  Sched. 3, para. 3 .... 28.25
  Sched. 4 .... 2.04, 15.104
    para. 15(17) 26.283
      (20) 26.283
    para. 18(3) 2.61, 13.61, 18.24
    para. 20(2)(a) 2.59
      (3)(a) 22.31
      (b) 22.31
    para. 52(2) 30.300
    para. 53(2) 2.15
  Pt I 26.61
  Pt II, ... 26.61, 26.77, 26.78,
      28.137, 28.139, 28.175
  Pt III 26.61
  Chaps 2, 3 ..... 28.137, 28.139,
      28.175
  Chap. 4 .... 28.137, 28.139
  Criminal Procedure (Con-
    sequential Provisions)
    (Scotland) Act (c. 40)... 2.24,
      26.314
    Sched. 4 .... 21.99
    para. 36 .... 2.24
    para. 50(10) 26.314
    para. 63(9) 2.22
    para. 97(7) 26.76
    Sched. 5 .... 5.29
  Proceeds of Crime (Scot-
    land) Act (c. 43)...... 26.110
  s. 17(1) 26.110
    (7) 26.110
  s. 28(1), (7), (8) 26.110
  s. 31(5) 26.110
  s. 33 .... 26.110
  Sched. 1, para. 1 .... 26.110
  Criminal   Procedure
    (Scotland) Act (c. 46)
  s. 7(1) 24.02
  s. 8 .... 1.38
    (1) 5.12
    (2) 5.13
  s. 50(1) 5.23
    (2) 5.23
  s. 58 .... 2.24, 26.310
  s. 59 .... 2.24, 26.310
  s. 61 .... 2.24
  s. 156(3) 16.13
    (4) 16.13
  s. 170 .... 2.130
  s. 204 .... 21.99
    (1) 2.22
  s. 207 .... 2.22, 2.24
  s. 225 .... 21.99
  s. 249 .... 3.34
  s. 250 .... 3.34
  s. 251 .... 3.34
  s. 252 .... 3.34
  s. 253 .... 3.34
  s. 267 .... 16.52
  s. 307(1) 2.22

1995 Disability   Discrimination
    Act (c. 50)........... 26.379
  s. 25(1) 26.379
    (4) 26.379
    (5) 26.379
  s. 26(1) 26.380
    (3) 26.380
  Sched. 3, para. 6(1) 26.379
  Pt III 26.379, 26.380
  Mental Health (Patients in
    the Community) Act
    (c. 52)
  s. 4 .... 26.305
  Criminal Injuries Compen-
    sation Act (c. 53)
  s. 7 .... 29.23
  Requirements of Writing
    (Scotland) Act (c. 57).. 15.56,
      26.107
  s. 2(1) 20.19
  s. 4(1) 26.107
    (2) 26.107
    (4)–(6) 26.107
  s. 5(6) 26.107
  s. 11 .... 8.56, 8.63
    (1) 18.42
    (3)(b)(ii) 20.19
1996 Defamation Act (c. 31)
  s. 12(2) 2.79, 2.105
  Licensing   (Amendment)
    (Scotland) Act (c. 36)
  s. 1 .... 26.252
  Deer   (Scotland)   Act
    (c. 58)......... 26.30, 26.31
  s. 27(2) 26.30
  s. 33(8) 26.31
1997 Firearms   (Amendment)
    Act (c. 5)
  s. 40 .... 26.183
  s. 41 .... 25.10, 26.83
  Sched. 2, para. 4 .... 26.183
  Planning (Listed Buildings
    and   Conservation
    Areas) (Scotland) Act
    1997 (c. 9)........... 26.399
  s. 42(1) 26.399
    (4) 26.399
    (5) 26.399
    (6) 26.399
  s. 45(6) 26.400
    (7) 26.400
    (8) 26.400
    (9) 26.400
  Social Security (Recovery
    of   Benefits)   Act
    (c. 27).... 16.30, 21.33, 21.36
  s. 3 .... 21.33
  s. 6 .... 21.33
  s. 15 .... 21.33
  s. 17 .... 21.33
  Sched. 2 .... 21.33, 21.34
  Protection from Harass-
    ment Act (c. 40)
  s. 8 .... 2.120
  s. 10(1) 2.120

TABLE OF STATUTORY INSTRUMENTS

1800 Act of Sederunt (March
11)
s. 4 .... 15.35
s. 7 .... 15.35
1806 Act of Sederunt
(February 6) 21.73
1809 Act of Sederunt
(June 22) 15.35
1820 Act of Sederunt
(February 1).......... 2.127
1839 Act of Sederunt (July 10)
s. 73 .... 15.19
s. 83 .... 16.97
paras 87–90 .... 21.03
1933 Act of Sederunt (February
3)
para. 2 .... 23.22
1935 Act of Sederunt (S.R. &
O. 1935 No. 756)
para. 1(1) 20.19
(4) 20.19
Act of Sederunt (July 19)
para. 1(2) 20.20, 20.21
(3) 20.20
1936 Act of Sederunt (March
18)............. 19.45, 19.46
Act of Sederunt (July 16)... 21.68
1937 Act of Sederunt (May 25)... 12.43
1948 Rules of Court R.C. 273(c).. 15.65
1950 Act of Sederunt (Sheriff
Court Rules Amend-
ment) (S.I. 1950 No.
1157)................ 10.54
1951 Act of Sederunt (Maintenance Orders Act
1950, Courts of Sum-
mary Jurisdiction,
Rules) (S.I. 1951 No.
552)
r. 2(3) 5.34
1954 Sheriff Court (Lan-
arkshire) Order (S.I.
1954 No. 712)
para. 11 .... 1.18
1963 Act of Sederunt (Rules of
Court Amendment)
(S.I. 1963 No. 380)..... 12.43
1968 Act of Sederunt (Confirmation of Executors)
(S.I. 1964 No. 1143)
para. 6(2)(b) 3.86
1965 Act of Sederunt (Rules of
Court, Consolidation
and Amendment)
(S.I. 1965 No. 321)
r. 85 .... 12.43
r. 164(c) 15.65

Act of Sederunt (Betting,
Gaming and Lotteries
Acts Appeals) (S.I.
1965 No. 1168)
para. 4 .... 26.41
1969 Minister of Technology
Order (S.I. 1969 No.
1498)
art. 2(1) 26.357
art. 5(6) 26.357
Preservation of Sheriff
Court Records Regu-
lations (S.I. 1969 No.
1756)................ 1.50
1970 Secretary of State for
Trade and Industry
Order (S.I. 1970 No.
1537)
art. 2(2) 26.357
art. 7(4) 26.357
Act of Sederunt (Firearms
Appeals) (S.I. 1970
No. 1984)
reg. 1 .... 26.184
Act of Sederunt (Altera-
tion of Sheriff Court
Fees) (S.I. 1971 No.
90)
Sched. 2, para. 7(iv) 19.18
para. 18(f) 2.29
1971 Sheriff of Chancery
(Transfer of Jurisdic-
tion) Order (S.I. 1971
No. 743.......... 1.12, 2.66
1972 Act of Sederunt (Emer-
gency Powers in the
Sheriff Court) (S.I.
1972 No. 220).......... 1.36
Hovercraft (Application of
Enactments) Order
(S.I. 1972 No. 971)
art. 8(2)(a) 26.208
Transfer of Functions
(Secretary of State
and Lord Advocate)
Order (S.I. 1972 No.
2002)................ 1.46
1973 Sheriff Courts (Scotland
Act 1971 (Transfer
Date) Order (S.I.
1973 No. 277)......... 1.49
Sheriff Court Houses
(Transfer) (Scotland)
Regulations (S.I. 1973
No. 402).............. 1.49
Firemen's Pension Scheme
Order (S.I. 1973 No.
966)
para. 68(1) 26.176

1973 Firemen's Pension Scheme
        Order—*cont.*
        (2) 26.176
        (3)(b) 26.176
1974 Union of Offices (Sheriff
        Courts and Legal
        Offices (Scotland) Act
        1927) Order (S.I. 1974
        No. 599). 1.21
     Act of Sederunt (Mainte-
        nance) Orders
        (Reciprocal Enforce-
        ment) Act 1972 Rules)
        (S.I. 1974 No. 929)
        para. 13(1) 5.34
     Sheriffdoms Reorganisa-
        tion Order (S.I. 1974
        No. 2087). 1.03
1975 Lord-Lieutenants Order
        (S.I. 1975 No. 428). 1.18
     Act of Sederunt (Com-
        missary Business) (S.I.
        1975 No. 539). 1.36
     Sheriff Court Districts
        Reorganisation Order
        (S.I. 1975 No. 637). 1.04
     Act of Sederunt (Interest
        in Sheriff Court
        Decrees and Extracts)
        (S.I. 1975 No. 948). 1.36
     Sheriff Court Districts
        (Amendment) Order
        (S.I. 1975 No. 1539). 1.04
1976 Sheriff Courts (Scotland)
        Act 1971 (Com-
        mencement No. 3)
        Order (S.I. 1976 No.
        236). 30.02
     Act of Sederunt (Proceed-
        ings under the Sex
        Discrimination Act
        1975) (S.I. 1976 No.
        374)
        para. 3 . . . . 26.362
     Act of Sederunt (Summary
        Cause Rules, Sheriff
        Court) (S.I. 1976 No.
        476). 30.02, 30.06, 30.07,
           30.12, 30.13, 30.72, 30.123,
           30.127, 30.128, 30.140, 30.143,
           30.201, 30.215, 30.225, 30.296
        Sched. 1 . . . . 30.16
        Sched. 1, Appendix 2 . . . 30.165
     Sheriff Courts (Scotland)
        1971 (Private Jurisdic-
        tion, etc.) Order (S.I.
        1976 No. 900). 30.02
     Act of Sederunt (Expenses
        of Party Litigants)
        (S.I. 1976 No. 1606). . . . 4.121
     Act of Sederunt (Proceed-
        ings under Sex Dis-
        crimination Act,
        1975) No. 2 (S.I. 1976
        No. 1851)
        para. 2 . . . . 26.368

1976 Fire Certificates (Special
        Premises) Regulations
        (S.I. 1976 No. 2003). . . 26.181
        reg. 12(1) 26.181
        (2) 26.181
        (4) 26.181
        reg. 14(1) 26.182
        (2) 26.182
        (3) 26.182
        reg. 16 . . . . 26.181
        Sched. 1, Pt 1 . . . . 26.181
     Offices, Shops and Rail-
        way Premises Act
        1963, etc. (Repeals)
        Regulations (S.I. 1976
        No. 2005)
        reg. 2 . . . . 26.122
        Sched. 26.122
1977 Fatal Accidents and Sud-
        den Deaths Inquiry
        Procedure (Scotland)
        Rules (S.I. 1977 No.
        191)
        r. 3 . . . . 27.07
        r. 4(2) 27.08
        (3) 27.08
        r. 5 . . . . 27.12
        r. 6 . . . . 27.12
        r. 7 . . . . 1.32
        (2) 27.09
        r. 9 . . . . 27.11
        r. 10(1) 27.13
        (2) 27.13
        (3) 27.13
        r. 11(1) 27.20
        (2) 27.21
        (3) 27.21
        r. 12 . . . . 27.12
        r. 16 . . . . 27.24
        r. 17 . . . . 27.24
        Sched.,
        Form 1 . . . . 27.07
        Form 2 . . . . 27.07
        Form 3 . . . . 27.08
        Form 4 . . . . 27.08
     Sheriff Court Districts
        (Amendment) Order
        (S.I. 1977 No. 672). 1.04
     Health and Safety (Enforc-
        ing Authority) Regu-
        lations (S.I. 1977 No.
        746)
        Sched. 2 . . . . 26.03
     Act of Sederunt (Proceed-
        ings under the Sex
        Discrimination Act
        1975) (S.I. 1977 No.
        973)
        para. 2 . . . . 26.368
     Act of Sederunt (Proceed-
        ings under Race Rela-
        tions Act 1976) (S.I.
        1977 No. 975)
        para. 2 . . . . 26.369
        para. 3 . . . . 26.376

1977 Act of Sederunt (Appeals under the Licensing (Scotland) Act 1976) (S.I. 1977 No. 1622).... 1.36, 26.255
para. 2 .... 26.255
para. 3(a) 26.255
      (b) 26.255
      (c) 26.255
Sheriff (Removal from Office) Order (S.I. 1977 No. 2046)......... 1.08

1978 Act of Sederunt (Summary Cause Rules, Sheriff Court) (Amendment) 1978 (S.I. 1978 No. 112)................. 30.06
Registration of Presumed Deaths (Prescription of Particulars) (Scotland) Regulations (S.I. 1978 No. 160)................ 20.15
Act of Sederunt (Presumption of Death) (S.I. 1978 No. 162)
para. 2(1) 20.08
      (2) 20.08
      (3) 20.09
Act of Sederunt (Betting and Gaming Appeals) (S.I. 1978 No. 229)..... 26.40
reg. 3 .... 26.38, 26.43
reg. 4 .... 26.38
reg. 5 .... 26.43, 26.44
reg. 6 .... 26.43, 26.44
reg. 8(1)(b) 26.47
      (c) 26.47
Act of Sederunt (Commissary Business) (Amendment) S.I. 1978 No. 1509)......... 1.36
Act of Sederunt (Summary Cause Rules, Sheriff Court) (Amendment No. 2) 1978 (S.I. 1978 No. 1805)............. 30.06

1979 Act of Sederunt (Suspension of Business) (S.I. 1979 No. 226)..... 1.36, 1.38
para. 2(4) 1.38
Act of Adjournal (Suspension of Sittings, etc.) (S.I. 1979 No. 232)...... 1.38
para. 2(4) 1.38
Act of Sederunt (Appeals under the Rating (Disabled Persons) Act 1978) (S.I. 1979 No. 446)
para. 2 .... 26.358
para. 3 .... 26.358
para. 4 .... 26.358

1979 Act of Sederunt (Commissary Business) (Amendment) (S.I. 1979 No. 1415)......... 1.36
Act of Sederunt (Appeals under the Licensing (Scotland) Act 1976) (Amendment) (S.I. 1979 No. 1520)....... 26.555

1980 Secure Tenancies (Proceedings for Possession) (Scotland) Order (S.I. 1980 No. 389)............... 26.216
Act of Sederunt (Summary Cause Rules, Sheriff Court) (Amendment) (S.I. 1980 No. 455)..... 30.06
Secure Tenancies (Proceedings for Possession) (Scotland) Order (S.I. 1980 No. 1389)............... 30.268

1981 Sheriff Courts (Scotland) Act 1971 (Summary Cause) Order (S.I. 1981 No. 842)......... 30.02
Act of Sederunt (Statutory Appeals) (S.I. 1981 No. 1591)............. 1.36
Transfer of Functions (Minister for the Civil Service and Treasury) Order (S.I. 1981 No. 1670)
art. 2(2) 26.368
art. 3(5) 26.368

1982 Act of Sederunt (Fees for Sheriff Court) (S.I. 1982 No. 652)
para. 2(2) 1.23
Act of Sederunt (Applications under the Matrimonial Homes (Family Protection) (Scotland) Act 1981 (S.I. 1982 No. 1432)... 22.106
para. 7 .... 22.107
para. 8 .... 22.107

1983 Registration of Establishments (Appeal Tribunal) (Scotland) Rules (S.I. 1983 No. 71)................. 26.282
Act of Sederunt (Interest in Sheriff Court Decrees or Extracts) (S.I. 1983 No. 409)...... 1.36
Act of Sederunt (Ordinary Cause Rules, Sheriff Court) (S.I. 1983 No. 747)................. 30.6
.r. 1 .... 5.93

1983 Act of Sederunt (Ordinary
     Cause Rules, Sheriff
     Court)—*cont.*
     r. 3(1) 9.41
     r. 8(1) 7.30
     r. 12(1)(b) 6.30
     r. 14(1) 4.95
     r. 27(3) 7.22
     r. 59A 14.71
     r. 59B 18.25, 22.55
     r. 64 .... 10.01
         (1)(a) 10.47
     r. 72(1) 15.43
     r. 72A 15.43
     r. 78 .... 10.01
         (3) 15.52
     r. 80 .... 10.01, 15.48
     r. 84A 12.04
         (7) 12.04
         (8) 12.04, 15.06
         (9) 15.06
         (10) 12.04, 15.06
     r. 89(1) 5.85, 17.03
         (3) 5.36
     r. 103(3) 23.13
     r. 107A 23.04
     r. 119 .... 5.40
     r. 120 .... 5.40
     r. 123(1) 21.66
     r. 142 .... 22.90
     Form A 9.41, 9.43
     Sheriff Courts Districts
     (Amendment) Order
     (S.I. 1983 No. 1028)..... 1.04
     Act of Sederunt (Expenses
     of Party Litigants)
     (Amendment) (S.I.
     1983 No. 1438)........ 4.121
     Control of Noise
     (Appeals) (Scotland)
     Regulations (S.I. 1983
     No. 1455)
     reg. 5 .... 26.169
     reg. 6 .... 26.170
     reg. 7 .... 26.171
     reg. 10 .... 26.169, 26.171
1984 Act of Sederunt (Fees for
     Sheriff Court) (S.I.
     1984 No. 233)......... 1.23
     Licensing of Venison
     Dealers (Application
     Procedures, etc.)
     (Scotland) Order (S.I.
     1984 No. 922)........ 26.31
     reg. 4 .... 26.31
         (11) 26.31
     Act of Sederunt (Com-
     missary Business)
     (Amendment) (S.I.
     1984 No. 969)......... 1.36
     Act of Sederunt (Adoption
     of Children) (S.I.
     1984 No. 1013)........ 28.07

1984 Adoption (Scotland) Act
     1978 Commencement
     Order (S.I. 1984 No.
     1050)............... 28.135
1985 Act of Sederunt (Solici-
     tors' Fees) (S.I. 1985
     No. 544)
     para. 3(1) 19.18
     Act of Sederunt (Con-
     sumer Credit Act
     1974) (S.I. 1985 No.
     705)
     Pt II 12.43
     Act of Sederunt (Appeals
     under the Rating
     (Disabled Persons)
     Act 1978) Amend-
     ment) (S.I. 1985 No.
     821)................ 26.358
     Sheriff Court Fees Order
     (S.I. 1985 No. 827)...... 1.23
     para. 2(1) 1.20
     para. 5(1) 13.47
     para. 32 .... 17.33
     Sched., Pt IV,
     para. 34 .... 1.26
     Act of Sederunt (Interest
     in Sheriff Court
     Decrees or Extracts)
     (S.I. 1985 No. 1179)..... 1.36
     Ionising Radiations Regu-
     lations (S.I. 1985 No.
     1333)
     Sched. 10, Pt II 26.181
     Act of Adjournal (Cir-
     cuits) (S.I. 1985 No.
     1534)
     para. 3(1) 1.12
1986 Act of Sederunt (Com-
     missary Business)
     (Amendment) (S.I.
     1986 No. 267)......... 1.36
     Act of Sederunt (Fees of
     Solicitors in the Sher-
     iff Court) (S.I. 1986
     No. 978)
     Sched., para. 14(f) 1.39
     Representation of the
     People (Scotland)
     Regulations (S.I. 1986
     No. 1111)
     reg. 42 .... 26.117
     Safety of Sports Grounds
     (Designation) (Scot-
     land) Order (S.I. 1996
     No. 1243)........... 26.157
     Act of Sederunt (Rules of
     Court Amendment)
     (S.I. 1986 No. 1937).... 16.53
     Act of Sederunt (Civil Juris-
     diction of the Sheriff
     Court) (S.I. 1986 No.
     1946)................ 30.06

1986 Act of Sederunt (Enforce-
      ment of Judgments
      under the Civil Juris-
      diction and Judg-
      ments Act 1982) (S.I.
      1986 No. 1947)
      para. 6(5) 5.34
             (10) 3.04
             (11) 3.04
      Act of Sederunt (Mis-
      cellaneous Amend-
      ments) (S.I. 1986 No.
      1966). 30.06
      Civil Jurisdiction and
      Judgements Act 1982
      (Commencement No.
      3) Order (S.I. 1986
      No. 2044). 3.01
1987 Act of Sederunt (Civil
      Legal Aid Rules) (S.I.
      1987 No. 492)
      r. 1(2) 4.117
      r. 3(1) .. 4.117, 8.12, 9.78, 9.107
          (2) 4.117, 8.12
             (b) 8.20
          (3) 4.117, 8.12
          (4) 4.117, 8.12
          (5) 4.117
1988 Act of Sederunt (Fees of
      Solicitors in the Sher-
      iff Court) (S.I. 1988
      No. 681)
      Sched., para. 14(f) .. 2.29, 2.31,
                                2.33
      Act of Sederunt (Small
      Claim Rules) (S.I.
      1988 No. 1976). 31.06,
                               31.10
      r. 13(5) 30.139
      Sched. 30.139
          Appendix 1 .... 31.06
          Appendix 2 .... 31.06
      Act of Sederunt (Amend-
      ment of Sheriff Court
      Ordinary Cause and
      Summary Cause
      Rules) (S.I. 1988 No.
      1978). 30.06
      Sheriff Courts (Scotland)
      Act 1971 (Private
      Jurisdiction and Sum-
      mary Cause) Order
      (S.I. 1988 No. 1993). 2.31,
                                30.02
      Small Claims (Scotland)
      Order (S.I. 1988 No.
      1999). 30.03, 30.18
      para. 4(2) 31.123
             (3) 31.123
      Act of Sederunt (Proceed-
      ing: in the Sheriff
      Court under the
      Debtors (Scotland)
      Act 1987) (S.I. 1988
      No. 2013). 1.32
      r. 6 .... 29.81

Act of Sederunt (Proceed-
      ing: in the Sheriff
      Court under the
      Debtors (Scotland)
      Act 1987)—*cont.*
      r. 8 .... 29.81
      r. 12 .... 26.129
          (1) 29.79
      r. 13 .... 29.78
      r. 15 .... 29.72
      r. 17 .... 29.81
      r. 19 .... 29.85
      r. 20 .... 29.82
      r. 26 .... 29.86
      r. 27 .... 29.87
      r. 31 .... 29.90
      r. 32 .... 29.90
      r. 35 .... 29.74
      r. 38 .... 29.42
      r. 40 .... 29.46
      r. 42 .... 29.52
      r. 45 .... 29.51
      r. 46 .... 29.54
      r. 47 .... 29.54
      r. 48 .... 29.54
      r. 50 .... 29.49
      r. 51 .... 29.49
      r. 53 .... 29.59
      r. 55 .... 29.60
      r. 57 .... 29.62
      r. 59 .... 29.61
      r. 60 .... 29.63
      r. 61 .... 29.64
      r. 63 .... 29.63
      r. 64 .... 29.63
      r. 66 .... 29.42
      r. 68 .... 29.02
      r. 72 .... 26.152
      Form 4 .... 29.81
      Form 5 .... 29.79
      Form 6 .... 29.79
      Form 9 .... 29.72, 29.80
      Form 10 .... 29.81
      Form 11 .... 29.81
      Form 26 .... 29.90
      Form 30 .... 29.42
      Form 32 .... 29.46
      Form 33 .... 29.46
      Form 34 .... 29.52
      Form 37 .... 29.51
      Form 38 .... 29.54
      Form 39 .... 29.54
      Form 40 .... 29.54
      Form 41 .... 29.49
      Form 43 .... 29.59
      Form 49 .... 29.62
      Form 54 .... 29.61
      Form 55 .... 29.63
      Form 56 .... 29.64
      Form 57 .... 29.64
      Form 61 .... 29.02
      Form 62 .... 29.02
      Act of Sederunt (Form of
      Charge for Late Pay-
      ment) (S.I. 1988 No.
      2059). 29.67

1988 Assured Tenancies (Forms) (Scotland) Regulations (S.I. 1988 No. 2109)

    para. 3 .... 30.268

    Sched. 30.268

    Form AT6 .... 30.268

1989 Civil Legal Aid (Fees) Regulations (S.I. 1989 No. 119)

    reg. 5(4) 27.23

Act of Sederunt (Amendment of Ordinary Cause and Summary Cause Rules) (Written Statements) (S.I. 1989 No. 436)......... 30.06

Civil Legal Aid (Scotland) (Fees) Regulations (S.I. 1989 No. 1490)

    reg. 5(4) 30.29

1990 Copyright, Designs and Patent Rules (S.I. 1990 No. 380)......... 2.46

Act of Sederunt (Amendment of Sheriff Court Ordinary Cause, Summary Cause and Small Claim Rules) (S.I. 1990 No. 661)......... 30.06

Act of Sederunt (Amendment of Sheriff Court Ordinary Cause, Summary Cause and Small Claim Rules) (No. 2) (S.I. 1990 No. 2105).... 30.06

1991 Act of Sederunt (Amendment of Summary Cause and Small Claim Rules) (S.I. 1991 No. 821)... 30.06, 31.06

Civic Government (Scotland) Act 1982 (Licensing of Houses in Multiple Occupation) Order (S.I. 1991 No. 1253)........... 26.289

Act of Sederunt (Messengers-at-Arms and Sheriff Officers Rules) (S.I. 1991 No. 1397)........... 1.27, 6.23

    r. 30 .... 29.89

Act of Sederunt (Proceedings in the Sheriff Court under the Model Law on International Commercial Arbitration) (S.I. 1991 No. 2214)

    para. 2 .... 26.33

1991 Access to Health Records (Steps to Secure Compliance and Complaints Procedures) (Scotland) Regulations (S.I. 1991 No. 2295)........... 26.378

1992 Act of Sederunt (Amendment of Ordinary Cause, Summary Cause and Small Claim Rules) (S.I. 1992 No. 249)... 30.06, 31.06

1992 Act of Sederunt (Judicial Factors Rules) (S.I. 1992 No. 272).... 1.22, 11.07, 20.13

    para. 4 .... 11.07

    r. 6(3) 1.22

    r. 7(2) 1.22

    r. 8 .... 1.22

    r. 11(2) 1.22

    r. 14 .... 1.22

    r. 19(5) 1.22

    (6) 1.22

    r. 29(2) 1.22

    Sched. 1.22

Act of Sederunt (Coal Mining Subsidence Act 1991) (S.I. 1992 No. 798)............ 26.318

    para. 3 .... 26.318

Act of Sederunt (Applications under Pt III of the Criminal Justice (International Co-operation) Act 1990) (S.I. 1992 No. 1007)

    para. 2 .... 26.111

    para. 3 .... 26.111

    para. 4 .... 26.111

Sheriff (Removal from Office) Order (S.I. 1992 No. 1677)......... 1.09

Act of Sederunt (Fees of Witnesses and Shorthand Writers in the Sheriff Court) (S.I. 1992 No. 1878).. 16.11, 19.64, 19.65

    Sched. 1 .... 19.59

    para. 8 .... 19.60

    para. 9 ... 16.19, 19.61, 19.65

    Note 8 .... 16.83, 16.103

    Note 9 .... 16.103

Child Support Act 1991 (Maintenance Arrangement and Jurisdiction) Regulations (S.I. 1992 No. 2645)

    reg. 3(1) 30.302

1992 Western Isles Islands Area (Electoral Arrangements) Order (S.I. 1992 No. 3323) 2.02

1993 Act of Sederunt (Interest in Sheriff Court Decrees and Extracts) (S.I. 1993 No. 769) 1.36, 9.93

Act of Sederunt (Fees of Solicitors in the Sheriff Court) (S.I. 1993 No. 898)

Sched., Table of Fees, Chap. 1, Pt 1, para. 1 . . . 7.10

Act of Sederunt (Child Support Act 1991) (Amendment of Ordinary Cause and Summary Cause Rules) (S.I. 1993 No. 919) 30.06

Act of Sederunt (Child Support Rules) (S.I. 1993 No. 920)

para. 2(1) 26.60

para. 5 . . . . 26.60

Act of Sederunt (Ordinary Cause Rules) (S.I. 1993 No. 1956) . . . 1.22, 30.06

Sheriff Court Fees Amendment (No. 2) Order (S.I. 1993 No. 2957) 1.23, 1.26

Act of Sederunt (Fees of Solicitors in the Sheriff Court) (Amendment and Further Provisions) (S.I. 1993 No. 3080) 30.220

Sched. 1 . . . . 19.18

Sched. 1, General Regulations,

reg. 1 . . . . 14.39, 19.48, 19.51

reg. 2 . . . . 13.47, 14.39, 14.67, 16.48, 19.33, 19.43, 19.48, 19.49

reg. 5 . . . . 30.220

(a) 14.39, 19.09, 30.220

(b) 14.39, 14.67, 19.18, 19.19, 19.21, 30.220

(c) 11.86, 13.03, 13.07, 14.07, 18.65, 19.09, 19.21

reg. 6 . . . . 19.46, 19.52, 19.53, 19.66

reg. 7 . . . . 19.43

reg. 8 . . . . 12.23, 19.11, 19.43, 19.47, 19.54

reg. 9 . . . . 19.11, 19.54

reg. 10 . . . . 13.34, 19.22

reg. 11 . . . . 19.56

reg. 12(a) 12.24, 19.43

(b) 12.21, 19.43

reg. 13 . . . . 19.58

Act of Sederunt (Fees of Solicitors in the Sheriff Court) (Amendment and Further Provisions)—*cont.*

reg. 14 . . . . 30.221

(a) 30.221

(b) 30.221

(c) 30.221

(d) 30.221

(e) 30.221

(f) 1.39, 2.31, 2.33, 19.48, 30.222

(3) 30.222

(g) 30.221

Sched. 1, Table of Fees,

Chap. I 19.48

Chap. II 19.48

para. 21(a) 17.32

Chap. III 19.48, 19.57

Chap. IV 2.31, 19.48, 30.220, 30.221

Act of Sederunt (Summary Suspension) (S.I. 1993 No. 3128) 24.11

para. 2 . . . . . . 2.78, 24.13, 24.14

para. 3(1) 24.14, 24.15

Act of Sederunt (Summary Court Application Rules) (S.I. 1993 No. 3240) 15.04

1994 Act of Sederunt (Fees of Sheriff Officers) (S.I. 1994 No. 392) 1.27

Act of Sederunt (Fees of Solicitors in the Sheriff Court) (Amendment) (S.I. 1994 No. 1142) 19.09

Act of Sederunt (Judicial Factors Rules) (Amendment) (S.I. 1994 No. 2354) 11.07

Meat Products (Hygiene) Regulations (S.I. 1994 No. 3082) 26.192

reg. 7(1) 26.192

(2) 26.192

1995 Judicial Pensions and Retirement Act 1993 (Commencement) Order 1995 (S.I. 1995 No. 631) 1.08

Civil Aviation (Air Travel Organisers' Licensing) Regulations (S.I. 1995 No. 1054)

reg. 6(2)(a) 26.36

(b) 26.36

reg. 7 . . . . 26.36

reg. 11(1) 26.36

(2)(a) 26.36

(5) 26.36

(a) 26.36

(d) 26.36

1995 Dairy Products (Hygiene)
(Scotland) Regu-
lations (S.I. 1995 No.
1372). 26.193
reg. 4 . . . . 26.193
reg. 6 . . . . 26.193
reg. 8(1) 26.193
(4) 26.193
(5) 26.193
Act of Sederunt (Fees of
Solicitors in the Sher-
iff Court) (Amend-
ment) (S.I. 1995 No.
1395). 19.09
Fees in the Registers of
Scotland Order (S.I.
1995 No. 1945)
Sched., Pt XII, Item 3 . . . 15.98
Air Navigation (No. 2)
Order (S.I. 1995 No.
1970)
para. 117(1) 26.37
(3)(a) 26.37
(6)(a) 26.37
(b) 26.37
(c) 26.37
(d) 26.37
para. 118(1) 26.37
Merchant Shipping (Port
State Control) Regu-
lations (S.I. 1995 No.
3128). 26.396
reg. 11 . . . . 26.396
(a) 26.396
Minced Meat and Meat
Preparations (Hy-
giene) Regulations
(S.I. 1995 No. 3205). . . 26.194
reg. 6(1) 26.194
(2) 26.194
1996 Sheriff Court Districts
(Alteration of Bound-
aries) Order (S.I.
1996 No. 1005). . . . 1.04, 2.02
Sheriffdoms (Alteration of
Boundaries) Order
(S.I. 1996 No. 1006). 2.02
Statutory Nuisance
(Appeals) (Scotland)
Regulations (S.I. 1996
No. 1076). 25.10, 26.345
reg. 2(1) 26.345
(2)(a) 26.345
(b) 26.345
(c) 26.345
(d) 26.345
(e) 26.345
(f) 26.345
(g) 26.345
(h) 26.345
(i) 26.345
(j) 26.345
(5) 26.346

1996 Act of Sederunt (Requirements of Writing)
(S.I. 1996 No. 1534)
para. 3(2) 26.107
Driving Licences (Com-
munity Driving
Licence) Regulations
(S.I. 1996 No. 1974). . . 26.382
reg. 100(1) 26.382
Act of Sederunt (Mental
Health Rules) (S.I.
1996 No. 2149)
r. 2 . . . . 26.307
(1) 26.301
(2) 26.301
r. 3 . . . . 26.307
r. 5 . . . . 26.306, 26.307
r. 6 . . . . . 26.301, 26.306, 26.307
r. 7 . . . . 26.307
r. 9 . . . . 26.305
r. 10 . . . . 26.305
r. 11 . . . . 26.305
Sched., Form 1 . . . . 26.301
Act of Sederunt (Family
Proceedings in the
Sheriff Court) (S.I.
1996 No. 2167). 11.07
para. 4 . . . . 26.79
Sheriff Court Districts
(Alteration of Bound-
aries) Amendment
Order (S.I. 1996 No.
2192). 1.04, 2.02
Act of Sederunt (Proceeds
of Crime Rules) (S.I.
1996 No. 2446)
r. 2 . . . . 26.110
r. 3(1) 26.110
r. 4 . . . . 26.110
r. 5 . . . . 26.110
r. 6(1) 26.110
r. 7 . . . . 26.110
r. 8(1) 26.110
Adoption Allowance
(Scotland) Regu-
lations (S.I. 1996 No.
3257). 28.82
Children's Hearings
(Scotland) Rules (S.I.
1996 No. 3261)
r. 22(7) 28.15, 28.23
(8) 28.15
Adoption Agencies
(Scotland) Regu-
lations (S.I. 1996 No.
3266). 28.12
reg. 7(4) 28.12
(5) 28.12
regs 9–12 . . . . 28.12
reg. 9 . . . . 28.64
reg. 12(3) 28.13
reg. 14 . . . 28.13, 28.137, 28.142
(1)(d) 28.13
(e) 28.13
reg. 15 . . . 28.13, 28.137, 28.142

1996 Adoption Agencies
(Scotland) Regu-
lations—*cont.*
  reg. 15(1) 28.13
    (2) 28.13, 28.15
  reg. 16 .... 28.17
  reg. 17(2) 28.14
  reg. 18(2) 28.15
    (3) 28.15
    (4) 28.15
    (5) 28.15
    (6) 28.15
  reg. 21 .... 28.139
  reg. 22(1) 28.64
    (2) 28.23
  Sched. 2 .... 28.12
  Sched. 4 .... 28.13
  Sched. 5 .... 28.13
  Sched. 6 .... 28.13
  Sched. 7 .... 28.13, 28.144
1997 Act of Sederunt (Child
Care and Mainte-
nance Rules) (S.I.
1997 No. 291).. 22.104, 28.07
  r. 1.3 .... 22.47
  r. 1.4(2) 28.07
  r. 2.1(3) 28.159
  r. 2.2 .... 28.128, 28.168
  r. 2.3 .... 28.124
  r. 2.5(1) 28.149
    (2)(a) 28.149
    (b) 28.149, 28.150
    (c) 28.149
    (x) 28.150
  r. 2.5(3) 28.148
  r. 2.6 .... 28.153, 28.154, 28.156
    (1) 28.142, 28.144
    (2) 28.144
  r. 2.7(1) 28.152
    (2) 28.152
    (3) 28.142, 28.147
    (4) 28.147
  r. 2.8(1) 28.152, 28.153
    (a) 28.143
    (c) 28.154
    (d) 28.154
    (e) 28.146, 28.154,
                    28.158
    (f) 28.154
    (g) 28.154
    (h) 28.154
    (k) 28.146, 28.150,
                    28.154
    (2) 28.152
    (a) 28.155, 28.156
    (b) 28.156
    (c) 28.156
    (d) 28.156
    (e) 28.156
    (f) 28.156, 28.156
    (g) 28.156
    (3) 28.156
  r. 2.9(1)(a) 28.157
    (b) 28.157
    (2) 28.157

1997 Act of Sederunt (Child
Care and Mainte-
nance Rules)—*cont.*
  r. 2.10 ... 28.145, 28.150, 28.172
    (1) 28.155
    (2) 28.155
    (5) 28.173
  r. 2.11(1) 28.158
    (2)(a) 28.158
    (b) 28.146, 28.158
    (3) 28.159
    (4) 28.158, 28.161,
                    28.164
    (5) ... 28.23, 28.159
  r. 2.12(1) 28.163
    (2) 28.152
  r. 2.13 .... 15.34, 28.159
    (1) 28.172
    (2) 28.172, 28.174
    (3) 28.173
  r. 2.14(1)(a) 28.170
    (b) 28.170
    (2) 28.171
    (a) 28.171
    (b) 28.171
    (c) 28.171, 28.196
    (d) 28.171, 28.196
    (e) 28.171, 28.196
  r. 2.15(1) 28.187
    (2) 28.187, 28.193
    (3) 28.187, 28.193
  r. 2.16 .... 28.193
    (1) 28.188
  r. 2.17 .... 28.193
    (1)(a) 28.189
    (b) 28.189
    (2) 28.189
  r. 2.18(1) 28.190
    (2) 28.190
    (3) 28.190
  r. 2.19(1) 28.194
    (2) 28.194
  r. 2.20 .... 28.192, 28.193
  r. 2.21(1) 28.57
    (2) 28.60, 28.63
    (c) 28.107
    (d) 28.67
    (e) 28.67
    (3) 28.66
    (c) 28.107
    (5) 28.67
  r. 2.23 .... 28.94
    (1) ... 28.72, 28.74, 28.80
    (2) 28.72
  r. 2.24(1) 28.55
    (2) 28.55
    (3) 28.55
    (4) 28.55
  r. 2.25(1) 28.68, 28.70
    (2) 28.68
    (4) 28.54
    (5) 28.54
  r. 2.26(1) ... 28.71, 28.72, 28.78
    (b) 28.70, 28.73, 28.75
    (d) 28.76, 28.90

1997 Act of Sederunt (Child
　　　 Care and Mainte-
　　　 nance Rules)—*cont.*
　　　 r. 2.26(1)(e) 28.23, 28.77
　　　　　　　 (f) 28.75
　　　　　　　 (2) 28.71, 28.79
　　　　　　　 (a) 28.68, 28.79
　　　　　　　 (b) 28.80, 28.83
　　　　　　　 (c) 28.81
　　　　　　　 (d) 28.81
　　　　　　　 (g) 28.81
　　　　　　　 (i) 28.81
　　　　　　　 (j) 28.82
　　　　　　　 (k) 28.82
　　　　　　　 (l) 28.83
　　　　　　　 (m) 28.82
　　　　　　　 (n) 28.83
　　　　　　　 (p) 28.81
　　　　　　　 (q) 28.81
　　　　　　　 (r) 28.81
　　　　　　　 (s) 28.81
　　　　　　　 (t) 28.83
　　　　　　　 (u) 28.80, 28.85
　　　　　　　 (3) 28.80, 28.86
　　　 r. 2.27(1)(a) 28.85
　　　　　　　 (b) 28.85
　　　　　　　 (2) 28.86, 28.105
　　　 r. 2.28(1) 28.88
　　　　　　　 (2) 28.68, 28.88
　　　　　　　 (3) 28.62, 28.88
　　　　　　　 (a) 28.88
　　　　　　　 (4) 28.88, 28.89
　　　　　　　 (a) 28.89
　　　　　　　 (b) 28.89
　　　　　　　 (c) 28.89
　　　　　　　 (d) 28.89
　　　　　　　 (6) 28.109
　　　　　　　 (7) 28.23, 28.92
　　　 r. 2.29 .... 28.96, 28.109
　　　 r. 2.30 .... 28.56
　　　　　　　 (1) 28.104
　　　　　　　 (2) 28.71
　　　 r. 2.31 .... 28.118, 28.130
　　　 r. 2.32 .... 28.117
　　　　　　　 (2) 28.117
　　　　　　　 (3) 28.117, 28.196
　　　 r. 2.33(1) 28.61, 28.131
　　　　　　　 (2) 28.131
　　　　　　　 (a) 28.61, 28.131
　　　　　　　 (b) 28.131
　　　　　　　 (c) 28.120,
　　　　　　　　　　　　 28.131, 28.196
　　　　　　　 (d) 28.131, 28.196
　　　　　　　 (e) 28.131, 28.196
　　　　　　　 (3)(a) 28.119
　　　 r. 2.34(1) 28.182
　　　　　　　 (2) 28.182
　　　 r. 2.35(1) 28.184
　　　　　　　 (2) 28.184
　　　 r. 2.36 .... 28.179
　　　　　　　 (1) 28.176
　　　　　　　 (2) 28.176
　　　　　　　 (3) 28.176
　　　 r. 2.39 .... 26.74
　　　 rr. 3.6–3.10 .... 26.61

1997 Act of Sederunt (Child
　　　 Care and Mainte-
　　　 nance Rules)—*cont.*
　　　 r. 3.16(2) 28.188
　　　 r. 3.19 .... 26.78
　　　 r. 3.20 .... 26.78
　　　 r. 3.21 .... 26.77
　　　　　　　 (2) 26.77
　　　 r. 3.49 .... 26.64
　　　 r. 21.15(2) 28.193
　　　　　　　 (3) 28.193
　　　 Chap. 2 .... 28.01
　　　　　　 Pt V 26.74
　　　 Chap. 3 Pt III 26.69
　　　　　　　 Pt IV 26.70
　　　　　　　 Pt V 26.75
　　　　　　　 Pt VI 26.67
　　　　　　　 Pt VII 26.64
　　　　　　　 Pt VIII 26.62
　　　　　　　 Pt X 26.68
　　　 Form 1 .... 28.142, 28.149
　　　 Form 2 .... 28.144
　　　 Form 3 .... 28.142
　　　 Form 4 .... 28.80
　　　 Form 5 .... 28.155, 28.173
　　　 Form 6 .... 28.174
　　　 Form 7 .... 28.88, 28.158
　　　 Form 8 .... 28.188
　　　 Form 10 .... 28.192
　　　 Form 13 .... 28.72
　　　 Form 14 .... 28.74
　　　 Form 15 .... 28.176
Sheriff Court Fees Order
　　　 (S.I. 1997 No. 687)
　　　 para. 2(1) 8.04
　　　　　　　 (3) 8.38
　　　 para. 4(1) 29.05
　　　 para. 5(1) 13.47
　　　 para. 6 .... 4.78
　　　 Sched. 1,
　　　　　 para. 16 .... 21.86, 21.87
　　　　　 para. 22 .... 8.34
　　　　　 para. 23 .... 8.47
Dairy Produce Quotas
　　　 Regulations (S.I. 1997
　　　 No. 733). 26.195
　　　 Sched. 3,
　　　　　 para. 1(1) 26.195
　　　　　 para. 19 .... 26.195
　　　　　 para. 20 .... 26.195
　　　　　 para. 21 .... 26.195
　　　　　 para. 22 .... 26.195
Children (Scotland) Act
　　　 1995 (Commence-
　　　 ment No. 3) (Amend-
　　　 ment and Transitional
　　　 Provisions) Order
　　　 (S.I. 1997 No. 744)
　　　 para. 5 .... 28.04
Deregulation (Betting
　　　 Licensing) Order (S.I.
　　　 1997 No. 947)
　　　 para. 5 .... 26.40

1997 Act of Sederunt (Fees of
     Shorthand Writers in
     the Sheriff Court)
     (Amendment) (S.I.
     1997 No. 1118)........ 19.59
     Act of Sederunt (Fees of
     Shorthand Writers in
     the Sheriff Court)
     (Amendment) (No. 2)
     (S.I. 1997 No. 1256).... 19.59
     Act of Sederunt Rules of
     the Court of Session
     Amendment No. 8
     (Early Disposal of
     Reclaiming Motions
     and Appeals) (S.I.
     1997 No. 2692)........ 19.06

1998 Act of Sederunt (Fees of
     Shorthand Writers in
     the Sheriff Court)
     (Amendment) (S.I.
     1998 No. 999)........ 19.59
1999 Small Claims (Scotland)
     Order (S.I. 1999 No.
     1999)................ 31.03
2000 Public Order (Prescribed
     Forms) Regulations
     (Northern Ireland)
     (S.I. 2000 No. 155).... 30.300
2001 Civil Jurisdiction and
     Judgments Order (S.I.
     2001 No. 3929)........ 30.16

TABLE OF SCOTTISH STATUTORY INSTRUMENTS

2000 Act of Sederunt (Sheriff
         Court Ordinary Cause
         Rules   Amendment)
         (Miscellaneous)
         (S.S.I. 2000 No. 239). . . 30.41
      Act of Sederunt (Summary
         Cause Rules) (S.S.I.
         2002 No. 132). . . 30.06, 30.07,
            30.09, 30.13, 30.113, 30.143,
            30.152, 30.154, 31.16, 31.17
      para. 3 . . . . 30.06
      para. 4 . . . . 30.06
      Sched. 1 . . . . 30.06, 30.09
      Sched. 2 . . . . 30.06
      Act of Sederunt (Small
         Claim Rules) (S.S.I.
         2002 No. 133). . . 30.03, 31.03,
            31.06, 31.10, 31.17, 31.31,
            31.75, 31.89, 31.94, 31.96,
            31.97, 31.100, 31.101, 31.102,
            31.110, 31.117, 31.122, 31.125,
                                       31.138
      r. 2.1(1) 31.13
         (2) 31.13
         (3) 31.13
      r. 3.1 . . . . 31.59
      r. 4.1(1) 31.36
         (2) 31.07, 31.36
         (3) 31.07
      r. 4.2 . . . . 31.37
      r. 4.3 . . . . 31.40
         (a) 31.40
         (b) 31.40
      r. 4.4 . . . . 31.38
         (3) 31.39
      r. 4.5 . . . . 31.43
      r. 4.6 . . . . 31.15
      r. 5.1(1) 31.07
         (2) 31.07
         (4) 31.08
         (5) 31.09
      r. 5.4(2) 31.52
      r. 6.1(1) 31.14
         (2) 31.14
         (3) 31.14
      r..6.2(1) 31.48
         (2) 31.49
      r. 6.3 . . . . 31.50
         (1)(a) 31.51
         (2) 31.51
         (3) 31.51
         (4) 31.47
      r. 6.4 . . . . 31.50
         (1) 31.52
         (2) 31.52
         (3) 31.52
         (4) 31.52
         (5) 31.52

2000 Act of Sederunt (Small
         Claim Rules)—*cont.*
      r. 6.4(6) 31.44
      r. 6.5 . . . . 31.45, 31.53, 31.65
         (14) 31.53
         (a) 31.45
         (b) 31.45
         (c) 31.47
      r. 6.6 . . . . 31.54
         (1)(a) 31.54
         (b) 31.54
         (5)(a) 31.46
         (b) 31.46
         (c) 31.47
      r. 6.7 . . . . 31.16, 31.52
      r. 6.8 . . . . 31.48
      r. 6.9 . . . . 31.56
      r. 6.10(1) 31.55
         (2) 31.55
      r. 6.11(1) 31.57
         (2) 31.58
         (3) 31.59
      r. 7.3(4)(a) 31.34
      r. 8.1(1) 31.60
         (2) 31.60
         (3) 31.60, 31.64
         (4) 31.60
      r. 8.2 . . . . 31.62
      r. 8.3 . . . . 31.63
      r. 8.18(2) 31.119
      r. 9.1(1) 31.41, 31.69
         (2) 31.67, 31.75
         (3) 31.76
         (4) 31.78
         (5) 31.76
         (6) 31.64, 31.77
         (7) 31.64, 31.77
         (8) 31.64, 31.77
      r. 9.2 . . . . 31.21, 31.30
         (1) 31.80
         (2) 31.81
         (3)(a) 31.81
         (b) 31.81
         (c) 31.81
         (4)(a) 31.82
         (b) 31.82
         (c) 31.82
      r. 9.3(2) 31.110
         (3) 31.110
         (4) 31.111
         (5) 31.111
         (a) 31.113
         (b) 31.111
      r. 9.3(6) 31.112
      r. 9.4(1) 31.114
         (2) 31.114
      r. 9.5(1) 31.84
         (2) 31.84

2000   Act of Sederunt (Small
     Claim Rules)—*cont.*

r. 9.5(3) 31.84
r. 9.6 . . . . 31.115
r. 9.7 . . . . 31.120
r. 9.8(1) 31.119
     (2) 31.119
     (3)(a) 31.121
       (b) 31.121
     (4) 31.121
r. 10.1 . . . . 31.07, 31.26
     (3) 31.26
r. 10.2 . . . . 31.27
r. 11.1(1) 31.41
     (a) 31.70
     (b)(i) 31.70
       (ii) 31.70
     (2) 31.71
     (3) 31.71
     (a) 31.71
     (b) 31.71
     (4) 31.71
     (5) 31.72
     (6) 31.73
     (7) 31.74
     (8) 31.64, 31.74
r. 11.8(7) 31.64
r. 12.1(1) 31.28
     (2) 31.29
r. 13.1 . . . . 31.30
     (5)(b) 31.30
r. 14.1 . . . . 31.31
r. 15.1 . . . . 31.17
     (2) 31.80
r. 15.2(1) 31.19
     (2) 31.20
     (3) 31.21
r. 16.1(1) 31.85
     (2) 31.85
     (3) 31.86
     (4) 31.86
r. 16.2 . . . . 31.88
r. 16.3 . . . . 31.23
     (1)(c) 31.23
     (2) 31.24
r. 16.4 . . . . 31.133
r. 17.1 . . . . 31.89
     (1) 31.89
     (2) 31.89
     (3) 31.89
r. 17.2(1) 31.90
     (2) 31.90
     (3) 31.91
     (4) 31.93
     (5) 31.92
r. 17.3 . . . . 31.95, 31.117
     (1) 31.95
     (2) 31.95
     (3) 31.95
     (4) 31.95
r. 17.4 . . . . 31.97
     (3) 31.97
r. 17.5 . . . . 31.98
r. 17.6 . . . . 31.99
r. 18.2(3) 31.93

2000   Act of Sederunt (Small
     Claim Rules)—*cont.*

r. 18.8(1) 31.97
r. 19.1(1) 31.103
     (2) 31.103
     (3) 31.104
r. 20.1(1) 31.106
     (2) 31.107
     (3) 31.108
     (4) 31.109
r. 21.2(1) 31.122
     (2) 31.122
     (3) 31.122
r. 21.3 . . . . 31.130
r. 21.4 . . . . 31.129
r. 21.5 . . . . 31.131
     (1) 31.132
     (2) 31.132
     (3) 31.132
     (4)(a) 31.132
       (b) 31.132
       (c) 31.132
r. 21.6 . . . 31.103, 31.128, 31.125
     (1) 31.125
     (2) 31.126
     (3) 31.127
     (4) 31.127
     (5)–(15) 31.128
r. 21.7 . . . . 31.134
r. 21.8 . . . . 31.134
r. 21.9 . . . . 31.135
r. 21.10 . . . . 31.136
r. 22.1 . . . . 31.68, 31.77
     (1) 31.07, 31.64
     (2) 31.68
     (3) 31.65
     (4)(i) 31.65
       (ii) 31.65
     (5) 31.67
     (6) 31.67
     (7) 31.66
     (8) 31.67
     (9) 31.68
     (10) 31.68
     (11) 31.68
r. 23.1 . . . . 31.139
r. 23.2 . . . . 31.140
r. 23.3 . . . . 31.141
r. 23.4 . . . . 31.142
r. 23.5 . . . . 31.138
r. 24.4(1) 31.32
r. 24.5 . . . . 31.33
r. 25.1 . . . . 31.25, 31.139
     (4) 31.139
r. 25.2 . . . . 31.25
Sched. 1 . . . . 31.06
     Chap. 6 . . . . 31.48
     Chap. 7 . . . . 31.34
     Chap. 8 . . . . 31.60, 31.61
     Chap. 18 . . . . 31.35
     Chap. 19 . . . . 31.102
     Chap. 20 . . . . 31.105
     Chap. 22 . . . . 31.64
     Chap. 24 . . . . 31.32

TABLE OF ORDINARY CAUSE RULES

OCR   1.1(1)................. 15.46
      (2) 15.46, 30.19
      1.2(2) 22.47
      1.3 .... 1.32
      (1) 26.154
      (2) 26.154
      2.1 ... 2.08, 5.93, 5.94, 5.95, 5.96,
            7.28, 8.04, 8.05, 8.34, 18.47,
            30.14
      (1) 5.93, 5.97, 9.41, 13.02,
            14.06, 14.09, 14.25, 18.56
      (2) 5.97
      3(1) 9.74
      3.1 .... 25.18
      (1) 9.14, 9.42, 9.45,
            9.46, 9.47
      (2) 9.50
      (3) 3.64, 9.101
      (4) 3.64, 9.101
      (5) 3.64, 6.33, 9.101
      (a) 9.14, 9.28
      (b) 9.14, 9.28
      (6) 6.33
      (7) 6.15, 9.49, 9.105
      3.2(1) 23.11
      (2) 23.11
      3.3(1) 6.07
      (2) 6.07
      (3) 6.14
      3.4 .... 3.101, 9.97
      3.5(1) 11.16, 11.18
      (2) 1.22, 11.17
      3.6 .... 6.11, 30.88
      (1) 6.11, 6.13
      (a) 25.19
      (b) 25.19
      (2) 6.12, 20.08, 30.88
      (3) 6.12, 30.88
      (4) 6.13, 30.88
      3.18 .... 18.80
      4.1(a) 21.86
      4.2 .... 25.19
      (1) 21.86
      (2) 21.87
      (3) 21.86
      5.1 .... 1.22, 5.21
      (1) 1.22, 6.08, 11.16
      (2) 6.08
      (a) 6.08, 23.16, 24.06
      (b) 6.08
      (c) 6.08
      (3) 6.07, 11.16
      5.2 .... 6.14, 6.30, 6.31, 6.45
      (1)(a) 6.14, 6.16
      (b) 6.14, 6.16
      (c) 6.14, 6.16
      (2) 6.14, 6.16
      (3) 6.30, 6.45
      (4) 6.23, 25.19
      (5) 6.28, 25.19

OCR   5.2(6).............. 6.28, 25.19
      5.3–5.6 .... 12.57, 25.19
      5.3 .... 15.66, 22.85
      (1) 6.19
      (2) ... 6.13, 16.08, 21.14, 30.88
      (3) 6.19, 16.08
      (4) 6.19, 6.45, 16.09
      5.4 .... 11.18, 15.66
      (1) 6.23, 6.26, 22.85
      (a) 6.24
      (b) 6.24, 6.40
      (2) 22.85
      (3) 6.27
      (b) 6.27
      (4) 6.27, 6.28, 6.30
      5.5 .. 6.29, 6.30, 6.31, 22.85, 29.68
      (1)(a) 6.29
      (i) 6.29
      (ii) 6.29
      (b) 6.30
      (i) 6.30, 7.12
      (ii) 6.30, 7.12
      (iii) 6.30, 7.12
      (iv) 6.30, 7.12
      (v) 6.30, 6.31, 7.12
      (c) 6.30, 6.31
      (2) 6.32
      (3) 6.32
      (a) 6.30
      (b) 6.30
      (5) 6.30
      (6) 6.29, 6.32
      (7) 6.32
      5.6 ..... 6.11, 6.33, 29.68, 30.105
      (1) 6.08, 6.11, 6.33, 6.34,
            6.35, 21.56
      (a) 6.34, 20.07
      (b) 6.35
      (2) 1.22, 6.34, 6.35
      (3) 6.36
      (4) 1.22, 6.34, 21.56
      (5) 6.35
      5.7 .... 25.18
      (1) 4.86, 4.95, 4.99, 4.101,
            6.40, 6.43
      (2) 4.86, 6.43
      5.8 .... 6.23, 11.18
      5.9 .... 5.51, 6.04, 6.47
      5.10(1) 6.04, 6.09, 6.15, 6.20,
            6.46, 8.06
      (2) 6.04, 8.06
      6.1 .... 11.22
      6.2 .... 11.23
      (1) 7.06, 11.23
      (2) 11.23
      7.1 .... 22.44
      7.2 .... 14.03
      (1) 2.11, 7.04, 7.06, 8.05

OCR   7.2(2)(a). 3.64, 7.12
             (b) 7.04
                  (ii) 7.04
                  (iii) 7.12
             (3) 2.14, 7.12
             (a) 7.12
             (b) 7.12
             (c) 7.12
             (4) 2.14, 7.04, 7.12
             (12) 22.69
      7.3(1) 7.02
          (2) 7.02, 7.03
          (3) 7.03
          (4) 7.03
          (5) 7.03
      7.4 . . . .   7.04, 7.10
      7.5 . . . .   7.18
      7.6 . . . .   9.78
          (1) 9.83, 9.93
          (a) 7.20
          (b) 7.20
          (2) 7.20
          (3)(a) 7.21
             (b) 7.21
      8.1 . . . .   8.05, 14.03
          (1) 1.22, 7.23, 7.25
          (a) 22.55
          (2) 7.23
          (3) 7.26, 7.29, 7.34, 7.35
          (4) 7.16, 7.27
          (5) . . .   7.36, 7.37, 18.10, 18.22,
                                                18.43
      8.8(2) 13.02
      9.1 . . . .   8.01, 8.05, 21.54
          (1) 1.22, 8.01
          (2) 8.06, 9.108
          (13) 8.24
      9.2 . . . .   5.41, 12.63, 21.54
          (1) 1.22, 8.07
          (2) 1.22
          (a) 8.07
          (b) 5.83, 8.07, 8.10
          (3) 8.31
      9.3 . . . . . .   8.10, 9.50, 9.67, 16.18
      9.4 . . . . . .   8.28, 8.31, 15.60, 21.54
      9.5 . . . .   5.43, 9.50, 30.142
          (1) 8.10, 8.10
          (2) 8.10
      9.6(1) 8.07, 8.18, 14.03
          (2) 8.24, 9.14, 9.46, 9.47,
                          9.106, 9.108, 9.109
      9.7 . .   8.24, 9.19, 9.22, 9.108, 9.109
      9.8 . . . .   21.54
          (1) 8.07, 8.30, 8.38
          (2) 8.28
          (3) 8.28
          (4) 8.30
      9.9 . . . .   21.54
          (1) 8.30
          (2)(a) 8.30
      9.10 . . . .   8.29, 21.54
      9.11 . . . .   21.54
          (1) 8.33, 8.39
          (2) 5.95, 8.34, 8.39, 14.06
          (3) 8.38
      9.12 . . . .   8.43, 10.11, 13.01, 18.61,
                          18.80, 21.11, 21.54

OCR   9.12(1)–(3). 8.49
          (1) 8.36, 21.59
          (2) 8.36, 21.59
          (3) 8.36, 8.39, 14.69
          (a) 8.42
          (b) 8.42
          (c) 8.42, 13.01
          (4) 8.44
          (5) 8.38, 8.52, 13.01
          (6)(a) 8.39
             (b) 8.39
          (7) . . .   8.36, 8.49, 14.07, 14.14
      9.14 . . . .   16.50, 30.154
          (1) 15.02, 16.01
          (2) 15.02, 16.01
          (3) 15.02, 16.01
      9.15 . . . .   21.54
      10.1(1) 8.45
          (2) 8.45
      10.2 . . . .   8.45
      10.3(1) 8.45
          (2) 8.45, 8.52
          (3) 8.45
      10.4 . . . .   8.46
      10.5(1) 8.47
          (a) 8.47
          (b) 8.47
          (2) 8.47, 10.54
          (3) 8.39, 8.47
      10.6 . . . .   8.47, 8.52, 13.01
          (1)–(3) 8.49
          (1) 8.49, 21.59
          (2) 8.49, 21.59
          (3) 8.49
          (a) 8.51
          (b) 8.51
          (c) 8.51
          (4) 8.49, 14.07, 14.14
      11.1 . . . .   8.11, 16.20
      11.2(1) 8.10
          (2) 5.74, 8.14
          (3) 8.14
      11.3(1) 8.14
          (2) 8.16
          (3) 4.119
          (a) 8.14
          (b) 8.14
          (4) 8.14
      11.4 . . . .   18.23
          (1) 5.100, 8.16
          (2) 8.16, 18.10
      11.5 . . . .   8.17, 16.55, 30.35
      11.6(1) . . .   8.13, 8.20, 14.43, 16.21
          (2) 14.43
          (a) 8.13
          (b) 8.13
          (3)(a) 8.13
             (b) 8.13
          (4) 8.13
      11.8 . . . .   30.235
      12.1 . . . .   5.83, 17.02
          (a) 5.83
          (b) 5.83
      12.2 . . . .   1.22
          (1) 2.03, 5.75
          (2)   5.84, 5.87, 19.05, 30.230,
                                              31.129

OCR	12.2(3).	16.104, 17.03, 17.25, 18.85, 18.90, 25.27
	(a)	8.63
	(4) . .	5.85, 11.83, 18.85, 18.90
	(5)	1.22, 2.03, 16.104
	(a)	5.36, 5.75, 18.47, 18.55
	(b)	17.33
	(ii)	5.36, 5.85
	(6)	1.22
	13.1(1)	12.15
	(2)	12.15
	(3)(a)	12.15
	(b)	12.15
	(4)	12.15
	13.2(1)	12.15
	(2)	12.15
	(3)	12.15
	13.80(1)	18.25
	14.1(1)	5.58
	14.2	5.58
	14.3(1)	5.59
	(2)	5.59, 25.23
	(c)	21.81
	(3)	5.59
	(4)	5.59
	(5)	5.69
	(6)	5.60
	(7)	5.59
	14.4	5.61
	(1)	5.61
	(a)	5.61
	14.5	5.61
	(1)(a)	5.62
	(b)	5.62
	(2)(a)	5.62
	(b)	5.62
	14.6	5.63
	14.7	5.60
	(1)	5.64
	(2)	5.64
	(3)	5.64
	14.8	5.60
	(1)	5.65
	(2)	5.65
	14.9	5.66
	14.10	5.60, 21.17
	(1)	5.67
	(2)	5.67, 21.17
	14.11	21.17
	(1)	5.68
	(2)	5.68, 21.81
	14.12	5.69
	14.13	21.17
	(1)	5.70
	(2)(a)	5.70
	(b)	5.70
	(c)	5.70
	(3)	5.70
	15(1)(b)	12.14
	(2)	6.20
	(4)	14.47
	15.1	22.50
	(1)	5.45
	(a)	14.64, 19.28
	(b)	13.03, 14.64
OCR	15.1(2).	5.46, 14.64
	(3)	5.46
	15.2	14.64, 15.101, 22.79
	(1)	5.47, 14.22
	(2)(a)	5.47
	(b)	5.47
	(a)	5.47
	(b)	5.47
	(4)	5.48, 5.51, 5.53
	(5)	5.48
	(6)	5.48
	(7)	5.47
	15.3	14.20
	(1)	5.49
	(c)	5.51
	(2)	5.49
	15.4	5.50, 5.81, 8.05, 14.47, 14.64
	15.5	30.37
	(1) . .	5.51, 8.05, 10.48, 14.24, 14.47, 14.64, 15.64
	(2)	5.51, 5.83, 17.02
	(3)	5.51
	(4)	5.51, 15.64
	(5)	10.48, 14.47, 15.64
	(a)	5.52
	(b)	5.52
	(6)	5.53
	(7)	5.53
	(8)	5.54, 15.64
	(9)	5.54
	15.6(1)(a)	30.41
	(b)	30.41
	(2)	30.41
	16.1(a)	14.02, 14.03, 14.14
	(b)	14.02, 14.03
	(c)	14.02, 14.03
	16.2	8.06, 8.16, 8.18, 14.03, 14.07, 14.14, 16.47, 16.48
	(1) . .	8.35, 11.61, 14.04, 16.48
	(a)	14.14
	(b)	5.91, 16.34
	(c)	13.07, 16.47
	(2)	11.78, 13.07, 14.02, 16.34, 16.47, 16.48
	(3)	13.07, 14.02, 14.04, 14.07, 16.47, 16.48
	16.3	5.93, 8.05, 8.18, 11.68, 14.02, 14.08
	17.1	14.72
	17.2(1)	14.72
	(2)	14.72
	(3)	14.72
	(4)	14.73
	(b)(ii)	21.91
	(5)	14.73
	17.3(1)	14.73
	(2)	14.73
	18(2)	7.20
	18.1 . . .	10.03, 10.13, 14.15, 21.13, 30.31
	(1)	8.26, 9.89
	(2)	8.26
	18.2	9.41, 9.41, 9.78, 10.01, 10.03, 10.06, 10.11, 10.22, 10.28, 10.29, 10.43, 11.86, 14.15, 16.96

OCR 18.2(1)................. 10.03
    (2) 9.41
      (a) 2.100, 9.83, 10.05,
                            30.43
         (i)–(iii) 10.08
         (i) 10.03, 10.13
         (ii) 10.03, 10.13
      (b) 4.85, 10.05
         (iv)–(v) 10.09
      (c) 2.100, 10.03, 10.05,
                            12.32
      (d) 4.36, 10.11, 10.11
      (d)(vi) 10.11
  18.3 .... 10.47
    (1)(a) 10.47
      (b)(i) 10.47
        (ii) 10.47
    (2) 10.49, 10.51
  18.4(1) 10.11
    (2) 10.11
  18.5 .... 10.11
    (1)(a) 10.11, 10.47
        (i) 10.11
        (ii) 10.11
      (b) 10.11
    (2) 10.11
    (3) 10.11
  18.6 ... 10.29, 10.31, 10.51, 11.86
  18.7(a) 10.43
    (b) 10.43
  18.8 .... 13.02, 13.12
    (1) 10.49, 13.02
    (2) 10.49, 13.02
  19.1 .... 12.39
    (2) 12.32
    (3) 9.45, 12.33
      (b) 9.46
      (c) 9.47, 9.126
  19.2
    (a) 12.33
    (1) 11.10, 11.36, 12.34
    (2)(a) 12.34
      (b) 12.34
    (3) 12.34
    (4) 11.10, 12.34
  19.2A 8.29, 8.33
  19.3 .... 2.33
    (1) 12.40
    (2) 12.40
  19.4(a) .. 2.33, 12.32, 12.35, 12.36
    (b) 12.32, 12.35
    (c) 12.32, 12.35
  20.1 .... 12.43, 12.44
    (1) 12.45, 12.49, 12.52,
              12.57, 12.62, 12.63
    (2) 12.42, 12.62
  20.2–20.6 .... 12.44, 12.62
  20.2(1) 12.54
    (2) 12.54
    (3) 12.54
  20.3 .... 11.10
    (1) 11.36, 12.56
    (2) 12.56
    (3) 12.56
    (4) 12.56
  20.4(1) 12.55

OCR 20.4(4)................. 12.58
  20.5(1) 12.59
    (2) 9.43, 12.60
      (a) 9.46
  20.6(1) 12.63
    (2) 12.63
    (3) 12.63, 12.65
  21.1(1) ... 4.31, 9.67, 9.69, 15.47,
                     16.18, 30.98
    (a) 8.10, 15.47
    (b) 5.59, 8.20, 15.47
    (c) 15.47
    (2) .. 9.67, 9.68, 15.46, 15.47,
                 15.48, 16.18
  21.2 .... 9.67, 15.47, 16.18
    (3) 14.21
  21.3 .... 2.42, 11.47, 12.68, 12.70,
                       14.46
    (1) 12.67
    (2) 11.44, 12.72
  22 .... 8.35, 8.38, 8.41, 8.42, 8.48,
         8.51, 13.02, 13.12, 13.22
  22.1 .... 8.48, 13.01, 13.02, 21.11,
                      21.62
    (1) 8.35, 8.48, 13.01
      (a) 9.67
      (b) 9.67
      (c) 9.67
    (2) 13.01
    (3) 8.35, 8.48, 13.02
    (4) 13.02
    (5) 8.38, 8.48, 13.01
  23 .... 10.11
  23.1 ... 12.41, 14.16, 14.27, 14.29,
                       30.197
    (1)(a) 14.16, 14.20
      (b) ... 14.16, 14.21, 14.22,
                    14.26, 14.30
    (2) 14.16, 14.21, 14.26
    (3) 14.16, 14.26, 14.25
  23.2 .... 30.199
    (1)(a) 14.20
  24.1 .... 18.72
    (1) 12.27
    (2) 12.27
  24.2(1) 12.28
    (2) 12.28
    (3) 12.28
  24.3 .... 12.28, 14.07
  25.1 .... 12.10, 12.13, 30.47
  25.2 .... 12.11, 12.13, 30.47
  26.1 ..... 2.04, 4.54, 13.51, 13.52,
               13.55, 25.21, 30.25
    (1) 13.54
    (2) 13.52
    (3) 13.53
    (4) 13.52, 13.53
    (5)(a) 13.55, 13.56
      (b) 13.55
    (6) 13.56
    (7) 11.25, 13.56
    (8) 13.55, 18.10, 18.45
  26.2(1) 13.66
    (2) 13.66
    (3) 13.66
  26.3 .... 13.67, 30.26

OCR 29.4.................... 13.02
   (1) 8.62
   (2) 8.62
   (3) 15.72
29.5 .... 8.54, 8.56
29.6(1) 8.61
   (2) 8.61
29.7 .... 15.34, 16.08, 30.179
   (3) 16.03, 16.13
   (4) 16.04, 16.08, 16.09
   (5) 16.11, 19.22
   (6) 16.10
29.8 .... 16.05, 30.182
   (1) 16.05
   (2) 16.05
29.9 .... 16.07, 30.179
   (1) 16.12
   (2) 16.12
29.10 .... 30.179
   (1) 15.34, 16.07, 16.15
   (2) 15.34, 16.06, 16.07,
                         16.13
29.11(1) 15.59, 16.20
   (2) 15.59, 16.22
29.12(1) 16.21
29.13 ..... 8.15, 8.14, 8.15, 16.19
29.14(1) 16.31
   (2) 16.31
   (3) 16.31
   (6) 16.31
29.15 .... 16.32, 16.34
29.16 .... 16.63, 16.64
29.17 .... 16.56
29.18 .... 15.36
   (1) 16.32, 16.88
    (a) 16.55
   (2) 16.34, 19.22
   (3) 16.34
   (4) 16.34, 19.22
   (5) 16.88
   (6) 16.55
   (7) 16.55
   (8) 16.55
   (12) 16.88
   (13) 15.36
29.19 .... 18.26
   (1) 15.76, 16.89, 18.10,
                         18.45
   (2) 15.76, 16.89
   (3) 16.89, 18.53
   (4) 15.76, 16.89
29.20 .... 16.95, 16.104, 17.01,
                         25.27
30.1 .... 1.22, 29.01
30.2 .... 1.22
   (1) 11.51, 17.31
   (2) 17.31, 21.68
30.3 .... 1.22, 9.92, 11.85
   (1) 9.92, 29.12
   (2) 9.92, 29.12
   (3) 29.12
30.4 .... 1.22, 29.05, 29.07
   (1) 17.24
    (a) 7.16
    (b) 29.07
     (iii) 11.85
    (c) 7.16

OCR 30.4(2).. 7.16, 11.85, 17.24, 18.55
   (3) 17.24, 29.09
   (4) 11.85
30.5 .... 1.22
30.6(1) 29.06
   (2) 29.06
30.7 .... 29.13
30.8(1) 29.07
   (2) 29.08
30.9 .... 30.238
31(1) 9.41, 18.55
31.1 .... 11.84, 18.19, 18.47
31.2(1) 18.19
   (2) 18.47
31.3 .... 18.60
   (1) 18.98
   (2) 18.98
31.4 ... 18.58, 18.60, 25.29, 22.90
   (1) 16.90, 18.57
   (2) 18.57
    (d) 5.85
   (3) 18.46, 18.58
   (4) 18.58
   (5) 18.58
   (6) 18.58, 18.71
   (7) 18.58
   (8) 1.22
31.5(1) 1.22, 18.60
    (b) 18.98
   (2) 18.60, 18.98
   (3) 18.60, 18.98
31.6 .... 18.07, 18.61
31.7 .... 18.61
31.8 .... 18.61
31.9 .... 18.40, 18.68
31.10 .... 18.69
    (d) 21.93
   (1) 11.08, 18.78
   (2) 11.08, 18.69
31.11 .... 18.65
32.1 .... 17.23, 19.04, 19.32
32.2 .. 12.41, 19.26, 19.28, 30.229
32.3(1) 1.22, 19.35
   (2) 19.35
   (3) 19.35
   (4) 19.36
   (5) 19.36
   (6) 19.37
32.4(1) 19.38
   (2)(a) 19.38
    (b) 19.38
   (3) 19.39
33.1 .... 14.72, 20.03, 22.02
   (1)(a)–(g) 14.14
    (a)–(h) 7.25, 22.54
    (h) 14.14
    (i)–(m) 14.14, 22.54
33.2 .... 22.06
   (2)(a) 22.06
    (b) 22.06
   (3) 22.06
33.3 .... 22.08
   (1)(a) 22.08
    (b) 22.08
   (2) 22.08
   (3) 22.08

OCR	33.4.	22.09
	33.5	22.10
	33.6(2)	22.11
	(3)	22.12
	(4)	22.13
	(5)	22.14
	33.7	8.18, 9.98, 16.47, 22.15, 22.23, 22.52
	(1)	22.16
	(a)	22.15
	(b)	22.15
	(c)	22.15
	(d)	22.15
	(e)	22.15
	(f)	22.15
	(g)	22.15
	(h)	22.15, 22.23
	(i)	22.15
	(j)	22.15
	(k)	22.15, 22.79, 22.80
	(l)	22.15
	(3)	22.16, 22.20
	(4)	22.15, 22.16
	(5)	22.16
	(6)	22.16
	(7)	22.15
	33.8	22.17
	33.9	22.18
	33.10	6.07, 6.14, 22.19
	33.11	6.14, 6.16
	(1)	22.19
	(2)	22.19
	33.12(1)	22.20
	(2)	22.20
	(3)	22.20
	(4)	22.20
	33.13	4.07
	(1)	22.21
	(2)	22.21
	(3)	22.21
	(4)	22.21
	33.14(1)	22.21
	(a)	22.22
	(b)	22.22
	(2)	22.22
	33.15	20.03, 22.79, 22.80
	(1)	22.23
	(2)	22.23
	(3)	22.23
	33.16	4.07, 4.23, 12.13, 22.46
	(1)	22.24
	(2)	22.24
	(3)	22.25
	(4)	22.25
	(5)	22.25
	(6)	22.25
	(7)	22.25
	(8)	22.25
	(9)	22.26
	33.17	22.27
	33.18(1)	22.32
	(2)	22.32
	(3)	22.32
	(4)	22.32
	(5)	22.32
	(6)	22.32
OCR	33.18(7)	22.32
	33.19(1)	22.33
	(2)	22.33
	(3)	22.33
	33.20	22.34
	33.21(1)	22.35
	(2)	22.35
	(3)	22.35
	(4)	22.35
	(5)	22.35
	(6)	22.35
	33.22	22.36
	33.22A(1)	8.08, 22.37
	(a)	8.08
	(b)	8.08
	(c)	8.08
	(2)	8.08, 22.38
	(3)	22.38
	(4)–(6)	22.38
	33.23	22.39
	33.24(1)	22.40
	(2)	22.40
	(3)	22.40
	33.25	22.41
	33.26	5.57, 22.42
	33.27	21.91, 22.43
	33.28	5.20, 14.03, 15.43
	(1)	22.46
	(2)	22.46
	(3)	22.46
	(4)	22.46
	33.29	22.48
	33.30	22.48
	33.31	7.04, 22.49
	33.32	22.50
	33.33	22.50
	33.34	8.02, 12.31
	(1)	22.52
	(a)	8.02
	(b)	8.02
	(c)	8.02
	(d)	8.02
	(2)	22.52
	(a)	8.02
	(b)	8.24
	(3)	22.52
	33.35	22.52
	33.36	5.42, 8.37, 8.50, 14.14, 16.47, 22.53
	33.37	8.37, 14.02, 14.03, 14.14, 22.53
	(1)	14.14, 22.54
	(a)	14.14
	(b)	14.14
	(c)	14.14
	(2)	8.49, 22.54
	(a)	14.14
	(b)	14.14
	(c)	14.14
	(d)	14.14
	(e)	14.14
	(3)	14.14, 22.54
	(4)	14.14, 22.54
	33.38	22.57
	33.39	22.57
	33.43	22.57

OCR		
33.44(1)	....	22.58
(2)	....	22.58
33.45(1)	....	22.58
(2)	....	22.58
33.46	....	22.71
(1)	....	22.59
(2)	....	22.59
(3)	....	22.59
33.47	....	22.60
(2)	....	22.61
33.48	....	22.60
33.49(1)	....	22.61
(2)	....	22.61
33.50	....	22.62
33.51(1)	....	22.63
(2)	....	22.63
(3)	....	22.63
33.52(a)	....	22.64
(b)	....	22.65
33.53(1)	....	22.65
(2)	....	22.65
33.55(1)	....	22.66
(2)	....	22.66
(3)	....	22.66
(4)	....	22.67
(5)	....	22.66
33.56	....	22.68
33.57(1)	....	22.69
(2)	....	22.69
33.58	....	22.71
(1)	....	22.70
(2)	....	22.71
(3)	....	22.71
(4)	....	22.71
(5)	....	22.71
33.59(1)	....	22.72
(2)	....	22.72
33.60	....	22.73
33.61	....	22.74
33.62	....	22.75
33.63	....	22.76
33.65	....	22.76
33.67(1)	....	22.77
(2)	....	22.77
33.68	....	22.78
33.69(1)	....	22.79
(2)	....	22.79
33.70(1)	....	22.80
(2)	....	22.80
33.71	....	22.81
33.72(1)	....	22.82
(2)	....	22.82
33.73(1)	....	22.83
(2)	....	22.83
33.74(1)	....	22.84
(2)	....	22.84
33.75	....	22.84
33.76(1)–(3)	....	22.85
(4)	....	22.85
33.77(1)	....	22.86
(2)	....	22.86
33.78(1)	....	22.87
(2)	....	22.87
(3)	....	22.87
(4)	....	22.87
33.79	....	5.20, 22.88

OCR		
33.80	....	5.20
(1)	....	22.89
(2)	....	22.89
33.81	....	18.25, 22.90
33.82	....	22.91
33.84(1)	....	22.92
(2)	....	22.92
(3)	....	22.92
(4)	....	22.92
(5)	....	22.92
33.85(1)	....	22.93
(2)	....	22.93
33.86(1)	....	22.94
(2)	....	22.94
33.87(1)	....	22.95
(2)	....	22.95
(3)	....	22.95
33.88–33.91	....	30.298
33.88	....	22.96
33.89	....	22.97
33.90	....	22.98
33.91(1)	....	22.99
(2)	....	22.99
33.92	....	22.100
33.93	....	22.100
33.94(1)	....	22.101
(2)	....	22.101
33.95	....	21.43, 22.102
34.1(1)	....	23.21
(2)	....	23.15
34.2(1)	....	23.16
(2)	....	23.16
34.3(1)	....	23.21
(2)	....	1.22, 23.21
(3)	....	23.21
34.4	....	23.19
34.5–34.9	....	23.12
34.5	....	23.09
(1)	....	30.282
(2)	....	23.13, 30.284
34.10(1)	....	23.04
(2)	....	23.04
35.2	....	21.54
35.3(1)	....	21.55
(2)(a)	....	21.55
(b)	....	21.55
35.4(1)	....	21.55
(2)	....	21.56
(a)	....	21.58, 21.60
35.5	....	6.07, 6.14, 6.16
35.6	....	6.14, 6.16
35.7	....	21.56, 21.57
35.8	....	8.03, 21.57
35.9	....	1.22, 5.41
(a)	....	21.58
(b)	....	21.58
(c)	....	21.58
35.10(1)	....	21.59
(2)	....	21.59
(3)	....	21.60
(4)	....	21.60
(5)	....	21.60
35.11(1)	....	21.61
(2)	....	21.61
35.12(1)	....	21.63
(2)	....	21.63

OCR 35.13(1) 21.64
  (2) 21.66
 35.14 . . . . 21.69
  (1) 21.62
  (2) 21.62
  (3) 21.62
 35.15(1) 21.66
  (2) 11.86, 21.66
  (3) 11.87, 21.66
  (8) 1.22
 35.16 . . . . 21.56, 21.57
 35.17(1) 21.68
  (2) 21.69
 35.18(1) 21.69
  (2) 21.69
 36.1–36.7 . . . . 4.40, 30.321
 36.1(1) 21.14
  (2) 21.14
 36.2 . . . . 21.14
 36.3 . . . . 9.98
  (1) 21.14
  (2) 21.14
 36.4(1) 21.15
  (2) 21.15
  (3) 21.15
 36.5 . . . . 21.16
 36.6(1) 21.17
  (2) 21.17
  (3) 21.17
  (4) 21.17
 36.7 . . . . 21.18
 36.8–36.10 . . . . 11.82
 36.8 . . . . 21.19
  (1) 21.19
  (2) 21.19
 36.9 . . . . 21.19, 21.19
  (1) 21.20
  (2) 21.20
  (3) 21.21, 21.25
  (4) 21.27
  (5) 21.19, 21.22
  (6) 21.27
  (7) 21.27
  (8) 21.19
 36.10 . . . . 21.19, 21.19, 21.28
  (a) 21.28
  (b) 21.28
 36.12(a) 21.30
  (b) 21.30
 36.13(1) 21.31
  (2) 21.31
  (3) 21.31
  (4) 21.31
 36.14–36.17 . . . . 5.21, 30.48
 36.14 . . . . 21.37, 21.38, 21.42
  (1) 21.37, 30.48
  (2) 21.38, 30.48
 36.15 . . . . 21.37, 30.48
  (a) 21.38
  (b) 21.39, 30.49
  (c) 21.40, 30.50
  (d) 21.41, 30.52
 36.16(1) 21.42, 30.54
  (2) 21.39, 21.40, 30.51
 36.17 . . . . 1.22
  (1) 21.40, 30.53

OCR 36.17(2) 21.40, 30.50
  (3) 21.40, 30.53
  (4) 21.40, 30.53
 37.2(1) 20.07, 20.12
  (2) 20.12
  (3) 20.07, 20.08, 20.18
  (4) 20.08
  (5) 20.08
  (6) 20.10
  (7) 20.10
 37.3 . . . . 20.09
 37.5(2) 20.18
  (3) 20.18
  (4) 20.18
 37.6(1) 20.13
 37.7 . . . . 30.327
 38.1–38.5 . . . . 30.63
 38.2(1) 13.70
  (2) 13.70
 38.3 . . . . 1.22, 13.70
  (1) 13.70
  (2) 1.22, 13.70
  (3) 1.22, 13.70
  (4) 13.70
  (5) 1.22
 38.4(1) 13.70
  (2) 13.70
 38.5(1) 1.22, 13.70
  (2) 13.70
  (3) 13.70
 40.6 . . . . 18.98
 50(5) 12.57
 57.5(1) 20.18
 69(2) 13.30
 71 . . . . 29.13
 83(1) 18.77
 145.1(2) 5.57
 Pt IV 21.27
 Chap. 2 . . . . 5.93
 Chap. 4 . . . . 15.42
 Chap. 5 . . . 5.47, 5.62, 8.13, 14.43,
       15.60, 19.65
 Chap. 6 . . . . 3.101
 Chap. 7 . . . . . . 8.06, 11.63, 22.44,
       22.69, 22.70
 Chap. 8 . . . . 22.55
 Chap. 9 . . . . 8.44
 Chap. 10 . . . . . . 8.44, 13.01, 21.54
 Chap. 11 . . . . 5.74
 Chap. 13 . . . . 23.24
 Chap. 14 . . . 5.56, 5.57, 5.58, 5.60,
   5.68, 5.71, 8.22, 11.77, 12.10,
   12.11, 12.19, 21.81, 23.24
 Chap. 15 . . . . . 5.45, 10.48, 10.51,
   11.64, 19.65, 25.16, 22.50,
          30.37
 Chap. 16 . . . . 30.200
 Chap. 17 . . . . 14.71, 14.72
 Chap. 20 . . . . 12.64, 30.143
 Chap. 24 . . . . . 13.03, 18.72, 22.44
 Chap. 28 . . . . 12.04
 Chap. 30 . . . . 29.01
 Chap. 31 . . . . 18.19
 Chap. 33 . . . . . 5.71, 22.01, 22.02,
   22.56, 22.68, 22.73, 22.74,
       22.77, 22.105

TABLE OF SUMMARY CAUSE RULES

SCR	2(2)...............	1.20, 3.64
	(3).................	3.64
	(4).................	3.64
—	3(2)................	3.101
—	5...................	5.93
—	16..................	1.22
	(1).................	5.37
—	18(4)...............	2.15
	(7).................	30.140
	(8).................	2.14
—	18A.................	2.14
—	19..................	1.22
	(1)............	5.37, 30.122
—	20..................	2.106
—	22..................	2.04
—	23(2)...............	13.47
—	24..................	1.22
—	24A.................	1.22
—	25..................	1.22
—	26..................	1.22
—	28..............	1.22, 30.201
—	36..................	1.22
—	38(4)...............	1.22
—	40(2)...............	1.22
—	41..................	2.42
—	45..................	1.22
—	46..................	1.22
	(2).................	30.215
—	47..................	1.22
—	48..................	1.22
—	51..................	1.22
—	52..................	1.22
—	55(5)............	2.11, 3.64

SCR	61..................	1.22
—	63..................	1.22
—	64..............	11.25, 21.47
—	65–67..............	21.03
—	68A.............	1.22, 29.10
—	69.............	23.12, 29.13
—	73(3)...............	1.22
—	74(3)...............	1.22
—	75..................	1.22
—	76..................	1.22
—	77–78..............	29.13
—	81..................	1.22
	(3)(b)..............	30.329
—	81A................	29.10
—	83(4)...............	1.22
—	85A(7)..............	1.22
—	86..................	1.22
—	88(1)...............	1.22
	(3).................	1.22
	(4).................	1.22
	(5).................	1.22
	(6).................	1.22
—	89..................	1.22
	(1)............	29.07, 29.10
	(2)............	29.06, 29.13
—	92(1)...............	5.37
	(2).................	1.22
	(3).................	1.22
—	93..................	1.22
—	96..................	1.22
—	97..................	1.22
—	Forms U1–U14.........	29.06

TABLE OF SUMMARY CAUSE RULES (2002)

5.12(2)................. 30.112, 31.58
    (3).................. 30.112, 31.59
6.1............................ 30.62
    (1)....................... 30.59
    (2)....................... 30.59
6.3(1).................. 30.60, 30.61
    (2).................. 30.60, 30.61
    (3)....................... 30.60
    (4)....................... 30.61
6.4(a)........................ 31.34
7.1.......................... 30.123
    (1)(a)............... 30.114, 31.60
       (b)............. 30.115, 30.118
    (2).............. 30.115, 30.123
    (3)...................... 30.115
    (4)...................... 30.114
       (a)................... 30.114
       (b)............. 30.114, 30.288
    (5).............. 30.114, 30.243
    (6)...................... 30.114
    (7).............. 30.115, 30.123
7.2........................... 31.62
    (1)(a)................... 30.118
       (b)............. 30.114, 30.120
    (2)...................... 30.118
    (3)...................... 30.118
    (4).............. 30.114, 30.118
    (5)......... 30.114, 30.119, 30.120
    (6).............. 30.119, 30.120
    (7).............. 30.118, 30.119
7.3........................... 31.63
    (1)...................... 30.121
8.1............. 30.136, 30.243, 30.307
    (1).......... 30.131, 30.134, 31.69
    (2)...................... 30.131
8.2–8.17......... 30.243, 30.307, 30.315
8.2............. 30.123, 30.157, 30.260
    (1)......... 30.134, 30.207, 30.316
    (2)...................... 30.134
    (3)...................... 30.135
    (4)...................... 30.136
    (5).............. 30.123, 30.136
    (6).............. 30.123, 30.136
    (7).............. 30.123, 30.136
8.3....... 30.127, 30.138, 30.140, 30.260
    (1)................ 30.137, 31.80
    (2)....................... 31.81
       (a)................... 30.138
       (b)................... 30.138
    (3)(a)............. 30.139, 31.81
       (b)............. 30.139, 31.81
       (c)................... 30.140
       (d)........ 30.141, 30.201, 30.202
    (4)................ 30.142, 31.84
8.4(1)....................... 30.151
    (2)...................... 30.151
    (3)(a)................... 30.151
       (b)................... 30.151
8.5(1)............... 30.152, 30.157
    (2)...................... 30.152
    (3)(a)................... 30.152
       (b)................... 30.152
8.6(1)....................... 30.154
    (2)...................... 30.154
    (3)...................... 30.154

8.7(1)(a)..................... 30.155
       (b)................... 30.155
    (2)...................... 30.155
8.8.......................... 30.153
8.9(1)............... 30.150, 30.214
    (2)...................... 30.150
8.11......................... 30.205
8.12......................... 20.206
8.13(1)...................... 30.207
    (2)...................... 30.207
    (3)...................... 31.115
       (a)................... 30.208
       (b)................... 30.208
8.14(1)............... 30.214, 31.118
    (2)(a)................... 30.215
       (b)................... 30.215
8.15........... 30.209, 30.212, 31.116
8.16......................... 31.117
    (1)........ 30.209, 30.211, 30.213
    (2)...................... 30.213
    (3)...................... 30.212
8.17................... 30.218, 31.120
8.18......................... 30.343
    (1).... 30.137, 30.140, 30.216, 30.217,
                               31.119
    (2)...................... 30.217
       (a)............. 30.217, 31.119
       (b)................... 30.217
    (3)...................... 30.217
8.2–8.17..................... 30.248
9.1............ 30.37, 30.278, 31.26
    (1)....................... 30.72
       (a)..................... 30.37
       (b)..................... 30.37
    (2)....................... 30.38
    (3)................ 30.37, 30.38
    (4)....................... 30.38
9.2........................... 31.27
    (1)(a)................... 30.41
       (b)................... 30.41
    (2)....................... 30.41
9.13......................... 30.152
10.1(1)...................... 30.132
    (2)...................... 30.132
    (3)...................... 30.132
    (4)...................... 30.132
    (5)...................... 30.132
11.1(1)............... 30.144, 30.147
    (2)............... 30.145, 30.148
    (3)............... 30.146, 30.148
11.2......................... 30.148
    (1)...................... 30.148
    (2)...................... 30.148
    (3)...................... 30.149
    (4)...................... 30.149
11.3......................... 30.146
    (1)...................... 30.145
    (2)...................... 30.145
13.1(1)............... 30.43, 31.28
    (2)................ 30.44, 31.29
       (e)................... 30.271
    (3)....................... 30.43
    (4)....................... 30.45
14.1......................... 31.30
    (1)....................... 30.46
    (2)....................... 30.46

14.1(3)(a).	30.46
(b).	30.46
(4).	30.46
(5)(a).	30.46
(b).	30.46
15.1.	31.31
(1).	30.47
(2).	30.47, 31.80
16.1.	30.24, 31.17
(2).	30.25, 30.137
16.2(1)(a).	30.31
(b).	30.31
(c).	30.31
(2)(b).	30.28
(a).	30.28
16.3.	30.26
17.1(1).	30.157, 31.85
(a).	30.156
(b).	30.156
(2).	30.156, 31.85
(3).	30.156, 31.85
(4).	31.86
(a).	30.157
(b).	30.157
(c).	30.157
(5).	30.157, 31.86
17.2.	31.87
(1).	30.158
(2).	30.158
17.3.	31.88
(1).	30.160
(2).	30.160
(3).	30.160
(4).	30.160
(5).	30.159
17.4.	31.88
(1).	30.161
(2)(a).	30.161
(b).	30.161
(3).	30.161
17.5.	30.35, 31.23
(1).	30.35
(c).	31.23
(d).	31.23
(2).	30.35, 31.24
17.6.	31.133
(1).	30.235
(3)(a).	30.235
(b).	30.235
(4).	30.235
18(3).	30.135
18.1.	30.152, 30.165, 30.316, 31.89
(1).	30.162
(2).	30.162
(3)(a).	30.162
(b).	30.162
(4).	30.162
(5).	30.162
18.2.	30.163, 30.174, 31.90
(1).	30.164
(2).	30.157, 30.166, 31.91
(3).	30.157, 30.165, 30.167, 31.93
(4)(a).	30.163
(b).	30.163
(5).	30.168, 30.174
18.3.	30.152, 30.316, 31.94
(1).	30.170
(2).	30.170
(3).	30.171
(4).	30.172
(5).	30.171
18.4.	31.95
(1).	30.174
(2).	30.168, 30.174
(3).	30.168, 30.174
(4).	30.168
(5).	30.174
18.5.	31.100
(1).	30.186, 30.188
(2).	30.186, 30.188
(4).	30.186
(5).	30.189
(6)(a).	30.189
(b).	30.189
18.6.	31.96
(1).	30.176
(2).	30.176
(3)(a).	30.177
(b).	30.177
(4).	30.177
(5).	30.177
(6).	30.178
18.7.	30.190, 31.101
(2)(a).	30.192
(b).	30.192
(c).	30.192
(d).	30.192
(e).	30.192
(3).	30.193
(4).	30.194
(5).	30.195
(6).	30.196
18.8.	31.97
(1).	30.180, 31.97
(2).	30.180
(3).	30.180
(4).	30.180
(5).	30.182
(a).	30.181
(b).	30.181
(i).	30.181
(ii).	30.181
(iii).	30.181
(iv).	30.181
(v).	30.181
(6).	30.181
18.9.	30.181, 31.98
(1)(a).	30.182
(b).	30.182
(2).	30.182
18.10.	31.99
(1).	30.183
(2).	30.184
(3).	30.184
(4).	30.184
(5).	30.184
19.1(1).	30.210
(2).	30.210
20.1(1).	30.63
(2).	30.63

20.2(1).	30.63	24.1(1).	30.37, 30.123, 30.125, 30.128,
(2).	30.64		30.130, 31.07
20.3(1).	30.65	(a)(i).	30.125
(2).	30.65	(b)(ii).	30.125
(3).	30.65	(2).	30.129, 31.68
(4).	30.65	(3).	30.124, 31.65
(5).	30.65	(4)(i).	30.124, 31.65
20.4(1).	30.66	(ii).	30.124, 31.65
(2).	30.66	(5).	30.126, 31.67
20.5.	30.65	(6).	30.126, 31.67
21.1(1).	30.197	(7).	30.125, 30.127, 31.67
(2).	30.198	(8).	30.126, 31.68
(3).	30.198	(9).	30.126, 31.68
(4).	30.198	(10).	30.126, 31.68
22.1(1).	30.201, 31.106	24.6(a).	30.278
(2).	30.204, 30.329, 31.107	(b).	30.278
(3).	30.202, 31.108	(c).	30.278
(4).	30.203, 31.109	25.1–25.3.	30.53
23.1.	30.73, 30.121, 30.136	25.1.	30.346
23.2.	30.219, 30.343	(1).	30.332
23.3.	30.198, 30.219, 30.343, 31.128	(2).	30.332
(1).	30.220, 31.126	(3).	30.333
(2).	30.224	(4).	30.333
(3).	30.224	(5).	30.65
(4).	30.224	(a).	30.334
(5).	30.225	(b).	30.334
(5)–(15).	31.128	(c).	30.334
(6).	30.225	(6).	30.65, 30.334
(7).	30.226	(7).	30.336
(8).	30.226	(8).	30.217, 30.333, 30.336
(9).	30.227	(9).	30.337
(10).	30.227	(10).	30.338
(12).	30.228	25.2.	30.346, 31.140
(13).	30.228	(1).	30.335
(14).	30.228	(2)(a).	30.339
(15).	30.229	(b).	30.339
23.4.	30.230, 31.129	25.3.	31.141
23.5(1).	30.231, 31.130	(1).	30.340, 30.346
(2).	30.231, 31.130	(2).	30.341, 30.346
23.6.	31.131	(3).	30.341, 30.346
(1).	30.232, 31.132	(4).	30.346
(2).	30.233, 31.132	(a).	30.342
(3)(a).	30.234, 31.132	(b).	30.342
(b).	30.234	(c).	30.342
(c).	30.234, 31.132	(5).	30.343, 30.346
23.7.	31.134	25.4.	30.330, 30.345, 31.142
(1)(a).	30.236	(1).	30.345
(b).	30.236	(2).	30.345
(2).	30.237	(3)(a).	30.345
23.8.	31.134	(b).	30.345
(1).	30.238	(4).	30.345
(2).	30.238	25.5.	31.138
(3).	30.238	(1).	30.331
(4).	30.238	(2).	30.331
23.9.	31.135	25.6.	30.330
(1).	30.239	(a).	30.344
(2).	30.239	(b).	30.344
23.10.	30.296, 31.136	(c).	30.344
(1).	30.240	25.7.	30.345, 30.346
(2).	30.240	(1).	30.347
(3).	30.240	(3).	30.347
(4).	30.240	26.1(1).	30.48, 30.54
(5).	30.240	(2).	30.48
(6).	30.240	26.2.	30.48
24.1.	30.9, 30.122, 30.128, 30.329	(a).	30.49
		(b).	30.50
		(c).	30.52

26.3(1)	30.54
(2)	30.51
26.4(1)	30.53, 31.32
(2)	30.50
(3)	30.53
(4)	30.53
26.5	30.57
29.2	30.114
27.1	30.243
27.2	30.243
27.3	30.244
27.4(1)(a)	30.244
(b)	30.244, 30.246
27.5(1)	30.244
(2)(a)	30.246
(b)	30.246
27.6(1)	30.247
(2)	30.247
27.7	30.243
(a)	30.248
(b)	30.248
27.8–27.10	30.248
27.8(1)	30.249
(2)	30.249
27.9	30.251
(1)	30.251
(a)	30.114, 30.243
(2)(a)	30.251
(b)	30.251
(3)	30.251
27.10(1)	30.253
(2)(a)	30.253
(b)	30.253
(3)	30.253
(4)	30.253
(5)	30.254
(6)(a)	30.254
(b)	30.254
(c)	30.254
27.11	30.252
27.12(1)(a)	30.250
(b)	30.250
(2)	30.250
(3)	30.250
28.1	30.255
29.1	30.258
29.2(1)(a)	30.259
(b)	30.259
(2)	30.259
(3)	30.259
(4)(a)	30.260, 30.277
(b)	30.260, 30.277
(c)	30.260
(5)	30.260, 30.278
(6)	30.260, 30.278
30.1	30.276
(1)	30.276
30.2	30.233, 30.276, 30.330, 30.344
(2)	30.276
(3)	30.277
(4)	30.277
30.3	30.262
30.4	30.281
30.5(1)	30.282
(a)	30.282
(b)(i)	30.283
30.5(1)(b)(ii)	30.283
(iii)	30.283
(2)	30.284
30.6(1)	30.263
(2)	30.263
31.1	30.286
31.2(1)	30.287
(2)	30.287
(3)(a)	30.287
(b)	30.287
31.3(1)	30.288
(2)	30.289
(3)	30.289
(4)	30.289
31.4	30.289
31.5	30.291
31.6(1)	30.290
(2)	30.290
31.7	30.286
32.1(1)	30.240, 30.296
(2)	30.297
(3)	30.296
32.2(a)	30.294
(b)	30.295
33.1	30.300
33.2(1)(a)	30.299
(b)	30.299
(2)	30.300
(3)	30.301
33.3(1)	30.303
(2)(a)	30.303
(b)	30.303
33.4(1)	30.304
(2)	30.305
34.1	30.307
(2)	30.307
(3)	30.307
(4)	30.307
34.2(1)	30.308
(a)	30.309
(b)	30.309
(c)	30.309
(2)(a)	30.310
(b)	30.310, 30.317
(3)	30.318
(4)	30.318
(5)(a)	30.311
(b)	30.312, 30.316
(6)	30.312
(7)	30.313, 30.317
34.3(1)	30.314
(2)	30.315
(3)	30.307
34.4(2)	30.316
(3)	30.316
(4)	30.316
(5)	30.316
(6)(a)	30.316
(b)	30.316
34.5(1)	30.317
(2)	30.317
(3)	30.317
(4)	30.317
34.6(1)	30.321
(2)	30.321

34.6(3)...................... 30.322
    (4)...................... 30.323
    (5)............... 30.323, 30.325
    (6)...................... 30.324
    (7)...................... 30.324
    (8)...................... 30.324
    (9)...................... 30.325
    (10)..................... 30.326
    (11)..................... 30.326
    (12)..................... 30.326
    (13)..................... 30.326
    (14)..................... 30.326
    (15)..................... 30.327
34.7(1)...................... 30.319
    (2)...................... 30.319
    (3)...................... 30.320
35.1......................... 31.25
    (1)....................... 30.36
    (2)....................... 30.36
    (3)....................... 30.36
35.2......................... 31.25
79(1)....................... 30.296
92.......................... 30.296
Chap. 5...................... 30.287
Chap. 6.................. 30.58, 31.34
Chap. 7............. 30.113, 31.60
Chap. 11.................... 30.143
Chap. 20..................... 31.35
Chap. 21.................... 31.102
Chap. 22.................... 31.105
Chap. 24.............. 30.136, 31.64
Chap. 25.................... 30.217
Chap. 26.............. 30.55, 31.32
Chap. 27.................... 30.243
Chap. 29.................... 30.257
Chap. 33.................... 30.298
Chap. 34.............. 30.308, 30.312
Form 1................. 30.67, 31.36
Form 1a... 30.81, 30.132, 30.241, 30.258,
            30.286, 31.40, 31.42
Form 1b... 30.81, 30.132, 30.241, 30.255,
            30.258, 30.286, 31.40
Form 1c......... 30.132, 30.241, 30.275
Form 1d...................... 30.81
Form 2...................... 31.36
Form 3...................... 31.36
Form 3a..................... 30.263
Form 3b..................... 30.263

Form 4................. 30.286, 31.36
Form 4a..................... 30.287
    (part 1).............. 30.287
    (part 2).............. 30.287
Form 5...................... 31.48
Form 5a..................... 30.246
Form 5b..................... 30.251
Form 7................. 30.242, 31.51
Form 8...................... 31.54
Form 9...................... 31.54
Form 10............... 30.308, 31.34
Form 10b.................... 30.314
Form 10c.. 30.308, 30.310, 30.317, 30.326
Form 10d.................... 30.323
Form 10e.................... 30.312
Form 10f.................... 30.319
Form 10g.................... 30.319
Form 11........... 30.89, 30.277, 31.60
Form 12..................... 31.62
Form 13.......... 30.106, 31.54, 31.62
Form 14.......... 30.107, 31.54, 31.74
Form 15................ 30.103, 31.90
Form 16............... 31.34, 31.97
Form 16a.................... 31.97
Form 17.............. 30.115, 30.259
Form 18.............. 30.118, 30.119
Form 18–18i................. 31.132
Form 19.............. 30.119, 31.134
Form 20.... 30.163, 30.189, 30.206, 31.64
Form 21......... 30.163, 30.189, 30.206
Form 22..................... 30.148
Form 23.............. 30.148, 30.149
Form 24..... 30.164, 30.165, 31.32, 31.90
Form 25..................... 30.193
Form 25a.................... 30.193
Form 26..................... 30.180
Form 26a.................... 30.180
Form 27..................... 30.64
Forms 28–28k................ 30.234
Form 29..................... 30.238
Form 30..................... 30.125
Form 31..................... 30.332
Form 32..................... 30.345
Form 33..................... 30.346
Form 35................ 30.53, 31.32
Form 36..................... 30.294
Form 37..................... 30.295
Form 40.4................... 30.346

TABLE OF SUMMARY APPLICATION RULES

SAR 2...................... 24.14
—   3(1)..................... 24.14
—   4........................ 25.18
    (1)..................... 25.18
    (2)..................... 25.18
    (8)..................... 25.18
—   5....... 12.04, 15.04, 15.87, 25.16
—   6........................ 25.17
    (2)..................... 25.17
    (3)..................... 25.17
—   7(1)..................... 25.19
    (2)..................... 25.19
    (3)..................... 25.19
    (4)(a)........... 25.19, 25.23
      (b)................... 25.19
    (5)............... 25.19, 25.23
    (6)..................... 25.19
    (7)..................... 25.19
    (8)..................... 25.19
    (9)..................... 25.19
    (10).................... 25.19
    (11).................... 25.19
—   8........................ 25.19

SAR 9........................ 25.19
—   10....................... 25.19
—   11....................... 25.19
—   12....................... 25.19
—   13....................... 25.19
—   14....................... 25.18
—   17(1).................... 25.19
    (2)................... 25.19
—   21............. 25.12, 25.21
    (3)................... 25.12
—   29........................ 3.64
—   30(1)............. 15.01, 15.87
    (2).................... 15.04
—   31....................... 25.16
—   32...... 12.04, 15.04, 15.87, 25.16,
                         25.23
—   Form 1.................... 25.18
—   Form 2............. 25.19, 25.23
—   Form 3............. 25.19, 25.20
—   Form 4............. 25.19, 25.23
—   Form 5................... 25.19
—   Form 6................... 25.19
—   Form 7................... 25.19

TABLE OF RULES OF THE COURT OF SESSION

RCS 1.3(4)..................... 11.37
—   2.1....................... 5.93
—   4.6(2)................... 14.43
—   4.14...................... 30.35
—   4.15(6).............. 5.87, 5.88
—   4.16(7).............. 5.87, 5.88
—   13.4...................... 6.13
—   14.2(c)................. 11.41
        (g)................... 11.40
—   16.1(1)................ 6.27
—   16.2.................... 6.30
—   16.4(6)................ 6.13
—   19.1.................... 7.04
        (2)(b)................ 8.06
—   19.2.................... 7.23
—   20.1.................... 8.06
—   22.3(6)............. 8.66, 13.42
—   23.3.................... 13.65
—   24.1(2)(a)............. 30.43
—   24.2(5)................ 10.23
—   25.2(1)................ 11.36
—   25.5(1)................ 12.35
        (2).................. 12.35
—   26.1.................... 12.43
        (2).................. 12.43
—   26.7(3)................ 12.64
        (4).................. 12.64
        (5).................. 12.62
—   26.31................... 11.36
—   29.1.................... 14.27
—   32.2(1)................ 13.64
        (2).................. 13.64
        (3)............. 13.64, 13.65
—   32.3............... 13.64, 13.66
—   32.4.................... 13.66
        (1).................. 13.64
        (2).................. 13.64
—   35.1.................... 15.20
—   35.3.................... 15.66
—   35.10................... 15.100
        (1).................. 13.65
        (2).................. 13.65

RCS 35.10(3)................. 13.65
        (4).................. 13.65
        (5).................. 13.65
—   35.11............. 15.20, 15.28
        (1)(c)............... 15.28
        (10)................. 15.31
—   36.1.................... 8.61
—   36.2(2)................ 16.03
—   36.8.................... 15.43
—   36.9.................... 16.51
        (2).................. 16.50
—   38.3(4)(e)............. 21.93
—   38.8(1)................ 18.65
        (3).................. 18.65
—   38.21................... 10.23
—   40.1(2)(c)(iii)......... 30.348
—   40.4(1)(b)(iii)......... 30.348
        (2).................. 30.348
        (3).................. 30.349
—   40.6.................... 18.98
        (1)(a).............. 30.349
        (b)......... 18.60, 30.349
        (2).................. 30.349
        (3).......... 18.98, 30.349
—   40.19................... 18.101
—   42.4(2)(b)(ii).......... 19.39
—   50.2(2)................ 20.08
—   53.8.................... 12.67
—   59.1(d)................ 11.37
        (3)(a).............. 11.37
        (b).............. 11.37
        (4).................. 11.37
        (5).................. 11.37
—   67.17................... 28.195
—   272..................... 18.20
—   Chap. 24............... 10.01
—   Chap. 26............... 12.43
—   Chap. 40.......... 18.98, 30.350
—   Chap. 58............... 18.01
—   Chap. 61............... 12.05
—   Form 13.2–B.......... 9.72, 9.84
—   Form 59.1–D............. 11.37

TABLE OF ABBREVIATIONS

(other than standard law reports)

Alexander's Abridgment	W. Alexander, *Abridgment of the Acts of Sederunt of the Lords of Council and Session*, Edinburgh, 1838; *Supplement*, Edinburgh, 1843.
Anton with Beaumont	A. E. Anton with P. R. Beaumont, *Private International Law*, 2nd ed., Edinburgh, 1990
Anton & Beaumont	A. E. Anton and P. R. Beaumont, *Civil Jurisdiction in Scotland*, 2nd ed., Edinburgh, 1995.
Bell, *Arbitration*	J. M. Bell, *Law of Arbitration in Scotland*, 2nd ed., Edinburgh, 1877.
Bell, *Comm.*	G. J. Bell, *Commentaries on the Law of Scotland and the Principles of Mercantile Jurisprudence*, 7th ed. by John McLaren, 2 vols, Edinburgh, 1870.
Bell, *Dict.*	W. Bell, *Dictionary and Digest of the Law of Scotland*, 7th ed. by G. Watson, Edinburgh, 1890.
Bell, *Prin.*	G. J. Bell, *Principles of the Law of Scotland*, 10th ed. by W. Guthrie, Edinburgh, 1899.
Bennett	S. A. Bennett, *Divorce in the Sheriff Court*, 5th ed., Edinburgh 1997.
Burn-Murdoch	H. Burn-Murdoch, *Interdict in the Law of Scotland*, Glasgow, 1933.
C.A.S.	Codifying Act of Sederunt, 1913.
Clive	E. M. Clive, *The Law of Husband and Wife in Scotland*, 4th ed., Edinburgh, 1997.
Currie	J. G. Currie, *Confirmation of Executors in Scotland*, 8th ed., by E. M. Scobbie, Edinburgh 1995.
Dicey and Morris	A. V. Dicey, *The Conflict of Laws*, 12th ed., under the general editorship of L. Collins, London, 1993.
Dickson	W. G. Dickson, *The Law of Evidence in Scotland*, 3rd ed. by P. J. Hamilton Grierson, 2 vols, Edinburgh, 1887.
Dobie	W. J. Dobie, *Law Practice of the Sheriff Courts in Scotland*, Edinburgh and Glasgow, 1948.
Dobie, *Styles*	W. J. Dobie, *Styles for Use in the Sheriff Courts in Scotland*, Edinburgh, 1891.
Dove Wilson	J. Dove Wilson, *The Practice of the Sheriff Courts of Scotland in Civil Cases*, 4th ed. by J. C. Dove Wilson, Edinburgh, 1891.
Encyclopaedia	*Encyclopaedia of the Laws of Scotland*, 18 vols, Edinburgh, 1926–52.

Encyclopaedia of Styles	*Encyclopaedia of Scottish Legal Styles*, 10 vols, Edinburgh, 1935–1940.
Ersk.	John Erskine of Carnock, *An Institute of the Law of Scotland*, 8th ed. by J. B. Nicholson, 2 vols, Edinburgh, 1871.
Fyfe	T. A. Fyfe, *The Law and Practice of the Sheriff Courts of Scotland*, Edinburgh and Glasgow, 1913.
Gill	B. Gill, *The Law of Agricultural Holdings in Scotland*, 3rd ed., Edinburgh, 1997.
Gloag	W. M. Gloag, *Law of Contract*, 2nd ed., Edinburgh, 1929.
Gloag & Henderson	W. M. Gloag and R. C. Henderson, *Introduction to the Law of Scotland*, 10th ed. by W. A. Wilson, A. Forten, Lord Rodgers, A. Paton, L. Dunlop, P. Hood and A. R. W. Young, Edinburgh, 1995.
Goudy	H. Goudy, *Law of Bankruptcy in Scotland*, 4th ed., Edinburgh, 1914.
Graham Stewart	J. Graham Stewart, *Law of Diligence*, Edinburgh, 1898.
Grant	*The Sheriff Court*, Report by Committee appointed by the Secretary of State for Scotland (Chairman: The Rt. Hon. Lord Grant, T.D.), Cmnd. 3248, Edinburgh, 1967.
Gretton	"Diligence and Enforcement of Judgments: Diligence" in *Stair Memorial Encyclopaedia of the Laws of Scotland*, Edinburgh, vol. 8.
Grieve	*Administration of Sheriffdoms*, Report by Committee appointed by the Secretary of State for Scotland (Chairman: The Hon. Lord Grieve, V.R.D.), Cmnd. 8548, Edinburgh, 1982.
Guild, *Arbitration*	D. A. Guild, *The Law of Arbitration in Scotland*, Edinburgh 1936.
Guthrie, *Sel. Ca.*	*Selected Cases Decided in the Sheriff Courts of Scotland*, collected by W. Guthrie, 2 vols, Edinburgh, 1879, 1894.
Halliday	J. M. Halliday, *Conveyancing Law and Practice*, 2nd ed. by I. J. S. Talman, 2 vols, Edinburgh, 1996 and 1997.
Halsbury	*Halsbury's Laws of England*, 4th ed., 56 vols, London, and subsequently updated.
Hume, *Lectures*	Baron David Hume, *Lectures on the Law of Scotland, 1786–1822*, ed. by G. C. H. Paton, 6 vols (Stair Soc. 5, 13, 15, 17, 18, 19), Edinburgh, 1939–58.
Innes of Learney	Sir Thomas Innes of Learney, *Scotts Heraldry*, 2nd ed., Edinburgh, 1956.
J.L.S.	*Journal of the Law Society of Scotland*.
J.R.	*Juridical Review*.
Kearney	B. Kearney, *An Introduction to Ordinary Civil Procedure in the Sheriff Court*, Edinburgh, 1982.

Lees, *Interlocutors*	J. M. Lees, *Notes on the Structure of Interlocutors in the Sheriff Court*, 2nd ed., Edinburgh and Glasgow, 1915.
Lees, *Pleading*	J. M. Lees, *A Handbook of Written and Oral Pleading in the Sheriff Court*, 2nd ed., Edinburgh and Glasgow, 1920.
Lewis	W. J. Lewis, *Sheriff Court Practice*, 8th ed., Edinburgh, 1939.
Lewis, *Evidence*	W. J. Lewis, *A Manual of the Law of Evidence in Scotland*, Edinburgh, 1925.
McBryde & Dowie	W. W. McBryde and N. J. Dowie, *Petition Procedure in the Court of Session*, 2nd ed., Edinburgh, 1988.
Macdonald	H. R. M. Macdonald, *A Guide to the Family Law (Scotland) Act 1985*, Bicester, 1986.
McGlashan	J. McGlashan, *Practical Notes on the Jurisdiction and Forms of Process in Civil Cases of the Sheriff Courts of Scotland*, 3rd ed. by H. Barclay, 1854.
Mackay, *Manual*	Ae. J. G. Mackay, *Manual of Practice in the Court of Session*, Edinburgh, 1893.
Mackay, *Practice*	Ae. J. G. Mackay, *The Practice of the Court of Session*, 2 vols, Edinburgh, 1877–79.
McKechnie Report	*Report of the Committee on Diligence* (Chairman: Sheriff H. McKechnie, Q.C., LL.D.), Cmnd. 456, Edinburgh, 1958.
Maclaren	J. A. Maclaren, *Court of Session Practice*, Edinburgh, 1916.
Maclaren, *Expenses*	J. A. Maclaren, *Expenses in the Supreme and Sheriff Courts of Scotland*, Edinburgh, 1912.
McLaren, *Wills and Succession*	John (The Hon. Lord) McLaren, *Law of Wills and Succession*, 3rd ed., Edinburgh, 1894; *Supplement* by D. O. Dykes, Edinburgh, 1934.
McNeill, *Adoption*	P. G. B. McNeill, *Adoption of Children in Scotland*, 3rd ed., Edinburgh, 1998.
Macphail, *Evidence*	I. D. Macphail, *Evidence*, Edinburgh, 1987.
Maher & Cusine	*Law and Practice of Diligence*, Edinburgh, 1990.
Maxwell	D. Maxwell, *The Practice of the Court of Session*, Edinburgh, 1980.
Maxwell Report	*Report of the Scottish Committee on Jurisdiction and Enforcement* (Chairman: The Hon. Lord Maxwell), Edinburgh, 1980.
Miller, *Partnership*	J. B. Miller, *The Law of Partnership in Scotland*, 2nd ed. by G. Brough, Edinburgh, 1994.
Nichols	D. I. Nichols, *The Family Law (Scotland) Act 1985*, 2nd ed., Edinburgh, 1991.
Nichols & Meston	D. I. Nichols and M. C. Meston, *The Matrimonial Homes (Family Protection) (Scotland) Act 1981*, 2nd ed., Edinburgh, 1986.

Nicholson, *Sentencing*	C. G. B. Nicholson, *Sentencing Law and Practice in Scotland*, 2nd ed., Edinburgh, 1992.
O.C.R.	Ordinary Case Rules, contained in the Sheriff Courts (Scotland) Act 1907, Sched. 1, as substituted by S.I. 1993 No. 1956 and subsequently amended as indicated in *Parliament House Book* updated to August 21, 1998.
Palmer	Palmer's *Company Law*, 23rd ed., London, 1982.
Paton & Cameron	G. C. H. Paton and J. G. S. Cameron, *The Law of Landlord and Tenant in Scotland*, Edinburgh, 1967.
R.C.S.	Rules of the Court of Session, contained in the Act of Sederunt (Rules of the Court of Session) (S.I. 1994 No. 1443) and subsequently amended as indicated in *Parliament House Book* updated to 1998.
Renton & Brown	Renton & Brown's *Criminal Procedure according to the Law of Scotland*, 6th ed. by G. H. Gordon and C. H. W. Gane, Edinburgh, 1996, and subsequently updated.
Scolag	*Scolag: The Bulletin of the Scottish Legal Action Group.*
S.C.R.	Summary Cause Rules, contained in the Act of Sederunt (Summary Cause Rules) 1976 (S.I. 1976 No. 476) and subsequently amended as indicated in *Parliament House Book* updated to August 21, 1998.
Scot. Law. Com.	Scottish Law Commission.
Sellar, *Forms*	G. Sellar, *Forms for Sheriffs and Sheriff-Clerks*, Glasgow, 1881.
Stair	James, Viscount of Stair, *The Institutions of the Law of Scotland*, 2nd ed., 1693, reprinted, ed. D. M. Walker, Edinburgh and Glasgow, 1981.
Stair Memorial Encyclopaedia	*The Laws of Scotland*, 25 vols, Edinburgh, and subsequently updated.
Stewart	W.S. Stewart, *Scottish Contemporary Judicial Dictionary*, Edinburgh, 1995.
Stoddart	C. N. Stoddart, *The Law and Practice of Legal Aid in Scotland*, 4th ed., Edinburgh, 1996.
Thomson	J. M. Thomson, *Family Law in Scotland*, 3rd ed., Edinburgh, 1996.
Thomson & Middleton	G. R. Thomson and J. T. Middleton, *Manual of Court of Session Procedure*, Edinburgh, 1937.
Trayner	J. Trayner, *Latin Maxims and Phrases*, 4th ed., Edinburgh, 1894.
Walker, *Civil Remedies*	D. M. Walker, *The Law of Civil Remedies in Scotland*, Edinburgh, 1975.

Walker, *Contracts*	D. M. Walker, *The Law of Contracts and Related Obligations in Scotland*, 3rd ed., London, 1995.
Walker, *Delict*	D. M. Walker, *The Law of Delict in Scotland*, 2nd ed., Edinburgh, 1981.
Walker, *Digest*	N. M. L. Walker, *Digest of Sheriff Court Practice in Scotland*, Edinburgh, 1932.
Walker, *Judicial Factors*	N. M. L. Walker, *Judicial Factors*, Edinburgh, 1974.
Walker, *Prescription*	D. M. Walker, *The Law of Prescription and Limitation of Actions in Scotland*, 5th ed., Edinburgh, 1996.
Walker, *Prin.*	D. M. Walker, *Principles of Scottish Private Law*, 4th ed., 4 vols, Oxford, 1988.
Walkers, *Evidence*	A. G. Walker and N. M. L. Walker, *The Law of Evidence in Scotland*, Edinburgh and Glasgow, 1964.
Wallace	W. Wallace, *The Practice of the Sheriff Court of Scotland*, Edinburgh, 1909.
Wilson, *Debt*	W. A. Wilson, *The Scottish Law of Debt*, 2nd ed., Edinburgh, 1991.
Wilson & Duncan	W. A. Wilson and A. G. M. Duncan, *Trusts, Trustees and Executors*, 2nd ed., Edinburgh, 1995.
Wilton	G. W. Wilton, *Company Law and Practice in Scotland*, Edinburgh and London, 1912.

STATUTES

1907 Act	Sheriff Courts (Scotland) Act 1907.
1971 Act	Sheriff Courts (Scotland) Act 1971.
CJJ Act	Civil Jurisdiction and Judgments Act 1982.

PART VII

SUMMARY CAUSES AND SMALL CLAIMS

CHAPTER 30

SUMMARY CAUSE PROCEDURE

I. INTRODUCTION

This chapter begins with the definition of a summary cause. It **30.01** continues with an outline of the statutory basis of the procedural rules. The next section is concerned with rules of general application to all summary causes. The procedural progress of a standard summary cause (*e.g.* a straightforward action for payment) from commencement to decree and enforcement thereof will then be examined. Subsequently the different forms of summary cause for which special rules have been provided will be considered. Finally the provisions for appeals will be dealt with.

II. DEFINITION OF SUMMARY CAUSE

The summary cause in its present form came into existence on **30.02** September 1, 1976, and is a creation of the Sheriff Courts (Scotland) Act 1971.[1] It replaced both the former summary cause procedure as defined in section 3 of the Sheriff Courts (Scotland) Act 1907 and the procedure in the sheriff's small debt court. Section 35(1) of the 1971 Act provides:

"The definition of 'summary cause' contained in paragraph (i) of section 3 of the Sheriff Courts (Scotland) Act 1907 shall cease to have effect, and for the purposes of the procedure and practice in civil proceedings in the sheriff court there shall be a form of process, to be known as a 'summary cause', which shall be used for the purposes of all civil proceedings brought in that court, being proceedings of one or other of the following descriptions, namely—

(a) actions for payment of money not exceeding £1,500 in amount (exclusive of interest and expenses)[2];

---

[1] Sheriff Courts (Scotland) Act 1971 (Commencement No. 3) Order 1976 (S.I. 1976 No. 236).

[2] When the 1971 Act was passed the sum stated in s. 35(1)(a), (b) and (c) was £250. Section 41 provides, *inter alia*, that the sum in these paragraphs may be altered by Order in Council. Before s. 35 of the Act came into force the sum was increased to £500 by the Sheriff Courts (Scotland) Act 1971 (Privative Jurisdiction, etc.) Order 1976 (S.I. 1976 No. 900). It was further increased to £1,000 by the Sheriff Courts (Scotland) Act 1971 (Summary Cause) Order 1981 (S.I. 1981 No. 842) and to £1,500 by the Sheriff Courts (Scotland) Act 1971 (Privative Jurisdiction and Summary Cause) Order 1988 (S.I. 1988 No. 1993). At the time of writing there are understood to be proposals for a further substantial increase of the sum to £5,000. It was at one time expected that this change would be effected at the same time as the Summary Cause Rules of 2002 came into force, but this has proved not to be the case.

(b) actions of multiplepoinding, actions of furthcoming and actions of sequestration for rent, where the value of the fund *in medio*, or the value of the arrested fund or subject, or the rent in respect of which sequestration is asked, as the case may be, does not exceed £1,500 (exclusive of interest and expenses)[3];

(c) actions *ad factum praestandum* and actions for the recovery of possession of heritable or moveable property, other than actions in which there is claimed in addition, or as an alternative, to a decree *ad factum praestandum* or for such recovery, as the case may be, a decree for payment of money exceeding £1,500 in amount (exclusive of interest and expenses)[4];

(d) proceedings which, according to the law and practice existing immediately before the commencement of this Act, might competently be brought in the sheriff's small debt court or were required to be conducted and disposed of in the summary manner in which proceedings were conducted and disposed of under the Small Debt Acts[5];

and any reference in the following provisions of this Act, or in any other enactment (whether passed or made before or after the commencement of this Act) relating to civil procedure in the sheriff court, to a summary cause shall be construed as a reference to a summary cause within the meaning of this subsection."

30.03   The above definition is subject to the qualification that certain types of case which would otherwise be conventional summary causes must be brought as small claims.[6]

30.04   Any proceeding (other than a small claim) which falls into one of the four categories covered by paragraphs (a) to (d) of section 35(1) of the 1971 Act normally must be brought as a summary cause.[7] It has been

---

[3] See n.2.

[4] *ibid*. All actions of removing must now be summary causes (see *Tennent Caledonian Breweries Ltd v. Gearty*, 1980 S.L.T. (Sh.Ct.) 71) except those brought under the Land Tenure Reform (Scotland) Act 1974, s. 9, which are to be ordinary causes (s. 9(6)). See Vol. 1, para. 23.05.

[5] Examples of proceedings covered by para. (d) are applications under the Tenancy of Shops (Scotland) Act 1949, s. 1 and actions for aliment brought under the Sheriff Courts (Civil Jurisdiction and Procedure) (Scotland) Act 1963, s. 3 (as substituted by the Family Law (Scotland) Act 1985, s. 23), where the amount of aliment sought does not exceed £35 per week in the case of a child under the age of 18 years or £70 per week in any other case.

[6] s. 35(2) of the 1971 Act (as substituted by the Law Reform (Miscellaneous Provisions) (Scotland) Act 1985, s. 18(1)) provides that there shall be a form of summary cause process to be known as a "small claim". This form of summary cause process is at the time of writing defined by the Small Claims (Scotland) Order 1988 (S.I. 1988 No. 1999). It consists of actions for payment of money not exceeding £750 in amount and actions *ad factum praestandum* and actions for the recovery of possession of moveable property where there is included as an alternative a claim for payment of such a sum. As in the case of summary causes, there are understood to be proposals for a substantial increase in this sum—in the case of small claims to £1,500. It was expected that this increase would come into effect at the same time as the new Small Claim Rules of 2002, but this has proved not to be the case. Small claims form the subject-matter of Chap. 31 of this volume.

[7] Actions for aliment falling within the scope of the Sheriff Courts (Civil Jurisdiction and Procedure) (Scotland) Act 1963, s. 3 (where the sum craved does not exceed £70 per week for the pursuer and £35 per week for a child) are competent as summary causes but are also competent as ordinary causes.

held in the sheriffdoms of Lothian and Borders and Grampian, Highland and Islands that an action which should have been a summary cause but which had mistakenly commenced as an ordinary action, was fundamentally null and must be dismissed.[8] The contrary view has been taken in the sheriffdom of North Strathclyde,[9] and should probably be preferred.[10]

An action *ad factum praestandum* which includes a crave for declara- **30.05** tor may be raised as an ordinary action.[11] Indeed, it is strongly arguable that such an action *must* be raised as an ordinary cause, as the summary cause legislation contains no provision for seeking declarator.

III. PROCEDURAL RULES—STATUTORY BASIS

The original rules of procedure in summary causes were contained in **30.06** the Schedule to the Act of Sederunt (Summary Cause Rules, Sheriff Court) 1976[12] (hereinafter referred to as "the 1976 Rules"). The 1976 Rules were amended on several occasions over the years,[13] but have now been completely revoked by the Act of Sederunt of March 1, 2002.[14] The present rules (hereinafter referred to as "the 2002 Rules") are contained in Schedule 1 to that Act of Sederunt. Appendix 1 to that Schedule contains the forms referred to in the Rules, and references to forms in this chapter are to the forms in that Appendix. Appendix 2 to the Schedule contains a glossary of legal terms. The Summary Cause Rules may conveniently be found in Volume I of the *Parliament House Book*,[15] in Division D. In contrast with the provisions of earlier procedural rules for summary causes, the 2002 Rules are entirely self-contained and there is no importing of certain Ordinary Cause Rules simply by cross-reference and a general statement of applicability. These rules, which will be examined in detail in this chapter, apply only to summary causes commenced after June 10, 2002. Actions raised prior to that date continue to be governed by the 1976 Rules.[16]

---

[8] *Tennent Caledonian Breweries Ltd v. Gearty*, 1980 S.L.T. (Sh.Ct.) 71, *supra*; *Fillets (Aberdeen) Ltd v. Aberdeen Harbour Board*, June 14, 1984, Sh. Stewart, Aberdeen Sh.Ct., unreported, in which it was held that an application under the Tenancy of Shops (Scotland) Act 1949, s. 1, commenced by way of initial writ and not summons was incompetent and should be dismissed. An appeal was marked in this case but it was abandoned.

[9] *Borthwick v. Bank of Scotland*, 1985 S.L.T. (Sh.Ct.) 49 in which it was held that an application under the Tenancy of Shops (Scotland) Act 1949, s. 1, raised as an ordinary action, was not fundamentally null and could be transferred from the ordinary to the summary cause roll.

[10] See Vol. 1, para 13.50.

[11] *Milmor Properties Ltd v. W. and T. Investment Co. Ltd* (Sh.Ct), 1999 S.C.L.R. 910 (Notes); 2000 S.L.T. (Sh.Ct) 2.

[12] S.I. 1976 No. 476.

[13] By S.I. 1978 No. 112; S.I. 1978 No. 1805; S.I. 1980 No. 455; S.I. 1983 No. 747; S.I. 1986 No. 1946; S.I. 1986 No. 1966; S.I. 1988 No. 1978; S.I. 1989 No 436; S.I. 1990 No. 661; S.I. 1990 No. 2105; S.I. 1991 No. 821; S.I. 1992 No. 249; S.I. 1993 No. 919; and S.I. 1993 No. 1956.

[14] Act of Sederunt (Summary Cause Rules) 2002 (SSI 2002 No. 132) (in these notes hereinafter referred to as "A.S. 2002"). Para. 4 and Sched. 2 revoke the 1976 Act of Sederunt and all amendments thereto.

[15] W. Green, 1982, looseleaf regularly updated by releases.

[16] A.S. 2002, para. 3.

30.07 Although the 2002 Rules are substantially different from the 1976 Rules, some decisions made by the courts under the latter rules are relevant to the former, and reference will be made to such decisions in this chapter.

IV. RULES OF GENERAL APPLICATION

Register of summary causes

30.08 The sheriff clerk must keep a register of summary cause actions and incidental applications[17] made in such actions.[18] The register is to be known as the "Register of Summary Causes".[19] It may be in electronic or documentary form.[20]

30.09 Into the register must be entered a note of all actions, together with a note of all minutes for recall of decree.[21] The register must contain the following particulars where appropriate:

(a) the names, designations and addresses of the parties;
(b) whether the parties were present or absent at any hearing, including an inspection, and the names of their representatives;
(c) the nature of the action;
(d) the amount of any claim;
(e) the date of issue of the summons[22];
(f) the method of service;
(g) the return day[23];
(h) the calling date[24];
(i) whether a form of response[25] was lodged and details of it;
(j) the period of notice if shortened or extended in accordance with rule 4.5(3)[26];
(k) details of any minute by the pursuer intimating that he does not object to an application for a time to pay direction[27] or time order,[28] or minute by the pursuer requesting decree or other order[29];
(l) details of any interlocutors[30] issued;
(m) details of the final decree[31] and the date of it; and
(n) details of any variation[32] or recall[33] of decree.

---

[17] For the meaning of "incidental application" see paras 30.37 to 30.40, *infra*.
[18] S.C.R., r. 5.1(1).
[19] *ibid*.
[20] S.C.R., r. 5.1(5).
[21] S.C.R., r. 5.1(2). S.C.R., r. 24.1 deals with recall of decree. See paras 30.122 to 30.130, *infra*.
[22] For summons see paras 30.67 to 30.70, *infra*.
[23] For return day see para. 30.75, *infra*.
[24] For calling date see paras 30.75. 30.114, 30.134 to 30.142, *infra*.
[25] For form of response see paras 30.84 to 30.87, *infra*.
[26] See para. 30.88, *infra*.
[27] See paras 30.116, 30.118 to 30.120, *infra*.
[28] See paras 30.117, 30.118, 30.120, *infra*.
[29] See para. 30.115, *infra*.
[30] "Interlocutor" is defined in the glossary in Appendix 2 to Schedule 1 of the A.S. 2002 as "the official record of the order or judgment of a court".
[31] For final decree see para. 30.219, *infra*.
[32] For variation of decree see para. 30.240, *infra*.
[33] For recall of decree see paras 30.122 to 30.130, *infra*.

Into the entry in the register for any action there must be placed **30.10**
details of any incidental application made in that action.[34] Such details
must include, where appropriate, (a) whether parties are present or
absent at the hearing of the application, and the names of their
representatives[35]; the nature of the application[36]; and (c) the interlocutor
issued or order made.[37]

The register must be authenticated in some appropriate manner by **30.11**
the sheriff in respect of each day any order is made or application
determined in an action.[38]

The register must be open for inspection during normal business hours **30.12**
without fee "to all concerned".[39] In the first edition of this book it was
suggested that the latter phrase (which appeared in the equivalent
provision of the 1976 Rules) meant that the register might be examined
only by persons having an interest in a particular summary cause action
and that it was not available for simply any member of the public who
wished to satisfy his curiosity. That opinion has not, so far as the editors
are aware, been challenged, and it is submitted that that is the intention
of the rule.

Dispensing power

In the 1976 Summary Cause Rules what is generally called "the **30.13**
dispensing power" was contained in the Act of Sederunt itself rather
than in the Schedule. Its terms were broadly similar to those of the
present power. In the 2002 Rules the power is contained in rule 3.1,
which provides:

> "(1) The sheriff may relieve any party from the consequences of any
> failure to comply with the provisions of these Rules which is shown
> to be due to mistake, oversight or other excusable cause, on such
> conditions as he thinks fit.
> (2) Where the sheriff relieves a party from the consequences of the
> failure to comply with a provision in these rules under paragraph
> (1), he may make such order as he thinks fit to enable the action to
> proceed as if the failure to comply with the provision had not
> occurred."

Although it is not specifically provided, it is submitted that this
dispensing power is conferred on the sheriff principal and sheriff alike.[40]

This power is in terms virtually identical to those of the dispensing **30.14**
power contained in the Ordinary Cause Rules 1993.[41] The reader is
referred to the comments on that power in Volume 1.[42]

---

[34] S.C.R., r. 5.1(3). For incidental application see paras 30.37 to 30.40, *infra*.
[35] *ibid.*, r. 5.1(3)(a).
[36] *ibid.*, r. 5.1(3)(b).
[37] *ibid.*, r. 5.1(3)(c).
[38] *ibid.*, r. 5.1(4)(a).
[39] *ibid.*, r. 5.1(4)(b).
[40] *Hardy v. Robinson*, 1985 S.L.T. (Sh.Ct.) 40. This was an appeal in an ordinary cause,
but there is no reason why the principle there enunciated should not be equally applicable
to a summary cause.
[41] O.C.R., r. 2.1.
[42] Vol. 1, paras 5.93 to 5.97.

30.15   The question whether or not to exercise the dispensing power in a summary cause has been held to be a question of law rather than of fact and thus to be the proper subject-matter of an appeal to the sheriff principal.[43] However it is suggested that, as in other cases involving an exercise of discretion, an appellate court would be slow to interfere with the decision of the judge of first instance.

Jurisdiction and competency

30.16   The basis of jurisdiction of the sheriff in a summary cause is no different from that in an ordinary cause. Thus the geographical jurisdiction is defined by section 4 of the Sheriff Courts (Scotland) Act 1907, and the various means by which a defender may be made subject to the jurisdiction are as set forth in the Civil Jurisdiction and Judgments Act 1982, especially Part III and Schedule 8.[44] Section 6 of the 1907 Act now applies only in so far as jurisdiction is not determined by Schedule 8.[45]

30.17   A sheriff has jurisdiction throughout the whole sheriffdom and not only in the sheriff court district to which he is appointed.[46] Theoretically therefore an action may be raised in any court within the sheriffdom. It is, however, a matter for the discretion of the sheriff whether he is prepared to deal with a case which would normally be brought in a different sheriff court district.[47] In practice an action is almost invariably brought in the sheriff court of the district appropriate to the defender or the subject-matter of the cause. It may be transferred to another court.[48]

30.18   Section 5 of the 1907 Act (which has been amended on several occasions)[49] extended the jurisdiction of the sheriff court to certain categories of action and it applies, where appropriate, to summary causes as to ordinary causes. It must be read in conjunction with section 35(1) of the Sheriff Courts (Scotland) Act 1971[50] and the Small Claims (Scotland) Order 1988 (or any subsequent Small Claims Order)[51] in order to ascertain the categories of proceeding which fall within the standard summary cause procedure. With the exception (already noted)[52] of actions for aliment, all the categories of proceeding mentioned in section 35(1) (which are not small claims) must be brought as summary causes and not as ordinary actions. Conversely, the scope of the summary cause is clearly defined by section 35(1), and any proceeding which does not fall within its limits (unless provided for by specific legislation) is not competent as a summary cause.

---

[43] *Webster Engineering Services v. Gibson*, 1987 S.L.T. (Sh.Ct.) 101.

[44] The original Sched. 8 has recently been substituted as a result of an amendment to the 1982 Act made by the Civil Jurisdiction and Judgments Order 2001 (S.I. 2001 No. 3929), although the changes are relatively minor.

[45] For jurisdiction generally see Vol. 1, Chaps 2 and 3.

[46] 1971 Act s. 7. See Vol. 1, para. 2.03.

[47] *Tait v. Johnston* (1891) 18 R. 606. See Vol. 1, para. 6.02.

[48] See paras 30.24, 30.25, *infra*.

[49] For details of the amendments see *Parliament House Book*, Div. D.

[50] See para. 30.2, *supra*.

[51] See para. 30.3 and n.6, *supra*.

[52] See n.7, *supra*.

Representation

A party to a summary cause who is not conducting his own case may **30.19**
be represented by an advocate, solicitor or "authorised lay representative".[53] "Authorised lay representative" is somewhat unhelpfully defined
as "a person to whom section 32(1) of the Solicitors (Scotland) Act 1980
(offence to prepare writs) does not apply by virtue of section 32(2)(a) of
that Act".[54] Section 32(2)(a) of the 1980 Act provides that section 32(1)
is not to apply to "an unqualified person if he proves that he drew or
prepared the writ or papers in question without receiving, or without
expecting to receive, either directly or indirectly, any fee, gain or reward
(other than by remuneration paid under a contract of employment)".
The position is thus that in order to qualify as an "authorised lay
representative" the person appearing on behalf of a party must not be
paid for so doing. A person purporting to be an authorised lay
representative for a party must cease to represent that party if the sheriff
finds that he is either not a suitable person to represent the party or is
not in fact authorised to do so.[55] An authorised lay representative may
"do all things for the preparation and conduct of an action as may be
done by an individual conducting his own action".[56] However, this is
subject to the qualification that, while an authorised lay representative
may always appear for a party at the first calling of the action, he may
appear thereafter only if the action is not defended on the merits or on
the amount of the sum due.[57] This latter provision is itself subject to the
qualification "unless the sheriff otherwise directs".[58] The sheriff may thus
direct that an authorised lay representative should not appear at any
calling of a case after the first, even though the action is undefended.

Person carrying on business under trading or descriptive name

A person carrying on business under a trading or descriptive name **30.20**
may sue or be sued in such trading or descriptive name alone.[59] If decree
is pronounced against such a person under the trading or descriptive
name, an extract of that decree is a valid warrant for diligence against
such a person.[60] Similarly an extract of a decree against such a person
proceeding upon any deed, decree arbitral, bond, protest of a bill,
promissory note or banker's note or upon any other obligation or
document on which execution may proceed and which has been recorded
in the sheriff court books is a valid warrant for diligence.[61]

Any document[62] in an action in which a person carrying on business **30.21**
under a trading or descriptive name sues or is sued in that name may be
served (a) at any place of business or office at which such business is

---

[53] S.C.R., r. 2.1(1).

[54] *ibid.*, r. 1.1(2).

[55] *ibid.*, r. 2.1(4).

[56] *ibid.*, r. 2.1(3).

[57] *ibid.*, r. 2.1(2).

[58] *ibid.*

[59] S.C.R., r. 5.2(1). But note that if that person is an individual and the basis of
jurisdiction against him is his domicile, that is normally his residence and *not* his place of
business: Civil Jurisdiction and Judgments Act 1982, s. 41(2), (3), (4).

[60] S.C.R., r. 5.2(2)(a).

[61] *ibid.*, r. 5.2(2)(b).

[62] *ibid.*, r. 5.2(3) specifies "a summons, decree, charge or other document following upon
such summons or decree".

carried on within the sheriffdom of the sheriff court in which the action is brought[63]; or (b) if there is no place of business within that sheriffdom, at any place where such business is carried on (including the place of business or office of the clerk or secretary of any company, corporation or association or firm).[64]

Intimation

30.22   Any provision in the Summary Cause Rules requiring papers to be sent to or intimation to be made to any party, applicant or claimant is to be construed as if the reference to the party, applicant or claimant included a reference to the solicitor representing that person.[65] The provisions discussed below relating to citation of defenders[66] apply equally to all cases of intimation where that is required by the rules.

Execution by sheriff officer—no need for endorsation by sheriff clerk

30.23   Any summons, decree, charge or other document following upon a summons or decree may be served, enforced or otherwise lawfully executed in Scotland without endorsation by a sheriff clerk and, if executed by a sheriff officer, may be executed either by a sheriff officer of the court which granted the summons or by a sheriff officer of the sheriff court district in which it is to be executed.[67]

Transfer to another sheriff court

30.24   Rule 16.1 provides:

> "(1) The sheriff may transfer an action to any other sheriff court, whether in the same sheriffdom or not, if the sheriff considers it expedient to do so.
> (2) If the sheriff is satisfied that the court has no jurisdiction, he may transfer the action to any sheriff court in which it appears to the sheriff that it ought to have been brought.
> (3) An action so transferred shall proceed in all respects as if it had been brought originally in the court to which it is transferred."

30.25   This rule is in wider terms than the equivalent rule in the Ordinary Cause Rules.[68] The sheriff is given virtually unfettered discretion. He may make the transfer *ex proprio motu* and not (as is normally the case in an ordinary cause) only on the motion of a party. The commonest reason for a transfer being sought is that it is discovered, after the action has been commenced, that the defender has changed his address. As in the case of an ordinary cause the sheriff has power to make a transfer even though the court in which the summary cause has been raised has in fact no jurisdiction.[69]

---

[63] S.C.R., r. 5.2(3)(a). But note that if that person is an individual and the basis of jurisdiction against him is his domicile, that is normally his residence and *not* his place of business: Civil Jurisdiction and Judgments Act 1982, s. 41(2), (3), (4).

[64] *ibid.*, r. 5.2(3)(b). But note that if that person is an individual and the basis of jurisdiction against him is his domicile, that is normally his residence and *not* his place of business: Civil Jurisdiction and Judgments Act 1982, s. 41(2), (3), (4).

[65] *ibid.*, r. 4.6.

[66] See paras 30.88 to 30.109.

[67] S.C.R., r. 5.8.

[68] O.C.R., r. 26.1. See Vol. 1, paras 13.51 to 13.56.

[69] S.C.R., r. 16.1(2).

Remit from Court of Session

In terms of the Law Reform (Miscellaneous Provisions) (Scotland) **30.26**
Act 1985, s. 14, the Court of Session "may in relation to an action before
it which could competently have been brought before a sheriff remit the
action . . . to the sheriff within whose jurisdiction the action could have
been brought, where, in the opinion of the court, the nature of the action
makes it appropriate to do so." This provision might, at least in theory,
result in an action which qualifies as a summary cause being remitted
from the Court of Session, although, given the pecuniary limit for cases
in the Court of Session, it is much more likely that such an action would
fall within the scope of the ordinary cause procedure.[70] The Summary
Cause Rules provide that on receipt of the process from the Court of
Session the sheriff clerk must (a) record the date of receipt in the
Register of Summary Causes, (b) fix a hearing to determine further
procedure on the first court day occurring not earlier than 14 days after
the date of receipt, and (c) forthwith send written notice of the date of
that hearing to each party.[71]

Remit between summary, small claim and ordinary rolls

Section 37 of the Sheriff Courts (Scotland) Act 1971[72] provides:　　　　**30.27**

"(1) In the case of any ordinary cause brought in the sheriff court
the sheriff—

(a) shall at any stage, on the joint motion of the parties to the
cause, direct that the cause be treated as a summary cause, and
in that case the cause shall be treated for all purposes
(including appeal) as a summary cause and shall proceed
accordingly; . . .

(2) In the case of any summary cause, the sheriff at any stage—

(a) shall, on the joint motion of the parties to the cause, and
(b) may, on the motion of any of the parties to the cause, if he is
of the opinion that the importance or difficulty of the cause
makes it appropriate to do so,

direct that the cause be treated as an ordinary cause, and in that
case the cause shall be treated for all purposes (including appeal) as
an ordinary cause and shall proceed accordingly:
Provided that a direction under this subsection may, in the case of
an action for the recovery of possession of heritable or moveable
property, be given by the sheriff of his own accord. . . .

(2B) In the case of any small claim the sheriff at any stage—

---

[70] O.C.R., r. 26.3 is the relevant rule. See Vol. 1, para. 13.67.
[71] S.C.R., r. 16.3.
[72] As amended by the Law Reform (Miscellaneous Provisions) (Scotland) Act 1980, s.
16(a) and the Law Reform (Miscellaneous Provisions) (Scotland) Act 1988, s. 18(3). The
relevant provisions of s. 37 are also discussed in Vol. 1, paras 13.45 to 13.50.

(a) may, if he is of the opinion that a difficult question of law or a question of fact of exceptional complexity is involved, of his own accord or on the motion of any party to the small claim;

(b) shall, on the joint motion of the parties to the small claim,

direct that the small claim be treated as a summary cause (not being a small claim) . . . and in that case the small claim shall be treated for all purposes (including appeal) as a summary cause (not being a small claim) . . .

(2C) In the case of any cause which is not a small claim by reason only of any monetary limit applicable to a small claim or to summary causes, the sheriff at any stage shall, on the joint motion of the parties to the cause, direct that the cause shall be treated as a small claim and in that case the cause shall be treated as a small claim for all purposes (including appeal) as a small claim and shall proceed accordingly.

(3) A decision—

(a) to remit or not to remit under . . .subsection (2B) or (2C) above; or

(b) to make, or not to make, a direction by virtue of paragraph (b) of, or the proviso to, subsection (2) above,

shall not be subject to review . . .

(4) In this section 'sheriff' includes a sheriff principal."

30.28 The power to direct that an ordinary action be treated as a summary cause is exercisable only on joint motion of the parties, and if such a motion is made the sheriff must grant it.[73] The initial writ is then deemed to be a summary cause summons[74] and the sheriff must specify the next step of procedure to be followed in the action.[75] It is suggested that the usual course would be to have the case call in the next most convenient summary cause court. The sheriff has no power under the rules to accede to a motion made by one party alone to make an ordinary cause a summary cause, no matter how justified he may consider that motion to be. On the face of it the case of *Borthwick v. Bank of Scotland*[76] might appear to be authority for the proposition that the sheriff has a discretion to grant a motion by one party that an ordinary cause be treated as a summary cause, but the facts of that case were special in respect that the "ordinary cause" never really came into existence as the action should all along have been a summary cause.

30.29 If both parties move the sheriff to direct that a summary cause be treated as an ordinary cause, the sheriff must grant the motion.[77] In such a situation it is a reasonable inference that the parties agree that the ordinary cause scale of expenses is appropriate.[78] If only one party makes such a motion, the sheriff has a discretion to grant it "if he is of the

---

[73] 1971 Act, s. 37(1)(a).
[74] S.C.R., r. 16.2(2)(b).
[75] *ibid.*, r. 16.2(2)(a).
[76] 1985 S.L.T. (Sh.Ct.) 49. See Vol. 1, para. 13.50.
[77] 1971 Act, s. 37(2)(a).
[78] *Forsyth v. John Dickinson Group Ltd*, 1984 S.L.T. (Sh.Ct.) 51. See Vol. 1, para. 13.47.

opinion that the importance or difficulty of the cause makes it appropriate to do so".[79] In *Hamilton District Council v. Sneddon*[80] the sheriff principal expressed the opinion that a remit to the ordinary roll would have been appropriate. That case involved allegations of improper behaviour on the part of public officials and could well be said to have been of "importance". Authorities on the meaning of "importance" and "difficulty" are not numerous, although the words are used in several different contexts in both primary and subordinate legislation.[81] It is suggested that an example of "importance" might be if the case in question were a test case. "Difficulty" might arise if the case involved complex questions of law or of fact. The decision whether any individual case is one of importance or of difficulty is entirely within the discretion of the sheriff and is not subject to review.[82]

The proviso to section 37(2) which empowers the sheriff to make a **30.30** direction of his own accord in respect of actions for recovery of heritable or moveable property is prima facie not confined to cases of "importance or difficulty". It is, however, submitted that this power ought to be used only in such cases. If a sheriff chose to exercise his power in any other sort of case there is in fact nothing which the parties could do about it as the exercise of the power is not subject to review.[83]

When the sheriff directs that a summary cause be treated as an **30.31** ordinary cause he must, at the time of making that direction, (a) appoint the pursuer to lodge an initial writ and intimate it to every other party within 14 days of the date of direction[84]; (b) appoint the defender to lodge defences within 28 days of the date of the direction[85]; and (c) fix a date and time for an options hearing, that date to be the first suitable court day occurring not sooner than 10 weeks after the last day for lodging the initial writ, or such lesser period as the sheriff considers appropriate.[86] The crave of the initial writ should not seek a remedy different from that contained in the claim of the summary cause summons,[87] although it would, of course, always be open to the pursuer to seek to amend the crave once the action had become an ordinary cause.[88]

At any stage in a small claim the sheriff may, of his own accord, or on **30.32** the motion of any party to a small claim, direct that a small claim is to

---

[79] 1971 Act, s. 37(2)(b).

[80] 1980 S.L.T. (Sh.Ct.) 36. It may be noted that the sheriff principal (Johnston, Q.C.) took the view that one or both of the parties should have made the motion to remit. In fact, as the action was one for the recovery of possession of heritable property, the sheriff might have remitted *ex proprio motu* in terms of the proviso to s. 37(2).

[81] For example "importance" in the Civil Legal Aid (Scotland) (Fees) Regulations 1989 (S.I. 1989 No. 1490), reg. 5(4); "importance or difficulty" in the 1971 Act, s. 37(1)(b), on which see *Mullan v. Anderson*, 1993 S.L.T. 835; 1993 S.C.L.R. 506 (overruling *Data Controls (Middlesborough) Ltd v. British Railways Board*, 1991 S.L.T. 426; 1991 S.C.L.R. (I.H.) 359).

[82] 1971 Act, s. 37(3)(b).

[83] *ibid.*

[84] S.C.R., r. 16.2(1)(a).

[85] *ibid.*, r. 16.2(1)(b).

[86] *ibid.*, r. 16.2(1)(c).

[87] *Monklands D.C. v. Baird* (Sh.Ct) 1987 S.C.L.R. 88.

[88] If the amendment is simply to alter the sum sued for, this may be done without formal amendment: O.C.R., r. 18.1. See Vol. 1, para. 8.26.

proceed as a conventional summary cause "if he is of the opinion that a difficult question of law or a question of fact of exceptional complexity is involved".[89] He is obliged to make such a direction if jointly moved to do so by the parties.[90] Whether there is a difficult question of law or an exceptionally complex question of fact is a matter for the sheriff to decide,[91] and there is no appeal against his decision.[92] In the case of a small claim the difficulty or complexity of the case may not become apparent until a relatively late stage.

30.33   If all parties agree, a case that is proceeding as a summary cause (or indeed as an ordinary cause) may be directed to continue as a small claim.[93] It is suggested that this is a direction which the sheriff will not often be invited to give looking to the limited scope for an award of expenses in a small claim.[94] Even though a direction that an action should proceed as a small claim may be made only on joint motion, it is, rather surprisingly, specifically provided that the sheriff's decision to give such a direction is not subject to review.[95]

30.34   More understandably, as the provisions for remitting causes on joint motion under either section 37(1)(a) or section 37(2)(a) of the 1971 Act are mandatory, there is neither provision for any form of review nor a statement that the direction is not subject to review. If a sheriff, in the mistaken view that he had a discretion in the matter, were to refuse such a motion, the frustrated parties would probably have no remedy under the summary cause provisions, given the limitations on the right of appeal.[96] An application to the *nobile officium* of the Court of Session might well be the only course open in such an improbable situation.[97]

Document lost or destroyed

30.35   Rule 17.5 applies to any summons, form of response, answers to counterclaim, third-party notice or answers to a third-party notice, Register of Summary Causes or any other document lodged with the sheriff clerk in connection with a summary cause.[98] The rule provides that if any such document is lost or destroyed, a copy thereof, authenticated in such manner as the sheriff may require, may be substituted and "shall, for the purposes of the action, including the use of diligence, be equivalent to the original".[99] Similar provisions apply to ordinary causes in the sheriff court[1] and to actions in the Court of Session.[2] The mode of authentication which the sheriff may require will, it is suggested, depend on the nature of the missing document. If it is something which was lodged by a party (*e.g.* a summons) a copy certified as accurate by the

---

[89] 1971 Act, s. 37(2B)(a).
[90] *ibid.*, s. 37(2B)(b).
[91] *cf.* the comments on "importance" and "difficulty" in para. 30.29, *supra*.
[92] 1971 Act, s. 37(3)(a).
[93] *ibid.*, s. 37(2C).
[94] See paras 31.124 to 31.129, *infra*.
[95] 1971 Act, s. 37(3)(a).
[96] See the 1971 Act, s. 38, discussed below at paras 30.328, 30.329.
[97] See, however, Vol. 1, para. 18.12 and the cases therein referred to.
[98] S.C.R., r. 17.5(1).
[99] *ibid*, r. 17.5(2).
[1] O.C.R., r. 11.5. See Vol. 1, para. 8.17.
[2] R.C.S., r. 4.14.

party or his solicitor would be appropriate. If, on the other hand, it is a document kept by the court (*e.g.* a register) the copy would be certified as correct by the sheriff clerk.

Electronic transmission of documents

The increasing use of electronic means of communication is recog- **30.36** nised in the Summary Cause Rules. It is provided that any document referred to in the Rules which requires to be (a) lodged with the sheriff clerk, (b) intimated to a party, or (c) sent by the sheriff clerk, may be in either electronic or documentary form.[3] However, the provision permitting electronic transmission does not apply to any certificate of execution of service, citation or arrestment, or to a decree or extract decree of the court.[4] If a document is in electronic form it may be lodged, intimated or sent "by e-mail or similar means".[5] The time of lodgement, intimation or sending is the time when the document was sent or transmitted.[6] This provision may cause some problems as the accuracy of any time stated on the transmitted document itself will depend on the accuracy of the clock in the sender's computer. It is suggested that, if the exact time of sending or transmission is of importance, an independent note thereof should be kept. If the document is lodged with the sheriff clerk by e-mail or similar means the sheriff may require any principal document to be lodged also.[7]

Incidental applications

The summary cause equivalent of the ordinary cause motion is an **30.37** "incidental application", which is the subject of rule 9.1. Except where otherwise provided,[8] any incidental application in a summary cause may be made either (a) orally with the leave of the sheriff during any hearing of the action[9] or (b) by lodging the application in writing with the sheriff clerk.[10] The procedure for written applications has some similarities to that for motions in ordinary causes,[11] but there are also some important differences between them.[12]

A written application may be heard only after two days' notice has **30.38** been given to the other party or parties.[13] Where the party receiving notice of a written incidental application intimates to the sheriff clerk and the party making the application that it is not opposed, the application need not call in court unless the sheriff so directs.[14] Such intimation must be made not later than noon on the day before the application is due to be heard.[15]

---

[3] S.C.R., r. 35.1(1).
[4] *ibid.*, r. 35.1(2)
[5] *ibid.*, r. 35.1(1).
[6] *ibid.*, r. 35.2.
[7] *ibid.*, r. 35.1(3).
[8] *e.g.* a minute under S.C.R, r. 24.1(1) (recall of decree).
[9] S.C.R., r. 9.1(1)(a).
[10] *ibid.*, r. 9.1(1)(b).
[11] O.C.R., Chap. 15. See Vol. 1, paras 5.44 to 5.55.
[12] For example, an ordinary cause motion does not call in court unless either opposition is intimated or the sheriff so directs (O.C.R., r. 15.5) whereas an incidental application must call unless there has been intimation that it is not to be opposed, and even then the sheriff may direct that it should call (S.C.R., r. 9.1(3)).
[13] S.C.R., r. 9.1(2).
[14] *ibid.*, r. 9.1(3).
[15] *ibid.*, r. 9.1(4).

30.39 Surprisingly, there appears to be no provision in the Summary Cause Rules for the fixing of a hearing of an incidental application or of intimation thereof to be given to parties by the sheriff clerk. It is therefore difficult to see how a party is to be aware of the date when an "application is due to be heard".[16] It must be assumed that on receipt of an incidental application in writing the sheriff clerk will at once intimate it to the other parties in the case and intimate to *all* parties, including the party who has lodged the application, the date when it will be heard unless there is intimation of no opposition and the sheriff does not require that a hearing takes place.

30.40 Details of all incidental applications must be entered in the entry for the action concerned in the Register of Summary Causes.[17] These details must include where appropriate (a) whether parties are present or absent at the hearing of the application and the names of their representatives, (b) the nature of the application, and (c) the interlocutor issued or order made.[18]

Sist

30.41 An incidental application to sist a summary cause must include a statement of the reason for the sist,[19] and the reason must be recorded in the Register of Summary Causes and on the summons.[20] If an action has been sisted the sheriff may, after giving parties an opportunity to be heard, recall the sist.[21] This provision gives a sheriff the opportunity to control the progress of an action, provided that he is made aware that the action has been sisted. It is suggested that sheriff clerks should keep a diary for sisted cases and ensure that they are brought to the attention of the sheriff at regular intervals—say every three months.

Amendment

30.42 The sheriff may "on the incidental application[22] of a party, allow amendment of the summons,[23] form of response,[24] counterclaim[25] or answers to a counterclaim[26] and adjust the note of disputed issues[27] at any time before final judgment is pronounced on the merits".[28] It should be noted that, differing from amendment in an ordinary cause, in a summary cause there is no requirement to lodge a minute of amendment along with the application to amend. The terms of the proposed amendment should be contained in the incidental application itself.

30.43 The rule states that amendment includes (a) increasing or reducing the sum claimed; (b) seeking a different remedy from that originally

---

[16] S.C.R., r. 9.1(4).
[17] *ibid.*, r. 5.1(3).
[18] *ibid.*
[19] S.C.R., r. 9.2(1)(a). *Cf.* O.C.R., r. 15.6(1)(a) inserted by SSI 2000 No. 239.
[20] *ibid.*, r. 9.2(1)(b). *Cf.* O.C.R., r. 15.6(1)(b) inserted by SSI 2000 No. 239.
[21] *ibid.*, r. 9.2(2). *Cf.* O.C.R., r. 15.6(2) inserted by SSI 2000 No. 239.
[22] For incidental application see paras 30.37 to 30.40, *supra.*
[23] For summons see paras 30.67 to 30.70, *infra.*
[24] For form of response see paras 30.84 to 30.87, *infra.*
[25] For counterclaim see paras 30.132, 30.133, *infra.*
[26] For answers to counterclaim see para. 30.132; *infra.*
[27] For note of disputed issues see para. 30.139, *infra.*
[28] S.C.R., r. 13.1(1).

sought; (c) correcting or supplementing the designation of a party; (d) enabling a party to sue or be sued in a representative capacity; and (e) sisting a party in substitution for, or in addition to, the original party.[29] These are, however, only examples of the scope for amendment, which is not, according to the rules, limited in any way.[30] The sheriff's discretion appears to be unfettered. In *Visionhire v. Dick*[31] Sheriff Principal Caplan commented with regard to the equivalent provision of the 1976 Rules:

> "I know of no rule or practice which on procedural grounds alone prohibits a complete re-statement of a case set out in the condescendence by way of adjustment and regrettably it is not unknown for this to happen. . . . I can see that a question could arise if a pursuer attempted to substitute a statement of claim containing what was really a totally different kind of claim."

In an undefended action[32] the sheriff may order the amended summons to be served on the defender on such period of notice as he thinks fit.[33] **30.44**

Where an amendment sists an additional or substitute defender the sheriff orders such service and regulates further procedure as he thinks fit.[34] **30.45**

Additional defender

Any person who has not been called as a defender may apply by incidental application for leave to enter the action as a defender and to state a defence.[35] His application must specify his title and interest to enter the action and the grounds of the defence which he proposes to state.[36] When such an application is lodged the sheriff must appoint a date for hearing the application,[37] and the applicant must forthwith serve a copy of the application and of the order for hearing on the parties to the action.[38] The sheriff may grant the application if, having heard the applicant and any other party to the action, he is satisfied that the applicant has shown title and interest to enter the action.[39] If the application is granted the applicant is treated as a defender.[40] The sheriff must forthwith consider whether any decision already taken in the action on the issues in dispute between the parties requires to be reconsidered in light of the terms of the application.[41] **30.46**

---

[29] S.C.R., r. 13.1(3).

[30] *cf.* O.C.R., r. 18.2(2)(a) and R.C.S., r. 24.1(2)(a): "an amendment . . . which may be necessary for the purpose of determining the real question in controversy between the parties".

[31] Sept. 18, 1984, Kilmarnock Sh.Ct., unreported.

[32] For undefended action see paras 30.113 to 30.121, *infra*.

[33] S.C.R., r. 13.1(2).

[34] *ibid.*, r. 13.1(4).

[35] *ibid.*, r. 14.1(1).

[36] *ibid.*, r. 14.1(2).

[37] *ibid.*, r. 14.1(3)(a).

[38] *ibid.*, r. 14.1(3)(b).

[39] *ibid.*, r. 14.1(4).

[40] *ibid.*, r. 14.1(5)(a).

[41] *ibid.*, r. 14.1(5)(b).

Sist of party

30.47   If a party dies or becomes legally incapacitated while an action is depending, any person claiming to represent that party or his estate may apply by incidental application to be sisted as a party to the action.[42] If a party dies or becomes incapacitated and the provision just referred to is *not* invoked, any other party may apply by incidental application to have the action transferred in favour of or against, as the case may be, any person who represents that party or his estate.[43]

Management of damages payable to persons aged 18 or over under legal disability[44]

30.48   Where, in an action of damages, a sum becomes payable, by virtue of a decree or an extra-judicial settlement, to or for the benefit of a person under a legal disability who is aged 18 years or over, the sheriff makes such order regarding the payment and management of that sum as he thinks fit.[45] The order is made on the granting of decree for payment or of absolvitor.[46] The Summary Cause Rules provide specifically for three possible orders which the sheriff may make,[47] but it is suggested that he is not confined to these three.[48]

30.49   First, the sheriff may order the money to be paid to either the Accountant of Court or the guardian of the person under legal disability as trustee to be applied, invested or otherwise dealt with and administered under the directions of the sheriff for the benefit of the person under legal disability.[49]

30.50   Secondly, the sheriff may order the money to be paid to the sheriff clerk of the sheriff court district in which the person under legal disability resides, to be applied, invested or otherwise dealt with and administered, under the directions of the sheriff of that district.[50] Where the sheriff so orders, the sheriff clerk must accept custody of the money.[51]

30.51   An application for directions from the sheriff under either of the two preceding provisions may be made by incidental application in the cause to which the application relates by any person having an interest.[52]

30.52   Finally, the sheriff may order the money to be paid directly to the person under legal disability.[53]

---

[42] S.C.R., r. 15.1(1). This provision is virtually identical to O.C.R., r. 25.1. See Vol. 1, para. 12.10.

[43] *ibid.*, r. 15.1(2). This provision is virtually identical to O.C.R., r. 25.2. See Vol. 1, para. 12.11.

[44] The corresponding rules for ordinary causes are O.C.R., rr. 36.14–36.17. See Vol. 1, paras 21.37 to 21.42.

[45] S.C.R., r. 26.1(1). *Cf.* O.C.R., r. 36.14(1).

[46] *ibid.*, r. 26.1(2). *Cf.* O.C.R., r. 36.14(2).

[47] *ibid.*, r. 26.2. *Cf.* O.C.R., r. 36.15.

[48] *cf.* Children (Scotland) Act 1995, s. 13(1), (2). See para. 30.56, *infra.*

[49] S.C.R., r. 26.2(a). *Cf.* O.C.R., r. 36.15(b).

[50] *ibid.*, r. 26.2(b). *Cf.* O.C.R., r. 36.15(c).

[51] *ibid.*, r. 26.4(2). *Cf.* O.C.R., r. 36.17(2).

[52] *ibid.*, r. 26.3(2). *Cf.* O.C.R., r. 36.16(2).

[53] *ibid.*, r. 26.2(c). *Cf.* O.C.R., r. 36.15(d).

The sheriff clerk's receipt in Form 35 is a sufficient discharge in **30.53** respect of money paid to him in exercise of any of the sheriff's powers under rules 26.1 to 26.3.[54] Any such money paid to the sheriff clerk may be paid out, applied, invested or otherwise dealt with by him only after such intimation, service and enquiry as the sheriff may order.[55] Any money invested by the sheriff clerk may be invested only in a manner in which trustees are authorised to invest by virtue of the Trustee Investments Act 1961.[56]

Where the sheriff has made an order under rule 26.1(1),[57] any person **30.54** having an interest may apply by incidental application for any other order for the payment or management of the money.[58]

The provisions just described apply to those under legal disability who **30.55** are over 18 years of age. The following paragraphs deal with the management of damages payable to children aged under 16 years as prescribed by section 13 of the Children (Scotland) Act 1995. There is an apparent *casus omissus* in respect of persons under legal disability who are aged 16 or 17 years as such persons are not covered either by Chapter 26 of the Summary Cause Rules or by section 13 of the 1995 Act. It is unfortunate that this omission, which has been apparent for several years,[59] has still not been rectified.

Management of money payable to children

The rules concerning damages payable to or for the benefit of a child **30.56** are similar to those that have just been described in respect of other persons under legal disability, but in the case of children the rules are contained in an Act of Parliament rather than in any court rules. Section 13 of the Children (Scotland) Act 1995 provides that where in any court proceedings a sum of money becomes payable to, or for the benefit of, a child under the age of 16 years,[60] the court may make such order relating to the payment and management of the sum for the benefit of the child as it thinks fit.[61] It goes on to provide that, without prejudice to the generality of the foregoing, the court may (a) appoint a judicial factor to invest, apply or otherwise deal with the money for the benefit of the child concerned, (b) order the money to be paid to the sheriff clerk or the Accountant of Court, or to a parent or guardian of the child, to be invested, applied or otherwise dealt with, under directions of the court, for the benefit of the child, or (c) order the money to be paid directly to the child.[62] Where payment is made to a person in accordance with an order under the foregoing provisions, a receipt given by that person is a sufficient discharge of the obligation to make payment.[63] The comments made in the preceding paragraphs

---

[54] S.C.R., r. 26.4(1). *Cf.* O.C.R., r. 36.17(1).

[55] *ibid.*, r. 26.4(3). *Cf.* O.C.R., r. 36.17(3).

[56] *ibid.*, r. 26.4(4). *Cf.* O.C.R., r. 36.17(4).

[57] See paras 30.48 to 30.52, *supra*.

[58] S.C.R., r. 26.3(1). *Cf.* O.C.R., r. 36.16(1).

[59] See comment in Vol. 1, para. 21.37.

[60] A child of or over the age of 16 is presumed to have full legal capacity: Age of Legal Capacity (Scotland) Act 1991, s. 1(1)(b). There appears to be a *casus omissus* in respect of persons under legal disability aged 16 or 17. See para. 30.55, *supra*.

[61] Children (Scotland) Act 1995, s. 13(1).

[62] *ibid.*, s. 13(2).

[63] *ibid.*, s. 13(3).

about payments to persons under legal disability other than children apply equally, *mutatis mutandis*, to payments to children, and are not repeated here.

30.57 If a court has made an order in a summary cause in terms of section 13 of the 1995 Act, any application by a person for an order for the administration of the child's property in terms of section 11(1)(d) of the 1995 Act must be made in writing.[64]

Arrestment

30.58 As will be described below, a summons or a counterclaim in a summary cause may be warrant for arrestment, either on the dependence or to found jurisdiction.[65] Chapter 6 of the Summary Cause Rules contains rules of general application referring to arrestments. These rules apply to arrestments used both before and after service.

30.59 An arrestment to found jurisdiction or an arrestment on the dependence of an action used prior to service ceases to have effect unless the summons for which it is warrant is served within 21 days from the date of execution of the arrestment.[66] The party using such an arrestment must report its execution forthwith to the sheriff clerk.[67]

30.60 If an arrestment on the dependence of an action or a counterclaim has been effected, the sheriff may order that it should cease to have effect if the party whose funds or property have been arrested either pays into court the sum claimed together with the sum of £50 in respect of expenses or finds caution to the satisfaction of the sheriff clerk in respect of these sums.[68] A party whose funds or property have been arrested may also apply to the sheriff to exercise his powers to recall or restrict an arrestment on the dependence with or without consignation or caution.[69] An application for recall or restriction is made by incidental application[70] which must be intimated to the party who instructed the arrestment.[71]

30.61 If payment into court is made in terms of rule 6.3(1) or the sheriff recalls or restricts an arrestment on the dependence in terms of rule 6.3(2) and any condition imposed by the sheriff has been complied with, the sheriff clerk must (a) issue to the party whose funds or property have been arrested a certificate in Form 16 authorising the release of any sum or property arrested to the extent ordered by the sheriff, and (b) send a copy of that certificate to the party instructing the arrestment and to the party who has possession of the fund or property which has been arrested.[72]

30.62 In all cases of arrestment in a summary cause, if a schedule of arrestment has not been personally served on an arrestee, the arrestment

---

[64] S.C.R., r. 26.5.
[65] See paras 30.77 to 30.79 and 30.132, *infra.*
[66] S.C.R., r. 6.2(1).
[67] *ibid.*, r. 6.2(2).
[68] *ibid.*, r. 6.3(1).
[69] *ibid.*, r. 6.3(2). For recall and restriction of arrestment generally see Vol. 1, paras. 11.28 to 11.33.
[70] See paras 30.37 to 30.40, *supra.*
[71] S.C.R., r. 6.3(3).
[72] *ibid.*, r. 6.3(4).

will be of no effect unless a copy of the schedule has been sent by registered post or first class recorded delivery to the last known place of residence of the arrestee if the arrestee is an individual.[73] If such place of residence is not known, or if the arrestee is a firm or corporation, the copy schedule must be sent (by registered post or first class recorded delivery) to the arrestee's principal place of business, if known, or, if the principal place of business is not known, to any known place of business of the arrestee.[74] The sheriff officer must certify that this has been done on the certificate of execution of arrestment and specify the address to which the copy of the schedule was sent.[75]

European Court

In terms of the Summary Cause Rules[76] a sheriff may make a **30.63** reference to the Court of Justice of the European Communities ("the European Court")[77] either on the application of a party or of his own accord.[78] A reference may be for either (a) a preliminary ruling under Article 234 of the E.E.C. Treaty, Article 150 of the Euratom Treaty or Article 41 of the E.C.S.C. Treaty, or (b) a ruling on the interpretation of the Conventions as defined in section 1(1) of the Civil Jurisdiction and Judgments Act 1982, under Article 3 of Schedule 2 to that Act.[79]

A reference must be in the form of a request for a preliminary ruling **30.64** in Form 27.[80] This is apparently the case even though the reference is for a ruling on the interpretation of the Conventions.

If the sheriff decides that a reference is to be made he must draft a **30.65** reference within four weeks.[81] The sheriff clerk must then send a copy of the draft reference to each party to the action.[82] Within four weeks of the copy of the draft having been sent to him each party may lodge with the sheriff clerk and send to every other party a note of any adjustments which he seeks to have made to the draft reference.[83] Within 14 days after the final date for lodging adjustments the sheriff, after considering any such adjustments, must make and sign the reference.[84] It may be noted that, differing from the provisions for adjusting a stated case in the summary cause appeal procedure,[85] no provision is here made for a hearing on the proposed adjustments. As soon as the reference has actually been made and signed the sheriff clerk must intimate this fact to each party.[86] A copy of the reference, certified by the sheriff clerk, must be transmitted by him to the Registrar of the European Court.[87]

---

[73] S.C.R., r. 6.1.
[74] *ibid.*
[75] *ibid.*
[76] There are similar provisions in the Ordinary Cause Rules (O.C.R., rr. 38.1–38.5). See Vol. 1, paras 13.68 to 13.70.
[77] S.C.R., r. 20.1(1).
[78] *ibid.*, r. 20.2(1).
[79] *ibid.*, r. 20.1(1). In terms of S.C.R., r. 20.1(2) the names of the treaties have the meanings assigned to them in Sched. 1 to the European Communities Act 1972.
[80] *ibid.*, r. 20.2(2).
[81] *ibid.*, r. 20.3(1).
[82] *ibid.*, r. 20.3(2).
[83] *ibid.*, r. 20.3(3).
[84] *ibid.*, r. 20.3(4).
[85] *ibid.*, r. 25.1(5) and (6). See para. 30.334, *infra.*
[86] *ibid.*, r. 20.3(5).
[87] *ibid.*, r. 20.5.

30.66   Once a reference has been made, unless the sheriff otherwise orders, the action must be sisted until the European Court has given a preliminary ruling on the question referred to it.[88] However, the sheriff may recall any such sist for the purpose of making an interim order "which a due regard to the interests of the parties may require".[89]

5. PRE-PROOF PROCEDURE IN A STANDARD SUMMARY CAUSE

Commencement of action

Form of summons

30.67   The initiating writ in a summary cause action is a summons. Rule 4.1 provides that a summons must be in Form 1. This form is appropriate for any type of summary cause and should be adapted by the pursuer or the pursuer's solicitor according to the nature of the action.

30.68   The first page of the form is headed "Summary Cause Summons" and continues "Action for/of". There are then eight numbered boxes. In box 1 should be inserted the name, address, e-mail address and telephone number of the sheriff court in which the action is raised. In box 2 the pursuer's name and address is inserted, and in box 3 similar information is given for the person against whom the action is being raised who may be, for example, a defender, an arrestee or the holder of property in an action of multiplepoinding. Box 3a is for the name and address of any interested person, *e.g.* a connected person in an action of reparation.[90] Box 4 is for the "claim",[91] *i.e.* the decree or other order sought. Box 5 is for the name, full address, telephone number and e-mail address of the pursuer's solicitor or representative (if any). Box 5a is for the details of fee in the case of a form sent electronically to the court.[92] Each of these boxes should be completed by the pursuer, his solicitor or his representative. Of course, in some cases it will not be necessary to complete every box. For example, if there is no party interested in the action other than the pursuer and defender box 3a will be left empty.

30.69   Box 6, which is to be completed by the sheriff clerk contains the warrant to serve the summons[93] together with the date of the return day[94] and the calling date.[95]

30.70   Page 2 of the form contains a box numbered 7 in which the pursuer must insert the statement of claim.[96] There is also a space on that page headed "FOR OFFICIAL USE ONLY" which is for the sheriff on the calling date[97] to note the issues of fact and law in dispute, the facts

---

[88] S.C.R., r. 20.4(1).
[89] *ibid.*, r. 20.4(2).
[90] See paras 30.321 to 30.327, *infra*.
[91] S.C.R., r. 4.1(2) provides that the form of claim may be in one of Forms 2 to 9 inclusive, depending on the nature of the action.
[92] See para. 30.36, *supra*.
[93] See para. 30.76, *infra*.
[94] See para. 30.75, *infra*.
[95] See paras 30.75, 30.114 and 30.134 to 30.142, *infra*.
[96] See paras 30.71 to 30.73, *infra*.
[97] See paras 30.75, 30.114 and 30.134 to 30.142, *infra*.

agreed and the reasons for any final disposal at the hearing on the calling date.

Statement of claim

Rule 4.2 provides: **30.71**

"The pursuer must insert a statement of his claim in the summons to give the defender fair notice of the claim; and the statement must include—

(a) details of the basis of the claim including relevant dates; and
(b) if the claim arises from the supply of goods or services, a description of the goods or services and the date or dates on or between which they were supplied and, where relevant, ordered."

The provisions of paragraph (b) of the rule should be especially noted.[98]

The requirement to give fair notice has been emphasised by the court. **30.72** "The test must be whether from reading the statement of claim and any documents referred to therein, copies of which are attached to the summons, the defender is given fair notice of the claim which is being made against him".[99] The same point has been made in other cases under the 1976 Rules, and the comments are equally applicable today.[1] If the statement of claim does not meet this basic requirement the action may not get off the ground as the sheriff clerk and sheriff may refuse to sign the summons.[2] Even if the summons were signed by the sheriff

---

[98] "It is not in my opinion enough if the defender is referred to a document which is not produced but is stated to be in his own possession. Nor do I think it enough if a statement is produced which contains only dates or invoice numbers or both and a note of the sum due", *per* Sheriff McInnes in *Bird's Eye Foods Ltd v. Johnston*, Feb. 3, 1977, Cupar Sh.Ct., unreported. In the case of actions brought by mail order catalogue companies against their allegedly defaulting agents there are conflicting decisions on the equivalent provision in the 1976 Summary Cause Rules. In *Littlewood's Warehouses v. Adam*, 1977, Edinburgh Sh.Ct. (reported in the commentary to *GUS Catalogue Order Ltd v. Oxborrow, cit. infra* at 1987 S.C.L.R. 617) the sheriff agreed to sign the summons. In *GUS Catalogue Order Ltd v. Oxborrow* (Sh.Ct) 1987 S.C.L.R. 615 the sheriff dismissed the cause as clearly incompetent because the statement of claim did not comply with the relevant rule. The statements of claim in both cases were virtually identical and gave no details of the goods supplied, the defender in each case having acted as an agent for the pursuers. In the *Littlewoods* case the defender never entered the process. In the *GUS* case the defender appeared at the first calling and claimed not to know which transactions the summons referred to. Despite having their action dismissed the pursuers did not appeal. The issue has therefore never been decided by a sheriff principal. It is submitted that *GUS* is to be preferred and that its ratio should be applied to the present rules.
[99] *per* Sheriff McInnes in *Bird's Eye Foods Ltd v. Johnston, supra.*
[1] For example: "Elaborate pleadings are out of place in a summary cause, but it seems to me that the rules call for each party to give to the other the minimum notice, albeit in a few words, of what he hopes to prove", *per* Sheriff Principal O'Brien in *Bennett v. Livingston Development Corporation*, Oct. 29, 1979, Linlithgow Sheriff Court, unreported. "The summary cause pleader does not require to present a case which can pass a relevancy test prior to proof. He only requires to give reasonable notice of his case and he ought also to bear in mind that it is in the essential nature of the summary cause procedure that the defender may not be legally represented", *per* Sheriff Principal Caplan in *Visionhire Ltd v. Dick*, Sept. 18, 1984, Kilmarnock Sheriff Court, unreported.
[2] See para 30.74, *infra.*

clerk, the action may be dismissed by the sheriff at the first calling in terms of rule 8.3(1) as clearly incompetent.[3]

30.73 The statement of claim should clearly state the basis on which the court has jurisdiction.[4]

Authentication of summons

30.74 Before the action can be commenced by service of the summons the summons itself must be properly authenticated. This gives it official status and enables the action to be entered in the Register of Summary Causes.[5] Authentication includes giving the summons a number. Normally the summons is "authenticated in some appropriate manner" by the sheriff clerk.[6] If the sheriff clerk refuses to authenticate the summons for any reason,[7] if the defender's address is unknown[8] or if the normal period of notice specified in rule 4.5(2)[9] is altered,[10] the sheriff, and not the sheriff clerk, must authenticate the summons "if he thinks it appropriate".[11] The sheriff clerk might refuse to authenticate the summons because, for example, he was doubtful about its competency or about whether the court had jurisdiction. Although the rules are silent on the matter, it is suggested that, where a sheriff clerk has refused to authenticate a summons, the pursuer or his solicitor should be given an opportunity of making representations before the sheriff as to why the summons should be authenticated.

30.75 Whether the summons is authenticated by the sheriff clerk or by the sheriff, the sheriff clerk must insert in the summons the date of the return day (the last day on which the defender may return a form of response[12] to the sheriff clerk)[13] and the calling date (the date set for the action to call in court).[14] The calling date is seven days after the return day.[15]

Effect of summons—arrestment

30.76 The authenticated summons is warrant for service on the defender.[16] The summons does not require to be endorsed by the sheriff clerk of the sheriff court district in which it is to be executed.[17]

---

[3] See para. 30.137, *infra*. "The next issue is whether lack of specification of a statement of claim is a question of relevancy or competency. Rule 2 [the 1976 equivalent to Rule 4.2(b)] is in mandatory terms. If it is not complied with in my opinion it will follow that the summons is not competent", *per* Sheriff McInnes in *Bird's Eye Foods Ltd v. Johnston*, *supra*. See also *G.U.S. Catalogue Order Ltd v. Oxborrow*, *cit supra*.

[4] S.C.R., r. 23.1, which provides, *inter alia*, that the sheriff must not grant decree against a defender unless it is clear from the terms of the summons that a ground of jurisdiction exists.

[5] See paras 30.08 to 30.12, *supra*.

[6] S.C.R., r. 4.4(1).

[7] *ibid.*, r. 4.4(1)(a).

[8] *ibid.*, r. 4.4(1)(b).

[9] See para. 30.88, *infra*.

[10] S.C.R., r. 4.4(1)(c).

[11] *ibid.*, r. 4.4(2).

[12] For form of response see paras 30.84 to 30.87, *infra*.

[13] S.C.R., r. 4.5(6)(a).

[14] *ibid.*, r. 4.5(6)(b).

[15] *ibid.*, r. 4.5(7).

[16] *ibid.*, r. 4.4(3)(a).

[17] *ibid.*, r. 5.8.

When the appropriate provisions are included in the summons, it may **30.77** also be warrant for (i) arrestment on the dependence of the action or (ii) arrestment to found jurisdiction.[18]

It is well established that, if the debt sued for is future or contingent, **30.78** warrant to arrest on the dependence is granted only in exceptional circumstances, *e.g.* that the defender is *vergens ad inopiam* or *in meditatione fugae*.[19] Until very recently the received wisdom was that warrant to arrest on the dependence in the case of an action to recover an existing debt did not raise any difficulties and was normally granted as a matter of course. However, this view may have to be reconsidered in the light of the Outer House decision in *Karl Construction Ltd v. Palisade Properties plc*,[20] in which it was held that a warrant for inhibition on the dependence had to be justified and should not be granted as a matter of course. It is therefore suggested that in all cases where a warrant to arrest on the dependence is sought, the sheriff clerk should refuse to authenticate the summons himself, thus enabling the sheriff to consider whether the statement of claim contains sufficient information to justify granting the warrant for arrestment. If there is not sufficient information in the statement of claim the sheriff may ask the pursuer or his solicitor to address him on the matter.

Arrestment to found jurisdiction may also give rise to difficult **30.79** questions and, again, it is suggested that the sheriff clerk should refuse to authenticate a summons in which a warrant for this form of arrestment is sought.

Copy summons

A copy of the summons is served on the defender. The form of this **30.80** copy depends on the nature of the summary cause. Various forms are prescribed in the summary cause rules.

In the case of an action for payment of money where a time to pay **30.81** direction or a time order may be applied for[21] the copy summons should be in Form 1a.[22] In every other action for payment of money the copy summons should be in Form 1b.[23] In all actions which are not for and which do not include a claim for payment of money (other than multiplepoindings) the copy summons should be in Form 1c.[24] For a multiplepoinding the copy summons should be in Form 1d.[25]

In the case of each copy summons the form contains the same boxes **30.82** numbered 1 to 7 mentioned above,[26] with the exception of box 5a

---

[18] S.C.R., r. 4.4(3)(b).

[19] *Symington v. Symington* (1875) 3 R. 205. On arrestment on the dependence generally see Vol. 1, paras 11.10 to 11.35.

[20] 2002 S.L.T. 312. Although this case was concerned with inhibition on the dependence of a Court of Session action, the principle enunciated therein, *viz.* that a diligence on the dependence had to be justified in every case because of its potential human rights implications, seems logically to apply equally to arrestment on the dependence in the sheriff court. See also *Barry D. Trentham Ltd v. Lawfield Investments Ltd,* May 3, 2002, O.H., unreported.

[21] For time to pay direction and time order see paras 30.116 and 30.117, *infra.*

[22] S.C.R., r. 4.3(a)(i).

[23] *ibid.*, r. 4.3(a)(ii).

[24] *ibid.*, r. 4.3(b).

[25] *ibid.*, r. 4.3(c).

[26] See paras 30.68 to 30.70, *supra.*

(details of fee in case of electronic transmission of summons to court). Box 6 contains only the date of the return day and the calling date. These boxes should all be completed by the pursuer, his solicitor or his representative before the copy summons is served on the defender.

30.83   The form of copy summons also contains a box numbered eight, which is where details of service are to be entered. These details include the place and date of service. Box 8 is to be completed by the person serving the summons who should sign it in the appropriate space.

Form of response

30.84   The second part of the copy summons includes what is referred to in the rules as the "form of response". As the name suggests, this provides the defender with an opportunity to respond to the summons. Section A of the form of response must be completed by or on behalf of the pursuer prior to service. This duplicates certain of the information contained on the front page of the copy summons, *viz.* the address of the sheriff court, the names and addresses of the pursuer and defender, the summons number, the date of the return day and the calling date. Section B of the form of response states the various options which are open to the defender. The defender is expected to indicate which of these options he wishes to take.

30.85   There is then provided in the case of all forms of response except for that contained in Form 1d (multiplepoinding) space for the defender who is defending an action to state his defence. This space has three headings: (1) state which facts in the statement of claim are admitted; (2) state briefly any facts regarding the circumstances of the claim on which you intend to rely; (3) state details of counterclaim, if any.[27]

30.86   Again, for all actions except multiplepoindings there is provided in the form of response a form of application for service of a third-party notice.[28]

30.87   Each form of copy summons contains a page of advice to a defender telling him how he may respond to the summons. In the case of an action for payment where a time to pay direction or a time order may be applied for (Form 1a) advice is also given about these, and there is included a form of application for a direction or order as the case may be, which provides an opportunity for the defender to give details of his financial resources.

Citation

Period of notice

30.88   A summary cause action proceeds after the appropriate period of notice of the summons has been given to the defender prior to the return day.[29] The "period of notice" is the period between the date of citation and the date of the return day. The periods of notice in

---

[27] For counterclaim see paras 30.132, 30.133, *infra*.
[28] For third-party notices see paras 30.143 to 30.149, *infra*.
[29] S.C.R., r. 4.5(1). For "return day" see para. 30.75, *supra*.

summary cause actions are identical with those in ordinary cause actions, *i.e.* 21 days where the defender is resident or has a place of business within Europe, or 42 days where he is resident or has a place of business outwith Europe.[30] As in the case of ordinary actions the sheriff may, on cause shown, shorten or extend the period of notice on such conditions as to the form of service as he may direct, but subject to a lower limit of two days.[31] Again as in the case of ordinary actions, provision is made for when the period of notice expires on a Saturday, Sunday, public or local holiday. In such cases it is deemed to expire on the first following day on which the sheriff clerk's office is open for civil court business.[32] As in the case of ordinary actions, where citation is by post the period of notice runs from the beginning of the day after the date of posting.[33]

Service of summons

With the copy summons served on the defender must be enclosed a **30.89** form of service in Form 11.[34] The envelope containing the service copy summons must contain nothing other than the summons, a response or other notice in accordance with the Summary Cause Rules, and any other document approved by the sheriff principal.[35] The purpose of this provision is to prevent unauthorised documents such as information from debt collecting agencies being sent to defenders. The power given to the sheriff principal to approve a document is new. It is expected that sheriffs principal will use it to permit the enclosure of information about advisory services which would be of assistance to the defender, such as the In-court Advice Project which exists in Edinburgh Sheriff Court.

After service has been effected a certificate of execution in Form 12 **30.90** must be prepared and signed by the person effecting service.[36]

Citation of a defender with an address in Scotland

A defender with an address in Scotland may be cited either by post[37] **30.91** or by sheriff officer.[38]

A. Postal citation

Postal citation is the commonest form of citation. It may be effected **30.92** by either registered letter or recorded delivery.[39] In practice recorded delivery is almost invariably used. Citation by recorded delivery is competent only if made by first class recorded delivery service.[40] Postal citation may be effected by a sheriff officer or by a solicitor.[41] The

---

[30] S.C.R., r. 4.5(2). *Cf.* O.C.R., r. 3.6(1). See Vol. 1, paras 6.11 to 6.13.

[31] *ibid.*, r. 4.5(3). *Cf.* O.C.R., r. 3.6(2), (3).

[32] *ibid.*, r. 4.5(4). *Cf.* O.C.R., r. 3.6(4).

[33] *ibid.*, r. 4.5(5). *Cf.* O.C.R., r. 5.3(2).

[34] *ibid.*, r. 5.3(1).

[35] *ibid.*, r. 5.9.

[36] *ibid.*, r. 5.3(2).

[37] Postal citation is permitted by the Citation Amendment (Scotland) Act 1882, s. 3 and the Recorded Delivery Service Act 1962, s. 1. See Vol. 1, paras 6.19 to 6.22.

[38] Citation by sheriff officer within Scotland is governed by S.C.R., r. 5.4. See paras 30.93 to 30.98, *infra*.

[39] Citation Amendment (Scotland) Act 1882, s. 3; and Recorded Delivery Service Act 1961, ss 1, 2 and Sched.

[40] S.C.R., r. 5.6(1).

[41] Execution of Diligence (Scotland) Act 1926, s. 4; and Solicitors (Scotland) Act 1980, s. 65(2).

envelope used must have printed or written on its outside a notice indicating that it contains a communication from the sheriff court concerned and stating that, if delivery cannot be made, it is to be returned immediately to the sheriff clerk.[42] The registered letter or recorded delivery receipt must be appended to the certificate of execution of citation.[43]

B. Citation by sheriff officer

30.93 In practice citation by sheriff officer is normally used only after postal citation has been attempted and has not succeeded. However, in certain cases it may be thought desirable to cite by sheriff officer without having attempted postal citation. In such cases the cost of citation by officer may not be allowed as a valid outlay which can be recovered from the defender, unless a satisfactory explanation is given by the pursuer as to why an attempt to cite by post was not made.[44]

30.94 Citation may be effected either by an officer of the sheriff court in which the action originated or by an officer of the sheriff court in whose district citation is to be carried out.[45]

30.95 A sheriff officer may cite a defender either by tendering the summons to the defender personally[46] or by leaving it in the hands either of an inmate at the defender's dwelling-place[47] or of an employee at the defender's place of business.[48] In terms of rule 5.4(2) if, and only if, the officer is unsuccessful in either of these two methods, he may "after making diligent inquiries" serve the summons by either depositing it in the defender's dwelling-place or place of business by letterbox or by other lawful means,[49] or by affixing it to the door of the defender's dwelling-place or place of business.[50] In either case the officer must also send by ordinary post a letter containing a copy of the summons to the address at which he thinks it is most likely that the defender may be found.[51] If the provisions of rule 5.4(2) are invoked the certificate of execution of citation[52] must state the mode of service previously attempted and the circumstances which prevented such service from being effected.[53]

30.96 The certificate of execution[54] must be signed by the sheriff officer[55] and must specify whether the service was personal or, if not personal, the mode of service and the name of any person to whom the defender's copy summons was delivered.[56]

---

[42] S.C.R., r. 5.6(2) and Form 15.
[43] *ibid.*, r. 5.6(3).
[44] See Vol. 1, para. 6.18.
[45] S.C.R., r. 5.8.
[46] *ibid.*, r. 5.4(1)(a).
[47] *ibid.*, r. 5.4(1)(b)(i).
[48] *ibid.*, r. 5.4(1)(b)(ii).
[49] *ibid.*, r. 5.4(2)(a).
[50] *ibid.*, r. 5.4(2)(b).
[51] *ibid.*, r. 5.4(3).
[52] See para. 30.90, *supra*.
[53] S.C.R., r. 5.3(4).
[54] See para. 30.90, *supra*.
[55] S.C.R., r. 5.3(3)(a).
[56] *ibid.*, r. 5.3(3)(b).

In all cases of citation by sheriff officer, except where the officer is **30.97** citing by post, he must be accompanied by a witness.[57]

There is no need for the sheriff officer who effects service actually to **30.98** have the original summons with him. If the firm employing the sheriff officer (*i.e.* the sheriff officers' firm, not the instructing solicitors) has in its possession the document concerned or a copy of it certified as correct by the pursuer's solicitor, the sheriff officer may serve the document on the defender without having the document in his possession, but must, "if required to do so by the person on whom service is executed and within a reasonable time of being so required" show the document or certified copy to that person.[58] Equally, the sheriff officer effecting service does not require to have in his possession a certified copy of the interlocutor allowing service. It is sufficient that he has with him a facsimile copy of that certified copy, and he must, if required, show that facsimile to the person on whom service is executed.[59]

Citation of a defender with an address outwith Scotland

Citation of a defender with an address outwith Scotland is governed **30.99** by rule 5.7.[60]

If the defender has a known home or place of business in England, **30.100** Wales, Northern Ireland, the Isle of Man, the Channel Islands "or any country with which the United Kingdom does not have a convention providing for service of writs in that country"[61] service may be either in accordance with the rules for personal service under the domestic law of the place in which the service is to be effected,[62] or "by posting in Scotland a copy of the document in question in a registered letter addressed to the person at his residence or place of business."[63] If service under this rule is effected outside the United Kingdom, Channel Islands or Isle of Man (*i.e.* in a country with which the United Kingdom does not have a convention providing for service of writs in that country), the pursuer must lodge a certificate to the effect that the form of service employed was in accordance with the law of the place where service was effected.[64] This certificate must be given by a person who is conversant with the law of the country concerned and who practises or has practised law in that country or is a duly accredited representative of the government of that country.[65]

If service is to be effected on the defender in a country which is a **30.101** party to the Hague Convention on the Service Abroad of Judicial and Extra Judicial Documents in Civil or Commercial Matters dated November 15, 1965[66] or the European Convention on Jurisdiction and

---

[57] S.C.R., r. 5.4(4).
[58] *ibid.*, r. 5.4(5)(a).
[59] *ibid.*, r. 5.4(5)(b).
[60] *ibid.*, r. 5.7(1).
[61] *ibid.*, r. 5.7(2)(b).
[62] *ibid.*, r. 5.7(2)(ii).
[63] *ibid.*, r. 5.7(2)(i). The recorded delivery service, as an alternative to registered post, is available only in the United Kingdom, the Channel Islands and the Isle of Man.
[64] *ibid.*, r. 5.7(10).
[65] *ibid.*, r. 5.7(11).
[66] On the Hague Convention and the parties thereto see Vol. 1, para. 6.30.

Enforcement of Judgments in Civil and Commercial Matters as set out in Schedule 1 or 3C to the Civil Jurisdiction and Judgments Act 1982,[67] there are five possible ways of effecting service.[68] These are:

(1) by a method prescribed by the internal law of the country where service is to be effected for the service of documents in domestic actions upon persons who are within its territory.[69] A certificate that the service was in accordance with the law of the place where service was effected, such as is described in the preceding paragraph, must be lodged.[70]

(2) by or through a British Consular authority at the request of the Foreign Office.[71] If service is effected in this way the pursuer must send a copy of the summons and warrant for service with citation attached with a request for service to be effected by the method indicated in the request to the Secretary of State for Foreign and Commonwealth Affairs.[72] He must also lodge "in process" a certificate of execution of service signed by the authority which has effected service.[73] This latter provision, it is suggested, means that the certificate should take the place of the certificate of execution of citation provided for by rule 5.3(2).[74] This method may be used only in exceptional circumstances if service is required in a country to which Council Regulation 1348/2000 on the Service in the Member States of Judicial and Extrajudicial Documents in Civil or Commercial Matters[75] applies.[76]

(3) by or through a central authority in the country where service is to be effected at the request of the Foreign Office.[77] If service is effected in this way the same provisions apply anent sending a copy of the summons and warrant to the Foreign Secretary and lodging a certificate of execution of service as in the case of service under rule 5.8(3)(b)[78] by or through a British Consular authority at the request of the Foreign Office.[79] This method too may be used only in exceptional circumstances if service is required in a country to which Council Regulation 1348/2000 on the Service in the Member States of Judicial and Extrajudicial Documents in Civil or Commercial Matters[80] applies.[81]

(4) where the law of the country in which the person resides permits, by posting in Scotland a copy of the summons and warrant in a registered letter addressed to the person at his

---

[67] See Vol. 1, para. 6.30.
[68] S.C.R, r. 5.7(3).
[69] *ibid.*, r. 5.7(3)(a).
[70] *ibid.*, r. 5.7(10), (11).
[71] *ibid.*, r. 5.7(3)(b).
[72] *ibid.*, r. 5.7(8)(a).
[73] *ibid.*, r. 5.7(8)(b).
[74] See para. 30.90, *supra*.
[75] [2000] O.J. L 160/37.
[76] S.C.R., r. 5.7(4).
[77] *ibid.*, r. 5.7(3)(c).
[78] *ibid.*, r. 5.7(8). For S.C.R., r. 5.7(3)(b) see immediately above.
[79] *ibid.*, r. 5.7(8).
[80] [2000] O.J. L 160/37.
[81] S.C.R., r. 5.7(4).

residence.[82] It may be noted that this method of service is, on the face of it, available only where the defender is a natural person who is cited at his residence as opposed to a place of business.

(5) where the law of the country in which service is to be effected permits, service by an *huissier*, other judicial officer or competent official of the country where service is to be made.[83] If service is effected in this way the pursuer must send a copy of the summons and warrant for service with citation attached "or other document" to the official in the country in which service is to be effected, with a request for service to be effected by delivery to the defender or his residence.[84] The pursuer must also lodge "in process" a certificate of execution of service by the official who has effected service.[85] This latter provision, it is suggested, means that the certificate should take the place of the certificate of execution of citation provided for by rule 5.3(2).[86]

If service is to be effected in a country with which the United **30.102** Kingdom has a convention on the service of writs in that country, other than the conventions and regulation referred to in the preceding paragraphs, this must be done by one of the methods approved in the relevant convention.[87]

Any document which requires to be posted in Scotland for the **30.103** purposes of rule 5.7 must be posted by a solicitor or sheriff officer.[88] The forms for citation and certificate of execution of citation are specified.[89] The registered letter or recorded delivery receipt must be appended to the certificate of citation.[90] On the face of the envelope used for postal service under this rule there must be written or printed a notice in the terms of Form 15.[91]

Every summons served under rule 5.7 and every citation and notice on **30.104** the face of the envelope referred to in rule 5.7(7)[92] must be accompanied by a translation in an official language of the country in which service is to be executed unless English is an official language of that country.[93] Such a translation must be certified as correct by the person making it.[94] The certificate must contain the full name, address and qualification of the translator and must be lodged along with the certificate of execution

---

[82] S.C.R., r. 5.7(3)(d).

[83] *ibid.*, r. 5.7(3)(e).

[84] *ibid.*, r. 5.7(9)(a).

[85] *ibid.*, r. 5.7(9)(b).

[86] See para. 30.90, *supra*.

[87] S.C.R., r. 5.7(5).

[88] *ibid.*, r. 5.7(6).

[89] *ibid.*, Forms 11 and 12 respectively.

[90] *ibid.*, r. 5.6(3). Although this rule (unlike S.C.R., r. 5.6(2)) is not repeated in S.C.R., r. 5.7, it seems logical that it should apply in *all* cases of postal citation, whether in Scotland or elsewhere.

[91] *ibid.*, r. 5.7(7). Form 15 intimates that the envelope contains a document from the sheriff court and requests that it be returned immediately to the sheriff clerk if delivery cannot be effected.

[92] See para. 30.103, *supra*.

[93] S.C.R., r. 5.7(12).

[94] *ibid.*, r. 5.7(13).

of citation.[95] The rule refers only to "an" official language. Its provisions would therefore apparently be satisfied in the case of a multilingual country, such as Belgium or Switzerland, if only one of the official languages were used, notwithstanding that that language might not be the one used in the part of the country in which service was being effected.

Citation of a defender whose address is unknown

30.105   If the defender's address is unknown the sheriff may grant warrant to cite the defender by publication of an advertisement in a newspaper circulating in the area of the defender's last known address[96] or by displaying a notice on the walls of court.[97] It should be noted that it is only the sheriff and not the sheriff clerk who may competently grant a warrant for citation by advertisement or notice on the walls of court. The provisions for citation in a summary cause where the defender's whereabouts are unknown are virtually identical to those for a similar contingency in an ordinary cause.[98]

30.106   The form of advertisement is that in Form 13.[99] It states that a summary cause has been raised by the pursuer against the defender and that if the defender wishes to defend he should immediately contact the sheriff clerk, whose telephone number, fax number and e-mail address must be given in the advertisement. A copy of the newspaper containing the advertisement must be lodged with the sheriff clerk.[1]

30.107   The form of notice for display on the walls of court is in Form 14.[2] It is in terms very similar to those of the newspaper advertisement described in the previous paragraph. It must be signed by the sheriff clerk or one of his deputes and must state the date when it was first displayed. A completed copy of the notice must be provided to the sheriff clerk by the pursuer.[3]

30.108   In the case of both newspaper advertisement and notice on the walls of court the period of notice is fixed by the sheriff and runs from the date of publication of the advertisement or display of the notice, as the case may be.[4] A service copy summons must be lodged by the pursuer with the sheriff clerk.[5] The defender may uplift it if he sees and responds to the advertisement or the notice.[6]

30.109   If the address of a defender cited by advertisement or notice on the walls of court becomes known after the action has commenced, the sheriff may allow the summons to be amended and, if appropriate, grant warrant for re-service subject to such conditions as he thinks fit.[7]

---

[95] S.C.R., r. 5.7(13).
[96] *ibid.*, r. 5.5(1)(a).
[97] *ibid.*, r. 5.5(1)(b).
[98] O.C.R., r. 5.6. See Vol. 1, paras 6.33 to 6.36.
[99] S.C.R., r. 5.5(1)(a).
[1] *ibid.*, r. 5.5(6).
[2] *ibid.*, r. 5.5(1)(b).
[3] *ibid.*, r. 5.5(5).
[4] *ibid.*, r. 5.5(2).
[5] *ibid.*, r. 5.5(3).
[6] *ibid.*, r. 5.5(4).
[7] *ibid.*, r. 5.5(7).

Effect of appearance by defender

A defender who appears in an action is not entitled to object to the **30.110** regularity of the execution of service or intimation, and his appearance remedies any defect therein.[8] However, a party who appears is not precluded from pleading that the court has no jurisdiction.[9]

Re-service

Rule 5.10 provides: "(1) If it appears to the sheriff that there has been **30.111** any failure or irregularity in service upon a defender, the sheriff may order the pursuer to re-serve the summons on such conditions as he thinks fit. (2) If re-service has been ordered in accordance with paragraph (1) or rule 5.5(7)[10] the action shall proceed thereafter as if it were a new action." The sheriff may make such an order either on the motion of the pursuer or *ex proprio motu*.

Return of summons

If any appearance in court is required on the calling date[11] in respect **30.112** of any party, the summons and the relevant certificate of execution of service[12] must be returned to the sheriff clerk not later than two days before that date.[13] If no appearance by any party is required on the calling date, only the certificate of execution of service need be returned to the sheriff clerk, and this too must be done not later than two days before the calling date.[14] Failure to return the summons or the certificate of execution by the appropriate date may result in dismissal of the cause.[15] The pursuer may, of course, seek to invoke the dispensing power contained in rule 3.1.[16] It is proper that he be given an opportunity to do so should he wish.[17]

Undefended action

The 2002 Rules contain a separate chapter dealing with undefended **30.113** actions.[18] Although "undefended action" is not specifically defined in the rules, the chapter covers (a) cases in which the defender has not lodged any form of response, (b) cases in which the defender has lodged a form of response admitting the claim, (c) cases in which the defender has lodged a form of response admitting the claim and applying for a time to pay direction or time order,[19] and (d) cases in which the defender has lodged a form of response admitting the claim and indicating an intention to attend court to apply orally for time to pay.

The general rule is that an undefended action should not call in **30.114** court.[20] However, this general rule does not apply to actions for recovery

---

[8] S.C.R., r. 5.11(1).
[9] *ibid.*, r. 5.11(2).
[10] *ibid.*, r. 5.5(7) is concerned with the situation in which the whereabouts of a defender which were previously unknown become known. See para. 30.109, *supra*.
[11] *ibid.*, r. 5.12. See paras 30.114, 30.134, *infra*.
[12] See para. 30.90, *supra*.
[13] S.C.R., r. 5.12(1).
[14] *ibid.*, r. 5.12(2).
[15] *ibid.*, r. 5.12(3).
[16] See paras 30.13 to 30.15, *supra*.
[17] *Calcranes v. Aberdeen Northern Transport*, 1978 S.L.T. (Sh.Ct.) 52.
[18] S.C.R., Chap. 7.
[19] For time to pay direction and time order see paras 30.116 and 30.117, *infra*.
[20] S.C.R., r. 7.1(1)(a).

of possession of heritable property[21] or actions for sequestration of rent,[22] both of which must call on the calling date even though no form of response has been lodged.[23] Actions of multiplepoinding[24] and actions of count reckoning and payment[25] have their own special rules. Where the defender has lodged a form of response admitting the claim and stating that he intends to apply orally for time to pay,[26] or where the pursuer has not accepted an application for time to pay lodged by the defender,[27] the case must call in court on the calling date.[28]

30.115 Subject to these exceptions, where the defender has not lodged a form of response and the pursuer has, before close of business on the second day before the calling date, lodged a minute in the prescribed form,[29] the case does not call in court, and the sheriff may grant decree with expenses against the defender if "satisfied that he does not intend to defend the action on the merits or on the amount of the sum due".[30] If the pursuer fails to lodge a minute the sheriff must dismiss the action.[31] If the sheriff is not prepared to grant the order sought by the pursuer in his minute, the sheriff clerk must fix a time and place for the pursuer to be heard thereon and must inform the pursuer of that time and place, and of the reason why the sheriff wishes to hear him.[32]

Time to pay direction

30.116 In terms of section 1 of the Debtors (Scotland) Act 1987 a defender in an action for payment may, in certain circumstances, apply for a time to pay direction. The cases in which such an application is not competent are set out in detail in section 1(5) of the 1987 Act and are beyond the scope of this chapter. In practice, in most straightforward summary causes for payment of money a time to pay direction would be competent. A time to pay direction is an order for payment either by instalments at such intervals as the court may order or as a lump sum after such period as the court may order.[33]

Time order

30.117 In terms of section 129 of the Consumer Credit Act 1974 in an action brought by a creditor or owner to enforce a regulated agreement or any security or to recover possession of any goods or land to which a

---

[21] S.C.R., r. 7.1(4)(a). For actions for recovery of possession of heritable property see paras 30.261 to 30.284, *infra*.

[22] *ibid.*, r. 7.1(4)(b). For actions of sequestration for rent see paras 30.285 to 30.291, *infra*.

[23] *ibid.*, r. 7.1(4).

[24] *ibid.*, r. 7.1(5) providing that S.C.R., r. 27.9(1)(a) is to be followed. See paras 30.243 to 30.254, *infra*.

[25] *ibid.*, r. 7.1(6) providing that S.C.R., r. 29.2 is to be followed. See paras 30.257 to 30.260, *infra*.

[26] *ibid.*, r. 7.2(1)(b). See para. 30.120, *infra*.

[27] *ibid.*, r. 7.2(4). See para. 30.119, *infra*.

[28] *ibid.*, r. 7.2(5).

[29] *ibid.*, r. 7.1(1)(b). The form is Form 17.

[30] *ibid.*, r. 7.1(7). This rule is rather oddly worded. It appears to provide for two possible situations: *either* the defender has failed to lodge a form of response; *or* the sheriff is satisfied that the defender does not intend to defend the action. However, it is suggested that it must be interpreted as set out in the text.

[31] S.C.R., r. 7.1(2).

[32] *ibid.*, r. 7.1(3).

[33] Debtors (Scotland) Act 1987, s. 1(1).

regulated agreement[34] relates,[35] a court may make a time order. A time order may provide for payment of any sum owed by such instalments as the court considers reasonable[36] and/or the remedying by the debtor or hirer of any breach of a regulated agreement (other than non-payment of money) within such period as the court may specify.[37]

Application for time to pay direction or time order

If a defender admits the claim but wishes to apply in writing for a time **30.118** to pay direction[38] (and also possibly recall or restriction of an arrestment on the dependence) or a time order[39] he should complete the form of response and return it to the sheriff clerk on or before the return day.[40] If the pursuer does not object to the defender's application he should intimate this fact before close of business "on the day occurring two days before the calling date", by lodging a minute in the prescribed form.[41] If the pursuer lodges such a minute the sheriff may grant decree in terms of the application for the time to pay direction.[42] This is done on the calling date in the absence of the parties and without the case calling in court.[43] If the pursuer fails to lodge a minute the sheriff may dismiss the action.[44]

If the pursuer is opposed to a written application for a time to pay **30.119** direction he must intimate this fact before close of business "on the day occurring two days before the calling date", by lodging a minute in the prescribed form.[45] There is no provision in the rules for intimation of this minute to be made to the defender, although in practice it is likely that the sheriff clerk will intimate to the defender the pursuer's opposition to the application. The case calls in court on the calling date, and the sheriff must decide whether to grant decree in terms of the application for the time to pay direction or in some other form.[46] There is no need for the parties to appear before the sheriff,[47] but it is clearly desirable for a party to appear if he wishes to make any representations to the sheriff. Where a defender has lodged a written application for a time to pay direction or time order and the pursuer fails to lodge either a minute stating that he does not object[48] or a minute opposing the

---

[34] In terms of the Consumer Credit Act 1974, s. 189 "regulated agreement" means a consumer credit agreement or consumer hire agreement other than an exempt agreement. In terms of the same section "exempt agreement" means an agreement specified in or under s. 16 of the 1974 Act.

[35] 1974 Act, s. 129(1)(c).

[36] *ibid.*, s. 129(2)(a).

[37] *ibid.*, s. 129(2)(b).

[38] See para. 30.116, *supra*.

[39] See para. 30.117, *supra*.

[40] S.C.R., r. 7.2(1)(a).

[41] *ibid.*, r. 7.2(2). The form is Form 18. It is not clear why the wording of this rule and of rule 7.2(4) (see para. 30.119, *infra*) is different from that of S.C.R., r. 7.1(1)(b) which provides for the pursuer's lodging of a minute for decree where there has been no form of response lodged (see para. 30.115, *supra*).

[42] *ibid.*, r. 7.2(3).

[43] *ibid.*

[44] *ibid.*, r. 7.2(7).

[45] *ibid.*, r. 7.2(4). The form is Form 19.

[46] *ibid.*, r. 7.2(5).

[47] *ibid.*, r. 7.2(6). Indeed the rule provides that the sheriff *shall* decide the application whether or not any of the parties appears.

[48] Form 18.

application,[49] the sheriff may dismiss the action.[50] It is suggested that this draconian step is unlikely to be taken very often and that a more probable disposal would be for the sheriff to grant the application for the time to pay direction or time order.

30.120 A defender may wish to make an oral application for a time to pay direction (and also possibly recall or restriction of an arrestment) or a time order rather than doing so in writing. He should intimate his intention by completing the appropriate part of the form of response.[51] In that event the case will call in court on the calling date and the sheriff must decide the application and grant decree accordingly.[52] The sheriff may hear and dispose of the case in the absence of the pursuer and may do so even if neither party appears,[53] although in the latter case he would have little alternative but to grant decree in favour of the pursuer provided he had lodged a minute in Form 17.[54]

30.121 In any undefended action the sheriff is not entitled to grant decree unless it is clear from the terms of the summons that a ground of jurisdiction exists.[55] If the summons in such an action has been served in a country to which the Hague Convention on the Service Abroad of Judicial and Extrajudicial Documents in Civil or Commercial Matters of November 15, 1965 applies, the sheriff must not grant decree until it is established to his satisfaction that the requirements of Article 15 of that Convention have been complied with.[56] The requirements of Article 15 are that decree should not be granted until it has been established that (a) the document was served by a method prescribed by the internal law of the state concerned, or (b) the document was actually delivered to the defender or to his residence by another method provided by the Convention.[57]

Recall of decree

30.122 Although the provisions for recall of decree apply to certain defended actions as well as to undefended actions, most applications for recall are made where an undefended decree has been granted. It is therefore appropriate that the subject should be dealt with in this part of the chapter.

30.123 In certain circumstances a decree may be recalled.[58] In terms of the 1976 Summary Cause Rules recall of decree could be applied for in the case of a defender against whom an undefended decree had passed and of a pursuer who had failed to attend a first calling at which the defender was present or represented.[59] These were the only circumstances in which recall of decree was competent. The present rule permits recall in

---

[49] Form 19.
[50] S.C.R., r. 7.2(7).
[51] *ibid.*, r. 7.2((1)(b).
[52] *ibid.*, r. 7.2(5).
[53] *ibid.*, r. 7.2(6).
[54] See para. 30.115, *supra.*
[55] S.C.R., r. 23.1.
[56] *ibid.*, r. 7.3(1).
[57] See Vol. 1, para. 3.56.
[58] S.C.R., r. 24.1.
[59] 1976 Rules, r. 19(1).

other circumstances also. A party may now apply for recall of a decree granted under rule 7.1 or rule 8.2(5), (6) or (7).[60] Rule 7.1 provides for the granting of a decree against a defender who fails to lodge a form of response[61] and also for the granting of decree of dismissal against a pursuer who fails to minute for decree.[62] Rule 8.2 applies to defended actions. Rule 8.2(5) provides for the granting of decree against a defender who has lodged a form of response but then fails to appear or be represented on the calling date.[63] Rule 8.2(6) provides for the dismissal of an action where the pursuer fails to appear or be represented on the calling date and the defender is present or represented.[64] Rule 8.2(7) provides for the dismissal of an action where all parties fail to appear on the calling date.[65]

A pursuer against whom decree of dismissal has been granted must **30.124** apply for recall within 14 days of the grant of decree.[66] A defender or third party against whom decree has been granted or a pursuer against whom decree in a counterclaim has been granted must normally apply for recall not later than 14 days after the execution of the charge or execution of arrestment or other intimation of decree, whichever first occurs.[67] Where an action has been served outwith the United Kingdom under rule 5.7[68] the minute for recall must be lodged "within a reasonable time after [the party] had knowledge of the decree against him or in any event before the expiry of one year from the date of that decree".[69]

All applications for recall are made by lodging with the sheriff clerk a **30.125** minute in Form 30.[70] The minute must explain "the party's failure to appear".[71] It may be assumed that this is intended to mean that an explanation for the failure should be given. The reason for this provision is obscure as the sheriff has no discretion to refuse an application for recall.[72] In the case of a defender against whom decree has been granted the minute must state his proposed defence.[73] In the case of a pursuer against whom decree in a counterclaim has been granted the minute must state his proposed answer to the counterclaim.[74]

When a minute for recall is lodged the sheriff clerk must fix a date, **30.126** time and place for a hearing on the minute.[75] Once a hearing has been fixed the party seeking recall must, not less than seven days before the date fixed for the hearing, serve on the other party a copy of the minute

---

[60] S.C.R., r. 24.1(1).
[61] *ibid.*, r. 7.1(7). See para. 30.115, *supra.*
[62] *ibid.*, r. 7.1(2). See para. 30.115, *supra.*
[63] See para. 30.136, *infra.*
[64] See para. 30.136, *infra.*
[65] See para. 30.136, *infra.*
[66] S.C.R., r. 24.1(3).
[67] S.C.R., r. 24.1(4)(ii).
[68] See paras 30.100, 30.101, *supra.*
[69] S.C.R., r. 24.1(4)(i).
[70] *ibid.*, r. 24.1(1).
[71] *ibid.*
[72] S.C.R., r. 24.1(7) provides that the sheriff *shall* recall the decree so far as not implemented.
[73] *ibid.*, r. 24.1(1)(a)(i).
[74] *ibid.*, r. 24.1(1)(b)(ii).
[75] *ibid.*, r. 24.1(5).

and a note of the date, time and place of the hearing.[76] On receipt of the copy minute any party in possession of an extract decree must return it to the sheriff clerk forthwith.[77] The lodging and service of the minute have the effect of preventing any further action being taken to enforce it by the party holding the decree.[78] If it appears to the sheriff that there has been any failure or irregularity in service of the minute he may order re-service on such conditions as he thinks fit.[79]

30.127 At the hearing the sheriff must recall the decree so far as not implemented.[80] The sheriff has no discretion in the matter. In a case proceeding under the 1976 Rules it was held in the sheriffdom of Tayside, Central and Fife that it is not necessary for the minute itself to be in court so long as the minuter is present or represented.[81] It is submitted that this is correct. After the decree has been recalled the hearing proceeds as if it were a hearing in terms of rule 8.3.[82]

30.128 In a case subject to the 1976 Rules the question was considered but not decided whether there was a right of appeal against a refusal by a sheriff to grant a motion for recall of decree where a minute had been properly lodged under the equivalent of rule 24.1(1).[83] As the granting of such a motion is mandatory where the minute has been lodged and served, cases of refusal to allow recall should be rare in the extreme. In an unreported case in Tayside, Central and Fife where recall had been refused, the sheriff principal held that the appeal was competent and allowed recall.[84] It is submitted that this is correct and that, in the unlikely event of a sheriff's refusing to grant recall, an appeal is competent and is bound to be granted. Otherwise the party seeking recall would be denied a remedy to which rule 24.1 clearly states he is entitled as of right.

30.129 Each party may apply for recall of a decree in the action on one occasion only.[85]

30.130 Where a party has failed timeously to lodge a minute in terms of rule 24.1(1) there is no reason in principle why it should not be open to him to move the court to exercise its dispensing power under rule 3.1 to allow the minute to be lodged late.[86] The sheriff's decision to refuse such a motion would, however, not be appealable to the sheriff principal as it would not be a "final judgment".[87]

---

[76] S.C.R., r. 24.1(6). The copy of the minute is in Form 30a.

[77] *ibid.*, r. 24.1(9).

[78] *ibid.*, r. 24.1(8).

[79] *ibid.*, r. 24.1(10).

[80] *ibid.*, r. 24.1(7).

[81] *Bell v. Thoro-Glaze Ltd*, Sept. 17, 1982, Sheriff Principal Taylor, Alloa Sh.Ct., unreported: "In my view one should not require a further implied condition of regularity, namely that the minute should be in court, because the minute contains no averments which the court has to consider. In this respect it is not like a reponing note, which contains explanations, and about which the court has to exercise a discretion".

[82] S.C.R., r. 24.1(7). For rule 8.3 see paras 30.137 to 30.142, *infra*.

[83] *W. Jack Baillie Associates v. Kennedy*, 1985 S.L.T. (Sh.Ct) 53.

[84] *Bell v. Thoro-Glaze Ltd, supra.*

[85] S.C.R., r. 24.1(2).

[86] See paras 30.13 to 30.15, *supra*.

[87] *W. Jack Baillie Associates v. Kennedy, supra.* For the competency of an appeal to the sheriff principal see paras 30.328, 30.329, *infra*.

Defended action

A defended action is one in which the defender has completed and **30.131**
lodged with the sheriff clerk a form of response[88] stating that he intends
(a) to challenge the jurisdiction of the court or the competency of the
action or (b) to defend the action (whether as regards the amount
claimed or otherwise) or (c) to state a counterclaim.[89] When the sheriff
clerk receives such a response from the defender he must intimate a
copy thereof to the pursuer.[90]

Counterclaim

A defender who intends to plead a counterclaim must state his **30.132**
counterclaim in the appropriate space in the form of response.[91] A
defender lodging a counterclaim may apply for warrant for arrestment
on the dependence in respect of the sum counterclaimed.[92] He does this
by appending to the counterclaim the words "warrant for arrestment
on the dependence applied for".[93] On receipt of a counterclaim in this
form the sheriff clerk, having consulted the sheriff and obtained his
agreement to the granting of the warrant,[94] writes thereon the words
"Grants warrant as craved" and authenticates it "in an appropriate
manner".[95] This warrant has the same effect as it would have had in a
summons.[96] A pursuer who intends to oppose a counterclaim must lodge
answers within seven days of the lodging of the form of response.[97] A
copy of the answers must at the same time be intimated to every other
party to the action.[98]

Under the pre-1976 summary cause procedure questions arose as to **30.133**
the effect of a counterclaim the crave in which was for a sum higher
than the summary cause limit. There are two conflicting decisions on the
matter, both given by sheriffs principal of Lanarkshire.[99] It is submitted
that, as was held in the later of these two cases, the fact that there is a
counterclaim for a sum higher than the summary cause limit should not
ipso facto make it incompetent for the cause to remain on the summary
cause roll. If a defender chooses to make his claim by way of a
counterclaim in a summary cause action, he must surely be deemed to
have accepted the summary cause procedure and its limitations. More-
over, the provisions of section 37(2) of the 1971 Act regarding the
transformation of a summary cause into an ordinary action[1] provide both

---

[88] See paras 30.84 to 30.87, *supra*.
[89] S.C.R., r. 8.1(1).
[90] *ibid.*, r. 8.1(2).
[91] Forms 1a, 1b and 1c. See paras 30.84 to 30.87, *supra*.
[92] S.C.R., r. 10.1(3). For arrestment on the dependence see paras 30.58 to 30.62 *supra*.
[93] *ibid.*, r. 10.1(4).
[94] See para. 30.78 and n. 20 *supra*.
[95] S.C.R., r. 10.1(4). The "appropriate manner" of authentication would, it is suggested,
normally be by signing and dating the warrant.
[96] *ibid.*, r. 10.1(5).
[97] *ibid.*, r. 10.1(1).
[98] *ibid.*, r. 10.1(2).
[99] In *Gottlieb v. Fons Potent Inkwell Ltd*, 1917 1 S.L.T. 331, it was held that the cause
should be remitted to the ordinary roll. In *Cleave and Son Ltd v. Letters & Co. Ltd* (1929)
45 Sh.Ct. Rep. 223, however, decree for a sum contained in a counterclaim and higher
than the summary cause pecuniary limit was held to be competent under summary cause
procedure.
[1] See paras 30.29 to 30.31, *supra*.

parties with the opportunity of seeking that the nature of the cause be changed.

Hearing—calling date

30.134   Where a defender has lodged a form of response in accordance with rule 8.1(1)[2] the case must call in court for a hearing.[3] The hearing takes place on the calling date,[4] which will have been stated in the copy summons served on the defender and which is seven days after the return day.[5]

30.135   The hearing may be continued by the sheriff to "such other date as he considers to be appropriate".[6]

30.136   A defender who has lodged a form of response in accordance with rule 8.1 must be either present or represented at the hearing.[7] If the defender, having lodged a form of response, fails to attend or be represented at the hearing at which the pursuer is present or represented the sheriff may grant decree against the defender in terms of the summons,[8] provided that it is clear from the terms of the summons that a ground of jurisdiction exists.[9] If the defender is present or represented at the hearing but the pursuer is neither present nor represented the sheriff must dismiss the action.[10] It may be noted that the sheriff is given no discretion in this situation.[11] Furthermore, if the defender has intimated a counterclaim in his form of response, the sheriff may grant decree in terms thereof.[12] If all parties fail to appear at the hearing the sheriff must "unless sufficient reason appears to the contrary" dismiss the action and any counterclaim.[13] In all these cases the decree granted may be recalled.[14]

30.137   If, at the hearing, the sheriff is satisfied that the action is incompetent or that there is a patent defect of jurisdiction, he must dismiss the action or, if appropriate, transfer it to another court in terms of rule 16.1(2).[15] An example of incompetence, which has already been referred to,[16] is that the statement of claim does not meet the basic requirements of such a document. The incompetence must be "patent on the face of the action".[17] The sheriff should state briefly the grounds of his decision.[18]

---

[2] See para. 30.131, *supra.*

[3] S.C.R., r. 8.2(1).

[4] *ibid.,* r. 8.2(2).

[5] *ibid.,* r. 4.5(7). For return day see para. 30.75, *supra.*

[6] *ibid.,* r. 8.2(3). Note that there is no limit placed on either the length of such a continuation or the number of times it may be made. Contrast this with the equivalent 1976 rule (r. 18(3)), which restricted a continuation to a maximum period of 28 days and to one occasion only.

[7] *ibid.,* r. 8.2(4).

[8] *ibid.,* r. 8.2(5).

[9] *ibid.,* r. 23.1.

[10] *ibid.,* r. 8.2(6).

[11] Contrast this with the recommended procedure in a summary application where the pursuer fails to appear or be represented at a first hearing. See Vol. 1, para. 25.20.

[12] S.C.R., r. 8.2(6).

[13] *ibid.,* r. 8.2(7).

[14] *ibid.,* Chap. 24. See paras 30.122 to 30.130, *supra.*

[15] *ibid.,* r. 8.3(1). For S.C.R., r. 16.1(2) see paras 30.24, 30.25 *supra.*

[16] See para. 30.72, *supra.*

[17] *per* Sheriff Principal O'Brien in *Shoker v. Buchanan,* Nov. 18, 1983, Edinburgh Sh.Ct., unreported.

[18] S.C.R., r. 8.18(1) which applies to the decision of a sheriff made at a hearing under rule 8.2 as well as to a decision made after proof.

If there is no problem about competency or jurisdiction the hearing **30.138** proceeds in accordance with the remaining parts of rule 8.3. The intention of the rule is that the sheriff should be interventionist. He must first ascertain the factual basis of the action and any defence and the legal basis on which the action and defence are proceeding.[19] Having done that he must seek to negotiate and secure settlement of the action between the parties.[20] This provision suggests that the sheriff should act as a sort of mediator or arbiter. It is perhaps open to question how many sheriffs, used as they are to adversarial procedures, have the skills necessary to fulfil this role. From the practical point of view, if the parties are represented by solicitors, the sheriff may consider continuing the hearing in order to enable the solicitors to negotiate.[21] If either of the parties is unrepresented the scope for this approach is more limited.

If the sheriff is unable to secure a settlement he must identify and **30.139** note on the summons the issues of fact and law which are in dispute.[22] This is a most important provision.[23] In order to comply with it the sheriff will almost certainly have to read the statement of claim and the form of response prior to the hearing, and at the hearing he will have to ask detailed questions of the parties or their representatives. The sheriff must also note on the summons any facts which are agreed.[24]

If it appears to the sheriff that the claim as stated or any defence **30.140** stated in response to it is not soundly based in law in whole or in part, he should hear parties on that matter and may grant decree in favour of any party.[25] This provision is to be welcomed. Under the 1976 Rules the sheriff was not permitted to consider any question of law until after the facts had been established,[26] which resulted on occasions in a case proceeding to proof even though the statement of claim or the defence was clearly irrelevant. The present rule provides that the sheriff should hear parties "forthwith",[27] which implies that he should do so at the first calling of the case. However, it is suggested that, unless the legal point involved is completely straightforward, it would usually be appropriate to continue the hearing to a later date. Whenever he makes his decision the sheriff must briefly give reasons for it.[28]

If the sheriff is satisfied that the claim and any defence have or may **30.141** have a sound basis in law and that the dispute between the parties depends upon resolution of disputed issues of fact, he must fix a diet of proof,[29] unless he is satisfied that the facts of the case are sufficiently

---

[19] S.C.R., r. 8.3(2)(a).

[20] *ibid.*, r. 8.3(2)(b).

[21] As has been pointed out above (para. 30.135 and n.6) there is no limit on the number of continuations nor on their length.

[22] S.C.R., r. 8.3(3)(a).

[23] *cf.* A.S. (Small Claim Rules) 1988, Sched., r. 13(5), which made provision for the sheriff to note disputed issues and which in some courts was more honoured in the breach than in the observance.

[24] S.C.R., r. 8.3(3)(b).

[25] *ibid.*, r. 8.3(3)(c).

[26] 1976 S.C.R., r. 18(7).

[27] S.C.R., r. 8.3(3)(c).

[28] *ibid.*, r. 8.18(1) which applies to the decision of a sheriff made at a hearing under rule 8.2 as well as to a decision made after proof.

[29] *ibid.*, r. 8.3(3)(d).

agreed. In the latter case he should "forthwith" hear parties on the merits of the action and may grant decree in whole or in part in favour of any party.[30] Again, there may be merit on some occasions in adjourning the case before hearing submissions on agreed facts.

30.142	If the sheriff fixes a proof the sheriff clerk makes up a folder for the case papers, and all documents in the case are placed therein.[31]

Third-party procedure

30.143	In the 2002 Rules, in contrast with the 1976 Rules, there is provision for the bringing of a third-party into an action.[32] The circumstances in which a third-party may be introduced in a summary cause are virtually identical to those relating to third parties in an ordinary cause.[33]

30.144	Thus, a defender may apply for an order for service of a third-party notice on a person who is not already a party to the action, if he claims either (a) that he has in respect of the subject-matter of the action a right of contribution, relief or indemnity against that person, or (b) that that person, whom the pursuer is not bound to call as a defender, should be made a party to the action along with the defender in respect that that person is either (i) solely liable, or jointly and severally liable with the defender, to the pursuer in respect of the subject-matter of the action, or (ii) liable to the defender in respect of a claim arising from or in connection with the liability, if any, of the defender to the pursuer.[34]

30.145	An application by a defender for an order for service of a third-party notice must be made at the time when the defender lodges a form of response unless the sheriff, on cause shown, permits a later application.[35] A defender applying for such an order may apply for warrant for arrestment to found jurisdiction or to arrest on the dependence as if the claim made by him had been made in a separate action.[36] A certified copy of the interlocutor granting warrant for arrestment is sufficient authority for its execution.[37]

30.146	A pursuer against whom a counterclaim is made and a third-party who is already in the action may also apply for an order for service of a third-party notice against a person in the same circumstances, *mutatis mutandis*, as apply to a defender as set out above.[38] A pursuer or third-party who applies for such an order has the same right to apply for a warrant to arrest to found jurisdiction or on the dependence as has a defender under rule 11.3.[39]

---

[30] S.C.R., r. 8.3(3)(d).

[31] *ibid.*, r. 8.3(4). *Cf*. O.C.R., r. 9.5. See Vol. 1, para. 8.10.

[32] S.C.R., Chap. 11.

[33] For third-party procedure in ordinary causes see O.C.R., Chap. 20 and Vol. 1, paras 12.42 *et seq.*

[34] S.C.R., r. 11.1(1).

[35] *ibid.*, r. 11.1(2).

[36] S.C.R., r. 11.3(1). It is suggested that such an application should be considered by the sheriff rather than the sheriff clerk. See para. 30.78 and n.6, *supra*.

[37] S.C.R., r. 11.3(2).

[38] *ibid.*, r. 11.1(3).

[39] *ibid.* It is suggested that such an application should be considered by the sheriff rather than the sheriff clerk. See para. 30.78 and n.6, *supra*.

The rules provide that all applications for an order for service of a **30.147** third-party notice should be made by incidental application.[40] However, as has been already noted,[41] the form of response for all actions except multiplepoindings contains a form of application for service of a third-party notice. This form should be used by a defender who applies for such an order. A pursuer or third-party already convened in the action who seeks an order should proceed by way of a conventional incidental application.

If the sheriff grants the application for an order for service of a third- **30.148** party notice he must (a) fix a date for a hearing at which he will regulate further procedure and (b) grant warrant for service on the third-party of (i) a copy of the summons, (ii) a copy of the grounds upon which it is claimed that the third-party is liable, and (iii) a third-party notice in the prescribed form and a copy of the prescribed form of response.[42] The party who has obtained the order for service of the third-party notice must, before the date of the hearing, lodge with the sheriff clerk a copy of the notice with the certificate of service attached.[43]

A third-party who seeks to answer the claim made against him must **30.149** lodge his form of response no later than seven days before the hearing referred to in the preceding paragraph.[44] On receipt of any form of response the sheriff clerk must intimate a copy thereof to the other parties to the action.[45]

Procedure prior to proof

Hearing parts of action separately

It is open to the sheriff, in any action which includes a claim for **30.150** payment of money, either of his own accord or on the application of any party, to order that proof on liability or some other specified issue should be heard separately from proof on any other issue and to determine the order in which the proofs are to be heard.[46] At the conclusion of the first proof the sheriff pronounces such interlocutor as he thinks fit.[47]

Remit to person of skill

A remit to a "person of skill, or other person, to report on any matter **30.151** of fact" may be made by the sheriff on application by any party or on joint application.[48] If the remit is made by joint application or of consent of all parties, the report of such person is final and conclusive with

---

[40] S.C.R., r. 11.1(1).
[41] See para. 30.86, *supra*.
[42] S.C.R., r. 11.2(1). The form of third-party notice is Form 22. The form of response is Form 23.
[43] *ibid.*, r. 11.2(2). This rule refers only to "the defender" but rule 11.1(3) provides that the provisions of rule 11.2 are to apply *mutatis mutandis* to a pursuer or a third party who has already been convened who has applied for a third-party notice in terms of S.C.R., r. 11.1(2).
[44] S.C.R., r. 11.2(3). The form of response is Form 23.
[45] *ibid.*, r. 11.2(4).
[46] *ibid.*, r. 8.9(1).
[47] *ibid.*, r. 8.9(2).
[48] *ibid.*, r. 8.4(1).

respect to the subject-matter of the remit.[49] Where the remit is made on the application of one party the expenses thereof must in the first instance be met by that party.[50] However, if the remit is made on joint application or of consent of all parties, the expenses must, in the first instance, be met by the parties equally unless the sheriff otherwise orders.[51]

Inspection and recovery of documents

30.152   The provision in the Summary Cause Rules for the inspection and recovery of documents is in terms very similar to those for the standard procedure in the Ordinary Cause Rules.[52] Within 28 days after the fixing of a proof each party must intimate to every other party, and lodge with the sheriff clerk, a list of the documents (which either are or have been in his possession or control) which he intends to use or put in evidence at the proof, including a statement of the whereabouts of those documents.[53] A party who has received such a list may inspect those documents which are in the possession or control of the party intimating the list at a time and place fixed by that party which is reasonable to both parties.[54] The provisions of this rule do not affect the law relating, or the right of a party to object, to the inspection of a document on the ground of privilege or confidentiality.[55] The right of a party to apply for a commission and diligence for recovery of documents or an order under section 1 of the Administration of Justice (Scotland) Act 1972 is preserved.[56]

Agreement of evidence

30.153   Where possible parties must agree photographs, sketch plans and any statement or document not in dispute.[57] It is open to question whether this rule is anything more than an expression of a pious hope, especially given the use of the words "where possible". The only sanction against failure to comply with it would presumably be an award of expenses against the recalcitrant party. However, if all parties have failed to take any steps to reach agreement it is difficult to see what the sheriff could do about it.

Exchange of lists of witnesses

30.154   Again, the provision in the Summary Cause Rules for the exchange of lists of witnesses is very similar to that for standard procedure in the Ordinary Cause Rules.[58] Within 28 days of the fixing of a proof each party must intimate to every other party, and lodge with the sheriff clerk, a list of witnesses, including any skilled witnesses, whom he intends to

---

[49] S.C.R., r. 8.4(2).
[50] *ibid.*, r. 8.4(3)(a).
[51] *ibid.*, r. 8.4(3)(b).
[52] O.C.R., r. 9.13.
[53] S.C.R., r. 8.5(1).
[54] *ibid.*, r. 8.5(2).
[55] *ibid.*, r. 8.5(3)(a).
[56] *ibid.*, r. 8.5(3)(b). For commission and diligence (S.C.R., r. 18.1) see paras 30.162 to 30.168, *infra*. For orders under the Administration of Justice (Scotland) Act 1972, s. 1 (S.C.R., r. 18.3) see paras 30.169 to 30.173, *infra*.
[57] S.C.R., r. 8.8.
[58] O.C.R., r. 9.14. See Vol. 1, para. 16.01.

call to give evidence.[59] This list must include the name and address of each witness and (where known) his occupation.[60] A witness who is not on a party's list may be called to give evidence by that party only if no other party objects, or, if any party does object, with leave of the sheriff.[61] The sheriff may grant leave on such conditions as he thinks fit.[62]

Exchange of reports of skilled witnesses

Not less than 28 days before the date of a proof a party who intends to **30.155** call a "skilled person" to give evidence must disclose to every other party in the form of a written report the substance of the evidence of such a person.[63] A copy of the report must also be lodged "in process".[64] Except "on special cause shown", a party may not call as a skilled witness any person the substance of whose evidence has not been so disclosed.[65]

Lodging of productions

A party intending to rely at a proof on any documents[66] or articles in **30.156** his possession, which are reasonably capable of being lodged in court must, no later than 14 days before the proof, lodge them with the sheriff clerk together with a list detailing the items lodged.[67] At the same time he must send a copy of the list to the other parties.[68] In addition a party lodging a document must send a copy of it to every other party unless it is not practicable to do so.[69]

Unless all parties consent or with the permission of the sheriff on **30.157** cause shown and on such terms as to expenses or otherwise as the sheriff considers proper,[70] only certain documents or articles may be used or put in evidence. These are: (a) documents or articles lodged with the sheriff clerk no later than 14 days before the proof in accordance with rule 17.1(1) as described in the previous paragraph[71]; (b) documents produced at a hearing under rule 8.2[72]; (c) documents produced under rule 18.2(2) or (3).[73]

Not later than 48 hours before the diet of proof a copy of every **30.158** production, marked with the appropriate number of process of the principal production, must be lodged with the sheriff clerk.[74] This copy is

---

[59] S.C.R., r. 8.6(1).
[60] *ibid.*, r. 8.6(3).
[61] *ibid.*, r. 8.6(2).
[62] *ibid.*
[63] S.C.R., r. 8.7(1)(a).
[64] *ibid.*, r. 8.7(1)(b).
[65] *ibid.*, r. 8.7(2).
[66] "Documents" in this context includes any affidavit or other written statement admissible under the Civil Evidence (Scotland) Act 1988, s. 2(1): S.C.R., r. 17.1(2).
[67] S.C.R., r. 17.1(1)(a).
[68] *ibid.*, r. 17.1(1)(b).
[69] *ibid.*, r. 17.1(3).
[70] *ibid.*, r. 17.1(5).
[71] *ibid.*, r. 17.1(4)(a). If the document was one to which rule 8.5(1) applies (see para. 30.152, *supra*) it must have been on the list lodged in accordance with that rule.
[72] *ibid.*, r. 17.1(4)(b). The hearing in terms of rule 8.2 is the first hearing in a defended action. See para. 30.134, *supra*.
[73] *ibid.*, r. 17.1(4)(c). Rule 18.2(2) relates to documents recovered under the optional procedure (see paras 30.164 to 30.168, *infra*). Rule 18.2(3) relates to documents recovered by commission and diligence (see paras 30.162, 30.163, *infra*).
[74] *ibid.*, r. 17.2(1).

for the use of the sheriff.[75] If the copy consists of more than one sheet, the sheets must be securely fastened together.[76]

30.159 Productions may be inspected within the sheriff clerk's office during normal business hours, and a party litigant may, where practicable, be provided with copies by the sheriff clerk.[77]

30.160 Productions may be borrowed subject to certain limitations. The general rule is that only a solicitor or his authorised clerk (for whom the solicitor is responsible) may borrow a production.[78] A party litigant or an authorised lay representative may borrow a production only with the permission of the sheriff and subject to such conditions as the sheriff may impose.[79] In either case a receipt for any production borrowed must be entered in the list of productions and the list must be retained by the sheriff clerk.[80] Any production borrowed must be returned to the sheriff clerk not later than noon on the day preceding the date of the proof.[81]

30.161 A solicitor who has borrowed a production and who fails to return it for any diet at which it is required may be fined a sum not exceeding £50 by the sheriff.[82] Such a fine is payable to the sheriff clerk.[83] It is recoverable by civil diligence.[84] There is no appeal against the imposition of this fine but it may, on cause shown, be recalled by the sheriff who imposed it.[85] Although it is not explicitly stated, it may be reasonably inferred that this rule applies equally to the case where a production has been borrowed by a solicitor's authorised clerk rather than by the solicitor himself. There is apparently no power given to a sheriff to fine a party litigant or authorised lay representative who fails timeously to return a production.

Recovery of evidence

Diligence for the recovery of documents

30.162 The provisions covering applying for and granting commission and diligence for the recovery of documents in a summary cause are similar to but simpler than those for the same processes in an ordinary cause.[86] At any time after service of a summons a party may apply to the sheriff by written incidental application for commission and diligence to recover documents.[87] In his application the party must list the documents which he wishes to recover.[88] A copy of the application must be intimated to every other party[89] and, where necessary, to the Advocate General for

---

[75] S.C.R., r. 17.2(1).
[76] *ibid.*, r. 17.2(2).
[77] *ibid.*, r. 17.3(5).
[78] *ibid.*, r. 17.3(3).
[79] *ibid.*, r. 17.3(4).
[80] *ibid.*, r. 17.3(2).
[81] *ibid.*, r. 17.3(1).
[82] *ibid.*, r. 17.4(1).
[83] *ibid.*, r. 17.4(2)(a).
[84] *ibid.*, r. 17.4(2)(b).
[85] *ibid.*, r. 17.4(3).
[86] For the provisions in an ordinary cause see Vol. 1, paras 15.50 to 15.83.
[87] S.C.R., r. 18.1(1).
[88] *ibid.*, r. 18.1(2).
[89] *ibid.*, r. 18.1(3)(a).

Scotland or the Lord Advocate (and if there is any doubt to both).[90] The Advocate General and the Lord Advocate are entitled to appear at the hearing of the incidental application.[91] The application may be considered by the sheriff with or without a hearing or the attendance of parties.[92] The sheriff may grant commission and diligence for the recovery of those documents in the list which he considers relevant to the action.[93] Although the rules are silent on the matter, it is suggested that it would be inappropriate for a sheriff to refuse to allow recovery of any document without giving an opportunity to the applicant to be heard on his application.

Execution of commission and diligence for the recovery of documents

The summary cause rules relating to the actual execution of a **30.163** commission for the recovery of documents are remarkably sparse. The only relevant provisions are contained in the rule headed "Optional procedure before executing commission and diligence".[94] At the commission the commissioner must administer the appropriate oath or affirmation to any clerk and any shorthand writer appointed for the commission.[95] He must then administer to the haver either the oath in Form 20 or the affirmation in Form 21.[96] It is suggested that thereafter the procedure described for an ordinary cause should be followed.[97]

Optional procedure

As in the case of ordinary causes, there is provision made in the **30.164** summary cause rules for the recovery of documents by an optional procedure without the execution of a full commission and diligence.[98] Any party who has obtained a commission and diligence may, at any time before executing it, serve on the haver (or on his known solicitor or solicitors) by first class recorded delivery post an order with certificate attached in Form 24.[99]

Form 24 consists of an order and a certificate. It requires the haver to **30.165** produce to the sheriff clerk within a specified time (i) the order itself, (ii) the certificate attached to the order, (iii) all documents within the haver's possession covered by "the specification which is enclosed",[1] and (iv) a list of these documents. It states that the documents may be delivered directly to the sheriff clerk or may be sent to him by registered or recorded delivery post. It further states that if confidentiality is

---

[90] S.C.R., r. 18.1(3)(b). Intimation is required where recovery is sought of documents belonging to or in the possession of the Crown or of records of the National Health Service. See Vol. 1, para. 15.60.

[91] S.C.R., r. 18.1(4).

[92] See paras 30.37 to 30.39, *supra.*

[93] S.C.R., r. 18.1(5).

[94] *ibid.*, r. 18.2. For optional procedure see paras 30.164 to 30.168, *infra.*

[95] *ibid.*, r. 18.2(4)(a).

[96] *ibid.*, r. 18.2(4)(b).

[97] See Vol. 1, paras. 15.73 to 15.79.

[98] For the optional procedure in an ordinary cause see Vol. 1 paras 15.66 to 15.71.

[99] S.C.R., r. 18.2(1).

[1] The reference to "specification" is perhaps a trifle unfortunate. That term is not used in S.C.R., r. 18.1, which relates to the granting of commission and diligence and which simply refers to a list. However, it is used once in S.C.R., r. 18.2(3), and "specification of documents" is defined in the glossary of terms in Appendix 2 to Schedule 1 to the Act of Sederunt.

claimed for any document it must still be produced but may be placed in a separate envelope marked "confidential". The certificate referred to is to be signed by the haver. In it he must certify either (i) that the documents which he has produced are all the documents which he possesses which "fall under the specification"[2] or (ii) that he has no such documents or (iii) that he believes that there are documents which are not in his possession which were last seen by him in the possession of a named person or company or (iv) that he knows of no documents.

30.166 Documents sent to the sheriff clerk in response to the order must be retained by him.[3] He must advise all parties to the action that the documents are in his possession and that they may be examined within his office during normal business hours.[4]

30.167 If the party who served the order is not satisfied that full production has been made "under the specification"[5] or that adequate reasons for non-production have been given, he may execute the commission and diligence in normal form[6] notwithstanding his adoption in the first instance of the optional procedure.[7]

30.168 All documents recovered under this optional procedure may be tendered as evidence at any hearing or proof without further formality.[8] The rules relating to confidentiality apply to such documents.[9] .

Administration of Justice (Scotland) Act 1972, s. 1

30.169 In terms of section 1(1) of the Administration of Justice (Scotland) Act 1972 the sheriff has power *inter alia* "to order the inspection, photographing, preservation, custody and detention of documents and other property (including, where appropriate, land) which appear to the court to be property as to which any question may relevantly arise in any existing civil proceedings before that court". In terms of section 1(1A) of the same Act the sheriff has power "to order any person to disclose such information as he has as to the identity of any persons who appear to the court to be persons who might be witnesses in any existing civil proceedings before that court".

30.170 So far as a summary cause is concerned an application for an order under section 1(1) or section 1(1A) must be made by incidental application in writing.[10] Along with the incidental application there must be lodged a specification of either "(a) the document or other property sought to be inspected, photographed, preserved, taken into custody, detained, produced, recovered, sampled or experimented with or upon as the case may be, or (b) the matter in respect of which information is sought as to the identity of a person who might be a witness or a

---

2 See n.1, *supra*.
3 S.C.R., r. 18.2(2).
4 *ibid.*
5 See comment in n.1, *supra*.
6 See para. 30.163, *supra*.
7 S.C.R., r. 18.2(3).
8 *ibid.*, r. 18.2(5).
9 *ibid*. The rules relating to confidentiality are S.C.R., r. 18.4(2), (3) and (4). See para. 30.174, *infra*.
10 S.C.R., r. 18.3(1).

defender.''[11] It is suggested that the reference to "defender" is otiose as the provision in section 1(1A) giving power to a sheriff to require disclosure of the identity of a potential defender applies only to proceedings which "appear to the court to be likely to be brought" and not to existing proceedings.

A copy of the specification must be intimated to (a) every other party **30.171** to the action, (b) any third-party haver, and (c) where necessary the Advocate General for Scotland or the Lord Advocate (and if there is any doubt, both).[12] The Advocate General and the Lord Advocate are entitled to appear at any hearing of the incidental application.[13]

If the sheriff grants the incidental application in whole or in part he **30.172** may order the applicant to find caution or to give some other security, as he thinks fit.[14]

The Summary Cause Rules are silent on how any order made in terms **30.173** of section 1 of the 1972 Act is actually to be executed. This is in contrast to the Ordinary Cause Rules which contain quite detailed provisions,[15] including the possibility of using the optional procedure.[16] It is suggested that the procedure should follow that for commission and diligence, *mutatis mutandis*.[17]

Confidentiality

Confidentiality may be claimed in respect of any evidence sought to be **30.174** recovered following either the grant of a commission and diligence or an order in terms of section 1 of the 1972 Act.[18] It may also be claimed in respect of any document recovered under the optional procedure provided by Rule 18.2.[19] If a claim of confidentiality is made the document or property concerned is enclosed in a separate sealed packet.[20] This packet may not be opened except by authority of the sheriff granted on an incidental application made by the party who sought the commission and diligence or order.[21] This incidental application must be intimated by the applicant to the party or parties from whose possession the items concerned were obtained.[22] Any party receiving such intimation is entitled to appear at the hearing of the application.[23]

Production of original documents from public records

Extracts of documents from public records are usually admissible in **30.175** evidence and sufficient for proof of the document concerned. However, in certain cases production of the original document is necessary, and

---

[11] S.C.R., r. 18.3(2).
[12] *ibid.*, r. 18.3(3).
[13] *ibid.*, r. 18.3(5).
[14] *ibid.*, r. 18.3(4).
[15] O.C.R., rr. 28.5, 28.6, 28.7. See Vol. 1, paras 15.84 to 15.92.
[16] *ibid.*, r. 28.5(2).
[17] For commission and diligence see paras 30.162, 30.163, *supra*.
[18] S.C.R., r. 18.4(1).
[19] *ibid.*, r. 18.2(5). For S.C.R., r. 18.2 generally see paras 30.164 to 30.168, *supra*.
[20] *ibid.*, r. 18.4(2).
[21] *ibid.*, r. 18.4(3).
[22] *ibid.*, r. 18.4(4). This rule refers only to "documents" and not to "property" even though both are mentioned in S.C.R., r. 18.4(2) which provides for the sealing up of allegedly confidential material. It is suggested that the rule should be interpreted as covering any item and not only documents.
[23] S.C.R., r. 18.4(5).

the Summary Cause Rules contain provisions for achieving this. These provisions are virtually identical to their equivalents for ordinary causes.[24]

30.176   A party seeking to obtain production of an original document from the keeper of any public record must apply to the sheriff by incidental application.[25] Intimation of this application must be made to the keeper of the record concerned at least seven days before the application is lodged.[26]

30.177   Special rules apply to public records kept by the Keeper of the Registers of Scotland or the Keeper of the Records of Scotland. In the case of these, if it appears to the sheriff that it is necessary for the ends of justice that an incidental application for production should be granted, he must pronounce an interlocutor containing a certificate to that effect.[27] The party applying for production may then apply by letter addressed to the Deputy Principal Clerk of Session for an order from the Court of Session authorising the relevant Keeper to exhibit the original of any register or deed to the sheriff.[28] With the letter must be enclosed a copy (certified by the sheriff clerk) of the sheriff's interlocutor containing the certificate that production is necessary for the ends of justice.[29] The Deputy Principal Clerk of Session must submit the letter of application to a Lord Ordinary in chambers.[30] If the Lord Ordinary is satisfied that the application should be granted he grants a warrant for production or exhibition of the original register or deed sought.[31] A certified copy of this warrant must then be served on the relevant Keeper.[32]

30.178   In all cases of production of an original document from any public register the expense of such production or exhibition must be met, in the first instance, by the party who made the original incidental application.[33]

Witnesses and havers

Citation of witnesses and havers

30.179   The provisions for citing witnesses and havers in a summary cause are similar but not identical to those in ordinary actions.[34]

30.180   The summons or the copy thereof served on the defender is sufficient warrant for the citation of witnesses and havers.[35] Each party is responsible for securing the attendance of his witnesses or havers at a

---

[24] O.C.R., r. 28.9. See Vol. 1, para. 15.98.
[25] S.C.R., r. 18.6(1).
[26] *ibid.*, r. 18.6(2).
[27] *ibid.*, r. 18.6(3)(a).
[28] *ibid.*, r. 18.6(3)(b).
[29] *ibid.*
[30] S.C.R., r. 18.6(4).
[31] *ibid.*
[32] S.C.R., r. 18.6(5).
[33] *ibid.*, r. 18.6(6).
[34] For ordinary actions see O.C.R., rr. 29.7, 29.8, 29.9 and 29.10 discussed in Vol. 1, paras 16.02 to 16.17.
[35] S.C.R., r. 18.8(3).

proof (or indeed any other hearing) and is personally liable for their expenses.[36] A witness or haver is entitled to not less than seven days' notice.[37] The form of citation is Form 26 and the certificate of execution of citation is in Form 26a.[38]

A solicitor may cite a witness or haver by registered post or first **30.181** class recorded delivery service.[39] Alternatively, a witness or haver may be cited by sheriff officer in a number of different ways.[40] He may be cited personally.[41] The citation may be left with a resident at the person's dwelling-place or an employee at his place of business.[42] It may be deposited in the person's dwelling-place or place of business.[43] It may be affixed to the door of the person's dwelling-place or place of business.[44] In the case of the last two methods of citation, the sheriff officer must, in addition, as soon as possible after citation, send a copy of the citation by ordinary post to the address at which he thinks it most likely that the person may be found.[45] Finally, the sheriff officer may send the citation by registered post or first class recorded delivery service.[46]

The provisions described in the two preceding paragraphs apply to the **30.182** citation of witnesses and havers by party litigants but there are additional requirements in respect of them.[47] First, a party litigant who wishes to cite witnesses for a proof must, not later than 28 days before the date of the proof, apply to the sheriff by incidental application for the sheriff to fix caution for expenses in such sum as the sheriff considers reasonable having regard to the number of witnesses he proposes to cite and the period for which they may be required to attend court.[48] The application should give full details of the witnesses whom the party litigant wishes to cite. Secondly, the party litigant must, before instructing a solicitor or a sheriff officer to cite any witness in conformity with rule 18.8(5), actually find caution in the sum fixed by the sheriff.[49] If a party litigant decides not to cite all the witnesses mentioned in his incidental application he may apply by a further incidental application for variation of the amount of caution.[50]

Witnesses failing to attend

A hearing is not to be adjourned solely on account of the failure of a **30.183** witness to appear unless the sheriff, on cause shown, so directs.[51] It is suggested that "cause shown" might properly be prayed in aid where a

---

[36] S.C.R., r. 18.8(2).

[37] *ibid.*, r. 18.8(4).

[38] *ibid.*, r. 18.8(1). Form 26 contains a note to the effect that the witness is entitled to claim for certain necessary outlays and loss of earnings. This note also states that a claim for payment of travelling expenses prior to attendance at court should be made to the person citing the witness.

[39] S.C.R., r. 18.8(5)(a).

[40] *ibid.*, r. 18.8(5)(b).

[41] *ibid.*, r. 18.8(5)(b)(i).

[42] *ibid.*, r. 18.8(5)(b)(ii).

[43] *ibid.*, r. 18.8(5)(b)(iii).

[44] *ibid.*, r. 18.8(5)(iv).

[45] *ibid.*, r. 18.8(6).

[46] *ibid.*, r. 18.8(5)(b)(v).

[47] *ibid.*, r. 18.9. *Cf.* O.C.R., r. 29.8. See Vol. 1, para. 16.05.

[48] *ibid.*, r. 18.9(1)(a).

[49] *ibid.*, r. 18.9(1)(b).

[50] *ibid.*, r. 18.9(2).

[51] S.C.R., r. 18.10(1).

witness has been competently cited and there is no explanation for his failure to attend.

30.184   The sheriff may grant a warrant for the arrest of a witness or haver who fails to attend.[52] The warrant is authority to have the witness brought to court.[53] Such a warrant is effective in any sheriffdom without further endorsation, and the expenses thereof may be awarded against the witness or haver.[54] The witness or haver who fails to answer a citation, having been offered his travelling expenses if he has asked for them, may be ordered by the sheriff to pay a penalty not exceeding £250.[55] Decree for payment of this penalty may be granted in favour of the party on whose behalf the witness or haver was cited.[56]

Evidence on commission

30.185   As in the case of ordinary causes there is provision in the Summary Cause Rules for evidence to be taken on commission in certain circumstances.[57] The provisions for summary causes are less complex than those for ordinary causes.

30.186   A party may apply to have a witness' evidence taken on commission to be retained until required if it is in danger of being lost[58] This might occur if the witness were dangerously ill or were about to go abroad. A party may also apply for the evidence of a witness to be taken on commission if (a) the witness is resident beyond the sheriffdom; (b) although resident within the sheriffdom, he resides at some place remote from the court in which the proof is to be held; or (c) the witness is "by reason of illness, age, infirmity or other sufficient cause" unable to attend the proof.[59] The evidence of a witness or haver who does not fall into any of the categories just described may be taken on commission "on special cause shown".[60]

30.187   A witness who is outside Scotland cannot be compelled to give evidence on commission unless the letter of request procedure has been followed.[61] However, in practice, a witness in England, Wales or Northern Ireland may be prepared to attend a commission and it is suggested that, rather than going through the somewhat cumbersome letter of request procedure, an application should be made in the usual way to take the evidence of such a witness on commission. If the witness is not prepared to attend, the provisions of sections 1 to 4 of the Evidence (Proceedings in Other Jurisdictions) Act 1975 may be used in combination with a letter of request.[62]

---

[52] S.C.R., r. 18.10(4).
[53] *ibid.*
[54] S.C.R., r. 18.10(5).
[55] *ibid.*, r. 18.10(2). Form 26 (form of witness citation) advises witness he may be fined if he fails to attend.
[56] *ibid.*, r. 18.10(3).
[57] For ordinary causes see O.C.R., r.r 28.10 to 28.13 discussed in Vol. 1, paras 15.18 to 15.40.
[58] S.C.R., r. 18.5(1).
[59] *ibid.*, r. 18.5(2).
[60] *ibid.*, r. 18.5(3).
[61] See paras 30.190 to 30.196, *infra*.
[62] See Vol. 1, para. 15.41.

In the case of any commission the sheriff may direct that the evidence **30.188** is to be taken by himself or by a commissioner.[63] The interlocutor granting the commission is sufficient authority for citing the witness to appear.[64]

Evidence taken on commission may be recorded by the sheriff (if he **30.189** himself is taking the evidence) or commissioner, or it may be recorded by a clerk or shorthand writer nominated by the sheriff or commissioner.[65] In the latter case the evidence may be recorded in narrative form or by question and answer as the sheriff or commissioner directs, and the extended notes of the evidence certified by the clerk or shorthand writer are held to be the notes of such oral evidence.[66] At the commission the sheriff or the commissioner as the case may be must administer the appropriate oath to any clerk or shorthand writer appointed for the commission.[67] The witness is put on oath or affirms in the appropriate form as at a proof.[68]

Letters of request

A letter of request is a request to a foreign court or tribunal, within **30.190** whose jurisdiction a witness resides or within whose jurisdiction evidence is to be recovered, for assistance in having the witness examined or other evidence recovered. For a country outwith the United Kingdom a letter of request will be effective only if it is a country with which the United Kingdom has entered into a convention for the taking of evidence.[69] If there is no such convention resort must be had to a commission in traditional form, but this is dependent on the explicit or implicit consent of the country concerned and the co-operation of the witness. The rule relating to letters of request in summary causes[70] is virtually identical to that for ordinary causes.[71]

Letter of request procedure is the only way of compelling a witness **30.191** outwith Scotland to provide evidence for a court in Scotland, although from the practical point of view, a witness in England, Wales or Northern Ireland may be prepared to attend voluntarily.[72] In the case of a witness in these countries who is not prepared to attend voluntarily an application to the appropriate High Court may be made in terms of section 1 of the Evidence (Proceedings in Other Jurisdictions) Act 1975, but here, as with countries outwith the United Kingdom, a letter of request is required to set the procedure in motion.

The rule relating to letters of request is concerned not only with a **30.192** request for the examination of a witness[73] but also with a request for: the inspection, photographing, preservation, custody, detention, production

---

[63] S.C.R., r. 18.5(1).
[64] *ibid.*, r. 18.5(2).
[65] *ibid.*, r. 18.5(5).
[66] *ibid.*
[67] *ibid.*, r. 18.5(6)(a).
[68] *ibid.*, r. 18.5(6)(b). The form of oath is Form 20 and that of affirmation Form 21.
[69] See Vol. 1, para. 15.42.
[70] S.C.R., r. 18.7.
[71] See O.C.R., r. 28.14 discussed in Vol. 1, para. 15.42.
[72] See para. 30.187, *supra.*
[73] S.C.R., r. 18.7(2)(a).

or recovery of, or the taking of samples of, or the carrying out of any experiment on or with, a document or other property[74]; the medical examination of any person[75]; the taking and testing of samples of blood from any person[76]; and "any other order for obtaining evidence".[77]

30.193 The application is made by minute in the prescribed form together with a proposed letter of request also in the prescribed form.[78] The form of letter of request is in three parts. Part A must be completed in all cases and gives details of the parties, the nature of the proceedings, the court in which they are being brought, the competent authority in the "requested state" and the evidence to be obtained or other judicial act to be performed. Part B is to be completed as appropriate and gives more detailed information about what evidence is to be obtained. Part C must be completed in all cases and specifies the date of the request together with the signature and seal of the requesting authority.

30.194 It is a condition of granting a letter of request that the applicant's solicitor or a party litigant, as the case may be, is personally liable in the first instance for the whole expenses which may become due and payable in respect of the letter of request to the court or tribunal obtaining the evidence and to any witness who may be examined; and the solicitor or party litigant must consign in court such sum in respect thereof as the sheriff thinks fit.[79]

30.195 Unless the court or tribunal to which a letter of request is addressed is in a country or territory where English is an official language or in relation to which the sheriff clerk certifies that no translation is required, the applicant must, before the issue of the letter of request, lodge in process a translation of the letter and of any interrogatories and cross-interrogatories into the official language of the court or tribunal.[80] It is suggested that the sheriff clerk might be prepared to certify that no translation (at least of interrogatories or cross-interrogatories) would be required where the witness to be examined spoke English.

30.196 The letter of request together with any interrogatories and cross-interrogatories with the relevant translations, if any, must be forwarded by the sheriff clerk to the Foreign and Commonwealth Office or to such other person and in such manner as the sheriff may direct.[81] In the case of letters of request addressed to the High Court in England or Northern Ireland the sheriff would, of course, direct that the letter of request should be sent to the relevant court and not to the Foreign and Commonwealth Office.

Abandonment of action

30.197 As in the case of an ordinary cause,[82] a pursuer may, before decree of absolvitor or of dismissal is granted, offer to abandon a summary cause.[83] The rule does not prescribe in what form an offer to abandon should be

---

[74] S.C.R., r. 18.7(2)(b).
[75] *ibid.*, r. 18.7(2)(c).
[76] *ibid.*, r. 18.7(2)(d).
[77] *ibid.*, r. 18.7(2)(e).
[78] *ibid.*, r. 18.7(3). The form of minute is Form 25 and that of the letter of request is Form 25a.
[79] *ibid.*, r. 18.7(4).
[80] *ibid.*, r. 18.7(5).
[81] *ibid.*, r. 18.7(6).
[82] O.C.R., r. 23.1. See Vol. 1, paras 14.20 to 14.30.
[83] S.C.R., r. 21.1(1).

made. It is suggested that it should be by way of incidental application which should include a request to the sheriff clerk to fix the amount of the defender's expenses.[84]

If the pursuer offers to abandon the action under rule 21.1(1) the **30.198** sheriff clerk, subject to the approval of the sheriff, fixes the amount of the defender's expenses in accordance with the rule governing the fixing of expenses,[85] and the action is continued to the first appropriate court occurring not sooner than 14 days after the amount has been fixed.[86] If, before that continued diet, the pursuer makes payment to the defender of the fixed amount of expenses, the sheriff must dismiss the action unless the pursuer consents to absolvitor.[87] If the pursuer fails to pay the fixed amount of expenses the defender is entitled to decree of absolvitor with expenses.[88]

In the summary cause rules, unlike the ordinary cause rules,[89] there is **30.199** no provision made for the abandonment of a counterclaim. It is submitted that it is always open to a defender to abandon a counterclaim at common law. Indeed, there seems to be no reason in principle why a pursuer should not also be able to abandon his claim at common law, although the method of abandonment in terms of the rules is to be preferred.[90]

Decree by default

The summary cause provisions for decree by default are simpler than **30.200** those for ordinary causes,[91] but the comments made in Volume 1 on the subject and especially on such matters as exercise of discretion are equally relevant to summary causes and should be referred to.[92]

In the case of a summary cause the sheriff may grant decree by default **30.201** if, after a proof has been fixed under rule 8.3(3)(d),[93] a party fails to appear at a hearing where required to do so.[94] This provision is a notable change from that in the 1976 Rules, which required a sheriff in cases of failure to appear to fix a diet at which the offending party could attend and explain his failure.[95] The change is to be welcomed as the old rule on occasions resulted in frustration and extra expense where a party was simply seeking to delay the passing of decree against him. Under the present rule the sheriff is not obliged to grant decree by default, but he is at least given the opportunity to do so.

The sheriff is also given a discretion to grant decree by default if a **30.202** party fails to implement any order of the court after a proof has been

---

[84] See para. 30.198, *infra.*
[85] S.C.R., r. 23.3 is the rule concerned. See paras 30.220 to 30.229, *infra.*
[86] *ibid.*, r. 21.1(2).
[87] *ibid.*, r. 21.1(3).
[88] *ibid.*, r. 21.1(4).
[89] O.C.R., r. 23.2.
[90] For abandonment at common law see Vol. 1, paras 14.18, 14.19.
[91] O.C.R., Chap. 16.
[92] See Vol. 1, paras 14.02 to 14.10.
[93] For S.C.R., r. 8.3(3)(d) see para. 30.141, *supra.*
[94] S.C.R., r. 22.1(1).
[95] 1976 S.C.R., r. 28.

fixed under rule 8.3(3)(d), although in this case he must give the offending party an opportunity to be heard.[96]

30.203   The sheriff is not entitled to grant decree by default solely on the ground that a party has failed to appear at the hearing of an incidental application.[97]

30.204   If all parties fail to appear at a hearing or proof where required to do so, the sheriff must "unless sufficient reason appears to the contrary" dismiss the action and any counterclaim.[98] It is suggested that the sort of factor which a sheriff might consider to amount to sufficient reason not to dismiss would be if travelling conditions to the court were difficult.

VI. PROOF

Conduct of proof

30.205   The general rule is that the pursuer must lead at the proof.[99] If any party seeks to depart from this rule he must lodge an incidental application to that effect not less than seven days before the diet of proof, and must intimate that application to all the other parties.[1] The sheriff has a discretion whether or not to grant the application.[2]

Oath or affirmation

30.206   The sheriff must administer the oath or affirmation in the prescribed form to each witness.[3]

Noting of evidence, etc.

30.207   Before the start of the proof the sheriff may make a note of any facts which have been agreed by the parties since the hearing held in terms of rule 8.2(1).[4] The parties may, and must if required by the sheriff, lodge a joint minute of admissions of the facts upon which they have reached agreement.[5]

30.208   The sheriff must make for his own use notes of the evidence led at the proof.[6] These notes must include a note of any evidence to the admissibility of which objection is taken together with a note of the nature of the objection.[7] The sheriff must retain his notes until after the disposal of any appeal.[8] In a case where no appeal has been taken, it might be thought that the sheriff need not retain his notes beyond the period within which an

---

[96] S.C.R., r. 22.1(3).
[97] *ibid.*, r. 22.1(4).
[98] *ibid.*, r. 22.1(2).
[99] *ibid.*, r. 8.11.
[1] *ibid.*
[2] As to the factors which a sheriff may take into account see Vol. 1, paras 8.64, 8.65.
[3] S.C.R., r. 8.12. The form of oath is Form 20 and that of affirmation Form 21.
[4] *ibid.*, r. 8.13(1). For the hearing in terms of rule 8.2(1) see paras 30.134 to 30.141, *supra.*
[5] *ibid.*, r. 8.13(2).
[6] *ibid.*, r. 8.13(3)(a).
[7] *ibid.* On objections to the admissibility of evidence see paras 30.209 to 30.213, *infra.*
[8] S.C.R., r. 8.13(3)(b).

appeal is competent.[9] However, given that a sheriff principal may, in exercise of the dispensing power, be prepared to allow an appeal to be marked late, it will be prudent for the sheriff to retain his notes for a reasonable period of time after a proof.

Objections to admissibility of evidence

If during the course of a proof a party objects to the admissibility of **30.209** any evidence and that line of evidence is not abandoned by the party pursuing it, the sheriff must normally allow the evidence to be led under reservation of the question of its admissibility.[10] At the close of the proof the sheriff hears submissions on the objection and decides whether or not the evidence is admissible.[11] There are two exceptions to this rule. First, the sheriff should sustain the objection and refuse to allow the evidence to be led if it is, in his opinion, clearly irrelevant or scandalous.[12] The second exception is where the objection is either to the admissibility of oral or documentary evidence on the ground of confidentiality or it is an objection to the production of a document on any ground. Such objection falls within the scope of rule 8.16(1).[13] In such a case the sheriff must rule immediately on the objection.[14]

An objection to a deed or other document on which a party relies to **30.210** support his case may be maintained without having to bring an action of reduction.[15] If such an objection is made and an action of reduction would otherwise have been competent, the sheriff may order the objector to find caution or to consign a sum of money with the sheriff clerk as security.[16]

Incidental appeal against rulings on confidentiality and production of documents

If in the course of a proof "a party or any other person" objects to the **30.211** admissibility of oral or documentary evidence on the ground of confidentiality or to the production of a document on any ground, he may, if dissatisfied with the ruling of the sheriff on the objection, express immediately his formal dissatisfaction with the ruling and, with leave of the sheriff, appeal to the sheriff principal.[17] This is the provision referred to above as one of the exceptions to the general rule whereby the sheriff must reserve his decision on any objection to admissibility until the end of the proof.[18]

Except for the circumstances described in this rule no other appeal **30.212** may be made during a proof against any decision of the sheriff as to the admissibility of evidence or the production of documents.[19] For practical

---

[9] For the period within which an appeal must be taken see paras 30.332, 30.348, *infra*.
[10] S.C.R., r. 8.15.
[11] *ibid.*
[12] *ibid.*
[13] See paras 30.211 to 30.213, *infra*.
[14] S.C.R., r. 8.15.
[15] *ibid.*, r. 19.1(1).
[16] *ibid.*, r. 19.1(2).
[17] *ibid.*, r. 8.16(1). The reference to "any other person" is to enable a person such as a haver who is not a party to the action to object to the admissibility of the evidence concerned.
[18] See para. 30.209, *supra*.
[19] S.C.R., r. 8.16(3).

purposes this means that there can be no immediate appeal against a sheriff's sustaining an objection on the ground that the evidence concerned is clearly irrelevant or scandalous, this being the only other situation in which a sheriff is entitled to make an immediate ruling on an objection.[20]

30.213 Any appeal to the sheriff principal in terms of rule 8.16(1) must be disposed of by him with the least possible delay.[21] Depending on the circumstances, either the proof could at once be adjourned until after the sheriff principal had heard and decided the appeal, or the sheriff could proceed to hear other evidence in the proof and then adjourn it to await the sheriff principal's decision.

Parties to be heard at close of proof

30.214 After all the evidence in the proof has been led the sheriff must hear parties on the evidence.[22] The actual wording of the rule is "all the evidence has been led relevant to the particular proof". This, it is assumed, is to take account of the possibility that the sheriff may have ordered that proof should be heard separately on different issues in terms of rule 8.9(1).[23]

30.215 After hearing parties the sheriff may either pronounce his decision immediately,[24] or he may reserve judgment.[25] Under the 1976 Rules which contained a similar provision[26] it was not unknown for a sheriff, having heard submissions, to adjourn a proof until the next day and then give his decision orally, thus avoiding having to produce a written judgment. There is no reason to suppose that such a procedure may not be adopted by sheriffs in appropriate cases under the present rules.

Sheriff's decision

30.216 If the sheriff pronounces his decision at the end of a proof he must briefly state the grounds for it, including the reasons for his decision on any question of law or of admissibility of evidence.[27] It is suggested that the sheriff should make it clear which facts he finds established and give reasons for doing so. He should in an appropriate case specifically comment on the credibility and reliability of witnesses.

30.217 If the sheriff reserves judgment he must produce his decision in writing within 28 days.[28] The judgment must be given to the sheriff clerk and must include a statement of his decision[29] and a brief note of the grounds for it including the reasons for his decision on any question of law or of admissibility of evidence.[30] The sheriff clerk must send copies

---

[20] S.C.R., r. 8.15, exception (a). See para. 30.209, *supra*.
[21] *ibid.*, r. 8.16(2).
[22] *ibid.*, r. 8.14(1).
[23] See para. 30.150, *supra*.
[24] S.C.R., r. 8.14(2)(a).
[25] *ibid.*, r. 8.14(2)(b).
[26] 1976 S.C.R., r. 46(2).
[27] S.C.R., r. 8.18(1).
[28] *ibid.*, r. 8.18(2).
[29] *ibid.*, r. 8.18(2)(a).
[30] *ibid.*, r. 8.18(2)(b), referring back to r. 8.18(1).

of the judgment to all parties to the action.[31] It may be noted that, even though the provision for the sheriff's producing his judgment within 28 days is *prima facie* mandatory, there is no sanction provided in the event of his failing to do so. It is improbable that he could make use of the general dispensing power in his own favour![32] However, it is suggested that, if there were good reason for the sheriff's being unable to comply with the 28 days' time-limit, it would be quite appropriate for him to apply to the sheriff principal for an extension of time by analogy with the provision in Chapter 25 of the Rules for the extension of various time limits in connection with appeals.[33] In the event of a sheriff's simply failing to produce his judgment within the time-limit the parties' remedy would appear to be an informal application to the sheriff principal asking him to take the sheriff to task.

Application for time to pay direction or time order in defended action

The procedure where a defender lodges an application for a time to **30.218** pay direction or a time order in an undefended action has already been described.[34] Even in a defended action it is competent for a defender to make similar applications provided that the criteria for granting the direction or order are satisfied.[35] The application may be made either in writing or orally.[36] If in writing it should be made by incidental application.[37] In whatever form, the application may be made at any time before decree is granted.[38] Although there seems to be no logical reason for the omission, the provision for seeking a time to pay direction or time order in a defended action does not apply to a pursuer where a defender has lodged a counterclaim.

VII. POST-PROOF PROCEDURE

Final decree

Final decree may be granted, where expenses are awarded, only after **30.219** expenses have been dealt with in accordance with rule 23.3.[39]

Expenses

The sheriff clerk, with the approval of the sheriff, assesses the amount **30.220** of expenses, including the fees and outlays of witnesses awarded in any cause.[40] Where a party has been represented by a solicitor this assessment is in accordance with the statutory table of fees of solicitors appropriate to the action.[41] At the time of writing the relevant table of fees is contained in Chapter IV of Schedule 1 to the Act of Sederunt (Fees of Solicitors in the Sheriff Court) (Amendment and Further

---

[31] S.C.R., r. 8.18(3).
[32] For the dispensing power see paras 30.13 to 30.15, *supra*.
[33] S.C.R., r. 25.1(8). See para. 30.333, n.78 and para. 30.336, n.90, *infra*.
[34] See paras 30.118 to 30.120, *supra*.
[35] S.C.R., r. 8.17.
[36] *ibid.*
[37] *ibid.*
[38] *ibid.*
[39] S.C.R., r. 23.2. For rule 23.3 see paras 30.220 to 30.229, *infra*.
[40] *ibid.*, r. 23.3(1).
[41] *ibid.*

Provisions) 1993.[42] The general regulations 1 to 13 in the Schedule apply *mutatis mutandis* to summary causes as to ordinary causes.[43] In particular regulation 5 empowers the sheriff to modify expenses[44] and to allow a percentage increase to cover the responsibility of the solicitor in the conduct of the case.[45]

30.221   Regulation 14 applies only to fees in summary causes. It provides that necessary outlays are allowed in addition to the fees allowed under Chapter IV.[46] Sheriff officers' fees and the costs of advertising are allowable as outlays in both undefended and defended causes.[47] No fee is allowable for attendance at a continuation of a first calling, whether the cause is defended or undefended, unless such a fee is specially authorised by the court.[48] In a defended cause, if a skilled witness has prepared his own precognition or report, one-half of the drawing fee is allowable to the solicitor for perusing it, whether or not in the course of doing so he revises or adjusts it.[49] In a defended cause no fees are allowed in respect of an account of expenses when the hearing on the claim for expenses takes place immediately on the sheriff's or sheriff principal's announcing his decision.[50] In all undefended reparation actions, in addition to the fee in item 1 of Chapter IV (for taking instructions, framing the summons, etc.) there are also allowable such fees for precognitions and reports as are necessary to permit the framing of the writ, together with necessary outlays in connection therewith.[51]

30.222   Regulation 14(f) provides for a percentage reduction in fees in respect of certain categories of summary cause. These reductions apply unless the sheriff, on a motion to that effect, otherwise directs. The only one relevant to a standard summary cause is that in an undefended action for recovery of possession of heritable property, there will be a reduction of 50 per cent.[52]

30.223   The summary cause table of fees contains no provision for fees payable to counsel. It has been held in Lothian and Borders (correctly, it is submitted) that, despite this omission, counsel's fees may properly be charged if the employment of counsel is sanctioned by the sheriff.[53]

30.224   A party litigant who would have been entitled to expenses if he had been legally represented may be awarded any outlays or expenses to which he might be found entitled by virtue of the Litigants in Person (Costs and Expenses) Act 1975 or any enactment under that Act.[54] A party who is or has been represented by an authorised lay representative[55] and who would have been entitled to expenses if he had been

---

[42] S.I. 1993 No. 3080.
[43] See Vol. 1, Chap. 19 on expenses generally.
[44] reg. 5(a).
[45] reg. 5(b).
[46] reg. 14(a).
[47] reg. 14(b).
[48] reg. 14(c).
[49] reg. 14(d).
[50] reg. 14(e).
[51] reg. 14(g).
[52] reg. 14(f)(3).
[53] *J. & A. Hastie v. Edinburgh D.C.*, 1981 S.L.T. (Sh.Ct.) 92.
[54] S.C.R., r. 23.3(2).
[55] See para. 30.19, *supra*.

legally represented may be awarded any outlays or expenses to which a party litigant might be found entitled.[56] A party, such as a limited company, which is not an individual, which is or has been represented by an authorised lay representative and which could not represent itself, is also in the same position as a party litigant, if it would have been found entitled to expenses if it had been legally represented.[57]

The sheriff clerk must hear the parties or their solicitors on the claims **30.225** for expenses including fees, if any, and outlays.[58] This hearing must take place immediately after the sheriff has pronounced his decision except where he has reserved judgment or has ordered that the hearing should take place at a later date.[59] In practice under the 1976 Rules the hearing on expenses before the sheriff clerk following a proof was usually postponed until a later date for reasons of convenience. It is probable that this practice will also be followed under the present rules.

If the hearing is not held immediately after the decision has been **30.226** pronounced the sheriff clerk must fix the date, time and place of the hearing and give the parties at least 14 days' notice thereof.[60] The party who has been awarded expenses must lodge his account with the sheriff clerk at least seven days prior to the date of the hearing and must, at the same time, send a copy of that account to every other party.[61]

After hearing parties on the claim for expenses, whether immediately **30.227** after the decision has been pronounced or at a later hearing, the sheriff clerk must fix the amount of expenses and report his decision to the sheriff for his approval in open court at a diet the date and time of which have been intimated to the parties.[62] A party who has any objections to the sheriff clerk's assessment of expenses must state them before the sheriff, and, after disposing of any such objections, the sheriff must pronounce final decree including decree for payment of expenses as approved by him.[63]

If any party fails to comply with any of the foregoing provisions (for **30.228** example by failing timeously to lodge an account of expenses) or if the successful party fails to appear at the hearing on expenses, the sheriff clerk must report the failure to the sheriff at a diet which he intimated to all parties.[64] At that diet the sheriff must, unless sufficient cause be shown, pronounce decree on the merits and find no expenses due to or by any party.[65] This decree is a final decree for the purposes of the summary cause rules.[66]

The Ordinary Cause Rules contain a provision permitting the sheriff **30.229** to allow a decree for expenses to be extracted in the name of the

---

[56] S.C.R., r. 23.3(3).
[57] *ibid.*, r. 23.3(4).
[58] *ibid.*, r. 23.3(5).
[59] *ibid.*, r. 23.3(6).
[60] *ibid.*, r. 23.3(7).
[61] *ibid.*, r. 23.3(8).
[62] *ibid.*, r. 23.3(9).
[63] *ibid.*, r. 23.3(10).
[64] *ibid.*, r. 23.3(12).
[65] *ibid.*, r. 23.3(13).
[66] *ibid.*, r. 23.3(14).

solicitor who conducted the cause.[67] In the Summary Cause Rules it is provided that the sheriff may, if he thinks fit, on the application of the solicitor of any party to whom expenses may be awarded, grant decree in favour of that solicitor for the expenses of the action.[68] The solicitor's application must be made at or before the time of final decree being pronounced.[69]

Correction of interlocutor or note

30.230   At any time before extract the sheriff may correct any clerical or incidental error in an interlocutor or note attached thereto.[70] There is an identical provision in the Ordinary Cause Rules.[71]

Consigned funds

30.231   In certain circumstances a party may have been ordered to consign money with the court or may voluntarily have agreed to do so.[72] Consignation is subject to the Sheriff Court Consignations (Scotland) Act 1893. Except to a limited extent in the case of a multiplepoinding, no decree or other order for payment of consigned money may be granted until there has been lodged with the sheriff clerk a certificate by an authorised officer of the Inland Revenue stating that all taxes or duties payable to the Commissioners of Inland Revenue have been paid or satisfied.[73] In the case of a multiplepoinding, decree or another order for payment may be granted even though all taxes or duties payable on the estate of a deceased claimant have not been paid or satisfied.[74] Apart from this, the general rule applies to multiplepoindings as to other actions.

Extract of decree

30.232   An extract is signed by the sheriff clerk and may not be issued until 14 days from the granting of the decree unless the sheriff orders an earlier extract.[75] A party seeking early extract should lodge an incidental application to that effect or may make an oral application at the time when decree is granted.

30.233   If an appeal has been lodged against the sheriff's decision an extract decree may not be issued until the appeal has been disposed of.[76] The only exception to this rule is where decree has been granted for recovery of possession of heritable property against a defender who is in possession of the property without right or title to possess.[77] In such a case the lodging of an appeal does not prevent issue of an extract decree.

30.234   An extract decree may be written on the summons or on a separate paper.[78] It may be in one of the Forms 28 to 28k.[79] An extract decree is warrant for all lawful execution.[80]

---

[67] O.C.R., r. 32.2.
[68] S.C.R., r. 23.3(15).
[69] *ibid.*
[70] S.C.R., r. 23.4.
[71] O.C.R., r. 12.2(2). See Vol. 1, paras 5.87 to 5.90.
[72] For consignation generally see Vol. 1, paras 11.43 to 11.51.
[73] S.C.R., r. 23.5(1).
[74] *ibid.*, r. 23.5(2).
[75] *ibid.*, r. 23.6(1).
[76] *ibid.*, r. 23.6(2).
[77] *ibid.* Rule 30.2 applies to such actions. See paras 30.276 to 30.278, *infra.*
[78] S.C.R., r. 23.6(3)(a).
[79] *ibid.*, r. 23.6(3)(b). Each form is appropriate to a different type of action.
[80] *ibid.*, r. 23.6(3)(c).

Documents to be retained by sheriff clerk

All documents or other productions which have at any time been **30.235** lodged or referred to during a hearing or proof must be retained by the sheriff clerk until either the expiry of the period during which an appeal is competent, or, if an appeal is lodged, the appeal has been disposed of.[81] If no appeal is lodged each party who has lodged productions must uplift them from the sheriff clerk within 14 days after the period for appealing has expired.[82] If an appeal has been lodged the party must uplift the productions within 14 days after disposal of the appeal.[83] If a production is not uplifted in conformity with these provisions the sheriff clerk must intimate to the party who has lodged it or to his solicitor if he has one, that if it is not uplifted within 28 days after such intimation, it will be disposed of in such manner as the sheriff directs.[84] Again this mirrors a provision in the Ordinary Cause Rules.[85]

Charge

In the case of a decree for payment of money the period of payment **30.236** to be specified in any charge is 14 days if the person on whom the charge is served is within the United Kingdom.[86] If that person is outwith the United Kingdom or his whereabouts are unknown the period of charge is 28 days.[87]

In respect of any form of charge other than for payment of money (*e.g.* **30.237** for delivery) the period for responding to the charge is 14 days.[88]

It may be that a pursuer desires to serve a charge on a defender whose **30.238** whereabouts are unknown. In that event the charge will be deemed to have been served on the defender if it is (a) served on the sheriff clerk of the sheriff court district where the defender's last known address is located and (b) displayed by the sheriff clerk on the walls of court for the period of the charge.[89] A sheriff clerk who receives a charge in this way must display it on the walls of court and it must remain so displayed for the period of the charge.[90] The period runs from the first date on which the charge is displayed.[91] On the expiry of the period the sheriff clerk endorses on the charge a certificate in Form 29 to the effect that the charge has been displayed and returns it to the sheriff officer by whom service was executed.[92] Again the summary cause provisions are identical with those for ordinary causes.[93]

Diligence in actions for delivery

In an action for delivery the sheriff may grant warrant to search for **30.239** and take possession of goods and to open shut and lockfast places,[94] but this warrant can apply only to premises occupied by the defender.[95]

---

[81] S.C.R., r. 17.6(1), (2).
[82] *ibid.*, r. 17.6(3)(a).
[83] *ibid.*, r. 17.6(3)(b).
[84] *ibid.*, r. 17.6(4).
[85] O.C.R., r. 11.8.
[86] S.C.R., r. 23.7(1)(a).
[87] *ibid.*, r. 23.7(1)(b).
[88] *ibid.*, r. 23.7(2).
[89] *ibid.*, r. 23.8(1).
[90] *ibid.*, r. 23.8(2).
[91] *ibid.*, r. 23.8(3).
[92] *ibid.*, r. 23.8(4).
[93] O.C.R., r. 30.9.
[94] S.C.R., r. 23.9(1).
[95] *ibid.*, r. 23.9(2).

Applications for variation of decree

30.240   In certain types of case, power is given to the sheriff by statute to vary, discharge or rescind a decree, or to sist or suspend execution thereon, without a new action having to be raised. A party seeking such an order must do so by lodging a minute to that effect in the original action.[96] On the lodging of such a minute by a pursuer the sheriff clerk grants warrant to cite the defender provided that the pursuer has returned the extract decree.[97] If it is the defender who lodges a minute for variation the sheriff clerk grants warrant to cite the pursuer ordaining him to return the extract decree.[98] The sheriff clerk may also, where appropriate, grant interim sist of execution of the decree.[99] The minute may normally not be heard in court unless seven days' notice has been given by the party lodging it to the other parties,[1] but this period may be shortened by the sheriff on cause shown to a period of not less than two days.[2]

VIII. SPECIFIC ACTIONS

A. Delivery

30.241   The form of copy summons in an action of delivery is Form 1c[3] unless the action includes a claim for payment of money, in which case the copy summons is in Form 1a or Form 1b depending on whether the defender may apply for a time to pay direction or time order.[4]

30.242   The claim for delivery is in Form 7.[5] This form contains an alternative claim for payment of money in the event of non-delivery. Such a claim would normally be made, but the form should be adapted according to the circumstances of the case.

B. Multiplepoinding

30.243   Chapter 27 of the Summary Cause Rules deals with actions of multiplepoinding which fall within the summary cause limits.[6] The summary cause provisions regarding multiplepoindings are broadly similar to those in ordinary causes.[7] The general scheme is that any challenge to the jurisdiction of the court or the competency of the action should be dealt with first. Then any objections to the fund or subject *in medio*

---

[96] S.C.R., r. 23.10(1). It should be noted that this rule does not apply to an application for variation of an award of aliment made under the Sheriff Courts (Civil Jurisdiction and Procedure) (Scotland) Act 1963, s. 3 (as substituted by the Family Law (Scotland) Act 1985, s. 23). In terms of S.C.R., r. 32.1(1) any application for such variation must be made by summons. See para 30.296, *infra*. Nor does the rule apply to any proceedings under the Debtors (Scotland) Act 1987 or to proceedings which may be subject to the provisions of that Act: S.C.R., r. 23.10(6).

[97] S.C.R., r. 23.10(2).

[98] *ibid.*, r. 23.10(3).

[99] *ibid.*

[1] S.C.R., r. 23.10(4).

[2] *ibid.*, r. 23.10(5).

[3] *ibid.*, r. 4.3(b). Form 1c is the standard form of copy summons where the action does not include a claim for payment of money.

[4] S.C.R., r. 4.3(a). See para. 30.81, *supra*.

[5] *ibid.*, r. 4.1(2).

[6] *ibid.*, r. 27.1.

[7] For ordinary cause multiplepoindings see O.C.R., Chap. 35 discussed in Vol. 1, paras 21.52 to 21.71.

should be disposed of. Finally, competing claims must be resolved. Because of the peculiar nature of such actions certain rules which apply to most summary causes do not apply to multiplepoindings. Thus rule 8.1 (return of form of response) does not apply.[8] Rules 8.2 to 8.17 (the standard rules in defended actions) apply only to a limited extent.[9] An action of multiplepoinding must call in court even though no party lodges a form of response.[10] In that case the actions proceeds in accordance with rule 27.9(1)(a).[11]

A summary cause of multiplepoinding may be raised by any party **30.244** holding or having an interest in or claim on the fund or subject *in medio*.[12] The pursuer must call as defenders all persons so far as known to him who have an interest in the fund or subject *in medio*.[13] If the pursuer is the holder of the fund or subject *in medio* he must in his statement of claim include a statement of the fund or subject.[14] If the pursuer is not himself the holder of the fund or subject, he must call the holder as a defender.[15]

A copy summons in Form 1d must be served on each defender.[16] This **30.245** contains a form of response which gives a defender an opportunity to challenge the jurisdiction of the court or the competency of the action, to object to the extent of the fund or subject *in medio* or to make a claim on the fund or subject.

If the pursuer is not the holder of the fund, the holder (who will have **30.246** been called as a defender[17]) must before the return day lodge with the sheriff clerk a statement providing (i) a statement of the fund or subject; (ii) a statement of any claim or lien which he may profess to have on the fund or subject; and (iii) a list of all persons known to him as having an interest in the fund or subject.[18] That statement must also be intimated to the pursuer, the other defenders and all persons listed in the statement as having an interest in the fund or subject.[19]

A defender who intends to challenge the jurisdiction of the court or **30.247** the competency of the action, to object to the extent of the fund or subject *in medio*, or to make a claim must complete and lodge with the sheriff clerk the form of response contained in the service copy summons, including therein a statement of his response which gives fair notice to the pursuer.[20] When the sheriff clerk receives this form of response he must intimate it to the pursuer.[21]

---

[8] S.C.R., r. 27.2(1).

[9] *ibid.*, r. 27.2(2). These rules apply only in accordance with rule 27.7 which is discussed in para. 30.248, *infra.*

[10] S.C.R., r. 7.1(5).

[11] *ibid.* See para. 30.251, *infra.*

[12] *ibid.*, r. 27.3.

[13] *ibid.*, r. 27.4(a).

[14] *ibid.*, r. 27.5(1).

[15] *ibid.*, r. 27.4(b).

[16] *ibid.*, r. 4.3(c).

[17] *ibid.*, r. 27.4(b).

[18] *ibid.*, r. 27.5(2)(a). The statement must be in Form 5a.

[19] *ibid.*, r. 27.5(2)(b).

[20] *ibid.*, r. 27.6(1).

[21] *ibid.*, r. 27.6(2).

30.248   If the form of response lodged by a defender includes a defence challenging the jurisdiction of the court or the competency of the action, rules 8.2 to 8.17 (the rules governing the procedure of an ordinary defended summary cause)[22] apply, with the necessary modifications, to the resolution of these issues.[23] The remaining rules peculiar to multiple-poindings (rules 27.8 to 27.10) come into play only when these issues have been dealt with.[24]

30.249   If the form of response lodged by a defender includes an objection to the fund or subject *in medio*, after disposing of any defence on jurisdiction or competency as described in the previous paragraph, the sheriff must (a) fix a hearing and (b) state the order in which claimants are to be heard at that hearing.[25] If there is no objection to the fund or subject or after any objection thereto has been disposed of, the sheriff may approve the fund or subject and, if appropriate, find the holder liable only in one single payment.[26]

30.250   At any stage in an action of multiplepoinding the sheriff may order that the fund or subject *in medio* be consigned with the sheriff clerk[27] or that the subject *in medio* be sold and the proceeds of sale so consigned.[28] After such consignation the holder of the fund or subject may apply for his exoneration and discharge.[29] On his exoneration and discharge the holder of the fund or subject may be allowed his expenses out of the fund and as a first charge thereon by the sheriff.[30]

30.251   After the disposal of any defence on jurisdiction or competency and of any objection to the fund or subject *in medio*, or if there is no such defence or objection, competing claims must be considered and rule 27.9 comes into play.[31] The sheriff must order claims in Form 5b[32] to be lodged within 14 days[33] and fix a claims hearing at which all parties may appear or be represented.[34] The sheriff clerk must intimate to parties the order for claims and the date and time of the claims hearing.[35]

30.252   If it appears to the sheriff at any stage of a multiplepoinding that there may be other potential claimants who are not parties to the action, he may order such advertisement or intimation of the order for claims as he thinks proper.[36]

30.253   At the claims hearing, if there is no competition between the claimants who appear, the sheriff may order the holder of the fund or

---

[22] See paras 30.134 to 30.142, 30.151 to 30.155 and 30.205 to 30.215, *supra*.
[23] S.C.R., r. 27.7(a).
[24] *ibid.*, r. 27.7(b).
[25] *ibid.*, r. 27.8(1).
[26] *ibid.*, r. 27.8(2).
[27] *ibid.*, r. 27.12(1)(a).
[28] *ibid.*, r. 27.12(1)(b).
[29] *ibid.*, r. 27.12(2).
[30] *ibid.*, r. 27.12(3).
[31] *ibid.*, r. 27.9(1).
[32] The form provides that the claimant should state the ground of his claim and include a reference to any document founded on in support thereof.
[33] S.C.R., r. 27.9(2)(a).
[34] *ibid.*, r. 27.9(2)(b).
[35] *ibid.*, r. 27.9(3).
[36] *ibid.*, r. 27.11.

subject, or the sheriff clerk if consignation has been made,[37] to make it over to the claimants "in terms of their claims or otherwise and subject to such provision as to expenses as he directs".[38] If there are competing claims, it is clear that the sheriff is expected to be interventionist in the same way as at a first hearing in any other summary cause.[39] He must attempt to resolve competing claims, and if he is unable to do so, he must fix the date, time and place for a further hearing[40] and regulate the nature and scope of the hearing and the procedure to be followed.[41] He may require that evidence should be led at this further hearing.[42] The sheriff clerk must intimate to all claimants the date, time and place of the further hearing,[43] although the necessity for this is not clear as it is implicit in the rules that all claimants should attend the claims hearing at which the further hearing is fixed.

At the conclusion of the claims hearing or of any further hearing the sheriff may either pronounce his decision immediately or may reserve judgment.[44] In the latter case he must give his decision in writing within 28 days and the sheriff clerk must forthwith intimate it to the parties.[45] In giving his decision, whether immediately or having reserved judgment, the sheriff must dispose of the action[46] and deal with all questions of expenses.[47] He may order the holder of the fund or subject *in medio*, or the sheriff clerk if there has been consignation, to make it over to such claimants and in such quantity or amount as he may determine.[48] **30.254**

C. Furthcoming

The form of copy summons for an action of furthcoming is Form 1b, which is the standard form for any action of payment where no application may be made for a time to pay direction or a time order.[49] The only special rule which applies to furthcomings is to the effect that the expenses of the action, including the expenses of the arrestment, are to be deemed to be part of the arrestor's claim which may be paid out of the arrested fund or subject.[50] **30.255**

If, as occurs not infrequently, citation of the common debtor has to be effected by newspaper advertisement,[51] it is desirable to indicate in the advertisement the nature of the action and to append a note to the effect that the arrestee is not personally indebted to the pursuer.[52] **30.256**

---

[37] See para. 30.250, *supra*.
[38] S.C.R., r. 27.10(1).
[39] See para. 30.138, *supra*.
[40] S.C.R., r. 27.10(2)(a).
[41] *ibid.*, r. 27.10(2)(b).
[42] *ibid.*, r. 27.10(3).
[43] *ibid.*, r. 27.10(4).
[44] *ibid.*, r. 27.10(5).
[45] *ibid.*
[46] S.C.R., r. 27.10(6)(a).
[47] *ibid.*, r. 27.10(6)(c).
[48] *ibid.*, r. 27.10(6)(b).
[49] *ibid.*, r. 4.3(a)(ii).
[50] *ibid.*, r. 28.1.
[51] In terms of S.C.R., r. 5.5(1)(a). See paras 30.105, 30.106, *supra*.
[52] See (1985) 30 J.L.S. 2.

D. Count reckoning and payment

30.257   In the Ordinary Cause Rules there are no special provisions for actions of count, reckoning and payment[53] However, in the Summary Cause Rules, although the rules for actions for payment of money apply generally, there are some rules directed specifically at count, reckoning and payment.[54]

30.258   The form of copy summons in an action of count, reckoning and payment is either Form 1a or Form 1b, depending on whether or not the defender may apply for a time to pay direction or time order.[55] The defender requires to adapt the form of response depending on whether or not he admits liability to account. If he admits such liability he must state that in the form of response.[56]

30.259   If the defender admits liability to account,[57] or if no response has been lodged within the appropriate time,[58] the pursuer must lodge with the sheriff clerk a minute in Form 17 before close of business on the second day before the calling date.[59] If the pursuer fails to lodge a minute the sheriff must dismiss the action.[60]

30.260   If in his form of response the defender challenges the jurisdiction of the court or the competency of the action, or if he defends the action on the basis that he denies liability to account, the case proceeds initially in the same way as any other defended summary cause.[61] If any such defence is repelled or if the pursuer has lodged a minute as described in the preceding paragraph, the sheriff must order that accounts should be lodged within 14 days and any objections to these accounts within such further period as he may direct.[62] He must also fix a date, time and place for an accounting hearing,[63] and regulate the nature and scope of the accounting hearing and the procedure to be followed.[64] The sheriff may require that evidence be led at an accounting hearing to prove the accounts and in support of any objection taken.[65] The sheriff clerk must intimate the date, time and place of the hearing to all parties.[66] It is suggested that, from the practical point of view, there would be merit in fixing a preliminary hearing after the lodging of accounts and objections as it will be very difficult for the sheriff to determine the nature and scope of the accounting hearing until he has seen both the accounts and the objections.

---

[53] For actions of count reckoning and payment as ordinary causes see Vol. 1, paras 21.02 to 21.11.

[54] S.C.R., Chap. 29.

[55] *ibid.*, r. 4.3(a).

[56] *ibid.*, r. 29.1.

[57] *ibid.*, r. 29.2(1)(b).

[58] *ibid.*, r. 29.2(1)(a).

[59] *ibid.*, r. 29.2(2). Form 17 is the standard minute in an undefended action. See para. 30.115, *supra.*

[60] *ibid.*, r. 29.2(3).

[61] *ibid.*, rr. 8.2 and 8.3 apply. See paras 30.134 to 30.142, *supra.*

[62] *ibid.*, r. 29.2(4)(a).

[63] *ibid.*, r. 29.2(4)(b).

[64] *ibid.*, r. 29.2(4)(c).

[65] *ibid.*, r. 29.2(5).

[66] *ibid.*, r. 29.2(6).

E. Actions for recovery of possession of heritable property

As has already been noted[67] all actions for the recovery of possession **30.261** of heritable property, with the exception of those brought under section 9 of the Land Tenure Reform (Scotland) Act 1974, must be brought as summary causes unless there is an alternative or additional claim for payment of a sum exceeding £1,500.[68] It has been held in Grampian, Highland and Islands that, even if an action for recovery of possession of heritable property includes a claim for interdict, it cannot be brought as an ordinary action.[69] It is, however, to be doubted whether this view is correct. It is probably the case that an action for recovery of possession of heritable property may be brought as an ordinary action if there is also a crave for a remedy which is not competent in a summary cause.[70] An action for recovery of possession of heritable property is not the appropriate form of action by the creditor in a heritable security in the event of the debtor's defaulting. Such a creditor has never been in possession of the property and therefore cannot *recover* possession.[71]

Effect of decree

Decree in an action for recovery of possession of heritable property **30.262** has "the same force and effect as (a) a decree of removing; (b) a decree of ejection; (c) a summary warrant of ejection; (d) a warrant for summary ejection in common form; or (e) a decree pronounced in a summary application for removing, in terms of sections 36, 37 and 38 respectively of [the Sheriff Courts (Scotland) Act 1907]".[72]

Notice of removal

Before an action for the recovery of possession of heritable property **30.263** can be commenced it may be necessary for the landlord to serve a notice of removal.[73] In the case of a tenancy to which sections 34, 35 and 36 of the 1907 Act apply[74] the form of notice is in Form 3a.[75] In the case of a tenancy to which section 37 of the 1907 Act applies[76] the notice is in form 3b.[77]

If the tenancy is of land exceeding two acres in extent leased under a **30.264** probative lease for three years or more, notice to remove must be given not less than one year nor more than two years before the termination of the lease.[78] If such a tenancy is for less than three years, the notice must be given not less than six months before the termination of the lease.[79]

---

[67] See para. 30.02, *supra*.

[68] 1971 Act, s. 35(1)(c).

[69] *Disblair Estates Ltd v. Jackson*, Nov. 23, 1982, Aberdeen Sh.Ct., unreported.

[70] See Vol. 1, paras 23.08 and 23.09.

[71] *Prestwick Investment Trust v. Jones*, 1981 S.L.T. (Sh.Ct.) 55. On this decision see Vol. 1, paras 23.03, 23.30, *supra*.

[72] S.C.R., r. 30.3.

[73] The precise circumstances of all cases in which a notice of removal is necessary are outwith the scope of this volume, and the reader should consult one of the specialist works on landlord and tenant or housing law.

[74] See paras 30.264, 30.265, *infra*.

[75] S.C.R., r. 30.6(1).

[76] See para 30.266, *infra*.

[77] S.C.R., r. 30.6(2).

[78] 1907 Act, s. 34(a).

[79] *ibid.*, s. 34(b).

30.265　　If the tenancy is of land exceeding two acres and there is no written lease, notice of termination of the tenancy must be given not less than six months prior thereto.[80]

30.266　　In all other cases where the lease is for one year or more, notice of termination of the tenancy must be given at least 40 days before May 15 or November 11, according to whether the termination of the tenancy is at Whitsunday or Martinmas respectively.[81]

30.267　　If a house or other heritable subject is let for less than one year the period for a notice of removal depends on whether the period of the lease is more or less than four months. If it is more, the period of notice is not less than 40 days.[82] If the period of the lease is not more than four months, the period of notice is either one-third of the period of the lease or 28 days, whichever is the greater.[83]

Notice of intention to take proceedings

30.268　　In most cases of leases of dwelling-houses a preliminary written notice of intention to take court proceedings must usually be served. The nature of this notice depends on the nature of the tenancy. In the case of public sector tenancies of dwelling-houses which are secure tenancies,[84] the landlord must serve a notice of intention to bring proceedings.[85] The notice must be in the prescribed form[86] and must specify the ground on which the action is being raised and the date after which proceedings may be commenced.[87] In the case of an assured tenancy (*i.e.* most private tenancies and housing association tenancies which are governed by the Housing (Scotland) Act 1988),[88] the provisions of section 19 of that Act apply. This provides *inter alia* that the notice of intention to bring proceedings must state the ground for doing so and particulars thereof.[89]

Scottish secure tenancy under the Housing (Scotland) Act 2001

30.269　　The Housing (Scotland) Act 2001 (hereinafter referred to as "the 2001 Act") contains radical provisions affecting leases of dwelling-houses These introduce a new form of tenancy to be known as a Scottish secure tenancy.[90] The general intention is to have the same provisions applying to all tenancies of dwelling-houses without any distinction between public and private sector leases. At the time of writing these provisions are not yet in force, but it is understood that it is intended to bring them

---

[80] 1907 Act, s. 36.

[81] *ibid.*, s. 37.

[82] *ibid.*, s. 38.

[83] *ibid.*

[84] As defined by the Housing (Scotland) Act 1987, s. 44.

[85] *ibid.*, s. 47(2).

[86] *ibid.*, s. 47(3). The form is as prescribed in the Secure Tenancies (Proceedings for Possession) (Scotland) Order 1980 (S.I. 1980 No. 1389), para. 2 and Sched.

[87] Housing (Scotland) Act 1947, s. 47(3).

[88] For the definition of "assured tenancy" see s. 12 of the 1988 Act.

[89] 1988 Act, s. 19(2) which applies to the grounds specified in Sched. 5 to the Act. The form of notice is as prescribed by the Assured Tenancies (Forms) (Scotland) Regulations 1988 (S.I. 1988 No. 2109), para. 3 and Sched., Form AT6.

[90] 2001 Act, s. 11. There is also to be a short Scottish secure tenancy as defined in s. 34. The provisions for recovery of possession relating to a Scottish secure tenancy apply generally also to a short Scottish secure tenancy.

into force on September 30, 2002. For that reason the provisions are discussed briefly here. However, the reader must be advised to ascertain the precise terms of the relevant commencement order and of the various regulations to be made relating to proceedings for recovery of possession.

Proceedings for recovery of possession in a Scottish secure tenancy **30.270** must be preceded by a notice of intention to take proceedings.[91] The notice is to be in a form prescribed by regulations and must specify the ground on which recovery of possession is sought and the date on or after which the landlord may raise proceedings.[92] The notice requires to be served not only on the tenant of the dwelling-house but also on "any qualifying occupier".[93] Before serving a notice the landlord must make such inquiries as may be necessary to establish "so far as is reasonably practicable" whether there are any qualifying occupiers and, if so, their identities.[94]

A qualifying occupier may apply to the court to be sisted as a party to **30.271** proceedings for recovery of possession, and, if he does so, the court must grant his application.[95] It is suggested that such an application should be made by incidental application.[96]

A requirement that it is reasonable to make an order for recovery of **30.272** possession applies in many cases of a Scottish secure tenancy under the 2001 Act[97] as it does under existing legislation.[98]

Again as under existing legislation,[99] the court is given power to **30.273** adjourn proceedings for recovery of possession in a Scottish secure tenancy for a period or periods "with or without imposing conditions as to payment of outstanding rent or otherwise."[1]

In the case where a Scottish secure tenancy has been abandoned by **30.274** the tenant the landlord may, in certain circumstances take possession of the house without any court proceedings.[2]

---

[91] 2001 Act, s. 14(2)(a).

[92] *ibid.*, s. 14(4).

[93] *ibid.*, s. 14(2)(a). "Qualifying occupier" is defined in s. 14(6) and means in general terms (a) a member of the tenant's family aged 16 years or over, (b) a sub-tenant, or (c) a lodger.

[94] 2001 Act, s. 14(3).

[95] *ibid.*, s. 15.

[96] *cf.* S.C.R., r. 13.1(3)(e) which provides for amendment of a summons to sist a party in substitution for, or in addition to, the original party, such amendment being by way of incidental application. See para. 30.45, *supra*.

[97] 2001 Act, s. 16(2)((a)(ii), (c)(ii). For the purposes of s. 16(2)(a)(ii) criteria of reasonableness are laid down in s. 16(3).

[98] Housing (Scotland) Act 1987, s. 48(2)(a) and Housing (Scotland) Act 1988, s. 18(4). See para. 30.279, *infra*.

[99] Housing (Scotland) Act 1987, s. 48(1) and Housing (Scotland) Act 1988, s. 20(1). See para. 30.280, *infra*.

[1] 2001 Act, s. 16(1). This is virtually identical to the terms of the Housing (Scotland) Act 1987, s. 48(1).

[2] 2001 Act, ss. 17, 18. In general terms the landlord must serve notices on the tenant and if there is no response to these notices the landlord is entitled to take possession of the house.

Form of claim

30.275   The form of claim in an action for the recovery of possession of heritable property is in Form 3.[3] The copy summons is in Form 1c[4] unless the pursuer is claiming payment of money as well as recovery of possession in which case the copy summons is in Form 1a[5] or 1b,[6] depending on whether or not the defender is entitled to apply for a time to pay direction. If the action is raised under section 38 of the 1907 Act (subjects let for less than one year)[7] it may be at the instance of a proprietor or his factor or any other person authorised by law to pursue an action of removing.[8]

Actions against defenders without right or title to possess

30.276   The normal rules about periods of notice and other periods of time apply to actions for the recovery of possession of heritable property with the exception of those covered by rule 30.2. This rule applies to actions for the recovery of possession of heritable property "against a person in possession of heritable property without right or title to possess the property",[9] but not to a person "who has or had a title or other right to occupy the heritable property and who has been in continuous occupation since that title or right is alleged to have come to an end".[10]

30.277   Where the name of the person in occupation of the property is not known and cannot reasonably be ascertained, the pursuer should call him as defender naming him as an "occupier".[11] In such a case the summons should, unless the sheriff otherwise directs, be served by sheriff officer in one of two ways.[12] In the case of a building the officer must affix a copy of the summons and a citation in Form 11 addressed to "the occupiers" to the main door or other conspicuous part of the premises and, if practicable, deposit a copy of each document in the premises.[13] In the case of land the officer serves the summons by inserting stakes in the ground at conspicuous parts of the occupied land and attaching to each a sealed transparent envelope containing a copy of the summons and a citation in Form 11 addressed to "the occupiers".[14]

30.278   In an action to which the rule applies the sheriff may, in his discretion, shorten or dispense with any period of time provided anywhere in the summary cause rules,[15] except in respect of the period for appeal which it is not competent to dispense with or shorten.[16] An application by a party to shorten or dispense with any period may be made orally, and the provisions of rule 9.1 for giving notice to the other party or parties[17] do

---

[3] S.C.R., r. 4.1(2).
[4] *ibid.*, r. 4.3(b). Form 1c is the appropriate form for any non-monetary claim.
[5] *ibid.*, r. 4.3(a)(i).
[6] *ibid.*, r. 4.3(a)(ii).
[7] See para. 30.267, *supra.*
[8] S.C.R., r. 30.1.
[9] *ibid.*, r. 30.2(1).
[10] *ibid.*, r. 30.2(2).
[11] *ibid.*, r. 30.2(3).
[12] *ibid.*, r. 30.2(4).
[13] *ibid.*, r. 30.2(4)(a).
[14] *ibid.*, r. 30.2(4)(b).
[15] *ibid.*, r. 30.2(5).
[16] *ibid.*, r. 25.6(a). See para. 30.344, *infra.*
[17] See para 30.38, *supra.*

not apply, although the sheriff clerk must enter details of any such application in the Register of Summary Causes.[18] As has a already been mentioned, the period for appeal may not be shortened or dispensed with,[19] even if there has been an early issue of extract,[20] but the lodging of a note of appeal does not operate so as to suspend diligence unless the sheriff directs otherwise.[21] Because of the serious implications of this rule (whose 1976 equivalent, which was in similar terms, has been the subject of critical comment)[22] it is suggested that a pursuer seeking to avail himself of its provisions should obtain the fullest possible information before making any application to the sheriff.

Reasonableness of decree

In certain cases, even though the tenant may be in breach of a **30.279** condition of the lease, the sheriff may not grant decree for recovery of possession unless he is satisfied that it is "reasonable" to do so.[23] In such cases the statement of claim should include an averment that it is reasonable for the court to grant decree.[24] The pursuer should be prepared to satisfy the sheriff of the reasonableness of granting decree, even if the defender is not present or represented when the case calls.

Adjournment

In terms of section 48(1) of the Housing (Scotland) Act 1987 the court **30.280** has power to adjourn proceedings for the recovery of possession of property let under a secure tenancy, for a period or periods "with or without imposing conditions as to payment of outstanding rent or other conditions". A similar power is conferred by section 20(1) of the Housing (Scotland) Act 1988 in respect of an assured tenancy, but without the reference to conditions. It is submitted, however, that it is quite competent for the court to adjourn under section 20(1) and to impose conditions in the same way as under section 48(1) of the 1987 Act.

Preservation of defender's goods and effects

If decree is granted in an action for the recovery of possession of **30.281** heritable property and the defender is neither present nor represented, the sheriff may give such directions as he deems proper for the preservation of the defender's goods and effects.[25]

Actions of removing where fixed term of removal

Rule 30.5(1) is in terms identical to those of Ordinary Cause Rule **30.282** 34.5(1).[26] The rule applies to leases where there is a fixed term of removal and which are not subject to section 21 of the Agricultural

---

[18] S.C.R., r. 30.2(6).

[19] *ibid.*, r. 25.6(a).

[20] *ibid.*, r. 25.6(b).

[21] *ibid.*, r. 25.6(c).

[22] *e.g.* in (1980) 45 SCOLAG Bul. 78.

[23] *e.g.* Housing (Scotland) Act 1987, s. 48(2)(a); Housing (Scotland) Act 1988, s. 18(4).

[24] *Gordon D.C. v. Acutt*, 1991 S.L.T. (Sh.Ct) 78.

[25] S.C.R., r. 30.4.

[26] See Vol. 1, para. 23.12. The terms of these rules to some extent mirror the provisions of the 1907 Act, ss. 34 to 37. See paras 30.264 to 30.266, *supra*.

Holdings (Scotland) Act 1991 (which requires a period of notice of not less than one or more than two years in respect of leases of land falling within the scope of that Act). An action of removing may be raised at any time against a tenant who has bound himself to remove by a writing dated and signed either within 12 months after the term of removal or "where there is more than one ish, after the ish first in date to remove".[27]

30.283 If the tenant has not so bound himself an action of removing may be raised at any time subject to certain limitations. In the case of a lease of lands exceeding two acres in extent for a period of three years and upwards, an interval of not less than one year nor more than two years must elapse between the date of notice of removal and the term of removal first in date.[28] In the case of a lease of lands exceeding two acres in extent, whether written or oral, held from year to year or under tacit relocation, or for any other period less than three years, an interval of not less than six months must elapse between the date of notice of removal and the term of removal first in date.[29] In the case of a house let with or without land attached not exceeding two acres in extent, of land not exceeding two acres in extent without houses, of mills, fishings, shootings and of all other heritable subjects except land exceeding two acres in extent, which are let for a year or more, 40 days at least must elapse between the date of notice of removal and the term of removal first in date.[30]

Caution for violent profits

30.284 In any defended action of removing the sheriff may order the defender to find caution for violent profits.[31]

F. Sequestration for rent

30.285 An action for sequestration for rent must be brought as a summary cause where the rent in respect of which sequestration is sought does not exceed £1,500.[32]

Summons

30.286 An action of sequestration for rent or in security of rent may be brought as a summary cause either before or after the term of payment.[33] The copy summons may be in Form 1a or 1b, depending on whether or not the defender may apply for a time to pay direction.[34] The statement of claim is in Form 4.[35] The summons is warrant for sequestration, inventorying and appraisal.[36] It is deemed to include authority, if need be, to open shut and lockfast places for the purpose of executing the warrant.[37]

---

[27] S.C.R., r. 30.5(1)(a).
[28] *ibid.*, r. 30.5(1)(b)(i).
[29] *ibid.*, r. 30.5(1)(b)(ii).
[30] *ibid.*, r. 30.5(1)(b)(iii).
[31] *ibid.*, r. 30.5(2). This rule is identical to O.C.R., r. 34.5(2). See Vol. 1, para. 23.13.
[32] 1971 Act, s. 35(1)(b). For sequestration of rent as an ordinary cause see Vol. 1, paras 23.14 to 23.24.
[33] S.C.R., r. 31.1.
[34] *ibid.*, r. 4.3(a)(i), (ii). See para. 30.81, *supra.*
[35] S.C.R., r. 4.1(2).
[36] Form 4.
[37] S.C.R., r. 31.7.

Appraisal and inventory

When the sheriff officer executes the warrant for sequestration he **30.287** must have the value of the effects in the property appraised by one person who may also be a witness to the sequestration.[38] The sheriff officer must give to or leave with the tenant an inventory or list of the sequestrated effects with the appraisal of their value in accordance with Part 1 of Form 4b.[39] Part 1 provides for the effects to be listed, described and valued. The tenant must also be given a notice in Form 4a.1[40] This advises the tenant of his rights under the Debtors (Scotland) Act 1987. The tenant must then be cited in accordance with Chapter 5 of the Summary Cause Rules.[41] After executing the sequestration the sheriff officer must prepare and sign the certificate of execution contained in Part 2 of Form 4b.[42] He must then return both parts of Form 4b to the sheriff clerk within seven days of execution of the sequestration.[43]

Further procedure

An action of sequestration for rent must call in court even though the **30.288** defender has not lodged a form of response.[44] After "hearing the cause" (which is in practice unlikely to involve any form of proof even though the defender has returned a form of response) the sheriff disposes of it as he thinks fit.[45] He may either recall the sequestration in whole or in part, or he may grant decree for the rent found due and grant warrant for the sale of the sequestrated effects.[46] He should also, if appropriate, grant decree for expenses.

Sale

If a warrant for sale is granted, the sale takes place by public roup at **30.289** such place as the sheriff may direct and after advertisement in a newspaper circulating in the district.[47] A copy of the warrant for sale must be displayed on the walls of the court which granted it until the sale has been concluded.[48] The sale is carried out by a sheriff officer or by such other person as the sheriff may direct.[49] If the proceeds of the sale exceed the total of the sum decerned for, the expenses awarded and the expenses of the sale, the surplus must be returned to the "owner".[50] This may raise difficult problems if the items sequestrated include the property of more than one person, as is possible. From the practical point of view every effort should be made to restrict the sale to items belonging to the tenant, if this can be done. If the owner of the items sold cannot be found, the surplus is consigned in the hands of the sheriff clerk.[51] If the effects sequestrated are not sold they must be

---

[38] S.C.R., r. 31.2(1).
[39] *ibid.*, r. 31.2(2).
[40] *ibid.*
[41] *ibid.* For citation under Chap. 5 see paras 30.89 *et seq.*, *supra.*
[42] S.C.R., r. 31.2(3)(a).
[43] *ibid.*, r. 31.2(3)(b).
[44] *ibid.*, r. 7.1(4)(b).
[45] *ibid.*, r. 31.3(1).
[46] *ibid.*
[47] S.C.R., r. 31.3(2).
[48] *ibid.*
[49] *ibid.*
[50] S.C.R., r. 31.3(3).
[51] *ibid.*

delivered to the creditor at the appraised value to the amount of the sum decerned for, the expenses of the action and the expenses of sequestration and sale.[52] Within 14 days of the date of the sale or of delivery the sheriff officer concerned must report to the sheriff clerk the proceedings in the sequestration and sale or delivery.[53]

Premises displenished

30.290 If it is reported to the court by the officer who has executed, or been instructed to execute, a warrant for sale, that the premises are displenished, the pursuer may apply for a warrant to cite the defender to a fixed diet at which the sheriff may make such order as he considers appropriate.[54] This order is likely to be a warrant entitling the pursuer to eject the defender and to re-let the premises. If a warrant to re-let is granted, any rent accruing thereafter is exigible only for such period as the tenant continues to occupy the premises.[55]

Recall of sequestration

30.291 If the tenant either pays to the landlord the rent due with the expenses of raising the summons and sequestrating, or consigns in the hands of the sheriff clerk the rent due together with a sum to cover expenses (as determined by the sheriff clerk), the sheriff clerk must recall the sequestration.[56] He does so by endorsing the original summons or the defender's copy of it to that effect.[57]

G. Actions for aliment for a spouse

30.292 The possibility of claiming aliment under the summary cause procedure in terms of section 3 of the Sheriff Courts (Civil Jurisdiction and Procedure) (Scotland) Act 1963 has already been noted.[58] The rules do not provide for a specific form of claim for such an action. It is suggested that the claim should be in the same form as the crave in an action for aliment in an ordinary cause.

30.293 It should be noted that very few actions of aliment for children are competent in the sheriff court, whether as summary causes or ordinary actions, as payments for the maintenance of children are now normally dealt with in terms of the Child Support Act 1991.[59] The provisions of the Summary Cause Rules relating to these exceptional cases where a court action in respect of aliment for a child *is* competent are dealt with in section H of this chapter. This section is relevant to applications for aliment for spouses.

Intimation

30.294 In an action for aliment where the address of the defender is not known to the pursuer and cannot reasonably be ascertained the pursuer must include in the summons an application for a warrant for intimation

---

[52] S.C.R., r. 31.3(4).
[53] *ibid.*, r. 31.4.
[54] *ibid.*, r. 31.6(1).
[55] *ibid.*, r. 31.6(2).
[56] *ibid.*, r. 31.5.
[57] *ibid.*
[58] See para. 30.02, n.5, *supra.*
[59] For a detailed examination of the provisions of the 1991 Act see Wilkinson and Norrie, *Parent and Child* (2nd ed., 1999), Chap. 14. For developments since then see Gloag and Henderson, *The Law of Scotland* (11th ed., 2001), para. 48.39.

to (i) every child of the marriage between the parties who has reached the age of 16 years, and (ii) one of the next of kin of the defender who has reached that age, unless the address of such person is not known to the pursuer and cannot reasonably be ascertained.[60] A notice of intimation in Form 36 must be attached to the copy of the summons intimated to any such person.[61] This notice informs the recipient of the fact that the action has been raised, requests him to inform the sheriff clerk in writing of the defender's address if he knows it and advises him that he may himself appear as a party if he wishes. The usual information about taking legal advice is also included.

In an action for aliment where the defender is a person who is **30.295** suffering from a mental disorder the pursuer must include in the summons an application for a warrant for intimation to the same persons as mentioned in the preceding paragraph and to the defender's guardian if one has been appointed.[62] A notice of intimation in Form 37 must be attached to the copy of the summons intimated to any such person.[63] This notice informs the recipient of the fact that an action has been raised and advises him that he may himself appear as a party if he wishes. The usual information about taking legal advice is also included.

Recall or variation of decree for aliment

Despite the terms of rule 23.10 (dealing with variation of decree by **30.296** minute),[64] rule 32.1(1) provides that an application for recall or variation of any decree for payment of aliment pronounced in the small debt court under the Small Debt Acts[65] or, in a summary cause under the 1971 Act must be made by summons. This means that a fresh summary cause action must be raised in such a case. In the first edition of this book it was surmised that the apparent conflict between the equivalent rules in the 1976 Summary Cause Rules was due to an oversight on the part of those drafting the Summary Cause Rules.[66] However, as these rules are in effect repeated in the present Summary Cause Rules it has to be assumed that there is some good reason for treating variation of decrees for aliment in a different way from variation of other decrees, although it is difficult to see what that reason can be.

Interim orders

In both actions brought under section 3 of the Sheriff Court (Civil **30.297** Jurisdiction and Procedure) (Scotland) Act 1963 and applications to vary aliment, the court has power to make such interim orders as it thinks fit.[67]

H. Actions for aliment for a child where competent in terms of the Child Support Act 1991

As has already been noted,[68] very few actions for aliment in respect of **30.298** a child are now competent in the sheriff court. The rules governing the actions which are still competent are contained in Chapter 33 of the

---

[60] S.C.R., r. 32.2(a).

[61] *ibid.*

[62] S.C.R., r. 32.2(b).

[63] *ibid.*

[64] See para. 30.240, *supra.*

[65] S.C.R., r. 32.1(3) defines "Small Debt Acts" as meaning and including the Small Debt (Scotland) Acts 1837 to 1889 and Acts explaining or amending the same.

[66] 1st ed., para. 25–172. The equivalent 1976 rules were S.C.R., rr. 92 (minute for variation) and 79(1) (variation of aliment to be by summons).

[67] S.C.R., r. 32.1(2).

[68] See para. 30.293, *supra.*

Summary Cause Rules. These are broadly similar to those contained in
the Ordinary Cause Rules,[69] but they have been updated to take account
of recent amendments to the 1991 Act. Claims for aliment which are still
competent in the sheriff court and therefore, within the appropriate
financial limits, as summary causes include: a claim by a child in excess
of the formula laid down in the legislation[70]; a claim for the expenses of
a child's education or training[71]; a claim for expenses in connection
with a child's disability where the child is in receipt of disability living
allowance or is disabled in terms of section 8(9) of the 1991 Act[72]; a
claim for aliment by a child against the parent with care.[73] A claim is also
competent by or in respect of a child where the habitual residence of the
child, the absent parent or the parent with care is outwith the United
Kingdom.[74] Other competent claims are: by a child against a step-
parent[75]; by a child against an adult who has accepted the child as a child
of the family[76]; by a child who is not a child within the meaning of
section 55 of the 1991 Act.[77]

Statement of claim in action containing claim relating to aliment of child

30.299   The statement of claim in a summons or counterclaim containing a
claim relating to aliment[78] to which section 8(6), (7), (8) or (10) of the
1991 Act applies[79] must state where appropriate: (i) that a maintenance
calculation[80] under section 11 of the 1991 Act[81] is in force; (ii) the date
of the maintenance calculation; (iii) the amount and frequency of
periodical payments of child support maintenance fixed by the maintenance calculation; and (iv) the grounds on which the sheriff retains
jurisdiction under the subsection concerned.[82] The summons or counterclaim must, unless the sheriff on cause shown directs otherwise, be
accompanied by any document issued by the Secretary of State to the
party, intimating the making of the maintenance calculation concerned.[83]

30.300   The statement of claim in a summons or counterclaim containing a
claim relating to aliment[84] to which section 8(6), (7), (8) or (10) of the

---

[69] O.C.R., r. 33.88 to 33.91 discussed in Vol. 1, paras 22.96 to 22.99. See also paras 22.11
and 22.12.

[70] Child Support Act 1991, s.8(6).

[71] *ibid.*, s. 8(7).

[72] *ibid.*, s. 8(8).

[73] *ibid.*, s. 8(10).

[74] *ibid.*, s. 44.

[75] *ibid.*, s. 3(1).

[76] *ibid.*

[77] The 1991 Act, s. 55 defines "child" for the purposes of the Act.

[78] S.C.R., r. 33.1 defines "claim relating to aliment as "a crave for decree of aliment in
relation to a child or for recall or variation of such a decree". The use of the term "crave"
is perhaps rather unfortunate in the context of a summary cause, where the summons
contains a claim rather than a crave.

·   [79] For the application of these subsections see para. 30.298, *supra.*

[80] S.C.R., r. 33.1 defines "maintenance calculation" as having the meaning assigned to it
in the 1991 Act, s. 54 as amended by the Child Support, Pensions and Social Security Act
2000, s. 1(2).

[81] As substituted by the Child Support, Pensions and Social Security Act 2000, s. 1(1).

[82] S.C.R., r. 33.2(1)(a).

[83] *ibid.*, r. 33.2(1)(b).

[84] *ibid.*, r. 33.1 defines "claim relating to aliment" as "a crave for decree of aliment in
relation to a child or for recall or variation of such a decree". The use of the term "crave"
is perhaps rather unfortunate in the context of a summary cause, where the summons
contains a claim rather than a crave.

1991 Act does *not* apply[85] must include a statement either that the habitual residence[86] of the absent parent, parent with care or qualifying child is outwith the United Kingdom, or that the child is not a child within the meaning of section 55 of the 1991 Act.[87]

The statement of claim in a summons or counterclaim which involves **30.301** parties in respect of whom a decision has been made in any application, review or appeal under the 1991 Act must (a) include statements to the effect that such a decision has been made and give details of that decision, and (b) unless the sheriff on cause shown otherwise directs, be accompanied by any document issued by the Secretary of State to the parties intimating that decision.[88]

Effect of maintenance calculations on court orders

Section 10 of the 1991 Act makes provision for the relationship **30.302** between maintenance assessments (now maintenance calculations) and certain prescribed court orders. The general purport of section 10 is that the court order will yield to the terms of the maintenance assessment. The prescribed court orders include any order made under the Family Law (Scotland) Act 1985 (which is the legislation providing for the obligation of a parent to aliment his or her child) as well as various other forms of maintenance order.[89]

Where a sheriff clerk receives notification that a maintenance calcula- **30.303** tion has been made, cancelled or has ceased to have effect so as to affect a prescribed order which had been made in a summary cause, he must enter in the Register of Summary Causes in respect of that order a note to that effect.[90] This note must state either that the order ceases or ceased to have effect from the date two days after the making of the maintenance calculation,[91] or that the maintenance calculation has been cancelled or has ceased to have effect.[92]

Effect of maintenance calculation on extract of alimentary decree

Where a decree relating to aliment is affected by a maintenance **30.304** calculation, any extract of that decree issued by the sheriff clerk must be endorsed with a certificate to the effect that the order so far as it relates to the making or securing of periodical payments to or for the benefit of a named child or children ceases to have effect from the date two days after the date of the making of the maintenance calculation.[93]

Where a decree relating to aliment has ceased to have effect on the **30.305** making of a maintenance calculation and that maintenance calculation is

---

[85] For the application of these subsections see para. 30.298, *supra.*
[86] Within the meaning of the 1991 Act, s. 3 as amended by the Children (Scotland) Act 1995, Sched. 4, para. 52(2) and S.I. 2000 No. 155.
[87] S.C.R., r. 33.2(2).
[88] *ibid.*, r. 33.2(3).
[89] Child Support Act 1991 (Maintenance Arrangement and Jurisdiction) Regulations 1992 (S.I. 1992 No. 2645), reg. 3(1).
[90] S.C.R., r. 33.3(1).
[91] *ibid.*, r. 33.3(2)(a).
[92] *ibid.*, r. 33.3(2)(b).
[93] *ibid.*, r. 33.4(1). For the precise terms of the certificate see the rule.

later cancelled or ceases to have effect, any extract of the decree issued by the sheriff clerk must be endorsed with a certificate to the effect that the order has been revived with effect from the date of cancellation or cessation of the maintenance calculation.[94]

I. Actions of damages for personal injury

30.306 Chapter 36 of the Ordinary Cause Rules applies to actions of damages for personal injury or the death of a person from personal injuries,[95] Chapter 34 of the Summary Cause Rules also deals with such actions. Although there are certain similarities between the two sets of rules there are sufficient differences between them to justify the Summary Cause Rules being considered quite separately.

30.307 Chapter 34 "applies to an action of damages for personal injuries or the death of a person from personal injuries".[96] "Personal injuries" includes any disease or impairment of physical or mental condition.[97] Rule 4.2 of the Summary Cause Rules (the rule dealing with the statement of claim) does not apply to such actions except for the requirement therein to give fair notice of the claim.[98] Rule 8.1 (the rule dealing with the form of response) does not apply at all.[99] Rules 8.2 to 8.17 (the rules applying generally to defended summary causes) apply with modifications.[1]

Statement of claim

30.308 The statement of claim in a Chapter 34 action must be in Form 10.[2] It may be noted that this is the only form of summary cause in which the detailed contents of the statement of claim are prescribed. Form 10 provides for the statement of claim being laid out in the same sort of way as that in which the condescendence in an initial writ in a similar type of action might be drafted. The first paragraph states details of the pursuer and, in a death action, the designation of the deceased and his or her relationship to the pursuer. Paragraph 2 states details of the defender. Paragraph 3 states the ground of jurisdiction. Paragraph 4 states the facts of the case. Paragraph 5 states the injuries suffered together with details of treatment received. Paragraph 6 states the legal basis of the claim. It may be noted that it is not necessary to include in the statement of claim the amount of damages claimed. This is done in a separate document called a valuation of claim.[3]

30.309 The statement of claim must contain a concise statement of the grounds of action, and the facts relied upon to establish the claim.[4] The pursuer's date of birth and, where applicable, his National Insurance number, must be stated.[5] In the paragraph dealing with treatment there

---

[94] S.C.R., r. 33.4(2). For the precise terms of the certificate see the rule.
[95] For a discussion of such actions as ordinary causes see Vol. 1, paras 21.12 to 21.36.
[96] S.C.R., r. 34.1(1). Such actions will be referred to henceforth as "Chapter 34 actions".
[97] *ibid.*, r. 34.1(2).
[98] *ibid.*, r. 34.1(3).
[99] *ibid.*
[1] *ibid.*, r. 34.1(4) provides that these rules are to apply only in accordance with S.C.R., r. 34.3(2), for which see para. 30.315, *infra*.
[2] S.C.R., r. 34.2(1).
[3] Form 10c. See para. 30.310, *infra*.
[4] S.C.R., r. 34.2(1)(a).
[5] *ibid.*, r. 34.2(1)(b).

must be stated the names of every medical practitioner from whom, and every hospital or other institution in which, the pursuer, or in an action in respect of the death of a person, the deceased, received treatment for injuries sustained or for disease suffered by him.[6]

Summons

With the summons a statement of valuation of claim must be lodged **30.310** (which must include a list of supporting documents) in Form 10c.[7] Form 10c provides for different heads of damages being stated together with details of what interest is being claimed. It requires the pursuer or his solicitor to give careful consideration to the question of damages before the action is raised. There must also be lodged with the summons either all medical reports then available to the pursuer on which he intends, or intends to reserve the right, to rely in the action, or a statement that there are no such medical reports.[8]

The summons may include an application for warrants for intimation **30.311** in so far as permitted under the Summary Cause Rules.[9] There might, for example, be intimation to a "connected person".[10]

The summons may also include a specification of documents in **30.312** Form 10e.[11] This specification contains the usual type of documents for which commission and diligence is sought in a Chapter 34 action, *e.g.* hospital records, employers' wages record, accident reports and the like. The provision for a specification at such an early stage of a case is to be welcomed. If the summons includes a specification it must, where necessary be intimated to the Lord Advocate or the Advocate General for Scotland and, if there is any doubt, both.[12]

The summons is served on the defender in the usual way, but, instead **30.313** of the standard form of response, Form 10b is used.[13] This gives the defender an opportunity to answer the pursuer's claim in detail, including the facts of the case and the heads of damage. The pursuer must also enclose with the defender's copy summons a copy of his valuation of claim.[14]

Defender's response

A defender who wishes to defend the action on any ground must **30.314** complete the form of response in Form 10b and lodge it with the sheriff clerk before the return day.[15] In the form of response the defender must state, in a manner which gives the pursuer fair notice, the grounds of fact and law on which he intends to resist the pursuer's claim together with a brief statement of the facts on which he relies in his defence.[16]

---

[6] S.C.R., r. 34.2(1)(c).
[7] *ibid.*, r. 34.2(2)(b).
[8] *ibid.*, r. 34.2(2)(a).
[9] *ibid.*, r. 34.2(5)(a).
[10] See paras 30.321 to 30.327, *infra*.
[11] S.C.R., r. 34.2(5)(b).
[12] *ibid.*, r. 34.2(6).
[13] *ibid.*, r. 34.2(7).
[14] *ibid.*
[15] S.C.R., r. 34.3(1).
[16] *ibid.*

30.315   If a defender lodges a form of response the normal procedure as provided for in rules 8.2 to 8.17 apply with the necessary modifications.[17]

Inspection and recovery of documents

30.316   Where the summons has included a specification of documents in accordance with rule 34.2(5)(b)[18] and the defender has lodged a form of response stating a defence to the action, the sheriff clerk makes an order granting commission and diligence for the production and recovery of the documents mentioned in the specification.[19] This order has the same effect as a sheriff's interlocutor granting commission and diligence.[20] If the defender or, where appropriate, the Lord Advocate or the Advocate General objects to the specification he must lodge an incidental application to that effect.[21] The incidental application must be lodged on or before the return day.[22] It is to be determined at the hearing held on the calling date in accordance with rule 8.2(1).[23] These provisions are without prejudice to the right of any party to apply for a commission and diligence for the recovery of documents in normal course[24] or for an order under section 1 of the Administration of Justice (Scotland) Act 1972.[25]

Statement of valuation of claim for party other than pursuer

30.317   As has already been stated, a pursuer must lodge a statement of valuation of claim with his summons and enclose a copy thereof with the defender's copy summons.[26] However another party to the case may also wish to make a claim for damages. He should do so by himself making a statement of valuation of claim (with a list of supporting documents) in Form 10c[27] and lodging it with the sheriff clerk.[28] A party who lodges such a statement must give written intimation to every other party of the statement and the list of documents contained therein.[29] The statement of valuation of claim must normally be lodged no later than 28 days before the date fixed for the proof.[30] A party who fails to lodge it by then will be liable to any other party for the expenses of proving the quantification of his claim unless the sheriff, on special cause shown, otherwise directs.[31]

Provisional damages

30.318   Section 12(2)(a) of the Administration of Justice Act 1982 provides that in certain circumstances a court may make a provisional award of damages. A pursuer who wishes to avail himself of this provision must

---

[17] S.C.R., r. 34.3(2).
[18] See para. 30.312, *supra*.
[19] S.C.R., r. 34.4(2).
[20] *ibid.*, r. 34.4(3).
[21] *ibid.*, r. 34.4(5).
[22] *ibid.*, r. 34.4(6)(a).
[23] *ibid.*, r. 34.4(6)(b). For the hearing under S.C.R., r. 8.2(1) see paras 30.134 *et seq.*, *supra*.
[24] *ibid.*, r. 34.4(4). For commission and diligence see paras 30.162, 30.163, *supra*.
[25] *ibid.*, r. 34.4(4). For orders under s. 1 of the 1972 Act see paras 30.169 to 30.173, *supra*.
[26] *ibid.*, r. 34.2(2)(b) and (7).
[27] *ibid.*, r. 34.5(1).
[28] *ibid.*, r. 34.5(2).
[29] *ibid.*, r. 34.5(3).
[30] *ibid.*, r. 34.5(4).
[31] *ibid.*

apply for an order under section 12(2)(a) of the Act by including in the summons a claim for provisional damages[32] in Form 10a.[33] This form provides for the purser's claiming a specific sum. The pursuer must include in it a statement that there is a risk that the pursuer will, as a result of the cause of action, develop serious disease or a deterioration of his condition in the future, and a statement that the defender is a public authority or corporation or is insured or indemnified in respect of the claim. These statements are to ensure that the claim for provisional damages complies with the requirements of section 12(1) of the Act. Similar statements should also be included in the statement of claim.[34]

A pursuer who has been awarded provisional damages in terms of **30.319** section 12(2)(a) of the 1982 Act may apply to the court for further damages. He does so by lodging with the sheriff clerk a minute in Form 10f.[35] The minute must include (a) a claim for further damages, (b) a concise statement of the facts supporting the claim, (c) an application for warrant to serve the minute on every other party and, where any such party is insured or otherwise indemnified, on their insurer or indemnifier if known to the pursuer, and (d) a request for the court to fix a hearing on the application.[36] On receipt of the minute the sheriff clerk fixes a date and time for the hearing. A notice of intimation in Form 10g, which includes details of the hearing, is then attached to every copy of the minute served on the parties.[37]

At the hearing the sheriff may determine the application or order such **30.320** further procedure as he thinks fit.[38]

Intimation to connected persons

As in the case of ordinary actions,[39] there is a rule for summary causes **30.321** relating to intimation to "connected persons",[40] which is intended to avoid a multiplicity of actions arising out of the death of a person. This rule applies to an action of damages in which, following the death of a person from personal injuries, either damages in respect of the injuries from which he died are claimed by the executor of the deceased, or damages in respect of his death are claimed by any relative[41] of the deceased.[42]

The pursuer must state in the summons either (a) that there are no **30.322** connected persons; (b) that there are connected persons being the persons specified in the application for warrant for intimation; or (c) that

---

[32] S.C.R., r. 34.2(4) provides that "provisional damages" means the damages referred to in the 1982 Act, s. 12(4)(a).

[33] S.C.R., r. 34.2(3).

[34] *ibid.*

[35] S.C.R., r. 34.7(1).

[36] *ibid.*

[37] S.C.R., r. 34.7(2).

[38] *ibid.*, r. 34.7(3).

[39] O.C.R., rr. 36.1 to 36.7. See Vol. 1, paras 21.14 to 21.18.

[40] S.C.R., r. 34.6(2) provides that "connected person" means a person, not being a party to the action, who has title to sue the defender in respect of the personal injuries from which the deceased died or in respect of his death.

[41] *ibid.*, r. 34.6(2) provides that "relative" has the meaning assigned to it in Sched. 1 to the Damages (Scotland) Act 1976.

[42] *ibid.*, r. 34.6(1).

there are connected persons in respect of whom intimation should be dispensed with on the ground either (i) that their names and whereabouts are not known to and cannot reasonably be ascertained by the pursuer, or (ii) that any such person is unlikely to be awarded more than £200.[43]

30.323   Where the pursuer knows the names and whereabouts of the connected persons he should include in the summons an application for a warrant for intimation to them.[44] A notice of intimation in Form 10d should be attached to the copy summons sent to the connected person.[45] This form gives notice of the action and states that the person concerned may be entitled to enter the action. It contains the usual information about seeking legal advice. Along with the copy summons must also be sent a copy of the statement of valuation of claim in Form 10c.[46]

30.324   Where the pursuer seeks to dispense with intimation to connected persons he must apply in the summons for an order for dispensation.[47] In determining whether or not to grant this application the sheriff must have regard to (a) the desirability of avoiding a multiplicity of actions, and (b) the expense, inconvenience or difficulty likely to be involved in taking steps to ascertain the name or whereabouts of the connected person.[48] If the sheriff is not satisfied that intimation should be dispensed with, he may (a) order intimation to a connected person whose name and whereabouts are known, (b) order the pursuer to take such further steps as he may specify in the interlocutor to ascertain the name or whereabouts of any connected person, and (c) order advertisement in such manner, place and at such times as he may specify in the interlocutor.[49]

30.325   If the name or whereabouts of a person in respect of whom intimation has been dispensed with subsequently becomes known to the pursuer, he must apply to the sheriff by incidental application for warrant for intimation to that person, and intimation will then be made as if it had been done at the outset of the action.[50]

30.326   A connected person may apply by incidental application to be sisted as an additional pursuer to the action.[51] Such an incidental application must seek leave of the sheriff to adopt the existing grounds of action and to amend the claim to include a claim by the connected person.[52] Along with the incidental application must be lodged a statement of valuation of claim (with a list of supporting documents) in Form 10c.[53] This statement must be intimated to the other parties to the action at the same time as the incidental application itself is intimated.[54] Answers to

---

[43] S.C.R., r. 34.6(3).
[44] *ibid.*, r. 34.6(4).
[45] *ibid.*, r. 34.6(5).
[46] *ibid.* For statement of valuation of claim see para. 30.310, *supra.*
[47] S.C.R., r. 34.6(6).
[48] *ibid.*, r. 34.6(7).
[49] *ibid.*, r. 34.6(8).
[50] *ibid.*, r. 34.6(9). Intimation is in conformity with S.C.R., r. 34.6(5). See para. 30.323, *supra.*
[51] *ibid.*, r. 34.6(10).
[52] *ibid.*, r. 34.6(11).
[53] *ibid.*, r. 34.6(13).
[54] *ibid.*, r. 34.6(14).

the incidental application must be lodged within 14 days from the date of intimation of the application.[55]

If a connected person to whom intimation has been made does not **30.327** apply to be sisted as an additional pursuer but subsequently raises a separate action against the same defender in respect of the same personal injuries or death, and would, apart from this rule, be awarded the expenses or part of the expenses of that action, he should not be awarded those expenses except on cause shown.[56] This rule is stated in quite general terms and is identical to a rule for ordinary causes.[57] However, it is possible that a connected person to whom intimation is given of a summary cause may consider that his claim is worth more than the summary cause limit. It is suggested that if he then raised an ordinary action rather than seeking to be sisted as an additional pursuer in the summary cause, he should not be penalised as to expenses if he were to be awarded damages of more than £1,500 or whatever the prevailing summary cause limit then was.

IX. APPEALS

Right of appeal

The right of appeal in a summary cause is limited. A party may appeal **30.328** to the sheriff principal from the final judgment of the sheriff on any point of law.[58] An appeal lies to the Court of Session on any point of law from the final judgment of the sheriff principal, if the sheriff principal certifies the cause as suitable for such an appeal.[59] Otherwise an interlocutor of the sheriff or of the sheriff principal is not subject to review.[60] There is authority for the proposition that there is no appeal to the sheriff principal "at common law" in a summary cause, even though the sheriff may have pronounced an incompetent interlocutor,[61] but the matter is not free from doubt.[62]

A sheriff's decision to refuse an adjournment is not a "final judgment" **30.329** against which an appeal lies, even though the result of the refusal of the adjournment is that the defender is assoilzied.[63] A dismissal under what

---

[55] S.C.R., r. 34.6(12).

[56] *ibid.*, r. 34.6(15).

[57] O.C.R., r. 36.7.

[58] 1971 Act, s. 38(a). "Final judgment" is defined in the 1907 Act, s. 3(h), and that definition is imported into the 1971 Act by s. 45(3) thereof. For a discussion of "final judgment" see Vol. 1, paras 18.33 to 18.37.

[59] 1971 Act. s. 38(b).

[60] *ibid.*, s. 38.

[61] *Gupta v. Laurie* 1994 S.C.L.R. 176, in which Lord Justice-Clerk. Ross, giving the opinion of the court (at 177D) stated that a sheriff principal has no common law jurisdiction to review an incompetent interlocutor. See also *L. Mackinnon & Son v. Coles*, Jan. 13, 1984, Sheriff Principal Bell, Aberdeen Sh.Ct., unreported, in which. the interlocutor sought to be appealed against was not a final judgment, and the appeal was therefore held to be incompetent. However, *cf. Bell v. Thoro-Glaze Ltd*, Sept. 17, 1982, Sheriff Principal Taylor, Alloa Sh.Ct., unreported; referred to at para. 30.329, *infra*.

[62] *Amplifaire Ltd v. The Chisholme Institute*, 1995 S.C.L.R. 11. See Vol. 1, para. 18.12.

[63] *Rediffusion Ltd v. McIlroy*, 1986 S.L.T. (Sh.Ct.) 33. There was no question of law directed to the correctness of the decree of absolvitor. The appellant's motion to be allowed to add such a question was refused by the sheriff principal. If such a question had been asked, the appeal would have been competent.

is now rule 22.1(2) (failure by all parties to attend a diet) is a "final judgment," and it has been held that it is a "point of law" whether the sheriff principal should exercise the dispensing power under what is now rule 3.1,[64] although the latter point is not free from difficulty. In the case cited the sheriff principal founded on the terms of the 1976 rule 81(3)(b)[65] as giving him scope to consider whether he should exercise the dispensing power. It is submitted that that rule was probably intended not to give the sheriff principal power to consider a point of law which could not have been argued before the sheriff (as no party appeared), but rather one which was not so argued. The present rules do not contain any rule equivalent to the 1976 rule 81(3)(b). The question has been raised whether a sheriff's refusal to grant a motion for recall of decree under what is now rule 24.1 would be a "final judgment" and hence appealable.[66] As such a refusal is incompetent it is submitted that there should be a right of appeal against it, and this has been held to be the case in an unreported decision in Tayside, Central and Fife.[67]

Special provisions for certain classes of appeal

30.330   There are special provisions for appeals in relation to time to pay directions,[68] and with respect to appeals in actions for recovery of heritable property to which rule 30.2 applies[69] (actions against persons in possession without right or title).[70]

Interim possession

30.331   Even though an appeal is taken against his judgment the sheriff has power to regulate all matters relating to interim possession; to make any order for the preservation of any property to which the action relates or for its sale, if perishable; to make an order for the preservation of evidence; or to make in his discretion any interim order which a due regard for the interests of the parties may require.[71] Any such orders may be reviewed by the appellate court only at the hearing of the appeal.[72]

Appeal to sheriff principal

30.332   A party who wishes to appeal to the sheriff principal must, not later than 14 days after the date of the final decree, lodge with the sheriff clerk a note of appeal in Form 31.[73] The note of appeal requests the sheriff to state a case and must set out the points of law upon which the appeal is to proceed.[74] At the same time as lodging his note of

---

[64] *Webster Engineering Services v. Gibson*, 1987 S.L.T. (Sh.Ct) 101. For the scope of the dispensing power see paras 30.13 to 30.15, *supra*.

[65] "The questions of law may relate to matters which were not raised during the proof or at the hearing thereafter".

[66] In *W. Jack Baillie Associates v. Kennedy*, 1985 S.L.T. (Sh.Ct.) 53, where the sheriff principal found it unnecessary to decide the question.

[67] *Bell v. Thoro-Glaze Ltd*, Sept. 17, 1982, Sheriff Principal Taylor, Alloa Sh.Ct., unreported. But see para. 30.328, *supra* on the sheriff principal's jurisdiction to review an incompetent interlocutor.

[68] S.C.R., r. 25.4. See paras 30.345, 30.346, *infra*.

[69] For actions to which rule 30.2 applies see paras 30.276 to 30.278, *supra*.

[70] S.C.R., r. 25.6. See para. 30.344, *infra*.

[71] *ibid.*, r. 25.5(1).

[72] *ibid.*, r. 25.5(2).

[73] *ibid.*, r. 25.1(1).

[74] *ibid.* Form 31.

appeal the appellant must intimate a copy of it to all the other parties.[75] The sheriff principal may exercise the dispensing power under rule 3.1[76] in the event of failure to intimate.[77]

Within 28 days[78] of the lodging of the note of appeal the sheriff must **30.333** prepare and issue a draft stated case containing (a) his findings in fact and law or, where appropriate, a narrative of the proceedings before him, (b) appropriate questions of law,[79] and (c) a note[80] stating the reasons for his decisions in law.[81] Where questions of admissibility of evidence have arisen, the draft stated case must contain a description of the evidence led at the proof to which these questions relate.[82] A copy of the draft stated case must be sent by the sheriff clerk to all parties.[83]

Within 14 days of the issue of the draft stated case any party may **30.334** lodge with the sheriff clerk a note of any adjustments he seeks to make to the draft stated case.[84] The respondent in the appeal may, within the same period, state any point of law which he wishes to raise in the appeal.[85] The note of adjustment and, where appropriate, point of law must at the same time be intimated to every other party.[86] The sheriff may, on the motion of any party or of his own accord, allow a hearing on adjustments and may provide for such further procedure prior to the hearing of the appeal as he thinks fit.[87] If he proposes to reject any proposed adjustment he must allow a hearing on adjustments.[88]

The lodging of a note of appeal by a party opens the appeal process to **30.335** all other parties, notwithstanding that they have not lodged separate appeals themselves.[89] All parties may, accordingly, propose adjustments to the stated case.

The sheriff must state and sign the stated case within 14 days[90] after **30.336** either (a) the latest date on which a note of adjustments has been or may be lodged or (b) the hearing on adjustments if there has been one.[91] Before doing so he must consider the note of adjustments and any representations made to him at the hearing.[92]

---

[75] S.C.R., r. 25.1(2).

[76] See paras 30.13 to 30.15, *supra*.

[77] *Renfrew D.C. v. Gray*, Oct. 2, 1985, Sheriff Principal Caplan, Paisley Sh.Ct., unreported.

[78] If the sheriff is temporarily absent from duty for any reason the sheriff principal may extend this period for such period or periods as he considers reasonable: S.C.R., r. 25.1(8).

[79] See para. 30.337, *infra*.

[80] In a case decided under the pre-1976 summary cause procedure it was held that the sheriff's note could not be looked to in order to modify findings in fact: *KHR Financings Ltd v. Jackson*, 1977 S.L.T. (Sh.Ct.) 6. This should apply equally to the present summary cause procedure. See Vol. 1, paras 5.86, 17.07.

[81] S.C.R., r. 25.1(3).

[82] *ibid.*, r. 25.1(4).

[83] *ibid.*, r. 25.1(3).

[84] *ibid.*, r. 25.1(5)(a).

[85] *ibid.*, r. 25.1(5)(b).

[86] *ibid.*, r. 25.1(5)(c).

[87] *ibid.*, r. 25.1(6).

[88] *ibid.*

[89] S.C.R., r. 25.2(1).

[90] If the sheriff is temporarily absent from duty for any reason the sheriff principal may extend this period for such period or periods as he considers reasonable: S.C.R., r. 25.1(8).

[91] S.C.R., r. 25.1(7).

[92] *ibid.*

30.337 The stated case signed by the sheriff must include questions of law framed by the sheriff arising from the points of law stated by the parties and such other questions of law as he may consider appropriate.[93]

30.338 The sheriff clerk must then put before the sheriff principal all the documents and productions in the case together with the stated case, send to all parties a copy of the stated case and inform them in writing of the date, time and place of the hearing of the appeal by the sheriff principal.[94]

30.339 After a notice of appeal has been lodged the appellant may not withdraw it without the consent of the other parties,[95] or by leave of the sheriff principal and on such terms as to expenses or otherwise as seem proper to him.[96]

30.340 The sheriff principal hears the parties or their solicitors[97] orally on all matters connected with the appeal including liability for expenses.[98] Any party may, however, move that the question of liability for expenses be heard after the sheriff principal has given his decision on the merits, and the sheriff principal has a discretion whether to grant such a motion.[99]

30.341 A party is entitled to raise only questions of law of which notice has been given except, on cause shown and subject to such conditions as to expenses or otherwise as the sheriff principal considers appropriate.[1] However, the sheriff principal may permit a party to amend any question of law or to add a new question.[2]

30.342 The sheriff principal may: adhere to or vary the decree appealed against[3]; or recall the decree appealed against and substitute another therefor[4]; or, if he considers it desirable, remit to the sheriff for any reason other than to have further evidence led.[5]

30.343 The sheriff principal may give his decision orally at the conclusion of the hearing.[6] Alternatively, he may reserve judgment, in which case he must give his decision in writing within 28 days, and the sheriff clerk must forthwith intimate it to the parties.[7] Surprisingly, there is no rule relating to the pronouncement of his decision by the sheriff principal equivalent to rule 8.18.[8] However, it is submitted that the

---

[93] S.C.R., r. 25.1(9).

[94] *ibid.*, r. 25.1(10).

[95] *ibid.*, r. 25.2(2)(a). The consent may be incorporated in a joint minute.

[96] *ibid.*, r. 25.2(2)(b).

[97] Although the rule refers only to solicitors it is of course quite competent (and indeed not unusual) for counsel to appear in an appeal to the sheriff principal.

[98] S.C.R., r. 25.3(1). For how the court deals with expenses see paras 30.22 to 30.229, *supra.*

[99] *ibid.*, r. 25.3(1).

[1] *ibid.*, r. 25.3(2).

[2] *ibid.*, r. 25.3(3).

[3] *ibid.*, r. 25.3(4)(a).

[4] *ibid.*, r. 25.3(4)(b).

[5] *ibid.*, r. 25.3(4)(c).

[6] *ibid.*, r. 25.3(5).

[7] *ibid.*

[8] S.C.R., r. 8.18 requires a sheriff to state the grounds of his decision. See paras 30.216, 30.217, *supra.*

sheriff principal, like the sheriff, should state the grounds for his decision. The sheriff principal's final decree, like the sheriff's, is pronounced only when expenses have been dealt with in accordance with rule 23.3.[9] The provisions of rule 23.3 apply to the sheriff principal as they do to the sheriff.[10]

Appeal in action for recovery of possession of heritable property under rule 30.2

Rule 30.2 applies to actions for recovery of possession of heritable **30.344** property against persons without right or title to possess.[11] The period for appeal in such an action may not be shortened or dispensed with,[12] and an appeal is competent within the period of appeal even though the decree may already have been extracted.[13] The lodging of a note of appeal does not operate so as to suspend diligence unless the sheriff directs otherwise.[14] Apart from these specialties the normal rules for appeals apply to such actions.

Appeals in relation to time to pay directions

Appeals relating solely to an application in connection with a time to **30.345** pay direction, whether to the sheriff principal or to the Court of Session,[15] are subject to a different procedure from that in other appeals.[16] Any such appeal is competent only on a question of law and with the leave of the sheriff.[17] An application for leave to appeal must be made in Form 32 to the sheriff against whose decision it is wished to appeal within seven days of that decision.[18] The application must specify the question of law upon which the appeal is to proceed.[19]

If leave to appeal is granted the appeal must be lodged in Form 33 **30.346** and intimated by the appellant to every other party within 14 days of the order granting leave.[20] The sheriff must state in writing his reasons for his original decision.[21] Rules 25.1 (note of appeal and stated case procedure), 25.2 (effect of appeal and abandonment), 25.3(2) and (3) (possibility of additional questions of law being raised at appeal) and 25.7 (certificate of suitability for appeal to Court of Session) do not apply to appeals relating solely to an application for a time to pay direction.[22] Rules 25.3(1) (sheriff principal to hear parties orally),[23]

---

[9] S.C.R., r. 23.2.

[10] For S.C.R., r. 23.3 see paras 30.220 *et seq.*, *supra.*

[11] See paras 30.276 to 30.278, *supra.*

[12] S.C.R., r. 25.6(a).

[13] *ibid.*, r. 25.6(b).

[14] *ibid.*, r. 25.6(c).

[15] The requirement for a certificate of suitability for appeal to the Court of Session does not apply to appeals in relation to time to pay directions. In terms of the Debtors (Scotland) Act 1987, s. 103(1), the 1971 Act, s. 38 (appeals in summary causes) does not apply to such appeals, and in terms of S.C.R., r. 25.4(2), r. 25.7 (application for certificate of suitability) does not apply to such appeals.

[16] S.C.R., r. 25.4 applies to such appeals: S.C.R., r. 25.4(1).

[17] Debtors (Scotland) Act 1987, s. 103(1).

[18] S.C.R., r. 25.4(3)(a).

[19] *ibid.*, r. 25.4(3)(b).

[20] *ibid.*, r. 25.4(4).

[21] *ibid.*

[22] S.C.R., r. 25.4(2).

[23] See para. 30.340, *supra.*

25.3(4) (powers of sheriff principal),[24] and 25.3(5) (sheriff principal may give decision at once or may reserve judgment)[25] apply to these appeals.[26]

Appeal to Court of Session

30.347 An appeal from the sheriff principal to the Court of Session requires a certificate of suitability from the sheriff principal.[27] To obtain such a certificate the appellant must lodge an application in Form 34 with the sheriff clerk within 14 days of the final decree.[28] The sheriff clerk must put the application before the sheriff principal who must decide whether to grant or refuse it after having heard the parties or their solicitors.[29] There are no criteria laid down as to what makes an appeal suitable for the Court of Session. It is suggested that the sheriff principal would require to be satisfied that there was a substantial and important question of law raised by the appeal.[30]

30.348 Rule 40.4 of the Rules of the Court of Session governs the appeal.[31] A note of appeal in Form 40.4 must be marked on either the written record containing the decision appealed against or on a separate sheet lodged with the sheriff clerk.[32] This must be done within 21 days after the sheriff principal has certified the suitability of the appeal.[33] The note of appeal must be signed by the appellant or his agent, bear the date on which it was signed, and, where the appellant is represented, specify the name and address of the agent who will be acting for him in the appeal.[34]

30.349 Within four days after an appeal has been marked the sheriff clerk must give written intimation of the appeal to every other party and certify that he has done so on the document on which the note of appeal was marked.[35] At the same time he must transmit to the deputy principal clerk the appeal process and any separate note of appeal.[36] On receipt of the appeal process the deputy principal clerk must mark the date of receipt on the case record and give written intimation of that date to the appellant.[37] A failure by the sheriff clerk or the deputy principal clerk to comply with the foregoing provisions does not invalidate the appeal, but the Court of Session may give such remedy as it thinks fit for any disadvantage or inconvenience thereby occasioned.[38]

---

[24] See para. 30.342, *supra.*

[25] See para. 30.343, *supra.*

[26] S.C.R., r. 25.4(5).

[27] 1971 Act, s. 38(b).

[28] S.C.R., r. 25.7(1), (2).

[29] *ibid.*, r. 25.7(3).

[30] Compare the criteria for granting leave to appeal: see Vol. 1, paras 18.50 to 18.54.

[31] R.C.S., 40.1(2)(c)(ii) applies Chap. 40 of the Rules of Court to appeals to which s. 38(b) of the 1971 Act applies. The procedure for an appeal to the Court of Session in a summary cause is similar to that for an appeal in an ordinary cause, for which see Vol. 1, para. 18.98.

[32] R.C.S., 40.4(2).

[33] *ibid.*, 40.4(1)(b)(iii). This rule refers to "the date on which leave was granted by the inferior court" but it is submitted that in this case "leave" must be interpreted as including the grant of a certificate of suitability.

[34] R.C.S., 40.4(3).

[35] *ibid.*, 40.6(1)(a).

[36] *ibid.*, 40.6(1)(b).

[37] *ibid.*, 40.6(2).

[38] *ibid.*, 40.6(3).

Further procedure in the Court of Session is beyond the scope of this **30.350** chapter.[39]

It should be noted that the Court of Session has no power, in terms of **30.351** either the Summary Cause Rules or the Rules of Court to allow amendment of or addition to the questions of law stated for the appeal to the sheriff principal. In the one summary cause appeal which has, at the date of writing, been the subject of a reported decision in the Court of Session it was held that the respondents could not raise an issue which had not been the subject of a question before the sheriff principal.[40]

---

[39] For details of the procedure see R.C.S., Chap. 40 as annotated in *Parliament House Book*, Vol. 2.

[40] *Verrico v. Geo. Hughes and Son*, 1980 S.C. 179.

CHAPTER 31

SMALL CLAIM PROCEDURE

I. INTRODUCTION

This chapter will, so far as possible, follow the same pattern as the **31.01** previous chapter. It begins with the definition of a small claim. It then describes the statutory basis of the procedural rules. The next section is concerned with a detailed examination of these rules apart from those relating to appeals. Finally, the provisions for appeals will be dealt with. Although the present Small Claim Rules are entirely self-contained, many of the provisions in these rules are similar or identical to those for conventional summary causes (*i.e.* summary causes other than small claims) or ordinary causes. In such cases, in order to avoid unnecessary repetition, the reader will be referred to the relevant paragraphs in the first chapter of this volume or in Volume 1.

II. DEFINITION OF SMALL CLAIM

The small claim came into existence on November 30, 1988 as a result **31.02** of an amendment to section 35 of the Sheriff Courts (Scotland) Act 1971.[1] Section 35(2) of the 1971 Act as so amended provides that "[t]here shall be a form of summary cause process, to be known as a 'small claim', which shall be used for the purposes of such descriptions of summary cause proceedings as are prescribed by the Secretary of State by order".

The current order provides that a small claim is an action for payment **31.03** of money not exceeding £750 (other than an action in respect of aliment or interim aliment or an action of defamation) and an action *ad factum praestandum* or an action for recovery of possession of moveable property where there is included as an alternative a claim for payment of such a sum.[2]

Legal aid is not available in relation to a small claim at first instance.[3] **31.04**

---

[1] Law Reform (Miscellaneous Provisions) (Scotland) Act 1985, s. 18(1) inserting new subss. (2) to (4) in 1971 Act, s. 35. Section 35(3) provides that no enactment or rule of law relating to admissibility or corroboration of evidence is to be binding in a small claim. Section 35(4) provides for the making of the order referred to in s. 35(2).

[2] Small Claims (Scotland) Order 1988 (S.I. No. 1999). At the time of writing it is understood that there are proposals to increase the financial limit for a small claim to £1,500 and to add to the category of case which may not be brought as a small claim actions of damages for personal injury. It was at one time expected that these changes would come into effect at the same time as the Small Claim Rules of 2002, but this has proved not to be the case.

[3] Legal Aid (Scotland) Act 1986, Sched. 2, Pt II, para. 3(c).

31.05   Although the small claim is a version of the summary cause, in this chapter the term "summary cause" will, unless otherwise indicated, be used to describe a conventional summary cause (*i.e.* a summary cause other than a small claim).

III. STATUTORY BASIS OF THE PROCEDURAL RULES

31.06   The original rules for procedure in small claims were contained in the Act of Sederunt (Small Claim Rules) 1988[4] (hereinafter referred to as "the 1988 Rules"). These rules were amended twice,[5] but have now been completely revoked by the Act of Sederunt (Small Claim Rules) 2002[6] except in relation to a small claim commenced before June 10, 2002.[7] The present rules are contained in the first Schedule to that Act of Sederunt. They may conveniently be found in Volume 1 of the *Parliament House Book*,[8] in Division D. As with the current rules for summary causes and in contrast with the 1988 Rules, the 2002 Rules are entirely self-contained and there is no importation of any of the Ordinary Cause Rules or Summary Cause Rules simply by cross-reference and a general statement of applicability. Appendix 1 to the first Schedule to the Act of Sederunt contains the forms referred to in the rules, and references in this chapter to forms are to the forms in that Appendix. Appendix 2 to the first Schedule contains a glossary of legal expressions similar to that in Appendix 2 to the first Schedule to the Act of Sederunt (Summary Cause Rules) 2002.[9]

IV. RULES OF GENERAL APPLICATION

Register of small claims

31.07   The sheriff clerk must keep a register of small claims and incidental applications[10] made in small claims.[11] This register is to be known as the "Register of Small Claims".[12] The provisions governing what must be entered into this register[13] are, *mutatis mutandis*, identical to those governing what must be entered into the Register of Summary Causes.[14] The only substantial differences are (a) that the reference to a minute for recall of decree in the case of a small claim is to Small Claim Rules, rule 22.1(1),[15] and (b) the reference to variation or recall of decree provides specifically that it is a variation or recall by virtue of the Debtors (Scotland) Act 1987.[16]

---

[4] S.I. 1988 No. 1976.

[5] By S.I. 1991 No. 821 and S.I. 1992 No. 249.

[6] SSI 2002 No. 133.

[7] *ibid.*, para. 3.

[8] W. Green, 1982, looseleaf regularly updated by releases.

[9] See para. 30.06, *supra*.

[10] "Incidental application" in a small claim, which is the subject of Small Claim Rules, r. 10.1 (see para. 31.26, *infra*) has the same meaning as in a summary cause (for which see paras 30.37 to 30.40, *supra*).

[11] Small Claim Rules, r. 5.1(1).

[12] *ibid.*

[13] *ibid.*, r. 5.1(2), (3).

[14] In terms of S.C.R., r. 5.1(2), (3). See paras 30.09, 3.10 *supra*.

[15] For recall of decree see paras 31.64 to 31.68, *infra*. The equivalent summary cause rule is S.C.R., r. 24.1(1).

[16] Small Claim Rules, r. 5.1(2)(n). The equivalent provision in the Summary Cause Rules (S.C.R., r. 5.1(2)(n)) simply refers to "variation or recall of decree".

The provisions for authentication and inspection of the register[17] are **31.08** identical to those for authentication and inspection of the Summary Cause Register.[18]

As in the case of the Register of Summary Causes,[19] the Register of **31.09** Small Claims may be kept in electronic or documentary form.[20]

Dispensing power

In the 1988 Small Claim Rules the dispensing power was contained in **31.10** the Act of Sederunt itself rather than in the schedule. In the 2002 Rules the power is contained in Rule 3.1, which provides:

(1) The sheriff may relieve any party from the consequences of any failure to comply with the provisions of these rules which is shown to be due to mistake, oversight or other excusable cause, on such conditions as he thinks fit.

(2) Where the sheriff relieves a party from the consequences of the failure to comply with the provision in these rules under paragraph (1), he may make such order as he thinks fit to enable the claim to proceed as if the failure to comply with the provision had not occurred.

These provisions are in terms identical to those in the Ordinary Cause **31.11** Rules and the Summary Cause Rules, and reference is made to the comments thereon in Volume 1 and in the previous chapter.[21]

Jurisdiction and competency

As a small claim is a form of summary cause the same rules regarding **31.12** jurisdiction apply to a small claim as to any other form of summary cause.[22]

Representation

A party in a small claim may be represented by an advocate, solicitor **31.13** or authorised lay representative.[23] However, differing from the rule for a summary cause,[24] the Small Claim Rules allow an authorised lay representative to act for a party throughout the whole proceedings.[25] If the sheriff finds that an authorised lay representative is either not a suitable person to represent the party or is not in fact authorised by him to appear, that representative must cease to represent the party.[26]

Persons carrying on business under trading or descriptive name

The Small Claim Rules contain provisions relating to persons carrying **31.14** on business under trading or descriptive names similar but not identical to those in the Summary Cause Rules. Such a person may sue or be sued

---

[17] Small Claim Rules, r. 5.1(4).
[18] S.C.R., r. 5.1(4). See paras 30.11, 30.12, *supra*.
[19] *ibid.*, r. 5.1(5). See para. 30.08, *supra*.
[20] Small Claim Rules, r. 5.1(5).
[21] Vol. 1, paras 5.93 to 5.97. Paras 30.13 to 30.15, *supra*.
[22] See paras 30.16 to 30.18, *supra*.
[23] Small Claim Rules, r. 2.1(1). *Cf.* S.C.R., r. 2.1(1).
[24] S.C.R., r. 2.1(2) restricts the scope of an authorised lay representative. See para. 30.19, *supra*.
[25] Small Claim Rules, r. 2.1(2).
[26] *ibid.*, r. 2.1(3).

in such trading or descriptive name alone.[27] An extract of a decree pronounced in a claim against such a person under such trading or descriptive name is a valid warrant for diligence against that person.[28] As in the case of a summary cause,[29] a summons, decree, charge, warrant or any other order or writ following thereon relating to such a person may be served at any place of business or office where business is carried on within the sheriffdom or, if there is no such place within the sheriffdom, at any place where such business is carried on.[30]

Intimation

31.15 The provision in the Small Claim Rules to the effect that intimation may be made to a party's solicitor if he has one[31] is virtually identical to that for a summary cause.[32]

Execution by sheriff officer—no need for endorsation by sheriff clerk

31.16 Rule 6.7 which provides for execution by a sheriff officer anywhere in Scotland without endorsation is identical to the equivalent provision in the Summary Cause Rules.[33]

Transfer to another court

31.17 There is in the Small Claim Rules a provision in terms virtually identical to that in the Summary Cause Rules dealing with transfer from one court to another.[34] The comments made in the previous chapter apply equally here.[35]

Remit between small claim and other rolls

31.18 At any stage of a small claim the sheriff (or sheriff principal)[36] may, if he is of opinion that a difficult question of law or a question of fact of exceptional complexity is involved, either of his own accord or on the motion of a party, direct that the small claim be treated as a summary cause or as an ordinary cause.[37] Whether a question of law is difficult or a question of fact is exceptionally complex is entirely a matter for the sheriff to decide.[38] If all the parties to the small claim move the sheriff to give such a direction, he has no discretion in the matter and must grant the motion.[39] In either case the small claim is thereafter to be treated as a summary cause or ordinary cause as the case may be for all purposes including appeal.[40] It is to be noted that the sheriff's power to give a

---

[27] Small Claim Rules, r. 6.1(1). *Cf.* S.C.R., r. 5.2(1). See para. 30.20, *supra*.

[28] *ibid.*, r. 6.1(2). *Cf.* S.C.R., r. 5.2(2). See para. 30.20, *supra*.

[29] S.C.R., r. 5.2(3). See para. 30.21, *supra*.

[30] Small Claim Rules, r.6.1(3). But note that if the person is an individual and the basis of jurisdiction against him is his domicile, that is normally his residence and *not* his place of business: Civil Jurisdiction and Judgments Act 1982, s. 41(2), (3), (4).

[31] Small Claim Rules, r. 4.6.

[32] S.C.R., r. 4.6. See para. 30.22, *supra*.

[33] *ibid.*, r. 5.8. See para 30.23, *supra*.

[34] Small Claim Rules, r. 15.1. The only distinction between this rule and S.C.R., r. 16.1 is that the word "claim" is used rather than "action".

[35] See paras 30.24, 30.25, *supra*.

[36] 1971 Act, s. 37(4) provides that throughout s. 37 "sheriff" includes a sheriff principal.

[37] *ibid.*, s. 37(2B)(a).

[38] See comments on "difficulty" in para. 30.29, *supra*.

[39] 1971 Act, s. 37(2B)(b).

[40] *ibid.*, s. 37(2B).

direction in the case of a small claim may in all cases be exercised of his own accord, whereas in the case of a summary cause, the power to remit to another roll may be exercised only on the motion of a party except in an action for recovery of possession of heritable property.[41]

If the sheriff directs that a small claim is to be treated as an ordinary **31.19** cause he must, when making the direction, (a) order the pursuer to lodge an initial writ and intimate it to every other party, within 14 days of the date of the direction, (b) direct the defender to lodge defences within 28 days of the date of the direction, and (c) fix a date and time for an options hearing, which date must be the first suitable court day occurring not sooner than 10 weeks, or such lesser period as he considers appropriate, after the last date for lodging the initial writ.[42]

If the sheriff directs that a small claim is to be treated as a summary **31.20** cause he must specify the next step in procedure.[43]

The power of a sheriff or sheriff principal to remit an ordinary cause **31.21** or a summary cause to the small claim roll[44] has already been commented on[45] and nothing further need be said here save that if such a remit is made, the case must call for a hearing in accordance with Small Claim Rules, rule 9.2.[46]

A decision to remit or not to remit under section 37(2B) or (2C) of **31.22** the 1971 Act is not subject to review.[47]

Document lost or destroyed

The small claim provision for the situation where a document has **31.23** been lost or destroyed[48] is virtually identical to that for a summary cause.[49] The only differences between the two provisions are (a) that in the case of a small claim one of the documents listed in the first part of the rule is a counterclaim[50] whereas in the summary cause rules the equivalent document is "answers to counterclaim"[51]; and (b) a third-party notice and answers thereto are mentioned in the summary cause rules[52] but not in the Small Claim Rules. This latter difference is not surprising as there is no provision in the Small Claim Rules for third-party procedure. The former difference is more puzzling as the provisions in the two procedures for lodging and answering a counterclaim are similar.[53]

Where any of the documents listed is lost or destroyed a copy, **31.24** authenticated in such manner as the sheriff may require, may be

---

[41] 1971 Act, s. 37(2). See para. 30.30, *supra.*
[42] Small Claim Rules, r. 15.2(1).
[43] *ibid.*, r. 15.2(2).
[44] 1971 Act, s. 37(2C).
[45] See para. 30.33, *supra.*
[46] Small Claim Rules, r. 15.2(3). For a hearing in accordance with Small Claim Rules, r. 9.2 see paras 31.75 to 31.82, *infra.*
[47] 1971 Act, s. 37(3)(a).
[48] Small Claim Rules, r. 16.3.
[49] S.C.R., r. 17.5.
[50] Small Claim Rules, r. 16.3(1)(c).
[51] S.C.R., r. 17.5(1)(c).
[52] *ibid.*, r. 17.5(1)(d).
[53] For counterclaim in a summary cause see paras 30.132, 30.133, *supra.* For counterclaim in a small claim see paras 31.70 to 31.74 *infra.*

substituted for and be equivalent to the original for all purposes of the action including the use of diligence.[54]

Electronic transmission of documents

31.25　　The Small Claim Rules contain rules relating to the electronic transmission of documents[55] which are identical to the equivalent rules in the Summary Cause Rules.[56] The comments made in the previous chapter apply equally to small claims.[57]

Incidental applications

31.26　　The small claim provisions for incidental applications[58] are the same as those for summary causes[59] with one exception. This is that in the case of a small claim a party who is not represented by a solicitor and who is not a partnership or body corporate, or who is not acting in a representative capacity, may require the sheriff clerk to intimate a copy of an incidental application to the other party.[60] Apart from that speciality the comments made in the previous chapter are as applicable to small claims as they are to summary causes with the substitution of a reference to the Register of Small Claims for a reference to the Register of Summary Causes.[61]

Sist

31.27　　The provisions for sisting a small claim[62] are virtually identical to those for sisting a summary cause[63] and the reader is referred to the previous chapter.[64]

Amendment

31.28　　As in the case of a summary cause,[65] in a small claim the sheriff may, on the incidental application of a party,[66] allow amendment of the summons,[67] form of response[68] or any counterclaim[69] and adjust the note of disputed issues[70] at any time before final judgment is pronounced on the merits.[71]

31.29　　In an undefended claim the sheriff may order the amended summons to be re-served on the defender on such period of notice as he thinks fit.[72]

---

[54] Small Claim Rules, r. 16.3(2), which is identical to S.C.R., r. 17.5(2). See para. 30.35, *supra*.

[55] *ibid.*, r. 25.1 and 25.2.

[56] S.C.R., r. 35.1 and 35.2.

[57] See para. 30.36 *supra*.

[58] Small Claim Rules, r. 10.1.

[59] S.C.R., r. 9.1.

[60] Small Claim Rules, r. 10.1(3).

[61] See paras 30.37 to 30.40.

[62] Small Claim Rules, r. 10.2.

[63] S.C.R., r. 9.2.

[64] Para. 30.41, *supra*.

[65] S.C.R., r. 13.1(1). See paras 30.42 to 30.45, *supra*.

[66] For incidental application see para. 31.26, *supra*.

[67] For summons see paras 31.36 to 31.40, *infra*.

[68] For form of response see paras 31.41, 31.42, *infra*.

[69] For counterclaim see paras 31.70 to 31.74, *infra*.

[70] For note of disputed issues see para. 31.81, *infra*.

[71] Small Claim Rules, r. 12.1(1).

[72] *ibid.*, r. 12.1(2). *Cf.* S.C.R., r. 13.1(2). See para. 30.44 *supra*.

Additional defender

There is provision in the Small Claim Rules as in the Summary Cause **31.30**
Rules for a person who has not been called as a defender to apply to the
sheriff for leave to enter an action as a defender and to state a defence.[73]
The small claim provisions are in terms virtually identical to those for
summary causes save that, if the application is granted the claim is to
proceed against him as if the grant of the application were the Hearing
in terms of rule 9.2.[74]

Sist of party

As in the Summary Cause Rules[75] the Small Claim Rules contain a **31.31**
provision for the sisting of a person in the event of a party's dying or
becoming legally incapacitated.[76] The small claim provisions are virtually
identical to those for summary causes, and the reader is referred to the
previous chapter.[77]

*Management of damages payable to persons aged 18 or over under legal
disability*

The small claim provisions for management of damages payable to **31.32**
persons aged 18, or over, under legal disability are virtually identical to
those for summary causes.[78] The only differences are (1) that in the small
claim provisions the term "claim" is used whereas in the summary cause
provisions the equivalent term is "action", and (2) the form of receipt by
the sheriff clerk is in Form 24 rather than Form 35.[79]

Management of money payable to children

The provisions of the Children (Scotland) Act 1995 described in the **31.33**
previous chapter[80] apply equally to small claims. If a court has made an
order in a small claim in terms of section 13 of the 1995 Act, as in the
case of a summary cause, any application for an order for the administration of the child's property in terms of section 11(1)(d) of the Act
must be made in writing.[81]

Arrestment

A small claim summons may be warrant for arrestment on the **31.34**
dependence or to found jurisdiction.[82] The provisions concerning arrestments in small claims are virtually identical to those for summary
causes.[83] The only differences are (1) that in the small claim provisions
the term "claim" is used whereas in the summary cause provisions the

---

[73] Small Claim Rules, r. 13.1. *Cf.* S.C.R., r. 14.1. See para. 30.46 *supra*.

[74] *ibid.*, r. 13.1(5)(b). For Hearing in terms of r. 9.2 see paras 31.75 to 31.82, *infra*. The reason for "Hearing" being spelt with a capital "H" is explained in para. 31.75, *infra*.

[75] S.C.R., r. 15.1.

[76] Small Claim Rules, r. 14.1.

[77] See para. 30.47 *supra*.

[78] Small Claim Rules, Chap. 24 is the equivalent of S.C.R., Chap. 26. See paras 30.48 to 30.55, *supra*.

[79] Small Claim Rules, r. 24.4(1). *Cf.* S.C.R., r. 26.4(1).

[80] See paras. 30.56, 30.57, *supra*.

[81] Small Claim Rules, r. 24.5.

[82] See para. 31.39, *infra*.

[83] Small Claim Rules, Chap. 7 is the equivalent of S.C.R., Chap. 6. See paras 30.58 to 30.62, *supra*.

equivalent term is "action", and (2) the certificate to be issued by the sheriff clerk authorising the release of arrested property is in Form 10 rather than Form 16.[84]

European Court

31.35   The provisions concerning references to the European Court of Justice in small claims are virtually identical to those for summary causes.[85] The only difference is that in the small claim provisions the term "claim" is used whereas in the summary cause provisions the equivalent term is "action".

V. COMMENCEMENT OF ACTION

Form of summons

31.36   The provisions in the Small Claim Rules relating to the summons are in terms virtually identical to those for summary causes. Thus a small claim is commenced by summons in Form 1.[86] The form of claim depends on the nature of the action.[87] If it is an action for payment only the claim is in Form 2; if it is an action for delivery the claim is in Form 3; and if it is an action for implement of an obligation the claim is in Form 4.

Statement of claim

31.37   The rule relating to the form of statement of claim in a small claim is identical to that for a summary cause.[88] Thus there is the same requirement for specification.[89]

Authentication of summons

31.38   Again the provisions for small claims and summary causes are identical.[90] The summons should normally be authenticated by the sheriff clerk, but, if he is unable or unwilling to do so, by the sheriff.[91]

Effect of summons—arrestment

31.39   The small claim rule relating to the effect of the summons is identical to the equivalent rule for summary causes.[92]

Copy summons

31.40   Again the provisions for small claims are identical to those for summary causes.[93] The form of copy summons depends on the nature of the action and whether or not the defender is entitled to apply for a time

---

[84] Small Claim Rules, r. 7.3(4)(a). *Cf.* S.C.R., r. 6.4(a).

[85] *ibid.*, Chap. 18 is the equivalent of S.C.R., Chap. 20. See paras 30.63 to 30.66, *supra*.

[86] *ibid.*, r. 4.1(1). The small claim Form 1 is identical to Form 1 for a summary cause save that the term "hearing date" is substituted for "calling date". *Cf.* S.C.R., r. 4.1(1). See paras 30.67 to 30.70, *supra*.

[87] *ibid.*, r. 4.1(2). *Cf.* S.C.R., r. 4.1(2). See para. 30.68, *supra*.

[88] *ibid.*, r. 4.2. *Cf.* S.C.R., r. 4.2. See paras 30.71 to 30.73 *supra*.

[89] *ibid.*, r. 4.2.

[90] *ibid.*, r. 4.4. *Cf.* S.C.R., r. 4.4. See paras 30.74, 30.75 *supra*.

[91] *ibid.*, r. 4.4(2).

[92] *ibid.*, r. 4.4(3). *Cf.* S.C.R., r. 4.4(3). See paras 30.76 to 30.79, *supra*. *N.B.* the comments made there on the advisability of the sheriff, rather than the sheriff clerk, considering whether to grant a warrant for arrestment on the dependence apply equally to a small claim as they do to a summary cause.

[93] *ibid.*, r. 4.3. *Cf.* S.C.R., r. 4.3. See paras 30.80 to 30.83, *supra*.

to pay direction or a time order.[94] However, there are only two different forms for small claims rather than the four for summary causes. If the action is for, or includes, a claim for payment of money and an application for a time to pay direction or time order may be made, the copy summons is in Form 1a.[95] In every other case it is in Form 1b.[96] These forms are similar to Forms 1a and 1b for summary causes,[97] but there are important differences which will be mentioned below in the paragraphs dealing with the defender's form of response.[98] As in the case of summary causes, the defender's copy of the summons in a small claim follows the same pattern as the principal summons with the addition of a space for details of service.

Form of response

The small claim form of response, although generally following the **31.41** pattern of that for a summary cause is not identical to it. The most significant difference is that in the case of a small claim there is no provision for the defender to state a defence in writing. A defender who wishes to defend an action simply indicates that fact in the appropriate box in section B of the copy summons and lodges it with the sheriff clerk on or before the return day.[99] However, if the defender wishes to state a counterclaim, there is provision for his doing so in writing on the form of response, although it is not mandatory for him to do so.[1]

As in the case of a summary cause, where the defender admits the **31.42** claim and is entitled to apply for a time to pay direction or a time order, the form of response gives him two options.[2] He may make written application to pay by instalments or by deferred lump sum by completing the appropriate part of the form giving details of his financial situation. Alternatively he may indicate on the form of response that he intends to appear or be represented in court to make such an application.

Citation

Period of notice

The periods of notice in a small claim are identical to those in a **31.43** summary cause, *i.e.* 21 days or 42 days.[3]

Service by sheriff clerk

Where the pursuer in a small claim is neither a partnership or body **31.44** corporate nor acting in a representative capacity, he may require the sheriff clerk to effect service of the summons on his behalf.[4] Such service is normally by first class recorded delivery,[5] but the pursuer may require

---

[94] Small Claim Rules, r. 4.3.
[95] *ibid.*, r. 4.3(a).
[96] *ibid.*, r. 4.3(b).
[97] See para. 30.81, *supra*.
[98] See paras. 31.42, 31.43, *infra*.
[99] Small Claim Rules, r. 9.1(1).
[1] *ibid.*, r. 11.1(1) provides that a counterclaim may be stated in writing on the form of response or orally at the Hearing of the claim.
[2] Form 1a, section B, boxes 1 and 2.
[3] Small Claim Rules, r. 4.5. *Cf.* S.C.R., r. 4.5. See para. 30.88, *supra*.
[4] 1971 Act, s. 36A.
[5] See para. 31.51, *infra*.

the sheriff clerk to instruct a sheriff officer to effect service. If he does so, the pursuer must pay the appropriate fee to the sheriff clerk.[6]

31.45   If service is on a defender with an address outwith Scotland,[7] the cost thereof must be borne by the pursuer[8] and the sheriff clerk must not instruct service until such cost has been paid to him by the pursuer.[9]

31.46   If the defender's address is unknown and service is by newspaper advertisement, the cost of that advertisement must be borne by the pursuer.[10] The sheriff clerk must not instruct any such advertisement until the pursuer has paid him the cost of the advertisement.[11]

31.47   If service is by the sheriff clerk, by whatever method, the pursuer may require the sheriff clerk to provide him with a copy of the summons.[12]

Service other than by sheriff clerk

31.48   Apart from the speciality described in the preceding paragraphs, the provisions for service of the summons in a small claim are very similar to those for service of the summons in a summary cause.[13] With the copy summons served on the defender must be enclosed a form of service in Form 5.[14] The restrictions on the contents of the envelope containing the service copy summons are the same as in the case of a summary cause.[15]

31.49   After execution of service a certificate of execution in Form 6 must be prepared and signed by the person effecting service.[16]

Citation of defender with an address in Scotland

31.50   Service may be either by post[17] or by sheriff officer.[18]

Postal citation

31.51   The summons may be served by first class recorded delivery post by the pursuer's solicitor, a sheriff officer or (in the circumstances described above)[19] the sheriff clerk.[20] On the face of the envelope there must be printed or written a notice in Form 7.[21] The relevant postal receipt must be annexed to the certificate of execution of service.[22]

---

[6] Small Claim Rules, r. 6.4(6).
[7] In terms of Small Claim Rules, r. 6.5 for which see para. 31.53, *infra*.
[8] Small Claim Rules, r. 6.5(14)(a).
[9] *ibid.*, r. 6.5(14)(b).
[10] *ibid.*, r. 6.6(5)(a).
[11] *ibid.*, r. 6.6(5)(b).
[12] *ibid.*, rr. 6.3(4), 6.5(14)(c), 6.6(5)(c).
[13] *ibid.*, Chap. 6 is the equivalent of S.C.R., rr. 5.2 to 5.12, for which see paras 30.89 to 30.112, *supra*.
[14] *ibid.*, r. 6.2(1).
[15] *ibid.*
[16] Small Claim Rules, r. 6.2(2). *Cf.* S.C.R., r. 5.3(2). See para. 30.90, *supra*.
[17] *ibid.*, r. 6.3.
[18] *ibid.*, r. 6.4.
[19] See paras 31.44 to 31.47, *supra*.
[20] Small Claim Rules, r. 6.3(1)(a).
[21] *ibid.*, r. 6.3(2). The notice states that the envelope contains a citation from the sheriff court and requires it to be returned immediately to the sheriff clerk if it cannot be delivered.
[22] *ibid.*, r. 6.3(3).

Citation by sheriff officer

The provisions for citation by sheriff officer in the case of a small **31.52** claim are virtually identical to those for a summary cause, and the reader is referred to the previous chapter.[23] As in the case of a summary cause, citation may be effected either by an officer of the sheriff court in which the action originated or by an officer of the sheriff court in whose district citation is to be carried out.[24]

Citation of a defender with an address outwith Scotland

The small claim provisions for citation of a defender with an address **31.53** outwith Scotland are identical to the summary cause provisions, and the reader is referred to the previous chapter.[25]

Citation of a defender whose address is unknown

Subject to some minor differences of detail the small claim provisions **31.54** for citation of persons whose address is unknown are identical to those for summary causes. The small claim provisions are contained in Rule 6.6.[26] The form of newspaper advertisement for a small claim is Form 8.[27] The form of notice for display on the walls of court is Form 9.[28] These forms are in terms similar to those of Summary Cause Forms 13 and 14 respectively, but both state that the defender may obtain the defender's copy summons from the sheriff clerk, something that does not appear in the summary cause forms.

Effect of appearance by defender

As in the case of a summary cause, a defender in a small claim who **31.55** appears is not entitled to object to the regularity of the execution of service or intimation, and his appearance remedies any defect therein.[29] A party who appears is not precluded from pleading that the court has no jurisdiction.[30]

Re-service

The small claim provisions for re-service[31] are identical to those for **31.56** summary causes[32] save that where the latter use the term "action" the former use the term "claim".

---

[23] Small Claim Rules, r. 6.4(1) is identical to S.C.R., r. 5.4(1), for which see para. 30.95, *supra*. Small Claim Rules, r. 6.4(2) is identical to S.C.R., r. 5.4(2) for which see para. 30.95, *supra*. Small Claim Rules, r. 6.4(3) is virtually identical to S.C.R., r. 5.4(3) for which see paras 30.95, 30.96, *supra*. Small Claim Rules, r. 6.4(4) is identical to S.C.R., r. 5.4(4) for which see para. 30.97, *supra*. Small Claim Rules, r. 6.4(5) is identical to S.C.R., r. 5.4(5) for which see para. 30.98, *supra*.

[24] Small Claim Rules, r. 6.7. Cf S.C.R., r. 5.8. See para. 30.94, *supra*.

[25] *ibid.*, r. 6.5 is identical to S.C.R., r. 5.7 apart from the fact that Small Claim Rules, r. 6.5(14) covers the situation where service is to be effected by the sheriff clerk (see paras 31.44 to 31.47 *supra*) for which there is no summary cause equivalent. For S.C.R., r. 5.7 see paras 30.99 to 30.104, *supra*.

[26] The equivalent rule for summary causes is S.C.R., r. 5.5. See paras 30.105 to 30.109, *supra*.

[27] Small Claim Rules, r. 6.6(1)(a).

[28] *ibid.*, r. 6.6(1)(b).

[29] *ibid.*, r. 6.10(1). *Cf.* S.C.R., r. 5.11(1). See para. 30.110, *supra*.

[30] *ibid.*, r. 6.10(2). *Cf.* S.C.R., r. 5.11(2). See para. 30.110, *supra*.

[31] *ibid.*, r. 6.9.

[32] S.C.R., r. 5.10. See para. 30.111, *supra*.

Return of summons

31.57   If someone other than the sheriff clerk has served the summons and the case requires to call in court for any reason on the hearing date[33] the pursuer must return the summons and the certificate of execution of service to the sheriff clerk at least two days before that date.[34] If the sheriff clerk has served the summons, he will, of course, already be in possession of both the summons and the certificate of execution of service.

31.58   If the case does not require to call in court on the hearing date, the pursuer is not required to return the summons but must return the certificate of execution of service to the sheriff clerk at least two days before that date.[35]

31.59   If the pursuer fails to comply with either of these requirements, the sheriff may dismiss the claim.[36] The pursuer may, of course, seek to invoke the general dispensing power.[37]

VI. UNDEFENDED ACTION

31.60   As in the case of summary causes, the Small Claim Rules contain a separate chapter dealing with undefended claims.[38] If the defender has not lodged a form of response,[39] the action does not require to call in court on the hearing date.[40] If the pursuer wishes to seek decree in terms of his claim or any other order, he must lodge with the sheriff clerk a minute in Form 11 before the close of business on the second day before the hearing date.[41] Where such a minute has been lodged the sheriff may grant decree or any other competent order sought in terms of the minute.[42] If the pursuer fails to lodge a minute the sheriff must dismiss the claim.[43] It will be observed that these provisions are similar but not identical to those for summary causes.[44]

31.61   The remaining provisions of Chapter 8 of the Small Claim Rules are identical to the equivalent provisions in the Summary Cause Rules save for different form numbers.

31.62   Rule 8.2 is concerned with an application for a time to pay direction or time order.[45] The form to be lodged by a pursuer who does not object to the application is Form 12. The minute objecting to the application is Form 13.

---

[33] For hearing date see para. 31.76, *infra*.
[34] Small Claim Rules, r. 6.11(1). *Cf.* S.C.R., r. 5.12(1). See para. 30.112, *supra*.
[35] *ibid.*, r. 6.11(2). *Cf.* S.C.R., r. 5.12(2). See para. 30.112, *supra*.
[36] *ibid.*, r. 6.11(3). *Cf.* S.C.R., r. 5.12(3). See para. 30.112, *supra*.
[37] In terms of Small Claim Rules, r. 3.1 See paras 31.10, 31.11, *supra*.
[38] Small Claim Rules, Chap. 8. *Cf.* S.C.R., Chap. 7. See paras 30.113 to 30.115, *supra*.
[39] For form of response see paras 31.41, 31.42, *supra*.
[40] Small Claim Rules, r. 8.1(1).
[41] *ibid.*, r. 8.1(2).
[42] *ibid.*, r. 8.1(3). He must be satisfied that the court has jurisdiction: Small Claim Rules, r. 21.1
[43] *ibid.*, r. 8.1(4).
[44] *cf.* S.C.R., r. 7.1(1), (2), (7). See paras 30.114, 30.115, *supra*.
[45] Small Claim Rules, r. 8.2 is identical to S.C.R., r. 7.2. See paras 30.118 to 30.120, *supra*.

Rule 8.3 deals with the granting of decree in claims to which the **31.63** Hague Convention or the Civil Jurisdiction and Judgments Act apply and is in terms identical to those of Summary Cause Rule 7.3.[46]

Recall of decree

The provisions for recall of decree in a small claim[47] are very similar to **31.64** those in a summary cause.[48] In the case of a small claim the decrees which may be recalled are those granted under (1) rule 8.1(3) (decree in favour of pursuer in undefended claim); (2) rule 9.1(6) (decree in favour of pursuer where defender has failed to attend Hearing); (3) rule 9.1(7) (decree in favour of defender where pursuer has failed to attend Hearing); (4) rule 9.1(8) (decree of dismissal where all parties have failed to attend Hearing); and (5) rule 11.1(8) (decree in favour of defender in a counterclaim where pursuer fails to attend continued Hearing fixed under rule 11.8(7)).[49] An application for recall is made by lodging with the sheriff clerk a minute in Form 20 explaining the reason for the party's failure to appear and, in the case of a defender or a pursuer seeking to answer a counterclaim, the proposed defence or answer.[50]

The time-limits for lodging a minute are the same as for summary **31.65** causes. Thus a minute by a pursuer seeking recall of a decree of dismissal must be lodged within 14 days of the granting of the decree.[51] A minute for recall by a defender or by a pursuer in respect of decree granted against him in a counterclaim must normally be lodged within 14 days of the execution of a charge or execution of arrestment, whichever first occurs following on the grant of decree.[52] If the action has been served outwith the United Kingdom under rule 6.5,[53] the minute must be lodged within a reasonable time after the party concerned had knowledge of the decree against him or, in any event, before the expiry of one year from the date of that decree.[54]

If the party seeking recall is neither a partnership or body corporate **31.66** nor acting in a representative capacity and is not represented by a solicitor, the sheriff clerk must assist him to complete and lodge the minute for recall.[55] The sheriff clerk must arrange service of the minute by first class recorded delivery post or, on payment of the appropriate fee, by sheriff officer.[56]

On the lodging of a minute for recall the sheriff clerk must fix a date, **31.67** time and place for a hearing.[57] When this has been done the party seeking recall must serve upon the other party a copy of the minute in

---

[46] See para. 30.121, *supra*.
[47] Small Claim Rules, Chap. 22.
[48] S.C.R., Chap. 24. See paras 30.122 to 30.130, *supra*.
[49] Small Claim Rules, r. 22.1(1).
[50] *ibid*.
[51] Small Claim Rules, r. 22.1(3). *Cf*. S.C.R., r. 24.1(3). See para. 30.124, *supra*.
[52] *ibid*., r. 22.1(4)(ii). *Cf*. S.C.R., r. 24.1(4)(ii). See para. 30.124, *supra*.
[53] See para. 31.53, *supra*.
[54] Small Claim Rules, r. 22.1(4)(i). *Cf*. S.C.R., r. 24.1(4)(i). See para. 30.124, *supra*.
[55] *ibid*., r. 22.1(7).
[56] *ibid*.
[57] Small Claim Rules, r. 22.1(5). *Cf*. S.C.R., r. 24.1(5). See para. 30.126, *supra*.

Form 20a together with a note of the date, time and place of the hearing.[58] At the hearing the sheriff must recall the decree so far as not implemented and the hearing then proceeds as a normal Hearing in a defended action in terms of rule 9.1(2).[59]

31.68   The other provisions of rule 22.1 are identical to their equivalents for summary causes. A minute for recall, when lodged and served, has the effect of preventing any further action being taken for enforcement of the decree concerned.[60] Any party in possession of an extract decree, if he receives a copy of a minute for recall, must return the extract forthwith to the sheriff clerk.[61] The sheriff may order re-service of the minute on such conditions as he thinks fit if it appears that there has been any failure or irregularity in service.[62] Finally, a party may apply for recall only once in the same action.[63]

VII. DEFENDED ACTION

31.69   A defended small claim is one in which the defender has completed and, on or before the return day, lodged with the sheriff clerk a form of response[64] stating that he intends (a) to challenge the jurisdiction of the court, (b) to state a defence (including where appropriate a counterclaim), or (c) to dispute the amount of the claim.[65]

Counterclaim

31.70   A defender who intends to state a counterclaim must indicate that intention on the form of response[66] He may actually state the counterclaim in writing in the form of response.[67] Alternatively he may state the counterclaim orally at the Hearing of the case.[68]

31.71   If the defender states his counterclaim in writing in the form of response he must send a copy of the form of response to the pursuer and any other party to the action.[69] Such a counterclaim may seek warrant for arrestment on the dependence or to found jurisdiction, in which case the sheriff clerk may authenticate it in some appropriate manner.[70] Alternatively, the defender may at the Hearing apply for the warrant to be authenticated.[71] In either case the authenticated warrant is valid for the

---

[58] Small Claim Rules, r. 22.1(6). *Cf.* S.C.R., r. 24.1(6). See para. 30.126, *supra*.

[59] *ibid.*, r. 22.1(8). *Cf.* S.C.R., r. 24.1(7). See para. 30.127, *supra*. For a Hearing under Small Claim Rules, r. 9.1(2) see paras 31.76 to 31.83, *infra*. The reason for "Hearing" being spelt with a capital "H" is explained in para. 31.75, *infra*.

[60] *ibid.*, r. 22.1(9). *Cf.* S.C.R., r. 24.1(8). See para. 30.126, *supra*.

[61] *ibid.*, r. 22.1(10). *Cf.* S.C.R., r. 24.1(9). See para. 30.126, *supra*.

[62] *ibid.*, r. 22.1(11). *Cf.* S.C.R., r. 24.1(10). See para. 30.126, *supra*.

[63] *ibid.*, r. 22.1(2). *Cf.* S.C.R., r. 24.1(2). See para. 30.129, *supra*.

[64] See paras 31.41, 31.42, *supra*.

[65] Small Claim Rules, r. 9.1(1). *Cf.* S.C.R., r. 8.1(1). See para. 30.131, *supra*.

[66] *ibid.*, r. 11.1(1)(a).

[67] *ibid.*, r. 11.1(1)(b)(i). See para. 31.41, *supra*.

[68] *ibid.*, r. 11.1(1)(b)(ii). For Hearing see paras 31.75 to 31.80, *infra*. The reason for "Hearing" being spelt with a capital "H" is explained in para. 31.75, *infra*.

[69] *ibid.*, r. 11.1(2).

[70] *ibid.*, r. 11.1(3)(a). But it may be advisable for the sheriff rather than the sheriff clerk to consider whether it is appropriate to grant a warrant to arrest on the dependence. See paras 30.78 and 31.39, *supra*.

[71] *ibid.*, r. 11.1(3)(b).

purpose for which it has been sought.[72] If the sheriff clerk refuses to authenticate a warrant the sheriff may do so.[73]

If a defender has indicated an intention to state a counterclaim orally **31.72** and does so, the sheriff may continue the Hearing to allow the pursuer to state an answer.[74]

A defender may state a counterclaim after the hearing or any **31.73** continuation thereof only with leave of the sheriff.[75]

If a counterclaim is stated orally at any Hearing at which the pursuer **31.74** fails to appear or be represented, the sheriff may note the counterclaim and its factual basis and continue the hearing to allow the pursuer to appear.[76] The sheriff clerk must intimate such a hearing to the pursuer in Form 14, which advises the pursuer that if he fails to appear or be represented thereat, decree may be granted in terms of the counterclaim.[77]

The Hearing

If the defender has lodged a form of response the case must call in **31.75** court for a hearing.[78] As this is such an important step in small claim procedure the term "Hearing" used in the Small Claim Rules is dignified by its first letter being a capital, and this practice will be followed in this chapter.

The Hearing is held seven days after the return day.[79] The defender **31.76** must attend or be represented at the Hearing, and the sheriff must note on the summons any challenge, defence or dispute stated by him.[80]

If the defender is not present or represented at the Hearing and the **31.77** pursuer is present or represented, the sheriff may grant decree against the defender in terms of the summons.[81] If the defender is present or represented and the pursuer does not appear or is not represented, the sheriff may dismiss the action.[82] If no party attends the Hearing the sheriff must, unless sufficient reason appears to the contrary, dismiss the action.[83] All these decrees may be recalled in terms of rule 22.1.[84]

A Hearing may be continued to such other date as the sheriff **31.78** considers appropriate if the claim is not resolved.[85]

Conduct of the Hearing

A small claim has traditionally been seen as a form of action in which **31.79** a certain degree of informality may be observed. For example, in many courts the sheriff does not wear a wig and gown and those appearing before him are similarly unrobed.

---

[72] Small Claim Rules, r. 11.1(3).
[73] *ibid.*, r. 11.1(4).
[74] *ibid.*, r. 11.1(5).
[75] *ibid.*, r. 11.1(6).
[76] *ibid.*, r. 11.1(7).
[77] *ibid.*, r. 11.1(8). This is one of the decrees which may be recalled. See paras 31.64 to 31.68, *supra*.
[78] *ibid.*, r. 9.1(2).
[79] *ibid.*, r. 9.1(3).
[80] *ibid.*, r. 9.1(5).
[81] *ibid.*, r. 9.1(6).
[82] *ibid.*, r. 9.1(7).
[83] *ibid.*, r. 9.1(8).
[84] See paras 31.64 to 31.68, *supra*.
[85] Small Claim Rules, r. 9.1(4).

31.80 A small claim Hearing is conducted in much the same way as the first hearing in a summary cause.[86] If the sheriff is satisfied that the claim is incompetent or that there is a patent defect of jurisdiction, he must dismiss the action or, if appropriate, transfer it to another sheriff court in terms of rule 15.1(2).[87]

31.81 Assuming that there is no problem about competency or jurisdiction, the sheriff must (a) ascertain the factual basis of the claim and any defence and the legal basis on which the claim and defence are proceeding, and (b) seek to negotiate and secure settlement between the parties.[88] If he cannot secure a settlement the sheriff must identify and note on the summons the issues of fact and law which are in dispute,[89] note on the summons any facts which are agreed,[90] and if possible reach a decision on the whole dispute on the basis of the information before him.[91]

31.82 If the sheriff decides that the dispute cannot be resolved without evidence being led the sheriff directs parties to lead evidence on the disputed issues of fact which he has noted,[92] indicates to the parties the matters of fact required to be proved (and may give guidance on the nature of the evidence to be led),[93] and fixes a "hearing on evidence" for a later date so that evidence may be led.[94] Although the hearing at which evidence is to be led in a small claim is not described in the Small Claim Rules as a "proof", that term is commonly used for such hearings and will be similarly used in this chapter for the sake of convenience.

Third-party procedure

31.83 It should be noted that there is no provision in the Small Claim Rules for any form of third-party procedure.

Procedure prior to proof

Remit to determine matter of fact

31.84 With the agreement of parties the sheriff may remit to "any suitable person" to report on any matter of fact.[95] It should be noted that this provision does not specify a "person of skill" unlike the equivalent rule for a summary cause.[96] If such a remit is made, the report of the person to whom the remit is made is final and conclusive with respect to the fact which was the subject matter of the remit.[97] A remit must not be made unless parties have previously agreed the basis upon which any fee payable to the person is to be met.[98]

---

[86] See paras 30.134 to 30.141, *supra*.

[87] Small Claim Rules, r. 9.2(1). *Cf.* S.C.R., r. 8.3(1). See para. 30.137, *supra*. For Small Claim Rules, r. 15.1(2) see para. 31.17, *supra*.

[88] *ibid.*, r. 9.2(2). *Cf.* S.C.R., r. 8.3(2). See para. 30.138, *supra*.

[89] *ibid.*, r. 9.2(3)(a). *Cf.* S.C.R., r. 8.3(3)(a). See para. 30.139, *supra*.

[90] *ibid.*, r. 9.2(3)(b). *Cf.* S.C.R., r. 8.3(3)(b). See para. 30.139, *supra*.

[91] *ibid.*, r. 9.2(3)(c).

[92] *ibid.*, r. 9.2(4)(a).

[93] *ibid.*, r. 9.2(4)(b).

[94] *ibid.*, r. 9.2(4)(c). The phrase "hearing on evidence" is perhaps an unhappy choice of wording as it normally connotes the submissions made by parties following a proof.

[95] *ibid.*, r. 9.5(1).

[96] S.C.R., r. 8.4. See para. 30.151, *supra*.

[97] Small Claim Rules, r. 9.5(2).

[98] *ibid.*, r. 9.5(3).

Lodging of productions

The rules for lodging productions for a proof in a small claim are **31.85** similar to those in a summary cause. A party who intends to rely on any document or article in his possession, which is reasonably capable of being lodged, must lodge it with the sheriff clerk together with a list detailing any item so lodged no later than 14 days before the proof and, at the same time send a copy of the list to the other party.[99] This rule covers any affidavit or other written statement admissible under section 2(1) of the Civil Evidence (Scotland) Act 1988.[1] In a small claim, unlike a summary cause, it is not necessary to send a copy of the lodged document itself to the other party.[2]

As a general rule the only documents and articles admissible in **31.86** evidence are those lodged as described above or at an earlier hearing and those recovered following the granting of a commission and diligence for recovery.[3] Otherwise documents (for some reason the rule does not mention "articles") may be used or put in evidence only with the consent of the parties or the permission of the sheriff and on such terms as to expenses or otherwise as to him seem proper.[4]

In a small claim there is no requirement for parties to provide the **31.87** sheriff with copies of their productions,[5] but if the productions are at all complex and copying would not be too expensive, provision of copies is a courtesy which would be much appreciated by the sheriff.

The provisions in the Small Claim Rules concerning borrowing of **31.88** productions[6] are virtually identical to those in the Summary Cause Rules.[7] The reader is referred to the comments in the previous chapter.[8] However, there is no provision for imposing a fine on a solicitor who fails timeously to return a production.[9]

Recovery of evidence

Diligence for recovery of documents

The small claim provisions for diligence for recovery of documents[10] **31.89** are somewhat simpler than those in the Summary Cause Rules.[11] At any time after service of the summons a party may make an incidental application in writing[12] to grant commission and diligence for recovery of documents.[13] The application must include a list of the documents

---

[99] Small Claim Rules, r. 16.1(1). *Cf.* S.C.R., r. 17.1(1). See paras 30.156, 30.157, *supra*.
[1] *ibid.*, r. 16.1(2). *Cf.* S.C.R., r. 17.1(2).
[2] *cf.* S.C.R., r. 17.1(3).
[3] Small Claim Rules, r. 16.1(3). *Cf.* S.C.R., r. 17.1(4). See para. 30.157, *supra*. For commission and diligence see para. 31.89, *infra*.
[4] *ibid.*, r. 16.1(4). *Cf.* S.C.R., r. 17.1(5). See para. 30.157, *supra*.
[5] *cf.* S.C.R., r. 17.2.
[6] Small Claim Rules, r. 16.2.
[7] *ibid.*, r. 16.2 is identical to S.C.R., r. 17.3 save that the latter used the term "the proof" where the form uses the term "any hearing".
[8] Para. 30.160, *supra*.
[9] *cf.* S.C.R., r. 17.4. See para. 30.161, *supra*.
[10] Small Claim Rules, r. 17.1.
[11] *cf.* S.C.R., r. 18.1. See para. 30.162, *supra*.
[12] For incidental application see para. 31.26, *supra*.
[13] Small Claim Rules, r. 17.1(1).

concerned.[14] The sheriff may grant commission and diligence to recover those documents in the list which he considers relevant to the claim.[15] As is the case in the Summary Cause Rules the Small Claim Rules are virtually silent on how a commission and diligence for the recovery of documents is actually to be executed. It is suggested that the procedure for executing a commission and diligence in an ordinary cause should be followed.[16]

Optional procedure

31.90   The optional procedure described for summary causes[17] has its equivalent for small claims, and the rules are very similar. A party who has obtained a commission and diligence for recovery of documents may serve by first class recorded delivery post on the haver (or his known solicitor or solicitors) an order with a certificate in Form 15.[18] Form 15 is in every way identical to Summary Cause Form 24, and the reader is referred to the previous chapter for a description of it and comments thereon.[19] For the unrepresented party who is neither a partnership or body corporate, nor acting in a representative capacity, there is the usual provision for service of the order and the certificate by the sheriff clerk on payment of the appropriate fee.[20]

31.91   Documents recovered in response to this procedure must be sent to and retained by the sheriff clerk, who must, on receiving them, advise the parties of that fact and that they may be examined within his office during normal business hours.[21]

31.92   Documents recovered by the optional procedure may be submitted as evidence without any further formality.[22] The confidentiality rules apply to such documents.[23]

31.93   If the party who served the order is not satisfied that full production of documents has been made or considers that adequate reasons for non-production have not been given, he may execute a commission and diligence in normal form.[24]

Administration of Justice (Scotland) Act 1972, s. 1

31.94   The Small Claim Rules contain no provisions for an application to be made for an order under section 1 of the Administration of Justice (Scotland) Act 1972.[25]

Confidentiality

31.95   The small claim provisions for confidentiality[26] are broadly similar to those for summary causes.[27] In a small claim confidentiality may be claimed for any document for whose recovery a commission and

---

[14] Small Claim Rules, r. 17.1(2).

[15] *ibid.*, r. 17.1(3).

[16] See Vol. 1, paras 15.73 to 15.79.

[17] S.C.R., r. 18.2. See paras 30.164 to 30.168, *supra*.

[18] Small Claim Rules, r. 17.2(1).

[19] See para. 30.165, *supra*.

[20] Small Claim Rules, r. 17.2(2).

[21] *ibid.*, r. 17.2(3). *Cf.* S.C.R., r. 18.2(2). See para. 30.166, *supra*.

[22] *ibid.*, r. 17.2(5).

[23] *ibid.*, applying Small Claim Rules, r. 17.3(3), (4). For confidentiality rules see para. 31.95, *infra*.

[24] Small Claim Rules, r. 17.2(4). *Cf.* S.C.R., r. 18.2(3). See para. 30.167, *supra*.

[25] *cf.* S.C.R., r. 18.3.

[26] Small Claim Rules, r. 17.3.

[27] S.C.R., r. 18.4. See para. 30.174, *supra*.

diligence was sought whether the document is produced before or after execution of the commission and diligence.[28] Where confidentiality is claimed the document in question must be enclosed in a separate sealed packet.[29] This packet may not be opened except by authority of the sheriff obtained on the application of the party who obtained the commission and diligence.[30] Before granting an application to open the sealed package the sheriff must offer to hear the haver of the document concerned.[31]

Production of original documents from public records

The Small Claim Rules contain no provision for obtaining original documents from the public records.[32] **31.96**

Citation of witnesses and havers

The small claim provisions for citation of witnesses and havers[33] are virtually identical to those for summary causes.[34] The reader is accordingly referred to the preceding chapter. The only notable difference is that, for a reason that is obscure, the provision prescribing the forms to be used comes as the third paragraph in the Small Claim Rules[35] whereas it appears first in the Summary Cause Rules.[36] The forms for small claims are Form 16 for the citation itself and Form 16a for the certificate of execution of citation.[37] **31.97**

As in the case of a summary cause, there are additional provisions for citation of witnesses by party litigants. The small claim provisions[38] are identical to those for summary causes[39] save that the term "hearing on evidence" is used in place of "proof". The reader is referred to the preceding chapter. **31.98**

Witnesses failing to attend

The small claim provision for a witness who fails to attend, having been duly cited,[40] is identical to that for summary causes.[41] The reader is referred to the preceding chapter. **31.99**

Evidence on commission

There is no provision in the Small Claim Rules for evidence of a witness to be taken on commission.[42] **31.100**

Letters of request

Similarly, there is no provision in the Small Claim Rules for obtaining evidence by a letter of request.[43] **31.101**

---

[28] Small Claim Rules, r. 17.3(1).
[29] *ibid.*, r. 17.3(2).
[30] *ibid.*, r. 17.3(3).
[31] *ibid.*, r. 17.3(4).
[32] *cf.* S.C.R., r. 18.6.
[33] Small Claim Rules, r. 17.4.
[34] S.C.R., r. 18.8. See paras 30.179 to 30.181, *supra*.
[35] Small Claim Rules, r. 17.4(3).
[36] S.C.R., r. 18.8(1).
[37] Small Claim Rules, r. 17.4(3).
[38] *ibid.*, r. 17.5.
[39] S.C.R., r. 18.9. See para. 30.182, *supra*.
[40] Small Claim Rules, r. 17.6.
[41] S.C.R., r. 18.10. See paras 30.183, 30.184, *supra*.
[42] *cf.* S.C.R., r. 18.5. See paras 30.185 to 30.189, *supra*.
[43] *cf.* S.C.R., r. 18.7, See paras 30.190 to 30.196, *supra*.

Abandonment of action

31.102   The provisions in the Small Claim Rules for abandonment of an action[44] are somewhat different from those in the Summary Cause Rules.[45]

31.103   A pursuer may offer to abandon the action at any time before decree is granted.[46] Although there is nothing in the rules providing how this offer should be made it is submitted that it should be by incidental application, either in writing or orally.[47] If a pursuer offers to abandon, the sheriff clerk must assess the expenses payable by him to the defender on such basis as the sheriff may direct subject to the provisions of section 36B of the 1971 Act and rule 21.6.[48] The action is continued to the first appropriate date not sooner than 14 days after the sheriff has given his direction.[49]

31.104   If the pursuer makes payment to the defender of the assessed amount of expenses before that continued diet the sheriff must dismiss the action unless the pursuer consents to absolvitor.[50] If the pursuer has not paid the assessed amount of the expenses before the continued diet the defender is entitled to decree of absolvitor with expenses.[51]

Decree by default

31.105   The small claim provisions for decree by default[52] are very similar to those for summary causes.[53]

31.106   If any party fails to appear or be represented at a hearing after a proof has been fixed the sheriff may grant decree by default.[54]

31.107   If all parties fail to appear or be represented at such a hearing, the sheriff must, unless sufficient reason appears to the contrary, dismiss the claim and any counterclaim.[55]

31.108   If, after a defence has been stated, a party fails to implement an order of the court, the sheriff may grant decree by default but must give the offending party an opportunity to be heard before he does so.[56]

31.109   As in the case of a summary cause, the sheriff may not grant decree by default solely on the ground that a party has failed to appear at the hearing of an incidental application.[57]

---

[44] Small Claim Rules, Chap. 19.
[45] S.C.R., Chap. 21. See paras 30.197 to 30.199, *supra.*
[46] Small Claim Rules, r. 19.1(1).
[47] For incidental application see para. 31.26, *supra.*
[48] Small Claim Rules, r. 19.1(2). For expenses generally and section 36B of the 1971 Act and Small Claim Rules, r. 21.6 see paras 31.123 to 31.128, *infra.*
[49] *ibid.*, r. 19.1(2).
[50] *ibid.*, r. 19.1(3).
[51] *ibid.*, r. 19.1(4).
[52] *ibid.*, Chap. 20.
[53] S.C.R., Chap. 22. See paras 30.200 to 30.204, *supra.*
[54] Small Claim Rules, r. 20.1(1). *Cf.* S.C.R., r. 22.1(1).
[55] *ibid.*, r. 20.1(2). *Cf.* S.C.R., r. 22.1(2).
[56] *ibid.*, r. 20.1(3). *Cf.* S.C.R., r. 22.1(3).
[57] *ibid.*, r. 20.1(4). *Cf.* S.C.R., r. 22.1(4).

VIII. HEARING ON EVIDENCE (PROOF)

Conduct of hearings generally

The Small Claim Rules specify that "a hearing shall be conducted as **31.110** informally as the circumstances of the claim permit".[58] It should be noted that this rule applies to *any* hearing and not only to "the Hearing". The procedure to be adopted at any hearing must be such as the sheriff considers (a) to be fair, (b) best suited to clarification and determination of the issues before him, and (c) gives each party sufficient opportunity to present his case.[59] The sheriff is thus given a high degree of discretion as to how he is to conduct any hearing.

Conduct of proof

It is further provided that before he starts to hear evidence the sheriff **31.111** must explain to the parties the form of procedure which he intends to adopt.[60] He should consider the circumstances of each party and whether (and to what extent) they are represented.[61] Having done so he must, if he considers it necessary for the fair conduct of the hearing, explain any legal terms or expressions which are used.[62]

Oath or affirmation

So far as the leading of evidence is concerned, although evidence is **31.112** normally to be given on oath or affirmation, the sheriff may dispense with that requirement if "it appears reasonable to do so".[63] The circumstances in which the requirement should be dispensed with are not immediately obvious, and it will be interesting to see whether this dispensation will be widely used.

Leading of evidence

It is specifically provided that, in order to assist resolution of the **31.113** disputed issues of fact, the sheriff may himself put questions to parties and witnesses.[64] It is suggested that this is simply giving formal recognition to a practice which many sheriffs have adopted with unrepresented parties for many years in all sorts of litigation.

If at any hearing a disputed issue is the quality or condition of an **31.114** object, the sheriff may inspect it in the presence of the parties or their representatives in court, or, if that is not practicable, at the place where the object is located.[65] The sheriff may also, if he considers it appropriate, inspect any place material to the disputed issues in the presence of the parties or their representatives.[66]

---

[58] Small Claim Rules, r. 9.3(2).
[59] *ibid.*, r. 9.3(3).
[60] *ibid.*, r. 9.3(4).
[61] *ibid.*, r. 9.3(5).
[62] *ibid.*, r. 9.3(5)(b).
[63] *ibid.*, r. 9.3(6).
[64] *ibid.*, r. 9.3(5)(a).
[65] *ibid.*, r. 9.4(1).
[66] *ibid.*, r. 9.4(2).

Noting of evidence

31.115   The sheriff must make notes of the evidence at a hearing for his own use and must retain them "until after any appeal has been disposed of".[67] In a case where no appeal has been taken, it might be thought that the sheriff need not retain his notes beyond the period within which an appeal is competent.[68] However, as in the case of a summary cause, given that a sheriff principal may, in exercise of the dispensing power, be prepared to allow an appeal to be marked late, it will be prudent for the sheriff to retain his notes for a reasonable period of time after a proof.

Objections to admissibility of evidence

31.116   The Small Claim Rules contain no provision for objection being taken to the admissibility of evidence.[69] This is not surprising in view of the terms of section 35(3) of the 1971 Act which provides, "No enactment or rule of law relating to the admissibility . . . of evidence before a court of law shall be binding in a small claim."

Incidental appeal against ruling on confidentiality and production of documents

31.117   Although the Small Claim Rules contain provisions regarding the confidentiality of documents,[70] there is no provision for any incidental appeal being taken against a ruling on confidentiality made by the sheriff.[71]

Parties to be heard at close of proof

31.118   It may be noted that there is no provision in the Small Claim Rules for parties making submissions to the sheriff after evidence has been led. This is in contradistinction to the Summary Cause Rules, where specific provision for submissions is made.[72] However, it is suggested that there is no reason why a sheriff should not be prepared to hear submissions, especially if the parties are legally represented.

Sheriff's decision

31.119   In most small claims the sheriff will be able to give his decision after hearing the evidence and any submissions which may be made. Indeed, this appears to be the intention of the Rules which provide that the sheriff "must, where practicable, give his decision and a brief statement of his reasons at the end of the hearing of a claim".[73] However, if it is not practicable for him to give his decision right away, he may reserve judgment.[74] If the sheriff does reserve judgment he must, within 28 days of the hearing, give his decision in writing together with a brief note of his reasons.[75] The sheriff clerk must send a copy of the judgment to the parties.[76]

---

[67] Small Claim Rules, r. 9.6. *Cf.* S.C.R., r. 8.13(3). See para. 30.208, *supra*.

[68] For the period within which an appeal must be taken see para. 31.139 *infra*.

[69] *cf.* S.C.R., r. 8.15. See paras 30.209, 30.210, *supra*.

[70] Small Claim Rules, r. 17.3. See para. 31.95, *supra*.

[71] *cf.* S.C.R., r. 8.16. See paras 30.211 to 30.213, *supra*.

[72] S.C.R., r. 8.14(1).

[73] Small Claim Rules, r. 9.8(1). Cf. S.C.R., r. 8.18(1). See para. 30.216, *supra*.

[74] *ibid.*, r. 9.8(1).

[75] *ibid.*, r. 9.8(2). *Cf.* r. 8.18(2). See para. 30.217, *supra*, especially the comment regarding the sheriff's failure to produce his judgment within 28 days.

[76] *ibid.*, r. 9.8(2).

Application for time to pay direction or time order in defended action

The small claim provision for applying for a time to pay direction or **31.120** time order in a defended action[77] is identical to that for a summary cause.[78] The reader is referred to the preceding chapter.

IX. POST PROOF PROCEDURE

Final decree

After he has given his judgment, whether at the conclusion of the **31.121** hearing or in writing at a later date, the sheriff must deal with the question of expenses and, where appropriate make an award of expenses.[79] The sheriff then grants decree.[80] This decree is a final decree.[81]

Decree for alternative claim for payment

The Small Claim Rules contain a provision for which there is no **31.122** equivalent in the Summary Cause Rules relating to the granting of decree for payment in certain actions. As has been mentioned above actions for delivery, recovery of possession of moveable property or implement of an obligation are competent as small claims if there is an alternative claim for payment of money not exceeding £750.[82] If decree has been granted in such an action and the defender has failed to comply with that decree, the pursuer may lodge an incidental application for decree in terms of the alternative claim for payment.[83] The pursuer must intimate the application to the defender at or before the time when he lodges it with the sheriff clerk.[84] The pursuer must appear at the hearing of the application.[85]

Expenses

In most defended small claims there is either no award of expenses or **31.123** an award of a fixed sum. This is because of the provisions of section 36B of the 1971 Act. Section 36B(1) provides that no award of expenses is to be made in a small claim in which the value of he claim does not exceed the sum prescribed in terms of that subsection.[86] Section 36B(2) provides that any expenses which the sheriff may award in any other small claim is not to exceed the sum prescribed in terms of that subsection.[87]

---

[77] Small Claim Rules, r. 9.7.

[78] S.C.R., r. 8.17. See para. 30.218, *supra*.

[79] Small Claim Rules, r. 9.8(3)(a). For expenses in a small claim see paras 31.123 to 31.128, *infra*.

[80] *ibid.*, r. 9.8(3)(b).

[81] *ibid.*, r. 9.8(4). *Cf.* S.C.R., r. 23.2. See para. 30.219, *supra*.

[82] See para. 31.03, *supra*.

[83] Small Claim Rules, r. 21.2(1).

[84] *ibid.*, r. 21.2(2).

[85] *ibid.*, r. 21.2(3).

[86] At the time of writing this prescribed sum is £200: Small Claims (Scotland) Order 1988 (S.I. 1988 No. 1999), para. 4(2).

[87] At the time of writing this prescribed sum is £75: Small Claims (Scotland) order 1988 (S.I. 1988 No. 1999), para. 4(3). However, it is understood that there are proposals to change this, if the financial limit for small claims is increased as mentioned in para. 31.03, n.2, *supra*. The proposed change is understood to be that where the value of the claim is £1,000 or less the prescribed sum will be £100 and where the value of the claim is greater than £1,000, the prescribed sum will be 10% of the value of the claim.

31.124   These provisions do not apply to a defender who has either (i) not stated a defence, or (ii) having stated a defence, has not proceeded with it, or (iii) having stated and proceeded with a defence has not acted in good faith as to its merits.[88] Nor do they apply to *any* party on whose part there has been unreasonable conduct in relation to the proceedings or the claim.[89] The provisions do not apply to expenses in an appeal to the sheriff principal.[90]

31.125   The detailed provisions in the Small Claim Rules therefore apply only to a limited category of cases.[91] These provisions are in most respects identical to those in the Summary Cause Rules.

31.126   The small claim rule relating to assessment of expenses by the sheriff clerk[92] is in the same terms as that for summary causes.[93]

31.127   A party who either represents himself or is represented by an authorised lay representative,[94] who would have been entitled to expenses if he had been represented by a solicitor or advocate, may be awarded any outlays or expenses to which he might be found entitled by virtue of the Litigants in Person (Costs and Expenses) Act 1975 or any enactment under that Act.[95] The same provision applies to a party which is not an individual, which could not represent itself, and which is represented by an authorised lay representative.[96]

31.128   The remaining provisions of rule 21.6 (the rule relating to expenses) are identical to those of Summary Cause Rules, r. 23.3, and the reader is referred to the preceding chapter.[97]

Correction of interlocutor or note

31.129   The small claim provision for correction of interlocutors or notes[98] is identical to that for summary causes and ordinary causes.[99]

Consigned funds

31.130   Small Claim Rules, r. 21.3, which relates to payment of taxes in the case of consigned funds, is in terms identical to those of Summary Cause Rules, r. 23.5(1), and the reader is referred to the preceding chapter.[1] As a multiplepoinding is not a competent form of action as a small claim, the saving for actions of multiplepoinding[2] does not appear in the Small Claim Rules.

---

[88] 1971 Act, s. 36B(3)(a).
[89] *ibid.*, s. 36B(3)(b).
[90] *ibid.*, s. 36B(3).
[91] Small Claim Rules, r. 21.6(1) emphasises this fact by providing that the remaining provisions of rule 21.6 apply only to those cases defined in s. 36B as exceptions to the general rule.
[92] *ibid.*, r. 21.6(2).
[93] S.C.R., r. 23.3(1). See para. 30.220, *supra*.
[94] For authorised lay representative see para. 31.13, *supra*.
[95] Small Claim Rules, r. 21.6(3), (4).
[96] *ibid.*
[97] Small Claim Rules, rr. 21.6(5) to (15) inclusive are identical to S.C.R., rr. 23.3(5) to (15) inclusive. See paras 30.225 to 30.229, *supra*.
[98] *ibid.*, r. 21.4.
[99] S.C.R., r. 23.4. O.C.R., r. 12.2(2). See Vol. 1 paras 5.87 to 5.90.
[1] See para. 30.231, *supra*.
[2] S.C.R., r. 23.5(2). See para. 30.231, *supra*.

Extract of decree

The small claim provisions for extract[3] are similar to those for **31.131** summary causes,[4] although expressed in slightly different terms.

An extract (which is signed by the sheriff clerk) may be issued only **31.132** after the lapse of 14 days from the granting of decree unless the sheriff grants an application for earlier extract.[5] An application for early extract is made by incidental application.[6] If an appeal has been lodged, the extract may not be issued until the appeal has been disposed of.[7] The extract decree may be written on the summons or on a separate paper.[8] It may be in one of Forms 18 to 18i, depending on the nature of the decree.[9] The extract is warrant for all lawful execution.[10]

Documents to be retained by sheriff clerk

The small claim provisions relating to retention of documents by the **31.133** sheriff clerk[11] are identical to those for summary causes,[12] and the reader is referred to the preceding chapter.[13]

Charge

The small claim provisions relating to charges[14] are virtually identical **31.134** to those for summary causes,[15] and the reader is referred to the preceding chapter.[16]

Diligence in actions for delivery

Small Claim Rules, r. 21.9 (which provides for the granting of a **31.135** warrant to search and open lockfast places) is in virtually identical terms to those of Summary Cause Rules, rule 23.9. The reader is referred to the preceding chapter.[17]

Applications for variation of decree

The terms of Small Claim Rules, r. 21.10, which relates to applications **31.136** in the same action for variation of a decree are identical to those of Summary Cause Rules, rule 23.10. The reader is referred to the preceding chapter.[18]

---

[3] Small Claim Rules, r. 21.5.
[4] S.C.R., r. 23.6. See paras 30.232 to 30.234, *supra*.
[5] Small Claim Rules, r. 21.5(1). *Cf.* S.C.R., r. 23.6(1).
[6] *ibid.*, r. 21.5(2). For incidental application see para. 31.26 *supra*.
[7] *ibid.*, r. 21.5(3). *Cf.* S.C.R., r. 23.6(2).
[8] *ibid.*, r. 21.5(4)(a). *Cf.* S.C.R., r. 23.6(3)(a).
[9] *ibid.*, r. 21.5(4)(b).
[10] *ibid.*, r. 21.5(4)(c). *Cf.* S.C.R., r. 23.6(3)(c).
[11] *ibid.*, r. 16.4.
[12] S.C.R., r. 17.6.
[13] See para. 30.235, *supra*.
[14] Small Claim Rules, rr. 21.7, 21.8. In the case of a small claim, where the defender's address is unknown, the certificate that a charge has been displayed on the walls of court is in Form 19.
[15] S.C.R., r. 23.7, 23.8.
[16] See paras 30.236 to 30.238, *supra*.
[17] See para. 30.239, *supra*.
[18] See para. 30.240, *supra*.

X. APPEALS

Right of appeal

31.137   The right of appeal in a small claim is even more limited than that in a summary cause.[19] In the case of a small claim an appeal lies only to the sheriff principal as it is specifically provided that there may be an appeal to the Court of Session from the final judgment of the sheriff principal only in the case of any summary cause "other than a small claim" and that an interlocutor of the sheriff or sheriff principal is not otherwise subject to review.[20]

Interim possession

31.138   The provisions in the Small Claim Rules relating to interim possession[21] are identical to those in the Summary Cause Rules.[22] The reader is accordingly referred to the preceding chapter.[23]

Appeal to sheriff principal

31.139   The provisions for appeals in small claims are virtually identical to those for appeals in summary causes. Rule 23.1 is the same as Summary Cause Rules, r. 25.1 save that there is no equivalent to Summary Cause Rules, r. 25.1(4) (appeal dealing with admissibility of evidence) as there are no rules in small claims relating to admissibility of evidence.[24] The reader is referred to the preceding chapter.[25]

31.140   Small Claim Rules, r. 23.2 (effect of and abandonment of appeal) is identical to Summary Cause Rules, r. 25.2. The reader is referred to the preceding chapter.[26]

31.141   Small Claim Rules, r. 23.3 (hearing of appeal) is identical to Summary Cause Rules, r. 25.3. The reader is referred to the preceding chapter.[27]

Appeal in relation to time to pay direction

31.142   As in the Summary Cause Rules[28] the Small Claim Rules contain separate provisions for appeals relating to time to pay directions.[29] The small claim provisions are *mutatis mutandis* identical to those for summary causes, and the reader is referred to the preceding chapter.[30] The only differences between the two rules are in respect of the numbers of the other rules referred to and of the numbers of the forms mentioned.

---

[19] For right of appeal in summary cause see paras 30.328, 30.329, *supra*.
[20] 1971 Act, s. 38 as amended.
[21] Small Claim Rules, r. 23.5.
[22] S.C.R., r. 25.5.
[23] See para. 30.331, *supra*.
[24] See para. 31.116, *supra*.
[25] See paras 30.332 to 30.343, *supra*.
[26] See paras 30.335, 30.339, *supra*.
[27] See paras 30.340 to 30.343, *supra*.
[28] S.C.R., r. 25.4.
[29] Small Claim Rules, r. 23.4.
[30] See paras 30.345, 30.346, *supra*.

Appeal to Court of Session

As has been pointed out there is no appeal to the Court of Session in **31.143** a small claim.[31] It is feasible that a small claim decree could be the subject of an action of reduction whether by way of judicial review or otherwise.[32] However, such speculation is beyond the scope of this volume.

---

[31] See para. 31.137, *supra*.
[32] See Vol. 1, para. 18.01.

INDEX

ABANDONMENT, 14.15–14.30
  after amendment of pleadings, 10.44
  appeals, 18.65
  common law, 14.18–14.19
  counterclaims, 12.40–12.41
  discretion of sheriff, 14.26–14.27
  expenses, 14.20, 14.23, 14.24, 14.25,
    14.30
  lis alibi pendens, 2.97
  minutes, 10.07
  plurality of parties, 14.28–14.29
  small claims, 31.102–31.104
  statutory procedure, consent to decree
    of absolvitor, 14.20
    decree of dismissal, 14.21–14.25
    summary causes, 30.197–30.199
ABATEMENT NOTICES, noise, 26.167–26.169
  nuisance, 26.341, 26.342
  appeals, 25.10, 26.167, 26.345
ABBREVIATIONS, written pleadings, 9.66
ABSOLVITOR, and dismissal, 13.16
  consent to decrees, abandonment of
    actions, 14.20
  extra-judicial settlements, 14.65
  motions, 14.25
  res judicata, 17.11
ABUSE OF PROCESS, 2.19
  amendment of pleadings, 10.60
  skeleton defences, 9.114
ACCESSORY PROCEEDINGS, 2.86
ACCIDENTS, *see also* FATAL ACCIDENT
  INQUIRIES
  employees' reports, confidentiality,
    15.54
  investigations, merchant shipping,
    26.392
ACCOUNTING, Actions, Jurisdiction, 2.32
ACTIONS *AD FACTUM PRAESTANDUM*, 2.84,
  21.75–21.82
  craves, 21.76–21.78
    alternative craves, 21.77
    delivery, 21.78
    precision, 21.76
  Crown proceedings, 4.57
  decrees, 21.80
    enforcement, 21.81
  interim orders, 11.82, 21.79
  jurisdiction, 2.31
  nature, 21.75
  small claims, 31.03
  summary causes, 23.02, 30.02, 30.05
ACTIONS FOR PAYMENT, 2.84
  count, reckoning and payment (*see*
    COUNT, RECKONING AND PAYMENT)
  decrees, 17.16–17.21
  foreign currencies, extracts, 29.12
  interim decrees, 11.82
  jurisdiction, 2.29–2.30
  solicitors' accounts, 21.72–21.74

ACTS OF COURT, 1.38, 1.39–1.40
ACTS OF SEDERUNT, 1.36–1.37
  procedures by summary application,
    25.01, 25.06
AD FACTUM PRAESTANDUM, see ACTIONS *AD*
  FACTUM PRAESTANDUM; ORDERS AD
  FACTUM PRAESTANDUM
ADDITIONAL PROCEDURE, 8.44–8.47
  procedure, 8.45
  purpose, 8.44
  records, closing, 8.47
    lodging open records, 8.46
ADDRESSES, disclosure, children freed for
  adoption, 28.148
  condition of amendment of
    pleadings, 10.31
  initial writs, 9.79
  unknown, citation, 6.08, 6.33–6.36,
    22.19
    family actions, 22.09, 22.15, 22.19
    simplified divorce procedure, 22.86
  written pleadings, signatures, 9.49
ADHERENCE, appeal judgments, 18.86
ADJOURNMENTS, appeal hearings, 18.72
  diets of proof, 16.56–16.57
    closing proof, 16.95
  recovery of possession in summary
    causes, 30.280
ADJUDICATIONS, 26.104, 29.92
  jurisdiction, 2.40, 23.01
ADJUSTMENT OF PLEADINGS, difference with
  amendments, 10.01
  extent permitted, 8.26
  object, 9.130
  open records, 8.29
  period, 8.30
  procedure, 8.28, 9.131–9.132
  purpose, 8.25
ADMINISTRATION, 1.44–1.50
  records, 1.50
  Scottish Courts Administration, 1.46
  Secretary of State, directions, 1.45
    intervention, 1.48
  sheriff court houses, 1.49
  sheriffs principal, 1.47
  statistics, 1.50
ADMINISTRATIVE PROCEEDINGS, 2.86
  appeals, sheriff's powers, 25.06, 26.01
ADMIRALTY ACTIONS, jurisdiction,
  2.74–2.76
  within Scotland, 3.85
  within UK, 3.71
ADMISSIBILITY OF EVIDENCE, appeals, 18.53
  fatal accident inquiries, decisions, 27.21
  irregular recovery, 15.105–15.106
  objections,
    small claims, 31.116
  recovery of documents, 15.53
  summary causes, 30.209–30.210

ADMISSIONS, drafting, 9.25–9.26
  general rule, 9.19
  implied, 9.20–9.24
  joint minutes, 16.28–16.31
ADOPTED CHILDREN REGISTER, 28.118
ADOPTION, agreements, 28.31–28.35
    dispensing with, 28.06, 28.34–28.35,
      28.59, 28.94
    evidence, 28.94
    step-parents, 28.74
    withdrawal, 28.75
    witnesses, 28.73, 28.94
  allowances, 28.82
  applications, *see* ADOPTION APPLICATIONS
  case law, 28.05
    Scotland and England, 28.06
  children subject to supervision
    requirements, 28.15, 28.21–28.23
  criteria, 28.08–28.11
    cultural and linguistic background,
      28.11
    race, 28.11
    religion, 28.11
    views of children, 28.10
    welfare of children, 28.09
  freeing for adoption, *see* FREEING FOR
    ADOPTION
  guardians, 28.29
  hearings, *see* ADOPTION HEARINGS
  jurisdiction, 2.57, 5.01, 28.36–28.39
  orders, *see* ADOPTION ORDERS
  parents, incapax, 28.28
    meaning, 28.24
    mothers, 28.25
    under 16, 28.28
    unmarried fathers, 28.26
  payments, 28.82
  placements, 28.02, 28.12–28.20, 28.138
    non-agency placements, 28.18–28.20
    pending revocation of freeing orders,
      28.194
  proceedings, 2.86, 22.104
    amicus curiae, 28.41
    nature, 28.01–28.02
    privacy, 5.20, 28.41
    timetables, 28.40
  register, 5.34
  relatives, 28.30
  rules of procedure, 28.07
  statutory regulation, 28.04
  welfare of children, 28.09, 28.83, 28.87,
    28.108
ADOPTION AGENCIES, 28.12
  reports, 28.64–28.67
ADOPTION APPLICATIONS, 28.42–28.134
  adoptable children, 28.43–28.44
  children, meaning, 28.44
  confidentiality, 28.104
    processes, 28.131, 28.196
  curators *ad litem*, appointment,
    28.68–28.71, 28.73, 28.95
    duties, 28.79–28.84
  expenses, 28.128–28.129
  forenames, 28.59
  habitual residence, 28.58

ADOPTION APPLICATIONS—*cont.*
  medical examinations, 28.107–28.108
  persons who may adopt, 28.45–28.53
    age, 28.48
    cohabitation, 28.46
    domicile, 28.50–28.51
    natural parents, 28.47
    previous applicants, 28.49
    step-parents, 28.52–28.53
  petitioners, protection of identity,
    28.55–28.56
  petitions, 28.57–28.61, 28.100
    documents, 28.60, 28.63
    lodging, 28.57–28.63
    service, 28.62
    two or more children, 28.61
  pleadings, 28.100–28.103
  proof, 28.109–28.115
  recovery of documents, 28.106
  referrals to principal reporter,
    28.124–28.125
  removal of children, applications,
    28.175–28.177
    return, 28.178–28.180
  reporting officers, appointment, 28.54,
    28.68–28.71
    duties, 28.72–28.78
  reports, adoption agencies, 28.64–28.67
    medical reports, 28.63
  views of children, confidentiality, 28.80,
    28.105
    obtaining, 28.85–28.87
ADOPTION HEARINGS, 28.88–28.99
  first hearings, disputed cases, 28.99
  further diets, 28.98
  further information, 28.96
  notices, 28.88–28.91
  remit to Court of Session, 28.97
ADOPTION ORDERS, 28.116–28.122
  amendments, 28.181–28.182
  appeals, 28.132–28.135
  contents, 28.117
  directions to Registrar General, 28.118,
    28.130
  extracts, 28.117, 28.196
  interim orders, 28.123
  nature, 28.42
  refusal, 28.126–28.127
    s. 11 orders, 28.121–28.122
  revocation, 28.183–28.184
  termination of supervision
    requirements, 28.119
  terms and conditions, 28.120
ADOPTION REGISTER, 28.172
ADULTERY, divorce actions, intimation,
  22.15
ADVERTISEMENTS, citations, addresses
    unknown, 6.34, 30.105–30.109
  declarators of death, 20.09
  multiplepoinding, 21.56
  race discrimination, 26.372
  sex discrimination, 26.366
ADVOCATES, deception, 16.42, 16.43
  diets of proof, attendance, 16.46–16.48,
    16.53

ADVOCATES, deception—*cont.*
  instruction, 12.21–12.23
  sanction of employment of counsel,
    12.21
    decision, 12.25
    interlocutors, 12.26
    motions, 12.24, 16.103
  standards of behaviour, 16.42–16.43
  taxation of accounts, 12.21
AFFIDAVITS, 15.43
  adoption proceedings, 28.112
  children proceedings, 22.43
  declarators, holograph wills, 20.20
  divorce actions, simplified procedure,
    22.88
  small claims, 31.100
  summary causes, 30.185–30.189
  undefended family actions, 22.46, 22.47
AFFILIATION, actions, 22.02
  jurisdiction, 2.56, 2.63
AFFIRMATIONS, *see* OATHS AND
  AFFIRMATIONS
AGE, adoptive parents, 28.48, 28.81
  legal capacity, 4.11, 4.22
  witnesses, commission and diligence,
    15.26
AGENCY, jurisdiction, foreign domicile,
    3.36
  within Scotland, 3.96
AGRICULTURAL HOLDINGS, 26.06–26.13
  arbitration, 26.06, 26.09–26.12
    stated cases, 26.10
  guardians, appointment, 26.08
  records of condition, 26.07
  removings, 23.07
AGRICULTURE, marketing boards, 26.04
  Meat and Livestock Commission, 26.05
  sanitary and washing facilities, 26.03
  statutory powers, 26.02–26.13
AIR, navigation, 26.37
  space, jurisdiction, 2.02
AIRCRAFT, arrestments, 29.28
  mortgages, register, 3.71, 3.87
ALIMENT, 22.02
  applications, divorce and separation
    actions, 22.57, 22.68–22.72
  arrestments, 29.29
    on the dependence, 11.11
  document production, evidence of
    financial resources, 15.49
  enforcement, civil imprisonment,
    26.125, 29.03
  initial writs, 22.10, 22.11, 22.12
  interim aliment, competency of appeal,
    18.39
  jurisdiction, 2.42, 2.56, 2.57, 2.59, 2.63
  orders, affected by maintenance
    assessments, 22.99
  small claims, 31.03
  summary causes,
    children, 30.298–30.305
    spouses, 30.292–30.297
ALL PARTIES NOT CALLED, 4.116, 9.118
  matters *pars judicis*, 4.36, 9.118

AMENDMENT OF PLEADINGS, 10.01–10.02
  after expiry of time-limits, changing
    basis of cases, 10.37–10.39
    curing of radical incompetence, 10.36
    damages for personal injuries,
      10.40–10.42
    principles, 10.34
    substitution of defenders, 10.35
  answers, 10.50
  appeals to sheriff principal, powers of
    sheriff, 18.79
  averments, proof, 10.45
  comptency, 10.02, 10.03–10.06
    inconsistency with earlier
      interlocutors, 10.06
  conditions, 10.02, 10.31, 10.53
    expenses, 10.02, 10.29–10.30, 10.53
  craves, 10.05, 10.13
  difference with adjustment, 10.01
  discretion, 10.02, 10.14–10.28, 10.37,
    10.38, 10.39
    appeals, 10.59
  effect, abandonment by pursuers, 10.44
    deligence on the dependence, 10.43
  instances, *see* INSTANCES
  leave, 10.01
  preliminary pleas, 10.55
  procedure, 10.46–10.59
    abbreviated, 10.56–10.57
    adjustments, 10.49
    appeals, 10.59
    further minutes of amendment, 10.58
    minor amendments, 10.46
    minutes, 10.47
    motions, 10.47–10.55
      hearings, 10.52–10.53
    oral amendments, 10.46
  small claims, 31.28–31.29
  summary causes, 30.42–30.45
  time-bar, 10.02, 10.32–10.42
  timing, 10.15–10.28
    after appeal, 10.28
    after closing of proof, 16.96
    appeal pending, 10.23
    at debate, 10.17
    at inquiry, 10.19–10.21
    before inquiry, 10.16, 10.18
    cases at avizandum, 10.22
    during appeal hearings, 10.24–10.27
    during hearing on evidence, 16.101
  undefended actions, 7.20–7.22
AMICUS CURIAE, adoption proceedings,
  28.41
ANIMALS, boarding establishments, 26.20
  cruelty, 26.15–26.18
  dangerous wild animals, 26.24
  deer, 26.30–26.31
  dogs, *see* DOGS
  health, 26.28
  offences, cancellation of licences, 26.21
  performing animals, 26.18
  pets, 26.19
  slaughter, 26.25–26.26
  statutory powers, 26.14–26.31
  zoo licensing, 26.29

ANNUITIES, government annuities, 26.322
ANSWERS TO CONDESCENDENCES,
    9.108–9.114
  adoption, 28.103
  amendments, 10.03
    minutes, 10.50
  jurisdiction, challenge, 9.108
  skeleton defences, 9.114
  third-party procedure, 12.60–12.62
APPEAL HEARINGS, 18.72–18.90
  adjournment, 18.72
  attendance of parties, 18.73
  decisions, adherence, 18.86
    dismissal, 18.86
    expenses, 18.87–18.89
    recall, 18.86
    remit to sheriff court, 18.86
    variation, 18.86
  judgments, 18.83–18.90
    findings in fact and law, 18.85
    identification of interlocutors, 18.84
    issue, 18.90
  powers of sheriff principal, 18.78–18.82
    amendment of pleadings, 18.79
    dispensing power, 18.78
    fixing of options hearings, 18.80
    further proof allowed, 18.81
  solicitors, withdrawal, 18.72
  speeches, 18.74–18.77
    expenses, 18.77
    preliminary pleas, 18.76
APPEAL PROCEDURE, abandonment, 18.65
  authorities, lists, 18.67
  before hearings, 18.57–18.67
  effect of appeals, 18.68–18.71
    powers of sheriff, 18.69
    respondents' appeals, 18.71
    review of prior interlocutors, 18.70
    suspension of decrees, 18.68
  hearings, *see* APPEAL HEARINGS
  motions, 18.64
  notes of appeal, 18.57
    grounds, 18.58
  notes of evidence, 18.63
  orders by sheriff principal, 18.61
  processes, return, 18.66
  reclaiming petitions and answers, 18.62
  requests for notes, 18.59
  sheriff clerks, duties, 18.60
APPEALS, 18.02
  abatement notices, 25.10, 26.345
  administrative decisions, building,
    26.50–26.52
    further appeals, 25.06
    sheriff's powers, 25.06, 25.07–25.11,
      26.01
  adoption orders, 28.132–28.135
  agriculture, functions of the Meat and
    Livestock Commission, 26.05
    health and safety at work, 26.03
    marketing boards, 26.04
  amendment of pleadings, 10.59
    appeal pending, 10.23
    during appeal hearings, 10.24–10.27
  approval of premises, meat
    preparations, 26.194

APPEALS—*cont.*
  arrestments on the dependence, recall,
    11.33
  building consents, 26.170
  byelaws, water works, 26.414
  caution for expenses, 11.61
  child support orders, 26.60
  children's hearings, 26.62
  contempt of court, 2.25
  counterclaims, 12.38
  Debtors Act 1987, 26.152
  decrees by default, 14.11–14.13
  decrees in absence, 7.19
  disposal of preliminary pleas, 13.25
  divorce, simplified procedure, 22.90
  driving licences, 26.383
  driving tests, 26.382
  education, attendance orders, 26.115
    placing requests, 26.115
    special education needs, 26.116
  electoral registration, 26.119
  entails, 26.263
  entertainment, cinemas, 26.159
    theatres, 26.155
  fire certificates, 26.178, 26.181
  fire service pensions, 26.176
  firearms, 25.10, 26.183
  fostering, 26.58
  freeing for adoption, 28.169
  friendly societies, 26.203
  from summary applications, *see*
    APPEALS FROM SUMMARY
      APPLICATIONS
  from tribunals, jurisdiction within
    Scotland, 3.87
    jurisdicton within U.K., 3.71
  housing, closing orders, 26.227
    control orders, 26.232, 26.236
    demolition orders, 26.227
    expenses, 26.243
    improvement orders, 26.219
    lodgings, 26.229
    overcrowding, 26.220
    prohibition orders, 26.220
    repair notices, 26.225
    standards of management, 26.228
  incidental appeals, discouragement,
    18.50
    rulings on evidence, 16.89–16.90
  industrial and provident societies,
    26.201
  interim decrees, 11.84–11.85
  interim interdicts, 21.93
  judicial references, 13.40
  jurisdiction, 18.03
  licences, air navigation, 26.37
    amusement machines, 26.47
    animals, 26.21
    aviation, 26.36
    betting, 26.38
    caravan sites, 26.161
    Civic Government Act 1982, 26.289
    diary products, 26.193
    dangerous wild animals, 26.24
    food, 26.191

APPEALS—*cont.*
  licences, air navigation—*cont.*
    gaming, 26.43
    guard dog kennels, 26.23
    nurses, 26.299
    riding establishments, 26.403
    vension dealing, 26.31
    zoos, 26.29
  liquor licensing, 26.252, 26.255
    Sunday opening, 26.254
  lost property, 26.293
  mental health, 26.304, 26.312
    community care orders, 26.305
    guardianship, 26.307
  merchant shipping, 26.394
  methylated spirits, sale, 26.402
  non-discrimination notices, race
      discrimination, 26.373
    sex discrimination, 26.364
  nuisances, 26.341
  offices and shops, 26.121
  pedlars' certificates, 26.401
  permits, amusement with prizes, 26.49
  poisons, 26.300
  pollution control, 26.164–26.169, 26.172
  principles, 18.100–18.117
    apportionment of liability, 18.115
    assessment of damages, 18.116
    awards of expenses, 18.117
    burden on appellants, 18.100
    judicial discretion, 18.110–18.114
    questions of fact, 18.103–18.109
    rehearings, 18.101–18.102
  property in police custody, 26.294
  public health, offensive trades, 26.35
    pests, 26.332
  public processions, 26.292
  rates rebates, 26.358
  recovery of documents, 15.65
  registration, child minders, 26.59
    lotteries, 26.48, 26.49
    residential establishments, 26.282
    slaughterhouses, 26.25
  remit to Court of Session, 13.60
  reponing, 7.36–7.37
  restraint orders, 26.110
  roads, 26.386
  safety certificates, 26.160
  sanction of employment of counsel,
      12.26
  sist, mandataries, 11.79
    processes, 13.81
  small claims,
    interim possession, 31.138
    rights of appeal, 31.137
    time to pay directions, 31.142
  stated cases, 26.13
  summary causes,
    interim possession, 30.331
    recovery of possession, 30.344
    rights of appeal, 30.328–30.329
  suspension of diligence, 24.15
  time to pay directions, 30.330,
      30.345–30.346
  to Court of Session, *see* APPEALS TO
      COURT OF SESSION

APPEALS—*cont.*
  to House of Lords, 18.99
  to sheriff principal, 1.11, *see* APPEALS TO
      SHERIFF PRINCIPAL
  warrants, installation of pipes, 26.298
APPEALS FROM SUMMARY APPLICATIONS,
    25.29–25.47
  common law applications, 25.29
  statutory applications, 25.30–25.47
    competency, 25.30
    finality, 25.32–25.35
    mode prescribed, 25.31
    no prescribed right, 25.36–25.47
APPEALS TO COURT OF SESSION, 18.91–18.98
  competency, 18.92
    final judgments, 18.94
    interlocutory judgments, with leave,
        18.96
      without leave, 18.95
    value, 18.93
  considerations, 18.91
  procedure, 18.98
  small claims, 31.143
  statutory provisions, 18.93–18.97
  summary causes, 30.347–30.351
APPEALS TO SHERIFF PRINCIPAL, advantages,
    18.07
  changes of sheriff principal, 18.09
  competency, 18.10–18.54
    appeals to other courts, 18.20
    divorce, 18.25
    fines for failure to return processes,
        18.23
    general rules, 18.10–18.12
    interlocutors, acted upon, 18.17
      extracted, 18.19
      incompetent, 18.12
      not subject to review, 18.16
      pronounced of consent, 18.15
    judicial references, 18.28
    matter *pars judicis*, 18.30
    new points, 18.13
    non-judicial acts, 18.29
    opinions in notes, 18.18
    recall of decrees in absence, 18.22
    remits in family proceedings, 18.24
    rulings on objections at proof, 18.26
    title to appeal, 18.21
    whether final judgments, 18.33–18.37
    withdrawal of concessions, 18.14
  considerations, 18.31
  history, 18.06
  judicial precedents, 18.08
  procedure, *see* APPEAL PROCEDURE
  small claims, 31.139–31.141
  statutory provisions, 18.32–18.37
  summary causes, 30.332–30.343
  with leave, 18.45–18.54
    against refusal, 18.49
    competency, 18.45–18.46
    general principles, 18.50
    in course of proof, 18.53
    judicial discretion, 18.51
    procedure, 18.47–18.48
    questions of law, 18.52

APPEALS TO SHERIFF PRINCIPAL, advantages
—*cont.*
  with leave—*cont.*
    statements of reasons, 18.54
    time-limits, 18.55–18.56
  without leave, 18.38–18.44
    interdicts, 18.38
    interim decrees, 18.39
    modes of proof, 18.42
    orders *ad factum praestandum*, 18.40
    recall of arrestments, 18.44
    refusal of reponing notes, 18.43
    sists, 18.41
ARBITERS, appointment, 26.01, 26.32
  clerks, 26.09
  judicial references, 13.35
  misconduct, 26.11
  removal, 26.11
  remuneration, 26.12
ARBITRATION, 26.32
  agricultural holdings, 26.06, 26.09–26.12
  awards, objections by way of exception,
    12.70
    setting aside, 26.11
  citation, havers, 25.04
    witnesses, 25.04
  expenses, 26.09
  friendly societies, 26.206
  jurisdiction, 2.47, 26.32
    exclusion, 2.99–2.102
    within Scotland, 3.107
  military manoeuvres, damages, 26.96
  mobile homes, 26.175
  roads, 26.386
  sist of processes, 13.76
  stated cases, agricultural holdings, 26.10
    dairy produce quotas, 26.195
AREA DIRECTORS, 1.25
ARMED FORCES, diligence against, 29.04
  lease renewal, 26.35
  military manoeuvres, compensation for
    damages, 26.96
  recovery of possession, 26.34
ARREST, powers, exclusion orders, 26.76
  matrimonial interdicts, 22.82
ARRESTMENTS, 29.14–29.39
  arrestable subjects, 29.16–29.29
    bank accounts, 29.17–29.20
    corporeal moveables, 29.27
    damages, 29.22–29.23
    partnership interests, 29.25
    payments due under contracts, 29.21
    rights under trusts and succession,
      29.26
    shares, 29.24
    ships, 29.28
  cargoes, 24.06
  competition with other diligences, 29.33
  Crown proceedings, 4.70–4.71
  earnings, *see* ARRESTMENTS OF EARNINGS
  effect, 29.30–29.35
  furthcoming, 29.37–29.39
  incompetent writs, 7.22
  jurisdiction, 2.78
    within Scotland, 3.98

ARRESTMENTS—*cont.*
  nature, 29.14–29.15
  non-arrestable subjects, 29.29
  prescription, 29.38
  priority, 29.32
  recall, 29.36
    appeals, 18.44
  ships, 24.06
  small claims, 31.34, 31.39
  summary causes, 30.58–30.62,
    30.76–30.79
  warrants, third-party procedure, 12.56
ARRESTMENTS OF EARNINGS, 26.144, 26.157,
    29.29, 29.40–29.65
  conjoined arrestment orders, 26.144,
    26.147, 26.149, 26.150–26.151,
    29.58–29.65
  current maintenance arrestments,
    26.144, 26.148, 26.149, 29.50–29.57
  earnings arrestments, 29.41
    commencement, 29.42
    duration, 29.47–29.49
    procedure, 29.43–29.46
    review, 29.46
  on the dependence, 11.15
  time to pay orders, 29.48
ARRESTMENTS ON THE DEPENDENCE,
    11.10–11.35
  breaches, 11.34
  competency, 11.11
  count, reckoning and payment, 21.04
  craves, 9.96, 11.16
  effect, 11.24–11.26
  jurisdiction, proceedings outside
    Scotland, 3.65
  nature of procedure, 11.10
  oppression, 11.26
  precepts, 11.17
  preventive procedures, 11.27–11.28
  recall, appeals, 11.33
    modern practice, 11.32
    nimious and oppressive arrestments,
      11.29
    on caution, 11.29
    title to sue, 11.31
  schedules and executions, 11.18–11.23
  service, 11.21–11.22
    arrestment prior to service, 11.23
  ships, 24.06
  subjects arrestable, 11.12–11.14
  subjects not arrestable, 11.15
  warrants, 11.16
    citation, 6.08
    counterclaims, 12.34
  wrongful arrestments, 11.35
ARRESTMENTS TO FOUND JURISDICTION,
    3.99–3.101
  citation, warrants, 6.08
  craves, 9.97
  ships, 24.05
ASSAULT, reparation, jurisdiction, 2.79
ASSESSORS, fatal accident inquiries,
    27.12
ASSIGNATIONS, leases, possession,
    26.265
  objections by way of exception, 12.70

ASSIGNEES, parties to litigation, 4.108
ASSISTED PERSONS, instances, 9.78
  noted in processes, 8.12
  parties to litigation, 4.117
ASSURED TENANCIES, 26.244
  leases, 26.249
  recovery of possession, 26.245–26.247
AUDIENCE RIGHTS, 1.32–1.33
AUTHENTICATION OF SUMMONS,
  summary causes, 30.74–30.75
AUTHORITIES, appeals to sheriff principal,
    18.08
  lists, 18.67
  debates, lists, 13.05
    not cited, 13.15
  hearings on evidence, 16.98
  notes, 17.29
AVERMENTS, answers, 9.109
    relevancy and specification, 9.113
  function, 9.07
  in minutes of amendment, proof, 10.45
  misleading, refusal of expenses, 19.11
  publication, before closing of records,
    8.32
  relevancy, 9.32–9.39
    alternative averments, 9.35–9.38
    deletion, 10.60
    scandalous averments, 2.15
    deletion, 10.60
  specification, 9.27–9.31
  third-party procedure, 12.54
AVIATION, 26.36
AVIZANDUM, 16.104
  fatal accident inquiries, 27.21
  summary applications, 25.26
AVOIDANCE TRANSACTIONS, family actions,
    applications, 22.65
    intimation, 22.15

BANK ACCOUNTS, arrestments, 29.17–29.20
  English and Scottish branches, 29.19
BANKERS' BOOKS, definition, 15.97
  recovery, 15.93–15.97
    expenses, 15.96
BANKRUPTCY, *see* SEQUESTRATION
BETTING AND GAMING, 26.38–26.49
  amusement machines, 26.47
  garding licences, 26.43–26.44
  lotteries, 26.48–26.49
  registration, clubs and miners' welfare
    institutes, 26.45–26.46
BIAS, declinature of jurisdiction,
    2.124–2.128
BILLS OF EXCHANGE, summary diligence,
    29.02
BLOOD TESTS, 15.103–15.104
BOATS, fishing boats, entry powers, 26.188
  hire, licences, 26.289
  houseboats, poinding, 26.132
BODIES, disinterring, expenses, 25.05
  warrants, 25.04, 25.05
BREACHES OF INTERDICT, concurrence,
  Lord Advocate, 4.67
    procurator fiscal, 21.96
  hearings, 21.97–21.98

BREACHES OF INTERDICT, concurrence,
  Lord Advocate—*cont.*
  initial writs, 21.96
  penalties, 2.80, 21.99
BRIBERY, declinature of jurisdiction, 2.126
BRUSSELS CONVENTION, 3.02, 3.04–3.66
  domicile, *see* DOMICILE
  interpretation, 3.04
  jurisdiction, consumer contracts,
    3.46–3.50
    counterclaims, 3.40
    declinature, 3.55–3.64
    exclusive, 3.23–3.28
    insurance, 3.41–3.45
    plurality of defenders, 3.38
    prorogation, 3.51–3.54, 3.78
    protective measures, 3.66
    provisional measures, 3.65
    rules, 3.03
    third-party proceedings, 3.39
  jurisdiction within Scotland, and
    Schedule 8 rules, 3.77
  scope, 3.05
BUILDING, 26.50–26.52
  consent, 26.170
BUILDING SOCIETIES, 26.53–26.54
  Building Societies Commission, 26.53
  winding up, 26.54
BUILDINGS, disinfecting, 26.327
BURDEN OF PROOF, 8.64
BURIAL GROUNDS, 26.55–26.57
  disinterring bodies, warrants, 25.04
    25.05
BUS SHELTERS, 26.281
BUSINESS NAMES, execution of citation,
    6.43
  partnerships, 4.96
  small claims, 31.14
  sole traders, 4.99
  summary causes, 30.20–30.21
BYELAWS, 26.286
  offensive trades, 26.35
  water, 26.414

CAPACITY OF PARTIES, 4.02–4.28
  children, 4.10–4.21
  curators *ad litem*, 4.23–4.27
  enemy aliens, 4.03
  foreign states, 4.04
  insane persons, 4.07–4.09
  international organisation, 4.06
  young persons, 4.21–4.22
CAR TAX, arrears, 26.153
CARAVAN SOES, entry powers, 26.162
  eviction orders, 26.163
  licences, 26.161
CARAVANS, poinding, 26.132
CARGOES, arrestments, 24.06, 29.14, 29.28
CARRIAGE BY AIR, jurisdiction, 2.02, 2.77
CATERING, late hours, licensing, 26.289
CATTLE, stray, warrants to sell, 25.04
CAUSES
  commencement, 6.06
  forms of process, changes, 5.03, 8.66

CAUTION, 11.43
  competency, 11.44–11.45
  condition of amendment of pleadings,
    10.31
  interlocutors, 11.46
  objections to documents, 12.72
  sequestrations for rent, 23.19, 23.20,
    23.21
  suspension of diligence, 24.15
  violent profits, 23.13
  witnesses, second diligence, 16.13
CAUTION FOR EXPENSES, 11.03
  amount, 11.60
  appeals, 11.61, 18.40
  bankruptcy, defenders, 11.55
    pursuers, 11.54
  bonds of caution, 11.65
  companies, 11.57–11.62
  discretion of the court, 11.52, 11.59
    special circumstances, 11.63
  grounds, 11.53
  nominal pursuers, 11.56
  procedure, 11.64–11.66
  time-limits, 11.62
CAVEATS, arrestments on the dependence,
  11.16, 11.27
  interim interdicts, 21.86
  sequestrations for rent, 23.16
  summary applications, 25.19
  suspension of diligence, 24.15
CELLULOID, storage, 26.329
CHANCERY, *see* SHERIFF OF CHANCERY
CHAROES FOR PAYMENT, 29.67–29.69
  executions, 29.68
  furth of Scotland, 29.68
  small claims, 31.134
  summary causes, 30.236–30.238
  whereabouts unknown, 29.68
CHARGING ORDERS, appeals, 26.50
  solicitors' expenses, 19.30–19.31
CHARITABLE COLLECTIONS, 26.297
CHILD ABDUCTION, international
  jurisdiction, 2.39
  registration of custody decision, 2.134
CHILD ASSESSMENT ORDERS, 22.104, 26.69
  legal aid, 26.279
CHILD MINDERS, registration, 26.59
CHILD PROTECTION ORDERS, 26.70–26.72,
  28.137
  legal aid, 26.279
CHILD SUPPORT PROCEEDINGS, 22.96–22.99
  and aliment orders, 22.99
  liability orders, 26.60
  maintenance assessments, 22.96
CHILD WELFARE HEARINGS, 8.08,
  22.37–22.38
CHILDREN, applications and orders,
  divorce and separation, 22.57
  Child Support Act 1991, 22.96–22.99
  damages for personal injuries, 21.43
    small claims, 31.33
    summary causes, 30.56–30.57
  defenders, 4.15–4.19
  disclosure of whereabouts, 22.39

CHILDREN, applications and orders,
  divorce and separation—*cont.*
  exclusion from court, 5.24
  exclusion orders, 26.75
  fostering, 26.58
  legal capacity, 4.12
  looked after by local authorities,
    contribution orders, 26.283
    freeing for adoption, 28.137, 28.141
  maintenance, mutual enforcement,
    22.104
  management of money, 22.102
  meaning, adoption proceedings, 28.44
  oaths and affirmations, 16.62
  parties to actions, 4.10–4.21, 4.118
  places of safety, warrants, 26.67
  proceedings, *see* CHILDREN'S
    PROCEEDINGS
  removal, applications, 22.40
CHILDREN'S PROCEEDINGS, 22.33–22.43
  affidavit evidence, 22.43
  applications, orders to disclose
    whereabouts of children, 22.39
    removal of children, 22.40
  child welfare hearings, 22.37–22.38
  expenses, 26.78
  identification of children, 5.29
  intimation to children, 22.23
  joint minutes, 22.42
  jurisdiction, 2.56, 2.59, 2.61–2.62
    within Scotland, 3.81
  legal aid, 26.279
  minimum intervention principle, 22.103
  referrals to principal reporter,
    22.100–22.101
  regulation, 22.104
  reporters, appointment, 22.35
  representatives, 26.77
  s. 11 orders, 22.38, 28.89
    alternative to adoption orders, 28.121
    divorce and separation actions, 22.57
    family actions, 22.73–22.76
    intimation, 22.15
    undefended actions, 22.49
  supervised contact orders, intimation to
    local authorities, 22.41
  views of children, 22.33, 22.103, 28.10
    recording, 22.34
  welfare of children, 22.103
CHILDREN'S HEARINGS, 22.101, 22.104
  adoption proceedings, 28.15, 28.21
  grounds of referral, 26.64–26.66
    appeals, 26.62
    legal aid, 26.279
    review, 26.68
CHILDREN'S REPORTER, referrals,
  22.100–22.101
  adoption proceedings, 28.124–28.125
CHURCH OF SCOTLAND, 26.80–26.88
  buildings, 26.82
    disposals, 26.88
    feuduties, 26.88
    transfer of rights, 26.86
  debtors, 26.87
  ministers, 26.80

CHURCH OF SCOTLAND—*cont.*
  stipends, 26.83
  teinds, fish teinds, 26.81
  valuation, 26.85
CINEMAS, licences, 26.159
CITATION, execution, *see* EXECUTION OF
    CITATION
  family actions, 22.19–22.21
  forms, 6.16
  summary applications, 25.19, 25.23
  warrants, *see* WARRANTS OF CITATION
CIVIL AVIATION, 26.36
CIVIL IMPRISONMENT, decrees *ad factum
    praestandum*, 26.126
  enforcement of aliment, 26.125, 29.03
CLOSED RECORDS, 8.39, 8.40–8.41
  additional procedure, 8.47
CLOSING ORDERS, 26.227
  compensation, 26.240
  superiors, entry powers, 26.242
CLUBS, licensing, permitted hours, 26.254
  registers, 5.38
  registration, 26.45, 26.256
COAL MINING, subsidence, 26.318
COAST PREVENTION, recovery of costs,
    26.89
COHABITATION, adoptive parents, 28.46
COMMISSARY PROCEEDINGS, 5.10
  administration, 1.38
  jurisdiction, 5.01
    within Scotland, 3.86
  registers, 5.38
COMMISSION AND DILIGENCE, evidence of
    witnesses, 15.18–15.42
  after proof allowed, 15.23–15.37
  applications, 15.20, 15.29
    decisions, 15.21
    grounds, 15.19, 15.23–15.28
    citation, 15.34
    expenses, 15.39
    in England and Northern Ireland,
      15.41
    interlocutors, 14.30
    interrogatories, 15.31
    mental illness, 15.27
    necessity, 15.24
    oaths, 15.35, 15.36
    outside Scotland, 16.17
    outside U.K., 15.42
    procedure, 15.30–15.37
      at diets, 15.35–15.36
      before diets, 15.32–15.34
    reports, 15.37
      use at proof, 15.38
    residence, 15.25
    sickness, age or infirmity, 15.26
    special cause shown, 15.28
    to lie *in retentis*, 15.19–15.22
  recovery of documents, *see* RECOVERY
    OF DOCUMENTS
COMMISSION FOR RACIAL EQUALITY,
    summary applications, 26.370
COMMON GOOD, disposal, 26.285
COMMON GRAZINGS, crofters, 26.02

COMMON PROPERTY, compulsory purchase,
    26.95
  division, jurisdiction, 2.55
  poinding, 29.73
  proceedings, 2.86
COMMONTIES, division, 23.37
COMMUNITY CARE ORDERS, 26.305
COMPANIES, arrestments on the
    dependence, 11.21
  caution for expenses, 11.57–11.62
  execution of citation, 6.40
    oversea companies, 6.41
  parties to litigation, 4.118
    investigated under Part XIV of 1985
      Act, 4.93
    liquidation, 4.90–4.92
    receivership, 4.88–4.89
COMPANY ADMINISTRATION, jurisdiction,
    2.45, 2.71–2.72
  exclusive jurisdiction, 3.25
    within Scotland, 3.84, 3.106
  proceedings, 2.86
COMPETENCE,
  small claims, 31.12
  summary causes, 30.16–30.18,
    30.137–30.138
COMPETENT AND OMITTED, 2.112–2.113
  preliminary pleas, 9.124
COMPULSORY PURCHASE, 26.92–26.107
  capital certificates, 26.92
  compensation, 26.240
    absent owners, 26.94
    assessment, 26.93–26.95
    listed buildings, 26.400
  listed buildings, 26.399
CONCURRENT JURISDICTION, 2.49–2.80
  admiralty actions, 2.74–2.76
  air, 2.77
  arbitration, 26.32
  bankruptcy, 2.70
  building societies, 26.54
  company administration, 2.71–2.72
  crime, 2.79–2.80
  death, declarators, 2.65
  diligence, 2.78
  family actions, 2.56–2.64, 22.03
  foreign domicile, 3.29–3.37
    agency, 3.36
    contract, 3.30
    delict, 3.33
    heritable property, 3.30
    maintenance, 3.31–3.32
    restitution for criminal acts, 3.34
    salvage, 3.37
  heritable rights, 2.53–2.55
  illegality, 2.79
  judicial factors, 2.68–2.69
  jurisdiction within U.K., 3.73
  moveable rights, 2.50
  obligations, 2.51
  partnerships, 2.73
  remit from Court of Session, 13.67
  rivers, 2.02
  succession, 2.66
  trusts, 2.44

CONDESCENDENCES, amendments, 10.03
  count, reckoning and payment, 21.05
  drafting, 9.99–9.103
  family actions, 22.06
  multiplepoinding, 21.61
  provisional damages, 21.30
CONFIDENTIALITY, admissibility of
    evidence, appeals, 18.53
  adoption, documents, 28.104, 28.131,
    28.196
    views of children, 28.80, 28.105
  bank accounts, 29.17
  communications, 15.03, 15.86
  freeing for adoption, 28.163,
    28.170–28.171
    children's addresses, 28.148
  recovery of documents, 15.54, 15.68,
    15.74, 15.101
  small claims, 31.95, 31.117
  summary causes, 30.174
CONFIRMATION OF EXECUTORS, jurisdiction,
  2.66
CONFISCATION ORDERS, compensation,
  26.110
CONJOINED ARREST ORDERS,
  29.58–29.65
  full payment, 29.63
  procedure, 29.60–29.61
  recall, 29.64
  requirements, 29.59
  termination, 29.64
  time to pay orders, 29.65
  variation, 29.62
CONJUNCTION OF PROCESSES, 13.42–13.44
CONSENT AND CONCURRENCE, pursuers,
  4.114–4.115
CONSIGNATION, 11.43
  competency, 11.44–11.45
  condition of amendment of pleadings,
    10.31
  custody of consigned money, 11.49
  effect, 11.48
  interim orders, competency of appeal,
    18.39
  interlocutors, 11.46
  judgments, 11.50
  multiplepoinding, 21.66
  objections to documents, 12.72
  small claims, 31.130
  summary causes, 30.231
  suspension of diligence, 24.15
  taxes and duties, 11.51
  voluntary, 11.47
CONSTITUTION, 2.84
CONSUMER CONTRACTS, jurisdiction,
  foreign domicile, 3.46–3.50
  within Scotland, 3.110
CONSUMER CREDIT, 26.213
CONSUMER GOODS, suspension orders,
  26.406
CONTACT ORDERS, 28.122
  supervision by local authorities, 22.41
CONTEMPT OF COURT, 2.18–2.25
  abuse of process, 2.19
  appeals, 2.25

CONTEMPT OF COURT—*cont.*
  breaches of interdict, 21.97
  failure to return processes, 8.16
  interlocutors, disregard, 5.91
  non-compliance with rules and orders,
    5.101
  procedure, 2.22–2.23
  publication of court proceedings, 5.30
  sanctions, 2.24, 2.80
  sheriffs, 1.16
  sheriffs principal, 1.13
  witnesses, refusal to answer questions,
    16.69
CONTINGENCY, processes, remit to Court
  of Session, 13.64
CONTINUATION, options hearings, 8.38
  procedural hearings, 8.52
CONTRACT, jurisdiction, 2.51
  consumer contracts, 3.46–3.50, 3.110
  employment, 3.92
  foreign domicile, 3.30
  within Scotland, 3.92
  payments due, arrestments, 29.21
  place of performance, 3.92
  sale, objections by way of exception,
    12.70
  several defenders, 4.45–4.47
CONTRIBUTION ORDERS, children looked
  after by local authorities, 26.283
CONTRIBUTORY NEGLIGENCE, award of
  expenses, 19.15
  damages for personal injuries, interim
    damages, 21.23
  form of decrees, 17.18
COPYRIGHT, jurisdiction, 2.46
CORPORATE BODIES, domicile, 3.13–3.20
  parties to actions, 4.83, 4.118
  names, 4.84–4.87
CORROBORATION, 16.76
  fatal accident inquiries, 27.14
CORRUPTION, declinature of jurisdiction,
  2.126
COUNT, RECKONING AND PAYMENT, 2.84
  answers, 21.10
  competency, 21.02
  condescendences, 21.05
  initial writs, 21.04
  liability admitted, 21.09
  liability disputed, 21.08
  objections, 21.10
    disposal, 21.11
  pleas-in-law, 21.06
  procedure, 21.03
    after defences lodged, 21.08–21.11
  summary causes, 30.257–30.260
  undefended actions, 21.07
COUNTERCLAIMS, 9.01, 12.29–12.41
  abandonment, 12.40–12.41
  appeals, 12.38
  competency, 12.29
  Crown proceedings, 4.60, 4.61, 4.62
  effect on prescription, 12.39
  expenses, 12.36, 12.38, 12.39
  family proceedings, 12.31
  form, 9.40, 12.33

COUNTERCLAIMS—*cont.*
  jurisdiction, foreign domicile, 3.40
    value, 2.33
    within Scotland, 3.109
  lodging, 12.32
  pleas-in-law, 9.126
  procedure, 12.32–12.41
  small claims, 31.70–31.74
  summary causes, 30.132–30.133
  tenders, 14.33
  warrants for arrestment on the
    dependence, 12.34
COURT DAYS, 5.11
COURT HOLIDAYS, 5.12
COURT OF SESSION, 1.01
  appeals, *see* APPEALS TO COURT OF
    SESSION
  decrees, *see* DECRESS
  jurisdiction, 2.37–2.48
    concurrent with sheriff court, *see*
      CONCURRENT JURISDICTION
    Crown proceedings, 4.55
    remit from sheriff courts, *see* REMIT TO
      COURT OF SESSION
    remit to sheriff courts, 13.67
CRAVES, actions *ad factum praestandum*,
    21.76–21.78
  alternative craves, 9.86
    decrees in absence, 7.08
  amendments, 10.05, 10.13
  ancillary craves, 9.88
  damages for personal injuries, 21.13
  declaratory actions, 20.04
  decrees in absence, alternative craves,
    7.08
    restrictions, 7.07
  division and sale, 23.38
  divorce, 22.05
  drafting, 9.82–9.85
  eventual craves, 9.87
  for expenses, 9.94–9.95
  for money, foreign currency, 9.91–9.92
    interest, 9.93
    lump sum, 9.90
    specific amount, 9.89
  for warrants, arrestments on the
    dependence, 9.96
    arrestments to found jurisdiction,
      9.97
    intimations, 9.98
  form, 9.45
  interdicts, 21.84
  provisional damages, 21.30
CREDIT, consumer credit, 26.213
  credit unions, 26.205
  extortionate credit bargains, 26.213
CREDITORS, judicial compositions,
    jurisdiction within Scotland, 3.83
CRIME, reparation, jurisdiction, 2.79, 3.34,
    3.94
CRIMINAL INJURIES COMPENSATION,
    arrestment, 29.23
CRIMINAL PROCEEDINGS, 26.108–26.110
  concurrent civil proceedings, exclusion
    of jurisdiction, 2.133

CROFTERS, common grazings, 26.02
CROSS-EXAMINATIONS, 16.73–16.77
CROWN OFFICERS, interdicts, 4.59
CROWN PRIVILEGE, 4.75
CROWN PROCEEDINGS, 4.52–4.81
  actions *ad factum praestandum*, 4.57
  arrestments, 4.70–4.71
    on the dependence, 11.21
  counterclaims, 4.60, 4.61, 4.62
  Crown privilege, 4.75
  death, declarators, 4.67
  decrees in absence, extracts, 7.17
  domicile, 3.22, 4.54
  enforcement of orders, 4.79–4.81
  expenses, 4.78
  form, 4.56–4.62
  instances, style, 4.66
  interdicts, 4.57, 4.59
  jurisdiction, 4.54–4.55
  meaning of 'Crown,' 4.53
  property, recovery, 4.58
  recovery of documents, 15.03, 15.86
    public interest, 4.72–4.75
  remit to Court of Session, 13.63
  representation, 4.63–4.69
  rules of court, 4.77
  set-off, 4.60, 4.61, 4.62
  shores, encroachment, 4.67
  special pleas, 4.76
CULTURAL BACKGROUND, adoption, 28.11,
    28.81, 28.156
CURATORS, 4.21, 4.22
CURATORS *ad litem*
    adoption proceedings,
      appointment, 28.68
      for parents, 28.73, 28.95
    duties, 28.79–28.84
    evidence, 28.113
    expenses, 28.128–28.129
    panels, 28.69
    reports, time-limits, 28.71
  appointment, 4.07, 4.13, 4.14, 4.18,
    4.20, 4.23
    community care orders, 26.306
    family actions, 22.24–22.26
    matters *pars judicis*, 2.15
    revocation of freeing orders, 28.188,
      28.193
    separation or divorce, 12.13
  discharge, 4.28
  expenses, 4.27
    tenders, 14.48
  freeing for adoption, appointment,
    28.149, 28.152
    functions, 28.156
    reports, 28.152, 28.156
  parties to actions, 4.23–4.27
  powers and duties, 4.24–4.26
CURATORS *BONIS*, appointment, during
    proceedings, 12.13
  jurisdiction, 2.62, 2.68
  pursuers and defenders, 4.07
CURRENCY, foreign, *see* FOREIGN
    CURRENCY
  poinding, 29.71

CURRENT MAINTENANCE ARRESTMENTS, 29.50
  commencement, 29.51
  procedure, 29.53–29.54
  recall, 29.55
  review, 29.54
  schedules, 29.52
  termination, 29.55–29.57
  time to pay orders, 29.56
CUSTODY, deaths, fatal accident inquiries, 27.04
  property or persons in police custody, 26.294

DAIRY PRODUCTS, licences, 26.193
  quotas, 26.195
DAMAGES, arrestments, 29.22–29.23
  assessment, review by appeal courts, 18.116
  death, several pursuers, 4.40
  negligence, relevancy of averments, 9.34
  payment to legally disabled persons, rules of court, 4.09
    small claims, 31.32
    summary causes, 30.48–30.55
  personal injuries or death, *see* DAMAGES FOR PERSONAL INJURIES
  several defenders, apportionment, 4.49
DAMAGES FOR PERSONAL INJURIES, 21.12–21.44
  amendment of pleadings, after expiry of time-limits, 10.32, 10.40–10.42
  children, 21.43
  craves, 21.13
  death actions, intimation, 21.14–21.16
    sist of pursuers, 21.17–21.18
  interest, 21.35–21.36
  interim damages, *see* INTERIM DAMAGES
  interim decrees, 11.82
  judgments, 21.44
  legal disability of payees, 21.37–21.42
    direct payments, 21.42
    judicial factors, 21.38
    sheriff clerks, 21.40
    trustees, 21.39
  limitation, 2.115–2.116, 12.51
  provisional damages, 21.29–21.32
    nature, 21.29
    procedure, 21.30–21.32
  recovery of documents, 15.56
  social security benefits, 21.33
  summary causes,
    inspection and recovery of documents, 30.316
    intimation to connected persons, 30.321–30.327
    provisional damages, 30.318–30.320
    response, 30.314
    scope, 30.307
    statement of claim, 30.308–30.309
    summons, 30.310–30.313
    valuation of claim, 30.317
DANGEROUS DOGS, 26.14
DATA PROTECTION, 26.377
DEAFNESS, party litigants, 16.68
  witnesses, 16.66

DEATH, *see also* FATAL ACCIDENT INQUIRIES
  actions for damages, intimation, 21.14–21.16
    limitation, 2.117–2.118, 10.40
    several pursuers, 4.40
    sist of pursuers, 21.17–21.18
  declarators, *see* DECLARATORS OF DEATH
  parties, 12.09
    sisting of representatives, 12.10
    transfer of causes, 12.11
  sheriffs, at proof, 16.41
DEBATES, 13.01–13.25
  allowance, 8.53
  amendments of pleadings at debate, 10.17, 13.14
  authorities, lists, 13.06
    not cited, 13.15
  circumstances, 13.01
  decisions, 13.15–13.25
    interlocutors, 13.23
  diets, attendance of parties, 13.07
    discharge before debates, 13.03
    speeches, 13.08–13.14
  document production, joint minutes, 13.05
  expenses, 13.07, 13.24
  preparation, 13.04
DEBTORS, protection, poinding, 29.81
DEBTS, arrestments on the dependence, 11.14, 11.15
DECLARATORS, actions, *see* DECLARATORY ACTIONS
  death, *see* DECLARATORS OF DEATH
  holograph wills, 20.19–20.22
  interim, 4.57
DECLARATORS OF DEATH, 20.06–20.18
  advertisements, 20.09
  circumstances, 20.06
  decrees, 20.13
    effect, 20.14
    intimation to Registrar General, 20.15
    recall, 20.18
    variation, 20.18
  defences, 20.10
  initial writs, 20.07, 20.08
  insurance, 20.16
  irrecoverable rights, 20.17
  jurisdiction, 2.39, 2.65
  Lord Advocate, 4.67
  minutes, 20.10
  proof, 20.12
  remit to Court of Session, 13.62, 20.11
DECLARATORY ACTIONS, 5.06, 20.01–20.22
  craves, 20.04
  defenders, 20.03
  jurisdiction, 2.32
    sheriff court, 20.02
  nature, 20.01
  precision, 20.05
DECLINATURE OF JURISDICTION, 2.124–2.129
  interest, 2.126–2.128
  procedure, 2.129
  relationship, 2.125

DECREES, 17.11–17.24
  absolvitor, *see* ABSOLVITOR
  ad factum praestandum, 21.80–21.82
    civil imprisonment, 26.126
  by default, *see* DECREES BY DEFAULT
  condemnator, *res judicata*, 17.11
  Court of Session, variation, 22.92–22.95
  dismissal, *see* DISMISSAL
  enforcement, 29.03
  errors, 17.14
  essentials, 17.13–17.15
  execution, 2.86
  extracts, 17.15, 30.232–30.234
  for expenses, 19.37
  for payment, 17.16–17.21
    contributory negligence, 17.18
    foreign currencies, 17.17
    instalments, 17.21
    interest, 17.19
    joint liability, 17.18
  in absence, *see* DECREES IN ABSENCE
  interdicts, 21.94
  multiplepoinding, 21.70
  small claims, 31.121–31.122,
    31.64–31.68
  summary causes, 30.129
  variation,
    small claims, 31.136
    summary causes, 30.240
    see also SUMMARY DECREE
  suspension, effect of appeals, 18.68
DECREES BY DEFAULT, 14.02–14.14
  and decrees in absence, 14.03
  appeals, 14.11–14.13
  at debates, 13.07
  circumstances, 14.04, 16.47
  discretion, general considerations,
    14.09–14.10
    prorogation, 14.08
  failure to appear at diets, 14.07,
    16.47–16.48
  failure to lodge, productions, 14.05
    records, 14.06
  family actions, 14.14, 22.54–22.55
  general rule, 14.02
  jurisdiction, 2.08
  nature, 14.03
  non-compliance with rules and orders,
    5.93, 5.101
  reduction, 14.13, 18.05
  small claims, 31.105–31.109
  solicitors, failures, 14.10
    withdrawal, 14.07
  summary causes, 30.200–30.204
DECREES IN ABSENCE, 7.01–7.19
  against children, 4.17
  against Crown, enforcement, 4.81
  and decrees by default, 14.03
  appeals, 7.19
  craves, alternative craves, 7.08
    restrictions, 7.07
  defenders furth of Scotland, 7.12
  effect, 7.19
  expenses, 7.10
  extracts, 7.15

DECREES IN ABSENCE—*cont.*
  finality, 7.18
  form, 7.15
  jurisdiction, 7.12
  late notices of intention to defend, 7.16
  matters *pars judicis*, 7.13
  minutes, 7.05
  powers of sheriff, 7.12
  procedure, 7.11–7.19
  recall, competency of appeal, 18.22
  reduction, 18.05
  removing, 23.05
  reponing, 7.23–7.35
  res judicata, 2.106, 7.19
  rules, 7.04
  several defenders, 7.09
  timing, 7.06
DEEDS, construction, awards of expenses,
  19.13
DEER, 26.30–26.31
DEFAMATION, caution for expenses,
  bankrupt pursuers, 11.54
  jurisdiction within Scotland, 3.93
  limitation of actions, 2.119
  reparation, 2.79
  small claims, 31.03
  tenders, 14.37
DEFECTS, housing in multiple occupation,
  26.229
  instances, amendments, 10.04
  pleadings, 9.41
  sewerage, 26.337
  systems of working, 27.18
DEFENCES, 9.01
  amendments, 10.03
  answers to condescendences,
    9.108–9.114
    skeleton defences, 9.114
  declarators of death, 20.10
  decrees in absence, reponing, 7.30
  drafting, 9.106–9.129
  form, 9.40, 9.43
  headings, 9.107
  lodging, *see* LODGING OF DEFENCES
  pleas-in-law, *see* PLEAS-IN-LAW
  signatures, 9.129
  time-limits, decrees by default, 14.03,
    14.08
  withdrawal, 8.23
DEFENDED ACTIONS, definition, 14.03
  small claims,
    abandonment of action,
      31.102–31.104
    confidentiality, 31.95
    counterclaims, 31.70–31.74
    decree by default, 31.105–31.109
    evidence on commission, 31.100
    failure of witnesses to attend, 31.99
    hearings, 31.75–31.82, 31.110–31.120
    letters of request, 31.101
    lodging productions, 31.85–31.88
    meaning, 31.69
    parties to be heard, 31.118
    public records, 31.96
    remit to determine facts, 31.84

DEFENDED ACTIONS, definition—*cont.*
　small claims—*cont.*
　　sheriff's decision, 31.119
　　third parties, 31.83
　summary causes,
　　abandonment of action,
　　　30.197–30.199
　　agreement of evidence, 30.153
　　citation of witnesses and havers,
　　　30.179–30.182
　　confidentiality, 30.174
　　counterclaims, 30.132–30.133
　　decree by default, 30.200–30.204
　　evidence on commission,
　　　30.185–30.189
　　exchange of skilled witness reports,
　　　30.155
　　exchange of witness lists, 30.154
　　failure of witnesses to attend,
　　　30.183–30.184
　　hearings, 30.134–30.142
　　inspection and recovery of
　　　documents, 30.152
　　letters of request, 30.190–30.196
　　lodging productions, 30.156–30.161
　　meaning, 30.131
　　noting evidence, 30.207–30.208
　　oath or affirmation, 30.206
　　objections to admissibility of
　　　evidence, 30.209–30.210
　　parties to be heard, 30.124–30.125
　　proof, 30.205
　　public records, 30.175–30.178
　　recovery of documents,
　　　30.162–30.173
　　remits to person of skill, 30.151
　　sheriff's decision, 30.126–30.127
　　specific issue hearings, 30.150
　　third-party procedure, 30.143–30.149
　　time to pay directions or orders,
　　　30.128
DEFENDERS, called for their interest, 4.116
　additional,
　　small claims, 31.30
　　summary causes, 30.46
　caution for expenses, bankrupts, 11.55
　children, 4.15–4.19
　citation, addresses unknown, 6.33–6.36
　declaratory actions, 20.03
　disclosure of identity, 12.02–12.04
　furth of Scotland, execution of citation,
　　6.29–6.32
　jurisdiction, 2.17
　mental disorder, family actions, 22.15,
　　22.21
　new defenders, amendment of
　　instances, 10.11–10.12, 10.35, 10.41,
　　12.07
　pleas, all parties not called, 4.116
　plurality, 4.41–4.51
　　abandonment of actions, 14.29
　　damages, 4.49
　　decrees in absence, 7.09
　　delict, 4.48==

DEFENDERS, called for their interest—*cont.*
　plurality—*cont.*
　　interim damages, 21.24
　　joint and several liability, 4.41, 4.42,
　　　4.47, 4.48
　　jurisdiction, 3.38, 3.109, 4.47
　　lodging of defences, 8.21
　　relief, 4.44
　　several wrongs, 4.50
　　tenders, 14.56–14.62
　　title to appeal, 18.21
　　transfers to other sheriff courts, 13.52
　substitution, after expiry of time-limits,
　　10.35
DELAY, avoidance, decrees by default,
　14.04
　judgments, 17.01
　judicial control, 5.98–5.100
DELICT, joint and several liability, 4.48
　jurisdiction, 2.51
　　foreign domicile, 3.33
　　within Scotland, 3.93
　place of harm, 3.93
DELIVERY, actions *ad factum praestandum*,
　21.78
　small claims, 31.135
　summary causes, 30.239, 30.241–30.242
DEMOLITION ORDERS, 26.227
　compensation, 26.240
　superiors, entry powers, 26.242
DESIGN RIGHTS, jurisdiction, 2.46, 3.26,
　3.27
　within U.K., 3.71, 3.108
DESIGNATIONS, instances, 9.79, 10.08
　written pleadings, signatures, 9.49
DIETS OF PROOF, additional proof,
　16.96–16.97
　adjournment, 16.56–16.57
　appeals in course of proof, 18.53
　attendance, 16.46–16.48
　calling of cases, 16.45
　closing proof, 16.94–16.95
　conclusion, 16.104
　discharge, 16.35–16.37
　fixing dates, 8.56, 30.141
　hearings on evidence, *see* HEARINGS ON
　　EVIDENCE
　inspections, 16.92–16.93
　meaning of diet, 14.07
　presentation of cases, 16.58
　procedure, 16.38–16.104
　proof in replication, 16.91
　publicity, 16.44
　recording of evidence, 16.55
　retiral of sheriff, 16.41
　role of advocates, 16.42–16.43
　role of sheriff, 16.38–16.41
　time, adoption proceedings, 28.110
　watching briefs, 16.49
　witnesses, *see* EXAMINATION OF
　　WITNESSES; WITNESSES
DILIGENCE, *see also* SPECIFIC DILIGENCES
　effect of reponing notes, 7.27
　jurisdiction, 2.78
　on the dependence, effect of
　　amendment of pleadings, 10.43

DILIGENCE—*cont.*
  proceedings, 2.86
  rents, assured tenancies, 26.247
  sisting, 24.15
  small claims, 31.89–31.93, 31.135
  summary causes, 30.162–30.173
    delivery actions, 30.239
  summary diligence, 29.02
  suspension, 2.85, 24.11–24.15
    appeals, 24.15
    caveats, 24.15
    competency, 24.11
    jurisdiction, 24.12
    nature of action, 24.11
    procedure, 24.14
DIPLOMATS, immunity, 4.05
DIRECTIONS, sheriffs principal, 1.38–1.40
  inherent jurisdiction, 2.07
DIRECTORS, parties to actions,
  receivership, 4.89
DISABILITY DISCRIMINATION, 26.379
DISCLAMATION, new parties, 12.19–12.20
DISCRETIONARY POWERS, *see also* JUDICIAL
    DISCRETION
  administrative authorities, scope of
    appeals, 25.08
DISCRIMINATION, disability discrimination,
  26.379
  race discrimination, 26.369–26.376
  sex discrimination, 26.362–26.368
DISEASES, infectious diseases, 26.326
  compensation, 26.334
DISMISSAL, abandonment procedure,
  14.21–14.25
  after proof, 17.11, 17.12
  appeal judgments, 18.86
  extra-judicial settlements, 14.65
  failure to lodge records, 8.34, 14.06
  parties failing to appear, 14.02, 14.04,
    14.07
  res judicata, 17.11
DISPENSING POWERS, fatal accident
    inquiries, 27.24
  jurisdiction, 2.08
  pleadings, defects, 9.41
  rules of court, non-compliance,
    5.93–5.97
  sheriff principal, appeals, 18.78
  small claims, 31.10–31.11
  summary causes, 30.13–30.15
  time-limits, appeals to sheriff principal,
    18.56
    leave to appeal, 18.47, 18.48
    licensing appeals, 26.255
DISTURBANCES, exclusion from court, 5.24
DITCHES, cleansing, 26.327
DIVISION AND SALE, 2.86, 23.37–23.43
  craves, 23.38
  matrimonial homes, 23.42–23.43
  nature of action, 23.37
  procedure, 23.38–23.41
DIVORCE ACTIONS, 22.02, *see also* FAMILY
    ACTIONS
  applications and orders, financial
    provision, 22.60–22.67
  relating to children, 22.57–22.59

DIVORCE ACTIONS—*cont.*
  competency of appeal, 18.25
  consent, notices, 23.32
    undefended actions, 22.44, 22.45
  initial writs, 22.05, 22.06, 22.08, 22.22
  jurisdiction, 2.39, 2.57, 2.58–2.60
    reduction, 2.39
  mandataries, sisting, 11.71
  mental disorder, rules of court, 4.07
  private hearings, 5.20, 5.22
  simplified procedure, 22.04, 22.83–22.91
    addresses unknown, 22.86
    appeals, 22.90
    challenge of jurisdiction, 22.87
    conditions, 22.83
    decrees, 22.89
    evidence, 22.88
    intimation, 22.85
    separation, 22.84
  sists, 22.27–22.31
DOCKS, 26.207–26.210, 26.212
DOCUMENTS, *see also* SERVICE
  as evidence, 15.44–15.46
    copies, 15.44
  debates, joint minutes, 13.05
  electronic transmission, 30.36
    small claims, 31.25
    summary causes, 30.36
  exception, 12.66–12.67
    cautions, 12.72
    competency, 12.68–12.71
    procedure, 12.72
    title and interest to object, 12.71
    types of documents, 12.70
  lodging of defences, 8.20
  lost documents, processes, 8.17
    small claims, 31.23–31.24
    summary causes, 30.35
  orders to produce, 12.02, 15.47–15.49
    applications, 15.01
    details of financial resources, 15.49
    documents founded on in pleadings,
      15.47
    powers of sheriff, 15.48
  preservation and inspection, court
    powers, 15.85
    orders, 15.91–15.92
  protective measures, 11.05
  processes, *see* PROCESSES
  productions, *see* PRODUCTIONS
  recovery, *see* RECOVERY OF DOCUMENTS
  rectification, 24.07
  retained by sheriff clerk,
    small claims, 31.133
    summary causes, 30.235
  summary causes,
    inspection and recovery, 30.152
  written pleadings, 9.67
    calls, 9.69
DOGS, dangerous dogs, 26.14
  licences, breeding, 26.22
    guard dogs, 26.23
DOMICILE, 3.06–3.64
  adoptive parents, 28.50–28.51
  corporations and associations, 3.13–3.20
    sheriff court jurisdiction, 3.17, 3.19

DOMICILE—*cont.*
  Crown, 3.22, 4.54
  declinature of jurisdiction, 3.55–3.64
  family proceedings, 2.58, 2.59
  general principle, 3.06
    qualifications, 3.23–3.64
      concurrent jurisdictions, 3.29–3.37
      consumer contracts, 3.46–3.50
      counterclaims, 3.40
      exclusive jurisdictions, 2.23–2.28
      insurance, 3.41–3.45
      plurality of defenders, 3.38
      prorogation, 3.51–3.54, 3.78
      protective measures, 3.66
      provisional measures, 3.65
      third-party proceedings, 3.39
    individuals, 3.07–3.12
      jurisdiction within parts of U.K., 3.08
      jurisdiction within Scotland, 3.09
      substantial connection, 3.07, 3.12
    jurisdiction within Scotland, 3.90
    matters *pars judicis*, 2.14
    trusts, 3.21
DOMINUS LITIS, 4.112–4.113
  expenses, cautions, 11.56
    recovery, 19.05
DRAINAGE, 26.257–26.258
DRIVING, licences, disqualification, 26.384
  large vehicles, 26.383
  tests, 26.381–26.382
DRUG TRAFFICKING, forfeiture, 26.11

EARNINGS, arrestments, *see* ARRESTMENTS
  OF EARNINGS
EDINBURGH SHERIFF COURT, commissary
  proceedings, 3.86
EDUCATION, 26.113–26.116
  attendance orders, 26.115
  exclusion orders, 26.114
  placing requests, 26.113
  special education needs, 26.116
ELECTIONS, expenses, 26.118
  local elections, 26.119
    disqualifications, 26.284
  registration of electors, 26.117
ELECTRONIC TRANSMISSION OF DOCUMENTS,
  small claims, 31.25
  summary causes, 30.36
EMBEZZLEMENT, reparation, jurisdiction,
  2.79
EMPLOYEES, precognitions, 15.08
  reports of accidents, confidentiality,
    15.54
EMPLOYERS, associations, parties to
  litigation, 4.100
  intimation, fatal accident inquiries,
    27.03
EMPLOYERS' LIABILITY, defective
  equipment, right of relief, 12.47
EMPLOYMENT, contracts, jurisdiction, 3.92
ENEMY ALIENS, litigation, 4.03, 4.118
ENERGY CONSERVATION, 26.124
ENFORCEMENT OF JUDGMENTS, 29.01–29.04
  adjudications, 29.92
  arrestments, *see* ARRESTMENTS

ENFORCEMENT OF JUDGMENTS—*cont.*
  Crown proceedings, 4.79–4.81
  exclusive jurisdiction, 3.28
  extracts, *see* EXTRACTS
  foreign courts, 29.02
  inhibitions, 29.91
  poinding, *see* POINDING
  registered deeds, 29.02
  summary diligence, 29.02
  warrant sales, *see* WARRANT SALES
ENMITY, declinature of jurisdiction, 2.126
ENTAILS, 26.259–26.264
  disposal of land, 26.285
ENTRY POWERS, 26.01
  caravan sites, 26.162
  control of pollution, 26.173
  disused tips, 26.317
  fire services, 26.177
  fishing boats, 26.188
  flood prevention, 26.91
  Inland Revenue, 26.250
  public health, 26.231
  reservoirs, 26.410
  river purification boards, 26.415
  sea-fishery officers, 26.188
  sewerage works, 26.340
  slaughterhouses, 26.27
  superiors, 26.242
  water works, 26.412
  weights and measures, 26.416
ENVIRONMENTAL PROTECTION, 26.190
  clean air, 26.343
  nuisance, *see* NUISANCE
EQUITY, division and sale, 23.37
  overriding time-limits, 2.121, 10.40
ERRORS, arrestments on the dependence,
  11.19
  correction in summary causes, 30.230
  instances, 9.78
  interlocutors, correction, 5.87–5.90
  reduction, 18.05
  registration of births, deaths and
    marriages, 26.360
  service copies, 6.15
  warrants of citation, 6.09
EUROPEAN CONVENTION ON HUMAN RIGHTS,
  adoption proceedings, 28.87
EUROPEAN COURT OF JUSTICE, *see also*
  REFERENCES TO EUROPEAN COURT
  jurisdiction, 13.68
EVICTION ORDERS, caravan sites, 26.163
EVIDENCE, admissibility, *see* ADMISSIBILITY
  OF EVIDENCE
  adoption proceedings, 28.01, 28.112
  agreement in summary causes, 30.153
  leading in small claims, 31.113–31.114
  recording
    small claims, 31.115
    summary causes, 30.207–30.208
  affidavits, *see* AFFIDAVITS
  blood tests, 15.103–15.104
  contents of notes, 17.27
  documentary, *see* DOCUMENTS
  expert evidence, 15.17
  hearings, *see* HEARINGS ON EVIDENCE

EVIDENCE, admissibility—*cont.*
insanity, 4.08
leading, 8.64
medical examinations, 15.102
notes, appeals to sheriff principal, 18.63
property, *see* PROPERTY
provisional damages, 21.30
publicity, close doors, 5.22–5.25
real evidence, 15.44–15.46
publicity, 5.26
recording, 16.32–16.34
diets of proof, 16.55
dispensing with, 16.33
summary applications, 25.25, 25.44
Scottish Solicitors' Discipline Tribunal,
26.278
undefended family actions, 22.46–22.47
witnesses, *see* WITNESSES
EXAMINATION OF WITNESSES, 16.59–16.90
by sheriffs, 16.39
concurring witnesses, 16.83
cross-examinations, 16.73–16.77
examinations-in-chief, 16.70–16.72
general rules, 16.60–16.61
interpreters, 16.65–16.68
leading questions, 16.71, 16.75, 16.78
oaths and affirmations, 16.62–16.64
objections, 16.84–16.90
incidental appeals, 16.89–16.90
recording, 16.88
rulings, 16.85, 16.100
competency of appeal, 18.26
timeous objections, 16.84
post examination procedure, 16.54
questions, 16.69
through the court, 16.80
recall, 16.81–16.82
re-examinations, 16.78–16.79
witnesses in court before examination,
16.52
EXCLUSION OF COMPETENT JURISDICTION,
2.88–2.135
arbitration, 2.99–2.102
competent and omitted, 2.112–2.113
concurrent criminal proceedings, 2.133
declinature, 2.124–2.129
failure to exhaust statutory remedies,
2.131
forum non conveniens, 2.89–2.93
jurisdiction clauses, 2.103
limitation of actions, *see* LIMITATION OF
ACTIONS
lis alibi pendens, 2.94–2.98
mora, taciturnity and acquiescence,
2.123
prescription, 2.114
recompense, 2.132
registration of custody decision, 2.134
res judicata, 2.104–2.111
statutory restrictions, 2.130
transfers and remits, 2.135
EXCLUSION OF JURISDICTION, 2.36–2.48
adjudications, 2.40
arbitration, 2.47

EXCLUSION OF JURISDICTION—*cont.*
company administration, 2.45
inhibitions, 2.41
intellectual property, 2.46
otherwise competent, *see* EXCLUSION OF
COMPETENT JURISDICTION
proving the tenor, 2.43
reduction, 2.42
status actions, 2.39
supervisory jurisdiction, 2.48
trusts, 2.44
EXCLUSION ORDERS, 22.104
children, 26.75
education, 26.114
EXCLUSIVE JURISDICTION, 2.11, 3.23–3.28
company administration, 3.25
enforcement of judgments, 3.28
heritable property, 3.24
intellectual property, 3.27
patents, 3.75
jurisdiction within Scotland, 3.111
prorogation of jurisdiction, 3.51–3.54,
3.78
public registers, 3.26
EXECUTION OF CITATION, 6.14–6.46
addresses known, 6.18–6.28
addresses unknown, 6.33–6.36
addresses known after citation, 6.36
display on walls of court, 6.35
granting warrants, 6.33
newspaper advertisements, 6.34
business names, 6.43
by sheriff officers, 6.23–6.28
certificates, 6.28
certificates, 6.45
companies, 6.40
oversea companies, 6.41
corporations, 6.42
defenders furth of Scotland, 6.29–6.32
documents to be served, 6.01
forms, 6.16
friendly societies, 6.44
local authorities, 6.39
Lord Advocate, 6.38
objections, 6.46
postal citations, 6.19–6.22
letters not returned, 6.20
letters refused, 6.22
letters returned, 6.21
service copies, 6.15
small claims, 31.16
address in Scotland, 31.50
address outwith Scotland, 31.53
by sheriff officer, 31.44–31.47, 31.52
effect of appearance, 31.55
other than by sheriff officer,
31.48–31.49
period of notice, 31.43
postal, 31.51
reservice, 31.56
return of summons, 31.57–31.59
unknown address, 31.55
witnesses and havers, 31.97–31.98
summary causes, 30.88
address in Scotland, 30.91

EXECUTION OF CITATION—*cont.*
  summary causes—*cont.*
    address outwith Scotland,
      30.99–30.104
    by sheriff officer, 30.93–30.98
    effect of appearance, 30.110
    postal, 30.92
  unknown address, 30.105–30.109
EXECUTION OF DEEDS, 26.103
EXECUTORIAL PROCEEDINGS, 2.86
EXECUTORS, confirmation, jurisdiction,
    2.66
  disposal of leases, 26.398
  parties to litigation, 4.105
  reponing, 7.24
EXHIBITION, 2.86, 24.01
EXPENSES, 19.01–19.02
  abandonment of actions, 14.20, 14.23,
    14.24, 14.25, 14.30
  adoption proceedings, 28.128–28.129
  amendment of pleadings, 10.02, 10.53
    condition, 10.29–10.30
    subsequent abandonment, 10.44
  answers to minutes of amendment,
    10.50
  appeals, against award of expenses,
    18.117
    betting licences, 26.39
    building decisions, 26.51
    gaming licences, 25.43
    housing, 26.243
    to sheriff principal, 18.77,
      18.87–18.89
  arbitration, 26.09
  awards, motions, 19.05
  caution, *see* CAUTION FOR EXPENSES
  childrens proceedings, 4.14, 26.78
  commission and diligence, evidence of
    witnesses, 15.39
    recovery of documents, 15.82
    witnesses outside U.K., 15.42
  consent and concurrence, 4.115
  counterclaims, 12.29, 12.36, 12.38
  craves, 9.94–9.95
  Crown proceedings, 4.78
    remit to Court of Session, 4.55
  curators *ad litem*, 4.23, 4.27
  debates, 13.07, 13.24
  decrees for payment, competency of
    appeal, 18.39
  decrees in absence, 7.10
  delay in proceedings, 5.100
  discretion of the court, 19.03
  domini litis, 4.113, 19.05
  extra-judicial settlements, 14.67
    rejected offers, 14.68
  fatal accident inquiries, 27.23
  freeing for adoption, 28.168
  furthcoming, 21.50
  interim awards, 11.86–11.89
    enforcement, 11.89
    modification, 11.88
    multiplepoinding, 11.87
  interlocutors, whether final judgments,
    18.36
  judgments, 17.23

EXPENSES—*cont.*
  judicial references, 13.39
  judicial remits, 13.34
  modification, 18.37
  motions, 5.55
  multiplepoinding, 21.71
  party litigants, 4.121
  procedure, 19.04–19.06
  recovery of documents, bankers' books,
    15.96
  remit to Court of Session, Crown
    proceedings, 13.63
  reponing, 7.35
  reservation, 16.104, 19.06, 19.16
    timing of extracts, 29.08
  rules, 19.07
    divided success, 19.14–19.15
    exceptions, 19.08–19.13
      construction of deeds, 19.13
      modification, 19.09–19.10
      successful parties' liability, 19.12
      successful parties refused expenses,
        19.11
    expenses in the cause, 19.17, 19.55
    failure to appear or proceed, 19.21
    percentage increases, 19.18–19.20
    solicitors, *see* SOLICITORS
  sisting of new parties, 12.18
  small claims, 31.123–31.128
  summary applications, 25.46–25.47
    disinterring bodies, 25.05
  summary causes, 30.220–30.229
  taxation, *see* TAXATION OF EXPENSES
  tenders, 14.38–14.39
    acceptance, 14.47–14.48
    non acceptance, 14.51–14.53
    plurality of defenders, 14.57, 14.58,
      14.60
  transfer of causes, 13.47
  transfer of interest to sue, 12.15
  withholding of admissions, 9.26
  witnesses, *see* WITNESSES
EXPERT EVIDENCE, 15.17
EXTRACTS, 17.15, 29.05–29.13
  adoption orders, 28.117, 28.196
  decrees for payment, foreign currency,
    29.12
  decrees in absence, 7.15
  execution, 29.13
  form, 29.06
  freeing orders, 28.170
  issue, 29.05
  nature, 29.05
  superseding extracts, 17.24, 29.11
  timing, 29.07–29.11
    reservation of expenses, 29.08
    small claims, 29.10
    summary causes, 29.10
EXTRA-JUDICIAL SETTLEMENTS, 14.31,
    14.63–14.68

FACTORIES, premises, alterations, 26.120
FAIR TRADING, 26.404–26.405
FAIRNESS, adoption proceedings, 28.87,
    28.108

FAMILY ACTIONS, 22.02–22.32, *see also*
  ADOPTION; AFFILIATION; ALIMENT;
  DIVORCE ACTIONS; FINANCIAL
  GROVISION; GUARDIANSHIP;
  LEGITIMACY; MATRIMONIAL HOMES;
  PARENTAGE; PARENTAL RIGHTS AND
  RESPONSIBILITIES; SEPARATION ACTIONS
  applications and orders, 22.56–22.82
    aliment, 22.68–22.72
    avoidance transactions, 22.65
    financial provision, 22.60–22.67
    matrimonial homes, 22.77–22.82
    relating to children, 22.56–22.59
    s. 11 orders, 22.57, 22.73–22.76
  avizandum, 16.104
  avoidance transactions, applications,
    22.65
    intimation, 22.15
  children proceedings, *see* CHILDREN
    PROCEEDINGS
  citation, 22.19–22.21
  condescendences, 22.06
  counterclaims, 12.31
  curators *ad litem*, appointment,
    22.24–22.26
  decrees by default, 14.14
  defended actions, 22.51–22.55
    attendance at options hearings, 22.53
    decrees by default, 22.54–22.55
    notices of intention to defend, 22.52
    reponing, 22.55
  evidence behind close doors, 5.20, 5.22
  form of process, 5.06
  initial writs, 22.05–22.14
  intimation, 22.15–22.17
    orders, 22.23
  judicial remits, competency of appeal,
    18.24
  jurisdiction, 2.56–2.64, 22.03
  notices, 22.22
    consent to divorce and separation,
      23.32
    intention to defend, 8.02
      child welfare hearings, 8.08
  private hearings, 5.20
  procedural hearings, attendance, 8.50
  productions, 22.18
  register, 5.34
  remit to Court of Session, 13.61
  reporting, 5.28–5.30
  sist of processes, 13.77
  sists, 22.27
    discretionary, 22.29
    mandatory, 22.28
  types, 22.02
  undefended, *see* UNDEFENDED ACTIONS
  warrants for intimation, addresses
    unknown, 22.09
  warrants of citation, 6.07, 6.08, 6.16
FAMILY MEDIATION, 22.36
FARMS, neglect, summary applications,
  25.04

FATAL ACCIDENT INQUIRIES, applications,
  27.07
  decisions, 27.14
    cause of death, 27.16
    contributory defects, 27.18
    delivery and distribution, 27.21
    precautions, 27.17
    relevant facts, 27.19
    time and place of death, 27.15
  discretionary inquiries, 27.02, 27.05
  dispensing powers, 27.24
  expenses, 27.23
  investigations, 27.06
  jurisdiction, 27.01
  legal aid, 27.10
  legislation, 27.02
  mandatory inquiries, 27.02, 27.03–27.04
    deaths at work, 27.03
    deaths in custody, 27.04
  notification, 27.08
  procedure, 27.11
    criminal proceedings, 27.13
    sheriff's powers, 27.12
    written statements, 27.13
  procurators fiscal, role, 1.30, 27.06
  representation, 1.32, 27.09
  review, 27.22
  service of documents, 27.24
FEES, *see also* TAXATION, accounts
  Crown proceedings, 4.78
  Law Society of Scotland, 14.67
  payment, 1.23
  personal liability of solicitors, 19.22
  regulation, 1.45
  small claims, 31.128
  summary causes, 30.220–30.229
FERRIES, 26.211
FEUDUTIES, church buildings, 26.88
  sequestrations for feuduties, 23.25
FEUS, grants, entailed estates, 26.262,
  26.264
FILMS, storage, 26.329
FINANCIAL PROVISION, 22.105
  applications, 22.02
    overseas divorces, 22.66
  evidence of financial resources,
    recovery of documents, 15.49,
    15.58
  jurisdiction, 2.42, 2.59
  orders, 22.60–22.64
FINANCIAL RECORDS, recovery of
  documents, 15.56
FINANCIAL SERVICES, jurisdiction within
  U.K., 3.71
FIRE CERTIFICATES, 26.178, 26.181
FIRE PRECAUTIONS, 26.178–26.180
  lodgings, 26.229
  modification of premises, 26.180, 26.182
  prohibition notices, 26.179
FIRE SAFETY, 26.160
FIRE SERVICES, entry powers, 26.177
  pensions, 26.176
FIREARMS, 26.183–26.185
  appeals, 25.10, 26.183
  destruction, 26.185
  prohibition, 26.184

FISHERIES, 26.186–26.189
  boats, entry powers, 26.188
  offences, entry powers, 26.188
    salmon poaching, 26.186
    sea fisheries, 26.187
  salmon, 26.189
FISHING DILIGENCE, 15.51, 15.53, 15.62,
    15.80, 15.84
  bankers' books, 15.95
FLOATING CHARGES, competition, with
    arrestments, 29.33
  with poinding, 29.83
FLOATING SHERIFFS, 1.06, 1.17
FLOOD PREVENTION, entry powers, 26.91
FOOD SAFETY, 26.190
  certificates, 26.191
  improvement notices, 26.191
  licences, 26.191
  meat, 26.192
  preparations, 26.194
FOREIGN CURRENCY, craves, 9.91–9.92
  decrees for payment, 17.17
  extracts, 29.12
FOREIGN LAW, written pleadings, 9.18
FOREIGN STATES, immunity, 2.17, 4.04
  jurisdiction, 2.36
FORUM NON CONVENIENS, 2.89–2.93
  exclusive jurisdiction, 3.53
  jurisdiction within Scotland, 3.78
  preliminary pleas, 9.120
  sist of processes, 13.79
FOSTERING, 26.58
FRAUD, documents, confidentiality, 15.54
    recovery, 15.62
  reduction of decrees, 18.05
FREEDOM, declarators, jurisdiction, 2.39
FREEING FOR ADOPTION, 28.135–28.174
  Adoption Register, 28.172
  appeals, 28.169
  applicants, 28.139
  children who may be freed,
    28.136–28.138
  children's addresses, confidentiality,
    28.148
  children's consent, 28.136, 28.149,
    28.156
  confidentiality, 28.163
    processes, 28.170–28.171, 28.196
  curators *ad litem*, appointment, 28.149,
    28.152
    functions, 28.156
    reports, 28.152, 28.156
  expenses, 28.168
  hearings, 28.158–28.161
    notices, 28.158
  necessity, 28.14, 28.92
  orders, 28.165–28.169
    extracts, 28.170
    revocation, 28.185–28.194
    sheriff's discretion, 28.160
    supervision requirements, 28.167
    terms and conditions, 28.166
  parental consent, 28.137, 28.140–28.145
  petitions, 28.149
  pleadings, 28.162

FREEING FOR ADOPTION—*cont.*
  proof, 28.164
  purpose, 28.02, 28.135
  reporting officers, 28.142, 28.144,
    28.146
    appointment, 28.147, 28.152
    functions, 28.153–28.155
    reports, 28.152
  reports, 28.150
  statutory requirements, 28.159
  timing, 28.14, 28.15
  unmarried fathers, 28.146, 28.150,
    28.154
    intimation of hearings, 28.158
  views of children, 28.156, 28.157
FRIENDLY SOCIETIES, 26.202–26.204, 26.206
  execution of citation, 6.44
  parties to litigation, 4.102
FURNITURE, control orders, 26.234
  Part VII tenancies, 26.273
FURTHCOMING, 21.45–21.51, 29.37, 29.39
  competing claims, 21.51
  expenses, 21.50
  jurisdiction, 2.78, 21.46
  nature of action, 21.45
  proceedings, 2.86
  raising actions, 21.47–21.49
  summary causes, 30.02, 30.255–30.256

GAMING, *see* BETTING AND GAMING
GOVERNMENT ANNUITIES, 26.322
GRANT REPORT, 1.44, 2.40
  inhibitions, 2.41
GRANTS, housing, 26.238
GRIEVE REPORT, 1.25
GUARDIANS, 28.29
  appointment, 26.79
    agricultural holdings, 26.08
    applications, 22.02
GUARDIANSHIP, 4.11, 26.307–26.308
  jurisdiction, 2.61, 2.68
    within Scotland, 3.82
  proceedings, 2.86

HAGUE CONVENTION, evidence abroad,
    15.42
  service of documents abroad, 3.56
    decrees in absence, 7.12
    execution of citation, 6.30
    methods, 3.57
    simplified divorce procedure, 22.89
HARASSMENT, limitation of actions, 2.120
HARBOURS, 26.207–26.212
HAVERS,
  citation,
    arbitration, 25.04
    small claims, 31.97–31.98
    summary causes, 30.179–30.182
    ratal accident inquiries, 27.08
    Scottish Solicitors' Discipline
      Tribunal, 26.278
  privilege, 15.03, 15.86
  recovery of documents, commission and
    diligence, 15.50, 15.73, 15.74
    expenses, 15.72

HAVERS—*cont.*
recovery of documents, commission and diligence—*cont.*
non-compliance, 15.71, 15.76
self-incrimination, 15.52, 15.73, 15.74
HEALTH AND SAFETY AT WORK, agriculture, 26.03
fatal accident inquiries, 27.03, 27.08, 27.09
HEARINGS, *see* ADOPTION HEARINGS; APPEAL HEARINGS; CHILDREN'S HEARINGS; HEARINGS ON EVIDENCE; OPTIONS HEARINGS; PROCEDURAL HEARINGS
HEARINGS ON EVIDENCE, 16.98–16.104
authorities, 16.98
role of sheriffs, 16.40
small claims, 31.75–31.82
conduct, 31.110–31.111
leading evidence, 31.113–31.114
oath or affirmation, 31.112
objections to admissibility, 31.116
parties to be heard, 31.118
recording evidence, 31.115
speeches, 16.99–16.103
amendment of pleadings, 16.101
concessions on matters of fact or law, 16.102
conclusions, 16.103
expenses, 16.103
summary causes
specific issues, 30.150
HERITABLE PROPERTY, actions, 5.06
jurisdiction, 2.53–2.55, 23.01
concurrent jurisdictions, 3.30, 3.73
exclusive jurisdiction, 3.24
within Scotland, 3.98, 3.102
Recovery of possession, *see* RECOVERY OF POSSESSION
HERITABLE SECURITIES, 1894 Act, 23.29–23.36, 26.97–26.102
appeals, 23.34
ejection of owners, 23.30, 26.98
expenses, 23.34–23.35
forfeiture of right of redemption, 23.32
leasing security subjects, 23.31, 26.99
notices calling up bonds, 23.36, 26.102
realising security subjects, 26.100
sale by *pari passu* security holders, 23.33, 26.101
1970 Act, 26.105
debtors, severe hardship, 26.274
modification, 26.240
recovery of possession, 23.03
intimation to security holders, 23.11
standard securities, 26.105
HIRE, contracts, objections by way of exception, 12.70
HIRE-PURCHASE, 26.213
contracts, objections by way of exception, 12.70
HOLIDAYS, fixing, 1.38
HOLOGRAPH WRITTINGS, wills, declarators, 20.19–20.22

HOMOSEXUALITY, 22.17
HONORARY SHERIFFS, 1.06, 1.17
appointment, 1.12
HOSPITAL RECORDS, recovery of documents, 15.56, 15.63
HOUSE OF LORDS, appeals, 18.99
HOUSEBOATS, poinding, 26.132
HOUSING, 26.215–26.249, *see also* ASSURED TENANCIES; SECURE TENANCIES
closing orders, 26.227
compulsory purchase, *see* COMPULSORY PURCHASE
control orders, 26.232–26.236
demolition orders, 26.227
grants, 26.238
housing action areas, 26.220
improvement orders, 26.219
leases, determination, 26.241
multiple occupation, defective condition, 26.229
licensing, 26.289
standards of management, 26.228
overcrowding, 26.230
prohibition orders, 26.220
public health, 26.231
repairs, *see* REPAIRS
superiors, entry, 26.242
HOUSING ASSOCIATIONS, rent limits, 26.271
HUMAN FERTILISATION, proceedings, 22.104
HYPOTHECS, sequestrations for feuduties, 23.25
sequestrations for rent, 23.14

IDENTIFICATION, children, 5.29
defenders, orders, 12.02–12.04
witnesses, 15.02–15.06
ILLEGALITY, matters *pars judicis*, 2.12
reparation, jurisdiction, 2.79
ILLEGITIMACY DECLARATORS, 22.02
initial writs, 22.13
ILLNESS, adjournments of proof, 16.57
witnesses, commission and diligence, 15.26
IMMUNITY, diplomats, 4.05
foreign heads of state, 4.05
foreign states, 2.17, 4.04
international organisations, 4.06
procurators fiscal, 1.31
sheriffs, 1.16
sheriffs principal, 1.13
IMPRISONMENT, breach of interdict, 21.99
breach of sequestrations for rent, 23.23
civil imprisonment, decrees *ad factum praestandum*, 26.126
enforcement of aliment, 26.125, 29.03
IMPROVEMENTS, entailed estates, 26.259, 26.263
protected tenancies, 26.276
INCEST, 22.17
INCIDENTAL APPLICATIONS,
summary causes, 30.37–30.41
INCIDENTAL ORDERS, divorce and separation, financial provision, 22.61

INCOME TAX, general commissioner, 1.12 (n. 51)
  records, recovery of documents, 15.56, 15.57
INCOMPETENCY, preliminary pleas, 9.121
  reduction of decrees, 18.05
INDECENCY, judicial reporting, 5.28
INDUSTRIAL ACTIONS, 1.36
  interim interdicts, 21.88
INDUSTRIAL AND PROVIDENT SOCIETIES, 26.197–26.201
  disputes, 26.200–26.201
  winding up, 26.199
INDUSTRIAL ASSURANCE COMPANIES, 26.196
INFECTIOUS DISEASES, 26.326
  compensation, 26.334
INFIRMITY, witnesses, commission and diligence, 15.26
INHERENT JURISDICTION, 2.05–2.25
  contempt of court, 2.18–2.25, 5.91
  definition, 2.05
  interlocutors, disregard, 5.91
  matters *pars judicis*, 2.09–2.17
    defenders, 2.17
    form, 2.14–2.17
    illegality, 2.12
    subject-matter, 2.11–2.13
  regulation of procedure, 2.07–2.08
  transfer of causes, 13.50
INHIBITIONS, 29.91
  jurisdiction, 2.41
INHIBITIONS ON THE DEPENDENCE, 11.36–11.42
  competency, 11.36
  effect, 11.39
  extinction, 11.40
  jurisdiction, proceedings outside Scotland, 3.65
  nature of procedure, 11.36
  prescription, 11.42
  procedure, 11.37–11.38
  recall, 11.41
INITIAL WRITS, 9.01
  amendments, 10.03
    effect, 7.21
  authentication, 9.105
  breaches of interdict, 21.96
  condescendences, 9.99–9.103
  count, reckoning and payment, 21.04
  craves, *see* CRAVES
  declarators of death, 20.07
  descriptions, 9.76
  divorce, 22.22
  drafting, 9.74
  family actions, 22.05–22.14
  form, 9.40
  headings, 9.75
  instances, *see* INSTANCES
  multiplepoinding, 21.55
  pleas-in-law, 9.104
  sequestrations for rent, 23.15
  service, *see* SERVICE
  style, 9.40
  summary applications, 25.18
    adjustment, 25.23

INLAND REVENUE, entry powers, 26.250
INSANITY, Evidence, 4.08
  parties to actions, 4.07–4.09, 4.118
INSOLVENCY, directors in receivership, parties to actions, 4.89
  evidence behind close doors, 5.23
  jurisdiction within Scotland, 3.83
INSTALMENTS, decrees for payment, 17.21
INSTANCES, 9.40
  amendments, 10.05, 10.07–10.12
    defects, 10.04
    new defenders, 10.11–10.12
    new pursuers, 10.09–10.10
  drafting, 9.78–9.81
  form, 9.44
  styles, Crown proceedings, 4.66
    dissolved partnerships, 4.98
    sole traders, 4.99
    trustees, 4.103
  summary applications, 25.18
INSURANCE, declarators of death, 20.16
  industrial assurance companies, 26.196
  jurisdiction, foreign domicile, 3.41–3.45
    within U.K., 3.72
  motor insurance, liability, 12.06
  policies, arrestments on the dependence, 11.14
  registered cattle insurance societies, 26.202
INTELLECTUAL PROPERTY, jurisdiction, 2.46, 3.26, 3.27
  within U.K., 3.71
  recovery of documents, 15.86
INTERDICTS, 2.84, 2.85
  appeals, to Court of Session, 18.96
    to sheriff principal, 18.38
  arrestments on the dependence, 11.27
  breaches, *see* BREACHES OF INTERDICT
  craves, 21.84
  Crown officers, 4.59
  Crown proceedings, 4.57, 4.59
  decrees, 21.94
  exclusion orders, 26.76
  interim, *see* INTERIM INTERDICTS
  jurisdiction within Scotland, 3.104, 21.83
  nature, 21.83
  remits to skilled persons, 21.95
  warrant sales, third-party property, 29.72
INTEREST, craves, 9.93
  damages, 16.103
  damages for personal injuries, 21.28, 21.35–21.36
    joint minutes, 16.30
  decrees for payment, 17.19
  tenders, 14.40–14.41
INTEREST TO SUE, 4.29, 4.33
  transfers, 12.14–12.15
INTERIM DAMAGES,
  personal injuries or deaths, 21.19–21.28
    applicability, 21.19
    conditions, 21.21
    contributory negligence, 21.23
    final orders, 21.28

INTERIM DAMAGES—*cont.*
  personal injuries or deaths—*cont.*
    hearings, 21.25
    interest, 21.28
    liability, 21.22
    motions, 21.10
    orders, 21.25–21.27
    several defenders, 21.24
INTERIM DECREES, 11.81–11.85
  appeals, 11.84–11.85
    competency, 18.39
  damages for personal injuries, 11.82
  interim awards of expenses, 11.86–11.89
  objectives, 11.03, 11.81
  timing, 11.83
INTERIM INTERDICTS, 21.85–21.93
  appeals, 21.93
  balance of convenience, 21.91
  conditions, 21.92
  duration, 21.90, 21.92
  effect of appeals, 18.68
  hearings, 21.89–21.92
  jurisdiction, proceedings outside
    Scotland, 3.65
  powers of the court, 11.04
  restrictions, caveats, 21.86
    trade disputes, 21.88
  suspension of diligence, 24.14
INTERIM ORDERS, actions *ad factum*
    praestandum, 11.82, 21.79
  adoption orders, 28.123
  matrimonial homes, applications in
    chambers, 5.21
  pending appeal, 11.08
  summary causes,
    aliment, 30.297
INTERLOCUTORS, 5.72–5.92
  actions *ad factum praestandum*, 21.80
  allowing debates, 8.53
  allowing proof, 8.54–8.55
  appeal judgments, identification of
    interlocutors reviewed, 18.84
  appeals to sheriff principal, acted upon,
    18.17
    extracted, 18.19
    incompetency, 18.12
    not subject to review, 18.16
    pronounced of consent, 18.15
    review of prior interlocutors, 18.70
  cautions, 11.46
  challenges, 5.92
  commission and diligence, evidence of
    witnesses, 14.30
  consignation, 11.46
  copies, 17.32
  correction, 5.87–5.90
  declarators of death, 20.13
  definition, 5.72
  disposal of preliminary pleas, 13.23
  effect, 5.91
  errors, reduction, 18.05
  form, 17.02–17.24
    orders, 5.77–5.82
    paper, 5.74

INTERLOCUTORS—*cont.*
  errors, reduction—*cont.*
    parties, 5.76
    signatures, 5.83–5.84
    time and place, 5.75
  identification of witnesses, 15.06
  issue, 17.31
  judgments, 17.02–17.24, 17.31–17.32
    appeals to Court of Session,
      18.95–18.96
    whether final judgments, 18.35, 18.94
  minutes, intimation, 5.66
  multiplepoinding, 21.67
  notes, 5.85–5.86
    grounds of decision, 5.85
  provisional damages, 21.30
  recall, 5.91
  reponing, 7.35
  sanction of employment of counsel,
    12.26
INTERNATIONAL CHILD ABDUCTION,
  jurisdiction, 2.39
INTERNATIONAL CO-OPERATION, customs
  and excise, 26.111
INTERNATIONAL ORGANISATIONS, immunity,
  4.06
INTERPRETERS, diets of proof, 16.65–16.68
INTERROGATORIES, commission and
  diligence, evidence of witnesses,
  15.31
INTIMATIONS, craves, 9.98
  family actions, 22.15–22.17
    addresses unknown, 22.09, 22.15
  potentially interested parties, 12.04
  small claims, 31.15
  summary causes, 30.22
  time-limits, prorogation, 14.08
IRRELEVANCY, averments, 2.15
  preliminary pleas, 9.122
IRRITANCIES, common law, 23.07
  declarators, jurisdiction, 2.53, 23.01,
    23.09
  feus, 23.09
ITINERANTS, jurisdiction within Scotland,
  3.91

JOINT AND SEVERAL LIABILITY, 4.41, 4.42
  contract, 4.45–4.47
  craves, 9.90
  delict, 4.48
  form of decrees, 17.18
  third-party procedure, 12.44
JOINT LIABILITY, 4.41
JOINT MINUTES, admissions, 5.57,
  16.28–16.31
    drafting, 16.29
    function, 16.28
    notices, 16.31
    style, 16.29
  childrens proceedings, 22.42
  description, 5.57
  documents at debates, 13.05
  extra-judicial settlements, 14.64
  multiplepoinding, 21.68

JOINT PROPERTY, arrestments, 29.29
  arrestments on the dependence, 11.15
  poinding, 29.73
JOINT WRONGDOING, 12.48
  interlocutors, 17.18
JUDGMENTS, appeals to sheriff principal,
    18.83–18.90
  competency of appeals, whether final
    judgements, 18.33–18.37
  decerniture, 17.09–17.12
  decrees, *see* DECREES
  delays, 17.01
  directions to court officers, 17.22
  enforcement, *see* ENFORCEMENT OF
    JUDGMENTS
  expenses, 17.23
  findings, in fact, 17.04–17.07
    in fact and law, 17.08
    in law, 17.08
  interlocutors, *see* INTERLOCUTORS
  notes, 17.25–17.30
  superseding extracts, 17.24
JUDICIAL ADMISSIONS, *see* ADMISSIONS
JUDICIAL DISCRETION, abandonment of
    actions, 14.26–14.27
  actions *ad factum praestandum*, 21.80
  adjournment of proof, 16.95
  adoption, dispensing with parental
    agreement, 28.35
    intimation of hearings, 28.89
    orders, 28.116
  amendment of pleadings, 10.02,
    10.14–10.28, 10.37, 10.38, 10.39
    appeals, 10.59
    new defenders, 10.41
    resulting from counterclaims, 12.32
  commission and diligence, 15.21
  conjunction of processes, 13.43
  decrees by default, 14.08–14.10
  diets of proof, inspections, 16.92
  disposal of common good, 26.285
  expenses, awards, 19.03, 19.07
    non acceptance of tenders, 14.52
  freeing for adoption, 28.160
  interim interdicts, 21.93
  leave to appeal, 18.51
  new diets of debate, 13.03
  oaths and affirmations, children and
    mentally defective persons, 16.62
  overriding time-limits, 10.40, 14.02,
    14.08
  references to European Court, 13.69
  review by appeal courts, 18.110–18.114
  rules and orders, non-compliance, 5.96
  sanction of employment of counsel,
    12.25
  sewerage, lines, 26.335
  sist of processes, 13.73
    recall, 13.83
  summary applications, 25.23
  transfer of causes, cause shown, 13.54
JUDICIAL FACTORS,
  appointment, applications, 22.02
    damages for personal injuries, 21.38
    pending litigation, 12.05
    preservation of property, 11.06–11.07

JUDICIAL FACTORS—*cont.*
  jurisdiction, 2.62, 2.68–2.69
  parties to litigation, 4.107
  partnerships, 26.319
  proceedings, 2.86
JUDICIAL REFERENCES, 8.66, 13.35
  appeals, 13.40
    competency, 18.28
  competency, 13.36
  decisions, 13.38
  expenses, 13.39
  procedure, 13.36–13.38
  statutory references, social security
    administration, 13.41
JUDICIAL REMITS, 8.66, 13.27–13.34
  competency, 13.29, 13.31
  expenses, 13.34
  family proceedings, competency of
    appeal, 18.24
  in place of proof, 13.28
  procedure after remit, 13.32
  reporters, appointment, 13.30
    procedure, 13.32
  reports, conclusiveness, 13.33
  timing, 13.31
  types, 13.27
JUDICIAL REVIEW, 18.01
  fatal accident inquiries, 27.22
JUDICIAL SETTLEMENTS, 14.31–14.63
JUDICIARY, 1.06–1.19
  sheriffs, *see* SHERIFFS
  sheriffs principal, *see* SHERIFFS
    PRINCIPAL
JURISDICTION, *see also* BRUSSELS
    CONVENTION; LUGANO CONVENTION
  adoption, 28.36–28.39
  appeals, 18.03
  civil causes, 1.01
  concurrent with the Court of Session,
    see CONCURRENT JURISDICTION
  Crown, 4.54–4.55
  declinature, by excluded jurisdictions,
    3.55–3.64, 3.113
  decrees in absence, 7.12
  definition, 2.01
  domicile, *see* DOMICILE
  European Court of Justice, 13.68
  exclusion, *see* EXCLUSION OF
    JURISDICTION
  exclusive, *see* EXCLUSIVE JURISDICTION
  family actions, 22.03
  fatal accident inquiries, 27.01
  furthcoming, 21.46
  heritable property actions, 23.01
  inherent, *see* INHERENT JURISDICTION
  interdicts, 21.83
  lawburrows, 24.02
  multiplepoinding, 21.53
  no jurisdiction, preliminary pleas, 9.119
    transfer to other sheriff courts, 13.53
  objections, 9.108, 9.119–9.120
  privative jurisdiction, 2.27–2.35
  protected tenancies, 26.277
  race discrimination, 26.376
  remedies, 2.81–2.87

JURISDICTION, *see also* BRUSSELS
   CONVENTION; LUGANO C
   ONVENTION—*cont.*
  sex discrimination, 26.368
  sheriff courts, 1.16
    appeals, 26.13
    declaratory actions, 20.02
  small claims, 31.12
  standard securities, 26.105
  summary applications, 25.12, 25.35
    appeals from, 25.37–25.41
    pleas, 25.19
  summary causes, 30.16–30.18,
    30.137–30.138
  supervisory, 2.48
  suspension of diligence, 24.12, 24.13
  territorial, 2.02–2.04
  value rule, 2.27–2.34
    actions *ad factum praestandum*, 2.31
    actions for payment, 2.29–2.30
    change of circumstances, 2.34
    counterclaims, 2.33
  within Scotland, *see* JURISDICTION WITHIN
    SCOTLAND
  within U.K., *see* JURISDICTION WITHIN
    U.K.
JURISDICTION WITHIN SCOTLAND, 3.77–3.113
  admiralty causes, 3.85
  agency, 3.96
  arbitration, 3.107
  arrestments, 3.98–3.101
  children, residence, 3.81
  civil claims in criminal proceedings,
    3.94
  commissary proceedings, 3.86
  company administration, 3.84, 3.106
  consumer contracts, 3.110
  contract, 3.92
  counterclaims, 3.109
  declinature, 3.113
  delict, 3.93
  exclusive jurisdiction, 3.111
  guardianship, 3.82
  heritable property, 3.98, 3.101
    securities, 3.105
  individuals, 3.09
  insolvency proceedings, 3.83
  intellectual property, 3.108
  interdicts, 3.104
  itinerants, 3.91
  maintenance, 3.95
  moveable property, 3.103
  plurality of defenders, 3.109
  prorogation, 3.112
  Schedule 8 rules, 3.77, 3.88–3.113
    and Brussels Convention, 3.77
    domicile, 3.90
    excluded proceedings, 3.79–3.87
    scope, 3.78
    special jurisdiction, 3.90–3.109
  status actions, 3.80
  third-party proceedings, 3.109
  trusts, 3.97
JURISDICTION WITHIN U.K., 3.69–3.76
  individuals, 3.08

JURISDICTION WITHIN U.K.—*cont.*
  Schedule 4 provisions, 3.69–3.70, 3.72
    concurrent jurisdictions, 3.73
    excluded proceedings, 3.71
JURORS, Lists, 1.12
JURY TRIALS, remit to Court of Session,
  13.59

LAND, acquisition, railways, 26.348–26.351
  drainage, 26.257–26.258
  registration, 26.106
LANDLORD AND TENANT, jurisdiction, 2.53,
  2.54
  exclusive jurisdiction, 3.24
LANGUAGE, adoption, 28.11, 28.81, 28.108,
  28.156
  diets of proof, 16.65
LAWBURROWS, 2.87, 24.02–24.05
  contravention, 2.80, 24.05
    Lord Advocate's concurrence, 4.67
  jurisdiction, 24.02
  procedure, 24.03–24.04
LEASES, assured tenancies, 26.249
  determination, 26.241
  disposal by executors, 26.398
  entailed estates, 26.261, 26.262, 26.263
  long leases, renewal, 26.106, 26.267
  modifications, control orders, 26.235
    Factories Act, 26.120
    fire precautions, 26.180, 26.182
    harbours and docks, 26.212
    offices, shops and railway premises,
      26.121
  possession of subjects, assignation in
    security, 26.265
  renewal, armed forces, 26.35
  repairing obligations, 26.223–26.224
  security subjects, 1894 Act, 23.31
  subjects under heritable securities,
    26.99
  validity, jurisdiction, 2.54
LEGAL ADVICE, privilege, 15.54
LEGAL AID, *see also* ASSISTED PERSONS
  applications, sist of processes, 13.74
  childrens proceedings, 26.279
  fatal accident inquiries, 27.10
LEGAL REPRESENTATION,
  small claims, 31.13
  summary causes, 30.19
LEGISLATION, written pleadings, 9.68
LEGITIMACY, declarators, 22.02
  jurisdiction, 2.39, 2.64, 20.03
LETTERS OF REQUEST, witnesses in
  England and Northern Ireland, 15.41
  witnesses outside Scotland, 16.17
  witnesses outside U.K., 15.42
LICENSING, air navigation, 26.37
  amusement machines, 26.47
  animals, breeding of dogs, 26.22
    dangerous wild animals, 26.24
    guard dogs, 26.23
    offences, 26.21
    slaughter, 26.25–26.26
  aviation, 26.36
  betting, 26.38

LICENSING—*cont.*
boat hire, 26.289
caravan sites, 26.161
cinemas, 26.159
Civic Government Act 1982,
26.288–26.291
dairy products, 26.193
driving, large vehicles, 26.383
food, 26.191
gaming, 26.43–26.44
housing in multiple occupation, 26.289
liquor, 26.252–26.256
permitted hours, 26.254
market operators, 26.289
metal dealers, 26.289
nurses, 26.299
private hire cars, 26.289
public entertainment, 26.289
riding establishments, 26.403
second-hand dealers, 26.289
sex shops, 26.291
small claims, 31.101
street trading, 26.289
summary causes, 30.190–30.196
taxis, 26.289
theatres, 26.155
venison dealers, 26.31
window dealers, 26.289
zoos, 26.29
LIFE ASSURANCE, arrestments, 29.21
LIGHTHOUSES, Commissioner of Northern
Lighthouses, 1.12
LIMITATION OF ACTIONS, 2.114
death, 2.117–2.118
harassment, 2.120
overriding time-limits, powers, 2.116,
2.118, 2.119, 2.121
personal injuries, 2.115–2.116,
10.40–10.42, 12.51
pleading, 2.122
LINLITHGOW SHERIFF COURT, records, 1.50
LIQUIDATIONS, applications, 2.84
competition, with arrestments, 29.34
with poinding, 29.83
jurisdiction, 5.01
within Scotland, 3.83
within U.K., 3.71
LIQUIDATORS, litigation, 4.90–4.92
sisting, 12.12
LIQUOR LICENSING, 26.252–26.256
LIS ALIBI PENDENS, 2.50, 2.94–2.98
foreign courts, 3.60
preliminary pleas, 9.120
LISTED BUILDINGS, compulsory purchase,
26.399
compensation, 26.400
LOCAL AUTHORITIES, citation, execution,
6.39
family actions, 22.20
intimation, family actions, 22.15
supervised contact orders, 22.41
reports, childrens proceedings, 22.35
LOCAL COUNCILLORS, disqualifications,
26.284
LOCAL GOVERNMENT, 26.284–26.287

LODGING HOUSES, removal, 26.327
LODGING OF DEFENCES, declarators of
death, 20.10
documents, 8.20
effect, 8.19
form, 8.24
multiplepoinding, 21.61
plurality of defenders, 8.21
sisting of defenders, 8.22
timing, 8.18
withdrawal, 8.23
LONG LEASES, renewal, 26.106, 26.267
LORD ADVOCATE, arrestments, 3.101
Crown proceedings, 4.63–4.69
declarators of death, 20.07, 20.08
discretion, fatal accident inquiries,
27.05
execution of citation, 6.38
multiplepoinding, 21.55
LOSS OF SOCIETY, assessment, appeals,
18.116
LOST PROPERTY, 26.293
LOTHIAN, sheriffdom, Chancery, 1.12, 1.21
LOTTERIES, 26.38, 26.48–26.49
LUGANO CONVENTION, 3.02
application, 3.03, 3.67
rules of jurisdiction, 3.68

MAILLS AND DUTIES, 2.84, 2.85
jurisdiction, 2.55
nature of action, 23.28
MAINTENANCE, *see* CURRENT MAINTENANCE
ARRESTMENTS; MAINTENANCE ORDERS
MAINTENANCE ORDERS, appeals,
references to European Court, 3.04
jurisdiction, 2.57, 2.63
foreign domicile, 3.31–3.32
within Scotland, 3.78
MALICE, declinature of jurisdiction, 2.126
MANDATARIES, liability, 11.73
parties to litigation, 4.124–4.127
requirements, 11.72
sist, *see* SIST OF MANDATARIES
MANDATES, production, condition of
amendment of pleadings, 10.31
MARCHES, fences, 23.44–23.46
jurisdiction, 2.55
proceedings, 2.86
MARITAL COMMUNICATIONS, privilege, 15.54
MARITIME CAUSES, 24.06
jurisdiction, 2.74–2.76
MARKET OPERATORS, licences, 26.289
MARKETING BOARDS, agriculture, 26.04
MARRIAGE, declarators, jurisdiction, 2.39,
20.03
MATRIMONIAL HOMES, 22.105–22.106
applications and orders, 22.02
family actions, 22.77–22.82
intimation, 22.15
dealings, 22.107
division and sale, 23.42–23.43
interim orders, applications in
chambers, 5.21
jurisdiction, 2.57
MATRIMONIAL INTERDICTS, powers of
arrest, 22.82

MATTERS *PARS JUDICIS*, 2.09–2.17, 17.28
    amendment, 10.04
    appearance of interested parties, 12.16
    calling of all parties, 4.36, 9.118
    competency, 9.121
        appeals, 18.30, 18.97
    decrees in absence, 7.13
    defenders, 2.17
    deletion of averments, 10.60
    form, 2.14–2.17
    illegality, 2.12
    service of writs, irregular service, 6.04
    subject-matter, 2.11–2.13
MAXWELL REPORT, 3.01, 9.108
MCKECHNIE REPORT, 2.41, 11.26
MEAT, hygiene directions, 26.192
    preparations, approval of premises,
        26.194
MEDICAL EXAMINATIONS, adoption
        proceedings, 28.107–28.108
    orders, 15.102
MEDICAL RECORDS, access, 26.378
    productions, 16.26
    recovery of documents, 15.56, 15.63
MEDICAL REPORTS, children subject to
        adoption proceedings, 28.63
MENTAL DISORDER, breaches of interdict,
        21.99
    Church of Scotland ministers, 26.80
    contempt of court, 2.24
    family actions, appointment of curators
        ad litem, 22.24–22.26
        citation, 22.21
        intimation, 22.15
    parents of adopted children, 28.28
    simplified divorce procedure, 22.83
    witnesses, commission and diligence,
        15.27
        oaths and affirmations, 16.62
MENTAL HEALTH, 26.301–26.314
    acting nearest relatives, 26.309
    admission to hospital, 26.301
        appeals, 26.304
        short-term detention, 26.302
    applications, register, 5.38
    community care orders, 26.305
    guardianship, 26.307–26.308
    prisoners, hospital transfers, 26.313
    restricted patients, 26.310–26.312
MENTAL WELFARE COMMISSION,
        intimation, family actions, 22.24
MERCHANT SHIPPING, 26.392–26.396
    accident investigations, 26.393
    deaths, jurisdiction, 27.03
    detention of goods, 26.392
    officers, inquiries into fitness and
        conduct, 26.393
MESSENGERS-AT-ARMS, acting in sheriff
        court proceedings, 1.28
METAL DEALERS, licences, 26.289
METHYLATED SPIRITS, sale, 26.402
MINERS' WELFARE INSTITUTES, registration,
        26.45
MINING, coal mining, subsidence, 26.318

MINISTERS, Church of Scotland, mental
        disorder, 26.80
    litigants, 4.68
MINORS, 4.21, 4.22
MINUTES, 5.56–5.71
    consent, 5.69
    declarators of death, 20.10
    description, 5.56–5.57
    form, 5.58
    hearings, no opposition, 5.65
        opposition, 5.68
    interlocutors, intimation, 5.66
    intimation, 5.61
        evidence, 5.63
        methods, 5.62
    joint minutes, *see* JOINT MINUTES
    lodging, 5.59
    notices of opposition, 5.67
    opposition, 5.64
    pre-1994 cases, 5.71
    procedure after grants, 5.70
MOBILE HOMES, 26.174
    poinding, 29.75
    caravans, 26.132
MORA, TACITURNITY AND ACQUIESCENCE,
        2.123
    pleas-in-law, 9.126
MOTIONS, consent, 5.50
    determination by sheriff clerks, 5.51
    expenses, 5.55
    hearings, 5.51–5.54
        fixing, 5.52
    interim damages, 21.10
    intimation, 5.47
    notices of opposition, 5.48, 5.49
    procedure, 5.44–5.46
MOTOR INSURANCE POLICIES, liability, 12.06
MOVEABLE PROPERTY, arrestments, 29.27
    arrestments on the dependence,
        11.13–11.14
    jurisdiction, 2.50
        within Scotland, 3.103
        within U.K., 3.73
MULTIPLEPOINDING, 2.85, 21.48, 21.51,
        21.52–21.71
    advertisements, 21.56
    arrestments on the dependence, 11.25
    citation, 6.07, 6.16
    claims, 21.61, 21.65
        disposal, 21.68–21.69
    competency, 21.52
    condescendences, 21.61, 21.65
        approval, 21.66
    decrees, 21.70
    defences, disposal, 21.63, 21.65
        lodging, 21.61
    expenses, 21.71
    hearing, 21.59
        first hearings, 21.60
        fixing, 5.41, 21.58
    initial writs, 21.55
        service, 21.56
    interim awards of expenses, 11.87
    interlocutors, 21.67
    issue, 17.31

MULTIPLEPOINDING—*cont.*
  jurisdiction, 21.53
  nature, 21.52
  notices of appearance, 8.03, 21.57
  objections, 21.61, 21.65
    disposal, 21.64
  preliminary pleas, 21.62
  summary causes, 30.02, 30.243–30.254

NAMES, parties to litigation, 4.84–4.87
NATIONAL ASSISTANCE, 26.280
NATIONAL SECURITY, evidence behind
  closed doors, 5.22, 5.25
NEGLIGENCE, damages, relevancy of
  averments, 9.34
NEW PARTIES, 12.07–12.18
  curators *bonis*, 12.13
  disclamation, 12.19–12.20
  expenses, 12.18
  liquidators, 12.12
  lodging of defences, 8.22
  permanent trustees, 12.12
  pursuers, damages for death,
    21.17–21.18
  representatives, 12.08–12.11
  transfer of interest, 12.14
NOBILE OFFICIUM, 1.36, 2.44
  commission and diligence, application,
    15.20
  interlocutors, correction, 5.88
    reduction, 18.01
NOISE, abatement notices, 26.167–26.169
  abatement zones, 26.171
  reduction notices, 26.171
NONAGE, limitation of actions, 2.116,
  2.118, 2.119, 2.120
NON-PARENTAGE ACTIONS, 22.02
  initial writs, 22.13
NOTES, appeal judgments, 18.83
  judgments, 17.25–17.30
    appeals to sheriff principal, 18.18
    authorities, 17.29
    evidence led, 17.27
  requests, 18.59
NOTICE, of appearance, multiplepoinding,
  8.03
  warrants of citation, calculation, 6.13
    period, 6.11–6.13
    variation, 6.12
NOTICES OF INTENTION TO DEFEND, 8.01
  effect, 8.06
  family actions, 8.02, 22.52
    child welfare hearings, 8.08
  late notices, 8.05
  payment of fees, 8.04
NUISANCE, abatement notices, 26.341,
  26.342
    appeals, 25.10, 26.167, 26.345
    noise, 26.167–26.169
  commercial waste, 26.165
  jurisdiction, 2.53
  proceedings against local authorities,
    26.328

NULLITY, summary applications, 25.35
NURSES, licensing, 26.299
NURSING HOMES, registration, 26.397

OATHS AND AFFIRMATIONS, commission
  and diligence, recovery of documents,
    15.73
  sheriffs, 1.14
  sheriffs principal, 1.07
  shorthand writers, 15.35
  small claims, 31.112
  summary causes, 30.206
  witnesses, 16.62–16.64
    commission and diligence, 15.36
OBJECTIONS, examination of witnesses,
  16.84–16.90
  rulings, 16.85, 16.100
    competency of appeal, 18.26
OBLIGATIONS, jurisdiction, 2.51
OCCUPANCY RIGHTS, matrimonial homes,
  23.43
OFFICE HOLDERS, 4.82
  actions, 4.82
OFFICES, statutory requirements, 26.121
OFFSHORE INSTALLATIONS, fatal accident
  inquiries, jurisdiction, 27.03
  notification, 27.08
OIL AND GAS, jurisdiction, within
  Scotland, 3.87
  within U.K., 3.71
OPEN RECORDS, 8.29
OPPRESSION, 2.94
  arrestments on the dependence, 11.26
    recalls, 11.30
  cross-examinations, 16.75
  inhibitions on the dependence, recall,
    11.41
  matters *pars judicis*, 2.15
  vexatious actions, 2.130, 4.122
OPTIONS HEARINGS, 8.36–8.43
  advising of imminent settlements, 14.69
  attendance, 8.37
    family actions, 22.53
  closed records, 8.39, 8.40–8.41
  continuation, 8.38
  fixing, 5.41, 5.42, 8.07
    after grants of minutes, 5.70
    powers of sheriff principal, 18.80
  options, 8.42
  purpose, 8.36
  timeous lodging of records, 5.95
ORDERS, before commencement of
  actions, powers, 12.02
  implementation, prorogation of
    time-limits, 14.08
  inherent jurisdiction, 2.07–2.08
  interlocutors, 5.77–5.82
  intimation to potentially interested
    parties, 12.04
  meaning, 4.56
  regulation of court procedure,
    1.38–1.40

ORDERS *AD FACTUM PRAESTANDUM*, appeals to Court of Session, competency, 18.96
  appeals to sheriff principal, competency, 18.40
  effect, 18.68
ORDINARY CAUSE RULES, 5.01
  incorporation into 1907 Act, 1.35
  non-compliance, dispensing powers, 5.93–5.97
  objectives, judicial control, 5.98
ORDINARY CAUSES, Definition, 5.05
  procedure, 5.06
  register, 5.32
  taxation of expenses, 19.48–19.50
  transfer from summary causes, 13.47
  transfer to summary causes, 13.46, 30.27–30.34
ORDINARY COURT, competent actions, 5.01
  definition, 5.02
  forms of process, 5.04–5.10
  proceedings, control, 5.98–5.102
  sittings, *see* SITTINGS
OUTLAYS, taxation of accounts, 19.56
OVERCROWDING, 26.230
OVERSEA COMPANIES, execution of citation, 6.41

PAPER, type, written pleadings, 9.50
PARENTAGE, declarators, 22.02
  jurisdiction, 2.39, 2.56, 2.57, 2.64, 20.02
PARENTAL CONTACTS, after adoption orders, 28.120
PARENTAL RIGHTS AND RESPONSIBILITIES, 4.11, 22.02, 28.24
  effect of adoption orders, 28.42
  step-parents, 28.52
  evidence behind close doors, 5.23
  jurisdiction, 2.56, 2.57, 2.61
  orders, 26.74
  proceedings, 22.104
  referral to family mediation, 22.36
  s. 11 orders, 28.89, 28.121, 28.122
  transfer to local authorities, 28.137, 28.139
    appeals, 25.38
  transfer to other agencies, 28.195
PARENTS, adoption, 28.24–28.28
PARS JUDICIS, *see* MATTERS *PARS JUDICIS*
PARTIES, *see also* DEFENDERS; PURSUERS
  assignees, 4.108
  assisted persons, 4.117
  attendance, appeal hearings, 18.73
    diets of debate, 13.07
    diets of proof, 16.46–16.48, 16.53
  bankrupts, 4.111
  capacity, *see* CAPACITY OF PARTIES
  companies, in liquidation, 4.90–4.92
    in receivership, 4.88–4.89
    investigated under Part XIV of 1985 Act, 4.93
  convenience, transfer to other sheriff courts, 13.52
  corporate bodies, 4.83
    names, 4.84–4.87

PARTIES—*cont.*
  Crown, *see* CROWN PROCEEDINGS
  death, *see* DEATH
  deceased, instances, 10.07
  domini litis, 4.112–4.113
  employers' associations, 4.100
  executors, 4.105
  failing to appear, dismissal, 14.02, 14.04, 14.07
  friendly societies, 4.102
  interest to sue, *see* INTEREST TO SUE
  judicial factors, 4.107
  mandataries, 4.124–4.127
  ministers, 4.68
  new parties, *see* NEW PARTIES
  recording in interlocutors, 5.76
PARTNERSHIPS, 4.94–4.98
  dissolution, 26.319
  domicile, 3.13
  interests, arrestments, 29.25
    arrestments on the dependence, 11.21
  jurisdiction, 2.73
    within Scotland, 3.83
  parties to litigation, 4.94–4.98
  proceedings, 2.86
PARTY LITIGANTS, 1.32, 4.118–4.121
  assistance from sheriffs, 16.39
  borrowing of processes, 8.14
  citation of witnesses, 16.05
  deafness, 16.68
  expenses, 4.121
  no understanding of English, 16.68
  prisoners, 16.16
PASSING-OFF, recovery of documents, 15.86
PATENTS, jurisdiction, 2.46, 3.26, 3.27
  within U.K., 3.71, 3.75, 3.108
PATERNITY, blood tests, 15.103
  examination of witnesses, 16.60
PATRIMONIAL LOSS, assessment, appeals, 18.116
PAYMENT, *see also* ACTIONS FOR PAYMENT
  charges for payment, 29.67–29.69
  due under contracts, arrestments, 29.21
PEDLARS, certificates, 26.401
PEERAGE CLAIMS, jurisdiction, 2.36
PENSIONS, arrestments, 29.29
  arrestments on the dependence, 11.15
  fire services, 26.177
  lump sums, applications, 22.15, 22.67
PERIODICAL ALLOWANCES, initial writs, 22.10
PERISHABLE GOODS, inspection, judicial remits, 13.31
  poinding, 29.79
  sale, interim orders, 11.08
  warrants to sell, sequestrations for rent, 23.19
    summary applications, 25.04
PERJURY, 16.64
PESTS, 26.331
PETITORY ACTIONS, 2.84, 5.06
  ad factum praestandum, *see* ACTIONS *AD FACTUM PRAESTANDUM*

PETITORY ACTIONS—*cont.*
damages for personal injuries or death, *see* DAMAGES FOR PERSONAL INJURIES
furthcoming, *see* FURTHCOMING
interdict, *see* INTERDICTS
nature, 21.01
payment, *see* ACTIONS FOR PAYMENT
PIERS, 26.207–26.211
PIPELINES, disputes, 26.357
PLEADINGS, *see* AMENDMENT OF PLEADINGS; WRITTEN PLEADINGS
PLEAS-IN-LAW, amendments, 10.03
count, reckoning and payment, 21.06
defences, 9.115–9.128
counterclaims, 9.126
merits, 9.125–9.127
mora, taciturnity and acquiescence, 9.126
order, 9.128
preliminary pleas, *see* PRELIMINARY PLEAS
prescription, 9.126
res judicata, 9.126
disposal, 17.10
form, 9.47–9.48
initial writs, 9.104
POACHING, salmon, 26.186
POINDING, 29.70–29.85
conjoining, 26.142
declarators of invalidity, 29.81
duration, 29.85
effect, 29.82
exempt property, 29.76
jurisdiction, 2.78
poindable property, 29.70–29.75
common ownership, 29.73–29.74
disputed ownership, 29.72
mobile homes, 29.75
procedure, 29.77–29.80
perishable goods, 29.79
reports, 29.80
schedules, 29.79
proceedings, 2.86
protection of debtors, 29.81
ranking, 29.83
recall, 29.81
second poindings, 29.84
summary applications, 26.129–26.143
valuation, 29.78
POINDING OF THE GROUND, 2.84, 2.85, 23.25, 23.26–23.27
POISONS, 26.300
POLICE CUSTODY, deaths, fatal accident inquiries, 27.04
property, 26.294
POLLUTION CONTROL, 26.164–26.173
household waste, 26.164
POLYGAMY, family actions, intimation, 22.15
POSSESSORY ACTIONS, 2.85
POST-MORTEM EXAMINATIONS, warrants, summary applications, 25.04
PRACTICE NOTES, 1.38, 1.39–1.40

PRECOGNITIONS, 15.07–15.16
absolute privilege, 15.16
contents, 15.11
employees, 15.08
fatal accident inquiries, 27.06
language, 15.13
nature, 15.07
obligations, 15.08
re-precognitions, 15.14
taking, 15.09–15.14
uses, 15.15–15.16
PRELIMINARY PLEAS, 9.116
all parties not called, 9.118
amendments, 10.55
appeal hearings, 18.76
competent and omitted, 2.112–2.113, 9.124
criticisms, 13.22
debates, 13.01–13.02
dismissal, 13.16
and decrees of absolvitor, 13.16
disposal, 13.15–13.25
appeals, 13.25
forum non conveniens, 9.120
incompetency, 9.121
irrelevancy, 9.122
lack of specification, 9.123
lis alibi pendens, 9.120
multiplepoinding, 21.62
no jurisdiction, 9.119
transfer to other sheriff courts, 13.53
notes of basis, 8.35, 8.48
preliminary proof, 8.60
proof before answer, 8.49
title to sue, 9.117
PRESBYTERY, witnesses, citation, 25.04
PRESCRIPTION, 2.114
actions of relief, 24.10
arrestments, 29.38
on the dependence, 11.25
Crown proceedings, 4.77
effect of counterclaims, 12.39
inhibitions on the dependence, 11.42
pleas-in-law, 9.126
PRESUMPTIONS, rebutting, leading of evidence, 8.64
PRICES, warrant sales, 29.89
PRISONERS, as witnesses, 16.16
mental health, hospital transfers, 26.313
PRIVACY, adoption proceedings, 5.20, 28.41
family actions, 5.20, 5.22
PRIVATE HIRE CARS, licences, 26.289
PRIVILEGE, absolute privilege, precognitions, 15.16
havers, 15.03, 15.86
professional legal advice, 15.54
witnesses, 15.03, 15.86
PROCEDURAL HEARINGS, 8.49–8.52
attendance, 8.49
family actions, 8.50
continuation, 8.52
options, 8.52
PROCEDURE
additional procedure, *see* ADDITIONAL PROCEDURE

PROCEDURE—*cont.*
control, 5.98–5.102
regulation, 1.34–1.43
acts of sederunt, 1.36–1.37
inherent jurisdiction, 2.07–2.17
orders and directions, 1.38–1.40
recommendations, 1.41
rules of practice, 1.42
rules of principle, 1.43
statutes, 1.35
PROCEEDS OF CRIME, 26.110
PROCESSES, 5.43, 8.09–8.17
assisted persons, 8.12
borrowing, 8.14–8.16
caption, competency of appeal, 18.27
conjunction, 13.42–13.44
contingency, remit to Court of Session,
13.64
custody, 8.14–8.15
folders, 8.10
minutes, *see* MINUTES
motions, *see* MOTIONS
new lodgings, delivery, 8.13
intimation, 8.13
paper type, 8.11
return, appeal procedure, 18.66
failure, fines, 5.100, 8.16, 18.23
sealing up, adoption, 28.131, 28.196
freeing for adoption, 28.170–28.171
PROCURATIONS FISCAL, 1.29–1.131
appointment, 1.29
civil court duties, 1.30
concurrence, breach of interdict, 21.96
breach of sequestration for rent,
23.23
immunity, 1.31
party to civil proceedings, 1.31
PRODUCTIONS, *see also* DOCUMENTS;
RECOVERY OF DOCUMENTS
admissibility, 16.24
agreed bundles, 16.23
borrowing, 16.19
commission and diligence, evidence of
witnesses, 15.37
copies, 16.21, 16.23, 16.24
failing to lodge, decrees by default,
14.05
family actions, 22.18
lists, 16.20
lodging, 16.18–16.27
documents for cross-examination,
16.25, 16.77
documents founded on in pleadings,
16.18
for proof, 16.20
intimation, 16.21
restriction on other productions,
16.22
small claims, 31.85–31.88
summary causes, 30.156–30.161
medical records, 16.26
preparation, 16.23
return, 16.27
Scottish Solicitors' Discipline Tribunal,
26.278
time-limits, prorogation, 14.08

PROHIBITION NOTICES, premises, 26.179
sport grounds, 26.158
PROMISSORY NOTES, arrestments on the
dependence, 11.15
summary diligence, 29.02
PROOF, adoption proceedings,
28.109–28.115
allowance, 8.54–8.65, 13.18–13.19, 13.21
before answer, 8.57–8.59, 13.20, 13.21
interlocutors, 8.54–8.55
appeals, 18.42
declarators of death, 20.12
diets, *see* DIETS OF PROOF
form, 8.63
freeing for adoption, 28.164
further proof, 16.96–16.97
powers of sheriff principal, 18.81
leading of evidence, 8.64
or judicial remit, 13.28
parties to be heard in summary causes,
30.124–30.125
preliminary matters, 16.01–16.37
preliminary proof, 8.60
liability or quantum, 8.61
preparation, 16.01
renunciation, 8.62
summary applications, 25.24, 25.25
summary causes, 30.205
third-party procedure, 12.64
PROPERTY, *see also* HERITABLE PROPERTY;
MOVEABLE PROPERTY
orders, summary applications, 25.04
preservation, 12.05, 15.46
court powers, 15.85
interim protective measures, 11.05
recovery, Crown proceedings, 4.58
orders, 15.84–15.92
transfer orders, intimation, 22.15
PROROGATION, of jurisdiction, 3.51–3.54,
3.78, 3.112
PROTECTED TENANCIES, 26.268–26.277
furniture, excessive price, 26.273
improvements, 26.276
jurisdiction, 26.277
Part VII contracts, 26.272
rateable value, 26.268
rents, 26.271
warrant sales, 26.276
security of tenure, 26.269–26.271
shared accommodation, 26.275
succession, 26.276
PROTECTION ORDERS, consumer credit,
26.214
PROTECTIVE PROCEDURES, interim
interdicts, *see* INTERIM INTERDICTS
interim orders pending appeal, *see*
INTERIM ORDERS
judicial factors, appointment, *see*
JUDICIAL FACTORS
objectives, 11.02
preservation of documents and
property, 11.05
PROTESTS OF BILLS, registers, 5.38
PROVING THE TENOR, jurisdiction, 2.43,
20.03

PUBLIC ENTERTAINMENT, licences, 26.289
PUBLIC HEALTH, 26.324–26.328
  buildings, disinfecting, 26.327
  celluloid storage, 26.329
  ditches, cleansing, 26.326
  housing, 26.231
  infectious diseases, 26.326
    compensation, 26.334
  lodging houses, removal, 26.327
  offensive trades, 26.35
  pests, 26.331
  proceedings against local authorities,
    26.328
  sewerage, 26.335–26.340
  upholstery materials, 26.333
PUBLIC INTEREST, due administration of
    justice, conduct of proceedings
    at proof, 16.38
  discharge of diets of proof, 16.37
  fatal accident inquiries, 27.05
  immunity, 15.55
  matters *pars judicis*, 2.09
    immunity, 2.16
  recovery of documents, 15.52, 15.86
    Crown documents, 4.72–4.75, 15.55
    income tax returns, 15.57
  sheriff's functions, 25.06
  withholding of information, 15.03
PUBLIC PROCESSIONS, 26.292
PUBLIC RECORDS, recovery of documents,
    15.98–15.99, 30.175–30.178
PUBLIC REGISTERS, exclusive jurisdiction,
    3.26
PUBLICITY OF PROCEEDINGS, 5.19–5.30
  applications in chambers, 5.21
  diets of proof, 16.44
  evidence, behind close doors, 5.22–5.25
    real evidence, 5.26
  exceptions, 5.20
  fatal accident inquiries, 27.12
  principle, 5.19
  reporting, 5.25, 5.28–5.30
  tape recordings, 5.27
PUPILS, 4.10
PURSUERS, caution for expenses,
    bankruptcy, 11.54
    nominal pursuers, 11.56
  consent and concurrence, 4.114–4.115
  new pursuers, amendment of instances,
    10.09–10.10
  damages for death, 21.17–21.18
  personal injuries actions, 10.42
  plurality, 4.38–4.40
    abandonment of actions, 14.28
    tenders, 14.54–14.55

RACE, adoption, 28.11, 28.81, 28.156
  discrimination, 26.369–26.376
    jurisdiction, 26.376
  inflammatory material, 26.109
RAILWAYS, accident inquiries, 26.353
  damages and charges, 26.347–26.353
  fire precautions, 26.356
  land acquisition, 26.348–26.351

RAILWAYS, accident inquiries—*cont.*
  premises, statutory requirements,
    26.121
  rolling stock, protection, 26.355
  works, accommodation, 26.353
    road repairs, 26.352
RATES, arrears, 26.152
  rebates, appeals, 26.358
RECEIPTS, objections by way of exception,
    12.70
RECEIVERSHIP, litigation, 4.88–4.89
RECOMPENSE, 2.132
  actions of relief, 24.09
RECORDS, books of court, 5.31–5.38
  act books, 5.36
    family proceedings, 5.34
    registers of deeds, 5.38
    registers of ordinary causes, 5.32
    registers of summary applications,
      5.33
    roll books, 5.35
    rolls, 5.39–5.42
    summary causes, 5.37
  closing, 8.39
  failure to lodge, decrees by default,
    14.06
    decrees of dismissal, 8.34
  for options hearings, 8.33–8.34
  health, access, 26.378
  preservation, 1.50
  processes, *see* PROCESSES
RECOVERY OF DOCUMENTS, adoption
    proceedings, 28.106
  bankers' books, 15.93–15.97
  commission and diligence, 15.50–15.83
    appeals, 15.65
    confidentiality, 15.54, 15.68, 15.74
    excerpts of books, 15.63, 15.70, 15.77
    execution, 15.73–15.74
    expenses, 15.82
    motions, 15.60
      disposal, 15.64
    non-compliance, 15.71, 15.76
    objections, 15.75
    optional procedure, 15.66–15.71
    outside Scotland, 15.83
    personal injury claims, 30.316
    procedure, 15.60–15.80
    professional assistance, 15.78
    public interest immunity, 15.55
    purpose, 15.51
    recoverable documents, 15.52–15.57
    relevance, 15.52, 15.53
    reports, 15.79
      use at proof, 15.81
    second commissions, 15.80
    self-incrimination, 15.52, 15.73, 15.74
    small claims, 31.89–31.93
    specification of documents, 15.60,
      15.61–15.63
    summary causes, 30.162–30.173
    timing, 15.58–15.59
  confidentiality, 15.101
  Crown proceedings, 4.72–4.75, 15.55,
    15.86

RECOVERY OF DOCUMENTS—*cont.*
orders, applications, 15.84, 15.87–15.89
  special reasons for refusing, 15.90
  court powers, 15.84–15.86
  execution, 15.92
  form, 15.91
productions in other processes, 15.100
public records, 15.98–15.99
Scottish Solicitors' Discipline Tribunal, 26.278
RECOVERY OF POSSESSION, 26.270
armed forces, 26.34
assured tenancies, 26.245–26.247
cautions for violent profits, 23.13
composite actions, 23.08–23.10
Conveyancing and Feudal Reform Act, 23.04
extraordinary removings, 23.07
farm workers, 26.270
heritable property, 2.85, 23.02–23.13
heritable securities, 23.03
Housing Act 1987, 23.06, 26.216
intimation, to security holders, 23.11
Land Tenure Reform Act, 23.05
protected tenancies, 26.269
secure tenancies, 26.216
Sheriff Courts Act 1907, 23.12
summary causes, 23.02, 26.215, 30.02, 30.261
  adjournment, 30.280
  appeals, 30.344
  caution for violent profits, 30.284
  effect of decree, 30.262
  fixed-term leases, 30.282–30.283
  form of claim, 30.275
  notice of proceedings, 30.268
  notice of removal, 30.263–30.267
  persons without right or title, 30.276–30.278
  preservation of defender's goods and effects, 30.281
  requirement of reasonableness, 30.279
  secure tenancies, 30.269–30.274
  undefended, 30.114
transfer of causes, 13.47
REDUCTION, 18.01, 18.05
decrees by default, 14.13
failure to follow practice notes, 1.40
failure to follow rules of practice, 1.42
interlocutors, consented, 5.81
jurisdiction, 2.42, 12.66, 23.01
minority, 4.19
orders for rectification of documents, 24.08
summary applications, 25.35
REFEREES, judicial references, 13.35
REFERENCES TO EUROPEAN COURT, 3.04, 13.68–13.70
discretion, 13.69
interim protective measures, 11.02
jurisdiction, 13.68
  within Scotland, 3.78
procedure, 13.70

REFERENCES TO EUROPEAN COURT—*cont.*
small claims, 31.35
summary causes, 30.63–30.66
REGISTER OF SMALL CLAIMS, 31.07
REGISTER OF SUMMARY CAUSES,
requirements and contents, 30.08–30.12
REGISTERED CATTLE INSURANCE SOCIETIES, 26.202
REGISTERED DESIGNS, jurisdiction, 2.46, 3.26, 3.27
within U.K., 3.71, 3.108
REGISTERS OF DEEDS, 5.38
registration procedure, 1.38
REGISTRATION OF BIRTHS, DEATHS AND MARRIAGES, 26.359–26.361
adoption, Adopted Children Register, 28.118, 28.130
directions, 28.118, 28.130, 28.134
cause of death, 27.21
correction, jurisdiction, 2.58
declarators of death, intimation, 20.15
RELATED ACTIONS, 2.93
foreign courts, 3.61
RELATIVES, acting nearest relatives, mental health, 26.309
adoption, 28.30
RELEVANCY, averments, 9.32–9.39
defences, 9.113
deletion of irrelevant averments, 10.60
preliminary pleas, 13.21
proof before answer, 8.58
recovery of documents, 15.52–15.53
RELIEF, actions, 24.09–24.10
RELIGION, adoption, 28.11, 28.81, 28.108, 28.156
REMEDIES, competency, 2.81–2.87
REMIT,
between ordinary rolls,
  small claims, 31.18–31.22
  summary claims, 30.27
summary causes,
  from Court of Session, 30.26
REMIT TO COURT OF SESSION, 8.66, 13.57–13.66
actions of declarators of death, 13.62
adoption proceedings, 28.38, 28.97
appeals, 13.60
by order of Court of Session,
  contingency, 13.64
  necessity, 13.65
circumstances, 5.03
Crown proceedings, 13.63
declarators of death, 20.11
family proceedings, 13.61
general provisions, 13.58–13.60
procedure, 13.66
REMITS TO SHERIFF COURT, appeal judgments, 18.86
from Court of Session, 13.67
REMOVING, 1907 Act, 23.12
cautions for violent profits, 23.13
extraordinary removing, 23.07, 23.09
jurisdiction, 2.53, 23.01
Land Tennure Reform Act, 23.05

RENTS, agricultural holdings, 26.09
   protected tenancies, 26.271
      warrant sales, 26.276
   sequestrations, *see* SEQUESTRATIONS FOR
      RENT
REPAIRS, housing, repair notices,
      26.225–26.226, 26.295
   obligations, short leases, 26.223–26.224
   roads, railway companies, 26.352
   secure tenancies, 26.218
REPONING, 14.11–14.12
   decrees in absence, 7.23–7.35
      appeals, 7.36–7.37
      applicants, 7.24
      competency, 7.25–7.26
      decisions, 7.34
      effect on deligence, 7.27
      expenses, 7.35
      hearings, 7.28
      initial procedure, 7.23
      no second reponing notes, 7.38
      reasons for failure to appear, 7.33
      relevant issues, 7.29–7.33
   family actions, 22.55
   refusal, appeals, 18.43
REPORTERS, appointment, judicial remits,
      13.30
REPORTING, proceedings, 5.25, 5.28–5.30
REPORTING OFFICERS, adoption
      applications, appointment, 28.68
      duties, 28.72–28.78
      evidence, 28.113
      expenses, 28.128–28.129
      panels, 28.69
      reports, time-limits, 28.71
   freeing for adoption, 28.142, 28.144,
      28.146
      appointment, 28.147, 28.152
      functions, 28.153–28.155
      reports, 28.152
REPOSITORIES, sealing, summary
      applications, 25.04
REPRESENTATION,
   small claims, 31.13
   summary causes, 30.19
REPRESENTATIVES, 4.106
   calling, 12.07, 12.08–12.11
   children's proceedings, 26.77
   Debtors Act 1987, 26.154
   fatal accident inquiries, 27.09
   parties to litigation, 4.106
   sisting, 12.07, 12.08–12.11
REQUIREMENTS OF WRITING, form of proof,
      8.63
   summary applications, 26.107
   wills, 20.19
RES JUDICATA, 2.104–2.109
   decrees, absolvitor, 17.11
      by default, 14.03
      condemnator, 17.11
      dismissal, 17.11
      in absence, 2.106, 7.19
   dismissal of cases at debates, 13.16
   evidence of closed records, 8.41

RES JUDICATA—cont.
   function of pleadings, 9.04, 9.10
   multiplepoinding, 21.70
   pleas-in-law, 9.126
   res noviter, 2.110–2.111
RES NOVITER VENTENS AD NOTITIAM,
      2.110–2.111
   further proof, 18.82
RESERVOIRS, entry powers, 26.410
RESET, reparation, jurisdiction, 2.79
RESIDENCE, habitual residence, adoption
      proceedings, 28.50, 28.58
      family proceedings, 2.58, 2.59, 2.62
   witnesses, commission and diligence,
      15.25
RESIDENCE ORDERS, 28.121, 28.122
   citation, 22.20
   intimation, 22.15
RESIDENTIAL ESTABLISHMENTS, registration,
      26.282
RESTITUTION, 2.84
RESTRAINT ORDERS, 26.110
RIDING ESTABLISHMENTS, licences, 26.403
RIGHTS OF AUDIENCE, 1.32–1.33
RIOTOUS ASSEMBLIES, 26.108
RIVER PURIFICATION BOARDS, entry
      powers, 26.415
ROAD TRAFFIC, driving disqualification,
      26.384
   driving tests, 26.381–26.382
ROADS, 26.385–26.391
   arbitration, 26.386
   new roads, works, 26.391
ROLLS OF COURT, 5.39–5.42
ROUPS, division and sale, 23.40
RULES OF COURT, crown proceedings, 4.77
   mental disorder, divorce, 4.07
      payment of damages, 4.09
      separation actions, 4.07
   non-compliance, dispensing power,
      5.93–5.97
RUNRIG, division, jurisdiction, 2.55

SAFETY CERTIFICATES, sport grounds,
      26.157, 26.160
SALMON FISHERIES, poaching, 26.186
   registration, 26.189
SALVAGE, jurisdiction, foreign domicile,
      3.37
SCANDALOUS AVERMENTS, 2.15
   deletion, 10.60
SCHOOL ATTENDANCE ORDERS, 26.115
SCOTTISH COURT ADMINISTRATION, 1.46
SEA, fisheries, 26.187
SEARCH WARRANTS, 26.01
   fishing boats, 26.188
   sex shops, 26.298
   unlicensed premises, 26.298
   VAT, 26.112
SECOND-HAND DEALERS, licences, 26.289
SECRETARY OF STATE FOR SCOTLAND,
      litigation, 4.68
SECURE TENANCIES, 26.215–26.218
   recovery of possession, 26.215–26.216
   summary causes, 30.269–30.274

SECURE TENANCIES—*cont.*
  repair works, 26.218
  variation of leases, 26.217
SECURITIES, jurisdiction within Scotland,
  3.105
SELF-INCRIMINATION, fatal accident
  inquiries, 27.13
  recovery of documents, 15.52, 15.73,
    15.74
  limits of privilege, 15.86
SEPARATION ACTIONS, 22.02
  applications and orders, relating to
    children, 22.57–22.59
  initial writs, 22.05, 22.06, 22.08, 22.22
  jurisdiction, 2.57, 2.58–2.60
  mental disorder, rules of court, 4.07
  notices of consent, 23.32
  private hearings, 5.20, 5.22
SEQUESTRATION, 5.10
  applications, 2.84
  bankrupts, litigation, 4.111
  competition, with arrestments, 29.34
    with poinding, 29.83
  for feuduties, 23.25
  jurisdiction, 2.70, 5.01
    within Scotland, 3.83
  permanent trustees, litigation, 4.110
  sisting, 12.12
  property, warrants to carry back, 25.04
SEQUESTRATIONS FOR RENT, 23.14–23.24,
    29.03
  appeals, effect, 18.68
  applications, 2.84
  breach, 23.23
    Lord Advocate's concurrence, 4.67
  care of effects, 23.19
  decrees, 23.21
  first deliverance, 23.16
  initial writs, 23.15
  inventories, 23.17
  nature of actions, 23.14
  opposition procedure, 23.20
  registration, 23.22
  summary causes, 30.02
    appraisal and inventory, 30.287
    form of summons, 30.286
    further procedure, 30.288
    premises displenished, 30.290
    recall, 30.291
    rent limit, 30.285
    sale, 30.289
    undefended, 30.114
  third parties, 23.24
  warrants to carry back, 23.18, 23.23
SERVICE, copies, 6.15
  documents, fatal accident inquiries,
    27.24
  documents abroad, 3.58
    Hague Convention, 3.56, 3.57
  initial writs, 6.04–6.06
    acceptance, 6.05
    declarators of death, 20.08
    execution of citation, *see* EXECUTION
      OF CITATION
    multiplepoinding, 21.56

SERVICE—*cont.*
  initial writs—*cont.*
    re-service, 6.47, 7.20
    summary causes, 3.80–30.83,
      30.89–30.90, 30.111
    warrants of citation, 6.07–6.10
  summary applications, 25.19
SERVICE MARKS, jurisdiction within
  Scotland, 3.71, 3.108
SERVITUDES, jurisdiction, 2.53
SESSIONS, 5.13
  fixing, 1.38, 1.47
SET-OFF, arrestments, 29.31
  Crown proceedings, 4.60, 4.61, 4.62
SETTLEMENTS, 14.31–14.70
  extra-judicial settlements, 14.31,
    14.63–14.68
    construction, 14.67
    disputes as to settlements, 14.66
    expenses, 14.67, 14.68
    joint minutes, 14.64
    rejected offers, 14.68
  information to the court, 14.69
  intimations, 14.70
  judicial settlements, 14.33–14.63
    tenders, *see* TENDERS
  sist of processes, 13.75
SEWERAGE, 26.335–26.340
  compensation, 26.339
  defects, 26.337
SEX DISCRIMINATION, 26.362–26.368
  jurisdiction, 26.368
SEX SHOPS, licensing, 26.291
  search warrants, 26.298
SHARES, arrestments, 29.24
  on the dependence, 11.14
SHERIFF CLERKS, 1.20–1.25
  advisory role, 25.03
  appointment, 1.21
  conditions of service, 1.21
  damages for personal injuries,
    payments to, 21.40
  duties and functions, 1.22–1.24
    appeal procedure, 18.60, 18.98
  fees, payment, 1.23
  help to party litigants, 4.119
  oaths, commission and diligence, 15.73
  qualifications, 1.21
  regional clerks, 1.25
  removal, 1.21
  signatures, interlocutors, 5.83
    warrants of citation, 6.08, 25.19
  transfers, 1.21
SHERIFF COURT AUDITORS, 1.26
  appointment, 1.12, 1.26
SHERIFF COURT DISTRICTS, 1.04
SHERIFF COURT RULES COUNCIL, 1.37
SHERIFF COURTS, administration, *see*
    ADMINISTRATION
  characteristics, 1.02
  choice, 6.02
  history, 1.01
  houses, 1.49
  privative jurisdiction, 2.27–2.35
  procedure, *see* PROCEDURE

SHERIFF OF CHANCERY, 1.12
  jurisdiction, succession, 2.66
  sheriff clerk, 1.21
SHERIFF OFFICERS, 1.27–1.28
  appointment, 1.12, 1.27
  citation of witnesses, 16.09
  executions, citation, 6.23–6.28
    objections by way of exception, 12.70
  registers, 5.38
  regulation, 1.27
  removal, 1.27
SHERIFFDOMS, 1.03–1.05
  boundaries, 1.03
SHERIFFS, 1.14–1.19
  appointment, 1.14
  control of proceedings, 5.98
  districts, 1.15
  floating sheriffs, 1.06, 1.17
  forms of address, 1.19
  honorary sheriffs, 1.06, 1.17
    appointment, 1.12
  judicial or administrative capacity,
    25.39–25.47
  jurisdiction, 1.16
  place of residence, 1.15
  powers, decrees in absence, 7.12
    summary applications, administrative
      decisions, 25.06, 25.07–25.11
  protection in exercise of duties, 1.16
  removal, 1.14
  retiral, during diets of proof, 16.41
  retirement age, 1.14
  role, at proof, 16.38–16.41
  salaries, 1.14
  temporary sheriffs, 1.06, 1.17
SHERIFFS PRINCIPAL, 1.07–1.13
  appeals, powers, 18.78–18.82
    right, 1.11
  appointment, 1.07
  court procedure, orders and directions,
    1.38–1.40
    recommendations, 1.41
  forms of address, 1.19
  functions, 1.11–1.13
    administration, 1.12, 1.47, 25.01
    sheriff officers, 1.27
  immunity, 1.13
  jurisdiction, 1.09
    declinature, 2.129
  protection in exercise of duties, 1.13
  ranking, 1.18
  removal, 1.08
  requirements, 1.08
  retirement age, 1.08
  salaries, 1.08
  temporary sheriffs principal, 1.06, 1.10
SHERIFF-SUBSTITUTES, 1.06
SHIPPING, jurisdiction, 2.02, 3.85
  merchant shipping, 26.392–26.396
SHIPS, arrestments, 24.06, 29.14, 29.28
  on the dependence, 11.13
  founding of jurisdiction, 3.11, 3.71
SHOPS, statutory requirements, 26.121
  tenancies, 26.266
SHORES, encroachment, Crown
  proceedings, 4.67

SHORT ASSURED TENANCIES, 26.244
SHORTHAND NOTES, extension, 17.01, 18.63
  role in appeals, 18.63
SHORTHAND WRITERS, oaths, commission
    and diligence, 15.35, 15.73
  recording of evidence, 16.32, 16.55
    instruction, 16.34
    payment, 16.34
SIGNATURES, defences, 9.129
  initial writs, 9.105
  interlocutors, 5.83
  warrants of citation, 6.08
  written pleadings, 9.49
SIST, 13.71–13.80
  appeals, 13.81, 18.41
  application for legal aid, 13.74
  arbitration, 13.76
  concurrent proceedings, 2.60,
    13.78–13.79
  diligence, 24.15
  discretion, 13.73
  family actions, 13.77, 22.07, 22.27
    discretionary, 22.29
    effect on interim orders, 22.31
    mandatory, 22.28
    recall, 22.30
  forum non conveniens, 13.79
  general rules, 13.71
  insanity, 12.13
  mandataries, *see* SIST OF MANDATARIES
  matrimonial homes, applications, 22.81
  new parties, *see* NEW PARTIES
  procedure, 13.72
  recall, 13.82–13.83
  settlements, 13.75
  small claims, 31.27, 31.31
  solicitors, decrees for expenses, 19.29
  summary causes, 30.41, 30.47
SIST OF MANDATARIES, 11.67–11.80, *see*
    also MANDATARIES
  appeals, 11.79, 18.41
  circumstances, 15.21
  conditions, 11.68
  discretion of the court, 11.69–11.71
  objectives, 11.67
  procedure, 11.75–11.79
  termination of mandates, 11.80
SITTINGS, 5.11–5.18
  civil days, 5.15
  civil sessions, 5.13
  court days, 5.11
  court holidays, 5.12
  fixing, 1.38, 1.47, 5.11
  incidental civil business, 5.16
  location, 5.18
  time, 5.17
  vacations, 5.14
SKILLED WITNESSES,
  summary causes,
    exchange of reports, 30.155
    remit to, 30.151
SLANDER, sheriffs, 1.16
  sheriffs principal, 1.13
SLAUGHTERHOUSES, registration, 26.25

SMALL CLAIM PROCEDURE,
additional defender, 31.30
amendment, 31.28–31.29
appeals, 31.137–31.143
arrestment, 31.34, 31.39
charges, 31.134
commencement of action,
authentication of summons, 31.38
citation, 31.43–31.59
copy summons, 31.40
form of summons, 31.36
statement of claim, 31.37
consigned funds, 31.130
correction of interlocutor or note,
31.129
damages,
to children, 31.33
to persons under legal disability,
31.32
decrees for alternative claims, 31.122
defended actions,
abandonment of action,
31.102–31.104
confidentiality, 31.95, 31.117
counterclaims, 31.70–31.74
decree by default, 31.105–31.109
evidence on commission, 31.100
failure of witnesses to attend, 31.99
hearing, 31.75–31.82
hearings, 31.110–31.120
letters of request, 31.101
lodging productions, 31.85–31.88
meaning, 31.69
parties to be heard, 31.118
public records, 31.96
remit to determine facts, 31.84
sheriff's decision, 31.119
third parties, 31.83
time to pay or orders, 31.120
delivery, 31.135
dispensing power, 31.10–31.11
documents,
lost or destroyed, small claims,
31.23–31.24
retained by sheriff clerk, 31.133
ECJ, 31.35
electronic transmission of documents,
31.25
execution, 31.16
expenses, 31.123–31.128
extract of decree, 31.131–31.132
final decree, 31.121
incidental applications, 31.26
intimation, 31.15
jurisdiction and competence, 31.12
recall of decree, 31.64–31.68
register, 31.7
remit between rolls, 31.18–31.22
representation, 31.13
sist, 31.27, 31.31
statutory basis, 31.6
trade or business names, 31.14
transfer to other court, 31.17
undefended actions, 31.60–31.63
variation of decree, 31.136

SMALL CLAIMS, introduction, 5.08
jurisdiction, 5.01
meaning, 31.02–31.05
summary causes, 30.02–30.03
transfer to other rolls, 13.48
SOCIAL SECURITY, administration, judicial
references, 13.41
benefits, arrestments, 29.29
damages for personal injuries, 21.33
recovery of benefits, joint minutes,
16.30, 21.33
SODOMY, 22.17
SOLATIUM, assessment, appeals, 18.116
SOLE TRADERS, 4.99
parties to litigation, 4.99
SOLICITORS, action for payment of
accounts, 21.72–21.74
attendance at diets of proof,
16.46–16.48
expenses, 19.22–19.31, *see also*
TAXATION OF EXPENSES
charging orders, 19.30–19.31
conduct of own cases, 19.24
from clients, 19.25
personal liability, 5.100, 19.22–19.23
remuneration from opposite parties,
19.26–19.31
taxation of accounts, 12.21, 12.23
failures, decrees by default, 14.10
intimation of summary causes, 30.22
mandates, 16.46
negligence, failure to raise actions
timeously, 21.19
rights of audience, 1.33
Scottish Solicitors' Discipline Tribunal,
26.278
withdrawal, 12.27–12.28
at appeal, 18.72
decrees by default, 14.07
SPECIFIC PERFORMANCE, *see* ACTIONS *AD
FACTUM PRAESTANDUM*
SPECIFICATION, averments, 9.27–9.31
defences, 9.113
preliminary pleas, lack of specification,
9.123
SPECIFICATION OF DOCUMENTS, 15.60,
15.61–15.63
SPECULATIVE DILIGENCE, 15.51, 15.53,
15.62, 15.80, 15.84
bankers' books, 15.95
SPORT GROUNDS, prohibition notices,
26.158
safety certificates, 26.157, 26.160
STAMP DUTIES, after stamping, sist of
processes, 13.80
deficiency, matters *pars judicis*, 2.16
STANDARD OF PROOF, breaches of interdict,
21.98
lawburrows, 24.04
rectification of documents, 24.07
STANDARD SECURITIES, jurisdiction, 26.105
STATED CASES, appeals from sheriff to
Court of Session, 26.13
arbitration, agricultural holdings, 26.10
dairy produce quotas, 26.195

STATED CASES—*cont.*
  caravan site licences, 26.161
  children's hearings, 26.63
  local elections, 26.119
  winding up of building societies, 26.54
STATEMENT OF CLAIM,
  small claims, 31.37
  summary causes, 30.71–30.73
STATEMENTS OF FACTS, form, 9.46
STATISTICS, Scottish Court Administration,
  1.50
STEP-PARENTS, adoption, 28.52–28.53,
  28.74
STREET TRADING, licences, 26.289
SUCCESSION, jurisdiction, 2.66
  proceedings, 2.86
  protected tenancies, 26.276
  rights of beneficiaries, arrestments,
    29.26
SUMMARY APPLICATIONS, 1993 Rules, 25.01
  absence of writs or parties, 25.20
  answers, 25.23
  appeals as, civic licensing, 26.290
    community care orders, 26.305
    firearms, 26.183
    further appeals, 25.06
    guardianship, 26.307
    licences, 26.38
    placing requests, 26.113
    safety certificates, 26.160
    sheriff's powers, 25.06, 25.07–25.11
  appeals from, *see* APPEALS FROM
    SUMMARY APPLICATIONS
  appointments, arbiters, 26.32
    valuators, 26.94
  child liability orders, 26.60
  citation, 25.19
  coal mining subsidence, 26.318
  common law applications, 25.01,
    25.03–25.05
  compensation, confiscation orders,
    26.110
  Conveyancing and Feudal Reform Act
    1970, 26.105
  defences, 25.23
  diets, 25.15, 25.26
  expenses, 25.46–25.47
  guardianship, 26.79
  hearings, form, 25.24
  heritable securities, severe hardship of
    debtors, 26.274
  identification, defenders, 12.04
    witnesses, 15.04–15.05
  initial writs, 25.18
    adjustment, 25.23
  judges, 25.13
  judgments, 25.27–25.28
  jurisdiction, 5.01, 25.12, 25.35
    pleas, 25.19
  leases, assured tenancies, 26.249
    modification, 26.239
    repairing obligations, 26.224
  licensing appeals, 26.255
  long leases, renewal, 26.106

SUMMARY APPLICATIONS—*cont.*
  meaning, 5.09, 25.01
  no hearings, 25.22
  nuisances, 26.342
    noise, 26.168
  orders, 25.16
  procedure, 25.13–25.36
    before hearings, 25.23
    first callings, 25.20–25.28
    hearings, 25.26
  proof, 25.24, 25.25
  protected tenancies, rateable value,
    26.268
    rent, 26.271
  public health, 36.324
  race discrimination, 26.369
  records of evidence, 25.25, 25.44
  recovery of documents, 15.84, 15.87,
    25.24
  register, 5.33
  registrar of births, deaths and
    marriages, 26.359
  requirements of writing, 26.107
  restraint orders, 26.110
  riotous assemblies, 26.108
  roads, 26.385
  rules, 25.14–25.17
  secure tenancies, repairs, 26.218
    variation of leases, 26.217
  sex discrimination, 26.362
  statutory applications, 25.01,
    25.06–25.11
  suspension orders, 26.406
  time-limits, 25.17
  tips, local authority notices,
    26.315–26.317
  transfers, to ordinary cause roll, 13.47,
    25.24
    to other sheriff court, 25.21
  warrants, installation of pipes, 26.298
SUMMARY CAUSE PROCEDURE,
  additional defenders, 30.46
  aliment,
    children, 30.298–30.305
    spouse, 30.292–30.297
  amendment, 30.42–30.45
  appeals, 30.328–30.351
  arrestment, 30.58–30.62, 30.76–30.79
  commencement of action,
    arrestment, 30.76–30.79
    authentication of summons,
      30.74–30.75
    citation, 30.88, 30.91–30.109
    form of response on summons,
      30.84–30.87
    re-service, 30.111
    return of summons, 30.112
    service of copy summons,
      30.80–30.83, 30.89–30.90
    statement of claim, 30.71–30.73
    summons, 30.67–30.70
  count reckoning and payment,
    30.257–30.260

SUMMARY CAUSE PROCEDURE—*cont.*
damages,
    payment to children, 30.56–30.57
    payment to legally disabled persons,
      30.48–30.55
defended actions,
    abandonment of action,
      30.197–30.199
    agreement of evidence, 30.153
    citation of witnesses and havers,
      30.179–30.182
    confidentiality, 30.174
    counterclaims, 30.132–30.133
    decree by default, 30.200–30.204
    evidence on commission,
      30.185–30.189
    exchange of skilled witness reports,
      30.155
    exchange of witness lists, 30.154
    failure of witnesses to attend,
      30.183–30.184
    hearings, 30.134–30.142
    inspection and recovery of
      documents, 30.152
    letters of request, 30.190–30.196
    lodging productions, 30.156–30.161
    meaning, 30.131
    noting evidence, 30.207–30.208
    oath or affirmation, 30.206
    objections to admissibility of
      evidence, 30.209–30.210
    proof, 30.205
    public records, 30.175–30.178
    recovery of documents,
      30.162–30.173
    remits to person of skill, 30.151
    specific issue hearings, 30.150
    third-party procedure, 30.143–30.149
delivery, 30.241–30.242
dispensing power, 30.13–30.15
documents,
    electronic transmission, 30.36
    lost or destroyed, 30.35
execution without endorsation by
    sheriff clerk, 30.23
furthcoming, 30.255–30.256
incidental applications, 30.37–30.41
intimation, 30.22
jurisdiction and competence,
    30.16–30.18, 30.137–30.138
multiplepoinding, 30.243–30.254
ordinary actions, 30.27–30.34
parties to be heard, 30.124–30.125
personal injury claims, 30.306–30.237
post proof,
    applications to vary decree, 30.240
    charges, 30.236–30.238
    consigned funds, 30.231
    correction of errors, 30.230
    delivery actions, 30.239
    documents retained by sheriff clerk,
      30.235
    expenses, 30.220–30.229
    extracts of decree, 30.232–30.234
    fees, 30.220–30.229
    final decree, 30.129

SUMMARY CAUSE PROCEDURE—*cont.*
recovery of possession, 30.261–30.284
references to ECJ, 30.63–30.66
Register, 30.08–30.12
remit,
    between ordinary rolls, 30.27–30.34
    from Court of Session, 30.26
representation, 30.19
sequestration for rent, 30.02, 30.114,
    30.285–30.291
sheriff's decision, 30.126–30.127
sist, 30.41, 30.47
statutory basis, 30.06
time to pay directions or orders, 30.128
trade or descriptive names, 30.20–30.21
transfer to sheriff court, 30.24–30.25
undefended actions,
    general rule, 30.114–30.115
    meaning, 30.113
    recall of decree, 30.122–30.130
    time to pay directions, 30.116–30.121
    time to pay orders, 30.117–30.121
SUMMARY CAUSES, books, 5.37
courts, 5.02
definition, 5.05, 30.02–30.05
introduction, 1.01, 5.07
jurisdiction, 5.01
march fences, 23.46
recovery of possession, 23.02, 26.215,
    26.270
rights of audience, 1.32
sequestrations for rent, 23.14
taxation of expenses, 19.48
transfers, from ordinary causes, 13.46
    to ordinary causes, 13.47
SUMMARY DECREE, 14.71–14.74
recall, 30.122–30.130
SUMMARY DILIGENCE, 29.02
SUMMARY WARRANTS, recovery of taxes,
    26.257, 29.02
SUMMONS,
authentication,
    small claims, 31.38
    summary causes, 30.74–30.75
form of response,
    small claims, 31.41–31.42
    summary causes, 30.84–30.87
small claims, 31.36
summary causes, 30.67–30.70
return of, 30.112
service of copy, 30.80–30.83,
    30.89–30.90
SUPERIORS, entry powers, 26.242
SUPERVISION REQUIREMENTS, children
    subject to adoption proceedings,
    28.15, 28.21–28.23
    intimations, 28.89
    termination, adoption orders, 28.119
    freeing orders, 28.167
SUSPENSION, 18.01, 18.04
decrees, effect of appeals, 18.68
diligence, 24.11–24.15
summary applications, 25.35
SUSPENSION ORDERS, consumer goods,
    26.406

SYSTEMS OF WORKING, defects, fatal accident inquiries, 27.18

TAPE RECORDINGS, court proceedings, 5.27
evidence, 16.32, 16.55
TAXATION OF EXPENSES, 19.04, 19.32–19.66
abandonment of actions, 14.30
actions for payment of solicitors' accounts, 21.72
advocates' fees, 12.21
auditors, 1.26
diets of taxation, 19.36
English solicitors, 19.57
extra-judicial settlements, 14.67
modes, 19.43–19.47
motions, 19.33
party and party, 19.43
solicitor and client, 19.44–19.46
nature, 19.32
outlays, 19.56
payment, 19.42
pre-litigation expenses, 19.52–19.53
procedure, 19.33–19.42
remit to auditors, 19.35
reports, approval and decree, 19.37
objections, 19.38–19.41
retaxation, 19.34
rules, 19.51–19.66
scales, 19.33, 19.48–19.50
solicitors' fees, 12.21, 12.23
tenders, 14.39
unnecessary expenses, 19.54–19.55
VAT, 19.58
witnesses, 19.59–19.66
present but not examined, 16.103, 19.60
skilled witnesses, 19.61–19.66
TAXES, payment, issue of interlocutors, 17.31
recovery, 26.152, 26.257, 29.02, 29.04
TAXIS, licences, 26.289
TEINDS, fish teinds, 26.81
fluctuating stipends, 26.83
valuation, 26.85
TELECOMMUNICATIONS, works, agreements, 26.320
TEMPORARY SHERIFFS, 1.06, 1.17
sheriffs principal, 1.06, 1.10
TENANCIES, *see* ASSURED TENANCIES;
LEASES; PROTECTED TENANCIES;
SECURE TENANCIES; TENANCY OF SHOPS
TENANCY OF SHOPS, 26.266
TENANTS-AT-WILL, conveyances, 26.106
TENDERS, acceptance, 14.46–14.48
dating of tenders, 14.48
decrees, 14.47
expenses, 14.47–14.48
minutes, 14.46
contents, 14.36–14.41
expenses, 14.38–14.39
interest, 14.40–14.41
form, 14.34–14.35
lapse, 14.45
lodging, 14.42–14.43
nature, 14.33

TENDERS—*cont.*
non acceptance, disclosure to sheriff, 14.49
expenses, 14.51–14.53
plurality of defenders, 14.56–14.62
Williamson tenders, 14.59–14.61
plurality of pursuers, 14.54–14.55
style, 14.36
withdrawal, 14.44
TERRITORIAL JURISDICTION, 2.02–2.04
THEFT, reparation, jurisdiction, 2.79
THIRD PARTIES, interests, matters *pars judicis*, 2.09
protection, actions of removing, 23.05
poinding, 29.72, 29.73
rectification of documents, 24.08
sequestrations for rent, 23.24
THIRD-PARTY PROCEDURE, 12.07, 12.42–12.65
advantages, 12.53
answers, 12.60–12.62
additional third parties, 12.62
counterclaims, 12.62
competency, 12.44–12.52
connected liability, 12.52
defenders' right of relief, 12.45–12.48
jurisdiction, 3.39, 3.109
object, 12.42
procedure, 12.54–12.65
averments, 12.54
judgments, 12.65
notices, 12.46, 12.55, 12.57–12.59
proof, 12.64
warrants for arrestment, 12.56
regulation, 12.43
small claims, 31.83
sole or joint liability, 12.49–12.51
summary causes, 30.143–30.149
TIED HOUSING, farm workers, recovery of possession, 26.270
TIME-LIMITS, amendment of pleadings, 10.32–10.42
appeals, to Court of Session, 18.98
to sheriff principal, 18.55–18.56
caution for expenses, 11.62
defences, 14.03
dispensing powers, 14.06, 26.255
discretion, 2.116, 2.118, 2.119, 2.121, 14.08, 14.09
personal injuries and deaths, 10.40
leave to appeal, 18.47
lodging productions, 14.05
lodging records, 14.06
summary applications, 25.17
TIME TO PAY DIRECTIONS, 26.127, 30.116, 30.218
appeals, 30.330, 30.345–30.346
applications, small claims, 31.120
TIME TO PAY ORDERS, 17.21, 26.128, 30.117
amendment of instances, 10.11
applications, 7.03, 30.118–30.121, 30.218
small claims, 31.120
citation, 6.07, 6.14, 6.16
response, 7.02

TIME TO PAY ORDERS—*cont.*
and conjoined arrestment orders, 29.65
consumer credit, 26.214
and current maintenance arrestments,
29.56
recall of earnings arrestments, 29.48
TIPS, local authority notices, 26.315
TITLE AND INTEREST TO DEFEND, 4.34–4.35
TITLE DEEDS, recovery of documents,
15.57
TITLE TO SUE, 4.29–4.32
arrestments on the dependence, recall,
11.31
date of actions, 4.32
definition, 4.30
preliminary pleas, 9.117
setting out, 4.31
transfers, 12.14–12.15
TRADE DISPUTES, 1.36
interim interdicts, 21.88
TRADE MARKS, jurisdiction, 2.46, 3.26,
3.27
within U.K., 3.71, 3.108
TRADE NAMES,
small claims, 31.14
summary causes, 30.20–30.21
TRADE UNIONS, 4.100
funds, political purposes, 26.123
parties to litigation, 4.100
TRADING INTERESTS, jurisdiction, within
Scotland, 3.87
within U.K., 3.71
TRANSCRIPTS, diets of proof, 16.55
TRANSFER OF CAUSES, 2.04
effect on arrestment on the
dependence, 11.25, 13.56
small claims, 31.17
summary causes, 30.24–30.25
to other rolls, 13.45–13.50
inherent jurisdiction, 13.50
ordinary causes to summary causes,
13.46
small claims, 13.48–13.49
summary causes to ordinary causes,
13.47, 25.24
to other sheriff courts, 6.03,
13.51–13.56
grounds, 13.52–13.54
procedure, 13.55–13.56
summary applications, 25.21
TRANSFERS OF PROPERTY, orders,
intimation, 22.15
TRANSPORT, contracts, jurisdiction, 3.49
TRANSUMPT, 2.86, 24.01
TRAVELLING EXPENSES, witnesses, 16.06,
16.11
TREES, lopping, 26.321
TRIBUNALS, appeals, jurisdiction within
Scotland, 3.87
jurisdiction within U.K., 3.71
TRUSTEES, 4.103–4.104
appointment, lapsed trusts, 26.407
arrestments on the dependence, 11.21
damages for personal injuries, 21.39
parties to litigation, 4.103–4.104

TRUSTEES—*cont.*
removal, 26.408
reponing, 7.24
TRUSTEES IN BANKRUPTCY, 4.110
parties to litigation, 4.110
TRUSTS, heritable property, completion of
title, 26.407, 26.409
jurisdiction, 2.44
foreign domicile, 3.21
prorogation of jurisdiction, 3.51,
3.53
within Scotland, 3.97
proceedings, 2.86
rights of beneficiaries, arrestments,
29.26
TUTORS, 4.11

UNCITRAL, Model Law on
International Commercial
Arbitration, 2.99
UNDEFENDED ACTIONS, 7.01
amendment of pleadings, 7.20–7.22
count, reckoning and payment, 21.07
decrees in absence, *see* DECREES IN
ABSENCE
family actions, 22.44–22.50
affidavits, 22.47
evidence, 22.46–22.47
procedure for decrees, 22.48
s. 11 orders, 22.49
small claims, 31.60–31.63
summary causes, 30.114–30.115
meaning, 30.113
recall of decree, 30.122–30.130
time to pay directions, 30.116–30.121
time to pay orders, 30.117–30.121
UNINCORPORATED ASSOCIATIONS, 4.101
domicile, 3.13
parties to litigation, 4.101
UNJUST ENRICHMENT, jurisdiction, 2.51
UNSOUND MIND, limitation of actions,
2.116, 2.118, 2.119, 2.120
UPHOLSTERY, materials, 26.333

VACATIONS, 5.14
VALUATION, appeal panels, appointment,
1.12
panels, appointment, 25.01
poinded goods, 29.78
VALUE ADDED TAX, arrears, 26.153
search warrants, 26.112
taxation of expenses, 19.58
VALUE RULE, appeals to Court of Session,
18.93
jurisdiction, 2.27–2.34
actions *ad factum praestandum*, 2.32
actions for payment, 2.29–2.30
change of circumstances, 2.34
counterclaims, 2.33
VEHICLES, driving licences, 26.383
VEXATIOUS LITIGANTS, 2.130, 4.122–4.123
VIEWS OF CHILDREN, adoption, 28.10,
28.80, 28.108
obtaining, 28.85–28.87
children proceedings, 22.33, 22.34,
22.103

VIEWS OF CHILDREN—*cont.*
  freeing for adoption, 28.156
    obtaining, 28.157
    revocation, 28.189
VIOLENT PROFITS, cautions, 23.13, 30.284

WARRANDICE, Crown proceedings, 4.76
WARRANT SALES, 29.86–29.90
  applications, 29.86
  sales, 29.89
    reports, 29.90
  warrants, contents, 29.87
    variation, 29.88
WARRANTS, apprehension of witnesses,
  16.13
  arrest, witnesses, 16.15
  arrestments, on the dependence,
    counterclaims, 12.34
    third-party procedure, 12.56
  citation of witnesses, 16.03
  installation of pipes, 26.298
  search, *see* SEARCH WARRANTS
  summary applications, 25.04, 25.19,
    25.23
WARRANTS OF CITATION, 6.07–6.10
  errors, 6.09
  form, 6.07
  period of effectiveness, 6.10
  periods of notice, 6.11
  signatures, 6.08
WASTE, commercial waste, 26.165
  controlled waste, 26.166
  household waste, 26.164
WATCHING BRIEFS, 16.49
WATER, unfit for human consumption,
  26.411
  works, 26.413
    entry powers, 26.412
WEIGHTS AND MEASURES, entry powers,
  26.416
WELFARE OF CHILDREN, adoption, 28.09,
  28.83, 28.87
  freeing for adoption, 28.156
  paramount principle, 22.103, 28.108
WILLS, holograph, declarators, 20.19–20.22
WINDING-UP, *see* LIQUIDATIONS
WINDOW CLEANERS, licensing, 26.289
WITNESSES, 15.02–15.43
  adoption agreements, 28.73
  age, 16.70
  arrest, 16.13
    warrants, 16.15
  citation, 16.02–16.17
    arbitration, 25.04
    by party litigants, 16.05
    cancellation, 16.10
    certificates, 16.09
    commission and diligence, 15.34
    form, 16.08
    necessity, 16.02
    notice period, 16.04
    penalities, 16.07
    presbytery, 25.04
    Scottish Solicitors' Discipline
      Tribunal, 26.278

WITNESSES—*cont.*
  citation—*cont.*
    small claims, 31.97–31.98
    summary causes, 30.179–30.182
    travelling expenses, 16.06
    warrants, 16.03
  commission and diligence, *see*
    COMMISSION AND DILIGENCE
  convenience, transfer to other sheriff
    courts, 13.52
  credibility, appeals, 18.103–18.109
  disclosure of identity, 15.01,
    15.02–15.06
    interlocutors, 15.06
    summary applications, 15.04–15.05
  enclosure, 16.51
  examination, *see* EXAMINATION OF
    WITNESSES
  execution of citation, 6.23
  expenses, 16.11, 19.59–19.66
    skilled witnesses, 19.61–19.66
    witnesses not called, 16.103, 19.60
  expert witnesses, 15.17
  failure to attend,
    small claims, 31.99
    summary causes 30.183–30.184
  fatal accident inquiries, citation, 27.08
    compellability, 27.13
  fees and expenses, 16.11
  imprisonment, 16.14
  incrimination, matters *pars judicis*, 2.16
  lists, 15.02, 16.01, 16.50
    exchange in summary causes, 30.154
  management at proof, 16.50–16.54
  oaths and affirmations, 16.62–16.64
    commission and diligence, 15.36
  outside Scotland, 16.17
  precognitions, *see* PRECOGNITIONS
  prisoners, 16.16
  privilege, 15.03, 15.86
  second diligence, 16.12
  skilled witnesses, meaning, 19.62
    remunceration, 16.103
WRIT OR OATH, 8.63
WRITTEN PLEADINGS, adjustment, *see*
  ADJUSTMENT OF PLEADINGS
  adoption, 28.100–28.103
  amendments, *see* AMENDMENTS OF
    PLEADINGS
  calls, 9.69–9.79
  definition, 9.01
  documents, 9.67
    calls, 9.69
  drafting, defences, *see* DEFENCES
    initial writs, *see* INITIAL WRITS
    styles, 9.72
    suggestions, 9.73
  form, 9.40
    addresses, 9.49
    craves, 9.45
    defects, 9.41
    description of pleadings, 9.43
    designations, 9.49
    heading, 9.42
    instances, 9.44

WRITTEN PLEADINGS, adjustment—*cont.*
 form—*cont.*
  paper type, 9.50
  pleas-in-law, 9.47–9.48
  signatures, 9.49
  statements of facts, 9.46
 functions, 9.03–9.12
  basis of procedural decisions, 9.09
  definition of issues, 9.03–9.04
  notice to opponents, 9.07
  notice to parties, 9.08
  notice to the court, 9.05–9.06
  res judicata, 9.10
 importance, 9.11
 language, 9.51–9.52
  abbreviations, 9.66
  poor expressions, 9.65
 legislation, 9.68
 pleaders' responsibility, 9.12
 rules, admissions, 9.19–9.26
  exceptions, 9.17
   foreign law, 9.18
  no evidence, 9.15
  no law, 9.16
  relevancy, 9.32–9.39

WRITTEN PLEADINGS—*cont.*
 rules, admissions—*cont.*
  specification, 9.27–9.31
  statement of facts only, 9.14
 summary applications, 25.23
 useful expressions, 9.53
  admitted, 9.59
  believed and averred, 9.54
  believed to be true, 9.60
  brevitas causa, 9.55
  denied, 9.62
  esto, 9.56
  explained and averred, 9.64
  not known and not admitted, 9.61
  quoad ultra, 9.63
  separatim, 9.57

YOUNG OFFENDERS, breaches of interdict, 21.99
 contempt of court, 2.22, 2.24
YOUNG PERSONS, parties to actions, 4.21–4.22

ZOOS, licensing, 26.29